An oil painting of Captain Robert Nairac GC, painted by Valarie Chilton in 1982. The portrait forms part of the Royal Military Academy (RMA) Sandhurst Collection, curated by Dr Anthony Morton. Reproduced with kind permission of the Ministry of Defence/Crown Copyright, 2015.

Cover image used with permission. © Press Association.

BETRAYAL

THE MURDER OF ROBERT NAIRAC GC

*"Some people are bound to die young.
By dying young a person stays young forever in
people's memory. If he burns brightly before he
dies, his light shines for all time."*
– Aleksandr Isayevich Solzhenitsyn

ALISTAIR KERR

For Julian Malins QC, without whose encouragement and advice this book would probably never have been written.

ISBN 1-903-499-85-2
978-1-903499-85-6

Printed and bound in the UK by PublishPoint
from KnowledgePoint Limited, Reading

FSC
www.fsc.org
FSC® C102342

The mark of
responsible forestry

CONTENTS

LIST OF ILLUSTRATIONS

On Slieve Gullion
for Douglas Carson

On Slieve Gullion 'men and mountain meet',
O'Hanlon's territory, the rapparee,
Home of gods, backdrop for a cattle raid,
The Lake of Cailleach Beara at the top
That slaked the severed head of Conor Mor:

To the south the Border and Ravensdale
Where the torturers of Nairac left
Not even an eyelash under the leaves
Or a tooth for MacCecht the cupbearer
To rinse, then wonder where the water went.

I watch now through a gap in the hazels
A blackened face, the disembodied head
Of a mummer who has lost his bearings
Or, from the garrison at Dromintee,
A paratrooper on reconnaissance.

He draws a helicopter after him,
His beret far below, a wine-red spot
Swallowed by heathery patches and ling
As he sweats up the slopes of Slieve Gullion
With forty pounds of history on his back.

Both strangers here, we pass in silence
For he and I have dried the lakes and streams
And Conor said too long ago: 'Noble
And valiant is MacCecht the cupbearer
Who brings water that a king might drink.'

*– by Michael Longley, used with permission from
his publisher Jonathan Cape*

FOREWORD

This is the story of a remarkable man, Captain Robert Nairac GC (1948-1977). It is not a history of the Troubles in Northern Ireland, nor of the British Army's involvement in them, which lasted officially from 1969 to 2007. There are good accounts of the Troubles available, written by people better qualified than I. Some, which I have consulted, are listed in the Select Bibliography. Likewise, this is not a conventional military biography: that would not be possible, given the nature of the subject – Nairac is an elusive figure who defies normal biographical methods. Moreover, although he was a soldier who died in the course of his military duties, Nairac passed less than five of his nearly twenty-nine years in the Army and two of those years are still shrouded in considerable secrecy. His police file has never been closed because the full story of his murder is not known and his body has never been found.

Although his deep interest in Ireland had started during his childhood, Nairac's direct involvement in Northern Ireland, first as a uniformed soldier and later as an undercover operative, only lasted from 1973 to 1977 and was not continuous. For most of 1975 and the first half of 1976 he was absent from the Province. As a result, many chapters and events of the Troubles are not covered in this book, because Nairac was not involved in them. On the other hand, because my primary interest is in Nairac the man, I have allowed space for an examination of his life before the Army: especially of his early life and studies at Ampleforth College and Oxford, which have been covered only briefly in other biographies.

I had two chief aims in writing this book. One was to disentangle the reality of Nairac from the thicket of legend and published disinformation that surround him. That would prove to be a formidable task: I believe that I have made useful progress, although I suspect that there may be still more to discover. Nairac has emerged as an even more complex and interesting person than I had anticipated, with his reputation intact and even enhanced. That is not necessarily true of the other people who played a part in his tragedy.

Following logically from the first aim, my other purpose was to get the impressions and memories of people who remembered Nairac, while they were yet alive: their testimony would be vital. If he were alive today, Nairac would have celebrated his 67th birthday on 31 August 2015. This comes as a slight shock, since he remains in our collective memory as a vigorous young man; he was only 28 when he was murdered. Some of his friends, enemies and other contemporaries, including some potentially important witnesses, are already dead, and not all from natural causes. In ten years' time very few of them will be left.

And the title: "Betrayal"? I think that is appropriate, because betrayal was a recurrent feature of Nairac's life, at least from Ampleforth onwards. He was betrayed by certain elements in the Army who used him for what he did and for too long, even before we arrive at the actual events of his murder in 1977. The murder was his life compressed into an apparently inevitable ending.

In the course of his short but eventful life Robert Nairac would suffer three major betrayals at the hands of people whom he should have been able to trust: the guilty parties on the first occasion were at his school. On the second occasion the Army had much to answer for, given that their acts and omissions had contributed to the chain of events that led to Nairac's murder. The third betrayal would occur several years after his murder, when Nairac's reputation would be subjected publicly to assaults as vicious as those visited upon his living body during the last hours of his life. This time the guilty people would be at the heart of British politics, but former Army officers would also play a part.

We should not however write off Nairac as "brief life and hapless". Life is not just about length of days; quality, rather than quantity, of life is what counts: he packed more into just under twenty-nine years than most of us manage in eighty. We can never know for certain what Nairac might have achieved, had he lived. But there are enough indications that he was an exceptional man who might well have become a distinguished or even a well-known one. He was definitely a hero but, apart from that, he was also thoroughly and engagingly human.

Alistair Kerr

PROLOGUE | THE CITATION

The war is ended on the Huai border, and the trading roads are open again;
Stray crows come and go cawing in the wintry sky.
Alas for the white bones heaped together in desolate graves;
All had sought military honours... (Chang Pin, 9th-10th centuries)

In February 1979 Captain Robert Laurence Nairac of the Grenadier Guards was awarded the George Cross (GC) posthumously for exceptional bravery in Ireland in 1977. The GC is of equal and supreme precedence to the Victoria Cross (VC) among British awards for valour *(Note 1)*.

The VC however is only ever awarded in wartime. Robert Nairac had been abducted from a bar in Northern Ireland on the night of 14-15 May 1977. He was never seen again. He had been engaged in undercover intelligence work at the time of his death, and there is evidence that he was brutally tortured and finally murdered under circumstances that have never been fully clarified. Although its location is known to a few people, his body has never been found. He is one of "the Disappeared" of the Troubles in Northern Ireland.

Nairac's parents, Maurice and Barbara Nairac, who had already lost their elder son David in tragic circumstances, received the George Cross from HM The Queen. She spoke with them for ten to fifteen minutes. The Queen, who was kind and sympathetic, said that a supportive family was a great help in times of stress and difficulty *(Note 2)*. They told her a little about their son. Afterwards Mrs Nairac said, "To know that one's son has done something to earn the George Cross makes one tremendously proud. To know how we feel you have to be the parent of a wonderful son like ours."

Whether Mr and Mrs Nairac knew it or not, the Queen had taken a close interest in Nairac's abduction and murder. That was to be expected: she is the Colonel-in-Chief of the Grenadier Guards. It is also highly likely that the Queen and Nairac had been acquainted. During his tour of Regimental duty with the First Battalion in 1975-76 he had been on duty at the royal residences, including Windsor Castle. According to a family member Nairac was invited to dinner by the Queen – who has an excellent memory for names and faces – along with a small number of other officers, while he was stationed at Windsor. Other Guards officers also recall occasionally dining with the Queen while on Castle Duty at Windsor. Sometimes visiting notables, such as the Archbishop of Canterbury, were also present.

In a letter from Major General John Swinton, Headquarters, Household Division, to The Queen's Private Secretary, Lieutenant Colonel Sir Martin Charteris, dated 26 May 1977, to be laid before Her Majesty, General Swinton reported that:

"There can be little doubt that he has been murdered. Furthermore, that he is likely to have suffered before dying... Robert Nairac was an outstandingly brave man fully aware of the risks he took and his death is a great loss to the Grenadier Guards and to The Household Division."

Nairac's GC was well-deserved: even the Provisional IRA had admitted his extraordinary courage when faced with his own death. However, although the original GC citation still exists and its authors' identities are known, the recommendation has vanished from the file in the National Archives at Kew, or was never there. No-one now admits to knowing exactly what it said, nor who signed it off. That is one of many mysteries surrounding Robert Nairac GC.

King George VI created the GC primarily to honour courageous civilian heroes, but military personnel may also receive it if the available military decorations are considered not to be adequate. They have done so in both peace and war-time. The GC was for example awarded to members of the Special Operations Executive (SOE) in the Second World War who had in some cases undergone terrible torture and displayed great heroism, as had Nairac. The citation reads:

"The Queen has been graciously pleased to approve the posthumous award of the George Cross to: Captain Robert Laurence Nairac (493007), GRENADIER GUARDS. Captain Nairac served for four tours of duty in Northern Ireland totalling twenty-eight months. During the whole of this time he made an outstanding personal contribution: his quick analytical brain, resourcefulness, physical stamina and above all his courage and dedication, inspired admiration in everyone who knew him. On his fourth tour Captain Nairac was a Liaison Officer at Headquarters 3 Infantry Brigade. His task was connected with surveillance operations. On the night of 14/15 May 1977 Captain Nairac was abducted from a village in South Armagh by at least seven men. Despite his fierce resistance he was overpowered and taken across the border into the nearby Republic of Ireland where he was subjected to a succession of exceptionally savage assaults in an attempt to extract information which would have put other lives and future operations at serious risk. These efforts to break Captain Nairac's will failed entirely. Weakened as he was in strength – though not in spirit – by the brutality, he yet made repeated and spirited attempts to escape, but on each occasion was eventually overpowered by the weight of the numbers against him. After several hours in the hands of his captors Captain Nairac was callously murdered by a gunman of the Provisional Irish Republican Army who had been summoned to the scene. His assassin subsequently said, 'He never told us anything.' Captain Nairac's exceptional courage and acts of the greatest heroism in circumstances of extreme peril showed devotion to duty and personal courage second to none."

The two-year delay in making the award was for two reasons. The Army needed to be quite sure that the IRA had learned nothing from Nairac during the last hours of his life, and the legal formalities in the UK and the Republic of Ireland, including the sentencing of those involved in his murder and an inquest, had to be completed first. Even Nairac's death certificate, issued in the Republic of Ireland on 16 October 1978, a year and a half after his murder, is unusual.

Firstly, it gives the wrong date for Nairac's murder. Exceptionally, it was issued in the absence of a body and the cause of death is given as "unknown: body not available for post-mortem examination". At the time of writing, in 2015, it has still not been found.

Robert Nairac was more than just a very brave man. He was an exceptionally intelligent and versatile officer whom the Army and England could ill afford to lose. He was a graduate of Ampleforth College, Oxford University, the Royal Military Academy, Sandhurst and the Army Staff College (Junior Division). He was expected to achieve rapid promotion by senior officers well-qualified to judge. As his Army obituary states:

"He quickly impressed everyone as being a young officer of the highest calibre and greatest potential. His intelligence and prowess on the sports field were apparent from his previous record: however, to these were added the more personal qualities of great charm, humility and willingness to learn from others which are not always found in people of his ability."

Charles Woodrow, who was one of three Grade 3 Operations Officers in 3 Brigade Headquarters and who knew Nairac well during his last tour in Northern Ireland (1976-77), wrote that: "The SAS Squadron, prior to [Robert's] abduction, was in Bessbrook Mill. Part of my job was to look after the needs of the SAS Squadron and I used to see him most days until he was murdered... As you can imagine Robert's abduction and subsequent murder was a terrible loss to his family, to all of us who worked alongside him, and to the Army, particularly in South Armagh, and is something I shall never forget."

Unusually for that time, Nairac was as well-liked and respected by warrant officers (WOs) and non-commissioned officers (NCOs) as he was by most of his commissioned brother officers. It is clear from NCO memoirs of the Troubles (Nicky Curtis' *Faith and Duty*, for example) that – rather alarmingly – many WOs and NCOs in Northern Ireland had little time for their Sandhurst-trained officers, whom they regarded as more of a liability than an asset in what was seen as "a corporals' war". Part of the problem was that the Sandhurst course at the time, with its emphasis on conventional warfare, was not really relevant to Northern Ireland, which was developing into an unconventional counter-insurgency campaign.

"Posing Ruperts" was one of the kinder expressions used for officers who came out of Sandhurst, and most officers had to work hard to earn the NCOs' respect; they accorded it late and grudgingly, if at all. These men, the backbone of the Army, are normally adept at smelling out posers, selfish careerists intent only on personal advancement, and bluffers who do not quite make the grade. Nairac more than made the grade. Nicky Curtis mentions with approval his "natural, officer-bred authority at odds with a squaddie's toughness in the eyes," and "the swagger of a soldier totally at ease with his own abilities." These are serious compliments: Curtis was a Sergeant at the time.

Or Tony Clarke in *Contact*: "I shake hands with the stocky guy with curly black hair, far removed from the normal type of Guards officer you usually meet. I take in the broken nose and the cheerful grin and think 'Thank God I haven't got one of those guys with a mouthful of marbles.'" Clarke was then a Parachute Regiment NCO.

A down-to-earth manner, with frequent use of the f-word; his great physical strength; his prowess at contact-sports; his boxer's broken nose, all helped to establish his credibility with other ranks. Despite rivalry between Regiments, this affection and respect extended to include non-Grenadier colleagues in other military formations, like Tony Clarke's Parachute Regiment and the Scottish Division, as well as the Brigade of Guards. His relationship with the SAS was more complicated. "Charismatic" is an over-used word these days, but in this context it is unavoidable: Nairac had charisma in spadefuls. He had exceptional leadership qualities. According to Brigadier David Woodford, Nairac had been recommended to receive a decoration in acknowledgement of his exceptional services at the end of his tour. This provides an interesting piece of evidence. Brigadier Woodford was not Nairac's Commanding Officer. If he instigated the MBE recommendation for Nairac, that is bureaucratic proof that Nairac was a Brigade staff officer. In the event Nairac would indeed receive a medal, but posthumously, under tragic circumstances. The Special Branch of the Royal Ulster Constabulary, whose relations with the Army had historically been characterised by distrust, had already in 1975 made him their own very personal award, in the form of an inscribed silver tankard (*Note 3*). If he had lived, Nairac would have returned to his Battalion a little later in 1977 in a glow of well-earned glory.

General Swinton further commented:

"Two extracts from his recent confidential report speak for themselves:

'It is to a major extent thanks to his efforts that the Security Forces now know more about the terrorists in South Armagh than at any previous point in the campaign.'

'His most valuable quality is his ability to understand the mentality and motivation of the Irish – this, coupled with his genuine interest and sympathy enable him to gain access to information not normally available to British soldiers.'"

This is high praise. Nairac's Army career had lasted for just under five years. He had been accepted for officer training while still an Oxford undergraduate, following an interview with the Grenadier Guards in September 1971. He passed his Regular Commissioning Board (RCB) without difficulty and was granted a regular commission. He was taken on strength (TOS) by his Regiment on 23 December 1971. He left Oxford at the end of the Trinity Term in July 1972 and went to the Royal Military Academy (RMA) Sandhurst for five months from September 1972. Only at this point can his Army career really be said to have begun. He had been a functioning Regimental officer since joining his Battalion in late January 1973. He did not come from an Army family and had no personal connection with the Grenadier Guards. Although he had been in the Combined Cadet Force (CCF) at Ampleforth, he had not even trained with the Territorial and Army Volunteer Reserve (TAVR) until January 1972, in his final year at Oxford when, after being awarded an Army university cadetship (a military scholarship), he had joined the Oxford University Officers' Training Corps, as he was obliged to do. Yet, once having decided to become a soldier, he adapted to the Army very successfully. He seemed to be one of nature's military men. Now, in May 1977, he was dead. His Army career might have been brief, but he had achieved a great deal in the short time available. He died a few months short of his twenty-ninth birthday, which would have fallen on 31 August 1977.

One troublesome recurrent question that remains is: why did Nairac take extreme risks and who, if anyone, authorised him to do so? Or perhaps that is the wrong question: risk-taking is an unavoidable aspect both of espionage and of soldiering; it is one of the factors that attract a certain type of man to the colours; especially to the Special Forces and to undercover work. Like Christopher Marlowe, Robert Nairac was one of those rare people who paradoxically live life to the full because they are not afraid to lose it. As the Harvard psychiatrist Ned Hallowell explains, risk is a prerequisite for this heightened state of existence:

"One must be willing to take risks. The lover must lay bare his soul and risk rejection and humiliation to enter this state. The athlete must be willing to risk physical harm, even loss of life, to enter this state. The artist must be willing to be scorned and despised by critics and the public and still push on. And the average person – you and I – must be willing to fail, look foolish, and fall flat on our faces should we wish to enter this state."

Soldiers are not the only people who take serious, premeditated risks. So do climbers. It is very risky indeed to attempt the north face of the Eiger at any time of the year – more than fifty have died in the attempt, yet people still do it. So do journalists. In 1993 Dan Eldon, an outstanding journalist and author, and three colleagues were beaten and stoned to death by an enraged Somali mob. Eldon was 23 years old at the time. It had been risky to enter Mogadishu immediately after a misdirected UN bombing raid in which over 70 Somali civilians had been killed, yet they did it. Ironically, they had hoped by bringing the raid and its outcome to the world's attention, to make a positive difference and to stop it happening again; just as Nairac had hoped to make a positive difference in Northern Ireland. But it is also to do with the challenge; with beating the odds. Nairac took calculated risks: one day he took one too many. However, he was aware of the risks that he ran; so equally were the superiors who sent him back to Northern Ireland in June 1976 on a fourth tour of duty, and who instructed him to give special attention to Drumintee.

In a classified Army paper written eighteen months before his death, Nairac had advocated the appointment of a dedicated Military Intelligence Officer

(MIO) based in South Armagh. When the Army took up his recommendation, he was appointed. He would have come under pressure to accept the job in any event because – among other reasons – the RUC Special Branch, some members of the SAS and others in Northern Ireland wanted him back. The fact that Nairac had recommended the appointment of an Intelligence Officer; that his proposal was adopted and that he was appointed, disposes of any suggestion that he was simply a Liaison Officer, not even of Field Rank, who had overstepped his job-description out of vanity, ambition or mischief, and paid the price. From Day One in June 1976, he was there in an intelligence role, whatever his official job-description may have been, and his appointment had been approved at a very senior level.

His intelligence function is unexpectedly confirmed by an IRA source cited by Martin Dillon in *The Dirty War*. According to this person, Nairac "worked in the way SAS people are trained to behave. He was involved, it seems, in an unusual method of intelligence-gathering. It follows that he probably had his own contacts and gathered information on which only the SAS acted. The guys who do hits, do hits, but he was someone who probably provided the intelligence on which hits or ambushes of IRA personnel are planned. The only thing which suggests that he might also have been required to shoot people is the presence in his room of a personal weapon. This suggests that he was required to do unattributable work; otherwise service-issue weapons would be sufficient. However his activities bear all the hallmarks of someone engaged in intelligence-gathering. He operated with more freedom than Army Intelligence or Special Branch would allow. The IRA knows that in the mid-1970s small intelligence-gathering units were established to provide specialist intelligence for the SAS. Nairac worked for one of those units and as such was not responsible to Army Intelligence proper but to MI5."

Martin Dillon's IRA source does not say that Nairac *was* SAS; only that he had apparently received appropriate SAS training, which we know to be the case. Nor does he seriously suggest that Nairac was a killer. The reference to Nairac's personal handgun is a red herring. It was possible legitimately to have a privately-owned weapon in Northern Ireland, provided that the RUC Divisional Commander had authorised it. This appears to have been the case. The gun was licenced. Other officers did so, too. In Nairac's case the explanation is probably unexciting. Nairac was a very good shot and took part successfully in competitions. Usually he used a rifle, but he was also proficient with small arms. The personal handgun is likely to have been a competition weapon.

A briefing paper by Nairac, written shortly before his death, *Talking to People in South Armagh,* remained in use until the Army's official peacekeeping role in South Armagh came to an end. Twenty years after his death the then Chief Intelligence Officer in South Armagh, Captain Rupert Thorneloe, was still distributing *Talking to People in South Armagh* to the resident battalion in 1996-97. Nairac's paper has its critics, but twenty-three years is a respectable life for any briefing document. In it Nairac makes some telling points, most of which were vindicated by later events. Among other things, he had concluded that the British Army could not defeat the South Armagh PIRA militarily. The war had to be fought on the basis of Intelligence; it would not be won by "out-ambushing or out-shooting the IRA". It is possible that this paper, or at least knowledge of its existence, came to the IRA's notice; in July 1977, two months after Nairac's death, they issued their own guidance in the form of a "flier" to civilians in South Armagh, telling them to say nothing to the Security Forces, on pain of death.

Rupert Thorneloe became fascinated by his distant predecessor's theories and methods, which some officers had dismissed as eccentric and reckless. Thorneloe, however, did not think so. Like Nairac, whom he somewhat resembled facially, he focused on studying the mindset of the border Irish Republicans. Like a field naturalist, he studied their habits and constructed charts of the relationships between the various IRA families. Like Nairac too, he recognised how helpful and informative the RUC Special Branch could be, if treated in the right way. Their friendship and co-operation could never be taken for granted. The charm was often reinforced by a gift of Black Bush whiskey, made by Bushmills. But it was whiskey well-spent; if well-disposed, the RUC could provide invaluable intelligence. The pledge of their friendship was heavy drinking; it was an Ulster male-bonding custom. Rupert Thorneloe, by then the Lieutenant Colonel of the First Battalion Welsh Guards, would in his turn be killed in action in Helmand in July 2009. Apart from his professional interest in Nairac, one of Thorneloe's friends has reported that Nairac exercised a romantic fascination over Rupert Thorneloe and still does over many other Guards officers from beyond the grave, even now.

One of Thorneloe's successors commented that, "Nairac lived and worked in a very different world to the one I inhabited in the 1990s in South Armagh. At first glance it looks as if he was reckless, but that doesn't take into consideration that it was relatively early in the campaign and the Security Forces in South Armagh were still finding their feet. Plus, many of the operating procedures we had were forged from the experiences of others, including Nairac."

"We are up against a sophisticated enemy, and we must prepare accordingly," wrote Nairac. "The IRA in South Armagh, and particularly Crossmaglen, are more professional and more successful than in other parts of Northern Ireland. Little of the South Armagh ideas or expertise has seeped through to the rest of the IRA. That is because of insularity of the units and the thick-headedness of the IRA in other regions."

Nairac also advised that soldiers who served in South Armagh should be hand-picked and specially trained. Everything they did "should be directed towards local contacts, amassing low-level Intelligence". He put into practice what he preached.

Later events have tended to vindicate Nairac. What eventually forced the IRA to the negotiating table was a combination of dwindling political support; internal corruption; a disillusioned younger generation and more effective pressure by the Security Forces north and south of the border. Above all, however, it was successful penetration of the IRA by the British Intelligence Agencies that made this possible. Nairac was in at the start of that process and made a serious contribution to the final result, although it would not occur until some twenty years after his own death.

Writers and journalists continue to speculate as to the true reason why Nairac was in the Three Steps Inn at Drumintee without backup on the night of 14 May 1977 and how he came to meet a brutal end in a field in the Republic of Ireland early the following day. As noted above, his body has never been recovered. Horrible stories about how it might have been disposed of have circulated. His parents died not knowing where he was buried; his surviving family and friends have never achieved closure. Police investigations continue sporadically. And the rumours keep proliferating; one of them being that Nairac is still alive somewhere, presumably in very deep cover.

It might have amused Nairac, who is said to have appreciated irony, that similar speculation persists around one of his boyhood heroes, T E Lawrence of Arabia: another enigmatic character of immense charm. Lawrence may well have been murdered by persons unknown, rather than dying in a simple motorcycle accident in 1935, as was thought at the time. The late Desmond Stewart constructed a compelling and plausible case in support of this thesis. Lawrence's youngest brother, A W Lawrence, also seems to have had his doubts. Both Nairac and Lawrence had engaged in undercover work. In both cases rumour suggests mysterious, political reasons for the murder or that the death was "staged," allowing Lawrence or Nairac to disappear and undertake fresh secret work under another identity for the British State, or to start a new life somewhere else. On "the Arab Street" a rumour persists that Lawrence really died as recently as 1968 in a villa in Tangier. A similar tale is told about Christopher Marlowe who, following his staged murder, is said to have beguiled his "posthumous retirement" abroad – in France or Navarre – by writing Shakespeare's plays: William Shakespeare merely produced them. If nothing else, these legends show how quickly romantic rumour and myth crystallised around these handsome, charismatic men (that word again). Indeed, they had started do so while Lawrence and Nairac were still alive, which makes the biographer's task especially difficult. What is the naked, unvarnished truth?

Robert Nairac has not simply passed into legend (*Note 4*). He has joined the ranks of famous historical murder mysteries, which fascinate later generations because they have never been solved. The list is long and is constantly being updated. What was the fate of the Princes in the Tower? Are the skeletons found in the Tower of London and ceremoniously entombed in Westminster

Abbey centuries after their alleged murder truly theirs? What, if it comes to that, happened to their "wicked" uncle, Richard III? Are the bones found in a Leicester car park really his? The DNA evidence is not conclusive. What really happened to Christopher Marlowe? Did he die in Deptford? What actually happened to Louis XVII? Could he have survived? Who was Jack the Ripper? Was he Virginia Woolf's cousin? How, why and when did T E Lawrence really die? What happened to Jim Thompson, the Thai silk king, when he vanished in Malaysia in 1967? Was he a CIA agent (*Note 5*)? The Irish poet David Wheatley treats Nairac as a metaphor for unsolved mystery: "Ach cá bhfuil uaigh Robert Nairac?!" (But where is Robert Nairac's grave?) Why truly was Robert Nairac where he was on the evening of 14 May 1977, apparently without backup?

CHAPTER 1 | THE MYTHS

Vera diu latitant, sed longo temporis usu emergunt tandem quae latuere diu.
(The truth, which was previously hidden, remains hidden for a long time; but
after a long time it emerges. Guillaume La Perriere, *Morosophie* 1553)

When I began researching for this book, the Grenadier Guards permitted me to study their files on Robert Nairac GC. That exercise was absorbing and moving. Among other things it brought home to me how widely and deeply Nairac had been respected, liked and admired, by all sorts of people. There were serious appreciations by superior officers writing in his annual Army confidential reports, all outstanding; the same from the Army Staff College (Junior Division), as well as more personal letters expressing grief and shock following his abduction, torture and murder in May 1977. They provided an insight into loss, personal grief and unbearable sadness, albeit suffused with love and pride. Above all, there was his impressive posthumous George Cross citation. There was a touching letter from his mother in which she expressed her intuition that he might still be alive somewhere, perhaps being held hostage. Barbara Nairac was not alone in this unfortunately vain hope. Many others, far more knowledgeable about the Army, Northern Ireland and the risks that he had been running, had difficulty in accepting that they would never again see boisterous, fun-loving, larger-than-life Robert, whose presence, when on top form, could light up the room and whose disappearance had left a painful void. On 9 June, three weeks after his disappearance, Brigadier David Woodford (Headquarters, 3 Infantry Brigade, Northern Ireland) wrote to Colonel Greville Tufnell, the Regimental Lieutenant Colonel of the Grenadier Guards:

"...I should have written to you earlier, but I have been hoping against all reason that Robert – tough and resourceful as we all knew he was – might have survived".

But he had not. There was another letter from Nairac's sister, written long after all hope of his survival had been extinguished, who donated Nairac's kit to his Regiment (Caps Forage Officer's 3; Caps Service Dress 1; Belts Sam Browne 3, etc). They still keep some items as sacred relics, such as his ceremonial scarlet No 1 Dress tunic, in the Guards Museum in Birdcage Walk. In the nearby Guards Chapel is the memorial window with, instead of a heraldic device, an engraving on glass of a falcon. Robert Nairac was a serious falconer: a famous and ferocious Hawk Eagle, Brimstone, to which he was deeply attached, outlived him. Nairac was also an exceptionally good shot and an accomplished angler. He had played rugby for the Second XV at Oxford, for the First XV at Sandhurst and had won four Boxing Blues in contests against Cambridge. He was an exceptionally strong man. He was an acknowledged expert on Ireland and Irish history.

Yet there were signs that there was another side to the handsome, dapper, accomplished and religious Guards officer. Since his death there had been serious and politically-motivated attempts by individuals like Ken Livingstone, Anthony Bradley (*Note 1*), Fred Holroyd, Colin Wallace (*Note 2*), and of course by Irish Republicans, to discredit him and darken his memory, accusing him of a range of unlawful activities, including murder. Given the implicit or explicit political agenda, I treated these allegations with caution. However even his friends referred to episodes in Nairac's life that would have raised military eyebrows, had the Household Division ever become aware of them. There were references to his membership of a decadent, drug-taking circle at Oxford and specifically to LSD abuse, to alcohol abuse and a love of violence for its own sake. Luke Jennings, the author of *Blood Knots*, a best-selling memoir mainly about angling, in which the young Nairac appears as the even more youthful author's mentor and the soul of kindness and generosity, mentions a few disquieting events, some of them narrated by Nairac himself, and speaks of "a life not fully under control". Jennings also mentions a tendency, noticeable as far back as 1967, and ten years before Nairac's murder, to act first and seek permission afterwards. Other writers like Anthony Bradley, the author of *Requiem for a Spy*, are bitterly critical of Nairac and of the system that produced him, as they perceive it, regarding him as a psychopath.

A further complicating factor was that within the wider Army, normal "green army" soldiers regarded "spooks" – those who served in any undercover or clandestine capacity in Northern Ireland – with a degree of suspicion. This category included Robert Nairac. Very few ordinary soldiers had any idea of what the spooks were doing or what their rules were. It followed that some, even most, of them thought that the spooks were up to no good. They were also jealous of their comparative freedom of action.

The people who in some respects seem to have known the young Nairac best, the monks of Ampleforth Abbey, while emphasising his academic and sporting successes, his leadership as Head of St Edward's House, his great integrity and his essentially good character, also expressed their fear that he would come to a sad end. One monk who had known him well said that he "was the SAS type", but with one or two fatal flaws. One of these was a tendency to become emotionally involved, which Nairac did, with Ireland.

One of his former tutors at Oxford wryly observed that if something could go wrong in Nairac's life, wrong it would go. In 1976 he had learned with alarm that Nairac was about to go back to Ireland to engage in undercover work. The strain of hubris that he had detected in Nairac's character boded badly for his future in that troubled, violent land. He feared the worst when in May 1977 he saw the newspaper placards, "Boxing Blue Killed". He knew, even before he opened his newspaper, that his worst fears had been realised.

Nairac's Oxford contemporary and friend Julian Malins QC commented:

"Robert was never going to make old bones. He was either going to fall off the North Face of the Eiger, be eaten by a shark or disappear into some inhospitable wasteland, of which Northern Ireland is a prime... example."

Or Luke Jennings, the friend of his youth, in *Blood Knots*: "The Little Owl, I would later learn, was the symbol of Athene, the Greek goddess of wisdom and war. And, when seen before sunset, of a death foretold". (*Note 3*)

Or Nicky Curtis, Nairac's Green Howard NCO friend: "There was the sickening feeling of an inevitability fulfilled... my gut feeling had been that it was a death waiting to happen".

Patrick Mercer, the former Conservative MP for Newark and a former Army officer, wrote something similar in a newspaper article:

"Robert's life was only ever going to end either in brilliant success or heroic death. The man was the very definition of charismatic".

Mercer, who survived nine tours of duty in Northern Ireland, also revealed that he had been with Nairac the night before he died. He added:

"Unfortunately, his bravery overreached itself".

These remarks were made or written after the tragedy had happened, with the sad wisdom of hindsight. To balance them, it should be noted that the mature Nairac – post-Oxford, post-Sandhurst and serving with his Regiment – was a somewhat different character from the incautious, unreliable schoolboy, assistant master and undergraduate whom the monks, Luke Jennings, the Dons and Nairac's fellow-students at Oxford had known. They hardly seemed to be the same person. People who encountered him at this period found him impressive: smart as a Guards officer proverbially is; well-informed, confident, articulate and highly professional, as well as immensely charming and radiating great warmth. His strong personality projected itself effortlessly, especially when lecturing or instructing, for which he had a natural talent. Stimulating, motivating leaders are all too few, but he was one and easily infected others with his energy and enthusiasm. In his mid-twenties he did not seem like a subaltern not long out of Sandhurst. To a superficial passing acquaintance at the School of Infantry he was not obviously marked for a tragic fate: rather, he was a man who was clearly going places. On the evidence of his annual confidential reports, the Army certainly perceived Nairac as an officer with a potentially great future ahead of him.

Patrick Mercer recalled that:

"I remember talking to him in the little canteen at the back of the RUC barracks in Crossmaglen. It seemed as if he had already lived a charmed and fascinating life – and as if he would be a distinguished and respected man in whatever path he chose to follow".

With the exception of Luke Jennings' *Blood Knots*, published in 2010, which concentrates on Nairac's pre-military youth and specifically on him as an angler and falconer, the best Nairac biography available to date is John Parker's *Death of a Hero*, published in 1999 and republished with new material in 2004 as *Secret Hero*. This biography however, limits itself almost exclusively to Nairac's military career, which lasted for less than five years (September 1972 to May 1977) out of just under twenty-nine. General Sir Michael Rose scathingly criticised it for inaccuracy, sensationalism and irrelevant padding in his review of 17 April 1999 in the English Catholic magazine *The Tablet*. He added, "Sadly, nowhere in the book does the deep spiritual nature of Robert Nairac emerge." This is correct: while John Parker and other biographers note Nairac's Roman Catholic faith, they seem to assume that it had faded or died as a result of his Northern Irish experiences. But was this really the case? Or did it remain central to his existence? The Benedictine monks, certain of whom remained his spiritual mentors even after he had left Ampleforth, certainly think so. A former officer who knew Nairac in Northern Ireland near the end of his life says that he could be "very Jesuitical, especially when expressing his views on duty and honour". So it would seem that he had not lost his faith or his moral standards. What was the truth about this man?

That would not be easy to establish. Some people, including his former Regiment, his old college at Oxford (Lincoln College) and the Ampleforth monks, were unexpectedly friendly and forthcoming. Thirty years after Nairac's death, some official papers had become available but there were still huge gaps in the story. Moreover, people in a position to talk often preferred not to. In some cases this was understandable. Because Robert Nairac's body has never been found, they had never achieved closure. Robert had left a terrible gap in their lives; his loss still hurt and they could not face going over it again. There was also a fear that there might be a factual basis for some of the dark rumours about him that, equally understandably, his surviving family and friends did not want to discuss. But more seriously, in the aftermath of the 1998 Good Friday Agreement there was a sense of official resistance, and not only in the UK, to reopening the case. Why rake that up again? Why upset our new friends the Irish Republicans? He's dead: just leave it alone! Anyway it was a long time ago and meanwhile the file has gone missing. Finally, in Ireland, or in some parts of it, the mention of Nairac still causes faces and doors to close. He was SAS; he was an enemy; he deserved everything that happened to him. Who cares about his family's feelings or where he is buried? Go away!

That Nairac is still controversial has been made evident on several occasions. Early in our correspondence a senior academic of Lincoln College, Oxford commented cautiously that "we are protective of our alumni's reputations; especially those who have been involved in controversy".

In 2013 a younger friend invited me to dinner at the Victory Services Club near Marble Arch in London. I went to the club from the Grenadier Guards' archive, where I had been doing research. My host was interested to hear what I had discovered that day. We were having pre-dinner drinks in the bar beneath the equestrian portrait of General Allenby. Almost everybody present in the bar would have had some connection, close or tenuous, with the Armed Services. Photocopied papers and photographs of Nairac were strewn on the table between us. We suddenly noticed that half of the people in that very large room had fallen silent and were clearly listening to our conversation. A large, muscular man with a very short haircut, who looked like a serving or former NCO, seemed to be making up his mind whether or not to beat me up. It was the mention of Nairac's name that had caused normally polite people within earshot eagerly to crane their necks, stop their conversations and openly listen to ours.

In 2014 a married couple of my acquaintance were drinking in a bar in Nairobi. This bar proved to be a watering hole of the Irish expatriate community. My friends fell into conversation with a beer-swilling Irishman with a thick South Armagh accent. The *craic* went smoothly and pleasantly until it emerged by chance that their son was serving in the British Army, in the Parachute Regiment. This did not go down well: the Irishman became abusive, damning the Brits, the Army, the Paras and above all Robert Nairac, repeating that "we", the Irish, had justifiably murdered him.

These encounters pointed to two things. Firstly, despite official reluctance to discuss Nairac, in certain circles it was evidently a claim to distinction to have had any kind of contact, however tenuous, with him. There were those who exaggerated, invented and repeated stories about him and their involvement with him. Secondly, because he was still the focus of so much emotion and controversy, it would prove incredibly difficult to get accurate information about anything that Nairac did, how he had lived or how he died. This proved to be correct: much that has been written about Robert Nairac, even by respectable authors and journalists, has turned out to be wrong.

Then there are the soldier memoirs of the Troubles. "No man but a blockhead ever wrote, except for money" said Samuel Johnson, and it is a safe generalisation that most modern British soldiers – certainly most other ranks – write about their experiences in order to achieve exactly that. Often this happens during a lean period of unemployment after leaving the Army. Andy McNab and Chris Ryan started out in that way, though they have gone on to greater things, including successful fiction writing. Since modern Army prose is concise, factual, accurate and unadorned, the former soldiers, on the instructions of their publishers, often employ ghost-writers.

The modern ghost-writer's brief is not simply to improve the author's prose style from plodding to readable; he or she is also employed to "sex up" the narrative with a view to maximising sales of the finished product. A few mentions of Nairac can still help to sell a book on the Troubles, by adding an extra pizazz to the narrative, even if the author in reality only met him for fifteen minutes or not at all. It follows that the accounts of Nairac in some military memoirs should be treated with care: for example there are a small number of lurid imaginary or embroidered episodes, including at least one involving Nairac, in Nicky Curtis' generally good Army autobiography, *Faith and Duty*. Curtis' former platoon commander confirms that these are the insertions of his ghost writer, at his publisher's request. So even contemporary accounts, or later accounts by contemporaries, had to be sifted carefully. They have been responsible for some Nairac myths.

These myths make a prospective biographer's task extra-difficult, even though Nairac died as recently as 1977. The fact that he has passed into folklore and fiction does not help. For example, in his "faction" novel *The Ultras*, Eoin McNamee insists that Nairac not only masterminded the infamous Miami Showband massacre of 1975 and was present when it happened, but that he personally carried out a number of other murders as well. Many readers seem to think that this novel is highly factual; it is not. Apart from errors about Nairac himself, it is also wildly inaccurate about falconry. No-one uses kites or vultures for hawking: certainly Nairac did not. *The Ultras* is inaccurate on other subjects too, but it is a novel; not history. Although it may be a good read, it is not a reliable source.

On the Irish Republican side, every successful Loyalist terrorist strike against Catholics or Republicans (*Note 4*) in the mid-1970s, and at least one by Republican terrorists against Protestants, is routinely laid at Nairac's door. The major crimes popularly attributed to Nairac are:

- 17 May 1974: The Dublin and Monaghan bombings. A large number of civilians were killed and injured in the course of these bombings within the Republic of Ireland;
- 10 January 1975: The Murder in the Irish Republic of IRA Staff Captain John Francis Green. A photograph of the dead man, said to have been taken by Nairac soon after killing him, is the piece of evidence on which Nairac's alleged guilt hangs;
- 31 July 1975: the Miami Showband massacre claimed the lives of members of one of Ireland's best and most popular boy-bands and of two Loyalist militiamen. Nairac has repeatedly been accused of planning this atrocity and of having been present when it occurred;
- 5 January 1976: The Kingsmills Massacre. On this occasion masked gunmen stopped eleven Protestant workmen travelling on a minibus, lined them up beside it, and shot them. One of the shot men survived, despite having been shot 18 times. A Catholic workman was unharmed;
- 15 April 1976: The Killing of IRA Staff Captain Peter Cleary, who was shot while trying to escape from SAS custody.

What is demonstrable from my research is that it was not humanly or physically possible for Nairac to have done these things, although none of this will deter conspiracy theorists. One journalist cynically put it that "If I had been planning to carry out a murder like that, I'd make damned sure that I had an alibi!" This is seemingly obvious, but Nairac's alibis appear to be cast-iron. Resourceful and intelligent though he undoubtedly was, it is hard to see how Nairac could have been in two places at once. Equally important is a comment by Julian Malins, who knew the youthful Nairac as well as anyone ever did:

"As a barrister, I meet quite a lot of murderers. It is part of my job. I am sure that Robert was not the type. He had some odd quirks, but was more of a masochist than a sadist. He had a dark side, but it was not [that]. Like Churchill, he suffered from 'the Black Dog' of depression at times. There was a gloomy, morbid side to his personality."

This is supported by a comment by Nairac's former Company Commander, Major Tom Lort-Phillips:

"He was a great all-round sportsman and very keen on boxing, but never a cruel and vindictive sort of person."

This view is echoed by other people who knew Nairac in the Army. He was a marksman: while they did not doubt that he would react quickly and with lethal effect in a fire-fight, to protect himself or others, he was not cold-blooded assassin material. His personal darkness was melancholy, not murderous.

Even though it is possible to demonstrate that Nairac could not have been involved in the crimes attributed to him, it has been argued that information supplied by Nairac to the RUC could still in some cases have got into the wrong hands and might have been used illegally by Loyalist paramilitaries like the UDA and the UVF, or even by the IRA. An objection to this theory is that in the 1970s the flow of information was almost exclusively in the other direction, from the RUC's Special Branch to the Army. During his third and fourth tours of duty in Northern Ireland, Nairac, in his role as a Liaison Officer, facilitated this process.

In 2003-4 the Republic of Ireland Government commissioned an inquiry chaired by a retired Supreme Court Judge, Mr Justice Henry Barron. Mr Justice Barron completed his investigation into the Dublin and Monaghan bombings in 2003 and concluded the inquiry in 2004. He had found no evidence of Robert Nairac's involvement. The Barron Inquiry did however find a chain of ballistic history linking weapons and killings under the control of a group of UVF and Security Force members, including RUC Special Patrol Group members John Weir and Billy McCaughey, that connected them to those alleged to have carried out the bombings. This Loyalist group was the Glenanne Gang. Incidents for which they were responsible "included, in 1975, three murders at Donnelly's bar in Silverbridge, the murders of two men at a fake Ulster Defence Regiment (UDR) checkpoint, the murder of IRA man John Francis Green in the Republic, the murders of members of the Miami Showband and the murder of Dorothy Trainor in Portadown in 1976. They included the murders of three members of the Reavey family (which helped to spark the Kingsmills massacre) and the attack on the Rock Bar in Tassagh". To date I have found no reliable evidence that Nairac even knew any members of the Glenanne Gang, although that cannot be completely ruled out; he had a very extensive network of acquaintances and contacts in Northern Ireland. Unexpected support for the view that Nairac had no involvement came recently from one of his Army contemporaries:

"There was an RTE programme aired last week [in June 2015] called *Collusion*. In short, it focused mainly on the FRU (Field Reconnaissance Unit or Force Research Unit, which was not formed until some years after Robert's time) and on the Glenanne Gang, about which there have been some Robert-related allegations. The programme contained an interview with one of the policemen involved and he made no mention at all of Robert. This was former Police Sergeant John Weir. He stated that there were a number of serving RUC officers who were part of the gang and I am certain that if there had been any link with Robert it would have come out in this programme. I think that it is quite telling that *no such claim was made*. Given that it is likely that the Glenanne [Gang] were responsible for the Seamus Ludlow shooting, which was also investigated by Michael Cunningham [*Micheal O'Cunneagan*], I think that leaves Robert pretty much in the clear. Any contemporary taint on Robert would appear to be based solely on his association with the area, rather than any association with people or events".

To complicate the picture further, some Loyalists believe that Nairac was a double-agent, or at least too sympathetic to the Nationalists – after all, he was a Catholic – and that successful Republican assassinations of their friends and relations can be blamed on information that Nairac had supplied to the IRA as part of some Faustian pact. In particular it has been suggested that Nairac was instrumental in setting up certain Ulster Defence Regiment (UDR) part-time soldiers, who were also Loyalists, in County Armagh for assassination by the IRA as a means to achieving his objective of infiltrating the Republican movement. The UDR soldiers all belonged to the Regiment's 2nd Battalion based in Co Armagh and operating in the Whitecross and Newtonhamilton areas in the 1970's. The son of one of the murdered UDR soldiers told *The Sunday Mirror* that his father's assassination had been orchestrated by Nairac. ''I am in no doubt that my father and at least four of his colleagues were set up by Nairac. He knew them individually, their movements, homes, everything. He set them up to be killed by the IRA. My father and his friends were sacrificed as a direct result of Nairac's efforts to infiltrate the IRA". Nairac is also alleged to have worked as a handler for a number of Loyalist paramilitaries. No convincing evidence of his involvement has ever emerged, but the rumours abound.

Several writers insist that Nairac was SAS. He was not, although in his last tour of duty he acted as Liaison Officer between them, 3 Infantry Brigade, other military units and the Royal Ulster Constabulary's Special Branch. He was usually referred to as the SAS Liaison Officer or SASLO. His formal relationship with the SAS is spelt out in his last Army annual confidential report:

"Captain Nairac has been the Special Air Service Liaison Officer at Headquarters 3 Infantry Brigade for 10 months. This task requires him to liaise closely with the Royal Ulster Constabulary (Special Branch), Brigade, unit and sub-unit headquarters. He also has special responsibility for the direction and continuity of Special Air Service Intelligence".

Nairac's office in Portadown was marked "SASLO". Some people still recall this. SASLO was one of Nairac's functions, but he was not a serving member of the SAS. He had some specialist SAS training; in anti-interrogation techniques, among other things, at Hereford, but so have many other soldiers who have not gone on to become SAS. The SAS have a training role towards the rest of the Army; Robert Nairac only ever belonged to the Grenadier Guards. That is why he is not commemorated on the SAS clock tower at Hereford, but in the Guards Chapel in Westminster. Moreover there is evidence that Nairac did not get on well with some members of that Regiment. While he was tough enough to have passed the physical and psychological parts of SAS Selection and had chimed extremely well with individual SAS officers and men, among them the then Major Michael Rose, the Selection interviews, in which both officers and other ranks participate as members of the interview board, could have posed a challenge. The fact that some other SAS officers and NCOs disliked and distrusted Nairac could have called into question his chances of success: "I couldn't work with that man" or "I just don't like him", from one member of the board would have been enough to exclude him. A former officer who knew and liked Nairac wrote: "I would agree with your assessment that Robert might well have been blackballed if he had attempted SAS Selection".

Then there are the "urban legends". One is that Nairac was the original of the fictional Captain Harry Brown in Gerald Seymour's best-selling novel, *Harry's Game*, later adapted as a TV mini-series starring Ray Lonnen. That is impossible. The novel was published in 1975 when Nairac was still alive, serving with his Regiment and not well-known. He only became famous after his death; Seymour never met him. Yet there are some striking parallels and *Harry's Game* now seems prophetic. At the time that Seymour wrote it, the story was fiction; later it became at least partially true. Another parallel is the rumour that Nairac, like Harry Brown, was of Irish descent; hence his emotional involvement with Ireland. He was not, although he might sometimes have given that impression. His origins are not in doubt. On his father's side he was French-Mauritian and Catholic. In some respects, including his appearance, Nairac was more southern French than English. His family can be traced to the Aveyron district of Languedoc, back to at least the sixteenth century. More recently his ancestors had lived in and near Bordeaux and latterly in Mauritius. His mother was English and Anglican, but of Scots and Welsh descent. Nairac never pursued postgraduate Irish Studies at Trinity College or University College, Dublin, though several authors firmly assert that he did. Although this is widely believed, he had no involvement whatever in the production of Ken Loach's 1969 classic film *Kes* (*Note 5*), nor did he supply any of the tame kestrels used in shooting the film. Nor, probably, did he as a very young man box a few rounds with the late Martin Meehan, who later became a senior IRA commander. Nor did he belong to the circle of old English Catholic Recusant families, although he knew some of them from his time at Ampleforth. He was never Head Boy at Ampleforth (*Note 6*), although he was Head of St Edward's House and a Monitor; nor did he abolish the caning of boys by Monitors: only the Headmaster could have done that. What he genuinely was and achieved is more interesting than the legends. Nevertheless it is easy to see why and how legends became attached to him, even while he was still alive. Like his friend Lieutenant Colonel "H" Jones VC, OBE, or like Lord Byron, with whom they both had something in common, he was a charismatic achiever, of whom almost anything could be believed: good or bad.

What might Nairac have done in the 1982 Falklands War, for example? "He would have won a VC without doubt. He was that sort of man", is the view of a former officer in the Parachute Regiment who knew Nairac well. There is agreement among his acquaintances that the fact that the Grenadier Guards were not in the event sent to the Falklands would not have stopped Nairac: he would have wangled his way there somehow. "H" Jones was going there as Commanding Officer of 2 Para: Nairac and Jones would have fixed up something between them. Jones was to join Nairac in Valhalla almost exactly five years after his murder. He would be killed in action at the Battle of Goose Green in May 1982, winning a posthumous Victoria Cross in the process.

No-one who met Nairac was ever indifferent to him. That may be one reason why he is still controversial. It seems that there were only three possible reactions:

- You became his friend – on his terms – and became deeply, permanently attached to him, even while recognising his fairly numerous irritating foibles and flaws. A large number of people, almost all of them men, fell into this category, from Peers to priests to policemen to poachers to private soldiers to ordinary people in England, Scotland, France and Ireland. Occasionally he would drive you up the wall. He often did not appear when you expected to see him and did appear when you did not; sometimes at midnight or very early in the morning – and would expect to be entertained at that hour with alcohol and conversation. One of his friends remarked about Nairac towards the end of his life that "Robert was in Northern Ireland but appeared irregularly [to see me in England] at odd hours of the night to unwind and gossip about life. He was a great if hopeless friend". The friend clarified that 'hopeless' in this context meant 'unreliable': "Like most of us in the days before mobile phones he was poor at letting one know when he was around and had a habit of turning up unannounced; and then he would disappear for months on end... None of this of course mattered, as one was always delighted to see him and enchanted by whatever adventure loomed";
- You disliked and distrusted him. Both socially and on duty you found him mysterious, incomprehensible, arrogant and impossible to get along with.

You worried about where his loyalties really lay. You were concerned about his unorthodox ways of proceeding. You thought that he was a security risk. This category included certain military colleagues, including some in the SAS;

• You were completely baffled by him. He was unlike anyone else you had ever met. Who is this guy and where is he coming from? This reaction is perfectly compatible with either of the above.

Maybe the Army should have the last word on him, for now: not from Nairac's memorial service eulogy, but from his Regular Commissioning Board (RCB) report; a comment written by Major General David Lloyd Owen in 1971 at the very start of Nairac's Army career, but less than six years before his murder:

"This is a high class young man... I believe that he will make a good all round Regular Officer; he has a lot of interests and is very good company."

This was accurate, albeit understated in a typically British way, but it was also praise by an immortal of the British military pantheon. David Lloyd Owen was one of the greatest-ever Special Forces soldiers and a disciple of Orde Wingate. During the Second World War he had commanded the Long Range Desert Group. Some military historians regard him as more influential than David Stirling himself. If that was Major General Lloyd Owen's considered assessment of the undergraduate Robert Nairac, we have to take it seriously.

It is tempting but potentially misleading to focus on Nairac's colourful "unconventionality" or "eccentricity". That is what his detractors, including certain politicians, authors and journalists have frequently done; usually as a prelude to making damaging allegations about his perceived lack of common-sense or moral scruple. It is an easy trap into which to fall: we think that we know where Nairac was coming from: that he was another flamboyant self-publicist like the late James Robertson-Justice or Nicholas Fairbairn MP, marketing himself like a "brand". The fact that he was a dandy and a falconer; was sometimes accompanied by spectacular birds – of the feathered variety – or by a spectacular Newfoundland dog – like Lord Byron (*Note 7*) – and that he was also deeply interested in the Middle Ages – like T H White, the eccentric author of *The Sword in the Stone* – lends colour to this perception.

Sir Michael Rose, however, made the important point in his 1999 review of John Parker's biography, *Death of a Hero,* in *The Tablet* that in many respects Nairac was very conventional. He was a churchgoing Christian. When not working undercover he dressed in a conservative, conventional way, like most Guards officers: suits from Savile Row, shoes by Lobb. He had a deep love for the traditions, discipline and history of the British Army; for British tradition in general, and for the British countryside. He chose to read History at Oxford at a time when fashionable people, even if they had attended distinguished Public Schools, often preferred to study the Social Sciences at new, more hip and "happening" universities like York, Keele and Kent. He chose the Army as his career at a time when it was not fashionable to do so. He chose to join a very conventional Regiment, the Grenadier Guards. His leisure pastimes: rugby, boxing, shooting and angling, were also conventional and as recently as 1939 or even later they would have been seen as normal activities of a gentleman of his class. Falconry might not have been, but it had been so in the past – for example, Oliver Cromwell, a middling country gentleman, was a keen falconer. Falconry virtually disappeared in Britain during the eighteenth century. Starting in the late nineteenth century, it experienced a modest revival in which Nairac participated. Had Nairac lived at an earlier period, before the First World War, he would no doubt have been outstanding in whatever career he chose to follow, but he would probably not have been seen as particularly eccentric. He was so perceived because he had no inclination to move with the times. He passed his short adult life in the late 1960s and 1970s: an era in which churchgoing had gone out of fashion; in which the traditions, discipline and history of the British Army evoked either fierce criticism or mockery, as did religion, self-discipline and idealism; an era in which standards had seriously slipped. Nairac wished to distance himself from it and to maintain the standards of a former age. Julian Malins concurs:

"I agree about his uniqueness as a character, but unique I think, only in the context of our time. He was a classic Romantic: Roman Catholic, full of knightly chivalry and personal quests for the Holy Grail and salvation etc., though honour and courage and self sacrifice..." *through*

For this reason Nairac stood out and appeared colourful and eccentric against the backdrop of the period in which he lived. However, his Catholicism apart, what Julian Malins wrote about Nairac could equally well have been written about most of the highly conventional young English officers, regular and volunteer, who in 1914 had eagerly and innocently welcomed the outbreak of the First World War.

Nairac was genuinely unconventional – original – as a soldier, in the sense that he was not afraid to challenge received military wisdom. He was a natural problem-solver: he had the ability to get to the heart of any problem; to "think outside the box" and identify unconventional solutions for new challenges. He also had the tact and political skills usually to persuade the authorities (including the RUC, as well as the Army) to adopt them. This was one of the things that the Army appreciated about him and it is reflected in the consistently excellent annual confidential reports that were written about him.

Over-emphasis of Nairac's alleged eccentricity renders much that has been written and said about him, especially by left-wing and Irish Republican writers, but also by some military critics like the late Clive Fairweather, wide of the mark. It would be difficult for most of Nairac's critics to draw his portrait in proper perspective even if their vision were not seriously distorted by political prejudice.

Nairac is not an easy subject to analyse and understand: in death, as in life, he is challenging. This mysteriousness may even have formed part of his charm. He may become more incomprehensible as time passes and he recedes further into the distance. This is because he belonged by temperament to a vanished age, the Edwardian, which had ended on 4 August 1914, thirty-four years before his birth. This was not a pose; it was just a fact. It may be explicable by his very conservative and religious upbringing in the 1950s; an upbringing against which he never showed any serious interest in rebelling. It might also reflect the fact that Ampleforth, like some other Public Schools, was still raising and turning out Edwardian empire builders after the British Empire had ceased to exist.

That lost Edwardian age was so near – well within living memory in 1948, when Nairac was born, and even in 1977, when he was murdered – and yet so far away. In Nairac's youth, prior to 1970, it was still possible to find worn Edwardian (and, less often, Victorian) penny coins in one's change, along with those of George V, George VI and Elizabeth II. Yet so much had happened since then: in 1914 Britain had been a great imperial power and the richest country in the world. Thirty-one years later, after two World Wars, it was bankrupt. Since then it has been struggling to find its feet again. A century after the Great War broke out, with our politically-correct witch-hunts and politico-religious fanaticism, we are in some respects closer in spirit to the seventeenth century than we are to the Britain of the optimistic and confident Edwardian age, seated amid peace, honour and plenty, and which seems very remote. Hardly any living person can now recall it at first hand (*Note 8*). Nevertheless, to begin to understand Nairac, we must try to view him through Victorian or Edwardian eyes. It is necessary to put aside all contemporary moral standards and principles: unfashionable abstract concepts like piety, duty, honour and patriotism were as real to Nairac as they had been to Gordon or Kitchener.

The questions that Nairac might have asked himself about his work in Northern Ireland would not have been: *Might I be violating this person's human rights? What are the official guidelines? Is this politically correct? Do I risk prosecution?* They would have been along these lines: *Can I, as a faithful son of the Church, in good conscience undertake this task? Is it in the best interests of my Sovereign and my country? Is it compatible with my duty and honour as an officer of the Grenadier Guards and a gentleman?* If in doubt he would have consulted a priest, preferably one of the Benedictine monks of Ampleforth. As a very traditional Roman Catholic, he believed in original sin and the Devil and had a fairly pessimistic view of humanity. His views were diametrically opposed to the fashionable consensus then, and even more so now, on a wide range of issues. He had no faith in comprehensive education, universal suffrage, the Social Sciences or the automatic progress of mankind, if indeed he gave them any thought at all.

Ironically, many of Nairac's posthumous critics, while sometimes showing ill-concealed disapproval of his Public School, Oxford and Sandhurst education, his membership of a Household Regiment and his inferred right-wing views, also seem to be tortured by a neuralgic class-consciousness that Nairac never for an instant knew: whatever else he may have been, Nairac was never a snob. These critics can neither understand nor empathise with his affectionate familiarity with his Guardsmen and other soldiers, with whom he used to box, play rugby and engage in horseplay, and who were devoted to him; nor with his immense pride in his Regiment, the Army and his status as an officer and gentleman. Nor do they grasp that, in addition to falconry, dry-fly fishing and shooting, which were upper-class pursuits, many of his other chosen pastimes, including swilling Guinness, singing in pubs, boxing, bare knuckle fighting, plain rough-housing and coarse fishing, were the literally coarse amusements of the common people, with whom he shared his enjoyment. At least one of his critics has professed to be shocked by Nairac's reported language, which was sometimes as foul as that of any squaddie, albeit pronounced in a cut-crystal Oxford accent. In the words of another soldier: "Gosh, we swear, we fight, and we fuck – how horrid!"

The Edwardian age was the last one in which imperialism, and its corollary of tough masculinity, were unashamedly celebrated in England. This means masculinity with all that that implies in the way of military virtues: duty, honour, stoicism, physical courage, exploration, conquest, cold baths and field sports. A quintessential Edwardian sportsman was Brigadier General Sir Claude Champion de Crespigny, Bart, who lived according to Spartan principles. Sir Claude wrote interesting sporting memoirs that Nairac would later read. Sir Claude greatly enjoyed shooting, riding, boxing, swimming, ballooning, sailing, hill-walking and "a cold tub before breakfast". In his view aristocratic sporting pleasures and military duty were closely linked. Unusually, Sir Claude had served in both the Royal Navy and the Army. He believed that every able-bodied male Briton had a moral obligation to help to defend his country by serving in the Armed Forces and could not be considered truly a man until he had done so. Members of the élite who declined to do this were, in Sir Claude's view, no better than the decadent pre-Revolutionary French nobility, dancing and laughing their way towards the precipice to the music of Gluck and Grétry. Sir Claude took pleasure in the successful military career of his extremely brave son, who served in the Anglo-Boer War of 1899-1902 and was twice recommended for the Victoria Cross. In the event Claude Champion de Crespigny Junior received the Distinguished Service Order (DSO) and Bar: i.e. the DSO twice over. These achievements Sir Claude attributed to the family enthusiasm for field sports:

"Men who have been good sportsmen at home are the men who will do best and show the greatest amount of resource when on active service."

Robert Nairac would have agreed. Although these sentiments might now sound dated and although some modern humanitarians may condemn both field sports and the Army, there is merit in Sir Claude's argument: accurate marksmanship, best acquired through game shooting and especially wildfowling, and marksmanship combined with cunning and the effective use of dead ground, essential for deerstalking, are equally applicable to, and necessary for, survival in the Infantry. Even angling has its place, if soldiers are living off the land while on campaign. So, at one time, had falconry and for the same reason; before accurate sporting guns became available, the falconers had supplemented the rations with game.

Books about falconry written in the Edwardian period are still consulted and quoted with respect today. Helen Macdonald, a modern falconer and author of the best-selling *H is for Hawk*, says of her first falconry books that "they were almost entirely written a long time ago, by bluff, aristocratic sportsmen who dressed in tweed, shot Big Game in Africa and had Strong Opinions... I was unconsciously soaking up the opinions of an imperial élite. I lived in a world where English peregrines always outflew foreign hawks, whose landscapes were grouse moors and manor houses, where women didn't exist. These men were kindred spirits". A similar process occurred with Nairac, who read many of the same books.

Elsewhere, Macdonald notes that: "falconers were a fellowship of men, a monkish élite, a 'small, tenacious sect' as Lord Tweedsmuir [*John Buchan's elder son, another falconer who favoured goshawks*] described them; who felt a love that ordinary people did not understand. It was a love that was not considered normal, and it was not something that they could help. Gilbert Blaine, the author of *Falconry*, published in 1936, wrote that 'deeply rooted in the nature of some individuals [exists] some quality which inspires a natural liking for hawks'". Today British and Irish falconers are numbered in their thousands but in Nairac's time they were indeed a "small, tenacious sect" of perhaps 300 falconers or less. Moreover the sect was divided into two unfriendly factions, affiliated either to the Hawking Club of Great Britain or to the British Falconers' Club, to which Nairac and his Oxford falconer friend Mark Allen belonged.

Another Edwardian phenomenon was the unapologetic celebration of male bonding (*Note 9*). Unfashionable as it may be today, this was of great importance to Robert Nairac, who is remembered by most of his male acquaintances as an outstandingly loyal and generous friend. Male bonding was celebrated in poetry as well as in prose; for example by the quintessential Edwardian poet, Hilaire Belloc. Belloc extolled his close friendships with "the men that were boys when I was a boy" and with his Oxford friends: "the best of Balliol loved and led me/ God be with you, Balliol men".

Rather like serving in the same Regiment, the activities of hunting, shooting and fishing with other men produce a bond unequalled in any other social interaction. It is an interesting coincidence that some of the most celebrated Edwardian sportsmen had in early life developed close bonds with their fathers or other older male relations, as Robert Nairac did. They tended to marry comparatively late in life, or not to marry at all. Nairac never married either and never seemed to be in danger of doing so although, had he survived, he might eventually have done so. Like Nairac, most of these sportsmen were also serious naturalists; some later became active in wildlife conservation and the creation of national parks. They sent seeds and specimens to Kew and other herbaria. The stuffed animals and birds that they shot enriched the collections of British natural history museums, including the Sunderland Museum, where the boy Nairac viewed them. Visits to such places kindled his wish to travel in Africa. He was to develop a strong affection for Kenya, a proverbially beautiful African country with which a certain type of romantic Englishman is apt to fall in love.

Nairac had a keen appreciation of beauty, although within the context of his own particular interests. This included landscapes, birds and fish, especially falcons and trout; his sister's collection of porcelain and his own weapons. A friend recalls a trip to a gunsmith in Gloucestershire to order a new stock for his gun. Nairac spent hours lovingly choosing a piece of wood with just the right grain.

All the Nairac family were talented; some of them were good linguists; some were musical and others were artistic. Some had a scientific bent: Robert Nairac's paternal grandfather, father and elder brother were impressively-qualified medical doctors. It is an interesting question how much of this rubbed off on Robert. Nairac was musical, played the guitar and had a good voice: he could sing Irish, Scots and Welsh folk songs beautifully, but he also liked belting out bawdy rugby songs. He was a skilful draughtsman, but he usually only drew or painted things that interested him, especially birds of prey and fish. A contemporary recalls his drawing a boxer (man, not dog) in the school art-room. The drawing was not anatomically perfect, but full of force, energy and life. While undoubtedly bright and well read, Nairac saw no intrinsic virtue in being intellectual, or in "deconstructing" a work of art. He was an intelligent man who had grown up in circumstances in which an appreciation of art, music and literature was taken for granted, but his personal taste for such things did not extend much beyond his own very particular interests. He would far rather have found himself on the rugby field, testing himself, than in a museum or gallery. If he enjoyed mediaeval art, the music of certain Classical and Romantic composers, or the poetical works of Chaucer, Malory and Tennyson, that was because they pleased him.

Nairac has been enshrined in the War Memorial Chapel at Ampleforth College, his old school, as a hero and martyr, along with Hugh Dormer DSO, the poet Michael Fenwick and Michael Allmand VC. All three had been exceptionally brave Amplefordian Catholic soldiers who died in action during the Second World War. Ampleforth's Combined Cadet Force now holds Nairac's dress sword, which is displayed in a glass case. There was formerly a Nairac Study Room at Sandhurst where, among other relics, copies of his medals were displayed. That no longer exists but there is a Northern Ireland Room in Victory Building, which is dominated by Nairac's portrait.

The Grenadier Guards keep an archive on Nairac, to which they rarely admit researchers. They also possess a number of his relics, including his bowler hat, still worn with plain clothes by Guards officers and now, in 2015, by almost nobody else. As well as the memorial window in the Guards Chapel, there is a memorial plaque in his village parish church at Standish and a heraldic stained glass memorial window in St Mary de Lode parish church, also in Gloucestershire, erected by the Royal Society of St George. Each year the local Branch of the Society holds a St. George's Day Service in Gloucester Cathedral, at which the Robert Nairac Youth Awards are presented by the Lord Lieutenant of Gloucestershire to young people who have demonstrated exceptional courage and integrity. These are among the remaining visible and tangible reminders of the enigma that was Robert Nairac (*Note 10*). no note!

There are other less-tangible reminders. If you are working or strolling near Wellington Barracks, Pirbright, Aldershot or any other base where the Grenadier Guards are stationed, you can sometimes hear the Regimental Band playing the stirring, sombre slow march *Nairac GC*. Colonel Stuart Watts, a former Grenadier Guards Director of Music, composed it. It was first performed by the massed bands at the Queen's Birthday Parade in 1991. It is a majestic march that was inspired by, and named in memory of, Robert Nairac. Some people find that it has the power to raise the hairs on the back of their neck the first time they hear it. On the second occasion it may move hearers even more deeply, if they are familiar with the main events of Nairac's military life. For it is a narrative piece of music, which loosely and briefly traces those events, ending with his murder by IRA supporters in 1977. It starts jauntily, with a swagger, but soon becomes dark, discordant and complicated. It ends with a brave display of trumpeted defiance; or possibly we are to understand that for Nairac, as for Mr Valiant-for-Truth in *The Pilgrim's Progress*, "he passed over, and all the Trumpets sounded for him on the other side". Impressive though it is, *Nairac GC* is also literally haunting; it conjures up the stain of a tragedy, and of a betrayal, that will not wash out.

CHAPTER 2 | THE MURDER, PART 1

Do not seek death. Death will find you.
(Dag Hammarskjöld)

Like much else in his short life, there is no consensus about what Robert Nairac was doing in the Three Steps Inn at Drumintee, County Armagh, late on the evening of Saturday 14 May 1977. It has been suggested that he had no business to be there, not having been authorised. That is not true. He was there in obedience to orders. He had sought authorisation in the correct way from the Brigade Major of 3 Infantry Brigade. This was Major Herbert "H" Jones of the Devon and Dorsets, who regretted giving it for the rest of his life. H's own life was also to end violently just over five years later, in the Falkland Islands. While making the supreme sacrifice H, who was by this time the Commanding Officer of 2 Para, would win the battle of Darwin and Goose Green, turn the tide of the Falklands War decisively in favour of the British forces and win a posthumous Victoria Cross (VC). His VC citation is as stirring as Nairac's George Cross citation. They had a lot in common.

H Jones and Robert Nairac were friends. Both were men of uncompromising integrity, who did what they thought was right "and to hell with the consequences". Both were original military thinkers who did not always do things by the book. To that extent were unconventional. However both were also career-orientated, professional and highly-regarded by most of their peers. Both of them had attended leading Public Schools: Eton in H's case; Ampleforth in Nairac's. Both enjoyed boxing. Both were slightly un-British: although both had been brought up in the UK, Robert Nairac's father was of French extraction and H Jones' was American. This gave them wider horizons than some of their contemporaries. Few people who knew them well doubted that both were destined for swift promotion. The proof of the pudding is in the eating: In 1979, two years after Nairac disappeared, H Jones was to be promoted Lieutenant Colonel. In 1981 he would receive the command of 2 Para. In 1982 he would be dead, but enshrined among the military immortals as a VC recipient.

In 1975 Robert Nairac, still aged 26 and only two years out of Sandhurst, was to have become Adjutant of the First Battalion Grenadier Guards; a position of serious responsibility (*Note 1*). According to his Army file, however, Nairac had spent so little time with his Regiment and so much time in Ireland (*Note 2*), that he was not in the event appointed. There were other unstated factors, including Nairac's own strong disinclination to accept the post. Instead, after a period training NCOs at Pirbright, he became the First Battalion's Reconnaissance Platoon Commander. At the time of his death, and following an unbroken series of exceptional annual confidential reports, he had been passed Fit for Immediate Promotion to the next rank (Major). "Fit for Immediate Promotion" normally means "fit for promotion as soon as a vacancy occurs" and not just when the seniority date rolls round. In this case the assessment bears the rider that the promotion should take effect as soon as possible. Nairac was to have been given command of a Company on his return from Northern Ireland in June 1977. He was also in line to receive a medal at the end of his tour for his outstanding service; probably an MBE on the Military List. Nairac knew about being passed Fit for Immediate Promotion and also the certainty of becoming a Company Commander. He should not have known about the recommendation for a medal but he might have got wind of it; he had good antennae.

Nairac's official job description from June 1976 to May 1977 was SAS Liaison Officer (SASLO) with 3 Infantry Brigade HQ, Northern Ireland (*Note 3*). He liaised between the Army, including the SAS, and the Royal Ulster Constabulary (RUC), including its Special Branch, while located mainly at Bessbrook Mill, a large former linen mill near Newry which the Army had taken over, fortified and used as a secure base, and where Nairac had a room. Intelligence was however at the heart of his "real" job. He had a number of Intelligence functions, which were not part of any normal Liaison Officer's job description. Given that he reported on some subjects directly to very senior officers, it is clear that he was more than just a Liaison Officer. This was not unusual, because Nairac was in reality a Military Intelligence Officer (MIO). MIOs often reported directly to the General Officer Commanding (GOC) and other senior officers whom they deemed "needed to know". Sometimes the mountain would come to Muhammad: the GOC would attend the MIOs' monthly meetings in person.

Again, unlike most Liaison Officers, Nairac also had an office at Headquarters in Lisburn, near Belfast. He had another office, or a share in an office, at Portadown. He moved between these three bases, so that it was sometimes difficult for colleagues to keep track of his movements. If he was not at one location, he was assumed to be at one of the others: sometimes he was at none of them. Furthermore, it has been suggested that he was working, on an informal basis, for or with one of the Agencies (MI5 or MI6), although confirmation of this is unlikely ever to be forthcoming. In the twenty-first century this would not normally be allowed: you may either work for the Army or for one of the Agencies, but not both. However, in Northern Ireland in the 1970s, it was different. An officer who served there at that time reports that helping MI5 and MI6 was unofficially "all but encouraged". Some people took the view that it was a potentially good career move. Moreover at that period many MI5 and MI6 officers had a background in the Armed Services; to come to their notice favourably while still in the Army could be helpful for a second career in one of the Agencies. There is nothing to suggest that Nairac was thinking along those lines; his commitment to the Army was deep. To his family, to some of his friends and in correspondence with his Regiment not long before his murder he had expressed his pleasure at the prospect of returning to normal

Regimental soldiering later in 1977. This was reasonable, given that his final tour of duty in Northern Ireland had proved to be very stressful; moreover he would be returning on well-deserved promotion.

A former Ulster Defence Regiment (UDR) officer who is not an uncritical admirer, but who seems to have known Nairac well, said from their first encounter it was obvious to him that Nairac was well trained in counter-surveillance techniques:

"He knew the ropes. He was clearly no ordinary Liaison Officer. He was much sharper than any others I had met. He asked very different questions. I soon realised this guy was not the 'rookie' that he wanted me to think he was."

This is independently confirmed by a former Captain in the Parachute Regiment, quoted by Desmond Hamill in *Pig in the Middle: the Army in Northern Ireland*:

"My soldiers had great respect for him. He knew what he was talking about and he knew his way round. He wrote some excellent papers about young people in the Ardoyne. He was always up to date with intelligence and was very good tactically."

H Jones, who was well-placed to judge, did not subscribe to a view that is often put forward, particularly in Press articles, but also by the late Colonel Clive Fairweather and some other former officers, that Robert Nairac was a maverick fool with a death-wish and more brawn than brains, who habitually took unacceptable risks. If he had thought that, H, who had strictly limited patience with fools, would not have liked and admired Nairac: he would have found a pretext to get him posted somewhere else. One of Nairac's former brother officers in the Grenadier Guards, interviewed in 1978 for a BBC Northern Ireland *Spotlight* programme, took a similarly positive line. In his view Nairac was not a rash risk-taker: if he took risks, they were calculated. Even as a student at Sandhurst on an Infantry exercise, faced with a tactical challenge, Nairac would adopt a potentially risky, original and unconventional solution. This would be one that the enemy were not anticipating and it usually worked. It is however a racing certainty that when Nairac sought authorisation to visit Drumintee on 14 May 1977, he did not tell H Jones that he intended to go alone and without backup. Jones would have taken it for granted that he would use backup, if only because he had done so when he went there the previous evening. This is confirmed by General Sir John Wilsey in his biography of H Jones: "Crucially, [Brigadier] Woodford and H were satisfied that Nairac always had adequate Special Forces backup from Bessbrook Mill", except that on that occasion he did not. It is also possible that H Jones was unaware that Nairac had in the past, no doubt for good reasons, more than once missed return and check-in deadlines. He had however always turned up eventually, none the worse for his adventures. When he failed to check in on time later that evening, it did not immediately set alarm bells ringing. By the time that the alarm was finally raised, six hours after it should have been, he was dead.

Due to the reluctance in 1921 of Lloyd George's Coalition Government to partition one of the historic six counties of Northern Ireland, South Armagh had remained within Northern Ireland and the UK and had not been permitted to join the Irish Free State. Following the Irish War of Independence, the Boundary Commission set up under the Anglo-Irish Treaty of 1921 to ensure that the new land border should "conform as closely as possible to the wishes of the population", had recommended that South Armagh should pass to the Free State. This did not happen, although in retrospect it is probably what should have happened. Resentment against the British Government, and against the Dublin Government that had accepted partition, had remained fierce ever since, making South Armagh a ready recruiting ground for the IRA. In 1919-22 there had been numerous murders of police, soldiers and civilians in the area. Much more recently, South Armagh had become officially recognised as the most dangerous posting for a British soldier anywhere in the world. This was still the case.

It is tempting to suggest that everything would have been fine if South Armagh had joined the Free State in 1921, but on past performance this was unlikely. Historically South Armagh has a problem not simply with the British authorities, but with authority in general. Disrespect for the Government of the day – for any government – is normal. Rebellion and any other type of crime, especially smuggling, is part of the way of life. But, had Armagh been partitioned in 1921, South Armagh would have become primarily the Free State's, and later the Republic's, problem, rather than the UK's. Even so, to judge from Toby Harnden's *Bandit Country*, whose historical background is well-researched, South Armagh would no doubt have remained a robbers' nest, a centre for cross-border smuggling and a focus of trilateral disagreement between London, Belfast and Dublin.

In the course of the Troubles, between 1970 and 1998, the South Armagh PIRA brigade would be responsible for the deaths of 165 members of the British Security Forces: 123 soldiers and 42 Royal Ulster Constabulary (RUC) officers. Most were young men, although they included Lieutenant Colonel David Blair, then commanding the First Battalion The Queen's Own Highlanders, who was forty years old at the time of his murder by landmine at Warrenpoint in 1979. Blair was vaporised; only his epaulettes were ever found. Seventeen other soldiers died with him. They died on the same day as Lord Mountbatten; another victim of the PIRA. Also in an older age group was the well-liked Roman Catholic RUC Inspector White, who was shot dead in his car a few miles from Forkhill, where he was stationed. In 1989 RUC Chief Superintendent Harry Breen and Superintendent Bob Buchanan were shot dead close to the border in South Armagh. They were the most senior RUC victims of the Troubles, on their way back from a high-level meeting with their Garda Siochana counterparts. Recent Garda reports have established that an Irish Republic policeman had colluded with the PIRA to arrange the ambush. In a separate category were the numerous part-time Ulster Defence Regiment (UDR) soldiers and former soldiers whom the IRA gunned down, blew up or disappeared.

By contrast, during this period only ten PIRA South Armagh Brigade members were admitted to have been killed. 6 were reportedly shot by the IRA as informers; 2 (James Lochrie and Sean Campbell) were killed in a premature explosion when a home-made landmine that they were constructing blew up, and 2 were admitted to have been killed by the British Army: not a great score. The last two men were important, however. One, Peter Cleary, an IRA Staff Officer, had been captured and later killed by the SAS while trying to escape on 15 April 1976. His story is erroneously believed by many to have a close relationship with Robert Nairac's. In reality Nairac had left Northern Ireland in April 1975 and did not return there until June the following year; he could not have been involved. The other important IRA victim was killed on 30 December 1990. This was Sinn Fein member and IRA volunteer Fergal Carraher, whom the Royal Marines killed near a checkpoint at Cullyhanna. His brother Michael Carraher survived, though he was badly wounded. He later became the commander of one of the South Armagh PIRA sniper squads.

The statistics quoted here are an IRA estimate and are certainly incomplete. They do not for example include Eugene McQuaid, who was blown up in 1974 by rockets he was transporting for the IRA, or PIRA volunteer Francis Jordan, shot dead by the Army in 1975 while planting a bomb, or PIRA volunteer Seamus Harvey, shot dead during a firefight with the SAS in 1977, although possibly by friendly fire.

Nor do they take account of the 75 assorted "civilians," of whatever persuasion, who also met violent death in, or in connection with, South Armagh in the course of the Troubles. Here are a few of them: seven-year-old Patrick Toner died when the IRA detonated a proxy car-bomb at Forkhill. A Protestant farmer, Hugh Clarke, was shot dead by the IRA on his tractor near Mullaghbawn. A Warrenpoint teacher, Liam Prince, was fatally injured when a soldier mistakenly opened fire after an IRA bomb attack near Drumintee. William Elliott, a Post Office worker, was shot dead by an IRA sniper, who had mistaken him for an RUC detective.

The South Armagh PIRA blew up Christopher Ewart-Biggs, the British Ambassador to the Republic of Ireland, in his car on 21 July 1976, soon after his arrival in Dublin. They stated that the Ambassador's murder was in retaliation for the shooting of Peter Cleary. In the only despatch that he was ever to write from Dublin: a short "First Impressions", Ewart-Biggs remarked perceptively that Ireland was a place where one should never mistake friendliness for genuine friendship. He might have added that Ireland is also one of those places where the past sometimes comes back to life. When it does, it usually proves lethal. Memories are long: "Now we'll get even for what your lot did to our lot in 1916," commented a local man in Crossmaglen to a newly-arrived Worcestershire and

Sherwood Foresters officer in 1976. Sixty years earlier, during the 1916 Easter Rising, the Sherwood Foresters had taken part in the Battle of Mount Street Bridge in Dublin, where they suffered heavy losses against a smaller force of Irish Volunteers. This skirmish was still vividly recalled.

Unlike North Armagh, there were relatively few large or significant Protestant communities in South Armagh. Nevertheless in the 1970s a number of Protestants still lived there but their lives were not easy. The IRA line was that Protestants should be tolerated provided that they did not become informers for the RUC or the Army. If they did, they would be killed; this applied equally to Catholics. But sometimes they were murdered anyway. Protestant farmers went about their work armed. Of the Orange Lodges in the area, one was a roofless shell even before the Troubles began: the IRA had burned it down in 1922 and no-one had ever ventured to repair it. The Tullyvallen Orange Hall among others had remained active until the IRA destroyed it in 1975, with considerable loss of life. Some Protestant church congregations were in terminal decline.

South Armagh was the one area in the six counties of Northern Ireland where, for various historical reasons and because of the poor quality of the land, the seventeenth-century "plantation" of Protestant English and Scots settlers had never properly taken root. It was still inhabited for the most part by deeply disaffected indigenous Irish people. The area had been anti-English and anti-British since at least the seventeenth century. It had long been the haunt of rebels and outlaws; all still proudly remembered by their descendants. A famous example is Count Redmond O'Hanlon (c. 1640 – April 25, 1681), the seventeenth-century *toraidhe* or *rapparee:* guerrilla, outlaw and highwayman. O'Hanlon was immortalised in folk tales that survive to the present day. The legends focus upon his Robin Hood-like ability to outwit the English Army, rob and terrorise the Anglo-Irish gentry. Writers and artists of the Romantic Era rediscovered him: Sir Walter Scott had considered writing a novel depicting O'Hanlon as an Irish Rob Roy. Although his title of Count was French - he had served in the French army with distinction - O'Hanlon was in reality a member of the old, dispossessed Celtic nobility and was probably the rightful Chief of Clan O'Hanlon. Ironically, in a narrative that is not exactly deficient in irony, he was murdered (like another famous Irish patriot, Michael Collins) not by the English but by his own side. In Poyntzpass, Co. Armagh, the local Gaelic football team is named "The Redmond O'Hanlons" in his memory. O'Hanlon is still a local hero. By the same token the modern descendants of informers and government spies are cold-shouldered. The South Armagh folk memory is long and unforgiving.

The area is dominated by Slieve Gullion. This mountain is the heart of the Ring of Gullion and the highest point (1,880 feet) in the county. On a clear day it offers spectacular views from the summit of places as distant as Dublin Bay and Wicklow. Villages around Slieve Gullion include Drumintee, Mullaghbawn, Lislea, Forkhill and Meigh. Slieve Gullion, a numinous place, plays a prominent role in Irish legend and history. Myths concerning Fionn Mac Cumhaill and Cu Chulainn are located there. Nairac knew these legends well. Redmond O'Hanlon was born at the foot of Slieve Gullion. By 1977 many British soldiers and RUC officers had met their deaths there: eighteen in 1973 alone, including three in a landmine explosion; another in a derelict house at Mullaghbawn. Robert Nairac's mortal remains are buried somewhere near Slieve Gullion, probably on the Irish Republic side of the border.

(handwritten margin note: ? doubtful)

"Bandit Country", the Army's nickname for the region, is accurate. In the South Armagh countryside the risk of ambush had forced the Army to rely heavily on helicopters, both to reconnoitre and to ferry troops. Foot patrolling was kept to a minimum; where it was unavoidable, helicopters were used to insert troops into the patrolling areas and evacuate them later. The Army operated a 'short tour of duty' policy. The advantage of this was that troops had an end-of-tour in sight and their exposure to stress and danger was of explicitly limited duration. The disadvantage was that the build-up of experience and local knowledge was also limited and the benefits of continuity were lost. Nairac, who had been in Northern Ireland for longer than anyone else, would supply the corporate memory.

Nairac had visited the Three Steps Bar and Lounge, to give it its full title, before. He was at an early stage in the process of becoming a "regular". When they were later interviewed by the police, some regulars recognised Nairac from photos, although the owner, Desmond McCreesh, said that he had definitely seen him only once, on 14 May 1977. McCreesh had thought that he was "a stranger". Nairac had previously passed undetected and almost unnoticed, which increased his confidence in going back yet again. In 1976 he had been given a briefing in which he had learned that the Three Steps was a known meeting place for Provos: Provisional IRA volunteers. His instructions were to infiltrate the premises; become one of the regulars; identify known PIRA members who drank there from the photographic records that he held, and make contacts. It went without saying that this could be dangerous: Nairac was not only likely to meet Provos, but everybody else in the bar would be a Republican sympathiser. In an area where everybody knew everybody else, any stranger could arouse interest or suspicion. Years later, Andrew Sanders, the co-author of *Times of Troubles: Britain's War in Northern Ireland*, learned from Belfast IRA volunteers to whom he was speaking about Nairac that even they, although IRA men, had stood out and felt conspicuous in South Armagh.

Clive Fairweather was later to remark to John Parker that Drumintee was a pretty remote place and "who in their right mind would ever go to Drumintee?" This was disingenuous: insignificant as it may look on the map, Drumintee was of special interest to the Security Forces. It was a hornets' nest of PIRA activity, as Fairweather must – or should – have known. The PIRA had regularly carried out major operations within a three mile radius of the village. These included a landmine explosion which had killed four soldiers, two other landmines which had killed an army explosives expert and a Private, and the shooting of a police constable and marksman. Everything favoured the PIRA, from the well-disposed population who informed, supported and protected them, to the intimacy with which the IRA knew the rugged, beautiful landscape, because they lived there, to the nearness of safe havens in the Republic a few miles away. In addition, the South Armagh PIRA included some of the most expert home bomb-makers anywhere on the planet. They were by far the most professional and dangerous Brigade of the IRA.

The Three Steps was a rebel shrine. It was and is an ugly modern bungalow with extensions, adapted as a bar. The RUC had burned down and demolished an older and larger pub, McGuill's Public House, on the same site in 1922. Commanding good fields of fire, the IRA had used it to ambush police patrols. In the nineteenth century there had been a soup-kitchen in the same building for victims of the 1845 Potato Famine. Murals on the Three Steps bar walls depict a Republican and Nationalist narrative of Irish legend and history. It was not a bar that any British soldier in his right mind would wish to frequent; even if the barman were willing to serve him, which was unlikely. Nairac would however be going there undercover, as Daniel or Danny McErlean, a visitor from Belfast. (In some accounts the name is given as McErlaine but this is not the correct or normal spelling. Nor is another variant, McElaine, found in the police notes.) If anyone should check on his story, they would discover that Danny McErlean was a real person, who lived, or had lived, in Belfast. A problem for Nairac's biographers is that there were two of them. Which one was Nairac impersonating on the night of his murder?

The elder Danny, then aged 24, had formerly lived in Belfast, where he worked as a motor mechanic. Since 1974 he had been on the run and had latterly moved to County Armagh, where he was living at the time of Nairac's death. It is not known for certain whether he and Nairac had ever met or were even aware of each other's existence, although that cannot be ruled out: Nairac was exceptionally well-informed. Danny was, or had once been, an Official IRA volunteer. The PIRA murdered this Danny McErlean in 1978, a year after Nairac. He was abducted and found shot dead outside Jonesborough the following day. Jonesborough is in the same Catholic parish as Drumintee, but that might seem to be the main, or even the only, link between the two killings. The PIRA stated that Danny was a criminal who had misused IRA guns for his own criminal purposes, and had thus been executed. The true reason could have been different. There are a few indications that Danny might have been suspected of collaboration with the late Robert Nairac. Given that Nairac was using that name, this theory is plausible.

The other Danny McErlean was then aged 21. He too had links to the IRA, although we do not know whether he ever became a fully-paid-up volunteer. His parents lived in Herbert Street, Ardoyne. He was known to Nairac from Nairac's days of doing outreach in Ardoyne in 1973. They had probably met at a sporting club for Catholic boys of that deprived area, where Nairac had coached the boys in boxing. He became friendly with many of them and with their Republican parents, despite being a British soldier. His Catholicism may have helped, although Nairac was also famously charming – the Irish were no less susceptible to this than anyone else. Moreover, he had helped the parents in practical ways, intervening on their behalf with the local authorities.

Nairac's outreach activity in Ardoyne in 1973 had an intelligence-gathering aspect. One result of it was a well-written paper classified Confidential, on the Fianna, the Irish Republican youth movement, to which many of his boxing pupils, including the younger Danny McErlean, belonged, and from which both branches of the IRA recruited volunteers. This is what he had to say about young Danny in 1973:

"His parents are honest Republicans. They are well respected decent people who are appalled that Danny is involved. Unfortunately he *is* involved. He is a very pleasant decent young lad who has been led astray. I hope that his father can keep control of him as it would be a great pity to turn him into a gunman. He does not wish to be left out, and the Fianna work on this – he is by no means dedicated and is not anti-SF (anti-Security Forces). I think that he can be detached and his father is sending him to England soonest."

It is not possible to be one hundred percent certain, but on balance it was probably the younger Danny McErlean whose identity Nairac stole, because he knew him well. There was a seven-year age difference, but Nairac was a youthful, even boyish, and exceptionally fit 28-year-old, who did not look his age. This Danny reportedly bore a superficial resemblance to Nairac. Both had dark curly hair. In 1977 both Nairac and the younger Danny McErlean were wearing facial hair, which can disguise the wearer's true age. The imposture was probably effective for most purposes. At a time when relations between the two wings of the IRA were exceptionally poisonous, it is conceivable that the fact that the two McErleans had links to the Official IRA, apart from anything that Nairac said or did, caused him to become the object of suspicion.

Nairac reportedly possessed a bogus Northern Ireland driving licence, and no doubt other documents, in Danny McErlean's name and bearing a Belfast address. Clive Fairweather stated that Nairac must have produced them, or had them produced, by himself: the Army would never have fabricated them for him, although in fact there was no need for the Army to have done so: Northern Ireland driving licences were not hard to come by. Unlike mainland Great Britain at that time, Northern Irish driving licences bore a photograph of the holder and were in effect used as ID cards. They had a blue cloth-bound cover with two paper pages. Blanks were easily obtained and the IRA would obtain them from contacts in the NI Civil Service. So did other people and there were many fakes in circulation. Nairac had left his British driving licence with other personal documents in the keeping of his uncle, Basil Dykes. He therefore had to drive around using a Northern Ireland licence, genuine or otherwise, and possessed more than one. Whichever licence he was using on 14 May 1977, it has never been found. The licence would have been on Nairac when he was kidnapped. It was not found in any of his rooms after his death and it was probably buried with him. Some accounts state that Nairac was using a slightly different name: Danny McAlevey. However, this seems not to be correct.

Nairac may have used McAlevey elsewhere and in other contexts; like an actor, he had multiple *personae*. They included military ones, as well as civilian, one being "Captain Charlie MacDonald of the Argyll and Sutherland Highlanders". He tended to use this *persona* when speaking to Loyalists. An acquaintance encountered him in this guise, with the Argylls in Scotland. He was taking part in an exercise as an observer or umpire. Interestingly, one (genuine) Argyll officer was heard to ask another: "Is that man really an Argyll?" To the Ulster Defence Regiment, which had been heavily penetrated by Loyalist paramilitaries, Nairac was known in 1976-77 as "Captain Charles Johnston". In addition to civilian "scruff order" disguises, he possessed a collection of Army headgear and other uniform items, which he would wear when he judged it right to do so. One of these hats was an SAS beret. This aroused the disapproval of genuine SAS men, who knew that he had not passed SAS Selection and had never been badged. Inquiries however revealed that Nairac had permission from "very high up" to adopt these disguises "when it was necessary for his work". If there was still any doubt, these permissions confirm that Nairac was more than just a simple Liaison Officer and that he was working for more than one master.

Various authors have told us that Nairac, under the name of "Danny McErlean", posed on 14 May 1977 as an Official IRA member, also known as a "Stickie," who had made Belfast too hot to hold him and who needed to escape discreetly to the Republic. He would need to know of a quiet minor or unclassified road to the frontier that would not take him near any checkpoints or patrols; he hoped to get local advice about this. His cover story was that he intended to meet Seamus Murphy – who is thought to have been the then most senior Official IRA officer in South Armagh – in the bar. In reality he was most unlikely to meet Murphy there. Seamus Murphy had renounced violence, was now working in local government and running an advice centre in Crossmaglen. As a result, he was no longer welcome in the Three Steps, which, as we have seen, was a Provo haunt. Nairac knew this; he had met Murphy on a number of occasions, although a Stickie newly arrived from Belfast could not be expected to be so well-informed. Murphy's brother Frank continued to drink there and was present on 14 May, but he had no affiliation with either wing of the IRA and was not the man whom Nairac hoped to meet. It seems odd that Nairac should have chosen a Stickie identity, given that he of all people was well aware of the animosity between the Official and the Provisional IRAs. However the information comes from the men who killed Nairac, not from him or a military colleague; it might not be entirely reliable.

On Saturday 14 May Nairac expected to meet a new contact or contacts. This is confirmed in an internal document, the Notes of a Meeting chaired by the Deputy Under-Secretary (Army) and attended by senior officials and military officers, at the Ministry of Defence (MOD) on 19 May, four days after Nairac's disappearance, when he was headline news. Nairac is described as having been "abducted while meeting sources at the Three Steps Inn in Drumintee". On leave in England in late 1976 and early 1977, Nairac had indicated to friends that he was close to a major intelligence breakthrough that would strengthen the Army's hand in South Armagh. Although he went into no detail, this could mean only one thing: that he believed that he had made tentative and indirect contact with a senior or well-informed PIRA source, who might be willing to become an informer and to reveal what he knew about the PIRA in South Armagh in exchange for a reward and a new identity. Nairac had apparently already been involved in the recruitment and evacuation of one informer, described in some detail in Nicky Curtis' book, *Faith and Duty*. He had been present in the Three Steps the previous evening, after speaking with a man outside Newry Courthouse and arranging to meet the contact, a third party, in the Three Steps. The contact, however, did not appear. According to witnesses, after drinking a Guinness and watching television for a while, Nairac had given up and left. On this occasion he had Army backup nearby, supplied by members of the COP Platoon of the Worcestershire and Sherwood Foresters.

The following day, Saturday 14 May, a caller with a strong South Armagh accent telephoned Bessbrook Mill twice, asking for "Bobby". This caller is presumed to have been Nairac's contact, ringing to apologise for having missed their meeting and to propose another date and time. The calls later proved to be untraceable. This suggests that they might have been made by a telephone engineer, or with his connivance, using a tap – which came in his maintenance kit – tapping onto the direct line into Bessbrook Mill from the telephone exchange or a junction-box, not from a private phone or call-box. Alternatively the tap could have been discreetly wired to an outside elevated telephone line. The telephone at Bessbrook Mill would still have rung normally. (The tap could of course have been stolen.) The caller has never been identified but he must have been the potential informer or someone speaking on his behalf.

The foregoing should not be interpreted as conclusive proof that Nairac was "set up" on 14 May. It is reasonable to infer that the caller, whoever he was, was nervous and being very careful. He did not want to be traced and identified by anyone. On the one hand, the untraceable way in which the call was made might suggest expert involvement, which in turn might suggest PIRA involvement. On the other hand, the manner of Nairac's abduction and death does not support this. Had it been a professional IRA kidnapping, the IRA would have taken Nairac away for a lengthy interrogation somewhere in the Republic and would not have killed him soon after his abduction without learning anything from him. That is the most persuasive evidence to date that the caller was benign; that Nairac was not set up and that his now-imminent murder was not premeditated by the IRA or anyone else. It simply happened, in a culture where mindless, homicidal mob violence with little or no provocation had become endemic and was seen as an appropriate response to anything even vaguely "suspicious". This had been the case in South Armagh not just since 1969 but for many decades; even for centuries. That mindset was not confined to South Armagh: the "Corporals Killings"; the brutal lynching of two off-duty soldiers in Belfast in 1988, is another, equally horrific example.

Nairac was not at Bessbrook Mill that afternoon. He had, against all the rules and without telling anyone, driven into the Republic of Ireland to go trout-fishing. That at least was his ostensible reason for visiting the Republic. According to a former fellow-soldier, Nairac took a third telephone call from the man after his return at teatime and again agreed to meet in the Three Steps later that evening. We shall never know what was said; Nairac spent the early part of the evening closeted in his room, preparing for his meet. He said very little about it to anyone else.

Nairac was co-located, and worked as a Liaison Officer, with the SAS and other military units. The SAS expected him to abide by their operating rules – which he did not always do. Had he done so, or had he really been SAS, the drama and tragedy of 14-15 May 1977 would not have happened. Had Nairac been carrying out an orthodox meet, he would have asked in advance for backup, in the form of a team of six men concealed near his place of rendezvous, well before his arrival. Nairac would have entered the bar, having agreed a pre-arranged radio signal with the backup signaller: typically, a faint double-click tapped out on a small radio concealed in Nairac's sleeve, every five minutes. It meant "everything's okay".

If the five-minute deadline was missed once, the backup team would prepare to move in. If a second five-minute deadline passed without a signal, they would act. Three men would have kicked down the front door of the pub, charged in and dealt with any PIRA men that they found inside. The other three would have covered the rear entrance in case there was any attempt to abduct Nairac that way. In addition to the external backup team, there would ideally have been another agent inside the pub, apparently unconnected with Nairac and ignoring him, but watching discreetly and ready to provide support or sound the alarm if required. In the event, this is not what happened. The SAS Operations Officer, Captain David Collett, stated that he had offered Nairac SAS backup, which could be organised in a few minutes. Nairac reportedly declined it. It was not that sort of mission, he said: he would only be away for a couple of hours and would be back by 11.30 pm.

In fairness to Nairac, the Army's, including the SAS's, textbook approach to backup was not ideal because the backup team, however discreet it was, and wherever it might be lurking, was far more likely to be spotted, identified and reported to the PIRA in South Armagh than anywhere else. Nairac was well aware of this and refers to it in his surviving military writings. As will become clear, the situation in that area and the threat posed by the South Armagh PIRA, were of a different order from those in the rest of Northern Ireland. The South Armagh PIRA was much more effective and sophisticated than its counterparts anywhere else. For example it often used sheepdogs to sniff out dug-in surveillance and backup teams: "undercover lurks", as they were then called. The local population were always vigilant and supportive of the IRA. Given the intense suspicion that unfamiliar faces could excite, it was preferable to operate alone if humanly possible. One stranger in a bar might be par for the course; two or more at a time might well arouse suspicion, except on a live band night. Then numerous "strangers" could be expected to be present, especially if the band was known to be a good one. Moreover the information that Nairac was seeking was for the SAS and other specialists' use, not the regular Army's. The SAS did not have its own intelligence-gathering capacity in Northern Ireland, so they relied on people like Nairac. There were very few similarly-qualified operatives available whom Nairac could have used as collaborators, to provide the right sort of cover that he would have required for an operation of this type. Secrecy was paramount: the fewer people who knew exactly what he was doing, the better. Nairac took very few into his confidence, and those he briefed on a strictly "need to know" basis. According to Martin Dillon in his book *The Dirty War*, Nairac's contacts, even with the RUC's Special Branch and military intelligence, were deliberately kept to a level that required liaison, but they were not developed operationally. It is now clear why.

Nairac's other reasons for not taking backup that night can only be conjectured: an obvious one is that he did not anticipate danger, or none that he could not deal with himself. He had after all been in the Three Steps before without mishap; without any incident at all. Another reason was that his contact had already shown himself to be very nervous. Explaining why he had not shown up the previous evening, he may well have said, "I realised that you had brought backup – others probably noticed it too – so I panicked and went home. Next time, come alone."

If it could be shown to be true, there might be a slight basis for the frequently-aired theory that Nairac was "set up" and that his abduction and murder were planned. If so, it would have been essential that Nairac should be induced to come alone, without backup. However the evidence is lacking. The only possible shred of supporting evidence is that witnesses saw him speak briefly with one of his abductors, Terry McCormick, early in the evening. We do not know what was said; McCormick has never revealed anything about it. It could have been something quite trivial, but Nairac might have gained the impression from it that this was the contact he was supposed to meet.

The last thing that Nairac wanted was for the SAS or any other soldiers to rush in while he was talking to his contact: that could easily happen. All that he would have to do was to miss the five-minute signal deadline through oversight, accident or gadget-malfunction and they would then charge in. The contact, and everyone else, would flee; the days, weeks or months spent cultivating him would be wasted.

A further factor may have been that Nairac's tour of duty was drawing to an end, the very next month. He had written to his Regiment a few weeks earlier, saying how much he was looking forward to his return to Regimental soldiering. He may have wished to tie up an intelligence loose end before handing over to his successor and leaving the Province. The imminence of his departure might have made him impatient, "boat happy" and therefore a little careless. Most of Nairac's former colleagues however stress that he was normally careful and cautious.

Nevertheless in some other acquaintances' view Nairac was a risk-taker. There is a curious link to falconry here. Helen Macdonald has pointed out that "Falconry was more like gambling, although the stakes were infinitely bloodier. At its heart was a willed loss of control. You pour your heart, your skill, your very soul, into a thing – into training a hawk, learning the form in racing or the numbers in cards – then relinquish control of it. That is the hook. Once the dice rolls, the horse runs, the hawk leaves the fist, you open yourself to luck and you cannot control the outcome. Yet everything you have done until that moment persuades you that you might be lucky. The hawk might catch her prey, the cards might fall perfectly, the horse might make it first past the post. That little space of irresolution is a strange place to be. You feel safe because you are entirely at the world's mercy. It is a rush. You lose yourself in it. And so you run towards those little shots of fate, where the world turns. That is the lure; that is why we lose ourselves, when powerless from hurt and grief, in drugs or gambling or drink; in addictions that collar the broken soul and shake it like a dog".

It is not far-fetched to link this aspect of Nairac's falconry to some of his other activities, which had included experiments with LSD at Oxford, hazardous sports and his dangerous undercover work in Northern Ireland, which in the end led to his death. Nairac had been living on adrenaline for months. He was still in his twenties and an adventurer, as many men tend to be at that age. One of his friends, a former Royal Marine officer, has explained what it felt like:

"Amongst other adrenaline-charged places, I served in Oman in the Dhofar War, and from my own experience that creates a sense of being able to do and risk anything; even 'walking on water.' I can quite understand Robert in that regard..."

That South Armagh was an adrenaline-charged place in 1977 is not in doubt. According to contemporary Press accounts, immediately prior to Nairac's abduction there had been repeated Provo threats to step up terrorist activity in the area because of the sustained presence and activity of the Security Forces.

Everyone was in a jumpy and trigger-happy state of "high alert": the SF, the IRA of both varieties, the Loyalist militias, their various supporters and ordinary civilians, just trying to get on with their lives.

What is now clear – although on this subject the informants are reluctant to be named – is that Nairac was in the Three Steps in obedience to orders. While he might be criticised for some of the things that he did and did not choose to do that fateful evening, like singing with the band and failing to use backup, some of the blame for the tragedy lies with the officers who issued those orders, rather than with Nairac who, if left to himself, only took calculated risks. This is also the view of others, including Martin Dillon. He may have only been a Captain, but clearly Nairac was an important operative; not just a Liaison Officer: being a Liaison Officer, a job that he did well, was his cover. Nor was he unique; just the first. As the Troubles unfolded, the use of undercover agents, sometimes posing as "ex-soldiers" or "deserters," claiming Irish Catholic ancestry and professing Republican sympathies, became a standard means of infiltrating the Republican paramilitaries. Nairac seems to have pioneered this strategy.

Stories that Nairac went to the Three Steps looking like an officer in plain clothes, in a sports jacket and cavalry twill trousers, with no attempt at disguise, are not correct. That evening he was "dressed down" in patched jeans or flared grey trousers, a shirt and pullover, either a donkey jacket or an anorak and workman's boots, or possibly scuffed suede desert boots (the accounts vary). He was also wearing a concealed 9mm Browning pistol with two magazines. This pistol had been modified for undercover use and was concealed in a shoulder holster that placed the gun under the left arm, so that it would not be detected by anyone brushing against him in a crowded location, such as a bar. So far, so good: but the night of 14 May was very warm and most people would be in shirt sleeves. Anyone who insisted on keeping his jacket on risked arousing suspicion; it might follow from this that he had a gun on him. Nairac did not, as has been alleged, leave his gun in his car. Latterly, even in England, he had been in the habit of always wearing it under his jacket. This gun was later found near the murder site in the Republic.

At 9.25 pm Robert Nairac left Bessbrook Mill in a red Triumph Toledo, a "Q Car" belonging to the Army, having told Captain Collett that he was going to the Three Steps in Drumintee and that he would be back by 11.30 pm. The Toledo was not unmarked but its number plate (CIB 4253) had been partially obscured by artfully-splashed "mud" – really cement – so that it could not easily be read. In addition the number plates of all pool cars were regularly changed. The car was fitted with a concealed microphone under the seat, a powerful radio (Callsign 48 Oscar) and a panic alarm button. Nairac called his base three times during his drive to Drumintee. At 9.58 pm he reported that he had arrived at his destination and that from now on, until the end of his meet, he would observe radio silence.

This was the last contact he would ever make.

Unlike the previous evening the bar was crowded, noisy and very lively. 150-200 people were present. As it was a Saturday night there was live music, provided by John Murphy's Band from Creggan. Because of the numbers the bar's owner, Desmond McCreesh, was sitting outside in his Mercedes, listening to the radio and making sure that everyone parked correctly. He was also alert to the possibility of car bombs being placed by Loyalists at his Republican bar and was checking the vehicles of anyone who looked suspicious. (Despite his care, McCreesh had already lost a teenage son, killed by a booby-trapped car-bomb. The bomb was probably an IRA bomb. Young Michael McCreesh died immediately; his companion Michael Gallagher was fatally injured.) McCreesh saw Nairac arrive, park at the furthest end of the car park from the pub, and then enter the bar. The car was backed into the parking space, ready to go, and facing the exit to the main road.

McCreesh checked the Toledo after Nairac had gone in. In his testimony to the RUC after Nairac's disappearance he said that apart from noting the mud/cement on the registration plates, he saw nothing that caused him concern. Empty cigarette packets were strewn on the back seat. The car was in need of a good valeting (*Note 4*). He later commented that he was sure that he had never seen the car before. That is quite possible: Nairac could have used other vehicles for his previous visits. Undercover officers never drove the same Q car two days running. McCreesh further stated that later in the evening he had also seen Nairac leaving – walking away from the bar towards his car, accompanied or closely followed by two other men – but he had thought nothing of it at that time.

Nairac entered the pub and shouldered his way to the bar. He ordered a pint of Guinness. Accounts of what happened next vary and are in some cases irreconcilable. However it is almost certain that Nairac did not succeed in meeting his contact. This leads to the next two questions: why had the contact once again not shown up? His failure to appear the previous evening might indicate that he was understandably nervous about doing so. Despite his telephone calls to Bessbrook Mill earlier that day, had he once again chickened out at the last moment?

Beside this must be set witness accounts that at one point in the evening Nairac had been seen talking earnestly to two men who were strangers to the bar's clientele. The two mysterious men have been identified as two of Nairac's killers: Maguire and McCormick. They were not really strangers, but were not regulars and had not been at the Three Steps often enough to be recognised by the owner and his staff. Was one of them Nairac's contact? Probably not, but the answer is not straightforward.

It is clear that Nairac did not know what his contact looked like – and vice-versa. For that reason and for simple security there had to be some kind of recognition signal. Soon after his arrival Nairac drew attention to himself by asking several people at the bar whether they had seen his packet of Major cigarettes, which had disappeared from the bar counter. This was presumably the recognition signal.

The response would have been something pre-agreed, such as "Sorry, here it is: my mistake", or "Try one of these; they're better". Although he made a fetish of his physical strength and fitness, Nairac both drank alcohol, especially Guinness, and was a moderate smoker of cigarettes; occasionally of a pipe. He had found that asking for a light was a good way of striking up a conversation with strangers. Major is a popular cigarette brand in Ireland, but is not readily available in the UK and was not Nairac's preferred or usual brand.

As a variation, some authors assert (notably Toby Harnden in *Bandit Country*) that Nairac reportedly seemed genuinely worried at the loss of his cigarette packet, although Major cigarettes were not expensive. They suggest that the packet, if it existed, might have contained a message or telephone number for the contact. However, it seems unlikely that Nairac would have left something so sensitive lying around. Moreover his contact, whoever it was, plainly knew how to reach him by telephone at Bessbrook Mill.

One small circumstance indicates that a recognition signal was involved. A woman who had been in the Three Steps the previous evening told the police that she remembered having seen Nairac there and had briefly spoken with him. She recalled that he had gone through exactly the same performance of the "lost cigarettes" on that occasion. This is too much of a coincidence to be an accident: Nairac was hoping that someone present would come out with the correct, pre-agreed response, but no-one did.

Either at this point or later, Nairac attracted the attention of the group of local Republicans who were to abduct and murder him, or help to murder him. They included Kevin Crilly, Danny O'Rourke, Pat Maguire, Gerry Fearon and teenager Thomas Morgan, all from Jonesborough; Michael McCoy from Forkhill; Owen Rocks from Killeavey; and Terry McCormick, who had recently moved to Jonesborough. All were Republicans and IRA sympathisers, but only two (O'Rourke and Fearon) were actually members of the PIRA, and they were very junior recent recruits. They were standing at the bar and were now watching Nairac closely.

There is no evidence to support a claim that is sometimes made, that a former boxing pupil from Belfast in 1973 was in the bar, recognised Nairac and tipped off the local PIRA, plausible though this theory may be. It is also possible, but to date unproven, that someone who simply knew him by sight from Ardoyne, which he had recently revisited in The Devon and Dorset's Regimental uniform, recognised him and became suspicious. Likewise it is quite true that because John Murphy's Band was highly-regarded and well-known, people might well have come to the bar that evening from further afield, including Crossmaglen, where Nairac had been in the habit of appearing in uniform and speaking to locals. He drank in pubs there and occasionally sang. It was therefore possible that someone from Crossmaglen might have seen and recognised him as a soldier. However the evidence of his assassins does not support any of these theories. They have repeatedly stated, including in court, that they had no idea who or what Nairac was, but had a hunch that he might be Army; specifically SAS, RUC, or something even worse: a Loyalist who was planning a strike against this Republican bar. It was a time of tit-for-tat murders and bombings by Loyalists and Republicans. In other words, while Nairac's carefully cultivated Belfast accent might have been good, it was possibly the wrong accent: more Shankill than Ardoyne. Less than a year after these events, some of his murderers confirmed to the BBC's Roisin McAuley their strong suspicion that he might have been a Loyalist paramilitary.

Owen Rocks subsequently claimed that Terry McCormick had told him, "We think that fellow at the bar is an SAS man. We're going to take him outside and give him a good hiding". Rocks said that he had then offered to help. Kevin Crilly and Daniel O'Rourke were also part of this conversation. However McCormick has not confirmed this. If true, this narrative suggests that, while violence was intended, murder was not. However there is other evidence to suggest that interrogation, which usually led to murder, was envisaged from the start and that McCormick was the ringleader. The accounts of the assassins are apt to be somewhat unreliable: they vary because most of them were arrested within a relatively short time of the murder and, having been caught, they were all keen to minimise their personal role in the killing and to shift as much blame as possible onto the others. Three went on the run in the USA and two, to date, are still there.

Of the men who would help to murder Robert Nairac, the most important witness is Terry McCormick, now apparently deeply remorseful for his actions:

"I am absolutely ashamed of what happened that night. I absolutely am disgusted with myself," McCormick said in 2007.

McCormick had been a serious amateur welterweight boxer and came from a family that had not historically been pro-IRA. His uncle and namesake, Terence McCormick, had served in the RAF in the Second World War, being killed in 1945. His name is on the war memorial in Larne. The younger Terry McCormick had recently moved from Larne to Jonesborough. He is almost the only one of Nairac's assassins who has been willing to speak about the murder other than in court, under cross-examination, and did so at some length to the BBC's Darragh McIntyre in 2007. He is a practicing Roman Catholic and has said that he prays for Robert Nairac every day: he has a lot on his conscience. Among other things, McCormick seems, with Maguire, to have been a prime mover in the plan to beat up Nairac, whether or not he expected it to end with his murder. He had also posed as a priest and tried to take Nairac's last confession, hoping to extract some useful information, minutes before the now badly-wounded man was murdered. This still troubles him. So does the fact that while he refused to shoot Nairac when ordered to do so, he did nothing to stop the murder, merely walking a short distance away to avoid witnessing the repulsive spectacle. His testimony is key to what happened next.

According to McCormick, Nairac, in his role as a counterfeit "Stickie," spoke to a girl to whom he confessed his bogus identity and asked whether she knew anyone who could help him find a discreet route into the Republic. The girl was surprised and suspicious and spoke to some men whom she knew to have PIRA links. They were, of course, McCormick and his friends. They too were suspicious, especially when they noticed that Nairac was keeping his jacket on during such a warm evening, and suggested that the girl should ask him to dance; if he did not take it off, she could put an arm round him to feel whether he was wearing a gun. Nairac laughingly said that he did not dance. The girl went back to the men and reported this: their suspicion deepened.

This account might be true but the girl has never been traced or identified. McCormick's story involving the girl has been widely accepted, but it is not corroborated by the others. It is quite possible that this part of his narrative is not true, or not completely true; an attempt to hide something else, perhaps to explain or justify what happened later. What seems to be generally agreed is that some people noticed that, on a very fine evening, Nairac insisted on keeping his jacket on and they wondered why.

How many times did Robert Nairac go to the lavatory on the last night of his life? This is not an irrelevant question as a number of unresolved issues depend on it. He had reportedly drunk one or two pints of Guinness. Most accounts state that he went there several times, more often than might be expected. On one of these visits two of his abductors, Kevin Crilly and Danny O'Rourke, alleged that they followed and challenged him to say who he was, while he was washing his hands. He reportedly answered in a Belfast accent that he was Danny McErlean and that he was in the bar to meet Seamus Murphy. However Terry McCormick firmly states that while it had been their intention to confront Nairac in the men's room, he never to his knowledge went there. Both accounts cannot be correct but Nairac's killers' testimonies frequently contradict each other. This leaves open the following questions: supposing that Nairac did in fact visit the lavatory several times,

- Did Nairac manage to meet his contact after all and exchange some information, verbal or written, while they were ostensibly washing their hands? In the light of what he did next, this seems unlikely;
- If Nairac had sensed impending trouble with which he might not be able to deal single-handedly, was he checking the windows in the lavatory, to see whether he could escape to his car that way? Again, it seems unlikely;
- But if so, why did he not accept the offer of Murphy's Band to leave in their vehicle at the end of the gig? They had sensed trouble brewing, but his later actions suggest that Nairac had decided he could deal with that himself. So, apart from the pints of Guinness, there must have been another reason for his reported visits to the lavatory.

The band-leader, John Murphy, was not present that night and his twenty-five-year-old son Sean was leading the band. Sean Murphy would go missing on 4 December 1981. He became one of the Disappeared, although not for long. He was found dead in his car when Dundalk harbour was dredged in July 1986. No cause of death has ever been established because his body was badly damaged and decomposed (berthing ships had crushed the car). But the inquest revealed that the car's ignition switch was in the off position. No paramilitary organisation has ever claimed responsibility for his murder but it is thought that the South Armagh PIRA killed him, for reasons known only to them. There is no firm evidence that Sean Murphy's death was linked to Nairac's killing, but it is a strange coincidence. Moreover, yet another Murphy, a band member, *had* tried to help Nairac to avoid the fight that preceded his kidnapping and murder. It is just possible that Sean Murphy was killed in error instead of Edmund Murphy. The IRA have made similar fatal mistakes.

Edmund Murphy, the band member in question, later recalled that he had seen Nairac with a group of five or six men in the bar. He added that he had seen him go to the lavatory more than once in a very short period. This conflicts with McCormick's testimony. His last visit was around 11.15 pm, after which Nairac did something that seems unwise, but may have been the only thing that he could think of. Nairac was musical. Not only did he play the guitar, but he had a good voice and knew many Irish songs by heart. He offered to sing along with the band and gave them the key in which he wanted to sing. Introduced by them as "Danny, the whole way from Belfast", he gave rousing renderings of two vintage Irish rebel songs, *The Broad Black Brimmer of the IRA* and *The Boys of the Old Brigade*. There was a lot of applause; so much, that the band invited him to stay on the rostrum and sing some more. Nairac was happy to oblige. After singing three more songs, he rejoined the men with whom he had been speaking earlier.

As with the Major cigarettes, it is possible that this was a recognition signal intended for Nairac's contact. This has been suggested by Michael Cunningham, the author of *The Nairac Affair*, published in 1981. If his contact was in the pub, he would now know for certain which of the drinkers was Danny McErlean/ Nairac. As far as is known, however, Nairac did not meet his contact as a result of this initiative. There is another equally plausible explanation for Nairac's decision to sing with the band: he simply could not resist doing so. Luke Jennings recounts the following incident in his book *Blood Knots*. It took place before Nairac joined the Army, while he was still at Oxford. The two friends had been successfully angling for trout near Ampleforth, where Jennings was a pupil, and at sunset had gone to a remote rural pub for a drink. Within a short time Nairac was the centre of attention. Despite the silence and stares that the entry of a stranger can provoke from the regulars of such country pubs, grinning his easy grin, he soon had the place at his feet.

"Pubs were Robert's theatre... He was at once the maverick toff, the life-and-soul raconteur, the poacher with a pocket full of trout. And while no-one completely believed in these *personae*, everyone at some level wanted to, because they seemed to stand for the old values and better times. All of this was less a matter of calculation – although calculation did enter into it – than of instinct. He wanted to make people feel good around him and he knew just how to do it. Later, there would be those who would express reservations about his need for centre-stage visibility and approbation. But that was later."

Nairac was to repeat this feat, not once but many times, in England, Scotland and in Ireland as well, including Belfast and even Crossmaglen, where he was known to be a soldier. His magic still worked, and at one level he literally was a magician, causing his audience to suspend disbelief; to see and hear what he wanted. However the outcome in Drumintee would not be so happy. We may legitimately ask why he, who was so enviably accomplished, should have needed this explicit "visibility and approbation"? We shall return to that later.

Although it may give an enjoyable adrenaline rush, centre-stage visibility carries obvious risks. To quote a different sort of entertainer and sporting star, the Irish-American wrestler Kevin Robert Kiley Junior, who wrestles under the name of Alex Riley:

"You're a total personality. From the moment you walk through the curtain, they see everything. You're not covered at all... they can see your face at all times... can catch the way you're feeling, what you say, the way you look, how you move at any moment once you start performing. It's very difficult to learn how you've always gotta be in character".

Nairac also had to be in character all the time when working undercover, not making a single mistake. But he seems to have slipped up.

Later Nairac went back to the band; not to sing but to talk with them as they were packing up. In the course of this conversation Edmund Murphy accidentally hit Nairac over the head with his guitar and apologised. The time was about 11.35 pm and the bar was emptying. As they were packing, Edmund Murphy noticed two men near the door who seemed to be waiting for someone. He guessed that this someone was Nairac. Sensing trouble, Edmund Murphy suggested that he should leave with the band but he refused the offer. Having stowed his equipment in the van, Murphy returned to the bar to be paid by McCreesh. It was now just before midnight. Murphy did not see Nairac again, but he did notice that the two young men, McCormick and Maguire, were still hanging around outside the bar; still apparently waiting for a third party to emerge. This suggests that Nairac was still inside the building. A little later, soon after midnight, Murphy heard and saw a scuffle at the far end of the car park. Four or five people seemed to be involved. He assumed that it was an "ordinary brawl." At this point the band drove away.

Nairac had been aware of the interest of the two men, one of whom was the former boxer McCormick and it probably did not bother him. Although only five foot ten, Nairac was an unusually strong man and a good middleweight boxer. He was not a pushover; still less "a lamb to the slaughter", to quote Clive

Fairweather. Moreover, he enjoyed roughhousing. Two incidents will serve to illustrate this.

Late one night, early in his time at Oxford, Nairac was followed by a gang of four skinheads. They saw a lone undergraduate "toff" walking back to his college and thought it might be fun to beat him up. They had picked on the wrong man.

The inevitable question came: "Want a fight, you bastard?"

"Yes!" was Nairac's cheerful reply. He was happy to punch it out.

Nairac put them all into Accident and Emergency. There was awkwardness with the Lincoln College authorities – soon forgotten – when the incident came to their notice. Other than that, Nairac came out of the incident undamaged.

Nairac's publisher friend Martin Squires (quoted in John Parker's *Secret Hero*) has described how, even after he had gone down from Oxford and was a serving Army officer, he would dress down in "scruff order" and get into fist-fights in Irish pubs in North London, roaring with laughter as he did so. Not that his fights were confined to North London; Squires once saw Nairac beat up a minicab driver in Kensington.

There is more than one story on record involving Nairac and a minicab driver who tried to overcharge him. He had the aggression and confidence to put the driver firmly in his place, which was out for the count, and a couple of half-drunken Micks should not prove too challenging. *Bring it on!* as Nairac might have said.

There could however be a completely different explanation for Nairac's nonchalant behaviour on this occasion. On balance this seems the more likely: a simple case of mistaken identity. He may genuinely have thought that one of the two men who had been waiting for him, and who were now following him to his car, was the key contact he should have met that evening. Something that McCormick had been seen to say or whisper to him in the bar earlier could have given him that wrong impression. Finally he was about to encounter his contact in the flesh and perhaps learn something important. Although they had arranged by telephone to speak in the bar, it had been exceptionally crowded and noisy; not ideal for an important and sensitive conversation. If the contact preferred to speak in the car park or at some other quieter location, that was fine by him. *Okay, let's go! Follow me.*

Normally footsteps in the dark, especially then, especially in Northern Ireland, would set alarm bells ringing, would make anyone nervous and put them on their guard. So Nairac must have been feeling cocky, confident and secure, thinking that he knew who he was dealing with. He walked on, confidently and unwittingly, towards his rendezvous with death, with Maguire and McCormick walking behind him.

CHAPTER 3 | THE MURDER, PART 2

Thou shalt seek me in the morning, but I shall not be.
(Job 7.21, Authorised Version)

Nairac should have returned to Bessbrook Mill at 11.30 pm on 14 May. At 11.45 pm he was fifteen minutes late and had not broken radio silence. Captain David Collett, the SAS Operations Officer (*Note 1*), was not yet seriously alarmed, given what he had heard about Nairac's track record of lateness. He checked again at midnight; still no sign of him. At this point Nairac should have made a mandatory radio check. He did not. He was now thirty minutes late. According to the rules, there was now no alternative to reporting that Nairac had failed either to return from his meet at the agreed time or to make contact, thereby activating the procedures which applied when a soldier had gone missing. HQ 3 Brigade and the Royal Ulster Constabulary (RUC) had to be informed. The RUC would inform the Irish Garda and they would then mount a joint search operation. Senior Army officers would also have to be notified and, if necessary, woken up. Captain Collett was reluctant to do this. At five minutes past midnight on 15 May Collett telephoned his Commanding Officer, Major John Sutherell, who agreed that they should wait a few more minutes.

But at fifteen minutes past midnight, 45 minutes after Nairac's agreed return time, there was still no word. Major Sutherell decided to consult Major Clive Fairweather, who was at that time GSO2 Int/Liaison, the General Staff officer responsible for intelligence based in Northern Ireland. It has never become clear whether Fairweather knew that Nairac had planned a meet in Drumintee for that particular evening. He later claimed that he had no idea. Clive Fairweather, who lived off-base near Lisburn, stated that he had been out to dinner with a male friend at a restaurant in Saintfield (County Down) near Belfast and had returned home at about 11.00 pm. Fairweather however could not be reached immediately. This suggests either that he had not in fact returned at 11.00 pm, but later, or that he had not gone directly home. He might for example have stopped off at a bar on the way. Although Fairweather was not on call or on duty that evening, it is odd that he was not contactable at all, given the job that he was doing. It would have been normal for him to carry a bleeper in the days before mobile phones and to give those who might need to contact him in an emergency the numbers of any restaurant or friends' houses at which he would be that evening. He had not done so. Nor had he arranged for another officer to cover for him during his absence at dinner, although this was to be expected if he was going out. At some point well after midnight, Fairweather finally received the message that Nairac had gone out alone without backup and had not returned from a meet. Nairac was now about an hour overdue.

Fairweather, on his own admission, had a drink problem. He admitted this long after he had left the Army and become HM Inspector of Prisons for Scotland. It is likely that, even if he had only been enjoying a convivial dinner, he had taken alcohol that evening – probably quite a lot. According to him, his drink addiction had started during his time in the King's Own Scottish Borderers, who at that period had something of an alcohol culture; in this they were far from unique among the Scottish Infantry. Too often the attitude was that to be a proper man, you had to be able to drink everyone else under the table. Fairweather's need to hit the bottle had, perhaps understandably, become more acute in stressful Northern Ireland, although at no stage does the Army seem to have noticed it officially. A former officer, who served under Fairweather in the early nineteen-nineties, when the latter was Chief of Staff at HQ 52 Brigade in Edinburgh, mentioned his very excessive drinking even at that late stage of Fairweather's Army career. Fairweather, who died in 2012, did not seek treatment or counselling during his Army service. This has a possible bearing on his actions and omissions in this story, as alcohol could have clouded his judgement at the time and affected his later recollection of what he had or had not done.

Fairweather, who had crossed swords with Nairac before, recalled that he had sometimes been late and missed deadlines in the past. Fairweather knew this because officers who offended in this respect were fined and Nairac had been fined more than once. Because raising the alarm would have involved getting senior officers out of their beds, the two officers agreed to do nothing for the time being. Hopefully Nairac would turn up. All of these delays, however reasonable or understandable, were fatal to Nairac. Strictly speaking, Collett broke the rules, Sutherell went along with this and Fairweather is beginning to appear in a curious light. If the missing officer had been someone he cared about, a member of his own Regiment or someone with whom he had not clashed, would he have delayed taking action for as long as he did? Again on his own admission (for example to John Parker, who quotes him in *Death of a Hero*), he cordially disliked and distrusted Nairac and Nairac had ridiculed and played practical jokes on him.

Nairac had crossed swords with Major Sutherell, too, over the SAS's killing of an important PIRA volunteer the previous January, whom he had wanted captured and kept alive for interrogation. Sutherell was a very correct and conventional officer, originally commissioned in the Royal Anglian Regiment, which he would later command. Two separate witnesses have said that Sutherell, like others who dealt with Nairac, never got the measure of him and never in reality managed him at all. He was only one year older than Nairac, and like many of his colleagues he was impressed by Nairac's exceptional knowledge and understanding of Ireland. Moreover Nairac had been in the Special Reconnaissance Unit (SRU, usually called NITAT (NI) at this period) in 1974-75, based at Castle Dillon. Sutherell's assumption seems to have been that Nairac knew what he was doing and that it was better to adopt a "hands-off" approach. According to a former colleague: "He (Sutherell) is a good bloke, decent and law abiding, wiry rather than strong, not your typical 22 SAS man: honourable, introverted, will always do his duty... He was confused about Robert: they were polar opposites, really." Another said: "He lacked confidence and needed always to be surrounded by stronger subordinates. None of this is critical – he's a good bloke".

In fairness to the SAS, there was no precedent of which they were aware for Nairac's disappearance. No other British officer had ever been abducted by the IRA in the course of the Troubles. It therefore seemed sensible to consult Clive Fairweather who, unlike Nairac, had been "one of them" and who claimed to have local knowledge. A further possible reason, advanced by Toby Harnden in *Bandit Country*, is that the SAS simply did not know what to do. Northern Ireland was alien territory to most of them and the operating rules were different from those which had applied in Oman. They were out of their depth. So they turned for guidance to Fairweather.

Some authors refer to Fairweather as an SAS officer. This is correct up to a point. He had served with the SAS in, among other places, the United Arab Emirates, Oman and Jordan. He was to serve with the SAS again. In 1980 he would play a role in the Iranian Embassy siege. He would be second-in-command of 22 SAS during the 1982 Falklands Conflict. However in 1977, as GSO2 Int/Liaison in Northern Ireland, he was not currently with the SAS and had formally reverted to his parent Regiment, the King's Own Scottish Borderers (KOSB). This might not have been obvious because, as GSO2 Int/Liaison, he seldom wore uniform. Despite his official KOSB status, it is probably accurate to say that Fairweather had kept a strong visceral loyalty to the SAS, where he still had friends. It is reasonable to assume that he would have been alert to any possible developments that might adversely affect the Regiment or its reputation, which a year earlier had received a battering over the Border incident on 5-6 May 1976.

Fairweather had wanted to bring Nairac under his control, which Nairac had successfully resisted. He and Fairweather had clashed, mostly over what Fairweather perceived as the lack of supervision of Nairac's activities. On his side Nairac was not inclined to take lessons from Fairweather, who had only arrived in Northern Ireland in January. Admittedly Fairweather had served there previously, but some years earlier. Nairac's knowledge of Ireland as a whole and of Northern Ireland and South Armagh in particular was deeper and more up-to-date than Fairweather's, as he may have implied in the course of their conversations.

At 1.00 am Fairweather agreed that the SAS should send up a helicopter. The crew reported seeing Nairac's car in the Three Steps car park. No other cars were there and the Toledo appeared to have been damaged. Soon afterwards an SAS ground team was sent in and reported signs of a struggle. Coins and cigarettes were scattered about: a lot of blood had been spilled on the gravel. They did not touch or investigate the car for fear that it might be booby-trapped. It was now fairly clear that Nairac must have been captured, taken south of the border and quite possibly killed. That would be bad enough, but Nairac had an encyclopaedic knowledge of the SAS's activities in South Armagh and elsewhere, as well as the RUC's. He had served four tours of duty in Northern Ireland and knew it better than anybody else in the Army. If he was still alive, being expertly tortured or drugged in a "safe house" in the Republic, he might reveal any amount of sensitive and compromising information. The fact that Nairac was an exceptionally tough man would not make much difference; it would simply take the IRA longer to break him and extract the information and he would still be shot at the end. His one chance of survival would be if the IRA decided to keep him alive as a potentially valuable hostage or to produce him in the Republic at a Press conference, to embarrass the British Government. Neither of these possibilities could be ruled out for the moment. Still the SAS did not report Nairac as being missing, nor did they inform senior officers or the RUC or activate emergency procedures. Why not? According to SAS Major C:

"[Nairac] had left us in a quandary. We weren't sure what he had been doing. He could have been screwing some lady, all sorts of things could have happened. There was very little we could do before first light because it might have been a come-on or the car could have been booby-trapped. We were left high and dry and Nairac had actually endangered the lives of a lot of our guys."

This was untrue. The SAS knew, because Nairac had told Captain Collett, that he would be at a meet; they knew exactly where he would be: at the Three Steps, and they knew that he had arrived there at 9.58 pm because he had radioed in at that time. They also knew that he was supposed to return at 11.30 pm and failing that, he should have made a radio check at midnight. When he failed to do so, they could have alerted a detachment of the Worcestershire and Sherwood Foresters who were stationed very near the Three Steps and asked them to investigate. We can dismiss the comment about "screwing some lady". Nor is it clear how Nairac had "endangered the lives of a lot of our guys," unless SAS Major C really believed that he had taken his Filofax with him when he went to the meet. Major C was later to make other hostile and dismissive comments about Nairac. The animosity between Nairac and certain members of the SAS was an important factor in his tragedy.

"There was very little we could do before first light", is not true either. There were many other things that the SAS, or Fairweather, could and should have done immediately, without waiting for first light. Their priority should have been to alert Brigade, who would alert the RUC. This was vital because if Nairac had been taken south of the border, the Irish police, the Garda Siochana, had to be involved immediately if there was to be any hope of rescuing him. The Garda refused to have direct contact with the British Army; all contact had to be made through the RUC. If the Irish Army was also to be involved, as in the event it was, it had to be activated through the Garda. All this took time, so time was of the essence – and time was being wasted. The SAS should also have alerted senior British Army officers.

A possible, albeit unsatisfactory explanation for the delay is that if any of Clive Fairweather's later comments can be relied upon at all, he had already given Nairac up for lost. "At this point it really became a search for his body," he observed laconically in an interview. Wrong again: in fact, Nairac was still alive at 1.00 am, but his hours were numbered. He seems to have been murdered at about 2.00 am, or fairly soon after that. For whatever reason, Nairac was posted as "missing, presumed dead" very soon after he disappeared. On 18 May he was already being referred to as "the late Captain Nairac" in MOD internal minuting.

It was not until 5.43 am – about six hours too late – that Fairweather finally took the decision to alert HQ 3 Brigade and through them the Royal Ulster Constabulary. By this time Nairac was definitely dead. The reason for this further delay has never been convincingly explained.

The timing of 5.43 am has been questioned. Evidence given at Kevin Crilly's (*Note 2*) trial in Belfast in 2011 seemed to indicate that the RUC may have opened a serious incident log at 4.30 am on 15 May on Nairac's being reported missing. If that was indeed correct, a concerned soldier acting on his own initiative must have alerted them; presumably someone other than Fairweather or Captain Collett. This could have been Nairac's close SAS friend, Tony Ball (*Note 3*), ringing from Hereford on his own initiative, with whom Fairweather had spoken briefly; even so, it was still far too late. At 4.30 am Nairac had been dead for two hours or more. This discrepancy cannot be otherwise easily explained.

Having handled the response to Nairac's disappearance badly, the Special Forces now quietly withdrew from involvement in the search operation and let the "green army" of conventional soldiers, with their greater manpower resources and their more numerous helicopters, take over. In Northern Ireland the search became a joint Army-RUC operation. In the Republic the Garda would shortly become involved too. So would the Irish Army (*an t'Arm*). The search for the missing officer would involve over 300 troops and 100 extra police officers in Northern Ireland alone. Numerous civilian volunteer searchers also took part on both sides of the border. Army foot patrols scoured the area around Drumintee and roadblocks were set up to check and monitor the movement of vehicles in the border area, which was now completely shut down on both sides. Up to twenty helicopters circled overhead.

Although Robert Nairac had personally been on good terms with the RUC Special Branch, relations between the RUC and the Army in general, including the SAS, were less cordial and trusting. Now the RUC were furious that they had not been alerted long before. It was difficult to explain why they had not been. The Irish Republic authorities, especially the Garda, would make similar angry complaints and the Irish Government would formally protest through diplomatic channels. Senior MOD officials now had to give an explanation to Ministers that would be both believable and acceptable. This would prove challenging. It would be a maniacally busy Sunday for all of them.

In the event the Army's official explanation was a masterpiece of disinformation. According to a letter classified Confidential and dated 24 May from the Ministry of Defence to the Northern Ireland Office, the Irish authorities had no grounds for complaint: "Captain Nairac's car was discovered at 0430; 3 Infantry Brigade were informed at 0500 and at 0615 they asked the RUC to inform the Garda. We presume that this was done shortly afterwards". Although this letter was signed off by a senior MOD official, it reflects Fairweather's line, expressed verbally then and later.

A misleading narrative had been put together by Fairweather and the SAS for Ministerial consumption – the timings are all-important:

- 10.00 pm: Nairac leaves Bessbrook Mill alone to meet a source, irresponsibly giving no indication of his destination. (He actually departed at 9.25 pm and arrived at the Three Steps before 10.00 pm) He has not told the SAS, Fairweather or anyone else where he is going or what he is planning to do.
- 11.30 pm: Nairac leaves the Three Steps pub accompanied by two men. He is never seen again. (In reality he left, having been kidnapped, sometime after midnight.)
- (Time unknown): Fears grow that Nairac may be missing. The SAS have no idea where to start looking. Fairweather authorises a helicopter search at first light. Search begins.
- 4.30 am: Allegedly by luck, Nairac's car is "discovered" in the Three Steps car park. There are signs of a struggle. A ground party is sent in who confirm the SAS's worst fears. Fairweather urgently consults 22 SAS in Hereford.
- 5.00 am: 3 Infantry Brigade are informed. (In reality, at 5.43 am)
- 6.15 am: 3 Infantry Brigade inform the RUC and ask them to inform the Garda.
- 9.00 am: Evidence of a "scuffle" is found in the pub car park.

So, according to this version of the narrative, the RUC and the Irish authorities were informed as soon as possible. This narrative, or a version of it, is fed to Ministers, who then unwittingly mislead Parliament and the public. A similar narrative is also sent to the Irish authorities through diplomatic channels.

The following is what actually happened:

Saturday 14 May 1977:
Prior to his departure, Nairac has sought and been given authorisation for his meet by 3 Brigade's Brigade Major, H Jones. Everybody who needs to know has been informed about where he is going, when and why.

9.25 pm: Nairac leaves Bessbrook Mill after a short conversation with the SAS Operations Officer, Captain David Collett. He reportedly declines an offer of SAS backup. He makes radio contact three times during his drive to the Three Steps.

9.58 pm: Nairac arrives at the Three Steps and radios to Bessbrook Mill that he is at his destination. He will now observe radio silence until after his meet. He enters the Three Steps.

11.30 pm: Nairac should have been back at base, according to his own estimate.

11.45 pm: Nairac is now 15 minutes late. Captain Collett starts to get uneasy but is not yet seriously alarmed.

00.00: Midnight mandatory radio check. Nairac fails to make contact and cannot be contacted. At this point the alarm should have been raised, but was not.

Sunday 15 May 1977:
Sometime after midnight: Nairac is attacked in the Three Steps car park. He loses his Browning pistol. He is beaten up, bundled into a car at gun-point and driven away.

12.15 am: Collett and his CO decide to contact Fairweather but have difficulty getting hold of him. When they finally do so, at an unknown time, Fairweather instructs them to do nothing.

1.00 am: Collett reports to Fairweather that there is still no sign of Nairac and there has been no radio contact. Fairweather sends up an SAS helicopter followed by an SAS ground party. He has a short conversation with Tony Ball and a longer one with persons unknown at 22 SAS, Hereford. Brigade, the RUC and the Irish authorities have still not been notified.

2.00 am or soon afterwards: Nairac is murdered.

4.30 am (there is some doubt about the timing and origin of this call): Someone, possibly Tony Ball, contacts the RUC. They reportedly open a Serious Incident file.

5.43 am: Fairweather finally informs Brigade. After a further delay Brigade inform the RUC. The RUC inform the Garda. Both police forces are furious at the delay that has been allowed to elapse before they were notified. The Irish authorities protest to the British authorities.

There is now an intensive search for Nairac on both sides of the Border. The PIRA dispose of his body. SAS officers ransack Nairac's room at Bessbrook Mill. His Army ID card, his ID discs (both of which carry details of his blood group) and his Filofax disappear. Highly classified files are found among his papers. These too are removed. So are other items, including "something very significant", which is never identified or produced in evidence. Shortly after this, Nairac's room is locked; no-one else is allowed to enter it again without authorisation. However, the evidence that it still contains has been contaminated.

Monday 16 May 1977. The PIRA announce that they have "executed" Captain Nairac after interrogation. They claim that he revealed a lot of information before he died. The first Press reports of his abduction appear. There is panic when the SAS let it be known that Nairac's Filofax, which contains details of many of his contacts, and of British Army officers who live off-base, is missing. The SAS and Fairweather claim repeatedly that "he has put a lot of our men's lives in danger". The RUC and the Garda ask the Army in Northern Ireland for details of Captain Nairac's blood group. The Army states firmly that it holds "no record" of his blood group.

Wednesday 18 May 1977. A misleading report about Nairac's last hours, as outlined above, is given to Ministers and others.

Thursday 19 May 1977. Captain Collett shows Nairac's room to Detective Sergeant Swanston. DS Swanston searches it and removes several items, including one of his hair brushes: some of his black hair is adhering to the bristles. Soon afterwards an SAS officer clears the room. He throws out or destroys a large quantity of "rubbish". No further investigation of this evidence is now possible.

There are important discrepancies between the official version of Nairac's last hours and what really happened; not least in the timings. The use of the word "discovered" when referring to Nairac's car is extremely misleading; it implies that no-one had a clue where Nairac had been; that a search for Nairac had begun soon after it was realised that he was missing; and that finally, after several hours, his car had been located at the Three Steps. But that was where it had been all along and the SAS knew this. Nairac had gone there on SAS business. It was from the Three Steps that he had radioed in for the last time: that should have been the first place to be investigated when the Army began to fear that Nairac was missing.

Nairac should have been reported missing, and the emergency procedures for that event activated, at the very latest when he missed the mandatory midnight radio check. At that point he was still at the Three Steps and would shortly be fighting off the mob. Sending up a helicopter at 1.00 am, followed by a visit by the SAS ground search party, was unnecessary and a waste of valuable time. The helicopter party registered the fact that Nairac's Q car had been damaged. This was confirmed by the ground party: the windscreen and a wing mirror had been shattered and the headlights broken. There was blood in and around the car. "Analysis is being carried out by the RUC Forensic Department", read a Secret Minute to the Minister of State from Defence Secretariat 10 (DS10). This was the Division within the Ministry of Defence (MOD) that during the 1970s was responsible for providing policy advice to Ministers and military staff concerning the Army's involvement in Northern Ireland and for playing a liaison role between the MOD and the Foreign and Home Offices. The Minute did not mention that the Army would not be co-operating with the RUC Forensic Department. Urgent requests for information about Nairac's blood group were being stonewalled.

A misleading account, classified Secret, of Nairac's last hours was given to Ministers on 18 May. This was essentially the Fairweather narrative. It was signed off by a Colonel with an illegible signature in GS MO4, MOD. According to this, "Captain Nairac was briefed at SAS HQ Bessbrook". This is the only known reference to any SAS briefing, as opposed to a very short conversation about backup with Captain Collett. If it had been true, which it probably was not, this detail might seem to provide additional confirmation that Nairac was about SAS business that evening. "It was established at 0900 hours that a scuffle had taken place in the car park of the pub", wrote the author of the report, with breathtaking understatement and inaccuracy: the timing is wrong by eight hours. "Scuffle" hardly covers the extreme violence involved; the extensive damage to the car, Nairac's copiously shed blood, and the teeth and hair found in the car park. The author of the briefing added that, "Two companies of 1 RRF (1st Battalion Royal Regiment of Fusiliers) have been deployed for search duties, but so far no further trace of Captain Nairac has been found." Nor would it be; the opposition had been given several hours' start. Roadblocks had not been put in place until 7.00 am, according to the MOD; much later, according to other sources.

Fairweather had indeed telephoned 22 SAS in the UK. Their ability to help was limited, given that they were in Hereford. At least some of Fairweather's consultation seems to have been about damage limitation and reputation management. His act of ringing them may also have been intended to deflect later criticism that he had done very little between 11.45 pm and 5.43 am. On the contrary: he had sent up a helicopter, followed by a ground search party, and he had called 22 SAS; although to very little purpose, as far as rescuing Nairac was concerned. Rescuing Nairac, as opposed to crisis-management, does not seem to have been high on Fairweather's list of priorities.

At Hereford, Major Tony Ball (*Note 3*), was very concerned for Nairac. He pressed to be allowed to return immediately to the Province to assist in the search. Ball had recently been serving undercover with Nairac in Northern Ireland and could have made a useful input. He said that he had a shrewd idea with whom Nairac had been in contact and who might have been involved in his abduction. However, Fairweather declined his offer of help. We shall never know what special information or expertise Tony Ball might have contributed; he was killed in 1981 in Oman, where he was working for the Sultan as Commander of the recently-founded Omani Special Forces, almost exactly four years after Nairac's death.

"Dan", a former Ulster Defence Regiment (UDR) soldier, who wishes to remain anonymous, was on duty in a UDR operations room the night that Nairac went missing.

"We knew from the radio traffic something major had happened. There was a lot of activity over at brigade in the early hours. When the helicopters went up at first light we knew someone had either been shot or was missing."

It was only later, when a photo of the missing Grenadier Guards officer was circulated, that he realised exactly with whom he had recently been working. He had known Nairac as "Captain Charles Johnston". The Army's reaction showed how important Nairac had really been.

Major H Jones would spend the next four days leading the search for Nairac, mainly from Bessbrook Mill. Personal factors increased the urgency of the operation for H. Nairac had become one of his closest Army friends. Hard man though he was, H's distress was evident at this time. He enlisted the help of Nairac's large Newfoundland dog, Bundle, who had a keen sense of smell, in the search for his master and he also asked his young son (now Brigadier Rupert Jones) to "pray for Robert, who is missing". Given the delay that had elapsed before emergency procedures were activated, H Jones feared the worst.

In Gloucestershire the news had to be broken privately to Nairac's parents. His uncle Basil Dykes (*Note 4*), who was Nairac's nominated next-of-kin, could not be located. The Army then "press ganged" the only available family member, Basil's younger daughter, to travel to Gloucestershire to help them to break the news to Maurice and Barbara Nairac. They drove her to Standish.

Meanwhile Basil and Mary Dykes were fishing with friends in the Pyrenees near Biarritz. It took several days to track them down. On receiving the news, Basil abandoned his holiday and drove straight to Standish to join his sister and brother-in-law. He never spoke a word throughout the long journey. A close bond had existed between him and his nephew. In Basil's words, "my wife and I had gone to France on the fateful day in May 1977 and it was some days before we were contacted through a friend living in France who did in fact know Robert through fishing with us".

It is unclear why Nairac had nominated Basil to the Army as his next-of-kin, given that his parents and two of his siblings were still alive. It is not normal Army practice to "cherry pick" next-of-kin. One of Nairac's former commanders has suggested that in Nairac's case it could have been because of the undercover job that he was doing. Basil Dykes would have understood what Robert was going through better than anyone else:

"My personal feeling is that he felt particularly close to this man who was not only his uncle, but also someone who resonated a hundred percent with Robert's temperament, and he felt that if he should be killed he would want Basil to be the first to know."

Before he left for Northern Ireland for the last time in 1976, Nairac had confided a box of personal papers, which included his British driving licence, to his uncle who had kept it in a secure place in his office. Apart from the licence, we know nothing whatever about the contents. Did they include a revelatory "in the event of my death" letter? The box still existed in 1992, when a family member saw it, but in 2014 a diligent search in the archive of Basil Dykes' former law office yielded nothing. The box and its contents had disappeared.

Nairac seems to have been more open with Basil Dykes about the risks that he was running in Northern Ireland than he was with his immediate family. One factor that may have drawn them together was that Basil's only son had gone to Canada at a young age and enjoyed it so much that he remained there for most of his working life, visiting his family in the UK irregularly. In his absence Basil welcomed the visits of his sporting, military nephew who was so like himself in many respects. After Nairac's parents moved to Gloucestershire in 1967, he and Basil Dykes saw a good deal of each other. Both were keen anglers; both were enthusiastic shots. Basil would sometimes ask his shooting hosts to include his nephew Robert in their invitations to him, which they were happy to do; he was good company and an excellent shot. They shot together for the last time a few months before Nairac's abduction and murder. When Nairac was murdered, according to his family:

"[Basil] was terribly cut up about Robert's death... he went out alone into the garden and sobbed his heart out. He, who was not a man given to tears. Besides being his sister's son, Robert had lived a life that Basil could admire and respect. Unlike his own son, far away, living a rather erratic, wandering life in Canada, Robert was there in the UK, a soldier, doing the 'right thing'. Although half Scottish and half Welsh, and an ardent Francophile to boot, Basil was very English at heart. For example, he admired Edward Heath... partly at least because he had commanded 'her Majesty's oldest Regiment' [the Honourable Artillery Company]... there was probably a bit of the old soldier thing in there too".

When it became clear that his family would never see Robert again, it was Basil who would reply to the many condolence letters. To at least one friend he wrote:

"The last thing Robert would have wished is that people should mourn for him. One must try and remember the example he set and do justice to his memory".

Long before Basil's death in 1992 and Barbara Nairac's in 1999, it would become painfully clear that many people on both sides of the Irish Sea were determined that justice should not under any circumstances be done to Robert Nairac or his memory. Some were Irish Republicans; others were British Left-wing politicians, but yet others were or had been in the British Army. From time to time his detractors still publish their views and their version of events in the media and online.

For a long time after his murder Nairac's mother was to cling to the hope that he might eventually turn up. She hoped that he might prove to have become a hostage, being held at a secret location. Her brother Basil had reappeared safe and well, weeks after being reported missing in action, at Dunkirk in 1940. Then, too, the family had prayed. Perhaps God would be gracious and answer their prayers once again? Maurice Nairac was not so optimistic. Less than two months earlier, in March 1977, as he ran Robert to the airport in his car, he had warned him that "you must be starting to get known there" and had asked Robert to take special care. Mr and Mrs Nairac had now lost both of their sons; both tragically and both in their twenties. Neither had been married nor left any descendants.

The media had started to take an interest – reporters were converging on Bessbrook and Drumintee – but the Army were not yet willing to release Nairac's name. All that they would confirm was that a Grenadier Guards officer was missing and was thought to have been kidnapped by the IRA. Far away in Yorkshire, hearing the news on the radio, the monks of Ampleforth Abbey had no doubt as to what had happened. They reacted immediately: "That's Robert Nairac!" They hastened to pray for him too. Like H Jones, they feared the worst. Their certainty that Nairac was the missing Grenadier Guards officer was based on more than a hunch or intuition. Nairac had remained in touch with some of the monks since leaving Ampleforth in 1966, just over ten years earlier. He still regarded certain of them as his spiritual counsellors or mentors. He had been more open with them about the reality of his work in Ulster and the risks that he was running, than he had been with his family.

No truthful account of Robert Nairac's murder can exonerate him from a degree of responsibility for his own tragedy. Given that he had orders to be at the Three Steps in Drumintee for his undercover work, his decisions not to use SAS backup and also to sing with the band were both questionable. On the other hand he had often visited Republican bars, including the Three Steps, and sometimes sung in them, without mishap; there was no reason to think that this evening would be any different. There is a view that others must share the blame, both in asking too much of Nairac and above all in the strange lack of urgency in their reaction when it became clear that he really was missing.

Nairac might have been saved, despite his errors of judgement, if the military authorities had reacted appropriately and quickly when they should have done: at 11.45 pm or midnight at the latest, for there was backup available very close to the scene of his abduction. Even though he had refused SAS backup, a detachment of the Worcestershire and Sherwood Foresters, which was about a surveillance task, was in the vicinity. According to the former Foresters Corporal who was the detachment commander, "at the time of his second visit we were a little further to the east [of the Three Steps] on a feature we called 799, which was the height of the feature, [where] we set up bashas for that night." The very same team had provided backup cover for Nairac at Drumintee the previous evening, so they knew the lie of the land. On that occasion their brief had stated that the Three Steps Inn and its car park were becoming of interest: they were to observe the area between 2000 and 0100 hours but only to get involved if they saw anything unusual happening. This would have covered fighting, such as would occur during Robert Nairac's abduction the following evening. Their instructions for 14 May were different and made no reference to the Three Steps.

The Foresters were not aware of what Nairac was doing and he may have been unaware that they were nearby. But if he had been, that might explain why he had declined SAS backup as being unnecessary.

The window of opportunity for Nairac's rescue was a narrow one but had the Foresters been alerted by midnight, they could have been with him within minutes. Even had he known about them, Nairac could not easily have alerted them to his danger, but others, notably the SAS detachment based at Bessbrook Mill, could and should have asked them to go and check the Three Steps. Sending them in would have been less costly than sending up a helicopter. The SAS did not do so; either they had forgotten the existence of the Foresters' detachment, which seems most unlikely, or – much more likely – they took a decision not to involve them. So the Foresters remained on Hill 799, unaware of the drama that was unfolding nearby.

Curiously, Ken Livingstone, many of whose pronouncements about Nairac have proved to be wildly inaccurate, seems to have picked up this detail: "Some have claimed that an Army unit was operating near the Three Steps pub where Nairac was captured by the IRA, and did not intervene to save him", he wrote in *The Independent* newspaper in 1999. That is partly true, but the Foresters did not intervene because they were oblivious to any danger. Livingstone's information is presumably hearsay from an Army source, but others got wind of it too. Some soldiers seem to have spoken remarkably freely to reporters immediately after Nairac's disappearance became public knowledge. On 17 May *The Scotsman*, for example, reported that:

"Colleagues said that Captain Nairac was an extremely able and very tough professional soldier who left as little to chance as possible. But he spoke with an Oxford accent and in a South Armagh pub he would 'stick out like a sore thumb' whenever he opened his mouth."

This was an odd and indiscreet comment by a soldier who was probably an officer. Given Nairac's acting ability and his practiced Irish accent, we know that this was not the case.

The Scotsman continued: "It is understood that Captain Nairac told his base at Bessbrook exactly where he was going and that some form of back-up was provided." (The latter statement was demonstrably untrue.) "What form this took is not being disclosed because of the risk to other soldiers carrying out similar tasks... Military sources said: 'It is reasonable to presume that he had been seen by a lot of local people who would know that he was a soldier, but people are not stuck out on their own. One of the rules we have around here is that support is available at all times.'" Except that it was not, on this occasion.

The surveillance operation by the Worcestershire and Sherwood Foresters on the night of Nairac's abduction was being carried out by members of the Close Observation Platoon (COP). These platoons were formed around the Recce Platoons of most Regiments stationed in the Province. Prior to a Northern Irish tour, each Regiment conducted a selection process for suitable candidates, who then underwent SAS-style training in covert surveillance, provided by the SAS. They became the COP Platoon. They were also armed with non-conventional SAS weaponry: Armalite rifles and Remington Wingmaster automatic shotguns.

Established early in 1977, and still a very recent innovation in May, COP Platoons provided static covert observation to support the police throughout the Province. The COPs were carefully selected and operated in extreme and dangerous conditions. Due to the necessary veil of secrecy which shrouded all covert operations, their successes usually went unpublicised. Officially the RUC tasked the COPs: in reality the SAS usually tasked them and their operations were closely linked to those of the SAS. In short, it is inconceivable that Captain Collett, the SAS Operations Officer, was not aware of the covert COP detachment's availability on the night of Nairac's abduction.

There was even further backup available. It would not have been necessary to abort the Foresters' surveillance mission, if that had been considered to be undesirable. The COP detachment on Hill 799 would have had its own COP backup waiting not far away in a state of high readiness in the event that they should run into trouble. This extra backup could easily have been mobilised without delay to look for and rescue Nairac.

What went wrong? Why did Captain Collett not ask the Foresters to order the COP detachment to go to the Three Steps and find Nairac? The only possible explanation is that Clive Fairweather, whose advice the SAS had sought, had told them not to alert the Foresters and to "keep this within the SAS".

Clive Fairweather was responsible for another strange omission, which could have cost yet more British lives. At his request the SAS ground team went into the Worcestershire and Sherwood Foresters' area without the Foresters being alerted. This has been confirmed by the former Foresters Corporal commanding the COP detachment and was completely contrary to security regulations in South Armagh. The area round Drumintee had been divided into two sectors known as North Railway and South Railway – infantrymen patrolling there waggishly called themselves "The Railway Children". Patrols in these sectors did not stray into each other's territory, nor did anyone else from the Security Forces. This was to ensure that friendly-fire incidents should not occur. If the patrols encountered armed men, they could be certain that they were enemy, and could open fire. Had the Foresters and SAS teams met, being unaware of each other's presence in the neighbourhood, there could have been a nasty accident. Fortunately they did not meet, but this was more by good luck than good management: the SAS ground team confined their researches to the immediate vicinity of the Three Steps.

At around midnight in the car park of the Three Steps there is yet another area of controversy over what actually happened. Nairac's assassins, all of whom had been drinking, gave conflicting testimony to the police and in court. Other eyewitness reports are likewise inconsistent. Although not an eyewitness, Clive Fairweather stated that Terry McCormick confronted Nairac at the bar and asked him outside for a fight. Nairac, nothing loath, left the bar. Maguire then held the pub door so that no-one else could get out and McCormick is then alleged to have thrown a scarf over Nairac's face from behind and started to lay into him, followed by Maguire and a mob of others. However this is completely false, except in one respect: McCormick and Maguire seem to have been the ringleaders in the attack on Nairac. Fairweather has proved overall to be an unreliable source of information. There are several reasons for this, some of which will be examined later.

According to more reliable accounts, the fight took place near Nairac's parked car as he was about to get into it. This matches the recollections of John Murphy's Band: as Nairac walked towards his car, two men followed or accompanied him. As noted elsewhere, as the Band were driving away just after midnight they saw what seemed to be a fight in progress at the far end of the car park, involving four or five people. This was not unusual, especially on a Saturday night; they drove off.

There definitely was a fight: Nairac was fighting for his life with a lynch-mob and successfully landing quite a few punches. The car park was covered with gravel and later a lot of blood was found to have soaked into it. Whatever had happened to Nairac, he had not gone down quietly. That evidence supports the musicians' testimony, so to a great extent does the testimony of the bar's owner, Desmond McCreesh; although there are discrepancies over the timing. Having paid the band their fee, Desmond McCreesh had resumed his vigil over the car park, which was emptying as the bar always closed at 1.00 am. He was again listening to the radio in his own car. Although it was dark, he later stated that he was sure that he had seen Nairac walking away from the bar into the car park with two other men two or three feet behind him at approximately 11.30 pm. McCreesh sat in his car for about ten more minutes but saw nothing out of the ordinary. This timing is incorrect and too early. It does not agree with John Murphy's Band's recollection, but McCreesh may simply have been wrong about the timing. There was no special reason for him to have noted the exact time that he left the car park and went back indoors.

The band, by contrast, who had been hired to play for a stated number of hours between designated times, would have been watching the clock. McCreesh's testimony might also suggest that the fight did not begin immediately when Nairac reached his car. There may have been some discussion, an altercation or a challenge first. According to his own account, McCreesh did not see what happened next, as at this point he left his car and walked back into the bar. He had gone inside before the fight began and it seems to have started in earnest fairly soon after midnight, or early on Sunday morning.

Nairac could have dealt with two men, even if one of them was a former boxer. However he was soon confronted by considerably more than two. Kevin Crilly,

Thomas Morgan, Gerard Fearon and Owen Rocks had followed McCormick and Maguire out of the pub. According to Rocks, he saw McCormick stop at his own car and take out a red and black scarf which he bound over his own face. (This is not confirmed by the others, but it may explain the curious reference to a scarf in Fairweather's misleading account of the fight.) He then walked up the car park after Nairac. Soon afterwards a fight began and McCormick shouted to his friends to "come on up". In the course of the fight Nairac drew, fumbled with and then dropped his Browning pistol *(Note 5)*, which fell to the ground. There was a shout of:

"The bastard's got a gun!"

Someone kicked it under the car, whence it was soon retrieved. According to his assassins, the sight of the gun really alarmed them; it seemed to confirm their suspicions that Nairac might be SAS or a Loyalist planning a strike. At this moment his fate was probably sealed.

Clive Fairweather, in his numerous statements to John Parker and the media insisted that Nairac had foolishly left his gun in the glove compartment of his car, or under the driver's seat, when he went into the Three Steps bar, and that he was trying desperately to get at it when the mob set upon him. This was not the case; he had it on him as usual, in his shoulder holster. Fairweather must have learned soon after the murder what had really happened and have known that Nairac had the Browning on him all the time, until it was taken from him. The assassins were agreed on that point. Why did Fairweather persist in repeating this disinformation long after the event? Fairweather's untruths about Nairac's having left his handgun in the glove compartment seem intended to discredit him, and their implication is serious. A soldier who left his Service handgun in an insecure compartment in his car while at a hazardous meet in what was effectively a war zone was both guilty of serious negligence, and personally to blame if he later found himself defenceless in the face of the enemy. It also raised serious questions about his judgement; he would be seen as his own worst enemy and a danger to others. It would follow that Nairac deserved everything he got.

Fairweather's portrayal of Nairac as someone who from vanity and ambition had greatly exceeded his modest terms of reference; the out-of-control maverick; the eccentric amateur spy; the naive romantic, the fool... has gained wide currency. Many people still accept it as an accurate picture. Others, who were in a position to know better, were restrained at the time by the Official Secrets Act and by more general military security considerations from making any statement to correct that impression. After the disaster had happened, it may have suited the Army in 1977 to downplay Nairac's importance, both to the IRA and the general public, and so to minimise their perception of the potential damage caused by his loss. If so, that was perhaps reasonable at the time, but that consideration can no longer apply in the twenty-first century.

As a corrective, an officer of the RUC's Special Branch who had known Nairac in 1974-5, observed to Martin Dillon, who quotes it in his book *The Dirty War*, that: "Robert was a professional and in no respect could he be considered naive. He was [then] working for a secret organisation (NITAT-NI), which was based in several parts of Northern Ireland." Writing on 30 May 1977 to Nairac's father, Brigadier David Woodward said: "I trusted him absolutely, and knew him to be a very experienced professional, who would never take a risk needlessly. We discussed this aspect of his work on several occasions, and I was each time reassured by his response – thoroughly sensible and down-to-earth, without the least sign of bravura". [He means "bravado."] A former UDR soldier who knew Nairac as "Captain Charles Johnston," commented that he had been on reconnaissance with him into the Republic, among other places, and that he knew the border area like the back of his hand. The words that he used to describe Nairac were: astute, clever, highly intelligent, competent, very professional and very adaptable.

There was no news on Sunday 15 May, but on Monday the PIRA issued a statement (*Note 6*). They claimed that they had killed Robert Nairac. "We arrested him on Saturday night and executed him after interrogation in which he admitted that he was an SAS man. Our intelligence had a number of photographs of him and he was recognised from them". This did not convince the Army – little reliance could be placed on anything that the PIRA said. Lies and disinformation were their normal currency. No corpse had yet been found. While the PIRA had "disappeared" quite a number of civilians, several of whose remains have never been found, they had never yet done this to a soldier. With a soldier their usual practice was to leave the body where he had been shot or blown up, or at a nearby roadside, as a warning. Moreover the Army knew that Nairac was not SAS. Finally, everyone who knew him also knew that he was "a tough bastard" and would not have broken so quickly. Had he been taken, he would have done his best to tough it out for at least 48 hours, during which time contacts could be alerted, codes changed, projects reviewed and if necessary aborted. It seemed on balance likely that Nairac was still alive, undergoing torture and interrogation somewhere in the Republic. To this extent the PIRA ploy was successful: a number of operations in whose planning Nairac had been involved, or which he had simply known about, were hastily halted or aborted because of fears that they might have been compromised. The Army could take no chances.

On Monday 16 May, speaking to the media on behalf of the family, Nairac's sister Rosemonde read a terse prepared statement:

"We are aware of the claims of the IRA to have murdered my brother although there has been no confirmation of this fact. We have been very moved by Cardinal Hume's appeal calling for my brother's safe return and we can only continue to hope and pray. Since he has always loved Ireland and the Irish it is ironic that he may have died while trying as a volunteer to contribute to peace in Ireland.

If he is dead he died trying to do what he felt and stated to be his duty. We are obviously shocked and do not wish to answer any detailed questions but we appreciate the restraint and sympathy of the Press."

While Nairac's family and civilian friends tried to keep up their hopes and continued to pray for him, his military friends, or those who knew Northern Ireland, were not optimistic. As one former soldier stated:

"Great shock when he disappeared but I think everyone knew we would never see him again. I remember the atmosphere in the Section that day, and indeed for... days to follow, was awful, until we had a pep talk from Major H Jones (soon to be Lt Col and die leading his Bn in the Falklands), who was then our Bde Ops Maj/Chief of Staff."

Jonathan Forbes, who in 1975 had taken over from Charles Fenwick as Adjutant of the 1st Battalion Grenadier Guards instead of Nairac, recalls:

"Rather as with the JFK assassination, I well remember where I was when I heard the dreadful news of his disappearance. It was somewhat after the event (on 2nd June 1977), but there was a good reason – I was in the Nanda Devi [National Park] in India with some Grenadier Guardsmen and others." He referred to Nairac as "that delightful, intelligent and fun brother officer I thought I knew in our relatively brief time serving together all those years ago. He was a remarkable man".

About the same time Luke Jennings, who was on a gap year in Australia, received by airmail a sheaf of Press cuttings from which he learned that Nairac, his boyhood friend and mentor, was missing, believed killed, in Ireland.

Nairac's angling friend, John Hotchkiss, recalls that: "I heard about Robert's death when I was fishing on Vancouver Island, British Columbia – my wife sent a piece to me which was in *The Evening Standard*. This was just before the Queen's Silver Jubilee celebrations."

Julian Malins, who had been aghast when Nairac had revealed to him at the Vincent's Club dinner in London in November 1976 that he was now working undercover (and was wearing his Browning in a shoulder-holster under his dinner-jacket to prove it) also feared the worst. He came from an Army family and knew more than most civilians about the risks of operating undercover in Northern Ireland. A formidable Silk, he admits that he wept when he got the news. He was far from being alone.

One friend who was profoundly affected by Nairac's murder was Lieutenant Colonel William Burke of the First Battalion Royal Irish Rangers, who is now a High-Church Anglican priest. As he related in his Remembrance Day sermon delivered to an Army congregation in St Anne's Cathedral in Belfast in November 2001, he had worked closely undercover with Nairac in Northern Ireland for sixteen months in 1974-75. Sometime after their return to England, their former Commander had asked to meet them. They learned that one of them was needed back in Northern Ireland, in South Armagh. In the event Nairac was chosen, partly because Colonel Burke was married, and Burke suddenly had a terrible premonition that Nairac would not survive his posting; so did his wife. The premonition proved to be correct; Burke received the news of Nairac's murder in Cyprus. Like many of Nairac's Army friends, he reacted with extravagant grief, drowning his sorrow in alcohol: "Even after a massive binge, he was still dead when I sobered up". This started Burke on a journey in the course of which he would leave the Army, abandon his atheist and rational beliefs, and eventually to become the priest that Nairac never had at his death. He still says Mass for him.

Nairac's former Commanding Officer, Lieutenant Colonel Richard Besly, learned about the murder in the following way: "I was sitting in my office at Horseguards Parade with a Corporal in the Intelligence Corps who was reading a newspaper. He suddenly said, 'I see they got him'. I said, 'What are you talking about?' He replied, 'Captain Nairac. Everyone at Bessbrook knew him and what he was up to'".

The comment about everyone at Bessbrook "knowing what he was up to" is not surprising, given the small size of the base and Nairac's coming and going in different orders of dress, while fresh faces were posted in every few weeks or months: rumours abounded. A more accurate comment would have been that "everyone *liked to think* they knew what he was up to", as in reality they probably did not know. Nevertheless this was not ideal for his personal security.

Another Army friend, Charles Woodrow, later wrote: "The (SAS) Squadron, prior to his abduction, was in Bessbrook. Part of my job was to look after the needs of the SAS Squadron and I used to see him most days until he was murdered... As you can imagine, Robert's abduction and subsequent murder was a terrible loss to his family, to all of us who worked alongside him, and to the Army, particularly in South Armagh, and is something I shall never forget."

There was damage to Army morale in Northern Ireland because Nairac had been so widely known, liked and respected by all ranks. To quote Brigadier Woodford again:

"I could only wish that we had had more time to develop what anyway became a firm friendship... which I shall always cherish. His intelligence, professional ability and toughness were apparent to everyone who knew him; equally, his less stern virtues made him the best of company – gaiety, vitality and a delightfully pointed sense of humour. Above all else, his selflessness and courage are what I shall remember."

Although a body of dissenting military opinion would emerge, this seems to have been a widely-held view of Nairac in the Army in Northern Ireland at the time of his murder. It seemed horribly wrong that this fate should befall such a likeable, friendly and promising officer. Nairac had continued to play rugby, for example, to the very end of his life, for the 3 Brigade Team against 8 Brigade. He was still a formidable, very fast player; an asset to his team. That kind of sporting prowess had helped to make him popular with all ranks; except, apparently, with the SAS. When reporting to Intelligence at Portadown, he invariably made time to speak kindly and affably to every soldier in the office: officers and other ranks alike. This might seem common courtesy, but not every visiting officer would do this. If not playing rugby with them, he would sometimes drink beer with the junior ranks on Saturday afternoons; they enjoyed his company. "He wasn't like other officers," said one former NCO. "He really was one of the boys". Nor was Julian Malins' reaction to Nairac's death unique. Soldiers who had known Nairac well candidly admit that they reacted in the same way. One of Nairac's Army friends recalled: "You know, some of my soldiers cried when they heard about his death." They were to weep unashamedly again at his memorial service in 1978; not many commissioned officers in Northern Ireland would have received this extreme and melancholy tribute. Nor would they have had a slow march composed in their memory by the Regimental Director of Music.

On 18 May there was a dramatic development. Two locals, described in one Press account as schoolboys on an angling trip, stopped a Garda Siochana patrol near the border between Newry and Dundalk. They had found bullet cases, bloodstains and signs of a struggle. They led the policemen to the spot near a bridge over the River Flurry on the edge of Ravensdale Forest in County Louth. Police found bloodstains on the grass in a corner of a field as well as under the parapet of the bridge. Silver and copper coins were found and there were further signs of a struggle. The bullet cases matched those that Nairac had had with him when he vanished. Later, more bloodstains, tufts of hair and teeth that were probably Nairac's were found. But none of his clothes or personal effects were discovered. The outlook did not look good for Nairac, but there was still no body to be seen.

On 20 May the English Catholic weekly *The Universe* quoted Cardinal Hume on Nairac, whom he had known well: "Robert was a fine and very courageous young man. I am deeply saddened. It makes me feel even more vividly what anguish and pain so many people have suffered in the long years of civil disturbance".

On 21 May the PIRA put out another announcement, this time in the Provisional newspaper, *Republican News*. They also sent a briefing to other newspapers, including *The Irish Times*. On this occasion the announcement took the form of a front page article in *Republican News*, and in most of the other newspapers that had received it, with the banner headline "SAS Captain Executed". It was accompanied by a photograph of Nairac in uniform, talking to young people in Ardoyne. At the time many readers assumed that this must have been taken during one of Nairac's two deployments in Belfast in 1973 and that he was wearing a Grenadier Guards beret with his combat uniform. In reality the picture had been taken by an IRA operative less than three months earlier; Nairac was clearly wearing the dark blue beret of the Devon and Dorsets. Since 1971 the Guards had worn a khaki beret. How a short-haired and clean-shaven Nairac had come to be back on patrol in Belfast in early 1977 is a separate story that will come later, in its proper place. The IRA's accompanying statement said that the picture was recent. The article continued:

"The elimination of Nairac is an obvious breakthrough in the war against the Special Air Service. Sources close to the IRA refuse to say how much detailed knowledge they now have of the SAS but they are obviously highly pleased with what Nairac has either given them or confirmed. IRA sources have revealed that Capt. Nairac was a high-ranking SAS officer. When arrested he had in his possession a Browning automatic with two magazines. He pretended that he had been in Canada and brought the gun home with him. When arrested, he gave as his identity that of a Republican Clubs' Member. This Stick [Official IRA] identity was broken almost immediately by an IRA officer. SAS morale must now be shattered as one of their most high-ranking officers has been arrested, interrogated, executed and has disappeared without a trace."

The last phrase at any rate was true: Nairac had disappeared, almost without a trace. It still seemed possible, even likely, that Nairac was alive and presumably being interrogated with refined cruelty in the Republic. It was equally possible that the PIRA really had killed him but were not producing the body, contrary to their usual practice, in order to provoke an atmosphere of paranoia and uncertainty in the Security Forces, in which numerous operations against the IRA would be abandoned. The PIRA may also have been hoping that a number of suspected informers who had been among Nairac's contacts would now lose their nerve and blow their own cover by rushing to seek protection from the RUC. The PIRA could then deal with them. Meanwhile the border area between the Republic and Northern Ireland remained effectively shut down, while the search for Captain Nairac, or his remains, continued and extended its geographical scope. All activities were affected, from churchgoing to farming to postal and grocery deliveries; including the activities of the Provisional IRA. Although the searchers never found Nairac or his remains, the Army, the RUC and the Garda did find a number of PIRA arms caches, ammunition dumps and other equipment. They made a number of arrests as a result. The PIRA were becoming more and more agitated.

The PIRA Press article was a clever mixture of truth and lies. Although the Army could not be sure of this, Nairac had not in fact revealed anything. Nor was he a member of the SAS; still less a "high-ranking" one. But he undoubtedly had a Browning pistol with two magazines on him when he disappeared. He had sometimes used a "Stick" identity, including on 14 May: usually one of the two Danny McErleans. The Browning pistol genuinely was produced in Canada; it was far easier for a private citizen to acquire one there or in the USA than in the UK, because the gun-licensing laws were more liberal. The Browning normally bore the stamp "Made in Canada". Part of Nairac's identity as "Danny McErlean" was that he had been working in Canada. That would explain both his possession of a Browning and anything odd about his Irish accent. Although

Nairac had never visited Canada, one of his cousins was living there; he probably knew enough about it to bluff his way, most of the time. It was now also very clear that someone in the IRA had recognised and photographed Nairac with the Devon and Dorsets in Belfast. No information on the photographer or the provenance of that photo is available: the IRA does not have a user-friendly Press Syndication Department.

Rumours continued to fly for the rest of May, some of which were PIRA disinformation. As they were intended to do, they wasted a lot of Army and RUC time and added to the atmosphere of uncertainty and paranoia. This was foreseeable and typical of the PIRA; especially in South Armagh. When they "disappeared" a civilian victim, they would not normally admit to having done so, even if it was clear to everyone else that they had. The line to take, when they commented at all, was the same as that used by Gerry Adams (the President of Sinn Fein) in his televised interview with BBC Northern Ireland's Darragh McIntyre about the Disappeared in 2013. It runs along these lines:

"We know nothing about it. This is the real world. People disappear for all sorts of reasons, often voluntarily. You shouldn't assume that, just because someone's disappeared, he was a victim of one or other lot of paramilitaries, or even that he's dead."

In the real world, in the Northern Ireland of the 1970s, that is exactly what one *would* have assumed, and one would usually have been right. The crime would occur; the victim would be shot, preceded by interrogation and torture; his or her remains would be buried secretly; those involved would say nothing. There would follow a series of carefully planted and nurtured rumours, which would send the police on both sides of the border on wild-goose chases, while the victim's family would be driven to distraction. The missing person would reportedly have been seen alive and well in Dublin, in Cork or on the British mainland. They had just telephoned a friend and left a message; an anonymous caller had received a postcard from them, posted in Liverpool... and so the weeks and months would trickle by with hope being extinguished, then suddenly and unexpectedly flaring into life and then being cruelly put out again. The act of disappearing someone was a very effective terror weapon. Not only the bereaved family, but whole communities could be demoralised in this way. No authentic, reliable information would ever be forthcoming. A similar fog of rumour and lies would now engulf and confuse the search for Captain Nairac.

One such report was a highly circumstantial account, attributed to two men out on an early fishing expedition, of a wounded man who resembled Nairac being picked up from the roadside near the border early on 15 May by three other men with noticeable English accents, and driven rapidly away. Needless to say, the car and its occupants were never traced. Nor were the two anglers, who were apparently never interviewed by the Gardai; this story may be a mix of fact and fiction. (Two young anglers genuinely had shown the Gardai bullet cases that they had found near Flurry Bridge.) This rumour may also be at the origin of one of the wilder Nairac legends: that his abduction was staged and that he was given a new identity so that he could go on serving British interests in some other capacity, somewhere else. This possibility was mooted later in 1977 during the trial in Dublin of one of Nairac's murderers by his defence counsel, Patrick McEntee. The court did not take the suggestion seriously, as it was not supported by the available evidence, and the Defendant was duly convicted of murder. Another equally circumstantial story concerned a report of some men putting a weighted corpse into a flooded quarry near Drumintee and then driving away. The Army sealed off the area and bomb-disposal experts searched it for booby-traps. The RUC then wasted days searching the flooded quarry: no corpse was ever found. A later story indicated that Nairac's body had been dumped near Forkhill at the spot where Peter Cleary had been killed the previous year, but it was never found there or anywhere nearby. In another, two men going early to work near Ravensdale Forest reportedly saw Nairac's corpse propped up against a dry-stone field wall. Later it had disappeared. But no-one seems to have interviewed the two men, if indeed they ever existed. Other stories related that Nairac had been buried in concrete under a construction site or fed to pigs.

The most horrific story of all is that Nairac's body had been taken to a nearby meat-processing plant (now closed and derelict), many of whose employees were affiliated to the PIRA. At a slack period when the management were not around, his body was processed, "like any other carcass". Although it now seems far-fetched, this story has been repeated many times, including by reputable journalists. Even the *Dictionary of National Biography* refers to the story: "Robert Nairac's body was never found. It is thought to have been destroyed at a local meat processing plant". There are four reasons why this may have seemed plausible at the time:

The first is that by 1977 many or most British people were willing to believe the worst of the IRA and of the Irish in general, just as they had been of the Japanese during World War II. They, and the British authorities, readily accepted this story. "The IRA were animals [human] enough to have done it," said a former brother officer in the Grenadier Guards. Secondly, in the days before DNA testing, it seemed to offer a good, although not perfectly fool-proof, way of disposing of a corpse. Thirdly, it is not in doubt that Nairac had been appallingly tortured before he was killed. If his body were found, the evidence of the atrocities that he had suffered and the public revulsion they would provoke could have constituted a serious propaganda setback for the IRA, so the body must not be found. Lastly, the story is repeated in *Killing Rage*, the memoirs of the late Eamon Collins (*Note 7*), a former PIRA operative who later turned "supergrass," and who was murdered in his turn in 1999. Surely Collins was in a position to know, if anyone was?

Collins was not. He never claimed any involvement in, or first-hand knowledge of, the Nairac murder. He did not know any of Nairac's killers. He had simply stayed for one night, a few years after the murder, while he was still in the PIRA and on the run, near Ravensdale with a grotesquely fat but physically strong and terrifying man, an IRA sympathiser, who lived alone in a remote farmhouse and who had worked at the meat-processing plant. The man had appalling table manners, ripping roast chickens apart with his bare hands and devouring them like an animal. The house was chilly, gloomy and filthy. Collins was relieved to depart the following day. Later another IRA volunteer in Dundalk told Collins that his former host was thought to be a psychopath and that "I think it was him that did the business on Nairac" – he had apparently disposed of the corpse by butchering and then processing it: "They treated him just like any other carcass". This IRA friend then told Collins the meat-processing factory story; which Collins, although a seasoned terrorist, found stomach-churning. But this story is double-hearsay, unverifiable and unreliable. Collins and his sinister host had never mentioned or discussed Nairac during his brief visit. Finally, the Garda Siochana had picked up the meat-processing story very quickly and investigated the factory soon after Nairac disappeared. They found no traces of human blood, bone or tissue, although despite this the story gained wide currency.

It is now clear that the PIRA invented the story because the intensive search for Nairac had shut down their operation in South Armagh and neighbouring parts of the Republic; they literally could not move. It was imperative to get the search called off: one way to do that was to make it believably clear that there was now nothing left to find. The authorities in both parts of Ireland bought the meat-processing factory story which, when it became public knowledge, had the additional benefit of demonstrating to an impressionable Irish public what scary people the South Armagh PIRA were – cross them and you'd end up like Nairac! Although the police files on Nairac's murder remained open, for this and other reasons the search operation was gradually wound down. The PIRA could breathe again, but they would need to take further decisive action before the operation would be abandoned altogether.

When the meat factory story hit the headlines, the feelings of Nairac's parents, wider family and friends are more easily imagined than described. Apart from Barbara Nairac, who had kept her Anglican faith, the Nairacs were a Catholic family. The decent, respectful treatment of a Christian corpse and its ceremonious interment following a Requiem Mass, are much more important to Catholics than to Protestants, or indeed to members of most other religions. The Church has only accepted cremation within recent years. Previously it had been regarded as un-Christian. Catholicism aside, the lack of a body to bury has prevented Nairac's family and friends from ever achieving closure.

Meanwhile, in the absence of a body no-one could be absolutely sure that Nairac was dead. As late as August 1977 a Scottish newspaper published an unconfirmed report that Nairac was being held prisoner in a remote area of Southern Ireland. This was what his mother had always privately believed, and his family's hopes were momentarily rekindled. It is not clear from what source the newspaper got this misinformation.

There is a further intriguing piece of information – or possibly disinformation. On his deathbed, Nairac's first Housemaster at Ampleforth, Father Jerome Lambert, told another monk that he had once been telephoned by a person claiming to speak for the PIRA. This person had assured him that Robert Nairac had a grave at a secret location and that the PIRA were willing to conduct Father Jerome there to see it. Presumably he would have been blindfolded and led to the spot. How he could possibly have been certain that the site that he would be shown was Nairac's grave, or any grave at all, we cannot know. Father Jerome reportedly said that he would have no dealings with the PIRA and hung up. He is said not to have been a completely reliable source of information. The other monk ambivalently observed:

"Jerome loved stories, but it was well said of him that 'The trouble with Father Jerome's lies is that they usually turn out to be true'".

What the IRA would gain from this exercise is unclear, unless they had planned to have a propaganda photo taken of Father Jerome praying at the graveside, to "prove" that they had some decent instincts and that the meat-processing factory story was not true. The telephone call might equally have been an unpleasant hoax. It is, however, possible that Father Jerome's story has a factual basis. It is now the view of the Independent Commission for the Location of Victim's Remains (ICLVR), as well as of a number of serious investigative journalists, that Nairac's body is buried within – at most – a ten-mile radius of the murder site, either inside or close to Ravensdale Forest. For many practical reasons, it has to be close by.

One reason for the uncertainty over the site of Nairac's grave is that the group of people who murdered him were not the same ones who disposed of the corpse. Most of the killers did not know, and did not ask, what had become of it, although Liam Townson, the PIRA volunteer who shot Nairac, may know. Of the people who buried Nairac, their number is diminishing with the passage of time. However, some younger people also know the location of Nairac's body. It may be that one of them will one day be moved to contact the ICLVR to reveal its whereabouts. Robert Nairac could then receive a solemn funeral, a Requiem Mass and finally be laid to rest.

So what really happened? After Nairac had lost his Browning, his position was precarious, to say the least, unless the Army and police moved quickly to find out where he was. We know, though he could not have known, that there was no likelihood of that happening given the involvement of Fairweather. While McCormick crawled around looking for, and finding, the Browning, the others crowded round to restrain and beat up Nairac. Then McCormick held the gun to Nairac's head and said:

"Don't move, you fucker, or I'll shoot you."

McCormick ordered Crilly and Morgan to fetch their cars and, according to Morgan, the other men started pulling Nairac's curly hair and kicking him. They forced Nairac into Crilly's bronze Cortina, with his own gun jammed between his shoulder blades. Crilly drove off with O'Rourke in the front passenger seat and Nairac in the back between McCormick and Maguire. These two seem to have been physically the strongest of the men and also the leaders of what had now become a kidnapping, evolving rapidly into a lynching. Morgan followed close behind in a second car, accompanied by Gerard Fearon. Both cars now headed for the Republic, a few miles away, by obscure minor roads where they were less likely to be stopped and checked by RUC or Army patrols.

They stopped beside the bridge over the River Flurry, where they forced Nairac out of the car while Crilly left with O'Rourke to fetch reinforcements. These would be Townson or "some of the Boys" meaning local PIRA volunteers. They may have simply been seeking orders from a senior PIRA officer on what to do next. If so, they should have waited. What they actually fetched was an executioner; a low-ranking hit man who was, by an evil chance, even more inebriated than they were. Meanwhile they began, on their own initiative, brutally to interrogate Nairac.

Morgan later said what he had seen:

"The soldier was sitting on his bottom with his back and head against the wall. He had his hands over his face as if he was trying to save his face. His mouth and nose were bleeding. McCormick was down on one knee beside the SAS man and was asking a lot of questions about who he was and all that. Fearon and Maguire were standing up and Maguire was pointing a gun at him." (This was Nairac's own Browning.)

What McCormick was asking was related to Nairac's alleged connections with Ardoyne. McCormick later indicated that while Nairac obviously knew Ardoyne well, he did not seem to know it quite as well as a native might be expected to. (This might be a retrospective explanation.) Nairac reportedly stuck to his story and never deviated from it. He never even revealed his real name. He was Danny McErlean from Belfast; he was an OIRA volunteer and would they leave him alone?

He gave them a telephone number in Belfast to ring, where someone would authenticate that he was who he said he was, but the call would never be made: mobile phones had not yet been invented. It was a lonely spot and there was no public telephone box nearby. Moreover the Republicans were probably rightly suspicious. The call would have put them in touch with a secret Army office where they would be questioned at length by people with genuine Belfast accents about whom they were holding, where and why. While they were answering these questions, it would be possible for listeners to work out where they were. While Maguire was writing down the telephone number on a cigarette packet, Nairac made an attempt to escape. He was again set upon. Morgan later told police that he had "kicked him in the balls" and went on kicking him when he fell. Maguire warned Nairac that if he tried to escape again, he would shoot him. McCormick continued the "interrogation."

Maguire asked Morgan to drive Fearon back to the Three Steps, pick up Fearon's 3.5 litre Rover, park it outside the Border Inn in Jonesborough and then come back to Ravensdale. This suggests that it was not yet 1.00 am. (If Clive Fairweather's recollection was reliable, the SAS helicopter crew went up at about that time and reported that Nairac's red Triumph Toledo was the only car left in the car park.) When they got back to Ravensdale they found that Nairac had been moved to the middle of a field, where a genuine, albeit very drunk, PIRA officer, Liam Townson, was clumsily trying to interrogate him. In Morgan's absence Nairac had managed to get his own gun back briefly and in the struggle had wounded one of his tormentors. On this occasion the Browning had fired. These repeated attempts to escape are remarkable evidence of Nairac's toughness and courage. Townson had a gun and was hitting Nairac over the head with it, while accusing him of lying. Townson had challenged Nairac to give the names of some "Stickies" – OIRA members – in Dundalk; Nairac could not. Townson kept saying that if he were a real OIRA volunteer, he should know who they were.

Even if Nairac had been a genuine OIRA operative from Belfast, he might well not have known. Much like the British Agencies, it was IRA policy to share information about each other on a strictly "need to know" basis. Townson, however, had been drinking all day and was not amenable to reason. He kept hitting Nairac over the head – pistol-whipping him – and giggling as he did so. Nairac was now lying on his side on the ground. He was in a bad way. He was still trying to protect his head with his hands.

Townson then got to his feet and announced to the men who were standing around that he was going to "take this fella over the fields and shoot him". He dragged Nairac to his feet and started to march him away from the group. They had only walked a short distance when a commotion broke out. Townson was screaming that the soldier had the gun. Nairac had made another bid to escape and had grabbed the revolver from Townson. However, he was now seriously weakened from the beatings that he had taken and was unable to make good his escape. Moreover the gun had jammed again. Townson laid the wounded man low with a vicious blow and seized the gun back from him.

The men then beat Nairac severely with fence posts and left him crying and whimpering, face down in the field, seriously injured and unable to move. His face was now covered with blood. Townson, whose authority had been dented by this *grand-guignol* fiasco and who had lost a lot of face, decided that the only way ahead was to "execute" Nairac.

Nairac asked for a priest. McCormick pretended to be one, hoping to elicit some useful information, but Nairac was not deceived: he would have recognised McCormick's voice – it had been badgering him since he had first been abducted.

He only said, "Bless me Father, for I have sinned" and then fell silent. Nairac's request for a priest was not an attempt to buy time. No cradle Catholic would call for a priest *in extremis* just for that reason. He called for a priest because he knew he was about to die. Whatever his private doubts might have been vis-a-vis his faith – assuming that he had any doubts – he was not taking any chances. Even that final favour was denied.

There is an important theological point here: in the Church's view the desire for mercy is contrition in itself and reconciles the sinner to the Church; so the simple phrase "Bless me Father, for I have sinned" was sufficient, regardless of his previous state of grace and faith. To the question whether Nairac died a good Catholic and in a state of grace, the answer is definitely "Yes".

From the evidence given in court, it seems clear that Townson used his own handgun to kill Nairac, rather than Nairac's own Browning, which Maguire had been holding (*Note 10*). There seems to be an IRA practice, or superstition, that a victim's own gun should never be used to kill him unless this is unavoidable. Townson's handgun was a .32 Harrington and Richardson (H&R) revolver, which he had brought to the scene. It is referred to as the murder weapon several times in the investigator's reports and also in the record of Townson's interview under caution. The subsequent forensic reports on both the H&R revolver and Nairac's Army issue Browning tend to support this. Townson admitted as much following his arrest. The Garda found both guns at the murder scene. All this evidence was aired at Townson's trial in Dublin.

Liam Townson had retrieved his own gun, the .32 revolver, and some ammunition from their hiding place before coming to interrogate Nairac. Unlike Nairac's gun, his was not well maintained. Townson had kept it concealed in a dry-stone dyke, which was not very dry, and the gun was rusty. Unlike the Browning with its magazine, this type of handgun has a revolving drum, which holds the rounds. Each time the trigger is pulled, the firing mechanism operates and the firing pin strikes one round, then rotates the drum so that the next round is lined up with the barrel, ready to be fired the next time the trigger is pulled. If the revolving drum was at all rusty, misfiring or even complete seizure would be likely to happen. If both the firing mechanism had been rusty and the ammunition badly maintained, the .32 could easily have allowed the trigger to be pulled several times before a round was properly struck. The part-struck or unfired rounds would not be automatically ejected from the revolver drum. Something along these lines seems to have happened.

It is quite likely that Townson, having experienced problems with his own gun, may now have tried to use Nairac's gun to kill him. However the Browning seems to have jammed again. Its jamming is one of the most mysterious aspects of the whole story. Townson screamed at his victim: "Fuck you, it's only blanks!"

He would have hardly shouted that at Nairac if he had been referring to his own gun, which he had loaded himself with real cartridges. That is also the view of Nairac's Green Howard friend Nicky Curtis (*Note 9*). Townson was wrong: blank ammunition would still have detonated and made a noise. The Browning *had* mysteriously jammed again: no detonation occurred.

Townson retrieved his own handgun, placed the barrel against Nairac's head and frantically pulled the trigger again and again. On the fourth attempt the gun fired. Nairac collapsed. Yet it is unusual – or unheard of – for an IRA executioner to use only one bullet. Normally a second round is always fired, to make certain. According to a Press report in the *Daily Telegraph* of 20 May 1977, several empty shells were found near the murder site on 18 May.

Townson had just killed the soldier who best knew and understood Ireland and who had been a friend of Ireland for most of his short life. He remained for a few minutes looking at the fallen man; then Maguire asked him whether Nairac was really dead. Townson said yes: he could "tell by the soldier's eyes" that he was dead. This statement has the ring of authenticity. When someone is killed, the eyes dim and go out like headlamps in a fog. They rarely close peacefully of their own accord but remain staring blankly: Townson evidently knew this. No war movie has ever satisfactorily reproduced this grim effect.

Townson has a difficult relationship with the truth: it is likely that Nairac's end was even more unpleasant than the basic, sanitised version that was aired in court, although that was bad enough. Nicky Curtis in *Faith and Duty* says: "They reportedly kicked him around like a football, threw him in a car, took him to the outskirts of the town, beat him some more with bricks and planks and then shot his body in every limb. Until there was nothing left to shoot."

Curtis, who had left the Army in 1976 and was working in the UK when Nairac was murdered, does not say what his source for this information was. It could be Army gossip. It is incorrect in at least three details: bricks and planks were not involved and Robert Nairac was done to death in a rural area, not on the outskirts of any town.

But the rest might possibly be true. This may be a reason why the PIRA are still so determined that Nairac's remains should never be found. Even if he is now only a skeleton, his broken bones might still reveal an appalling story. Ken Wharton, the author of *Wasted Years, Wasted Lives: The British Army in Northern Ireland*, a critically acclaimed account of the Troubles, mentions that "one theory is that he was tortured with electric drills and angle grinders – that the IRA could not allow his terrible injuries to be made public". Wharton does not give the source for this, nor does he explain how the assassins could have arranged this means of torture at short notice in the open country, far from an electric power-point. Other versions that appeared in the Press at the time suggested that Nairac had been murdered in a lonely ruined farmhouse. That too is incorrect.

"Bless me, Father, for I have sinned", may have been Nairac's last spoken words, but it is depressingly easy to imagine the unspoken thoughts that must have coursed through his brain between the tidal waves of pain during his final moments:

God give me strength... Why has no-one come to look for me? Okay, I should have taken backup: I see that now! But they knew where I was going. They knew when I was supposed to get back to Bessbrook Mill. They must have realised that something bad had happened when I missed the midnight radio check. Didn't they raise the alarm then? What has gone wrong?

Nairac loved life and had everything to live for. His twenty-ninth birthday would fall on 31 August. Whether he celebrated it at home with his family or in the Mess with brother officers, there would have been much to celebrate. In less than five years of Army life he had achieved a great deal. His promotion to Major was now assured, although the precise timing was not yet known. He was definitely going to become a Company Commander (*Note 10*) on his return to the UK.

Platoon Commander to Company Commander and Acting Major in four years, before his twenty-ninth birthday, was excellent progress. Nairac already held the General Service Medal. He might conceivably have heard a rumour about his prospective second medal. He was due to return in a very few weeks to his Regimental family, the Grenadier Guards, who were eager to get him back. He wanted to go hawking again with Brimstone, the hen Hawk Eagle, to go fishing in Scotland in August and wildfowling on the Severn estuary in the autumn. He had many friends to catch up with. But it was now sickeningly clear that none of this was going to happen. They were going to kill him; the only thing left was to die bravely. *In manus tuas, Domine, commendo spiritum meum... (Note 11).*

Later, in court, Townson would pay a kind of tribute to Nairac: "He never told us anything. He was a great soldier."

Above: The Three Steps Inn, Drumintee, from whose car park Robert Nairac was abducted on the night of 14-15 May 1977. Used with permission ©Victor Patterson.

Below: Civilian volunteers join in the search for Nairac's body in Ravensdale Forest. Used with permission ©Victor Patterson.

Irish Republic Police stand on Flurry Bridge, near Ravensdale Forest, where Nairac was brutally interrogated by PIRA supporters. Used with permission ©Victor Patterson.

CHAPTER 4 | NEW TO EARTH AND SKY

The baby new to earth and sky,
What time his tender palm is prest
Against the circle of the breast,
Has never thought that "this is I":
But as he grows he gathers much,
And learns the use of "I," and "me,"
And finds "I am not what I see,
And other than the things I touch."
So rounds he to a separate mind
From whence clear memory may begin,
As thro' the frame that binds him in
His isolation grows defined.
(Alfred, Lord Tennyson)

It is now time to go back to the start of Robert Nairac's strange life journey and retrace the path that led him, via England, from the tropical Mascarene Island of Mauritius to violent death in a field in Ireland, at the hands of an intoxicated mob of low-level IRA supporters: men who were designated in the Army slang of the day as "pond life".

As noted earlier, the published material on Nairac includes references to his background and education couched in implicitly critical or disapproving terms. Rather as some journalists like to refer often, and frequently irrelevantly, to Prime Minister David Cameron's Etonian education and membership of the Bullingdon Club at Oxford, so Nairac's critics like to emphasise that he was not merely a Guards Officer in an "élite Regiment"; he was "a public schoolboy". He had attended an "élite school", the "Catholic Eton". He was "Oxbridge educated" and had enjoyed a "privileged upbringing".

All of this was true, up to a point. However such references, taken out of context, might suggest that Nairac came from a rich and rarefied noble background, like the giddy Catholic aristocrat Sebastian Flyte in Evelyn Waugh's novel *Brideshead Revisited*. The reality was different: he had more in common with Sebastian's conventional bourgeois friend, Charles Ryder, except that Ryder only became a Catholic in early middle age; an age that the cradle Catholic Nairac would never know.

Robert Nairac came from a respected middle-class family. Over several centuries the Nairacs had been achievers; first in Languedoc, then in the Bordeaux region and more recently in Mauritius, where Robert's ancestors had played an important role in pre-independence colonial society, serving as Chief Justice and in other prominent positions. There was a strong medical tradition in the Nairac family: Robert's father Maurice and his paternal grandfather had both, against considerable competition, won scholarships to study Medicine in England. Mauritius was then a British colony, although prior to 1810 it had belonged to France, so Maurice Nairac regarded himself as British, even though he was of French descent and French was his first language. Robert's father was a surgeon and his paternal grandfather and his elder brother were physicians. His Scots maternal grandfather had been another physician. His Welsh maternal grandmother was a former nurse. Nairac's mother was a talented musician, an Associate of the Royal College of Music. His sister Gabrielle, another musician, played and taught the clarinet. His sister Rosemonde became a well-known ceramics designer, examples of whose work are held by the Victoria and Albert Museum. His uncle, Basil Dykes, was a successful lawyer and a decorated Territorial soldier. Robert Nairac therefore had a number of positive family role models to emulate while growing up. Robert himself was to show definite signs of linguistic, musical and drawing ability, among other things.

In 1946 Robert's parents, who had first met in England, moved with their three eldest children to Maurice's native Mauritius, where he practised general medicine. They would remain in Mauritius for three years. Barbara Nairac gave birth to a further son on 31 August 1948, who was christened Robert Laurence. For career-related reasons, the family left Mauritius in July 1949 and returned to England, where Maurice would practice as an ophthalmic eye-surgeon at the Sunderland Infirmary. Robert attended a local day school until the age of eight; he then went to Gilling Castle School, a feeder school for Ampleforth College in Yorkshire. Between the ages of twelve and eighteen he was a pupil at Ampleforth: initially in College, the junior school, and later in St Edward's House.

It is striking how normal, conventional and ordinary Nairac's background was, at least until he went to Ampleforth. It was not the obvious background for an original military thinker. He had been born in Mauritius, which is an attractive tropical island, the habitat of beautiful or striking endemic species like the Pink Pigeon, the Purple Swamp Hen and the extinct Dodo, and the scene of Bernardin de Saint-Pierre's famous novel, *Paul et Virginie*. However, although Nairac relations still live there, Robert left it at less than one year old and probably had no memories of the place. Nor does he come across as the sort of person who would enjoy *Paul et Virginie,* which is a beautiful, mannered novel. It tells the fate of a simple child of nature corrupted by the artificial standards that prevailed on the eve of the 1789 Revolution among the French upper classes. The young Nairac preferred to read Kipling, Henty or Haggard.

Far from living in a stately home or rural manor house during his childhood, Robert Nairac passed his early youth in suburban Sunderland; then part of County Durham, now Tyne and Wear. Sunderland was not a romantic place. In the nineteenth and twentieth centuries it was famous for heavy industry, notably ship-building. Ships had been built there since the fourteenth century. Coal mining started in the seventeenth. In the twentieth century glass-making was a major employer; Sunderland was the home of Pyrex Glass until 2007, when the factory closed. Ovenproof Pyrex products had been manufactured there for 85 years and general glassware had been produced at the site for over 150 years. During the twentieth century, as the former heavy industries declined, electronic, chemical, paper and motor manufacturers replaced them. The Sunderland public transport network was enhanced in 1900 by an electric tram system. The trams were gradually replaced by buses during the 1940s before finally being axed in 1954, when Robert Nairac was six years old. He would have remembered the trams; children of that generation enjoyed riding on them; they were more fun than buses.

In the 1950s many areas of Sunderland were in a mess, though the town was starting to recover. Sunderland had suffered from unemployment during the economic depression of the early 1930s. World War II had caused its industry to revive, but at a high cost. As a heavy industry town that built ships, Sunderland became a target of the German Luftwaffe, which caused the destruction of, or damage to, 4,000 homes, and devastated industry. The devastation was there for all to see, well after the war had ended. More interestingly, for a family that included two active sons, Sunderland seems to have been a very sporting place; even sports-mad. Its local soccer team, Sunderland AFC, has been in the Football League since 1890 and is still (just) in the Premier League. Sunderland was and still is also noted for high-class amateur soccer, rugby, cricket, boxing and athletics. Possibly due in part to this early pervasive sporting influence, Robert Nairac was motivated later to become proficient in rugby, soccer, running and other sports.

Sunderland, especially in the drab, rationed 1950s, may not have been the most inspiring place, but it had several advantages. The Nairacs were comfortably off and lived in Thornhill Gardens, which had not been bombed. This leafy suburban street then consisted of Victorian and Edwardian detached and terraced houses with large gardens and open country readily accessible not far away. Robert Nairac was to develop a deep and abiding love of the countryside. Since those days Sunderland has expanded; the countryside is now further away; some of the bigger houses have been replaced by flats, but it remains a desirable address. Maurice Nairac and his children were practicing Roman Catholics, although Barbara Nairac had remained an Anglican. This caused no friction within the family: the parents respected each other's religion. Being, and behaving like, a Christian was perhaps in the final analysis even more important than the denomination. It seems to have been a religious, harmonious family. The Nairacs would no doubt have endorsed Sunderland's motto, "Nil Desperandum, Auspice Deo", loosely translated as "Never Despair, Trust in God."

In some parts of England Roman Catholicism is, or was, seen as un-English, alien and even threatening; practiced chiefly by immigrants from places like Ireland, Poland and Italy. That was not however the case in County Durham and the neighbouring Northern English counties, where a number of areas had remained faithful to the Catholic Church despite the Reformation, and were living reminders of an authentically ancient English Catholic tradition. Close to Sunderland numerous monastic remains and local place-names like Monkwearmouth and Bishopwearmouth recalled a time when Catholicism had been the norm. Importantly for a family of four children, there were good schools available in the region. One of these was Ampleforth College in North Yorkshire, run by the Benedictine monks of Ampleforth Abbey. It possessed more than one "feeder school" for younger boys.

If there was anything odd about Robert Nairac's early life it is this: to us his upbringing now seems conventional but very old-fashioned, with an emphasis on making your own entertainment through reading, natural history and sport, including country sports like angling and shooting. Seen from the perspective of the twenty-first century, it looks more like an Edwardian than a post-World War II childhood. Even this may not be as odd as it now appears: it simply reflected his parents' and many other parents' choice. Numerous other children born around the same time had a similarly conservative upbringing. Some would rebel; others did not. The fifties, which can be said to have lasted from the Conservatives' election victory of 1951 until their defeat in 1964 or from the Korean War to the rise of the Beatles, were also a small-c conservative era: especially in the early-to-mid 1950s. Many British people of all classes wanted to "get back to normal" after the stresses, strains and shortages of World War II, which the Labour Government had prolonged between 1945 and 1951 by the continuation of the war economy, with rationing, heavy taxation, travel restrictions, the regulation of almost everything and National Service. "It was like living in an occupied country," said Evelyn Waugh to his friend Frances Donaldson.

The continuing post-war austerity in the UK was not even imposed or endured to any good purpose. It was at least partly ideologically-driven. The West German Finance Minister, Ludwig Erhard, engineered an economic miracle out of rubble by slashing taxes: Labour achieved exactly the opposite result between 1945 and 1951 by crushing the British entrepreneurial and innovative spirit under crippling taxation and endless regulations. The top rate of taxation was 98%; death duties were ratcheted up twice in four years. By contrast with renascent West Germany, which rose like the Phoenix from its ashes, hardly any new wealth-creators arose from the mess of post-war Britain. Defeated West Germany, Japan and even (temporarily) Italy bounced back and regained their pre-war prosperity. So did France. Britain however failed to do so to anything like the same extent. The UK's recovery after 1951 was slow, modest, fragile and always at risk from international crises and domestic industrial action by the Trade Unions. This may be attributed at least in part to the reluctance of Conservative Governments from 1951 to 1964 and from 1970 to 1974, to dismantle the structures that Labour had left in place and de-nationalise the economy. Some politicians, notably R A Butler, realised that a bold and innovative approach to the economy was required but he was not supported by his serving Prime Ministers. By an evil consensus between the leaders of industry (nationalised and otherwise) and the Trade Union bosses, the available resources were poured into propping up ailing sunset industries with which both were comfortable, and not developing new technologies of which both were suspicious. Research and development were neglected. This was in contrast to what was happening in Germany, France, Italy, other European countries and Japan.

"Back to normal" for many people meant back to what had been comfortingly normal before 1939 or, better still, prior to 1914. That however was not a realistic option. World War II, and what had amounted to an American occupation from 1942 to 1945, had severely disrupted traditional British culture and behavioural patterns. The UK was now far poorer than it had been in 1914 or even in 1939. The cost of living had risen steeply. Servants were hard to find, even if you could afford to employ one. Britain might possess a symbolic independent nuclear deterrent, but it was no longer an independent imperial power running its own foreign policy. It had been mortgaged to the USA: the Suez crisis of 1956 made that clear. In 1960 the collapse of the Paris "four-power summit" of the USA, the USSR, France and the UK, whose purpose had been to avert nuclear war, of which Prime Minister Harold Macmillan had been the main instigator and in which he had invested much political capital, showed that the UK now counted internationally for relatively little. Its views could be, and increasingly would be, disregarded by the USSR, the USA and France. "It is ignominious; it is tragic; it is almost incredible", wrote Macmillan in his diary. He was so upset that he then retired to bed to lose himself in *Dombey & Son*.

But it was not incredible: it was the predictable consequence of the UK's loss of empire; even more of its loss of economic power and, above all, of the diminution of its military muscle; the ability to intervene effectively in distant parts of the world, which is still the main qualification for a seat at the top table in any international context. Without it, no-one listens; domestic prosperity, "moral authority" of the Swedish variety and skilled diplomacy are not a substitute. Harold Macmillan, like many other British people, had continued to cherish the comforting illusion that the UK, by the skilful use of smoke and mirrors, could continue to play the part of "a great power," dealing on equal terms with the USA and USSR, as it had done as recently as the Second World War. However events had shown that the Emperor now had very few clothes. "The public", wrote a commentator, "which, particularly in England, has been snuggling cosily into 1910, is being bumped and banged into the icy air and blows and counterblows of the 1960s." British people, on the Left and the Right, had great difficulty in adjusting to their reduced status. They would remain in denial for years to come.

Despite this, a measure of prosperity returned, thanks to the optimistically-named "Butler Boom", after the aforementioned R A Butler, who served as

Chancellor of the Exchequer from 1951. There was a conscious and deliberate attempt to return, at least superficially, to the reassuring old ways by many people, including Robert Nairac's parents. The 1950s were the Indian summer of British establishment life. This applied equally to the Army. In 1947, in time for HRH Princess Elizabeth's wedding to Lieutenant Philip Mountbatten RN, the Household Regiments went back to wearing Home Service Clothing with scarlet or blue tunics for public duties. Prior to that date they had been wearing wartime khaki. According to the tailors Gieves & Hawkes, the reason for this was that due to wartime and post-war shortages, tailors, finishers and accoutrement makers had simply not been able to access the required materials for certain parts of, or even for entire, full-dress uniforms since the 1930s. Between 1947 and the Queen's coronation in 1953 other Regiments would follow them, although in some cases the restoration of full-dress uniform was limited to the Regimental band and a token Colour Party. Also in 1947 their Regimental Adjutants instructed Guards officers serving in London, when not on duty and therefore not in uniform, to revert to wearing pre-war plain clothes, including bowler hats, dark suits and a certain type of overcoat, and to carry rolled umbrellas when appearing in public. Informal dress would no longer be acceptable. Contemporary photographs show them looking like their grandfathers half a century earlier. Robert Nairac would for a few years wear this Edwardian version of plain clothes when in London in the 1970s. The Adjutants also wrote to retired and former Guards officers, instructing them to do the same; most of them did so without demur. Many non-Guards men followed their sartorial lead; Savile Row tailors and others obliged by popularising this new, formal "look" (*Note 1*).

It was a time of hats for men as well as for women; of dark suits and stiff detachable shirt collars; of formality and of good manners. In 1956 the London Season revived, complete with Royal Ascot, presentations at Court (*Note 2*) and "coming out" balls for debutantes. "Society is cocking a tentative snook at the masses", fumed the Left-wing *New Statesman (Note 3)*. However the masses did not read *The New Statesman*. It had, and still has, an illustrious but small readership. It did not reflect the mood of the moment, which favoured having fun. That mood was perfectly captured by Julian Slade and Dorothy Reynolds' funny and light-hearted musical *Salad Days*, which had opened in Bristol and quickly transferred to the London West End in 1954. Like much else at that time, *Salad Days* was initially run on a shoestring budget, with a piano rather than an orchestral accompaniment. Nevertheless it ran for 2,283 performances. Many women stopped wearing trousers, which reminded them of the war years, and began to dress elegantly again. For a while church-going increased and became the norm for many; it certainly was for the Nairacs, who were regular attenders at Mass. To many who were alive then, 1963, the last full year of the Conservative "fifties" when Nairac was an impressionable fifteen-year-old, looks in retrospect like the last year of sanity, as an earlier generation had looked back to 1913.

There was another side to this nostalgic picture. The 1950s were not unreservedly an age of innocent *Salad Days* fun. For anyone who did not want to conform or could not, because they were the wrong race, were homosexual or their faces did not fit, life could be difficult. Homosexual men were still prosecuted as vigorously as they had been in Oscar Wilde's time, under the same legislation. Every now and again a new scandal would detonate to remind the public of this. The distinguished mathematician and Enigma code-breaker Alan Turing was prosecuted for homosexual acts in 1952 and died two years later, probably by his own hand. In 1954 Peter Wildeblood, Lord Montagu of Beaulieu and his cousin Michael Pitt-Rivers were imprisoned on flimsy evidence for alleged homosexual offences. For those who were perceived to practice questionable morality, short of fleeing the country altogether, there was only one place to go: cosmopolitan London, where a more relaxed code prevailed; at least in some Bohemian quarters like Chelsea, Soho and Fitzrovia, where exciting new developments in the arts, literature and morals, and stimulating, creative people, were to be encountered. The late Dan Farson has written engagingly in his autobiography, *Never a Normal Man,* about London's Bohemia at this period and its intelligent, witty, abrasive characters like Francis Bacon, Muriel Belcher and John Deakin.

1958 also saw the UK's first race riots, in which Teddy Boys played a prominent role, but that was in London. In Sunderland nothing as jolly or exciting as Soho's Colony Room or the Gargoyle Club was on offer. This did not trouble the Nairacs, however. There were other amusements. It would be years before they even installed a television set and their children were encouraged to read instead. The young Robert became an avid reader, especially of boys' adventure stories. His favourites included G A Henty, whose novels for children typically revolved around boys or young men living in an interesting, troubled period of history. These periods ranged from classical antiquity through the Crusades to more recent conflicts like the 1745 Jacobite Rebellion, the American Civil War and British colonial wars. Henty's young heroes were intelligent, courageous and resourceful but also displayed Christian virtues like honesty and modesty. They were rarely accompanied by a heroine. When there was one, her role was to be saved from danger. Henty, a fervent imperialist, was fortunate to die in 1902; twelve years before the world that he had celebrated went up in smoke. His novels are still popular with many Christian parents and home-schoolers because of the traditional virtues that they seek to inculcate in their young readers and because they are an excellent way of painlessly introducing children to the study of History. Henty's history is normally accurate. He is particularly good when describing events like the Crimean War, at which he had been present in person, either as an Army officer or a journalist.

Robert Nairac would become and remain interested in History, but in a selective way: not all periods appealed equally to him. The Middle Ages, an age of faith, did appeal. One of his Tutors at Oxford was to write that Nairac was "a mediaevalist at heart". By contrast, the reforming Victorian age bored him, with the important exception of British colonial and other wars. Only at Oxford would he become interested in the eighteenth century Age of Reason. Partly because of this selective approach, when he came to read History at Oxford where a broader and deeper approach was required, Nairac experienced problems. Apart from Henty, other authors whose works the young Nairac appreciated were H Rider Haggard and Rudyard Kipling. Haggard's novels, of which *King Solomon's Mines* is the best-known, are mainly set in Africa and are outstandingly bloodthirsty; as a result, children love them. Kipling's novel *Kim (Note 4)*, arguably his best novel, which is based on the life of a real secret agent in imperial India, became and remained one of Nairac's favourite books. Although he appeared to be Indian and spoke Indian languages fluently, the hero, Kim O'Hara, was really the orphan son of an Irish soldier. He was also a master of disguise who became a trusted secret servant of the Raj. Kim's cockiness, courage, resourcefulness and sense of fun clearly appealed to Robert Nairac: Kim was a kindred spirit.

A less Christian influence than G A Henty's heroes was Bulldog Drummond, the creation of H C McNeile (1888-1937), a prolific novelist and former soldier who wrote under the pen-name of "Sapper". Drummond attracted the detestation of the literary Left, for whom he became a hate-figure: "an unspeakable public school bully", according to the Anglo-Irish Poet Laureate Cecil Day-Lewis (Sherborne and Wadham College, Oxford). Curiously, this disapproval has not extended to anything like the same extent to comparable heroes like The Saint, Biggles and James Bond. In 1999, exuding fastidious and politically-correct disapproval, T J Binyon, a distinguished biographer of Pushkin but a less-distinguished literary critic, wrote of Drummond:

"[Sapper's] work, with its reactionary political views, anti-Semitism and curious blend of chivalry and brutality, is scarcely acceptable to the modern reader".

That is arrant nonsense, as well as being unhistorical. Bulldog Drummond is still read and enjoyed. The well-informed modern reader is able to place Bulldog Drummond in his historical context, which is the turbulent immediate aftermath of the Great War. This included the brutal and merciless Russian Revolution and Civil War, the murder of the Russian Imperial Family and many other Russians, and the Anglo-Irish War of 1919-21, followed by the Irish Civil War of 1921-22. As any historian could confirm, Drummond had many reasons for feeling reactionary. His "anti-Semitism" seems to have consisted mainly of an awareness that a number of leading Bolsheviks were of Jewish or partly-Jewish origin; which they were, including Lenin himself and Trotsky and so had been Karl Marx: that is simply fact. There are Jewish villains in some of the Drummond stories (e.g. *The Black Gang*) but they are outnumbered by Gentile villains. Careful study however shows that the characters of other contemporary writers, including Agatha Christie, also often exhibit the unthinking xenophobia of that period, so Drummond is not exceptional. The late Ion Trewin, editor, author and publisher, considered that, at any rate in the 1920s and 1930s, Drummond was perceived "simply as an upstanding Tory who spoke for many of his countrymen".

The reader will presumably also understand that fictional characters do not necessarily express their authors' considered moral or political views. For example, P G Wodehouse's languid hero Psmith claimed to be a Communist and addressed his friends as "Comrade", but we do not usually think of Wodehouse as a Bolshevik. We first meet Bulldog Drummond through an advertisement, which he placed in the Press in 1919:

"Demobilised officer, finding peace incredibly tedious, would welcome diversion. Legitimate if possible; but crime, if of a comparatively humorous description, no objection. Excitement essential."

Drummond received 45 replies. While it aroused his respectable servant's disapproval, Drummond's advertisement was guaranteed to appeal to most boys and many men who bought the book. Captain Hugh Drummond DSO MC is of interest, among other reasons, because he is one of James Bond's ancestors. The young Ian Fleming had enjoyed the works of both Sapper and Somerset Maugham, whose Ashenden spy stories are based on Maugham's own experiences as a source-handler in Geneva during the First World War. Both of their influence can be detected in the James Bond novels. The first four Bulldog Drummond novels pitted Drummond against the international criminal Carl Peterson, who became his arch-enemy. Peterson, a prototype Bond villain, was a master of disguise and used several aliases. He was satisfyingly and painfully killed at the end of the fourth novel, *The Final Count.* Unlike Drummond, Peterson was not married but had a slinky, sinisterly beautiful mistress, Irma, who smoked Sobranies in a long cigarette-holder. An archetypal 1920s vamp, elegant and villainous, Irma was clearly very bad news.

Captain Drummond was physically very strong. Although he predated the foundation of the SAS Regiment by more than twenty years and his creator died before the SAS was founded, Drummond's Great War experiences had given him capabilities akin to those of an SAS soldier (*Note 5*). One was stealth: "he could move over ground without a single blade of grass rustling." Drummond had the ability to kill and incapacitate others silently and easily: "he could kill a man with his bare hands in a second." During his time on the Western Front he would go on solitary, and presumably unauthorised, raids across No-man's Land to murder Germans. Drummond was proficient in unarmed combat and boxing and was a crack shot. He would have hated to be called intellectual but his native intelligence allowed him to equal and beat his opponents. In his post-war adventures Drummond was joined by several of his ex-Army friends. He was "a brutalized ex-officer whose thirst for excitement is also an attempt to re-enact the war".

If some of this sounds curiously familiar, perhaps it should. Several of Nairac's former friends have suggested that Bulldog Drummond might have influenced him in his keen interest in contact sports like boxing and in physical fitness, in his choice of the Army as a career and in his decision to volunteer for undercover work in Northern Ireland. This might be so, although it is impossible to prove. It is a matter of record that Nairac became an exceptionally fit and strong young man, like Bulldog Drummond. But was Bulldog Drummond indirectly responsible for Nairac's early death? That seems to be carrying amateur psychology much too far. Yet this was apparently the view of his elder sister Gabrielle, quoted in Toby Harnden's *Bandit Country*. Gabrielle travelled to Ireland seven years after her brother's murder to see the places where he had been abducted and killed. She reportedly said:

"Robert certainly stuck his neck out. He was a bit dotty like that. He thought he could get away with it, but in a way we all do. As a small boy he had read Bulldog Drummond, so you can imagine his approach."

In the interest of fairness and balance, Nairac's Oxford friend Julian Malins does not agree. He believes that the Christian and idealistic Henty, rather than the brutal Bulldog Drummond, was a much more important influence on Nairac.

Nairac's reading tastes were to mature beyond Henty and Sapper. Malins describes Nairac as well-read. The adult Nairac's literary interests were eclectic. He continued to enjoy Kipling. He enjoyed reading T E Lawrence, especially *The Seven Pillars of Wisdom*. Like Lawrence, he developed an interest in the Crusades and other mediaeval wars. There are however some curious, capricious gaps in Nairac's interests; that is often the case with autodidacts. For example, despite his deep interest in T E Lawrence and in the Crusades, Sir Mark Allen, who knew Nairac at Oxford, says that he never showed the faintest interest in the Arabs, Arab culture or even in Arabian falconry techniques. He was only mildly interested when Allen showed him an Arabian falcon that he had acquired. In addition to being an Arabist, Mark Allen is the author of *Falconry in Arabia*.

Anything mediaeval was likely to be well-received, which included mediaeval romances like Malory's *Le Morte d'Arthur*. So was anything on Ireland: history, biography, poetry, folklore or legend. Nairac read works of general history and biography, if only because they were relevant to his studies. In due course he would graduate to the novels of R S Surtees, John Buchan, Evelyn Waugh and Simon Raven. He read extensively about natural history and field sports. Nairac is one of the very few people known to have read every single volume of the Badminton Library of Sports and Pastimes – one of which is devoted to *Coursing and Falconry* – and to have remembered most of what he had read. He was familiar with the writings of T H White, who shared his interest in the mediaeval period, although he preferred *The Goshawk* above *The Sword in the Stone*. This is unsurprising in a boy and man who would become devoted to falconry.

Little information of interest is available on Nairac's early schooling, probably because it was so ordinary and conventional. From a day school he passed to Gilling Castle, one of the feeder schools for Ampleforth College. It is now Ampleforth's Preparatory School. From there in 1960 he moved to College, the junior house of Ampleforth. All the evidence suggests that he was at that time a bright, motivated little boy with a lively imagination, happy to lose himself in G A Henty's novels or Arthurian legends, but equally happy to play sport; almost any sport, with a serious interest in natural history and keeping a variety of animals as pets.

I have found little evidence to support the theory put forward by some biographers (Anthony Bradley, for instance) that the young Nairac was a military maniac, who was determined from an early age to join the Army, and if possible the Special Forces, with a view to killing numerous people. There was no tradition of military service on his father's side. Basil Dykes, his maternal uncle, had an adventurous war between 1939 and 1946, but that had been Territorial Army and wartime service: Basil had not studied at Sandhurst and was never a regular soldier. In civil life he was a lawyer. Insofar as Nairac the schoolboy had any clear plans for adult life, his immediate priority was to get into either Oxford or Cambridge to read History and, having got there, to play a lot of sport. Thereafter he seems to have favoured becoming a school teacher. There is evidence of this on his Lincoln College file, and other evidence from his time teaching at Avisford School in 1967-68, that indicates that he might have made a very good schoolmaster.

Nairac's leaving report from Ampleforth states under Future Career: "Law – Solicitor?" This probably represented a school careers adviser's suggestion, rather than Nairac's personal inclination. It might also reflect the fact that Basil Dykes was a country solicitor. No doubt a place could have been found for Nairac in his law office if he had decided to follow that path. Whatever the reason, the suggestion implies a lack of understanding of what made Robert tick. It aroused merriment and disbelief among Nairac's surviving friends: "He'd have died of boredom", said one. "Flamboyant barrister just possibly, but solicitor? No way!" said another. Julian Malins, who read Law at Oxford and did become a barrister, said that Nairac had never shown the slightest interest in the Law. However the Army was not mentioned, either, until much later. When Nairac left school in 1966 the Army might not have seemed an especially good career option, given that it had shrunk dramatically in response to the end of the Empire and of National Service, and was still shrinking. Following the 1957 Defence White Paper, many Regiments had been amalgamated between 1958 and 1960. Further cuts and amalgamations would take place in the 1960s and early 1970s.

Even if they have no intention of joining the Army later, most boys enjoy playing soldiers, whether with a group of friends or with model figurines. Robert Nairac was no exception. He was born in 1948, soon after the Second World

War, during a militarised period of British history. Conscription had been a fact of British life for almost a decade and showed no sign of ending any time soon. In 1948, the year of Nairac's birth, the Malayan Emergency began and would continue until 1960. In 1950 the Korean War broke out; it would last until 1953. This was a UN operation to which the UK contributed 100,000 troops as part of the First Commonwealth Division, with troops from Canada, Australia, New Zealand and India. Of these 100,000, 1,000 were killed (some by friendly-fire); a further 1,000 were posted missing in action or taken prisoner during the conflict; 2,000 were wounded. In 1952, when Nairac was four years old, the SAS would be re-founded to confront the Chinese Communist insurgents in Malaya. There followed a series of other "emergencies" in *inter alia* Kenya, Cyprus, Borneo and Yemen. Although call-ups officially ended on 31 December 1960, the last National Servicemen did not hand back their boots until May 1963. Nairac could not have escaped the influence of that period. He developed an interest in military history, although that interest tended to focus on periods prior to the twentieth century, including the Middle Ages. Luke Jennings recalls his lecturing with panache at Avisford School during his gap year as an Assistant Master on such subjects as the Crimean War and the Indian Mutiny, giving vivid and gory descriptions of field surgery without anaesthetic and of the Cawnpore Massacre. No matter: many small boys have ghoulish tastes and his young pupils seem to have thoroughly enjoyed his lectures. By contrast, the political causes of these two conflicts were treated in a fairly perfunctory way.

Ampleforth was a very military school in those days, for various reasons including National Service. Nairac trained with the Combined Cadet Force (CCF) at Ampleforth and became a Cadet Under-Officer. He sat and passed his Army Proficiency Certificate (APC; the former Cert A). This included Tactics, Shooting, Drill and Map Reading. At that period however CCF was compulsory for all pupils and Nairac could not easily have avoided it, even if he had wished to. There is no evidence that he ever had any serious military interests at Oxford, other than as part of his History course, until his final (fourth) year. He seems to have decided on an Army career after a lot of hard thinking during the long summer vacation of 1971.

Looking back to Sunderland in the 1950s, Robert Nairac benefited from a strong and stable family. He was the youngest of four children: a much-desired second son and an amusing, adorable little brother, with a much older brother and two older sisters. All of them were accomplished; Robert was expected to become successful and accomplished in his turn. Once more, there is something slightly atypical or old-fashioned. In modern English families, boys are normally closer to Mother and girls to Father. In Robert Nairac's case, his closest bond seems to have been with his father, who is remembered as an exceptionally kind and gentle person, for whom Medicine was a vocation, not just a profession. More than once in the coming years Maurice Nairac would have to intervene with the authorities on behalf of his beloved but wayward younger son: "my boy Robert", as he referred to him in correspondence, even in Robert's twenties. Maurice has been described as "a devout Catholic and a purist trout fisherman who disdained all methods but the upstream dry fly". He tied his own fishing flies. He was a keen horticulturist, who cultivated delicious miniature melons in his greenhouse and grew Pattisons, a rare kind of squash native to Mauritius, from seeds sent to him by relations there. He claimed to be shocked to learn that one of his relations had bought tomato plants for her greenhouse, instead of growing her own from seed, as he did. The science of growing things fascinated Maurice.

As his specialisation, Maurice became a distinguished eye-surgeon, pioneering new surgical techniques and publishing numerous articles on eye surgery in learned journals. Despite the many calls on his time, Maurice Nairac took an Edwardian paternal interest in his sons' upbringing, introducing them to country sports. Initially these were angling, especially dry-fly fishing, and shooting, at both of which Robert was to excel. There was a tradition of angling on both sides of Nairac's family. Not only was his father a dry-fly angler; Robert's great-grandfather on his mother's side, Martin Woosnam, had been a keen salmon fisherman. His uncle, Basil Dykes, was a serious trout angler, although he only took to it in later life. To these Robert eventually added falconry, in which Maurice also took a friendly interest.

Maurice Nairac was less Francophile than his son Robert. Although he was a Mauritian French speaker, of impeccable French descent with numerous French relations, his loyalty was to the British Crown. He was also a sincere and conservative Roman Catholic, who passed on to his sons his loyalties and his prejudices. Robert seems to have liked France, enjoying visiting French cousins, and spoke the language very well.

This book is not a hagiography: although he was basically a good person, Robert Nairac was not a saint, or not a conventional one, although he was a hero. His father, however, does seem to have had saintly qualities. One of his nephews said:

"I went to see Uncle Maurice when he was dying of cancer aged about eighty. We usually spoke French together. I sat with him for a while and, after a silence, staring out of the window, he said 'J'ai eu une parfaite vie'. I was stunned. He'd lost both sons in unhappy circumstances; his only son-in-law had dropped dead from a heart attack aged fifty, and yet he was looking back on his life and thinking it perfect. I couldn't figure it out at all, but thought: 'Well, good, if that's how he feels, so be it, thank goodness he's not bitter at the end. Many would be.'"

In parallel with field sports, Maurice encouraged an interest in natural history. Robert became a good field naturalist, specialising in ornithology. As a logical extension to this, he kept a private menagerie of pet animals, including a snake, a polecat-ferret (a ferret with normal polecat markings, as opposed to an albino), a buzzard and kestrels. In some respects the young Robert Nairac sounds rather like the young Gerald Durrell, the author, naturalist and zoo-director, who had also kept numerous animals as pets, but Nairac was better educated and more religious.

A cousin recalls that: "Once there was a wounded blackbird (maimed by a cat I think) in their garden in Sunderland. I went to get David's BSA airgun in order to put the thing out of its misery. But Robert got into an awful pet about finishing it off, really squalling, so I didn't!"

The outcome – whether Nairac nursed the bird back to health or whether the cat later finished it off – is now forgotten.

Latterly hawks supplanted other animals, as Robert Nairac had become a serious falconer. Strictly speaking, he became an austringer: a falconer who specialises in goshawks. Although Nairac is known to have flown a buzzard, an eagle and long-winged falcons, including peregrines, which belonged to other people, he preferred goshawks and their equally ferocious smaller relations, sparrowhawks.

A second "significant other" in Robert Nairac's life was his maternal uncle, Basil Dykes, who had been born in 1911 near Kidderminster. Basil was articled to one of his Welsh Woosnam uncles in his law practice in Solihull, near Birmingham. He passed his Law Society exams, qualified as a solicitor and joined the firm of Russell & Orme in Ledbury, a market town in Herefordshire, soon becoming a partner. Perhaps to add interest to his life, by 1936 Basil had joined the Territorial Army and started to train as a soldier in his spare time.

Surviving photos show two different aspects of Basil: later ones depict a bespectacled and benevolent-looking man who appears to be exactly what he was: a respected country solicitor living at Colwall in the Malvern Hills and with an office in Ledbury. He looks the sort of person who might be featured in *Amateur Gardening* magazine, having won first prize for his delphiniums in the Mid-Worcestershire Flower Show. When his daughter, Nairac's cousin, became engaged to be married, her attractive and demure portrait occupied the title page in *Country Life*. In addition to being an angler, Basil was an excellent shot. Some of his clients, who were rich landowners, would invite him to shoot over their estates. Like his nephew, Basil Dykes was widely liked and respected but a hard man to know. He was affable, charming, gentlemanly, but not much of a joiner. He belonged to the Rotary Club, but only because that was the right thing for a solicitor in a small country town to do. Unlike his nephew, he was reserved and not at all boisterous. One of his former legal colleagues recalls that "No matter who you talk to, even today, you won't hear a bad word spoken about Basil Dykes". He added that Basil was a very kindly man who had been most welcoming when he first joined the practice. But in the final analysis the kind and charming Basil remains as elusive and hard-to-fathom in death as he was in life. This amiable man was also very secretive.

Earlier photographs of Basil, taken in the 1930s and 1940s, show a keen-looking officer in battledress or No 2 Service Dress; quite unlike the solicitor of later years.

Although he was never in the Regular Army, Basil was the nearest thing to a career soldier in Robert Nairac's immediate family. On 18 April 1936, at the age of 25, he had been commissioned as a Second Lieutenant in the 7th (Territorial) Battalion of the Worcestershire Regiment, having previously been a Cadet Sergeant in the Clifton College Officers' Training Corps. His Commission, which survives, was signed by King Edward VIII, making it something of a rarity. Basil Dykes was gazetted Lieutenant on 1 July 1939, two months before the outbreak of war and was soon promoted to Captain. He served through the Second World War in various capacities and ended it as an Acting Major. Unusually, when he was discharged from active service in 1946, the Army Council granted him the honorary rank of Major, which he had the right to use from the day of his demobilisation. This is confirmed both by a letter from the War Office and in the Gazette. (Basil seldom, if ever, after leaving the Army, called himself "Major Dykes".)

Basil Dykes' war got off to a bad start. In January 1940 he was sent to France and then to Belgium with the British Expeditionary Force (BEF). In June 1940 he was caught up in the BEF's retreat to Dunkirk. The Low Countries had been overrun, France was collapsing and the BEF had been cut off in a small and indefensible enclave around the Channel Ports. The BEF had tried to counter-attack. They were not successful and now they were waiting to be evacuated. We should be grateful for Hitler's vanity. If Hitler had been prudent and had listened to his Generals, he would have finished off the BEF at that point by sending in General Guderian and his tanks. Fortunately for the BEF, Hitler was convinced that he knew better and did not follow the Generals' advice. The BEF was not in the event annihilated.

However things were quite bad enough. When weather permitted, the Luftwaffe would strafe and bomb the beaches. The RAF's fighter-planes were not numerous enough to prevent them. British corpses were floating face-down in the shallows. All the BEF's heavy equipment had to be abandoned, together with stores, ammunition and fuel. Between 10 May and 22 June, when France surrendered, the BEF lost 68,000 soldiers killed, wounded, missing or captured. Basil's family were told that he had been posted "missing, believed killed or taken prisoner".

This was not in fact the case. Basil, a twenty-eight-year-old recently-gazetted Captain, was now the Acting Company Commander of C Company of his Battalion. With the remains of his Company Basil had managed to get aboard the very last Royal Navy ship to leave Dunkirk. He was one of a total of 338,226 soldiers who were successfully evacuated. Although his own account, *Dunkirk, a Memoir*, is written in terse Army language and modestly underplays his own role, it is clear that Basil showed presence of mind and leadership in getting many of his men back to England through an amphibious evacuation under heavy fire. No Mention in Despatches would ever be forthcoming but Basil had unquestionably been very brave. He laconically concluded his account: "The ship raced on and at 2.30 am on June 3rd we were disembarking across the decks of another destroyer in Dover Harbour". He then took leave to visit his family. They had not given up hope; they had prayed for his safety, as they would pray again when Robert Nairac went missing in 1977. In 1940 God answered their prayers and Basil walked in, unannounced.

After his return Basil was emotionally and physically exhausted, unable to sleep and probably suffering from Post Traumatic Stress Disorder (PTSD), although recognition of this condition lay many years in the future. Possibly for this reason, and because he seems to have been a good linguist, Basil was soon afterwards transferred from the Infantry to the Army Intelligence Corps. A new phase of Basil's war was about to begin. From the Army Intelligence Corps he joined MI5 on 24 November 1941. His next posting was as a Regional Security Liaison Officer in Birmingham. MI5 have provided few details of his work for them, but he was entrusted with some very sensitive inquiries. He was the first person to express concern about the reliability of the German-born British theoretical physicist Dr Klaus Fuchs. In 1943 Captain Dykes minuted: "Surely the point is whether a man of his nature who has been described as being clever and dangerous should be in a position where he has access to information of the highest degree of secrecy and importance?" At that time his warning seems to have been disregarded, but Basil was right: Fuchs turned out to be a Soviet spy.

Basil transferred to Counter-Espionage in London in March 1944. His family believe that part of his work at this time was training French spies. In August 1944 he left MI5 to join the Supreme Headquarters Allied Expeditionary Force (SHAEF). This was the headquarters of the Commander of Allied Forces in North-West Europe from late 1943 until the end of the Second World War and was based at Teddington in Middlesex. Basil served in France, Italy and Germany. Basil's British medals, which survive, include the Italy Star and the Germany Star, along with the 1939-45 Star and the General Service Medal, but little is known about his service in Italy and Germany.

Basil was now engaged in military intelligence-gathering and source-handling. He spoke fluent French, had a great love of France and a number of friends there, so his secret work in France is perhaps not surprising. After his death his family found in a drawer in his desk the citations of two French decorations that General de Gaulle had conferred on Basil in his capacity as President of the Provisional Government of the French Republic. These were the *Médaille de la Reconnaissance Nationale* (literally, the Medal of National Gratitude) for "exceptional military services rendered in the course of operations for the liberation of France." The other was the *Croix de Guerre* (the French War Cross). This medal is awarded to soldiers who have distinguished themselves by acts of heroism during combat with the enemy. The citation, while short on specifics, indicates that Basil had been attached to the French General Staff as a Liaison Officer. He had carried out his duties with great conscientiousness and in a comradely spirit under conditions that had been "often difficult". He had made an important contribution to "operations against the common enemy". Precisely what Basil had done against the common enemy has been hard to establish; even today the French authorities are reticent on the subject.

Basil never spoke to his family about his war service, other than his time as an Infantry officer in 1939-40, about which he also wrote. Long after 1945 he considered that he was still constrained by the Official Secrets Act. They were nevertheless aware that he had been involved in some branch of Military Intelligence. He was more forthcoming with his nephew Robert Nairac, especially after he had signed up for the Army. As an Army officer, Nairac would have signed the same Act. Nairac mentioned to one or two brother officers that he had a respected older relation who had had an exciting career as a secret agent during the Second World War. This, he implied, had sparked his own interest in undercover work.

After the war Basil's spirit of adventure was still alive. He proposed to emigrate and become a farmer in Africa. However his wife Mary was opposed to this, so Basil went back to being a solicitor in Ledbury: this was probably not the life that he would have chosen for himself. He varied his existence with travel, shooting and fishing. He briefly and vicariously lived adventurously though his nephew's all-too-short military career. Basil seems to have been a sympathetic mentor who was an important influence on his nephew and he was definitely hero material. Although he would have winced at this description, during the war Basil had come close to being a James Bond in real life. So Nairac had a heroic uncle who had been a soldier and a secret agent, with whom he would inevitably compare himself and whom he felt he ought to emulate.

Nairac had a further hero against whom to measure himself. This was his elder brother, David. While it is clear that a strong bond existed between the young Robert and his father, it is more difficult to measure the impact that Robert's elder brother had on him, although he certainly did make an impact. We can only guess at how close they were. David was a decade older than Robert; he almost belonged to an earlier generation. It is likely that he was named after his maternal grandfather, Dr David Dykes. (Basil Dykes' first name was also David, although he rarely used it.) Born in 1937, David, like Robert, bore Laurence as his middle name. Like Robert, he was sent away to be educated: first to Avisford School, where Robert would later spend his gap year teaching, and then to Ampleforth College, to which he had won a scholarship. He would however have been at home for at least some of the time during the academic holidays. He only spent four years at Ampleforth, as many bright boys did, but he made his mark there. David left in 1955 aged almost eighteen to start the intensive and demanding medical course at St Bartholomew's Hospital (Bart's), the oldest and most prestigious of the London teaching hospitals, founded in 1123. At Bart's David performed so well as a medical student that on graduation in 1960 he was offered a post on the staff of the hospital, which is an unusual distinction. This must have caused his father particular pleasure.

From the surviving records at Ampleforth it is clear that David was a parent's and a teacher's dream pupil. He seems never to have done anything wrong, other than to fail an Italian exam, which was hardly central to his science studies. Handsome, upright, honourable, academically brilliant, good at games, his Housemaster in St Cuthbert's House, Fr Sebastian Lambert, later described him in this way:

"A boy of very sound character, most conscientious and energetic – a splendid example of public spirit. He was always a hard worker and reached a high standard in his work. In every way he was most satisfactory, thoroughly reliable, honest and straightforward".

David Nairac achieved a more than respectable spread of academic passes, especially in Science subjects, including a Distinction in Chemistry. He also played in the First XV at rugby; was a first-class shot; a Monitor, a Cadet Sergeant in the CCF and other admirable achievements. He left Ampleforth covered in glory and bound for further glory. While clearly a splendid man and a credit to his family and his school, he was going to be a hard act for his younger brother to follow: especially if, like Robert, that brother was not endowed with a scientific intellect.

A cousin describes David thus:

"Robert's older brother David was a lovely guy, good-looking, utterly charming, played the guitar and used to sing us slightly risqué songs. I remember one about a girl thinking about becoming a prostitute in London: "Curzon Street, Curzon Street, are your pavements really paved with gold?" or something like that. He had the happy knack of treating me, and all young kids, like equals, though he was much older. I loved him. We so looked forward to his unfortunately rare visits. I almost feel like crying now to think of such a lovely life vanishing, paf, just like that".

Suddenly David was no longer there. As the *Ampleforth Journal* for 1962 records, David, by now an Assistant to the House Physician at Barts, contracted a rare virus in the course of his duties and died on the feast day of his patron (St Laurence), 10 August. He was 24 years old. Fit and healthy young man though he was, it attacked him with frightening speed; myocarditis (inflammation of the heart muscle) set in. He was dead within 48 hours. Any one of a number of viruses could have had this effect and we do not know which one was involved. There was no autopsy. There was no time for deathbed farewells. Maurice Nairac travelled from Sunderland to identify the body and apply for the death certificate.

It is reasonable to assume that Robert was badly affected by losing his only brother. He seldom mentioned him thereafter, even to close friends. His Army friends were surprised to discover, in most cases only after Robert's own death, that he had ever possessed a brother. However he could hardly have forgotten

David, even if he had wished to. In September 1962 Robert, who had passed two years in College, would move into St Edward's House. This was only seven years after David's departure from the school. At Ampleforth there were reminders of David. He was present in team and cadet force photos; his name was recorded as the winner of major prizes and distinctions. At home he would be remembered often, even if he was rarely mentioned. From this point Robert became the Nairac heir; the repository of his parents' and siblings' hopes and ambitions. The onus was on Robert to make a name for himself; to achieve what his brother never now could, and in some subliminal way to compensate his parents for David's loss. He would try hard to do so for the rest of his short life. Fifteen years remained to him: in that time he would achieve a remarkable amount, against considerable odds.

It was a great responsibility to place on the shoulders of a boy of fourteen and was in fact unrealistic. Robert might one day equal or surpass David's sporting achievements, but academically there was no competition. Robert Nairac was not stupid: he seems to have had a good IQ (*Note 6*), but his was not a scientific mind. The subjects at which he excelled, and which he was to study to A Level, were Arts subjects such as French, Latin, and History. Although he also achieved a good spread of O Levels, including some science subjects, there was no question of his following his father and David into the medical profession. He would have to find other ways to impress his parents and make his mark. Meanwhile, a month after David's death, Robert was about to move into St Edward's House at Ampleforth, and come under the care of the eccentric Fr Jerome Lambert, in a vulnerable emotional state of mind; not the ideal circumstances for confronting what would prove to be, to put it mildly, a challenging experience. For good or ill, Ampleforth would mark him permanently. If David's death was the first real crisis that Robert had known, Ampleforth would shortly deliver a second home-grown crisis of its own, with lasting consequences. We shall examine this in due course.

So far little mention has been made of Nairac's mother, née Barbara Dykes, or of his maternal heredity. Yet this is important. Obviously his mother's brother Basil Dykes was a major influence on Robert Nairac for the whole of his short life. Although the Dykes family appeared to be very English, Anglican and conventional, they were not: Basil and Barbara Dykes' parents were Scots and Welsh. This means that Robert Nairac was not really English or Anglo-Saxon at all. On his father's side he was Gascon, Catholic, Latin and volatile; on his mother's he was a Celt; talented, artistic and mystical. Not only would his mother have helped to form Robert's character but her Welsh mother, née Vida Woosnam and known to her relations as "Mumsie", lived with the Nairacs during the last years of her life. She was reportedly a strong character; she has been described as small, lively and fast-talking. She could play the part of the "sweet little old lady" to perfection but could also reportedly be "a right royal pain in the backside!" She had endured a difficult childhood involving a disliked stepmother and half-siblings, which might explain this. Mumsie could also be kindly, witty, fun; occasionally outrageous, and was apparently much loved by her grandchildren.

Humour apart, she sounds a lot like her grandson Robert Nairac. The "mischief-gene" seems to have come from her. So did his taste for the finer things in life, his ability as a raconteur, actor, mimic and linguist. A family member commented that:

"Re Robert's 'posh Malone' put-on accent, we as a family have always been good mimics and I think the gene came from Mumsie. She was quite a raconteur and used to embellish her stories by imitating those she was telling you about. Basil could do a good Brummie accent too, after his years in Solihull. Rosemonde can do a fine Geordie amongst others, besides speaking German, Italian and French".

The same cousin mentioned that "I, too, always had a good French accent despite never speaking it till I was 16 and have been complimented on my accent by natives in my smattering of German, Italian and Spanish. Inherited mimicry, you see."

Robert Nairac could also mimic a good Geordie accent, acquired from a much-loved cleaning lady in Sunderland. He too seems to have had little difficulty in picking up new languages. Having a good ear for languages often goes with having an ear for music, which Nairac also possessed. And, like his grandmother, he was a brilliant raconteur.

Nairac's mother, Barbara, was completely different. She was reportedly "very proper, very English, though perhaps with a faint echo of Scotland in her speech; quite formal and serious in outlook". Barbara took after her father, who was a serious-minded Scottish doctor. When one of her nephews, aged about sixteen, came to stay with the Nairacs, she arranged for him to visit a coal mine, because she thought it was educational. It took him a very long time to clean off the coal-dust afterwards. Barbara was a very positive person; always looking for the good in things, always keen to do something useful. She would have need of this positive attitude. She lived through, and somehow rose above, four great personal tragedies: she outlived her sons, both of whom she lost young in tragic circumstances; her only son-in-law, who died of a heart attack not long after Robert's murder; her brother and her husband, who died of cancer. She was stoical, as was Robert.

Barbara Nairac could never quite accept the fact of Robert's death in 1977, probably because his body was never found. She had a little shrine in the hall with his portrait and the GC medal. She must have looked at it every day. For years she continued to hope that somehow he might have survived and would one day walk through her door, as Basil had in 1940. She died in 1999, still not knowing what had really happened to Robert.

Sometimes Nairac's Celtic heritage would show through his veneer of Englishness. After a few drinks, he was quite likely to sing Welsh songs. It is not evident to what extent he had mastered the Welsh tongue; his grandmother only spoke limited Welsh. But it is possible to sing songs in any language beautifully, without really understanding the words – opera singers frequently do so. Given this strong Celtic influence, Robert Nairac's later empathy with the Irish is more readily understandable. In their long history the Scots and the Welsh spent almost as much time resisting English invasion as did the Irish; in the case of the Scots, rather more successfully. Once again, the half-Scots, half-Welsh Basil Dykes played an indirect role. His wife Mary was an Irish Catholic, born and raised until the age of ten in Dungarvan, County Waterford. Her parents left Ireland for England after 1922 as a result of the original Troubles; her father was working for the British Government as a colonial civil servant. Soon after their departure their house was burned down. Despite this, Mary Dykes had remained very Irish in outlook. It is highly likely that Mary, who had known Nairac from his childhood, told him stories about Ireland, taught him Irish songs and awakened his interest in her country. On one occasion Mary took Nairac night-fishing while he was visiting her and Basil. Nairac was driving an open-topped sports car and the pair of them drove through the summer night singing Irish songs at the top of their voices. Well into her nineties Mary had an excellent memory and could recall and recite song lyrics faultlessly. This aunt by marriage on his mother's side was the nearest thing that Nairac could have produced to a genuinely Irish ancestor.

While Nairac was at Ampleforth his parents moved upwards and southwards. His father became a consultant surgeon at the Gloucestershire Royal Hospital in Gloucester: an improvement on Sunderland Infirmary in both financial and social terms. This dictated a move from County Durham to the Cotswolds in rural Gloucestershire. Maurice Nairac was now able to buy part of a subdivided large, ancient manor house: Master's Keep in the village of Standish, near Stonehouse and about twelve miles from Gloucester. The manor house is said once to have formed part of a monastery. It was a great area in which to engage in field sports, including fishing, shooting and, in due course, falconry. It was within easy striking distance of London. The move also placed the Nairacs within easy reach of Basil Dykes in Worcestershire. Sunderland was now just a memory, although Robert Nairac would continue to study in the North of England at Ampleforth until 1966 and would often revisit it in later years, to call on the monks and see other friends. He loved the Yorkshire moors as much as he did the rolling countryside of Gloucestershire, or the mountains, moorlands and lochs of the Hebrides. The British countryside was Nairac's natural habitat, as it was Hilaire Belloc's:

The spring's superb adventure calls
His dust athwart the woods to flame;
His boundary river's secret falls
Perpetuate and repeat his name.
He rides his loud October sky:
He does not die. He does not die.

If Nairac hated the twentieth century, how much more would he have hated the twenty-first, and what we have done to our countryside, sliced up by motorways and increasingly built over?

One of the many positive aspects of Nairac's character was his immense capacity for love and loyalty: it needed an outlet. It was often deflected onto unexpected people and objects. One of these would be the Army, for which he developed a great and lasting love; another was Ireland, which became his nemesis. Yet another was birds of prey, with which he may be said to have had a mystical love affair that ended only with his death.

Nairac's interest in falconry was stimulated at an early age by reading T H White's *The Goshawk* and nurtured in Ireland while staying with his Amplefordian friends the Morris brothers, who were keen falconers. His interest received further encouragement after the Nairacs moved to Gloucestershire. Not far from his parents' house was Newent, where the then Falconry Centre (now the International Centre for Birds of Prey (ICBP)) was the brainchild of its first Director, Philip Glasier (*Note 7*), the "Pope" of British falconry. During the Second World War Glasier had instructed Hugh Dormer, the future DSO, then a Sandhurst cadet, in falconry. The Centre opened in 1967. In addition to its educational work as a specialised zoo, the Centre began successfully breeding birds of prey in captivity, including species threatened in the wild. The Centre also offered courses in falconry for those who wanted to learn how to train, fly and hunt with birds of prey. Philip Glasier trained Nairac in falconry: he could have wished for no better tutor. However, even in 1967 Nairac clearly was not a complete falconry novice; he had kept a hawk while still at Ampleforth. He continued to keep them while teaching at Avisford and later, while studying at Oxford. Whenever he had the chance he would continue to fly hawks; including an eagle, in the Army. The falconer Martin Jones recalls that:

"Harris Hawks first came to the UK in the late sixties and we used to take students from Newent hawking moorhens with them around the local ponds. When Robert accompanied us, which he did on several occasions, he was his usual gung-ho self and had the majority of them jumping in to flush, himself in the lead, even though some of the ponds had a fair leavening of agricultural effluent."

Nairac was never afraid to get down and dirty: it would stand him in good stead as a future Infantry officer. Philip Glasier, who died in 2000, was to dedicate his monumental and magisterial work *Falconry and Hawking*, published in 1978, the year after Nairac's murder, to Captain Robert Nairac. The ICBP Director is now Glasier's daughter, Jemima Parry-Jones MBE, who liked Nairac and remembers him well, although she was a young girl when he was killed.

After joining the Army Nairac kept his hawks at the Centre. The famous, beloved hawk eagle, Brimstone, was in fact Philip Glasier's property although Nairac often flew her, mostly against gamebirds in Scotland. Apart from Brimstone,

Nairac also flew a buzzard, goshawks, sparrow-hawks and kestrels, and he almost certainly flew peregrines and lanners belonging to Philip Glasier. In Ireland he flew peregrines and peregrine hybrids that belonged to John Morris, which he bred in captivity.

The birds that Nairac would keep at Oxford, though not simultaneously, were an intimidating goshawk and irritable sparrow-hawks. Most sparrow-hawks are irritable: they are fiery, difficult birds; tremendous to fly, but rarely have any respect for the person flying them and are apt to go absent without leave. Goshawks, much larger cousins of the sparrow-hawk, share many of the same characteristics and are even more challenging to train.

Although his hawks are one of the reasons why Nairac stood out and is remembered by many Oxford contemporaries, he was not the only falconer of his generation at Oxford. At least one Don and two other undergraduates, both of whom knew Nairac, were also falconers. One was Robert Kenward, now Professor Robert Kenward of the Centre for Ecology and Hydrology. At that time he was an undergraduate of Christ Church and sometimes tethered his hawks in Christ Church Meadow. Like Nairac, he favoured goshawks. The other contemporary was Mark Allen, now Sir Mark Allen KCMG, Arabist and Fellow of St Antony's College, who was reading Arabic at Exeter College at the same time that Nairac was reading History at Lincoln College.

Patrick Mercer, who was later MP for Newark and who knew Nairac while they both were in the Army, once asked Nairac whether it was difficult to train a bird of prey to impose his will on a wild bird.

"He said he found it easy. But Nairac was so charismatic that he could have found it easy to impose his will on most people. In truth there was something of the bird of prey about him."

If so, Nairac must have been an exception. Most people find training a hawk hard and stressful work, requiring the patience of Job (*Note 8*), as does dry-fly angling, which was another of Nairac's favourite sports.

Why falconry? Luke Jennings explains: "To anyone who has immersed himself in the traditional rituals of field sports and experienced the near-mystical sense of place and history that can accompany them... such associations will be less surprising. Put simply, the swooping hawk, the belling stag and the rising trout connect you with nature, whose rhythms and laws are unchanging. There is no pity here, and no sentimental narrative (*Note 9*); only the knowledge that you are part of a continuum. But for a man who feels himself out of sympathy with his times, that knowledge is everything."

T H White, whose books Nairac enjoyed, also experienced a sensation of time-travel when he finally graduated as a falconer. Like Nairac, he was steeped in the Middle Ages; he too preferred goshawks. "I thought it right that I should be happy to continue as one of a long line", he mused. He felt a strange affinity with an Assyrian falconer depicted in an ancient bas-relief. Visiting the site of a mediaeval village with his hawk, he felt a psychic kinship with the vanished villagers, buried somewhere nearby in an obliterated churchyard, to whom a hooded hawk on a falconer's wrist would have been an everyday sight. J Wentworth Day (1899-1983), author, broadcaster, wildfowler and fox-hunter, who celebrated the English countryside in his writings, went hawking with the British Falconers' Club in the 1920s. He wrote that, "with the wind in your face, the hawk on your fist, you may know that you are, for a brief space, an heir of the ages. A minor page of history has turned back a thousand years". Helen Macdonald, the author of *H is for Hawk*, agrees: "History collapses when you hold a hawk".

There is no question that Nairac did feel out of sympathy with his times. As Luke Jennings expresses it, "The outgoing persona that he presented to the world was balanced by a deep seriousness and introspection. Although barely an adult, he felt himself out of step with the spirit of the times." But it follows that men such as these, whether they are innovators ahead of their time, like Desiderius Erasmus or Charles Darwin, or those looking back to a former and better time, like Evelyn Waugh or Matthias Grunewald, cannot expect to feel comfortable in the present, and Robert Nairac often did not. At the same time, he was conscious of, and fascinated by, the continual march of History.

Chapter 5 | Ampleforth, Setbacks and Achievements

In my younger and more vulnerable years my father gave me some advice that I've been turning over in my mind ever since. 'Whenever you feel like criticizing anyone,' he told me, 'just remember that all the people in this world haven't had the advantages that you've had.' (F. Scott Fitzgerald, *The Great Gatsby*)

Ampleforth College was to leave an indelible impression on Robert Nairac. For that reason a closer look at Ampleforth is in order. First, the history: Ampleforth Abbey, the College's parent foundation, occupies a special place in the hearts of English Catholics because it is the spiritual successor of the great Benedictine monastery of Westminster Abbey. Its history could be argued to extend backwards well beyond the formal foundation of the modern Abbey in 1802, to at least 1049, when Edwin, the first known Abbot of Westminster, was elected. It is a living reminder of the rich heritage of Catholic England, before the stripping of the altars and the extinguishing of the candles. Knowing Robert Nairac, he would have been moved by this thought.

Although Henry VIII had dissolved the English Benedictines in the 1530s, one Benedictine monastery was briefly re-established: the Benedictines returned to Westminster Abbey under the Catholic Queen Mary Tudor, twenty years later. In 1558; after only one year, Mary's half-sister Queen Elizabeth I dissolved the monastery again. By 1607 only one of the Westminster monks was left alive; Fr Sigebert Buckley. A skilled lawyer arranged for him to accept as new members of his community a few Englishmen, already monks, and so he passed on to them all the rights and privileges of the ancient English Benedictine Congregation. In 1608 some of these English monks took up residence at the abandoned church of St Laurence in Dieulouard, near Nancy in Lorraine, then an independent Duchy within the Holy Roman Empire; later incorporated into France under Louis XV. They started to restore it and it became their church. That is why Ampleforth Abbey is dedicated to St Laurence and not to St Peter, as Westminster Abbey is. The penal laws against Catholics meant that monasteries and Catholic priests were illegal in England. Nevertheless many of the monks were given permission to vary their vow of stability and leave their monasteries to work secretly, at some risk to themselves, as missionary priests in England.

In the late eighteenth century Protestants and Catholics discovered that there now existed something far worse than each other: atheistic revolutionary Frenchmen. Before long the Pope and King George III would be allies; the Pope would recognise the House of Hanover as the lawful monarchy of Great Britain; and George III would be subsidising the impoverished Cardinal of York, also known as Prince Henry Benedict Stuart (*Note 1*) and the last of the

Royal Stuarts, who was the Dean of the College of Cardinals and whom the Revolution had ruined. In 1792 the English monks, and any other religious who could manage it, fled from France to avoid the escalating anti-clerical violence of the Revolution. Suddenly, more than two centuries after the Reformation, Protestant England once more seemed a safe and acceptable place to settle. The penal laws against Catholics were being eased and in 1829 Catholics would be fully emancipated. About the same time Fr Anselm Bolton had taken up residence in a lodge at Ampleforth. He had been the chaplain to Lady Anne Fairfax at Gilling Castle, two miles away. Much later Gilling Castle became Ampleforth's preparatory school. It was there that Robert Nairac would study before proceeding to Ampleforth College. Lady Anne had built Ampleforth Lodge for Fr Anselm just before she died, but in 1802 Fr Anselm handed the house over to his brethren to be their new monastery. In 1803 the school from Lamspringe, another of the English monasteries abroad, reopened as Ampleforth College. Their schools had been an important feature of English Benedictine life in exile. Many English Catholic Recusant (*Note 2*) families had sent their sons to be educated there during penal times; not a few of these boys had become monks and priests. This close relationship was to continue when the monks returned to England. During the next century monks continued to work both in the College (which then had about seventy boys), and on the urban missions.

In 1900 the major monastic houses became independent Abbeys with their own elected Abbots. At this time Ampleforth was a community of just under 100 monks. The first Abbot of Ampleforth was Fr Oswald Smith, who continued in office until his death in 1924. He was succeeded as Abbot by Fr Edmund Matthews, who appointed Fr Paul Nevill as Headmaster of the school. Under the leadership and guidance of these two men, the school was transformed from a modest provincial school into a great public school for Catholics. The middle and upper class Catholic families formed the backbone of the College. Nevertheless, compared with, for example Eton or Winchester, Ampleforth College is a recent newcomer.

Ampleforth College was part of an ambitious project. According to Madeleine Bunting, whose father, the sculptor John Bunting, was an Amplefordian, its purpose was to reintroduce Catholicism into the heart of the English establishment; ultimately leading to nothing less than the conversion of England, for which Nairac and Ampleforth boys prayed every Sunday, as they (like any other catholic parish) sang hymns like *Faith of Our Fathers*:

Faith of our fathers, Mary's prayers
Shall win our country back to Thee;
And through the truth that comes from God,
England shall then indeed be free.

The monks lived by a reading of history based on Ampleforth's roots in native Northern English Catholic Recusancy. This was that English Catholicism was even more authentically English than the Church of England, tracing its spiritual lineage back to the earliest days of British Christianity. Unlike some Roman Catholic institutions, Ampleforth's origins were firmly English, owing little to southern Europe. The tenuous connection with Westminster Abbey, which had once hung on one man's life, that of Fr Sigebert Buckley, was strongly emphasised; among other places in the new Abbey's heraldry. Far from being unpatriotic or un-English, modern English Catholicism embodied the best that had been salvaged from the brilliant English mediaeval past.

Reminders of that past were not far to seek. Nearby stand the ruins of Byland Abbey, once a great Cistercian monastery. The empty and broken frame of the great rose window of the abbey church is a symbol of the Wheel of Fortune, a terrible reminder of the precariousness of human existence or, as Madeleine Bunting puts it: "ominously silhouetted against the sky, as eloquent to new generations as it was to its builders, both prediction and epitaph". In the words of Eliot:

... nothing lasts, but the wheel turns,
The nest is rifled, and the bird mourns;
That the shrine shall be pillaged, and the gold spent,
The jewels gone for light ladies' ornament,
The sanctuary broken, and its stores
Swept into the laps of parasites and whores.

That is more or less what happened. The loot that fell to the Crown as a result of the dissolution of the monasteries made Henry VIII very briefly the richest Prince in Christendom. However he wasted most of this windfall in futile wars against the King of France.

The monks' argument is not without merit. It is possible to argue that Protestantism, not Catholicism, was the exotic foreign invader. It was certainly a destructive one, responsible for the wreck of our mediaeval artistic and architectural heritage. The austere Reformer John Calvin of Geneva wrote a well-argued defence of the destruction of religious works of art: they encourage men to venerate created objects and distract them from adoration of the Creator. Calvin is now known to have had a considerable influence on the early phase of the English Reformation under Henry VIII and Edward VI. That influence was exercised on Archbishop Cranmer and other genuine Protestants who were King Henry's political allies. Henry himself remained basically a Catholic, but without the Pope. Notwithstanding the efforts of the Lollards, Wycliffe and Calvin, English Catholicism had been in a healthy state on the eve of Henry VIII's assault on the Church. Even foreign enemies: French travellers, for example, commented favourably on the piety and devotion of the English. It followed that, when the Henrician Reformation began, the reaction of most people was not, as Victorian Liberal historians have led us to understand, approval and gratitude, but grief and rage. This was particularly the case with the dissolution of the monasteries. There is plenty of evidence from primary sources (private letters, for example) for this. However the opposition to King Henry had been taken by surprise. They were not sufficiently organised or united. They were defeated. The English Reformation was a long, slow process, driven forward by political factors. At least once, it went into reverse. It was forced through against the natural conservatism and piety of the people. But forty years later it was complete and apparently irreversible, for the reason that later generations of English people allowed themselves to be persuaded, in the teeth of contemporary evidence, that their ancestors had truly desired this outcome, shouting "Vivat Rex" or "God save the King", depending upon how well-educated they were, as each new "reform" was enacted.

In the interest of balance and in fairness to the Victorian Liberal historians, who were, apart from Lord Acton, Protestants, the prospects of the re-conversion of England had been greatly reduced by a number of Catholic "own goals". Notable among these was the disastrous five-year reign of Mary Tudor. During this period (1552-58) Mary had some 284 Protestants burned at the stake for heresy, including 56 women. 30 others died in prison. This is probably a conservative estimate. The Protestant martyrs included men of intellectual distinction and sanctity like Archbishop Cranmer, Bishops Ridley and Latimer (all Cambridge men; all burned at Oxford) and Bishop Robert Ferrar (burned at Carmarthen), as well as numerous ordinary people. In 1685 Louis XIV of France revoked the Edict of Nantes: England received an influx of French Protestant refugees bearing horrible tales of persecution and forced conversion. Twenty-five percent of modern native English people, and significant numbers of Scots, Welsh and Irish, have a Huguenot ancestor. Whenever in later centuries the question of relaxing the penal laws against Roman Catholics was mooted, folk-memories of the fires of Smithfield and of Louis XIV provoked an understandable and furious reaction in many Protestants. These memories were a decisive factor in the expulsion of the Catholic convert King James II and VII in 1688 and in the ruthless pacification of the Scottish Highlands after the 1745 Jacobite rebellion. They also informed England's treatment of Ireland, most of whose inhabitants remained obstinately Catholic, despite being given every inducement to convert.

From the late nineteenth century there existed a connection between Ampleforth College and the Armed Forces (*Note 3*). English Catholics had something to prove. In the past: in the Elizabethan era and again in the Jacobite rebellions of 1690, 1715, 1719 and 1745, some English, Scots and Irish Catholics had sided with a foreign would-be invader (usually Spain or France) in attempts to overthrow the established monarchy, government and church. The popular and Protestant view is expressed in the libretto of Handel's

Occasional Oratorio, commissioned to celebrate the final defeat of the Stuart cause at Culloden in 1746:

Tyrants, whom no cov'nants bind,
Nor solemn oaths can awe,
Strove to enslave the freeborn mind,
Religion, liberty, and law.

Hence Ampleforth's compulsory CCF and emphasis on patriotism. Latter-day English Catholics had to demonstrate their patriotism: they did so, in both World Wars. The lists of names – and of awards for gallantry – on the war memorials at Ampleforth, Stonyhurst and Downside tell their own story. In the process the Catholics acquired a reputation for being exceptionally brave and disciplined soldiers. Their fervency of belief probably helped; there was no room for the intellectual doubt often entertained by Protestantism.

There was however a subtler connection between Ampleforth, English Catholicism and the Armed Forces. It seemed to run in the Recusant DNA. This was the connection with undercover and clandestine military operations, at which Amplefordians have seemed to excel. It is related to the heritage of the Catholic past: to what had happened during the centuries of the penal laws, when English Catholics had often lived a cloak-and-dagger existence, with priests disguised as something else, because they were outlaws; priests concealed in priests' holes, because any priest ordained abroad after 1559 and discovered in England was deemed to be a traitor, his host a felon, and both were put to death; the Mass being celebrated in secret, because it was banned; sons being smuggled out of the country to be educated abroad, often seeking careers there in the service of Catholic sovereigns (*Note 4*) like the Holy Roman Emperor, the King of Naples or the Grand Duke of Tuscany; and, after 1688, surreptitious support for the exiled Stuart dynasty. All of which was extremely dangerous if discovered; secrecy and evasion were vital. Given that his father was of French origin, with Huguenot as well as Catholic ancestors, and that his mother was an Anglican, Robert Nairac could not have qualified as an heir of the English Catholic Recusant tradition. Nevertheless he identified strongly with that tradition.

From this it was a short step to the secrecy and adventure of modern unconventional warfare. It was very different from the industrial warfare of the first half of the twentieth century and it connected with much older warrior traditions of courage and skill. Colonel David Stirling, the co-founder of the SAS (*Note 5*), was a Catholic and an Amplefordian. But he was not unique, there were numerous others. Whether or not Robert Nairac was conscious of his elder brother's lingering presence at Ampleforth, there could be no avoiding Hugh Dormer's ghost or those of other Catholic warriors of the Second World War.

John Bunting's War Memorial Chapel on the moors near Ampleforth is a *chapelle expiatoire*. It is his tangible expression of gratitude and atonement to the dead of the Second World War, in which he was slightly too young to have served. Everyone who has visited it comments on the striking effigy that dominates the small chapel: not a recumbent crusader knight but an Airborne Division soldier, complete with nailed boots. The presiding Saints or Worthies are not St George or St Michael but three Ampleforth military heroes: the poet Michael Fenwick (Gurkha Rifles), killed in Kowloon in 1941; Michael Allmand VC (Chindits), killed in Burma in 1944; and Hugh Dormer DSO (Irish Guards), killed in France in 1944. The effigy bears Hugh Dormer's features. All three had been deeply committed Catholics, all had been very brave and patriotic; all had shown considerable intellectual and literary promise, never to be fully realised. In 1977 a fourth would be added and commemorated in the shrine: Robert Laurence Nairac (Grenadier Guards), later GC.

Long before John Bunting had placed the first stone of his chapel, Hugh Dormer was well on the way to unofficial canonisation at Ampleforth. His *War Diary*, which has literary merit and is still in print, was often read at the boys' annual retreat. Dormer was a charismatic individual, a member of one of England's oldest Recusant families. He is seen as a role model for later generations of Amplefordians, who are still inspired by him to join the Army. Like him, they often prove to have a penchant for undercover operations. It is possible that Robert Nairac, reading the *War Diary*, was inspired to follow in Dormer's footsteps. They had much in common: Dormer was a very tough man; a good boxer, an excellent shot and a keen falconer. Like Nairac, he loved East Africa, where he had passed part of his childhood on a farm near Mount Kenya. He was also a man of enormous integrity and a pious, mystical Catholic. Dormer, had he survived, might have become a priest. He was hesitating between the Church and the Foreign Service when war broke out in 1939. He had been studying Modern Languages at Oxford with a view to becoming a diplomat. Dormer led undercover operations to assist the French Resistance and strike at the economic base of the German war effort in France. In some respects he seems uncannily like Robert Nairac, although they were not related and Nairac was not born until four years after Dormer's death in 1944. He was however familiar with the *War Diary* and some of the same monks taught them both.

Similar things were written about Dormer after his death in battle to those that would be written about Nairac after his murder: "He had an infectious zest for everything, whether it was a formal debate or an informal cricket match with a neighbouring village ... his men knew that they had in him a young, brilliant and trusted leader ... the high spiritual ideals which he always upheld were assiduously practiced by him as a matter of course ... the inspiring but only too short life of this splendid young Englishman..."

Dormer had an exalted and at times frightening view of his military vocation, expressed in his *War Diary*, which sometimes seems almost to amount to a death-wish: not suicidal but a coherently-expressed longing for a meritorious and heroic martyrdom:

"The sublime moments of sacrifice on the battlefield are what bind men together for eternity!"

Dormer eventually returned from undercover work to Regimental soldiering. One passage of the *War Diary*, in which he explains why he did this, seems curiously prophetic and relevant to Nairac:

"Guerrilla fighting often breeds a race of soldiers who love war and can only live in a violent, restless and destructive atmosphere ... each individual eager for revenge against his own political enemies ... And another of my reasons for returning to my Regiment had been the fear of being asked to do things that I did not agree with ... One's initiative can lead one into some very strange decisions, following the insidious principle of total warfare, that the ends justify the means."

Whether consciously or not, this was echoed in one of Nairac's last letters to his Regiment, written a few weeks before his death, in which he expressed his pleasure and relief at the prospect of returning to conventional Regimental soldiering. What Nairac wrote could have been mere formal politeness; on the other hand Nairac, like Dormer, may well have seen the light, because he expressed a similar view in private conversations with friends like Tom Lort-Phillips and with family members. Nor is it hard to see why. Ineluctably, given the unspoken assumption that the end does indeed justify the means, working undercover in the secret world is apt to involve half-truths, outright lies and betrayals. As an NCO who knew Nairac well said: "A lot of dirty tricks were employed by both sides." That world is not an ideal environment for high-minded, religious young men of integrity, steeped in the mediaeval past. It can prove deeply disorientating and inevitably brings them into strange company. This seems to be confirmed by an email from Nairac's former brother officer, Jonathan Forbes:

"I have never knowingly met any of Robert's family [but] I did discover this weekend that I had written to his parents in Feb '79, when his [posthumous] GC award was announced. I have copies of replies from his uncle Basil Dykes and his mother. The latter (22 Apr '79) confirms what you have already picked-up, in that she says, '...I know he was looking forward to being back with the Battalion.'"

Not everyone whose parents sent them to Ampleforth College has responded positively to its high-minded religious and military ethos. The actor Rupert Everett (who is the son of an Army officer) in his memoir *Red Carpets and Other Banana Skins*, states that, apart from the school theatricals, in which he shone, he hated the place. He describes Ampleforth as "a drizzly Dickensian village nestling against the steep wooded banks of a huge and beautiful valley on the Yorkshire moors". He admits that the daily religious services and the church music were impressive; Everett was a chorister. However, he provides some informed insights into the College as it was a few years after Nairac had left it. "You felt as if you belonged to something big; and the plan was that you left Ampleforth a raunchy eighteen year old boy bursting with testosterone, a fully formed empire builder with the added twist of a Catholic agenda. After ten years of prep and public school you were part of the gang; and if you weren't, then you were a freak or a fairy. Luckily for me, I was both." Robert Nairac had no wish to be perceived as either of those things, but he would turn out to be a good actor in a different context. Meanwhile the Empire was fast disappearing.

Almost all the published accounts of Robert Nairac emphasise that he was a successful schoolboy at Ampleforth: a Monitor and Head of St Edward's House, with an enviable record of sporting successes; that he achieved sufficient A-Level passes to get himself into Oxford, where he enjoyed yet more sporting successes, graduated and soon afterwards began his military career in a distinguished line Regiment. Amplefordian comment tends to support this impression. "He was the sort of boy who was good at everything," said Father Patrick Barry, who had been Headmaster of Ampleforth while Nairac was a pupil there and was still in that office when Nairac was murdered in 1977. Father Barry's statement, made in the spirit of *de mortuis nihil nisi bonum* (Speak only good about the dead), was however rather misleading. It has resulted in a perception, shared uncritically by most Nairac biographers, that Nairac not only enjoyed a "privileged" and expensive Public School upbringing but that he also had a very easy time; that his life until his murder was a story of continual and almost effortless achievement. At Ampleforth sporting triumph succeeded sporting triumph. He got into Oxford, played a lot more sport, graduated successfully, went through Sandhurst to join a top line Regiment, the Grenadier Guards, and later (according to some writers) the SAS. In addition, he was good-looking, charming and a charismatic leader. All this, in the eyes of a certain type of Left-liberal reader, is enough to damn him and even cause them to say "serve him right".

The reality was different. While there were achievements, Nairac had a hard time and suffered setbacks, both at Ampleforth and at Oxford. He had difficulty getting into Oxford at all. He failed on the first attempt in 1966, was deeply upset about that, received coaching and got accepted on the second attempt in 1967. He did not get into the college of his choice, but into one much lower in the pecking order. Oxford was not plain sailing when he finally got there in October 1968. He suffered a nervous breakdown, took four years to complete a three year BA degree course, only achieved a Third and did not do himself justice academically. Admirably, after each setback he picked himself up, dusted himself off and went on to achieve something. But Nairac's life seems only to have "come together" when he went to Sandhurst after graduating belatedly from Oxford in 1972. By that time he had less than five years left to live.

There is one exception to the bland accounts of other authors. Luke Jennings, whose angling memoir *Blood Knots* devotes considerable space to the young

Nairac, gives a more disquieting account. For example, he refers to an occasion when he and Nairac had been angling for eels. Jennings was about to go to Ampleforth and Nairac, who was a few years older, was briefing him about the challenges and pitfalls that he could expect to face there. At that time all the Housemasters and many of the specialist teachers were monks. A few were saints. Most were decent and fair-minded men, many were excellent teachers. Some were amusingly eccentric. Nairac's first housemaster, for example, had been in the habit of shooting at rabbits from his study windows, posing a certain risk to the humans too. There were, however, a very few who needed to be approached with caution. They were at least potentially paedophile. Even though they rarely allowed their desires to assume a physical form, it was best to be aware. Ampleforth might be set amid an idyllic Claude landscape but there were some serpents lurking in this rural paradise.

Well-run contemplative monasteries have been described as staging posts on the frontiers of Paradise. The vast majority of monks, friars and nuns lead exemplary lives. Nevertheless logically in every barrel there is likely to be the occasional rotten apple: for example, people who joined their Order for the wrong reasons or in response to family pressure and not as a proper vocation. Well within living memory, pious parents of large Catholic families liked to "give a son to the Church" regardless of that son's personal inclination or whether he really had a vocation. Sometimes he did not have a true vocation. These men were among the ones who were most likely later to go seriously wrong.

Nairac was right. Long after his murder, Ampleforth and one of its feeder schools would be damaged by revelations of a paedophile scandal that had been successfully concealed at that time. Evidently Nairac knew about this, but the matter did not become public knowledge for many years. Inevitably the College came in for criticism, not least over its secrecy at the time. There are detailed contemporary Press accounts available from 2005.

That is the background against which Robert Nairac's adolescent trauma would occur. The important difference is that Nairac was the victim, not of paedophile teachers, but of sadistic older boys; or rather young men, aged seventeen to nineteen. At that period Heads of Houses, who were responsible for discipline, were allowed to inflict corporal punishment for serious demeanours by caning a boy. A very small minority of other monitors, it seems from reports, abused it.

Unfortunately some of them were to be found in St Edward's House, to which Robert Nairac went in September 1962, a month after his brother's sudden death, still in shock and therefore in a vulnerable state of mind. The phenomenon was not confined to St Edward's House. It occurred in at least one other House where Nairac's best friend from Ampleforth, who is still alive, reportedly had an equally bad time. Their friendship was partly founded on shared suffering. What is extraordinary in retrospect is that while this abuse continued, everyone or almost everyone in the House was aware of it. The rabbit-shooting Fr Jerome

Lambert may not have been; or else he turned a blind, or at least an ineffectual, eye to it. Among the boys who were not directly concerned, the ongoing drama of stalking and capture was followed with amused or excited interest, like a TV soap-opera. What would happen in next week's episode?

For this part of the narrative we must rely entirely on the comments of people who were at Ampleforth at about the same time as Nairac and who do not wish to be identified for fairly obvious reasons. One man preferred not to speak at all; the memory was evidently still too painful. Nairac himself was always extremely reticent about what had really happened to him. Moreover it all happened a very long time ago; even very painful memories eventually fade. It follows that this evidence is hearsay and that the resultant picture may be incomplete.

In *Blood Knots* Luke Jennings depicts what happened to Nairac as Flashman-like physical bullying. Jennings mentions that Nairac grew pale and tense when he related these experiences to him and that his speech became very clipped. Physical bullying would have been bad enough: what actually happened seems to have been worse than *Tom Brown's Schooldays*.

Nairac later indicated, in one of his rare comments on the subject that the violence was sexual in nature, although he refused to go into any detail. Aged 14, he was already a very handsome boy, small for his age, and a prime target. There were only a few ways in which the victims could handle this, given that an appeal to authority was not likely to be effective and that the schoolboy code of honour viewed an appeal to parents to be taken away as a discreditable last resort.

Whatever the precise detail, it is clear that something very bad happened to Nairac at the age of fourteen, soon after the death of his elder brother and his arrival in St Edward's House; something that caused his father to take action with the College authorities. Nairac spoke to very few people about this but some of them have spoken recently. What happened upset him enormously at the time, caused him to suffer a crisis of confidence and impacted on his studies. It also impelled him to take boxing lessons and generally toughen himself up. He had pressing reasons for doing so. He did not say to himself, "I'd like to try that sport; it looks rather exciting!" He took up boxing as a matter of survival, to defend himself against senior boys at Ampleforth and said so to more than one interlocutor. In the event he would prove to be very good at boxing, representing both Ampleforth and Oxford in major competitions, captaining both teams and becoming a Boxing Blue, but that was probably a fortuitous bonus. It took time to train himself up to the necessary, lethal standard. Meanwhile his first few terms in St Edward's House were miserable.

It would have been good to report that Nairac fought the good fight and won entirely by his own determined efforts. However that would not be literally true: as indicated above, his father became involved. When Nairac went home at the end of one school term his father, a highly perceptive man, recognised that he was not himself and had been deeply upset by something. Nairac later said that, "He asked me what the matter was, and I burst into tears and told him everything." Maurice Nairac took action with the College authorities and was evidently satisfied with the assurances that he received. Robert was not removed. Once again, there was no public scandal; no media coverage. Fr Lambert subsequently withdrew from being a Housemaster and moved to an industrial parish. He was replaced by a very different kind of monk in the person of Fr Edward Corbould, who successfully re-imposed discipline. Amplefordians of that generation have nothing but praise for this dedicated schoolmaster and priest. Fr Edward was to remain a friend and spiritual influence until Nairac's early death.

In the interest of balance, it should be recorded that many of his former pupils, and not a few non-Catholics, also held Fr. Jerome Lambert in high regard: An Anglican friend wrote after his death: "A man of depth and sure faith, he stood by his creed, but finding others shared it he responded liberally". A man of unusual experiences, he had played as a child at Rievaulx with the future Prime Minister Harold Wilson, who called him "Ozzy Lambert"; his baptismal name was Oswald. Once (in 1944) he found a beached German submarine. However he seems also to have been slightly unworldly and to have had difficulty in imagining that people whom he knew and liked might be capable of acts of premeditated wickedness.

This was not a promising start in the senior school. However Nairac not only survived but would ultimately succeed and excel, by guts and determination. In due course he too became a Monitor and Head of St Edward's House. Instead of revelling in his chance to inflict corporal punishment, he firmly declined to do so as a matter of principle. He is remembered for his charismatic leadership; for his kindness to unhappy junior boys and for making a special effort with people whose faces did not fit. As an adolescent, Nairac was unusually good at looking after, and keeping control of, younger children. He was sometimes invited to children's parties for that reason, as he seemed able to keep them happy and in order by a mixture of great good humour and authority. He never "talked down" to younger people but tried to engage their interest. Nairac also became a wing-forward at rugby. His exam results, while not as distinguished as those of his elder brother, were perfectly respectable: at O-Level he passed English Language, English Literature, History, Latin, French, General Science and Biology. At A Level he secured four passes: History A, General Papers B, French C, Latin D. He became a cadet Under-Officer in the CCF. According to his father, writing in 1967, he had also become a very good shot and an excellent dry-fly fisherman. His other interests included falconry, ornithology, classical and traditional jazz music. Luke Jennings recalls that he also enjoyed some melancholy early Beatles music like *Norwegian Wood*.

If male on male rape is what happened to Nairac at Ampleforth, he was never explicit about it. It must however have been something along those lines. Psychologists tell us that rape is all about power and control; not about sex. This may be true, but the victims might be forgiven for thinking that sex is exactly what it is about. The experience can put them off sex for good, or for a very long time, which is what seems to have happened to Nairac. It has recently proved to be a serious problem in the US military (53% of all intra-military rape victims turned out to be male), although it was rarely reported because the male victims were too embarrassed to do so. Nor were the authorities necessarily sympathetic if they did.

"It makes you do a complete about-face in the way that you view the world," said one victim, who was twenty years old when he was assaulted in 2000. "Really, it's a day-to-night experience."

"You have an environment that values strength and values the warrior ethos," says Nate Galbreath, the senior civilian adviser to the Pentagon's Sexual Assault Prevention and Response Office. "And, of course, when any man is sexually assaulted, they really wonder whether or not they fit into this warrior culture. But what we're trying to get across to men is that warriors not only know how to fight, they also know how to ask for help."

Former US servicemen described long-lasting impacts, including depression, anxiety, flashbacks and substance-abuse. All of these things were to happen to Nairac.

Given this background, Nairac's black moods of morose, morbid depression and fatalism, in one of which he is said to have predicted his own death in Ireland ("I have a horrible feeling that this place is going to be my destiny"); even his collection of gruesome scene-of-the-crime photos of dead Irish terrorists, become more easily understandable.

Mary Price, a young woman friend of Nairac who, to her embarrassment, was discovered, interviewed and presented to the public by the *Daily Mail* as "the girlfriend" after Nairac's murder, once saw him in this state. It was at Oxford, just after he had taken his Finals, in which he probably knew that he had not done himself justice. "A group of us later went out to supper. He sang a strange mixture of Welsh and Irish rebel songs and became quite morose – and that was before he had even embarked on his curious mission." Mary added that this was the one occasion on which she had seen him express genuine feeling.

There were other side-effects: Nairac, like T E Lawrence, developed a taste for sado-masochism, with the emphasis on masochism. Lawrence liked to be flogged: according to people who knew him at Oxford, Nairac positively enjoyed being beaten up in the boxing ring. This made him a feared opponent. Other men might be concerned about brain injury or damage to their youthful good looks; not Nairac. He was happy to slug it out, and if necessary to be punished, to the bitter end. He normally won anyway. When his nose was broken, he did not bother to have it re-set. If he got "cut" and started bleeding during a match, he would apply a plaster and carry on. Amateur boxing was at that time more dangerous and painful than it is today. In modern amateur boxing matches it is obligatory to wear a regulation helmet to protect the head. The gloves are more extensively padded, and several ounces heavier as a result. The rounds are of shorter duration. The risk of major damage is greatly reduced, as is the excitement. These developments have made it possible for women to start boxing. They even do so in the OUABC; a development that Nairac, it is safe to say, would have hated.

No-one can come through a season in Purgatory such as Robert Nairac endured at the age of fourteen without experiencing some after-effects. These were both good and bad. On the positive side, Nairac developed a strong dislike of seeing other people being badly treated. He was on the side of the underdog. It made him a very good, caring Head of House. In due course he would become a very good, caring Army Platoon Commander, for whom the welfare and morale of his men was paramount; they sensed this and appreciated it. Their comments after his death make that clear. In 1973 he would stand up for the Catholics of Ardoyne who had suffered discrimination by Belfast City Council. They were grateful for this and still had positive memories of Nairac in 1977. Clearly his experiences at Ampleforth are relevant.

This sympathy for the underdog influenced Nairac's attitude to Ireland, which he perceived as a small, defeated but romantic country, which had suffered cruelty and injustice over much of its history. Nairac identified with the Irish. Thanks to his Irish Amplefordian friends Redmond and John Morris, the sons of Lord Killanin, he had the opportunity to pass holidays in Ireland, based at their father's houses in Dublin and County Galway. John Morris in particular, later a famous falconer and breeder of falcons, encouraged him in that sport. Unspoiled Ireland was a great place for angling, falconry and shooting. Nairac fell in love with it: he learned the history, learned the songs and went out of his way to befriend the people. This love went beyond simple affection for a place where one has spent happy holidays. Some people found it strange, given that Nairac had no Irish ancestry or any close family connection. His friend Martin Squires wrote that, "he had this unnerving relationship with Ireland, the history, the accent". Another friend, SAS Major B (quoted by John Parker), said, "He had a very strong and curious affinity, in the strangest possible way, towards the IRA ... He also had a great feeling for the whole of Ireland ... His interest went very much deeper, and in a more diverse fashion, than most soldiers posted to their tours of duty in Ireland ever had."

It is easy with hindsight to see that this odd, one-sided love affair with the Irish led to his eventual murder. But no-one could have predicted this when the love affair began, while he was still at school, before the Troubles started. Nairac was not even contemplating joining the Army at that point. His family did not share his interest, amounting almost to an obsession, in Ireland. They might however have warned him that falling in love with an alien people, a culture, a country or a place is likely in the end to prove unrequited and unrewarding. Karen Blixen's disillusioned cry when, ruined and bereaved, she had to leave Kenya forever in

1931 still rings true today: "What business had I ever to set my heart on Africa?" For Africa, one might equally well read Ireland.

It speaks volumes for Nairac's generosity of spirit that he appears to have forgiven his tormentors and Ampleforth College. He bore no animosity towards his first housemaster, Fr Jerome Lambert, who by his lack of leadership had arguably let him (and others) down badly. At no stage did he ever turn against Ampleforth, the Benedictines or the Church. To the end of his life he remained a loyal Amplefordian. He would return to the College from time to time to call on younger friends like Luke Jennings and to visit the monks like Fr Edward Corbould who had been his mentors. Luke Jennings describes Nairac at the time that he left Ampleforth as a Catholic of almost mediaeval intensity, for whom country pursuits and spiritual transcendence were lyrically, and occasionally bloodily, entwined. The single-minded dedication with which he pursued the difficult arts of dry-fly casting and falconry now seems almost religious.

However there were other consequences. To the surprise of people who had only known the assured, cocky Nairac of the Grenadier Guards, when they learned about it years later, he experienced a severe crisis of self-confidence as a result of the abuse he had suffered. To a boy who aspired to emulate the masculine virtues of his literary and historic heroes, it seemed that his own masculinity, to which he attached great importance, had been horribly compromised by what had happened to him. Boxing, rugby and other macho activities would help to expiate that. From now on he had to be fitter, stronger, tougher and braver than everyone else. Throughout his short life Nairac would set himself challenges, which were sometimes hazardous, to reassure himself about his physical and mental toughness and courage. It was possible to guess where this might lead: one day he might accept a challenge too many. If it had not been dangerous undercover work in Ireland, it could have been K2 (a Himalayan peak with a high climber-fatality rate) or an expedition down the Blue Nile. I believe that this would have been the case even if Nairac had, like Frederick Spencer Chapman (the wartime Force 136 (SOE) soldier and author of the guerrilla warfare classic, *The Jungle is Neutral*), stuck to his original plan and become a schoolmaster. While teaching brilliantly at Gordonstoun or somewhere similar, Nairac would still have sought dangerous challenges: expeditions or extreme sports, during the academic vacations.

Add to this a natural gambler's temperament and it looks like potential trouble. The mature Nairac is known to have made fairly frequent (and sometimes ridiculous) wagers with other officers, and to have enjoyed a day at the races. Julian Malins recalls: "I knew several heavy gamblers at Oxford. I do not think that Robert gambled [then] but he had a really daredevil attitude to life, so he definitely had the personality to take a bet that he could do something dangerous or difficult. So he would take risks. Superstitious people, e.g. the Chinese, or very religious people, e.g. the Irish, are often heavy gamblers because they believe that God is involved in everything they do, including bringing them luck. So he had the background for gambling." Nairac was both deeply religious and at times superstitious.

Meanwhile damage had been done and it affected Nairac's academic performance. His school reports from Ampleforth, although generally good, contain a frequent refrain of "could do even better." Writing to support his university application in 1966, the Headmaster, Father Patrick Barry, wrote, among generally favourable remarks, that, "he lacks intellectual toughness and would do much better if he had a higher opinion of himself", and "He has the basic ability to get a Second in History but there is some doubt whether he has the drive and determination to do really well". Also: "He is inclined to under-rate himself but his success in A-Levels has increased his confidence". While true, this seems somewhat disingenuous on Fr Barry's part. Because of Maurice Nairac's intervention, he must have had some idea about the real reason for Nairac's serious loss of self-confidence.

While in an ideal world it might be true that "warriors not only know how to fight; they also know how to ask for help", and although his father was a well-connected medical man, Robert Nairac seems neither to have been offered, nor to have sought, any psychiatric counselling for what happened to him at Ampleforth. He would probably have seen it as an admission of weakness – as at that time would the Army. A referral did not look good on your CV. He seems to have been in denial: he tried to put aside the memory of what had happened to him, rather than deal with it. Like his brother's early death, it was seldom if ever mentioned, but equally it was not forgotten. It would come back to haunt him and would jeopardise his chances of graduating from Oxford with Honours. In the academic year 1970-71 Robert Nairac would suffer a nervous breakdown. Although there were other complicating factors, this was probably, at least in part, the delayed result of what had happened to him at Ampleforth. The demons could no longer be avoided: he had to confront them.

It may seem impertinent to subject the fragments that survive of a life like Nairac's to amateur analysis. But we must make the effort if we are even partly to understand what made this complex man tick. The challenge is that Nairac, who was one of nature's actors, had no great wish to be fully understood by anyone; least of all by his close friends and family. He probably expressed his most important questions and fears only in the privacy of the Confessional. In this respect too, he was very un-modern. There are relatively few windows into his soul and as a result he tends to defy normal biographical methods. It is often easier to illustrate him by an anecdote, a chance encounter or a racy quotation. Then, suddenly, he comes to life and into focus. For a few minutes we can see him, grinning his easy grin, smiling at us through the smoke like that ambiguous god of Delphi, Apollo Loxias.

The sad part of this story is that Nairac really had every reason to feel confident. He was an exceptional man with enviable qualities. Intelligence, courage and integrity are uncommon; even to have one of these is enviable. He had all three, plus good looks, charm and leadership, although at this stage of his life he might not have recognised this. One of his falconry friends, Martin Jones, commented that he could have made a success of anything, provided that it interested him. Fr Edward Corbould wrote:

"He has an extraordinarily attractive personality with almost boundless enthusiasm, generosity and good humour. A person of great moral integrity. His very qualities leave him with a certain naivety and lack of balance or judgement. A born leader with something of the quality of the winner of the VC."

This positive assessment of Nairac would be fully borne out during his time in the Army and echoed in his Army confidential reports. But that is evidently not how Nairac perceived himself at that time, and having a positive view of oneself is a prerequisite for having self-confidence. He still seemed to regard himself as flawed; damaged goods, and we now know why. Yet the damage had not been his fault. Another related result of Nairac's abuse at the hands of the Monitors was a need for reassurance. His fiercely competitive drive for success at boxing, fly fishing, shooting and team games was part of this. But it went a lot further. As noted in Chapter 2, Luke Jennings refers to his compulsive "need for centre-stage visibility and approbation". This took the form of acting a part to an enthralled audience: the maverick toff; the jolly poacher with trout to give away; the life-and-soul raconteur; the brilliant singer of folk-songs. Typically this would happen in a pub, and it was usually a great success: Nairac would soon have the place at his feet. Some might call this "showing off". Jennings however makes a subtler analysis. "He wanted to make people feel good around him and he knew just how to do it." This is confirmed by an Army friend of Nairac, who says that: "I think that you are absolutely right about Robert 'playing to the gallery'. It was part of his charm, and probably was driven not only by a desire to impress but also a need to please."

In this respect Nairac had much in common with the great entertainers of the past: Charlie Chaplin, for example. Chaplin and his rivals wanted, for reasons rooted in their heredity or upbringing, to make others feel good and to win their affection. Yet they did not give much away. In the final analysis they were often enigmatic and un-knowable. Chaplin and his famous character "the Tramp" were very different people, but Chaplin impersonated the Tramp brilliantly. The real Chaplin was far less likeable than the Tramp, who rescued fallen women, lost children, lost animals and did other good deeds. Nevertheless, long after Chaplin's death, we willingly go along with the imposture and laugh happily at his mainly silent, slapstick black-and-white films, as he intended. The real Chaplin's misdemeanours are forgotten: we only remember the Tramp.

A perceptive former officer who was not a close friend but had encountered Nairac a few times in the course of his work commented that, "He was a master of being whatever his audience wanted him to be; of blending in and making friends by hitting the right note with anyone and everyone. Then he would get what he wanted from them ... He would be clever enough to know when and under what circumstances to approach you."

In other words, like a great actor, Nairac knew instinctively what his audience wanted to see and experience, and then played it back to them. He succeeded brilliantly, basking in the amused approval of his fans in his chosen theatre of pubs and bars. But again, with the wisdom of retrospect, this was a very early step towards his murder after just such an evening in a bar in Drumintee in May 1977. As Eliot reminds us,

... Any action
Is a step to the block, to the fire, down the sea's throat
Or to an illegible stone: and that is where we start

Except that Nairac does not have even an illegible headstone.

Conscious role-playing is one thing: rock-stars, spies, barristers and actors do it all the time, but there was a further and separate development which was less desirable. This too was probably related to Nairac's trauma at Ampleforth. As he grew older, Nairac showed all the signs of developing a "shadow personality," which was not simply one of the charming or amusing public personae that he liked to project. It could be very un-charming indeed and it was not under his control. There are numerous historical examples of this, although the most famous one is fictional. It typically occurs in stiflingly conformist, very religious, societies and is not peculiar to Catholicism. An individual who is fundamentally unable to conform to many of his society's (or his family's, his religion's or his school's) demands and expectations may consciously or subconsciously separate and disown those elements of his personality that he perceives as unacceptable. These may include his sexuality. They may also include past bad experiences or personal acts of wickedness about which he is in denial. A problem is that the "evil twin" does not go away. He is always there; the lurker at the threshold. He may develop into a separate "person," who can suddenly and startlingly take over when the individual is drunk; under the influence of drugs; disorientated by some stressful experience or merely experiencing a pleasurable "high". In the past such dramatic personality changes were often put down to enchantment or demonic possession. It goes without saying that this is unhealthy. It can take years of therapy to re-integrate the two personalities.

The obvious, albeit extreme, example of this phenomenon is *The Strange Case of Dr Jekyll and Mr Hyde*. It is no coincidence that the novella's author, Robert Louis Stevenson, was a Scot whose maternal grandfather was a Presbyterian Minister. The Reverend Dr Lewis Balfour, with whom the schoolboy Stevenson passed almost every weekend, was a well-meaning but stern man and a terror to back-sliding parishioners. For his young grandson, "his strictness and distance ... oppressed us with a kind of terror". As a young man R L Stevenson himself had led a "Jekyll and Hyde" existence. He was a reluctant Law student by day and frequenter of Bohemian literary circles, opium dens and houses of ill fame in the Old Town and Leith (Edinburgh's port) by night. It was necessary for him to lead a double life: had his family been aware, they would definitely not have approved.

A real Jekyll-and-Hyde was a man who is often compared with Robert Nairac. The most-decorated British soldier of the Second World War, Lieutenant Colonel Robert Blair "Paddy" Mayne (1915-55) was one of the co-founders of the original SAS Regiment. He replaced David Stirling as Commanding Officer when the Germans captured Stirling in 1943. Mayne was an enormous man, six feet two or three, and weighed about 15 stone of solid muscle. He was a fervent Northern Irish Protestant and Unionist, who disliked and despised Roman Catholics. Despite this prejudice, his best friend in the Army and perhaps the love of his life, Eoin McGonigal, was a Catholic. Mayne was highly literate, often to be found with his head in a book, reading dark and complicated poets like A E Housman. Mayne was himself a complex and secretive man. Like Nairac, he suffered from terrible moods of "Black Dog" depression. Like Nairac, he was a boxer, winning the Irish Universities' heavyweight championship and reaching the final in the British Universities' championship. Mayne was also an outstanding rugby player; he was capped six times for Ireland and once for the British Lions. He made his name as a lock-forward against the Springboks in the Lions' 1938 rugby tour. In the course of this legendary tour Mayne absented himself from a formal black-tie event to go hunting – still in evening dress. The following morning, muddy and tattered but still wearing his black tie, he dumped on the Lions Captain's bed his trophy: a bloodstained dead Springbok (antelope, not rugby player).

Mayne when sober has been described as a shy and modest man; sensitive and good at empathising with others. He has also been described as gentle, considerate and intelligent. Like Nairac he was an inspirational military leader, totally devoted to the soldiers under his command. Like Nairac, there is abundant evidence of the respect and affection in which his NCOs and men held Mayne. "No matter how bad things looked, once Paddy appeared it was *magic*."

Mayne under the influence of alcohol or powerful emotion was another matter entirely: a complete "Mr Hyde". His "shadow personality" was terrifying. David Stirling, a very brave man, spoke with awe of Mayne's "satanic rages" and admitted that at times he had found his friend Paddy frightening. Mayne's size and strength made him extremely dangerous; he had a homicidal streak. Under the influence, he would beat a man to pulp for little or no reason. His victims included the Chindit Mike Calvert; himself no mean boxer and unarmed combatant. One drunken evening, Mayne very nearly killed him; he was hospitalised. There is a falconry term for this state of mind: a falcon in killing mode is said to be "in yarak". This expression may derive from a Farsi word meaning "super-alert, hungry but not weak, and ready to kill". Some of the things that Mayne in yarak allegedly did to enemy soldiers would these days cause him to be investigated, but he was a brilliant – wartime – leader.

Peace did not agree with him. Paddy Mayne lived on for ten unhappy years after 1945. The holder of a wartime commission and a solicitor by profession, he returned after the war to his law practice in Northern Ireland but it gave him little satisfaction. He continued to play rugby. In the words of his biographer Martin Dillon, he was "at odds with an uncongenial and unprofitable [peacetime] world, so stale and out of tune after the wild, annihilating rapture of the one he had known" in the wartime SAS. He was often involved in brawls and was jailed at least once. At four o'clock one morning in 1955, after drinking with a friend, he crashed his sports car and killed himself. He was just forty. Despite all of this, Paddy Mayne was the right man at the right time in 1941 and again in 1943. He was definitely a hero. Here a point is demonstrated: we should not expect heroes to behave like saints; they are quite different animals.

Paddy Mayne was a well-documented example of a Jekyll-and-Hyde with a dark "shadow personality". As such, a comparison of the two men may help to cast light on some aspects of Robert Nairac's character. However, we should be cautious. Although Mayne plainly had some characteristics in common with Nairac: for example, they both boxed and played rugby, it would be going much too far to suggest that the resemblance must perforce extend into other areas. This is an error that some Irish Republican and other writers have made: possibly because, like Nairac, Mayne posthumously became a hate-figure for them. Because Mayne was probably homosexual as well as homicidal; has been judged to be a violent "borderline psychopath"; was a sado-masochist with the emphasis on sadism, and had shown himself to be a ruthless and bloodthirsty warrior, it follows that Nairac must have been all of these things too, and that therefore he must have been capable of, and guilty of, the numerous crimes that Republicans have tried to lay at his door. But it does not follow at all; it is a *non-sequitur*. Nairac probably knew about Mayne's military career from his private reading but Mayne and Nairac were not genetically related, nor did they ever meet. (Nairac was seven years old when Mayne was killed.) Mayne existed in his own right; he is not the key that will help us to decode Nairac, his emotions and motives in their entirety. There is no complete key to Nairac; no Rosetta Stone that will suddenly make everything about him, his motivation, his actions and character, crystal-clear. Certain aspects of Nairac will always be enigmatic. To find him in some respects unknowable is not a defeat; merely an acknowledgement of the realities of the human condition.

The "shadow personality" is the only way in which can be explained the occasional, startling and violent lapses of Robert Nairac, who was fundamentally a good person, whose kindness and generosity are well-attested. At times, and especially under the influence of alcohol, a different and more brutal man seemed to inhabit his body. Martin Squires again: "He had this thuggish side to him that I could not figure; very buoyant." These lapses include his delight in non-

Queensberry Rules violence; occasional spectacular rages; heartless practical jokes; pub fights and the beating-up of mini-cab drivers. In the Army, on one occasion Nairac threatened to punch his Grenadier soldier-servant, Guardsman David Webster, for not doing what he was told. The soldier-servant decided to get his punch in first, got duffed up and then locked up. He remained loyal to Nairac and to his memory, despite this incident.

One of Nairac's Army contemporaries recalls that a visit to an Irish Republican pub in Kilburn, London with Robert resulted in some interesting use of the fists when he contributed to the musical entertainment of the evening with a spirited rendering of "The Sash" ("The Sash My Father Wore," a Loyalist song commemorating the victory of King William III in the Williamite War in Ireland in 1690). There was a brief moment of stunned silence before the place erupted with a roar: bottles, chairs and punches were launched in their direction. There followed a splendid battle. Nairac and his friends gave a good account of themselves before beating a tactical retreat. The friends were shaken by the experience but Nairac considered this to be hilarious fun, excellent sport and was in very high spirits.

The Jekyll-and-Hyde aspect of Nairac's personality explains some of the contradictory accounts of him that have been given by people who knew – or thought that they knew – him. Nairac's lapses were relatively infrequent, although they seem to have become more frequent as he grew older. Fortunately for them, many of his friends never experienced "Mr Hyde". Their accounts of Nairac depict him as being, in the words of one of his former Tutors, a "young man who in some respects had embodied Chaucer's *parfait knight*". The same thing had happened more than a century and a half earlier with Lord Byron; another Jekyll-and-Hyde character with whom Nairac had more than a little in common. There were people who never saw Byron's wicked and self-destructive side and had difficulty in believing that it existed. One such group was to be found in the Armenian monastery of San Lazzaro near Venice, where Byron studied Armenian and collaborated with a monk on the compilation of the first Armenian-English dictionary and grammar. To this day the monks of San Lazzaro will not hear a word against Byron. Their predecessors had experienced only the charm, the friendship, the intelligence and the learning: never the cruelty, violence and despair.

Only slightly less antisocial was Nairac's tendency, when the shadow self had taken over, to tell "whoppers," and act the braggart; something that was normally alien to his character. Nairac's humour was usually kindly, understated and genuinely funny. In "Mr Hyde" mode, however, Nairac enjoyed shocking people and "winding them up", often by telling dreadful and untrue stories about himself in order to appal them. These stories may well have included his alleged "confession" to Major Fred Holroyd of having murdered IRA Staff Captain John Francis Green in the Republic. If so, Holroyd swallowed the story, hook, line and sinker, and later relayed it to Ken Livingstone MP, who caused acrimonious exchanges about it in the House of Commons a decade after Nairac's death. Nairac seems anyway to have taken a mischievous delight in misleading the solemn and gullible Holroyd, while Ken Livingstone, gullible in a different way, was clearly desperately eager to believe anything, however improbable, to the discredit of the Army, the SAS and Nairac. The "whoppers" also include Nairac's statements to friends in London near the end of his life that he had successfully penetrated the IRA and was now a Brigade Commander. These remarks, probably made under the stimulus of alcohol, horrified those friends who believed them and were no doubt intended to. Not all his interlocutors did believe them. Julian Malins is dismissive: "I do not think that that can be true. He might have said it in his cups".

Somewhere between the antisocial and the merely amusing was Nairac's penchant for "romantic autobiography", in which embarrassing events would be embroidered and turned into hilarious or dashing escapades. One example was his "confession" to Luke Jennings that he had been rusticated from Oxford University for LSD abuse. As a result, he would have to go back to Lincoln College for a fourth year to complete his BA degree. This was not true. College records show that Nairac kept all his terms at Lincoln. No disciplinary action against him is recorded anywhere on his file: fortunately, because, had any such event been recorded, it could have jeopardised his chances of obtaining an Army commission when he came to be vetted in 1971. His nervous breakdown in academic year 1970-71, which should have been his final year, was the main reason for his taking a fourth year to complete a three-year degree course. However Nairac obviously preferred to depict this essentially medical decision to his younger friend as a disciplinary matter: it was preferable to appear wicked or reckless rather than weak or vulnerable. Likewise he claimed, as part of his case for being allowed back for a fourth year, that all his study notes had been lost when his car was stolen. The car was later recovered; the notes were never seen again. Nairac later boasted to Jennings that his study notes had never existed, or that the missing notes had been his A Level History notes from Ampleforth, which we now know not to have been the case. Jennings believed him, having no reason not to, and committed these stories to print, where they have not enhanced Nairac's posthumous reputation. This was not normal behaviour for Nairac. He was by nature an honest and truthful person. But, in a certain mood, he would do and say these things.

Here there is a strong similarity with T E Lawrence (*Note 6*); another practitioner of romantic autobiography. On one occasion, soon after Lawrence had left Bernard Shaw's (GBS) country house, Shaw's Corner at Ayot St Lawrence, having been "shooting a line," an exasperated Charlotte Shaw, who normally liked Lawrence very much, said to GBS: "He's such an INFERNAL liar!"

GBS corrected her: Lawrence was "an actor". That was different from being a mere liar. Nairac was certainly an actor; a good one. As result, he was not an easy person to know truly; apparently this was how he preferred it. But then he did have a genuine dark secret – his ordeal at Ampleforth – to cover up. This haunted him, just as T E Lawrence's illegitimacy had haunted Lawrence. Lawrence had a further guilty secret: his homoerotic sado-masochism, which might have caused him to face criminal charges, had it become known during his lifetime. These guilty secrets caused both men to edit the truth about themselves. In neither case could they be blamed for what had happened to them, but they still felt uneasy about it.

Jemima Parry-Jones says that there is at least one important exception to this generalisation: Nairac's alleged but non-existent Irish antecedents. These stories were probably part of his cover, as well as (perhaps) containing an element of wish-fulfilment. They may include the rumours of his having boxed with the late Martin Meehan and having studied at Trinity College, Dublin. "Robert was generally a very truthful man, although he had to be discreet, even misleading, about his work. However he may well have put out misleading disinformation in the context of his work, e.g. pretending to be of Irish descent. He had had relevant training with the Army. Given his work, he may well have posed as an Irishman or a Brit of Irish descent. His in–depth knowledge of Ireland and Irish history could easily have made people think that he had been born there."

Nairac had *some* characteristics in common with Byron, Paddy Mayne and particularly with T E Lawrence. Of all his historic and literary heroes, Nairac most closely resembled Lawrence. Both found endless fascination in studying the Middle Ages. As a boy Lawrence read the same mediaeval romances that Nairac would later enjoy. Lawrence's bedroom walls were papered with brass-rubbings: near-life-size images of mediaeval knights, ladies and clergy, reproduced from their funeral brasses. Both read Modern History at Oxford. Both were autodidacts, studying subjects that were not part of their curriculum. Both had a tendency to "cherry pick" their favourite subjects. In the military context Lawrence, like Nairac, was sometimes described by his detractors as reckless and arrogant, although others firmly denied these charges. Both had, or at least claimed to have, limited time for the opposite sex. Both of them had great charm. Both could be a fantastically loyal and generous friend. Both had a tendency to bend the rules; both were naturally clever and secretive. Both had a strange emotional relationship with Ireland. There were however some important differences. Lawrence disliked team games intensely; Nairac loved them. Nairac was very religious; Lawrence was not. Moreover, in the case of Lawrence, given Nairac's private cult of him, some of Nairac's resemblances to him might have been subconsciously or consciously cultivated. One of his colleagues in NITAT (NI) in 1974-75 was heard to say: "He thinks he's Lawrence of bloody Arabia!"

Comparison with others, especially with other soldiers, can helpfully cast some light on Nairac. However, there are dangers inherent in carrying this process too far. Such comparisons run the risk of consigning Nairac to a particular "type" of Bohemian soldier-romantic. That would be reductive of the great originality and individuality that was his essence. In the final analysis Nairac was not exactly like anybody else.

What the foregoing demonstrates is simply this: Robert Nairac was a hero and he had a certain amount in common with other heroes. The classical definition of a hero is a person who puts himself at risk for the benefit of others; that is what Nairac did, on many occasions. According to SAS Major B, "It is entirely right to describe him as a hero, regardless of those particular traits that others may consider foolhardy, or even a weakness. I have nothing but good feelings for him." Sam Martin, the author of *How to be a Hero*, a humorous book, adds that essential qualities for heroes include "chivalry, confidence, subtlety, charm, bravery and honesty. Add a bit of culture, intelligence, brute strength, sexiness and wit and you're almost there." That is a pretty good sketch of Robert Nairac.

CHAPTER 6 | GETTING TO OXFORD

I may not be there yet, but I'm closer than I was yesterday. (Author unknown)

Robert Nairac left Ampleforth College in December 1966 at the age of eighteen, but he would be past twenty before he went up to Oxford in October 1968. He would suffer at least one major setback before he reached his chosen university.

In 1966 Nairac's immediate challenge was to get into Oxford in the first place. His academic qualifications were respectable and other universities had accepted him on that basis. One of these was London University (Bedford College), which, then as now, set high entry standards. However Nairac had set his heart on Oxford. Here he faced two additional hurdles. Good A-Level passes were not enough. Oxford had its own entrance examinations, held in December. At that time the colleges were looking for bright, original thinkers. The entrance exam was appreciably stiffer than A-Levels. However it gave candidates the opportunity to shine by writing a paper on their chosen special subject, no matter how obscure. This counted for much more than their A-Level results; a good essay could compensate for a mediocre haul of A-Levels. If you were the best at something, and it did not really matter what, you had a chance of getting into Oxford. Julian Malins, for example, chose to write about witchcraft, although witch trials were only tangentially relevant to his future Law studies. He passed successfully and was accepted by Brasenose (BNC), his preferred College.

The second hurdle was the college interview. In the late 1960s the collegiate system devolved considerable authority and autonomy to the member colleges of the University of Oxford. This has been to some extent eroded in recent decades and further diluted by gender and diversity policy considerations, but the college interview remains important. All colleges had their own distinctive ethos, which they were keen to preserve and strengthen. Balliol College had a reputation, forged in the Victorian era, for intellectual brilliance. BNC was hearty and athletic. Christ Church was grand, aristocratic, and political and had produced thirteen Prime Ministers. It was also W H Auden's old college. Magdalen College was both aristocratic and intellectual: its alumni included Oscar Wilde, Sir Compton Mackenzie and the future King Edward VIII, as well as Cardinals Thomas Wolsey and Reginald Pole. Smaller colleges like Hertford (Evelyn Waugh's old college) or Worcester were worthy, poor but academically sound. It was not enough to be bright: a successful candidate had to be able to bring something special to the college. Most colleges sought to maintain a balanced intake of undergraduates. There was a place for Scholars (scholarship holders), who were often from humble backgrounds. Colleges actively sought brilliant Scholars and Commoners to win Firsts and enhance the college's reputation within and beyond the university. They also looked for good athletes who were not necessarily the brightest students but who would maintain or improve the college's rowing capability and ideally propel it to Head of the River. Large, muscular American, Australian and Canadian Rhodes Scholars were particularly welcome for that reason. The same applied to a lesser extent to cricket, rugby, boxing and other sports. There were other, less easily-definable, criteria. They often amounted to: "He may not be Einstein but I think he'd be good for the college", or alternatively "I just don't think that he'd fit in".

At some colleges local and regional connections still counted for a good deal. Jesus College – T E Lawrence's old college – was still definitely the Welsh college. (Lawrence had been born in Tremadog, which allowed him to qualify as Welsh.) Exeter College had historic links with the Channel Islands and Lincoln College still maintained a connection with Lincolnshire. In addition certain colleges nurtured historic links with the older Public Schools but these did not include the Catholic and relatively recently-founded (1803) Ampleforth College. The links often took the tangible form of scholarships reserved for pupils of those schools. Winchester was linked to New College. Both had been founded by William of Wykeham, Bishop of Winchester. Westminster School was formally linked to Christ Church, Oxford and Trinity College, Cambridge. Eton had ties with Christ Church and with King's College, Cambridge.

Most of these factors did not favour Nairac. No Oxford college had a special relationship with Sunderland or Mauritius. Ampleforth had no special or long-standing connection with any particular Oxford college, although quite a number of Amplefordians had studied at Oxford. Hugh Dormer, for example, had been an alumnus of Christ Church.

The Headmaster of Ampleforth, Father Barry, had advised Nairac to set his sights on Trinity College. Trinity was one of the grander Oxford colleges. Sir Thomas Pope (*circa* 1507–1559) had founded it in 1555. A pious Roman Catholic with no surviving children, Sir Thomas saw the foundation of an Oxford college as a means of ensuring that he and his family would always be remembered in prayers and Masses by its members. Pope was a trusted Privy Councillor of the Catholic Queen Mary Tudor. It was Mary who granted him her royal approval and the Letters Patent for his new foundation. The College Statutes set out rules for a simple, quasi-monastic life of religious observance and study but it is unlikely that any Catholic Masses for the repose of Sir Thomas' soul and those of his family ever took place. Queen Mary died and Queen Elizabeth I came to the throne in 1558. Sir Thomas died in January 1559. It is possible that the association with the pious Sir Thomas Pope appealed both to the Headmaster and to Nairac himself, as may have the fact that a Pre-Reformation foundation on the same site, Durham College, had belonged to the Benedictine Order. A fragment of Durham College survives, incorporated into the later buildings.

Trinity College survived the Elizabethan Reformation by becoming Anglican and it soon forgot Pope's plans for holy and studious austerity. In 1664 the Fellows elected Ralph Bathurst to the Presidency and a time of expansion began.

Bathurst wanted to attract the nobility to his college; he sought as a priority to provide suitably luxurious accommodation. In 1668 a two-story building (part of today's Garden Quadrangle) was completed with elegant panelled rooms and accommodation for servants to a design by Sir Christopher Wren, who was one of Bathurst's friends. Expansion continued through the eighteenth and nineteenth centuries on an ever-grander scale. The college became rich and exclusive. It would produce some formidably intellectual alumni like Cardinal Newman, Lord Acton the historian and Kenneth Clark the art historian. However Trinity was usually regarded as a "hearty" sporting college. A Merton College friend who slightly preceded Nairac at the university has described Trinity at that period as "a den of public school slouches, which would for that reason have been ideal for Nairac: the brilliant and thrusting went next door to Balliol". It might appear that Nairac, as a good all-round sportsman, was a potentially suitable candidate for Trinity College.

So why did Trinity not accept Nairac? One reason may have been that Nairac had no family or other connection with the college. In 1966 and for long afterwards, Trinity was a difficult college to enter if you did not have the right, ideally family, connections. More than a decade after Nairac had left Oxford, the son of a friend, wishing to follow his father to Trinity, was told:

"We'd love to take you, given that your father and grandfather were here. But we almost certainly cannot take you if you insist on reading PPE (Philosophy, Politics and Economics). There are too few places and the competition is too stiff. Could you see your way to reading Zoology?"

That year Zoology was less eagerly subscribed than PPE. Fortunately he could see his way to reading that subject and he had the necessary science passes. He settled into his ancestors' college for three happy years, rowed for the college and graduated as a zoologist, although that had not been his original plan.

Another reason may have been that Trinity had a very successful Boat Club, for which it sought good oarsmen, who were welcome even if they did not have a family connection. Nairac did not row; however, given his prowess at rugby, boxing and other sports and the fact that he had been Head of St Edward's House at Ampleforth, he might still have secured admission to Trinity if he had been on good interview form on the day. Unfortunately he was not, and his lack of self-confidence evidently let him down. As Maurice Nairac wrote in 1967, Robert had written a fair paper in the exam, but had had a "rotten" interview at Trinity and had been rejected. Worcester and Hertford Colleges, to which he had also applied, did not accept him either. He was "completely put out" and, several months later, was still "frightfully upset about it". Oxford, and by extension Cambridge, seemed as far away as ever.

Nairac left Ampleforth just before Christmas 1966, having returned for an extra term to prepare for and sit the Oxford entrance exams. He had expected to go up to Oxford in October 1967, but clearly that was not now going to happen.

He had no interest in going to London, or to any of the other non-Oxbridge universities that had accepted him. He had made arrangements to pass a "gap half-year" teaching History and French as an uncertified Assistant Master at the Catholic Avisford School from January to June 1967. He decided to go ahead with this, even though his future after Avisford was uncertain. While at Avisford he acted as an extra Games Master: he coached the boys in rugby, soccer, cricket, tennis, boxing and swimming. To a few boys who were interested, he gave extra-curricular instruction in falconry and angling. One was Luke Jennings; he was often Nairac's sole pupil for these subjects, which involved spending long hours out of doors, sometimes in horrible weather. At Avisford Nairac was a complete success; he was a natural teacher and mentor. This experience turned his thoughts towards teaching as a career. He made a favourable impression on the Headmaster of Avisford, Michael Jennings, who was Luke Jennings' father. Mr Jennings encouraged Nairac to try again for Oxford in December 1967. He offered him employment at Avisford until he should succeed. As a result Nairac's teaching gap year extended itself from January 1967 to June 1968. Encouraged during term-time by Mr Jennings, Nairac received extra tuition and coaching at home during the academic holidays, with a view to going up to Oxford in October 1968. By then he would be twenty years old, slightly older than most other first-year undergraduates. This was not evident, however: Nairac always looked, and sometimes acted, younger than his age. Julian Malins was surprised when, years later, he learned that Nairac had been two years older than him. He had perceived Nairac as an inexperienced younger brother for whom he should look out.

In his book *Blood Knots*, Luke Jennings describes the youthful Nairac as he appeared in 1967 at Avisford, with not-uncritical affection. He refers to Nairac's deeply religious side; to his occasionally profound melancholy; to his perfectionism, but also to his subversive side. This included teaching English public schoolboys to sing IRA rebel songs like *The Broad Black Brimmer* at after-supper sing-songs – admittedly, they were Catholics and the Troubles had not yet begun, although they were about to do so – and a general tendency to act first and seek permission afterwards. This earned him the odd severe reprimand from the senior staff, the details of which he was always happy to relay to Luke Jennings and his friends. For the most part, however, his fellow teachers were as taken with him, and as susceptible to his charm, as were the boys.

Meanwhile Nairac was no closer to getting into Oxford. It was time for Maurice Nairac to take action once more on behalf of "my boy Robert". Although the Nairacs had no close family connection with the University, Maurice's brother André was friendly with the Rector of Lincoln College, Dr (later Sir) Walter Oakeshott, who was Rector from 1954 to 1972. Mr Nairac had made an initial approach to Lincoln in 1966, before his son's A-Level results were known, but the response had not been encouraging. Now, however, equipped with an A in

History and a B in General Papers, Robert looked a more credible candidate. Maurice Nairac sought and was granted a private meeting with Dr Oakeshott in May 1967. In due course, having discussed his candidature with the Senior Tutor, Dr Owen, Dr Oakeshott concluded that Robert "does not look at all a bad bet" and wrote to Maurice Nairac that he should be encouraged to sit the Oxford entrance exam again in December 1967, this time giving Lincoln College as his first preference. He now appeared "a very reasonable candidate and we think that his chances will be better than 50/50." However Dr Oakeshott could not guarantee a place at that stage. Maurice Nairac clearly had misgivings, given that Robert still had the firm offer of a place at Bedford College, London. In his view this was worth following up: Robert, however, was not to be moved. Bedford College dated only from 1849. It was now co-educational, but had until recently been a women's college. For Robert it had to be a good, ancient men's college at either Oxford or Cambridge. Michael Jennings was also active on Robert's behalf, writing to the Senior Tutor at Lincoln giving Robert a strong recommendation "academically, in games, and as an excellent young man in general." He asked that he should be considered for an Old Member Scholarship. Although the college promised to do so, nothing came of this initiative. When Nairac finally went up to Oxford in the Michaelmas Term of 1968 (*Note 1*), it would be as a Commoner, not a Scholar.

Given Nairac's continuing fascination with Ireland, why he did not try for a place at Trinity College, Dublin (TCD), as some writers – and alumni of TCD – seem to be convinced that he did? TCD is architecturally distinguished and possesses one of the most magnificent libraries in Europe. Moreover TCD then still regarded itself as a British university. It was relatively easy at that time for British people with no close, or no Irish connections to obtain a place there, especially if they were good at team sports. An acquaintance who was an accomplished all-round sportsman and who would in due course represent TCD at inter-university level was told, "Find yourself an Irish grandmother and two A-Levels and I'll get you in!" Somehow he managed to acquire all three, and got in. Robert Nairac had the advantages that he was not only a sporting star, but he had a genuine family connection with TCD; other Nairacs, albeit distant Protestant cousins, had graduated from TCD in the past. So had numerous other distinguished people, including Sheridan Lefanu, Oscar Wilde (for his first degree), Bram Stoker, Lord Dunsany, J P Donleavy and a shoal of Irish and Anglo-Irish authors, bishops, aristocrats and politicians. On the social scale TCD was regarded as being almost on a par with Oxford and Cambridge. It was delightfully old-fashioned: in some respects life at TCD was like life at Oxford as it had been before the Second World War. The BA degree course was four, instead of three, years long, which meant less pressure of work on the undergraduates. Nairac would have been able to study Irish History to his heart's content and, given his insatiable interest in that subject, he might have achieved a First or a good Second Class Honours degree. There would be plenty of opportunity for sport, including rugby and he could have seen his Irish friends often. But there is no indication that this ever crossed his mind. He never did any postgraduate work at TCD or at any other Irish university either, despite the assertions of more than one writer that he did. Officials at TCD and the National University of Ireland have confirmed this.

The legend of Nairac at TCD may have arisen from one of two possible misconceptions. Firstly, he undoubtedly applied to Trinity College, Oxford and Trinity College, Cambridge in 1966 and 1967 respectively and therefore confusion could have arisen between the three Trinity Colleges. Secondly, it is conceivable that a previous researcher has confused him with one of his distant relations, the Dublin-based Protestant Nairacs, who genuinely had graduated from TCD, although this would have been somewhat before Robert Nairac's time. These Dubliner Nairacs were part of the Huguenot diaspora whose ancestors had fled from France after the revocation of the Edict of Nantes 1685. Other branches of the Nairac dynasty became established in the Netherlands and North America for the same reason. The senior branch, who remained in Bordeaux, reverted to being Catholic (or in certain cases pretended to do so). This is the branch to which Robert Nairac belonged. The exiled Nairacs seem to have prospered. They remained in touch with the senior branch and established branches of the family companies where they eventually settled. The Dublin company was called Nairac & Collins, sugar importers and refiners.

The key phrase above is *almost on a par*. TCD still would not have been Oxford. Nairac was only satisfied with the best, to be part of the best, and to be with the best. Hence Oxford. Hence his membership of Vincent's Club, hats from Lock & Co, boots and shoes from Lobb. Hence haircuts at Trumper's. So, when in 1972 he joined the Army, for Nairac it had to be either the Coldstream or the Grenadier Guards. Had he ever become a City gentleman – an improbable scenario – Nairac would have had to join the Drapers' and Mercers' Company, because it is the first among the ancient City Livery Companies. His dead brother David was probably similar in this respect. For him it had to be St Bartholomew's Hospital Medical School: the oldest and most famous in the world. Having got into the Grenadier Guards, Robert Nairac would be very happy indeed. That he might have performed better at a different university or that he might have been temperamentally better-suited to the less aristocratic Royal Marines or the Parachute Regiment, would not have entered his head.

If this seems snobbish, it was – but in a rather innocent way. Coming from a family of high achievers, Nairac was concerned with achievement, excellence and the trappings of excellence. "Trappings" sometimes had a literal application, extending to physical accessories as well as to things like membership of the University of Oxford or the Grenadier Guards. Luke Jennings records that Nairac, then aged eighteen or nineteen, had bought himself a Dunhill pipe from that firm's finest and most expensive range: "the only possible option, in his book. His conversation was full of such absolutes. A certain product was the *ne plus ultra*, identifying its owner as one of the elect". This applied to guns and trout rods, too.

As far as people were concerned, Nairac was refreshingly free, most of the time, from English class- and rank-consciousness. The exception to this generalisation was his fascination with the nobility, or with their dashing style. It is probably accurate to say that Nairac's nose had been pressed against the aristocracy's window throughout his early youth. Many British people share this harmless fascination: it keeps numerous stately homes and the National Trust in business. It assured the success of Evelyn Waugh's *Brideshead Revisited,* both the original novel and the television adaptations. It has made Julian Fellowes, the creator of *Downton Abbey,* a rich man.

Despite their enjoyment of field sports, despite Maurice Nairac's elevation to consultant surgeon and despite the move from suburban Sunderland to a manor house in Gloucestershire, Robert Nairac's family were definitely middle-class. They were not armigerous. His eighteenth-century French ancestors had been wealthy Bordeaux ship owners and merchants, including slave-traders. At its height, under the *ancien régime* about one-third of the Bordeaux slave trade was in the Nairac family's hands. They were also deeply involved in the closely related sugar importing and refining business. They became active in politics. A Nairac had sat as Deputy for Bordeaux in the 1789 session of the *états généraux,* whose convocation marked the start of the French Revolution. The impressive neoclassical Hotel de Nairac in Bordeaux, then their principal town house and now a court building, and the Chateau de Nairac at Barsac with its well-known vineyard testify to the Nairacs' former wealth and importance. By the nineteenth century that wealth had dwindled. For several generations before him Robert Nairac's male ancestors had been doctors and lawyers; in some cases distinguished ones.

Robert Nairac however had studied at Ampleforth. There he had mixed with the survivors of the old Recusant gentry and nobility, whose culture, values and folklore he had eagerly absorbed. His shooting, angling and falconry, and especially his friendship with Lord Killanin's family, had given him a limited entree into their aristocratic world; he wanted more. Nairac may have hoped that by going up to Oxford and excelling at sport there, he might achieve full membership of the club. This eluded him, although he befriended some aristocrats, who included Viscount Cranborne, the present Marquess of Salisbury and at that time an undergraduate of Christ Church.

In 1967 Nairac once again applied to Oxford, specifying his course preferences as: L1, L3 and L7 (all Lincoln College); Mg1 (Magdalen College); and O1 (Oriel College). He also applied for places at Bedford College, London (again); Trinity College, Cambridge; Bristol, Exeter and Aberystwyth Universities. This time he had a much better interview. On 20 December 1967 the Senior Tutor of Lincoln College wrote to inform Nairac that he had been successful and offered him a place for the Michaelmas Term of 1968. He accepted three days later. Meanwhile Nairac would continue to teach at Avisford School until the 1968 long summer vacation. Following the vacation, part of which would be spent in Ireland, he would start at Oxford in October. He would by then be twenty years old and, to quote Napoleon, "to understand the man, you have to know what was happening in the world when he was twenty".

What was happening as Nairac approached his twentieth birthday on 31 August 1968? As far as the UK was concerned, it was a depressing and unedifying spectacle. This is important because it affected the way in which Nairac saw the world: in the words of the hymn-writer Henry Francis Lyte, "Change and decay in all around I see".

In April 1964 the Chief of the Imperial General Staff (CIGS), the Army's professional head, Field Marshal Sir Richard Hull, dropped "Imperial" from his title because it no longer had any meaning. The British Empire was fast evaporating. In the same month the three historic Cabinet Ministerial Posts representing the Armed Services were abolished. These were the First Lord of the Admiralty (Navy), the Secretary of State for War (Army) and the Secretary of State for Air (RAF). A single new Secretary of State for Defence replaced them. This reflected the continuing contraction of both the Empire and the Armed Forces and the ending of National Service the year before.

By 1964 the Conservatives had been in power for thirteen years. The Labour Party scraped into office on 15 October that year with a small majority of four seats, following the Profumo scandal (*Note 2*), which had severely dented the Conservatives' responsible, respectable image. Even so, having shed Prime Minister Harold Macmillan and Secretary of State for War John Profumo, the Party had been experiencing a modest revival under Sir Alec Douglas-Home, whose personal integrity and expertise, particularly in foreign affairs, were not in question. The 1964 election was close-run; it was also arguably a stolen election. Labour had made exaggerated allegations that national security had been compromised as a result of Profumo's affair with Christine Keeler, who was alleged also to have had an affair with a member of the Soviet Embassy. She may or may not have done so. Her admission that she had was made months after the scandal had detonated; some authors regard her testimony as unreliable. In any event, national security had not been compromised. Stephen Ward, the osteopath who had introduced them, was not a Soviet spy-master and Mrs Profumo (the actress Valerie Hobson) did not divorce Mr Profumo. It was a storm in a teacup, exaggerated by the media. When Profumo resigned, it was not due to any security consideration but because he had knowingly lied to Parliament about his relationship with Miss Keeler. That was, and still is, a resigning matter.

The 1964 general election was the first in which image, specifically TV image, rather than substance or manifesto commitments, counted. The BBC threw its weight behind Labour. The Director-General, Hugh Greene, a brother of the novelist Graham Greene, was openly keen for Labour to win and may have delivered the small majority that it needed to achieve power. His methods included exposing Prime Minister Douglas-Home to hostile and discourteous interviewers, while treating Labour speakers favourably; unflattering lighting of Douglas-Home, so as to make him look old, tired and skeletal; even – at the Labour Leader Harold Wilson's request – postponing a popular evening TV programme, so that it should not deflect working-class Labour voters, who enjoyed watching it, from going to the polls. Wilson had reportedly explained to Greene that *Steptoe & Son* "might cost him up to ten seats", coming as it did between the hours of Northern English high tea and going to the pub. After the briefest internal discussion, the BBC kindly obliged.

The new Prime Minister, Harold Wilson (*Note 3*), came into office, as many years later would Tony Blair, speaking grandiloquently of a "New Britain" and promising to transform British society with references to "the white-hot heat of technology." It was typical of Wilson, who had no scientific credentials, to employ a metaphor more appropriate to the technology of the first industrial revolution, 200 years earlier. It gradually became clear that Wilson had no plan, other than to stay in office. He often drifted. He had no compass; no weight of ideological baggage; plenty of tricks and slogans but few ideas and, in the final analysis, no achievements. His Cabinet colleague Dennis Healey considered that Wilson was a man who had "neither political principle nor sense of direction". His presence in Parliament over a lengthy period demonstrates simply that he was a politics-addict and had a certain plausibility that beguiled the electorate. His sole good deed was to resist American pressure to involve Britain in the Vietnam War, which the Army had told him was unwinnable.

Nevertheless, like a glob of exceptionally viscous bubblegum, Labour would cling to power for eleven of the next fifteen years, at one point (1966-70) with a large majority; more usually with a very small – and for several months in 1974, no – majority. From 1977-79 Labour only managed to survive in office with Liberal support. There was a short Conservative restoration under Edward Heath from 1970 to 1974. The period of 1964-79, ending with Margaret Thatcher's first election success, represents the twentieth-century nadir of Britain's national morale, political, economic and military fortunes and of its international prestige.

For most of that period Harold Wilson was the Leader of the Labour Party. He is seldom mentioned today, yet he won four general elections. Few Prime Ministers have been in office for so long (1964-70 and 1974-76) but had so little to show for it. Wilson has joined Addington, Derby, Liverpool, Campbell-Bannerman, Bonar Law, Ramsay MacDonald and Callaghan in the lumber-room of forgotten British Prime Ministers. Yet at the time he was a hate-figure for right-wing writers and thinkers, some of whom believed him to be in the pay of the Soviet Union, while others speculated in the media about the chances of success of a military coup against Wilson's government. One was the journalist and novelist Constantine Fitzgibbon. Yet another was Colonel David Stirling, the ageing, but still active co-founder of the original SAS Regiment and owner of a private military company (PMC). Excited rumour suggested that MI5, MI6, the SAS, senior Army officers, members of the Royal Family and others in "the Establishment" were seriously interested in a coup. So, it was thought, might be some foreign powers, including the government of South Africa.

In reality, all of this was highly unlikely. "The Establishment" in the sense of a close network of influential people; movers, shakers and fixers who all knew each other, had attended the same schools and universities, belonged to the same clubs and were disproportionately represented in Parliament, the Church of England, the Royal Household, the upper ranks of the Armed Forces, the Civil Service, MI5, MI6, the City of London, the learned professions, the senior judiciary and of course the Conservative Party, had ceased to exist. Already becoming decadent and weakened by the loss of many brilliant young men in the Great War, its last successful coup had been the removal of the controversial King Edward VIII in 1936: not necessarily a bad thing. The Second World War had delivered its *coup de grace*. Its last gasp had been the "Indian summer" of the early-to-mid-1950s. The British Army had not engaged in *coups d'état* since the seventeenth century. The Royal Family had not intervened politically to any purpose since Edward VII. MI5 and MI6 were at that period highly unlikely to collaborate effectively on anything: least of all on an illegal coup d'état.

Many of the published articles and letters were written tongue-in-cheek; only a chump would have taken them seriously. Although he was admittedly implicated in two not very serious coup initiatives against the governments of Libya and the Seychelles, which came to nothing, Colonel Stirling was at this stage a notable mischief-maker and practical joker. It was part of the "fun" side of his character, which is amply attested by his former friends. The thought that the Labour leadership might be collectively in disarray as a result of his pranks would have delighted him. Nevertheless the response of Wilson and the wider Labour Party was paranoid. What they had read and heard seemed to suggest that there was an advanced and well-laid "Establishment plot" against them. This is confirmed by the remarks of, among others, Mrs Marcia Williams after Labour lost the 1970 election. From time to time a few unreliable sources such as Peter Wright's book, *Spycatcher,* would seem to confirm this; at least they did if you were an eager conspiracy theorist. Labour's paranoia would last for decades. It was to impact on Nairac during his life and after his death.

A future development, coming after 1968, of the "Establishment plot" theory was that there was a conspiracy, involving among others MI5 and elements of the Army, to escalate what was by then the already serious situation in Northern Ireland into full civil war by a series of carefully-timed strikes against both Republicans and Loyalists. Once law and order had completely broken down, this would permit the Army to wage all-out war on the IRA, dispensing with peacetime restraints; outshooting and out-ambushing them, and in the process discrediting the Labour Party, causing it to lose the next election. Although there are those on the British Left and among Irish Republicans who still take this theory seriously, there is no evidence of any such plot. Nevertheless, logically it should follow that there has to have been a military mastermind – probably a member of the SAS – to coordinate and execute the plan: someone trained in sabotage and assassination, a martial Machiavelli devoid of moral scruple, who positively enjoyed mayhem; a mighty shadow looming large behind every event but never clearly seen. Unlikely as it must now appear, this is the role in which some people, including writers like Michael Cunningham (Miceal O'Cuinneagain), Anthony Bradley and Eoin McNamee, have sought to cast Robert Nairac. In Cunningham's words in the Foreword to his self-published *The Nairac Affair*, he offers:

"A brief examination of some of the events in South Armagh and North Louth in the period 1976-77 involving Captain Nairac of the 22nd Special Air Service (SAS) Regiment. This Regiment caused untold suffering on both sides of the Irish Border. The unjust conviction of two young Catholic men, from South Armagh, for murder, bears testimony to the evil influence of Captain Nairac and his fellow SAS men. This evil appears to have permeated every sector of the legal process North and South."

For sweeping inaccuracy and wild supposition, this Foreword cannot be bettered; nor does the rest of the book disappoint. Nevertheless some people took it seriously at the time. When these theories began to be aired, Nairac was safely dead and could not comment or sue. The "two young Catholic men" allegedly unjustly convicted for murder were Nairac's assassin, Liam Townson, and John Anthony McCooey, convicted for the multiple Tullyvallen Orange Hall murders.

History rarely misses its cue. On 24 January 1965, a few months after Labour's election victory and almost twenty years after the end of the Second World War, Sir Winston Churchill, the last of the great Victorians, died at the age of ninety-one. Although this came as no surprise, it was still a shock: a colossus had disappeared. Born in full imperial sunlight in 1874, he had lived to see night fall. A Member of Parliament continuously from 1900 to 1964, for nine of those years (1940-45 and 1951-55) Churchill had been Prime Minister. In June 1964, old, ill and leaning on two sticks, he had made his last bow to the Speaker of the House of Commons. On 30 January 1965, a grim and bitterly cold day, his State funeral took place, marked by antique ceremony and sombre pomp. In the funeral procession from Westminster Hall to St Paul's Cathedral, Churchill's black-clad female relations rode in horse-drawn carriages. Lady Churchill was heavily veiled, as had been the custom in Churchill's youth. His male relations, in dark overcoats and black top-hats, walked on foot. They looked like Edwardians; figures from a distant and more distinguished past. Artillerymen, muffled in heavy Victorian-style greatcoats, fired gun salutes. Military bands played solemn music. Among the many soldiers lining the route in the freezing air was a detachment of the King's Own Scottish Borderers commanded by Lieutenant Clive Fairweather. The giant candlesticks standing around the catafalque in St Paul's, "the parish church of the Empire", had been used at Wellington's State funeral. The great Duke had been the last commoner before Churchill to be so honoured. Monarchs, Presidents and other notables swelled the congregation. Even President de Gaulle of France, whose relations with Churchill had often been strained, was there.

More than two centuries earlier the vaults of St Paul's had echoed to *Te Deums* sung in honour of the victories of Churchill's ancestor, the First Duke of Marlborough, over the French. At that time Britain's rise to empire, riches and military glory had seemed unstoppable. Now they heard the desolate Last Post sounded on a cavalry trumpet. To many who watched the ceremony, it seemed to be the Empire's funeral, as well as Churchill's. There was an implicit finality in the slow, heavy tread of the soldiers and the rhythm of the funereal music. The curtain had come down for the very last time on an era of British greatness and achievement. What, if anything, did the future hold for the British?

It was not only people on the political Right who felt this foreboding: Richard Crossman, at that time a Labour Cabinet Minister, wrote in his diary: "It felt like the end of an epoch, possibly even the end of a nation". Half a century later, that seems a perceptive judgement. Another commentator wrote after the funeral: "This was the last time that London would be the capital of the world. This was an act of mourning for the imperial past. This marked the final act in Britain's greatness". As Wordsworth once put it, referring to the extinguishing of the Venetian Republic in 1797:

Men are we, and must grieve when even the Shade
Of that which once was great is passed away.

It was understandable that people like Nairac should look back to the Edwardian British Empire, in which Churchill had first become a prominent politician, with nostalgia and regret. The UK's new leaders did not share this nostalgia. They considered that they had nothing to learn from the past and felt nothing but contempt for people who wanted to cling to Britain's traditions. This applied equally to the Conservative Leader, Edward Heath, who was elected in 1965 and was in some respects "a Tory Mr Wilson", and to Wilson's Ministers like Crosland and Jenkins. The period of 1965-7 has been described by John Campbell, Roy Jenkins' biographer, as "coinciding with the height of Beatlemania, the miniskirt, the contraceptive pill and 'Swinging London', but also with the Rolling Stones, the drug scene and the first [anti-] Vietnam War demonstrations ... [It] now appears, for good or ill, a turning point in the social history of the country – a halcyon time of personal liberation or the onset of national decadence". It was indeed a turning point. Even if this was not clear at the time, in retrospect the verdict has to be: the onset of potentially terminal national decadence. In 2015 Dominic Sandbrook, writing in *The Daily Mail*, described 1965 as "the year that old Britain was wrecked". Again, it is no wonder that Nairac so disliked the age in which he lived.

In November 1965, Ian Smith, the white Prime Minister of Rhodesia, Britain's last remaining major African colony, determined to resist British and Commonwealth pressure to concede majority rule, would declare independence unilaterally (UDI). Although the UN General Assembly had sanctioned British use of military action to enforce majority rule as a prelude to formally granting independence, nothing would happen. White Rhodesia continued to exist until 1979, periodically defying the British Government and the Commonwealth (*Note 5*). Its eventual fall would be brought about by other factors than British military intervention. One of Nairac's future friends, Lord Richard Cecil, would become involved in the Rhodesian bush war, which would cost him his life.

In 1966 the last Secretary of State for the Colonies, Frederick Lee, resigned and was not replaced. His diminished former Ministry was subsumed into the Foreign Office. As the Empire was progressively dismantled, almost every year, starting in 1947, the Union Flag was being lowered somewhere for the last time. At independence celebrations in colony after colony, garish new flags were being raised amid fanfares. Large areas of former colonial territory, soon to be called "the Developing World" or "the Third World", now entered an era of jet travel, Swiss bank accounts and gold bullion chamber-pots for the ruling élite amid growing poverty, overpopulation, environmental degradation, ethnic conflict and political instability for almost everybody else. By 1967 the decolonisation process was largely complete. Except for Southern Rhodesia, Aden and Hong Kong, the UK had divested itself of most of its major colonial responsibilities. It had yet to find another, post-imperial, role. Apart from its role as a NATO partner and its permanent seat on the UN Security Council, which reflected its former status during the Second World War, Britain now belonged to no important international grouping. President de Gaulle had vetoed the UK's attempt to join the EEC, which was the EU's predecessor. The Empire had gone. The Commonwealth was of no importance. At times it seemed like a liability: an anti-British organisation. The Commonwealth has reinvented itself since those days.

1967, when Robert Nairac entered his twentieth year, is distinguished for one reason; a slightly fraudulent one. It is designated in works of popular history as "the only year of peace since 1945". In every other year since World War II (runs the narrative) British troops have been deployed on active service somewhere in the world, often in a counter-insurgency role. But in 1967 there were fewer British troops serving abroad than at any time in living memory. The Borneo counter-insurgency campaign had ended in 1966. No important military action involving the UK, we read, was happening anywhere in the halcyon year of 1967. This was not literally true, although 1967 might have been slightly more peaceful for the UK than any year since then.

It was certainly not true of South Arabia, usually referred to as Aden after its capital, one of Britain's last remaining important Dependent Territories. A mutiny by the British-trained Aden Armed Police in mid-1967 had led to a massacre of British troops. The town of Aden went out of control. Lieutenant Colonel Colin Mitchell of the Argyll and Sutherland Highlanders became famous when, in July 1967, he successfully re-occupied the Crater District of Aden, which nationalist insurgents had taken over. Mitchell's action in Crater was of interest to Nairac because it was latter-day Henty. It is often referred to as "the Last Battle of the British Empire". The event made Mitchell a popular hero but, apart from Mitchell and his men's heroism, the end of British rule in Aden was not an edifying story.

The courage shown by British soldiers, colonial officials and police officers on the ground in Aden contrasted sharply with the moral cowardice and lack of scruple of the UK's political leaders. The achievements and sacrifices of the Armed Forces to restore order were wasted. After the Argyll and Sutherland Highlanders and others had reasserted control at considerable cost in soldiers' lives, Harold Wilson suddenly lost his nerve. He precipitately announced the abandonment of the colony, the evacuation of the British community and the withdrawal of British forces. This duly took place on 30 November 1967.

According to the journalist Brian Barron, who was present, betrayal and melodrama marked Britain's undignified exit from Aden. Of all the various end-of-empire sagas, this was the saddest, the most abject. Whoever chose the tune of "Fings Ain't Wot They Used T'Be" for the military band bidding farewell to the last Governor, when he departed with undignified haste from the RAF base, evoked exactly the right note of seediness and frayed national self-belief. Britain withdrew, abandoning moderate allies to their fate and the colony to civil war. Twenty-three years of police-state thuggery followed, with the Soviet KGB replacing the British. After Aden and the rest of the South had merged with North Yemen, there would be yet another destructive civil war in the 1990s.

The abandonment of Aden and the withdrawal of British forces alarmed Britain's Arab Gulf State allies, with whom the UK had long-standing defence agreements. The Foreign Office expended considerable effort in reassuring them that there would still be a British military presence in the region and that treaty commitments would be honoured. The following year, 1968, again without prior consultation, Wilson suddenly announced the withdrawal of all British forces east of Suez and the winding–down of the Near East Command. Britain lost face; its Arab allies felt betrayed; the Foreign Office had been made to look untruthful. The UK's international prestige plummeted further. In the event a low-key British military presence, including that of the SAS in Oman, had to be preserved or reinstated. These Prime Ministerial antics can only have reinforced Nairac's detestation of the period of British history through which he was living.

Meanwhile, the North Yemen Civil War, in which the UK was covertly involved, would smoulder on until 1970. The UK had also become involved, less covertly, in the Oman (Dhofar) counter-insurgency campaign, which would last until 1979. Since 1965 Rhodesia had been in a state of successful rebellion, although there were no plans for the Army to intervene there. Hong Kong was a neuralgic subject with China, so British troops were stationed there. The same was true of Belize (the former British Honduras) and Guatemala, ditto Gibraltar and Spain. There was still a British garrison in Libya, and would be for another three years. The Cold War, which kept a large number of British troops stationed in West Germany, was ongoing. Much nearer home, Northern Ireland was not quiet. Stimulated, among other things by memories of the 1916 Easter Rising whose fiftieth anniversary fell in early 1966, Irish Republicanism was stirring again. Both the IRA and its Ulster Protestant equivalent, the UVF, were being revived. The past was coming to life again. Although the Army would not become involved until 1969, the scene was being set for conflict in Northern Ireland, although Britain's political class seemed blithely or apathetically unaware of this.

Elsewhere there was enough non-British military action to keep war correspondents gainfully employed. Israel and several Arab States fought a very short (six-day) war from 5 to 10 June 1967: Israel won. The Vietnam War continued, with no end in sight. So did various small wars in Africa, one of which was the Nigerian Civil War, also known as the Biafra War, which lasted from 1967 to 1970. So 1967 was not in reality a year of peace, even for the UK.

With the exception of the Arab-Israeli War, the sputtering conflicts of 1967 would pale into insignificance by comparison with the events of the following year. 1968, the year of Nairac's twentieth birthday as well as of his arrival in Oxford, was exceptionally turbulent: it was marked by massive, often violent, civil rights demonstrations in several countries, including the USA. The most important event of 1968 was the Soviet invasion of Czechoslovakia, following the Czech government's announcement of a programme of reform that included amendments to the constitution of Czechoslovakia that would have brought back a degree of political democracy and greater personal freedom. The world's attention, however, was focused on France, which was Nairac's ancestral territory and where he still had friends and relations. The May 1968 events, *les événements de mai*, were a volatile period of unrest with strikes and the occupation of factories and universities across France. When it materialised, the strike proved to be the largest ever declared in France, and the first nation-wide wildcat strike. The unrest successfully disrupted France's advanced economy. It almost caused the fall of President de Gaulle's government. The student occupations and strikes initiated across France encountered forceful resistance from university administrators and the police. The government's attempts to quell those strikes by force inflamed the situation, leading to street battles between students and the police in the Paris Latin Quarter; and the old university quarter, near the Sorbonne, followed by the spread of general strikes and occupations throughout France.

"The Sorbonne," wrote Eugene Pelletan, "shines from the heights through the early mists like the dawn of intelligence. It is there that the French Revolution was really born, thence its point of departure..."

There is a factual element in this rodomontade: the 1968 protestors did indeed see themselves as part of a revolutionary tradition stretching back through the revolutions of 1870, 1848 and 1830 to 1789 and even earlier. History seemed to be repeating itself. The protests reached such a pitch that Ministers feared civil war or revolution. In retrospect, although not at the time, this seems an unlikely outcome. Nevertheless President de Gaulle lost his nerve and fled to a French military base in Germany. Having recovered it, on his return he dissolved the National Assembly and called new parliamentary elections for 23 June 1968. In France the violence evaporated almost as quickly as it had arisen. The end result was almost nil. Workers went back to their jobs. When the elections took place in June, the Gaullist Party and its allies emerged even stronger than before, although de Gaulle himself was to resign in 1969, following what he perceived as an insufficiently positive referendum result.

Sympathetic or imitative action occurred in other countries, including the USA and the UK, where the London School of Economics (LSE) in particular became a hotbed of Left-Wing dissent and protest. Nairac was probably right in deciding that he would not have enjoyed life at London University. Apart from a few ritual sit-ins and occupations of university buildings, which annoyed town and gown alike, the University of Oxford stayed aloof from the tragicomedy. As the satirical radio show *Listen to This Space* put it in the refrain of an amusing topical song, "Oxford isn't like the LSE." Elsewhere, at one point West Germany seemed likely to follow France into chaos. In the USA African-Americans asserted their civil rights. The civil rights leader Martin Luther King and Senator Robert Kennedy were both assassinated. As a footnote, Robert Nairac's native Mauritius became independent within the Commonwealth on 12 March 1968.

In 1968 Nairac took little interest in the political events that were occupying the media's attention, although he could not totally ignore them. He felt no sympathy with the revolting French students or with their various grievances. As Nancy Mitford, who was living in France, summed it up at the time: "They were out for a rough-up and they got it. Nobody was killed and now they are behaving like babies who have been slapped. It's not very dignified." In all the four years that he spent at Oxford Nairac never showed any interest in politics or even made a serious political remark, although some of his friends were politically active, and he never went near the Oxford Union. In 1970 his Tutor in Political Thought would write of him: "Political Thought, requiring a good deal of abstract thinking, is not really his métier." He was a small-c conservative; a "Queen and country" man and most of the time he left it at that.

However Ireland was a special case. Given his Irish interests, Nairac followed events there with closer attention. In 1968 Northern Ireland too was the scene of organised protest, although it seemed like a minor sideshow at the time. There were protests everywhere, even in London. Why should Northern Ireland be any different? The Northern Ireland Civil Rights Association (NICRA), formed in Belfast on 29 January 1967 and initially including some Unionist politicians, was created to campaign on such issues as discrimination against Roman Catholics in employment and housing, the gerrymandering of electoral boundaries and other issues. Poor housing, high unemployment and institutionalised discrimination had led to protests. To this extent there was a parallel with the disadvantaged, and effectively disenfranchised, African-Americans. The difference was that the moribund IRA, based in Dublin, saw this as an opportunity to acquire a new *raison d'être* and to challenge and topple the Belfast Government. It now prepared to infiltrate and subvert the Civil Rights organisations, misappropriating their funds to buy weapons and deliberately promoting confrontation and violence. Inspired by the Civil Rights campaigners in America, the first Northern Irish protests had taken the form of marches. The marches were initially peaceful but they soon triggered – or appeared to trigger – a series of violent clashes with police and Loyalists; these provoked a rapid rise in the number of sectarian attacks within the Province; exactly what the IRA wanted.

From then on the IRA was increasingly in control of events, although this was not immediately obvious. When it did become obvious, many people abandoned the Civil Rights movement. In October 1968, while Nairac was settling into Oxford, a Civil Rights march in Londonderry ended violently. Later in October People's Democracy and The Derry Citizens' Action Committee would be established. Matters deteriorated further in 1969. In January, People's Democracy organised a march from Belfast to Londonderry. Ominously, riots started in Londonderry even before the marchers had arrived. When they did, Loyalists attacked them. In January and February 1969 Catholics in the Bogside barricaded themselves in. In April Northern Ireland Prime Minister Terence O'Neil resigned. The scene was now set for the Troubles to begin in earnest. In 1969 the first British troops would be sent into the Province, supposedly as a temporary measure, to back up the civil power and keep the two sides apart. The first Army victim, Gunner Robert Curtis, was killed in February 1971. Two years later, in 1973, Nairac would be sent to Belfast with his Battalion. As one of his former commanders later wrote, Nairac had come to see Northern Ireland as a major challenge for his generation. So did other young aspirant Army officers.

This is an appropriate point at which to pause and consider what Nairac did during his academic vacations from Ampleforth and later Oxford. Sometimes he travelled. He visited Kenya at least once, probably at the invitation of one of several white Kenyan boys then studying at Ampleforth, and fell in love with the country. Sometimes he helped Martin Jones to train apprentice falconers. He often visited his friends the Morris brothers in Dublin and Galway. He explored Ireland thoroughly. In the words of one of Nairac's former school friends, Ireland "was instilled in his psyche with a kind of romantic intensity". In the course of his Irish explorations he sought out and spoke with the elderly survivors of the Easter Rising, the Irish War of Independence and the Irish Civil War. Many of them had been, or still were, members of the IRA. Later, in Northern Ireland, Nairac would establish his street-credibility in conversation with Republicans by referring to his links with these veteran heroes of the past. Some at least of his Republican and Nationalist interlocutors were very impressed. Later he also mentioned this interesting connection to his acquaintances in the SAS. They were far less impressed and viewed it as a yet another symptom of Nairac's general unsoundness.

Nairac had French relations on his father's side, whom he visited at their house near Narbonne. He did a lot of fishing in England, sometimes with Luke Jennings as companion. He spent time in Scotland too: angling, shooting and hawking. He became an enthusiastic wildfowler on the Severn estuary. This sport, involving rising long before dawn on sub-zero winter mornings to wade in freezing mud, often to lie in it and, in the dawn twilight, to ambush fast-flying, wary wild ducks and geese (widgeon, shoveller duck, teal, white-fronted geese) which present a challenging target at any time, is for very tough, very good marksmen; not for wimps. The Gloucestershire Wildfowlers' Association, of which Nairac was once a keen and supportive member, annually awards a Robert Nairac Trophy to the person who has done the most that year to help or advance the club. It was due to his passion for wildfowling that Nairac came to acquire his huge Newfoundland dog, Bundle, which would outlive him. Newfoundlands, which enjoy swimming, make ideal retrievers for wildfowl.

Lest Nairac should appear as an irresponsible and indiscriminate destroyer of wildlife, the following anecdote is supplied by one of his cousins:

"Another time, when Robert was about 18 I think, he took me duck hunting on the Severn estuary. He was a great shot (they'd moved to Standish by then). Anyhow, we saw nothing until this solitary duck suddenly appeared and flew straight over me, a sitter. I lined it up and was just about to fire when Robert cried out: 'No, don't shoot! It's a Merganser!' I was very irritated. I'd gotten up at about four to go with him and we hadn't bagged so much as a feather. I'd never even heard of Mergansers! It escaped into the pale dawn and we went home empty handed."

Nairac's point was that the handsome Red-Breasted Merganser (*Mergus serrator*), a fish-eating duck, was at that time quite rare in England. The Merganser had been persecuted because of its alleged impact on trout and salmon stocks. Moreover it tastes disagreeable, due to its diet of fish. The most palatable wild ducks are those like the Mallard, the Gadwall, the Pintail and the Widgeon, which eat a mainly vegetarian diet. They are the ones worth shooting.

Nairac's favourite pastimes: falconry, dry-fly angling and shooting, were costly. In addition, he ran a car even before he went up to university. Although his father was comfortably-off, Nairac preferred not to ask him for more financial support than was absolutely necessary. From time to time he was therefore obliged to seek a vacation job. Predictably, he did something a bit different: Nairac worked as a construction worker on Sir Robert McAlpine building sites (*Note 6*) around London. To his pleasure, many of his fellow-labourers turned out to be Irish. He went with them after work to Irish bars in Kilburn, one of London's oldest Irish colonies. Kilburn was also an area where the IRA was starting to establish itself and to set up "safe houses", although Nairac is unlikely to have known much about that (*Note 7*). If he rubbed shoulders with IRA operatives at that time, it was unwittingly and in the pub. In Kilburn, which he grew to know well, he enjoyed drinking Guinness, singing and rough-housing. It was an Irish home from home. Sinister implications have been read into this activity by some authors. These are that Nairac had been talent-spotted by one of the Agencies, presumably MI5 or MI6, probably while still at Ampleforth, and was already, as an undergraduate, being groomed as a future undercover agent and assassin for use against Irish Republicans: "so he moved like a sly imperial fox among the exiled Paddies, keeping the cover story wide and flexible..." according to Anthony Bradley's fanciful account. It follows that his work on building sites "must" have been part of his training.

With respect, this is nonsense. The Agencies do not recruit schoolboys. They are not even very keen on undergraduates; they prefer potential recruits to have work experience. At that time Nairac had no firm career plans. Insofar as he had any, they inclined towards teaching, as we have seen, rather than the Army or anything undercover. He did not, as has been alleged, continue to work on building sites after he had joined the Army, although when off-duty or on leave in the UK he would continue to go slumming, drinking, and sometimes getting into fights, in Kilburn.

The explanation of Nairac's construction work is simple: money, lots of it, to fund his expensive hobbies. Labouring on building sites was well paid at that time. It had to be, as it was physically very demanding. Because the labourers were always paid in cash, it was possible to avoid declaring it to the Inland Revenue. Most undergraduates, even rugby players, were not sufficiently strong and did not have the stamina to do this work. However, for the few who were tough enough, it was the best-paid vacation work available. Nairac was tough enough. So was his friend Julian Malins, who worked as a hod-carrier on Ministry of Public Buildings and Works construction sites. Apart from the money, as an additional bonus the heavy and gruelling work kept the young men very fit. Given this background of manual labour, it is easy to see how

Nairac was later able to impress his Guardsmen with arm-wrestling and other feats of strength.

It was also in Kilburn that Nairac became involved in bare-knuckle fighting. This was and is against the law. All fights, unless held under the Amateur Boxing Association (ABA) or some other licence and contested in accordance with the Queensberry Rules as now enacted by the British Boxing Board of Control, are illegal and have been for many years. However professional bare-knuckle fights still take place, often in the back-rooms of pubs. If you wish to watch one or to take part, it is a matter of knowing the right people. The sport is exciting and dangerous, the prize money significant. Like the sums paid to construction workers, it is paid in cash: it is possible (indeed, prudent) not to declare it to the tax authorities. Nairac's participation did not surprise the few friends to whom he mentioned it. Nairac was a skilful mover in the ring, weaving and ducking and with a good and generally effective guard. His great strength was that he positively lapped up punishment. Bare-knuckle fighting is extremely painful and risky; Nairac's appetite for pain and his ability to endure it would make him a disheartening opponent in any bare-knuckle fight.

Unless you have spent months hardening your hands and knuckles (the old professional boxers had ways of doing this in brine or pickle), hitting someone, especially head shots, with your bare knuckles is as dangerous to the puncher as to the recipient, so bare-knuckle fights tend to be mostly conducted with body punches, where endurance and pain tolerance would have given Nairac a good edge. At any rate, he seems to have found it financially worthwhile.

Nairac fought for money in country fairs on more than one occasion. Oxford friends recall his occasional participation at country shows and remember seeing him later with bruised knuckles or a black eye. As a bonus, he was once again connecting with the English past: in this case with the world of the Regency Corinthian gentleman pugilists.

Nairac was never anything other than an amateur boxer, albeit a very skilled one, but he had considerable admiration for professional boxers like Henry Cooper. He evidently knew some of them; a former Grenadier Guards brother officer recalls Nairac, while serving in London, going out one evening to dine with Joe Bugner.

Nairac also fought for money in the Republic of Ireland. He once ran out of funds while on holiday there as an undergraduate, but was reluctant to ask his father or friends for help. At a country fairground the owner of a boxing show was offering five pounds as prize money to anyone who could go three rounds with one of the "house stable" of boxers. Five pounds went a long way in the late 1960s and early 1970s. Nairac took off his shirt, got into the ring, knocked out the man put up against him and damaged him so severely that the pugilist was rendered *hors de combat* for the foreseeable future. Nairac had won his five pounds, but the show was now one pugilist short. This was most inconvenient.

Nairac was offered the job of replacing the unfortunate man as a member of the booth's "staff" for the remainder of the summer. He accepted and travelled around Ireland with the fair. This kept him in food and beer for the rest of his holiday, but damage to several among the many parts of him that at one time or another got broken (nose, jaw, cheek-bone…) resulted from this experience.

Nairac's later trips to Kilburn while serving in the Army, when he posed as an Irishman, speaking with an Irish accent and still getting into fights, were of concern to his friends. They reasonably feared that he would be "spotted" by the IRA in Kilburn. His friend Lord Salisbury has raised the possibility that he might have been, and that intelligence about him could have been passed from Kilburn to the South Armagh PIRA. Not long before his death in 1977 Nairac spent a short leave with the Cecils in their house in Chelsea. In Lord Salisbury's words, "Robert spent his last night on this side of the water in what is now my house in London when he was, perhaps with hindsight rather imprudently, nosing around in Irish communities in Kilburn." Nairac's friends predicted that he would be recognised as a soldier or something equally unwelcome, and get into a situation in Kilburn very similar to the one into which he got in Drumintee on 14 May 1977. Not long before his murder, following a rough and exciting evening in Kilburn, Martin Squires told him bluntly, "Robert, you are going to get rumbled one day, chum", and "You'll be recognised somewhere along the line, either here in London or back in South Armagh." That was a reasonable fear, but there is no evidence that the IRA ever spotted Nairac in Kilburn, although he was a frequent visitor. A former brother officer recalls "going to the Memphis Belle pub in Kilburn with Robert when we were based in Chelsea Barracks. It was a well-known Irish Republican meeting place where, late at night, one would join in rousing choruses of *The Men Behind the Wire*" (*Note 8*).

In the event the people who would murder Nairac in May 1977 were, as we have seen, a bunch of thuggish amateurs who had no idea who he was, but just felt that "there was something not quite right" about "Danny McErlean." Their initial suspicion was that he was a Loyalist paramilitary on a recce; which might suggest that by that time his Belfast accent sounded pretty authentic.

Chapter 7 | This Side of Paradise

And now in proud LINCOLN, the star of the Turl
We see our three heroes the banner unfurl
Drink death to the Commies, the queers and the left
Who lurk in dark Balliol of banner bereft.
(Robert Nairac in *The Imp* magazine, 1969.
This seems to commemorate an undergraduate prank.)

He had a tough exterior, which covered a sensitive nature.
(Dr V H H Green on Nairac, after his murder in 1977)

As a freshman Robert Nairac was required to go up to Oxford to begin residence a week earlier than second- and third-year men, at the start of the Michaelmas Term of 1968. This means that he would have moved into Lincoln College in the first week of October or even slightly earlier. Lincoln was a small college, to which Nairac went because he could not get in elsewhere, but that college would prove to offer some real compensations. One of these would be his friendship with the distinguished History Tutor, the Reverend Dr Vivian H H Green. Lincoln was a smaller college, and therefore a friendlier place, than Trinity. It was not dominated by aristocrats bearing famous names – which Nairac probably regretted – nor by arrogant rich men's sons. Nairac would not be rubbing shoulders with future Prime Ministers or other movers and shakers. Nevertheless, although he might not have fully appreciated this at the time, Nairac was fortunate to have secured a place at Lincoln.

Lincoln College is authentically ancient. Richard Fleming, Bishop of Lincoln, had founded the College in 1427 and named it after his cathedral as "The College of the Blessed Mary and All Saints, Lincoln, in the University of Oxford, commonly called Lincoln College". A Plantagenet, King Henry VI, was then on the throne, albeit precariously. Lincoln, straddling Turl Street in the heart of the city and the university, is a late mediaeval architectural gem. As such, it would have appealed to the mediaevalist Nairac. The College's comparative poverty in earlier centuries has had the fortunate result that it was never rebuilt: the original pattern and fabric can still be seen, with many interiors almost unaltered, as they were in Nairac's time and for several centuries before that. In a few corners it is almost possible to fantasise that the Reformation never happened, so thoroughly and authentically fifteenth-century has the College remained. In recent decades the historic core of the College has been extended into neighbouring streets and areas to cope with the expanding demands of a modern university, but the main focus remains its beautiful original buildings. Lincoln is such a perfectly-preserved archetypal Oxford college that it has served as the backdrop of at least three episodes of the *Inspector Morse* television series, based on Colin Dexter's Oxford detective novels.

Lincoln College, for all its antiquity and beauty, was not high in the pecking order of Colleges at that time; it came well below Christ Church, Magdalen and Trinity in social terms. Although it had produced some heavyweight scholars, and despite the presence of the Rector, Dr Walter Oakeshott – a distinguished Malory scholar and discoverer in 1934 of the Winchester manuscript of Malory's *Le Morte d'Arthur* – and Dr Vivian Green, the College was not famous for scholarship, sporting prowess or flamboyance. Perhaps not entirely justly, other Oxonians then perceived it as a cosy place for the gentle and unambitious. If that perception was to any extent correct, Nairac was not a typical Lincoln man of that era.

Despite not being large, rich or grand, Lincoln had nurtured a surprising number of famous Fellows and alumni over the centuries. In the seventeenth century a notable alumnus was William Davenant, the distinguished playwright and Ben Jonson's successor as Poet Laureate. In the eighteenth, John Wesley had been a Fellow. Methodism could be said to have been born in Lincoln College. Edward Thomas, the First World War poet, author of numerous writings about the English countryside and a kindred spirit to Nairac, had been a History Scholar at Lincoln in the 1890s. He was killed during the Battle of Arras in 1917. More recently the MI6 officer and novelist David Cornwell, better known as John le Carré, had read Modern Languages at Lincoln in the 1950s and achieved a brilliant First. Another 1950s graduate was Chukwuemeka "Emeka" Odumegwu-Ojukwu, subsequently President of the breakaway "Republic of Biafra", whose secession caused the Nigerian Civil War of 1967. This war was still in progress when Nairac went up to Oxford in 1968. Nairac would be in excellent historic company.

There were to be other compensations at Oxford. For example Nairac would be elected to the exclusive, and exclusively masculine, Vincent's Club: "a happy breed of men" as it describes itself. The criteria of membership are not simply sporting success but "all-round qualities; social, physical and intellectual qualities being duly considered". Nairac's personal charm and sporting prowess made him supremely clubbable. "We elect primarily on character," wrote the 1992 President, Stephen Sparrow. "We value the relaxed atmosphere up here; we feel that members should be able to welcome and talk to any old member who may drop in". Prominent past members of Vincent's had included Cecil Rhodes, King Edward VIII and Noel Godfrey Chavasse VC and Bar, MC, an Olympic athlete and one of only three people ever to be awarded the Victoria Cross twice. Like Edward Thomas, Chavasse was killed 1917. Another former member was the celebrated Charles Burgess Fry (1872-1956), usually known simply as C B Fry. Strikingly good-looking, a polymath and all-round sportsman, he is best remembered for his career as an England cricketer. He excelled at other sports too, including rugby, running, tennis, football, shot-putting and ice-skating. Nevertheless Fry experienced occasional setbacks: although academically brilliant, he had a nervous breakdown at Oxford and achieved only a mediocre degree. In 1894, while still an undergraduate, Fry achieved the ultimate late

Victorian and Edwardian accolade: a caricature by "Spy" in *Vanity Fair* magazine, which was in reality a handsome straight portrait. In the picture Fry is wearing Oxford rowing kit. A contemporary wrote: "Charles Fry could be autocratic, angry and self-willed: he was also magnanimous, extravagant, generous, elegant, brilliant – and fun". Captain (RNVR) C B Fry, as he eventually became, sounded very like the future Captain Robert Nairac. Once again Nairac would be in good historic company.

Founded in 1863, Vincent's Club had not changed much since C B Fry's time, or considerably earlier. It was a congenial time-warp for someone as firmly out of sympathy with his era as Nairac. The undergraduate membership is limited to 150 (originally 100) at any given time and once elected members remain members for life. In addition to functioning as a gentlemen's club at Oxford, where it has its own premises, Vincent's holds an annual dinner in London in November. This dinner is the largest regular gathering of Oxonians outside Oxford. Women are still not admitted as members, although they may now be introduced as guests on certain evenings. When Nairac joined they were not permitted to set foot in the Club at all; he was one of the leaders of the opposition to relaxing this rule. When the motion was carried, he seems to have accepted it with good grace.

Nairac was never a member of any of the hedonistic clubs which wax and wane at Oxford depending on the particular generation, and each of which claims to be the successor of the Hellfire Club, which, based at Brasenose, flourished in the eighteenth century. So he was not a member of The Grid (The Gridiron) or of The Phoenix or The Assassins, or The Bullingdon – which was going through a phase of unfashionable eclipse in Nairac's day. Unlike Vincent's, the public and the media are well aware of the reputation of those clubs. Had Nairac ever been a member of any of them, he would have been typecast forever in the popular imagination as an upper-class, muscle-bound thug and vandal who habitually drank to excess. Even so, there have been attempts by his critics and enemies to depict him in exactly this light.

Nairac would play for the Greyhounds Rugby Team (the Oxford University Second XV, originally a separate rugby club). He was very proud of having done so. Julian Malins makes a pertinent observation on this:

"An example on the rugby field was to get a 'Greyhound' ... when I came to pick the team with David Badenoch (the Greyhounds Secretary) for the 1970 match against the Cambridge LX club, I picked Nairac, even though he was not in the best 3 wing forwards and even though he was [at that moment] injured, because I took the view that what mattered was how things would be 40 years on when who won or what the score was, would long be forgotten, and it was everything to him. I somehow knew that he was one of those flaming torches that life, one day, snuffs out. I thought his 'Greyhound' would give him pleasure in his last moments..."

It would be good to think that it might have done so, even for one fleeting second, given the appalling circumstances of Nairac's early death, but we shall never know. Nairac himself seems to have had an intuition that he might die young. One drunken evening at Oxford, he recited his own imaginary epitaph to a friend, who recalls it. A few years later, some of it would prove to be uncannily prescient.

Neither military glory nor scholarship was uppermost in Nairac's mind when he arrived at Oxford in October 1968. His priority was sport: specifically to join the Oxford University Amateur Boxing Club (OUABC) (*Note 1*). He was in for a disagreeable surprise. Unknown to him, he was also about to embark upon one of the most important friendships of his life. The then Captain of the OUABC lived in Trinity College. From him Nairac learned, in fairly basic language, that the boxing club, which had been in financial difficulties and was suffering from lack of interest by the rising generation, had just been dissolved: end of story. "Now you bugger off!" The Captain was on the point of notifying his Cambridge counterpart. Given that the OUABC was disbanding, the 1969 Oxford-Cambridge Varsity Match, which was scheduled for March 1969, would have to be cancelled. This was a shock, as the OUABC was famous, had been in existence for more than eighty years and the Varsity Match had been a celebrated annual event since 1897. Shortly afterwards the Captain received a visit from another freshman, Julian Malins, who was reading Law at Brasenose. He too was given short shrift. However the Captain also mentioned that Malins was the second person to call on him that day, asking about the Boxing Club. Who, asked Malins, was the first?

"Someone called Nairac, at Lincoln."

As Julian Malins related it to John Parker long after Nairac's murder, "Within a minute, we had met. Within five, we were friends, and before the sun had set, we had recruited a team, revived the club and kept the fixture with Cambridge. It was, indeed, action this day."

Nairac became Captain of the revived Club. In the OUABC Captain's book is written Nairac's account of the revival: "I decided to get a team together, try and get permission to revive the Club, get Blue recognition and box Cambridge. Looking back on it, I think it was mad."

Malins wrote: "Robert, you were not mad. You were a star".

Although the Club was revived in 1968, the lengthy formalities were not completed until shortly before the Varsity Match of 1969. As a result, different accounts give either 1968 or 1969 as the date of the OUABC's re-foundation.

Nairac's next pressing task was to use all his charm to persuade Alf Gallie, the OUABC Coach, to remain in Oxford to coach the revived club. Gallie agreed, provided that Nairac could succeed in raising a team in time to keep the Varsity Match with Cambridge: he succeeded and Gallie remained. The club survived and is still in existence. Nairac would gain four Blues for Boxing: a Blue being a distinction awarded to university athletes for competing in certain sports at the highest level. At Oxford and Cambridge, this means representing one of these universities against the other.

The OUABC boxing team of this period would include a number of future celebrities. In addition to Nairac and Julian Malins, the members included David Heathcoat-Amory, a future Conservative MP and Minister; Alasdair McGaw, a future actor and companion of Derek Jarman; and one of Evelyn Waugh's sons, James, who was considered to be the most stylish boxer in the OUABC.

The OUABC was not helpful to Nairac's studies at Oxford. This was not simply a matter of the time spent training for, arranging and travelling to matches. The Club was seldom financially healthy for long: Nairac spent a lot of time fundraising and was fortunate in having an able administrator to help him. This was a diligent, likeable undergraduate called John Leyden. A "boxing club groupie", though not a sportsman himself, Leyden was an extremely efficient organiser and "nuts and bolts man". Nairac was a member of the club for four years and either Captain or Secretary for nearly three, with the exception of a short interval when he was told to stop boxing by his doctors, and in his final year. In March 1970, according to a Press article, "the superbly fit" Nairac took part successfully in a Varsity match against a formidable Cambridge opposition. In the Varsity Matches of 1969 and 1970 Nairac had boxed at light-middleweight. He would go up to middleweight for 1971 and 1972. In November 1971 he was ordered by his doctors to give up boxing for good after suffering concussion on the rugby field. He had twice been seriously concussed at rugby; had insisted on boxing the next day and had sulked when he was forbidden. Nairac appeared to agree to this, but in 1972 he somehow managed to obtain medical clearance from an Army doctor – he was now commissioned and the holder of a university cadetship – to start boxing again. He successfully took part in a Varsity match against Cambridge on 9 March 1972. He had previously been successful in Varsity bouts in 1969 and 1971. Nairac would continue to box and play rugby at Sandhurst and in the Army, despite the reservations of his doctors, whom he had to consult fairly frequently about his injuries, and of some of his friends.

The effects of Nairac's concussions might have been more profound than was realised at the time. Although there is no medical consensus on the long-term effects of repeated concussion on the brain, it is generally regarded as a bad thing. In some cases it can result in a form of dementia in later life, including memory loss and confusion. A number of famous pugilists have ended in this state. Since Nairac was murdered in his twenties, we cannot know whether he might have suffered in this way in late middle age. Even when the symptoms of a concussion appear to have gone, the brain is still not yet 100 percent normal, according to Dr. Maryse Lassonde, a neuropsychologist and the scientific director of the Quebec Nature and Technologies Granting Agency. Concussion causes temporary loss of brain function leading to cognitive, physical and emotional symptoms, such as confusion, vomiting, headache, nausea, depression, disturbed sleep, moodiness, and amnesia. Nairac did sometimes show depression, moodiness and forgetfulness, although these characteristics became less noticeable after he joined the Army. Occasionally he showed poor judgement. At this distance in time one hesitates to dogmatise, especially given that Nairac was also suffering the after-effects of his abuse at Ampleforth and had been experimenting with LSD, but concussion could have been a contributory cause of these. It might go some way towards explaining his uneven exam results and some of the stranger decisions that he took. Moreover Nairac had sustained his worst concussions on the rugby pitch, not in the boxing ring: in other words, from contact with unpadded parts of other people's anatomies, not with padded boxing gloves.

There is another aspect to Nairac's sporting activities that has never been flagged-up. Nairac's sporting career made him an ephemeral Oxford celebrity. Or not completely ephemeral: he is commemorated in Lincoln College and is still remembered by the OUABC as a heroic figure of the distant past who saved the club. He is pictured on their website. As a result of his boxing and rugby playing, he achieved quite a high media profile while he was still at university, being often mentioned and pictured in the local Press, especially the *Oxford Mail* and university publications; less often in the national Press. This was not ideal for a future undercover officer. The IRA are known to have done their research thoroughly, trawling the media and their archives for information, including Regimental magazines, where they would note carefully which officers were described as being "detached for duties with Special Forces" and keep copies of any available photos for future reference. They might have done so in Nairac's case, although we cannot be sure. Yet neither at the time when he decided on a military career in 1971, nor when he decided to go undercover for the first time in 1974, does anyone in the Army, including Nairac, seem to have thought of this.

Much as he liked Nairac, Malins was not star-struck. Like many barristers, he is an acute judge of character and is observant about people. He probably displayed these attributes even when he was at Oxford and, in his view, Nairac was a mixture. He was not very experienced in the ways of the world and in some respects he came across as a bit naïve, romantic and very idealistic. But in other ways he was very experienced. For example, he knew, or understood instinctively, a great deal about motivation, leadership and man-management. He was very adept at getting his own way and carrying others along with him and his knowledge of subjects that interested him, like shooting, dry-fly fishing, boxing, Ireland and falconry, was remarkable. For those subjects he had a prodigious and accurate memory. Malins says that he also had a premonition about Nairac: that he would not enjoy his company for very long.

"I always foresaw a tragic early end for him too. We all saw that coming. He was 'a candle that burned too brightly'. He reminded me a bit of Scott of the Antarctic."

Apart from rugby and boxing, Nairac would continue to run cross-country, to fish, shoot and practice falconry during his time at Oxford. Many contemporaries remember him because he kept a hawk and could sometimes be seen flying it round Oxford.

Contrary to legend, Nairac did not keep a hawk in his room in Lincoln College; the College Statutes did not permit this. The years in which Nairac shared his lodgings with birds of prey were 1969-70, when he lived on Boar's Hill. Then, his hawks lived in his bedroom and roosted on top of the wardrobe. In 1971-72 Nairac was again living out of college and shared his rooms with hawks and a pet owl. At other times the birds lived elsewhere. Nairac and his friend Mark Allen both kept their hawks at St Benet's Hall, usually shortened to "Benet's", one of the Permanent Private Foundations of Oxford University and an off-shoot of Ampleforth Abbey. A Catholic Hall, it had been founded in 1897 so that younger English Benedictine monks could study for secular degrees at Oxford while continuing to function as monks. Today most of the inhabitants are lay undergraduates, although there still are some monks, and normal monastic services take place in the chapel. It is in all but name a small Oxford college, run on mediaeval lines. The then Master, the Reverend James Forbes OSB, was a great friend of Nairac, who had first met him while he was teaching at Ampleforth. Forbes granted Nairac and Mark Allen honorary membership of Benet's, so that in effect they belonged to two colleges. They often dined at Benet's and spent time with "Jimmy" Forbes, who was always good for a drink before dinner and a malt whisky after it. Forbes allowed them to keep their hawks and falcons in an outbuilding, which was transformed into a makeshift mews. More exotic and warmth-loving falcons from India and Arabia (Allen's Indian Red-headed Merlin, for instance) lived behind the High Altar of the chapel, which was the warmest place in the Hall.

There has been discussion about which species of hawk Nairac kept at Oxford. According to Julian Malins, it varied; although only one hawk was ever present at any given time with Nairac, he would change hawks quite often. He had a car and would sometimes drive home to Gloucestershire, even during term-time, to see his parents and visit Philip Glasier at Newent, leaving with one hawk and returning with another. Both goshawks and sparrowhawks accompanied him at Oxford at different times. One of Nairac's party tricks was to place a piece of raw steak on the bridge of his nose and allow his large, ferocious female goshawk which, had it wished to, might have pecked out his eyes, to swoop down from its perch and take it. Others would then be invited as a dare to repeat this feat. It required a steady nerve and he did not get many takers; Julian Malins was one of this select group.

Sometimes the goshawk would get Nairac into trouble. One day Allen and Nairac were taking her for a walk in the Parks at Oxford. The goshawk flew up into the top of a tree and refused to come down. Nairac decided to walk on and pretend that he was going to leave her there. The idea was that the hawk would take alarm and come flying after him; she did not. Suddenly there was a bloodcurdling sound; they turned round to see the goshawk standing on the back of an old lady's lapdog, which was screaming with fright and pain, as the hawk dug her claws into it. She had decided that the Yorkie would make a good snack. Nairac rescued the dog, which was traumatised but unharmed. It soon calmed down, but its owner did not. It took quite a while, and all of Nairac's charm, to soothe her ruffled feelings.

Nairac's twenty-first birthday fell during the Summer Vacation of 1969. He would pass most of that vacation in Ireland, engaged in angling and falconry. This vacation would also be the occasion of Nairac's first, and almost only known, romance: a chaste and honourable love for a strikingly beautiful Irish girl from Galway, who is still alive. Both of them were young, shy and devout Roman Catholics. There was no sequel, but his Irish friends say that Nairac was definitely emotionally involved on that occasion. Because the relationship did not develop further, the female icon could remain on her pedestal and be idealised for a few years longer. Typically, Nairac never mentioned this episode to any of his Oxford friends.

Nairac did not join the Oxford University Officers' Training Corps (OTC) or any other Volunteer Reserve unit. His military interests, apart from studying the Crusades and Military History, had become dormant. This should not come as a surprise, except to writers who regard Nairac as having always been "army barmy". He had numerous extra-mural activities. He could not possibly have fitted in the commitment that the Territorial Army, of which the OTC was part, then required: parades and training on Wednesday evenings and Saturday mornings; shooting practice some weekends and two weeks' Annual Camp in the summer. Moreover he had had several years of compulsory CCF at Ampleforth. He had probably decided to give military training a rest; for a while, anyway.

In some respects, although on balance Nairac probably enjoyed his time at Oxford, it suited him less well than Ampleforth had, or the Army would. The reason is that, unlike some other intelligent men, he throve on a highly structured existence. This was no doubt the result of having studied at Ampleforth, a college run by monks, attached to a monastery, with a highly organised daily timetable, including attendance at religious services, compulsory CCF and games, keeping periods of potential idleness to a minimum. If his day was tightly organised, as with:

0530 hours, run
0700 hours, breakfast
0830 hours, parade
0900 hours, tactics
1030 hours, Tactical Exercise without Troops (TEWT)... etc.

Nairac would be perfectly happy, in his element, and would perform well. The trouble with Oxford is that undergraduates are left very much to their own devices. They are expected to be self-starters; to work out, and stick to, their own routines of study, exercise and relaxation. The weekly tutorials are compulsory and must be prepared for; lectures are not, and how much time undergraduates choose to devote to unsupervised study in the library or the privacy of their rooms is up to them. At this stage of his life Nairac, left to himself, did not manage his studies well and had too many competing interests, mostly sporting ones. Julian Malins says that he never knowingly saw Nairac do a stroke of work for his degree. "Lack of application", echoes another former friend. This is not entirely borne out by his Tutors' comments, however. Nairac evidently read copiously about subjects that really interested him, like Mediaeval History, and much less on those that did not. As a result, he did not do himself justice academically. Yet sporting excellence also requires a degree of planning, preparation, practice and commitment; in other words, discipline. Nairac was capable of delivering these for the OUABC, the Greyhounds and even more so for dry-fly angling, shooting and falconry. So why did he not deliver it for the History School?

There were multiple reasons. One was that throughout his life and even in the Army, about which he cared passionately and which in general he enjoyed, Nairac showed a tendency to "cherry-pick": to become enthusiastic about, and to master brilliantly, subjects that interested him, while avoiding or neglecting those that bored him and making it clear that he found them boring. Lincoln's then Chaplain and History Tutor commented that, "While ... he shone at Mediaeval History, he had not much interest in modern times."

Unfortunately for Nairac, the Oxford BA Honours Modern History Course covered the whole period from 284 to 1939 AD (or CE). The course included a paper on a foreign language. Not all of this was of equal interest to Nairac. It was obligatory to study English History (1, 2 and 3) and General History (1, 2 and 3), which meant in effect European History, with brief excursions into the Americas and elsewhere. Also obligatory was Political Thought (Aristotle, Hobbes and Rousseau, with a fleeting examination of other philosophers like Marx) and Latin, in order to read historic documents in the original. There was virtually no scope for the study of Irish History (which had to be studied elsewhere); limited scope for Military History, although that did form a single module of Nairac's degree course, and too close a concentration on his favourite Middle Ages was simply not possible at undergraduate level. Some historic periods and Political Thought, for example, did not interest Nairac at all. Those subjects got neglected.

Another factor was that the culture of Oxford at that time did not favour swotting. Here is Julian Malins again, quoted by John Parker in *Secret Hero*:

"The Oxford class of 1968 was good-looking, confident and unlike any previous generation since the 1930s. We came after austerity and before the shadow of stress had fallen on the young. We parked our cars on Radcliffe Square. We dined at the Elizabeth. The sun shone and the girls were sensational. *Work was not on the agenda* (author's italics) ... Undergraduates were chosen by different criteria in those days ... Even against such a backdrop, Robert stood out. He was the most handsome of his generation. He had a terrific aura. No-one could be in his presence without feeling the better for it. That is a great and rare gift. He never once indulged in a biting or satirical jest, which is always remembered by the victim long after it has been forgotten by the speaker ... Robert was a romantic, an enthusiast, simple-hearted, brave; a charismatic leader and quite without guile..."

Not everyone viewed Nairac in such a positive light. One of his Tutors later wrote that "not all his contemporaries greatly liked him, for some thought him too arrogant, but I found him charming and attractive." The Don in question also referred to Nairac as one of his most interesting pupils. The charge of arrogance is odd, set against the numerous testimonies to Nairac's friendliness and kindness, such as Julian Malins' comment quoted above. In this context Luke Jennings has remarked that "I can imagine that Robert's charisma and straight-arrow Catholic conscience could well have made him enemies at Oxford". Nairac was no killjoy but in the late "swinging sixties" his Christian conscience might have made him appear priggish and disapproving in the eyes of people who were enjoying the permissive society. Nairac however would have known, and agreed with, Izaak Walton's dictum on this subject: "The person that loses their conscience has nothing left worth keeping".

Julian Malins evidently never encountered Nairac in "Mr Hyde" mode. Possibly "Mr Hyde's" appearances were rarer at that time than in later years. Here he is again:

"And then ... I see Robert in the ring ... he was fast. He had a lovely style; he was fluid and he never seemed to retreat. I do not recall that he was ever beaten but, if he was, it must have been a crooked verdict, no doubt at Cambridge! I fought him once in a bare-knuckle fight which was the main attraction at a riotous summer party held on the college barge. We were roared on by the Fancy and though he gave me at least a stone, I took some terrible punishment."

"I see him as the Greyhounds' open side wing forward, springing across the pitch at Grange Road to tackle the Cambridge winger in the corner."

The preceding vignettes could almost be quotations from Compton Mackenzie's Oxford *bildungsroman, Sinister Street,* which is set in the Edwardian period. It was published on the eve of the First World War. Like Nairac, the hero, Michael Fane, played rugby and other manly sports, although he also had an aesthetic side. Similarly, Michael was devout at school; less so at Oxford. A High-Church Anglo-Catholic, he was clearly heading Rome-wards, and possibly cloister-wards, by the end of the novel. Scott Fitzgerald thought *Sinister Street* a masterpiece, which he tried to emulate in his own university novel, *This Side of Paradise.* Max Beerbohm said of *Sinister Street*: "There is no book on Oxford like it. It gives you the actual Oxford experience. What Mackenzie has miraculously done is to make you feel what each term was like." The main difference is that Nairac had no Lily

Haden in his life: perhaps on balance fortunately, because the beautiful heroine of *Sinister Street* turned out to be shallow, promiscuous and worthless. Yet more than eighty years and two World Wars separate Malins' reminiscences of 1970s Oxford, given in the late 1990s for John Parker's benefit, from the publication of Mackenzie's novel: Nairac and Malins' generation now seem like throwbacks. They were the last of a long line. Their type was far more common before the terrible negative eugenics of the Great War had taken effect. Soon after their time Oxford would change beyond recognition. Among other things, women would invade the famous old men's colleges, one by one. Men would also be admitted to the former women's colleges. It was the end of an era.

Although his friendship with Malins was to endure to the end of Nairac's life, Nairac sometimes put it under strain. At Oxford he proved to be very disorganised: "reliably unreliable," according to Malins. He often forgot appointments and, when he did remember, was frequently late. On one dreadful occasion he forgot to post the application forms of members of the OUABC who wished to take part in an important international boxing competition, to which they had been looking forward. Nairac had been walking around with the forgotten and un-posted envelopes in his pocket for days. As a result several members of the boxing team missed their chance of international fame on that occasion. Yet they forgave him.

Malins and Nairac had become so friendly that, had Malins not possessed a brother, he would have asked Nairac to be his best man when he got married. Typically, when invited to be an usher instead, Nairac pleasantly asked:

"I hope that you won't mind if I'm late?"

The date and time of the ceremony had not even been decided at that point, but it was a racing certainty that Nairac would indeed arrive late.

While they were sharing rather grand student lodgings on Boar's Hill, Nairac proved to be a disconcerting house-mate. Like Kipling's *The Cat that Walked by Himself*, Nairac would appear and disappear unpredictably, rarely giving any indication of what he had been doing or with whom. For all that anybody ever knew, he could have been at Mass, in the Bodleian Library, fishing, jogging, or about some other mysterious business: he never said. Some of the time he was at St Benet's Hall, but it much later emerged that during some at least of these absences he had been drug-tripping. He would continue this secretiveness in the Army, to the consternation of those responsible for his backup and security. Irritating at Oxford, in the Army context this was unprofessional and potentially put his and other people's lives at risk. It was not however a factor in his murder in May 1977. Nairac kept his friendships in separate, watertight compartments and did not mention the friends; far less introduce them, to each other. Only Nairac saw the whole picture. He seems to have run his friendships very much as undercover agent handlers run their "sources"; they were unaware of each other's existence and of each other's connection with Nairac. If they became aware, it was by accident, usually years later. This was an oddly furtive way for such a warm-hearted, extravert fellow to behave. For example, Julian Malins never met Redmond or John Morris. He was similarly unaware until many years later that Nairac had been acquainted with Duncan Fallowell of Magdalen College and his circle of LSD-experimenters. He knew nothing whatever about Nairac's own experiments with LSD. Malins has commented that:

"Taking drugs would have been a challenge to him, but he would have definitely kept it a secret from me, as I would not have picked him for the Greyhounds XV (I was Captain) if I had known that his fitness was compromised in any way by drugs and he would have known that … also, he knew that I completely despised drugs."

When their two house-mates started experimenting with marijuana, Nairac joined Malins in earnestly trying to dissuade them. He put on a very convincing performance; he seemed genuinely to disapprove. Yet LSD, with which he was then experimenting in private, is potentially much more dangerous, if less-addictive, than marijuana, as Nairac presumably knew. What else was he keeping secret from his friend Malins? Quite a lot, it now seems. For example, Malins was never told about Nairac's honourable but emotional romance with the Irish girl during the long vacation of 1969. Did he enjoy leading a double life, even then? Apparently the answer is yes. At times Nairac may have seemed to his Oxford contemporaries, and still sometimes seems to his posthumous biographer, a little like God, as Omar Khayyam mystically envisaged Him:

> Hidden you live, inscrutable as ever –
> A person sometimes, but sometimes a place,
> Showing this costly spectacle to no one –
> You, the sole audience and the actor too.

A later quatrain of Khayyam's *Rubaiyat* contains the lines:

> Raise the bowl high, like tulip-cups at Nauroz,
> And if the moon-faced one has time to spare
> Drink gloriously deep, for brutal Time
> Will strike you down with never a warning yell.

Nairac seems to have known and enjoyed this poem, probably in the well-known Edward Fitzgerald translation, and he quite often drank 'gloriously deep'.

Nairac had told the interview board members, when he attended his Lincoln College interview in December 1967, that he intended to teach. Naturally that would have to be at a good private sector boys' school like Avisford. To do this he would ideally need to achieve a Second Class Honours degree. He was still talking about teaching as late as January 1971, although by then he was definitely looking at other options. From his time teaching at Avisford in 1967-68 it was clear that Nairac was a natural and gifted teacher of young boys aged eight to sixteen and that he enjoyed it. Teaching older boys History and other subjects at a more advanced level would probably not have been his forte. But, as time went by at Oxford, he became familiar with a wider world of people, places and points of view. His horizons expanded; so too, in slower time, did his ambition. In Julian Malins' view, by the end of 1969 or the beginning of 1970, Nairac had privately decided that being a schoolmaster would not give him the scope for achievement that he craved.

Julian Malins was indirectly responsible for Nairac's getting into the Army and into the Grenadier Guards. Malins' father was a senior Army Chaplain. At that time he was still in the Army; Nairac met him on a number of occasions. The Malins, father and son, often talked to him about the Army.

By helping Nairac to resurrect the OUABC in 1968, Malins had unintentionally helped to turn Nairac's thoughts towards a possible military career; although it would be some time – the summer of 1971, in fact – before Nairac did anything about it. Boxing and the Army go together like bacon and eggs (*Note 2*); the revived OUABC started to have matches with Service boxing teams, including against the Royal Military Academy, Sandhurst. Nairac enjoyed those evenings at Sandhurst, which were very grand, with the ring set up in one of the main halls. Often the hall in question would be the Indian Army Memorial Room in Old College. A former chapel, this impressive room boasts a gigantic cascade of a chandelier, several stained glass windows and oil portraits of, among others, General Sir Charles James Napier, General Sir Sam Browne, Field Marshal Viscount Slim and Field Marshal Sir Claude Auchinleck. Senior officers would sit in the front rows in armchairs wearing full mess kit, drinking brandy and smoking cigars; cadets, also in uniform, filling the rows behind them and hoarsely cheering on their boxers. It was an Edwardian, or even Regency, spectacle. Like falconry, it appealed to Nairac's love of the British past.

There was another Malins connection – another Proustian coincidence – which Nairac would have relished. It was a connection with Lawrence of Arabia. Julian Malins had grown up partly in colonial West Africa, where his father was *en poste* during his military career. T E Lawrence's youngest brother, Professor A W Lawrence (1900-1991) (*Note 3*), was at that time Professor of Archaeology at the University College of the Gold Coast (now Ghana), where he had established the National Museum and was Secretary and Conservator of the Monuments and Relics Committee. The Lawrences and the Malins became friends. The young Julian Malins had once found on the beach a curiously carved stone cylinder with a spiral inscription in an unknown script, which he presented to Lawrence for the Museum. A W Lawrence was the only one of Lawrence of Arabia's four brothers who closely resembled him, both in appearance and manner. This included the famously disconcerting high-pitched giggle and the mischievous teasing. He had a fund of interesting stories, including some about, and at the expense of, his Plymouth Brother and Chindit cousin Orde Wingate, but he seldom mentioned his famous elder brother "Ned", although he was the Executor of T E Lawrence's literary estate. A W Lawrence was also the only Lawrence brother to have married and left descendants. Given that Professor Lawrence was to live until 1991, it would be satisfying to report that Nairac had met his hero's brother through Julian Malins, but this never happened; the Malins and Lawrence families had lost touch after leaving Ghana. Nor, it appears, did Nairac ever attempt to meet the widow of T E Lawrence's close friend, Colonel Stewart Francis Newcombe, who is mentioned in *The Seven Pillars of Wisdom*, although she was living in North Oxford at that time.

Some Oxford and Cambridge Dons have always acted as talent spotters for the Agencies and their predecessors (at Cambridge, for the Soviet KGB as well). This has been going on since at least Christopher Marlowe's time. It has been alleged that Nairac was recruited by one of the Agencies, MI5 or MI6, while at Oxford or even earlier, but there is no reason to think that this is true. Given that Nairac was an athlete and sportsman who had represented the university as well as his own college and was a public figure at Oxford, unmistakable wherever he was, the Agencies' Oxford talent-spotters would have been unlikely to have considered recruiting him. Apart from that, there were his disorganisation, his uneven academic performance and other negative factors. Nairac could not have worked officially (as opposed to occasionally and unofficially) for one of the Agencies and for the Army simultaneously. He was still a serving Army officer when he was killed in 1977. If Nairac had genuinely been recruited by either MI5 or MI6, his career would already have been mapped out for him and he would have shown none of the anxiety and uncertainty about his future that he clearly experienced in 1970-71; nor could he have joined the Army. One possible explanation of this legend is Nairac's extremely tenuous connection with John Le Carré, who was also an alumnus of Lincoln College, although he had graduated with a First in Modern Languages twelve years before Nairac matriculated.

At least one Don taught both John Le Carré and Nairac. This was the Reverend Dr Vivian H H Green: Fellow, History Tutor and Chaplain of Lincoln College, later Sub-Rector and finally Rector from 1983 to 1987. In 1995 John le Carré revealed that Dr Green had been a model for his fictional spymaster George Smiley. It is tempting to suggest that Dr Green must therefore have been a talent spotter for MI5 and/or MI6 and have influenced both of his famous pupils towards undercover work. However this would be wrong. The former Attorney General, Dominic Grieve MP, who was Dr Green's godson and who wrote his 2005 obituary in *The Independent*, states firmly that Dr Green had no personal connection with espionage or counter-espionage. George Smiley has more than one original: he is composite, as characters in fiction usually are. Smiley in his role as secret agent is based on the late Lord Clanmorris, who genuinely worked for MI5. John le Carré had, however, borrowed many of Dr Green's mannerisms, interests and his appearance for George Smiley. Dominic Grieve confirmed to me that Dr Green had known Robert Nairac and had tutored him. This is borne out by references in college files. Grieve remembers Dr Green making a reference to Nairac in very positive terms. He had found him warm-hearted, engaging and boisterous. Dr Green had later been surprised to learn about Nairac's undercover work, because he had not associated him with such a role. This seems to rule out any suggestion that Nairac was recruited by one of the Agencies while at Oxford or that Dr Green was the talent spotter who recruited him.

It is a matter of record that one of Nairac's Oxford friends joined the SIS (MI6), rose to a senior position as Head of Counter-Terrorism and was at one point tipped as a future Director ("C"). This was Sir Mark Allen. As noted earlier, Allen was reading Arabic in Exeter College, which is next door to Lincoln College, while Nairac was reading History at Lincoln. He and Nairac had much in common. They shared an interest in T E Lawrence, with whom both Nairac and Allen have sometimes been compared. Both were falconers and both kept falcons while at Oxford. Both were devout Roman Catholics.

So Nairac had a friend in MI6. This may be at the origin of some of the stories that Nairac himself was recruited by one of the Agencies, presumably encouraged by Mark Allen. There is no truth in this rumour: Mark Allen never saw Nairac again after they left Oxford; they lost touch completely. From Oxford he went to Jordan for a year to study and perfect his Arabic. After further training in London he was posted to the Gulf, seldom returning to the UK. Allen was fortuitously in England visiting his parents-in-law when Nairac was murdered in 1977. He learned about it on the television news. Later he heard a version of the events that ended with Nairac's body having been fed to pigs. Having read accounts of Nairac's last months, Allen became strongly critical of the way in which the Army had managed his friend Robert in South Armagh.

Airey Neave MP, Margaret Thatcher's Shadow Northern Ireland Secretary, whom an IRA splinter-group, the INLA, murdered in March 1979, has also been mentioned as a person who might have recruited Nairac to MI5 or MI6. This seems to be a mistake: they never met. Neave never worked for MI5 or MI6, of which he was a mordant critic. He wanted to reform them. Had he lived, he might have been allowed to do so. Neave had served in the disbanded MI9, which was a department of the War Office. Between 1939 and 1945 MI9 was tasked with aiding resistance fighters in enemy-occupied territory and rescuing Allied servicemen who found themselves behind enemy lines. This may be the factual basis of the legend that Neave, by now an MP, was, nearly thirty years later, also "a secret agent". Finally, Neave, who was a very political person, and Nairac, who had almost no interest in Westminster party politics, do not come across as obvious soul-mates. On 17 May 1977, in the immediate aftermath of Nairac's murder, Neave would call for an all-out attack on the "godfathers" of the IRA. However he did so in his capacity as Shadow Northern Ireland Secretary and not as a former friend of Nairac. Neave's hawkish stance would lead to his own murder in the House of Commons car park two years later. Slack security at the Palace of Westminster would make this surprisingly easy.

There is a further possible explanation for the rumours of Nairac's having been an MI5 or MI6 agent. In the Army anyone who is engaged, even temporarily or peripherally, in clandestine or undercover special duties is referred to indiscriminately as a "spook". To the rest of society "spook" means MI5 or MI6, but in the Army it has a wider and less precise meaning. Army "spooks" are also known as "secret squirrels". This seems perfect for Nairac, given his tendency to hoard objects and information.

An examination of Nairac's college file shows that his academic performance was mixed. In the Michaelmas Term of 1968 he is marked down for Prelim Latin Translation as "scrappy and inconsistent, yet he seems to know enough for his work to be better than this." As for his History Prelim: "I suspect that he is both muddleheaded and disorganised, but he (or possibly 'this;' the writing is almost illegible) should pass." It is the same message as at Ampleforth: "could do much better." Apart from that, Nairac had encountered another challenge. Because of Lincoln's small size, first-year men were often asked to share a room. Nairac found his room-mate unacceptable. He wrote formally to ask Dr Oakeshott to change his room. He had found this person's outlook on life "wholly incompatible with my own." In December the College was able to offer Nairac another room, not shared, for the next two terms.

For the next two years Nairac's progress would continue bumpily. But most of his Tutors seem to have been captivated by his charming personality and he evidently got away with much more than might have been tolerated in a less-prepossessing undergraduate. One theme, which re-emerges later at Junior Staff College, is that Nairac performed far better in oral discussion in Tutorials than he did on paper. Tutors in various subjects wrote:

"His ideas are sometimes perverse."

"A charming person with a wide range of wholly non-academic interests and a most refreshing unconventionality of viewpoint, academically and otherwise. A quick mind, although lacking in discipline and application. I am sure that he will benefit from continued presence in the University, and it may well benefit from him." (English History I)

"He has worked well and shown interest but there remain a good many gaps to be filled in." (English History II)

"A mixed report, but an exceptionally pleasant pupil to teach." (Political Thought)

"A mediaevalist at heart ... very ready to participate in discussion." (English History II)

"He reads widely and produces vigorous essays. I think that in his determination to restore idealism to the centre of historical interpretation in the mediaeval period, he often does less than justice to the arguments of economic or political motivation. But he is always lively and interesting to teach." (General History III)

However in 1970 there were signs that something was going seriously wrong. Nairac took up and then dropped a Special Subject (Gregory VII and Henry IV). He put on a brave face and did not confide in his friends, but it was more difficult to conceal his growing state of anxiety and almost suicidal depression from the more experienced Dons. Most of them, especially Dr Green, showed him sympathy and understanding:

"It has in fact been a bad time for Nairac – personal problems, depression, and a fading interest in his subject, all of which have caused him considerable anxiety." (Political Thought)

"Mr Nairac has only recently come to me after what has undoubtedly been an unnerving and disrupting term for him. At the moment he is reading conscientiously and producing adequate essays." (English History III)

Most explicitly, on 15 November 1970 a senior Don reported to the Senior Tutor that there were "special circumstances that make it reasonable to grant Nairac a fourth year, to finish his degree in 1972 and not in 1971." These included "a period of psychological trouble which momentarily had a devastating effect on his work and life;" the theft of his car and the loss of all his notes; "a period of History chosen to study this term proved to be a mistaken choice; the fault was not entirely his" (presumably he had been badly advised). "There is immense ground to make up. It would not be impossible for [some men] to recover in the time available, but I fear that for a man of Nairac's psychological make-up this may be out of the question." He continues: "Nairac wants to teach; he does feel that a Second is desirable. Whether he will get a Second or not is, of course, another question. He has consulted his father and his uncle and a number of other friends and counsellors; and they have all advised him to stay on, if the College permits, and make a bid for a Second, rather than to accept the Third (or even Pass) degree, which would be his lot in June."

The reality had to be faced: Nairac would need a fourth year at Oxford if he were to get even a half-decent degree. For that he would require funding: a county grant to cover the extra year. Once more Maurice Nairac stepped in and lobbied the Gloucestershire County Education Office for the necessary extra funding to enable Robert to continue his studies. So did Lincoln College, which stood firmly behind Nairac. On 19 November 1970 the College notified Nairac that his request to be allowed to take a fourth year, so as to take the Final Honour School in Modern History in June 1972, had been approved. Hopefully the County Education Office funding would also soon be approved. It was. This was a reprieve, but it had been achieved at some cost to Nairac's still fragile self-esteem.

Now should be the moment to consider what had gone wrong. Clearly Nairac was suffering severe psychological problems. He himself was always either silent or misleading about this subject. The Senior Tutor of Lincoln College, writing in early 1971 to the County Education Office in Gloucester supporting his application for a further year's funding, stated that:

"Nairac, through no fault of his own, suffered a number of serious setbacks to his work in the last three years. His car, which contained all his notes, was stolen and the notes have not been recovered. The choice of special subject for him was not satisfactory. Sending him to an outside Tutor (i.e. outside Lincoln College, in another college) had not worked out. *Although at first sight a hearty extrovert, he is in fact highly strung* [author's italics] and all these problems have upset him a good deal. At the end of last year he asked us if we would permit him to have a fourth year before taking Final Honours Schools. He is keen to be a schoolmaster and his Tutors think that he should be able to get a Second, but that, if he were to tackle Schools [Finals] this summer, he would be very unlikely to do so."

Not all of Nairac's Tutors were convinced that this concession to him was justified but Nairac had "such charm and, where Mediaeval History was concerned, such enthusiasm" that Dr Vivian Green warmly supported his request and carried the day. Nairac took no degree exams in 1971. Julian Malins and other close friends sat their Final Schools and ceremonially graduated in June that year (or at some later date more convenient to them; there are usually several options), after which they then left Oxford to start their careers.

The Senior Tutor's letter says more about the symptoms than the causes of Nairac's nervous breakdown. I am certain that Nairac's joke to Luke Jennings, that the notes had never existed, or that they were his old study notes from Ampleforth, was not true. The loss of all his Oxford study notes would have been a serious, although not an insuperable, setback. He would still have had more than half a year in which to make good the loss and revise. He still had his texts. But reading between the lines, the theft of his car and the loss of the notes seem to have come as the final straw at a time when Nairac was for other reasons going through a very dark period of his life. Where to begin?

It is stressful at the best of times to belong to a high-achieving, upwardly-mobile family, however loving. Members of such families tend to suffer from anxiety and depression due to the high hopes and expectations that their parents and others have invested in them. There is every reason to believe that this was the case with Nairac; especially after his elder brother's death. This is borne out by the comment of his friend Martin Jones:

"Robert was a great guy and a very brave man, but he was always trying to prove himself to his father, especially after the tragic death of his elder brother David. He drove himself to the limit and took too many risks in an attempt to show himself worthy."

An extreme example of this behaviour is the Stephen family, of which the author Virginia Woolf (née Stephen) was a member. In the nineteenth century the Stephen family, who descended from a transported Scots felon whose convict ship had been wrecked on the south coast of England, had risen rapidly to become Dons, barristers, High Court Judges, Knights and Baronets.

This vertiginous rise to success, riches and eminence took its psychological toll. Virginia's father, Sir Leslie Stephen KCB, a former Cambridge Don, author, critic, alpinist and first Editor of *The Dictionary of National Biography* (in which Robert Nairac would one day feature posthumously), was a conscientious father, ambitious for his offspring, but also a gloomy and controlling man, who was probably a manic-depressive. He wore out two wives and dominated his children, so it was a relief to them when he died. Sir Leslie Stephen's brother, Sir James Fitzjames Stephen, Baronet, a High Court Judge, went mad and had to retire from the bench. There had been serious accusations of his unfairness and bias in the murder trials of Israel Lipski in 1887 and of Florence Maybrick in 1889. By early 1891 his incapacity to exercise his judicial functions had become a matter of public discussion and Press comment and he resigned in April 1891. Sir James's son and Virginia's cousin, James Kenneth Stephen, a handsome and distinguished scholar and athlete at Eton and Cambridge, a published poet and friend of HRH the Duke of Clarence, also suddenly went mad and eventually starved himself to death in a private lunatic asylum. At a time when patients who refused to eat were usually force-fed, no-one tried to stop him. Some biographers have suggested that it was grief at Clarence's early death that led to Stephen's suicide. That is possible: Clarence died in January, and J K Stephen in February, 1892. His family however believed that the trigger of J K Stephen's madness was an accidental blow on the head by a sail of a windmill. There is an oblique reference to this incident in Virginia Woolf's 1931 novel, *The Waves*. Whatever the cause, J K Stephen became so eccentric that he was one of several candidates suspected of having been Jack the Ripper. That may be why he was permitted to commit suicide by fasting. Other members of the Stephen dynasty seem to have shared this death-wish. Virginia Woolf's nephew, Julian Bell, got himself avoidably killed in the Spanish Civil War in 1937. Virginia herself suffered from severe bouts of mental illness throughout her life. She committed suicide in her turn in 1941.

If we exclude suicide, there are two possible responses to this kind of moral pressure. One is to rebel: to kick over the traces; to refuse to conform any longer to the family's expectations and to do your own thing. At this stage the rebellious child, if at university, may change his course and/or place of study for something more congenial; he may also commit some other act of rebellion like "coming out" as homosexual, "dropping out" as a hippie, which may include experiments with drugs, contracting a wildly unsuitable marriage, departing for some distant ashram or doing something really extreme like joining the French Foreign Legion. Those who did this at that period enjoyed the Legion, at least in retrospect, but at the time their conformist families were very concerned, as the aspirant legionnaires no doubt intended.

Another possible response is to try even harder. This is what Nairac did. Not only will the child now be under intense pressure of work; he will also be haunted by the worry that he has to keep up an act; something at which Nairac was normally good. But the fear remains: "If only my parents knew what I am really like: if they realised that I am not the Goody Two-Shoes that they imagine or desire me to be; that I have lost my religious faith; that I am homosexual; that I do not want to join my father's profession or the family firm; that I actually hate playing cricket but keep it up to impress them, how upset they would be". These are random examples, not all necessarily applicable to Nairac, but giving a general idea.

Family pressures definitely seem to have been a factor with Nairac. Apart from his parents' and siblings' expectations, he was constantly competing with his dead brother while simultaneously trying to compensate his parents for David's loss through his own accomplishments. David represented a standard against which Nairac had come to measure himself. He was now approaching David's age at the time of his death (24), but he had to recognise that, except on the sporting field, he had failed even to come close to matching David's achievement. Mary Price has something to say about this:

"I think that the tragedy of his brother's death had a very bad effect on him. From then onwards, he felt he had to make up for it and threw himself in a maniacal fashion into rugger and boxing despite having had a bad accident in the latter and being told to give it up. This maniacal energy led, I believe, to his quite unnecessary death in Ireland that must have been so hard for his family to bear."

Here again there is an odd note. Although it is clear that his family's, especially his father's, good opinion was important to Nairac, according to Mary Price "He had a lovely family but never communicated with them". This is a slight exaggeration. However, reliable witnesses from Nairac's time at Oxford say that his parents very rarely visited him there, nor did they ever attend his sporting matches or boxing contests. Julian Malins' parents, by contrast, usually turned up to watch him, even if he had not notified them of an imminent match. On his side, Nairac was never a great letter-writer. He kept in touch with his friends fitfully, by telephone and occasional unexpected visits. However he quite often visited his family, including during term-time. This was not difficult; Oxfordshire and Gloucestershire are neighbouring counties and Nairac possessed a car. He also visited his uncle Basil Dykes in Worcestershire. The male bond between Basil and his nephew was deep and endured to the end of Nairac's life. The demands of Army life meant that his family saw less of Nairac after he had left Oxford and joined the Grenadier Guards.

A factor of which Mary Price was not aware was his abuse at Ampleforth, shortly after David's death. That would have been enough to cause emotional problems in any sensitive young person. However, it was something that he rarely, if ever, mentioned. This seems now to have come back to haunt him. Facing it may have forced him to confront some other unpalatable truths about himself.

A further complicating factor was Nairac's experimenting with LSD or lysergic acid diethylamide. According to one of his former Tutors, Nairac had fallen in with a drug-taking circle, but the sensationally unpleasant symptoms following a bad "trip" with LSD made him vow to abstain thereafter. Although Nairac left no written account of his involvement in drug abuse, we have Duncan Fallowell's account of the circumstances under which he came to introduce Nairac to LSD. Fallowell is a distinguished critic, novelist and travel writer who was an Oxford (Magdalen College) contemporary of Nairac and is quoted in *Days in the Life*, Jonathon Green's account of 1960s culture in the UK.

"In 1970 I took a lot of LSD ... I had a group of about a dozen people around me and we would take it regularly. This group didn't form by a process of decision; it actually formed because of an excitement that was generated by this closed group. Among them, funnily enough, were some boxers. Robert Nairac, who was later chopped up by the IRA, was part of my little group. I was in bed one day with [Nairac's] favourite boxing blue [Alasdair McGaw] and we'd taken acid, not really having sex but sort of tripping. Having sex on acid was not easy. There was a knock on the door and this guy jumped out and answered and it was Nairac, with two heavies, saying 'Are you in there with that shit Fallowell?' Then I heard this whispering at the door, but I was so at home with acid by this stage that I could actually separate the hallucinations from the facts very easily. Then I saw him at the end of the bed, twirling a swagger-stick, wearing a chocolate suit with white stripes, a flower in his button-hole, and two heavies: it looked like the Marquess of Queensberry come to get Oscar Wilde. And with as little justification. He was furious, but he didn't beat me up in the end, he actually wanted to join the group and take acid. He was one of those good-looking, conceited men who might have liked to be gay, but he went to a Catholic school and this makes life a problem for anybody. So he eventually joined us for some of our acid trips..."

This is a very strange story: how much of it is true? A "stick, swagger" was among the kit handed over to the Grenadier Guards by Nairac's family after his murder and is still preserved as a relic by them. It might be the same stick. On the other hand at least one detail seems to be hallucinatory. None of Nairac's Oxford friends recalls his ever possessing a chocolate-coloured suit with white stripes; let alone wearing a flower in his button-hole. Nor can they imagine his wishing to possess such a suit; it was not his style. At Oxford Nairac dressed in a tweedy, Barbour-jacketed, informal and countrified fashion, verging at times on the scruffy. He became a dandy only later, after he joined the Grenadier Guards, as Guards officers are apt to do. One would very much like to know who exactly the "heavies" were and why Nairac, an accomplished boxer, should have thought that he needed to bring them along to support him. What did the heavies do next? Did they remain to sample LSD with Nairac or did they just go away?

This account is capable of at least two interpretations: either that Nairac had wanted to rescue Alasdair McGaw, a promising boxing Blue, from Fallowell's decadent, drug-taking circle, who sound like a twentieth-century version of Comus and his crew or, as Fallowell seems to imply, that Nairac was in love with McGaw and had come to fetch him away out of possessive jealousy. Either way, Nairac evidently did not succeed and ended by taking LSD with the rest. According to Fallowell, "he ... joined us for some of our acid trips and liked it very much. He was rather silent, but when pressed just said 'the room is full of green birds.'"

Nairac was a keen ornithologist and a roomful of green birds is very aesthetic and Firbankian, but Fallowell's account is not the whole truth. There is more. In March 2011, following the publication in 2010 of the first edition of *Blood Knots*, the late Judge Richard Lowden approached the author, Luke Jennings. He had a curious tale to relate. In 1970 Lowden had been in residence at Keble College. One night, Nairac, who had been LSD tripping, roused him at 3 am, white-faced and shaking, saying that he had just met the Devil. Nairac was so convinced of the unutterable evil that he had encountered that he had determined to report everyone involved, including himself, to the authorities, regardless of the consequences to his own career. Nairac's "straight-arrow Catholic conscience" had reasserted itself. This was a serious step for him to take. In the 1970s drugs like LSD were not simply illegal: the Army, the Civil Service and other employers regarded their recreational use as constituting as high a security risk as past ties with the Communist Party, Russian or East German ancestry, or homosexuality. Nor would it have gone down well with most private sector boys' schools.

This story, had it become widely known, would have torpedoed Nairac's chances of ever having a career in the Armed Forces. That did not happen because, although the Army vetted Nairac on two separate occasions, and this included interviews with Dr Oakeshott and other Dons who had known Nairac, Dons of that generation did not see it as fair to reveal undergraduates' embarrassing, but hopefully ephemeral, youthful indiscretions to their prospective employers, so they said nothing about it. Had the Army become aware, "we would not have been happy", as Nairac's former Adjutant, Lieutenant Colonel Conway Seymour, has attested. The episode eventually became public knowledge in March 2010, long after Nairac's murder, in the context of the publication of the first edition of *Blood Knots*. By that time Nairac's drug-tripping was of only historic interest. Even so, it created a minor sensation. The London *Evening Standard* gave it the headline "Oxford Highs of a Latter-Day Hero".

What Nairac seems to have done next was to drive through the darkness to Ampleforth to make his confession to, and seek the counsel of, one of the monks. We shall never know what was said as it would have been under the seal of the

Confessional. Luke Jennings has written that, while visiting him at Ampleforth in 1971, Nairac had told him that he had admitted what he had done to the Lincoln College authorities; he had been sent down for a term but he had managed to keep the matter quiet. Luckily, he was to be allowed to continue his studies. He hoped to join the Army. This was not entirely true. As stated earlier, there is no evidence of rustication, or of any other disciplinary action against him, on his college file. Jennings adds that "No-one else who knew about this incident has ever spoken out". They would have been ill-advised to do so for all sorts of career-related reasons.

Neither could have known it, but this was to be the last occasion on which Jennings was ever to set eyes on his friend and mentor. As he recounts it in *Blood Knots*, he was stopped just after breakfast outside his House. A car horn sounded.

"It was Robert, and he was moving on. As I went down the steps, he leant out of the car and skimmed something towards me through the air. It was a flat green tin printed with the words 'Loch Leven Eyed Fly Box.' Inside were rows of hand-tied dry flies: Mayflies, Ginger Quills, Red Spinners, Blue-Winged Olives, Iron-Blue Duns and Black Gnats. I looked up. He grinned, waved and was gone."

It is unlikely that LSD-tripping alone caused Nairac's nervous breakdown. That had been slowly building up over eight years and was a disaster waiting to happen, but LSD was probably the catalyst that precipitated the crisis. It might also have a bearing on other things that happened to Nairac later in his life.

LSD belongs to the hallucinogen family of drugs. This synthetic drug was first produced in 1938 by a Swiss scientist who was investigating the medical uses of a fungus that grows on various types of grass. After accidentally swallowing a small amount of the drug, the scientist experienced an intense and terrifying distortion of his sensory perceptions, which he compared to being possessed by a demon; this sounds very like Nairac's experience. In general, the long-term effects of LSD involve the brain and psyche rather than the body. For example, they do not affect the drug-taker's ability to play sport. Frequent users may experience episodes of psychosis, or severely altered perceptions, for years after they have ceased taking the drug. References to LSD "flashbacks" are common in popular culture. But the clinical term for repeated, drug-induced psychotic episodes – hallucinogen persisting perception disorder (HPPD) – is less well known. The psychotic disturbances associated with HPPD may last for months or years, and it is not always possible to reverse the effects of HPPD simply by quitting the drug. According to the Cleveland Clinic the exact effect of LSD on the brain remains unknown, but the drug may affect the brain's response to serotonin, a neurotransmitter that affects the emotions, moods and perceptions. A person who has been using LSD for any length of time may experience some of the signs and symptoms of hallucinogen abuse:

- Intense mood swings and emotional disturbances
- Hallucinations (seeing or hearing things that are not there, like a roomful of green birds)
- Recurrence of hallucinations after they have stopped taking the drug ("flashbacks")
- Changes in the way they perceive time and space
- Changes in the way they perceive themselves
- Overwhelming fear or depression
- Severe paranoia.

Nairac did occasionally show some of these symptoms. Some users report having aesthetic, mystical experiences while under LSD's influence. However, because it is impossible to predict or control the type of experience that a person may have, they are just as likely to have a terrifying hallucination as a spectacular or enlightening one. That is what happened to Nairac when he "met the Devil". These episodes may recur later, interfering with their social and professional lives and putting them at risk from anxiety, depression and – in extreme cases – suicidal thoughts. Nairac ceased taking LSD when he was twenty-two. He was murdered when he was twenty-eight and during the intervening six years it is quite possible that he was still from time to time experiencing the after-effects of LSD. Again, they could have affected his behaviour and his judgement. Nairac's terrible bouts of depression could have been caused or exacerbated by LSD.

Nairac never mentioned any of this to Julian Malins, who would not have been sympathetic. Malins' comment, some thirty-odd years after Nairac's murder, was that he could believe that Robert had experimented with drugs, as he had an inquiring mind. He was not surprised that he had encountered the Devil: "The Devil is precisely the sort of person whom I would expect to appear to Robert, as he believed strongly in the Devil!" It was all down to Nairac's Catholic upbringing which, in Malins' view, had "seriously screwed up Robert". Among other things it had taught him to believe that pain and suffering equalled righteousness and virtue (Christ, after all, had suffered); whereas pleasure, especially sexual pleasure, equalled sin and vice.

Interestingly, the author F. Scott Fitzgerald, also the product of a devout Catholic upbringing, had a very similar experience. This also involved a terrifying encounter with the Devil. Fitzgerald fictionalised it in his first novel, *This Side of Paradise*. This experience was supposed to have been due to alcoholic excess rather than drug abuse, although Fitzgerald's description sounds remarkably like a bad drugs trip. There is a further parallel with Scott Fitzgerald, and with his fictional hero, Amory Blaine, who came to believe that evil and sex were virtually synonymous. This begs the question: Did Nairac read Scott Fitzgerald, and was he influenced by *This Side of Paradise*? Julian Malins thinks it highly likely: "I feel sure that Robert would have read Scott Fitzgerald, though at this distance in time, I cannot recall talking about it with him". Fitzgerald's other famous novel, *The Great Gatsby*, was at that time an English Literature set text. Nairac is likely to have read it for O-Level English; this could have led him to read some of Fitzgerald's other works. He was in any case well-read. So, could Scott Fitzgerald's description of an encounter with the Devil have been "played back" to Nairac while he was under the influence of LSD, possibly several years after he had read the novel? Yes, it could have been and it probably was.

There was a connection between Nairac's renunciation of LSD and the loss of his History notes. He had "turned Queen's Evidence" and reported the full facts of the LSD parties to his own college authorities. They had informed the colleges of Nairac's erstwhile fellow LSD-trippers, whom he had named and who were probably more severely punished by their college authorities than Nairac was by Lincoln College. Certainly they did not forgive his defection: they took revenge. According to a well-informed former Don, it was they, or some of them, who stole Nairac's car and destroyed his History notebooks; presumably with a view to making him more likely to fail Final Honours Schools. That was by no stretch of the imagination the act of gentlemen. It could be an additional reason why this is an episode that none of them now wishes to discuss.

Duncan Fallowell seems to be the originator of some at least of the persistent stories that cast doubt on Nairac's heterosexuality. As we have seen, Fallowell has admitted to having introduced Nairac to LSD at Oxford. "I introduced Bob to acid," he said. "At the time I was having a relationship with Nairac's protégé, Alasdair McGaw, who later went to live with the film director Derek Jarman. I'm sure Alasdair would have told me if Bob had been sent down for LSD. Perhaps it was for something else." (Londoner's Diary, *The Evening Standard,* 25 March 2010). Here and in the vignette quoted by Jonathon Green in *Days in the Life,* Fallowell, who identifies as homosexual or bisexual, makes his suspicions clear. Not only does he refer to Alasdair McGaw as Nairac's "protégé" and "his favourite Boxing Blue": he adds that Nairac was "one of those good-looking, conceited men who might have liked to be gay, but he went to a Catholic school and this makes life a problem for anybody". This is tantamount to saying that Nairac really *was* homosexual but had been inhibited – at least initially – from practicing by his strict Roman Catholic upbringing. Fallowell declined to elaborate, maintaining that he had nothing to add to what he had already written. However, common acquaintances assert that he has been more explicit in private, indicating that he · and Nairac had been bitter rivals for the affection of Alasdair McGaw.

It is clear from his *obiter dicta* that although Fallowell and Nairac were acquainted and took acid together on more than one occasion, they were not close friends. Remarks like "Robert Nairac, who was later chopped up by the IRA", and "one of those good-looking, conceited men who might have liked to be gay", are hardly friendly. Given that Nairac had apparently wanted to beat up Fallowell at the start of their acquaintance, this may be understandable. It is probably correct to say that

Fallowell still views Nairac with considerable ambivalence and therefore might not be a totally dispassionate witness on this subject.

It has not been possible to trace Alasdair McGaw or to discover whether he is still alive, so his side of the story is unavailable. However Press reports of his career as an amateur boxer make it clear that he was not a contemptible man. Although his photos appear to show a slightly epicene but still handsome and (at one period) long-haired poet of the late nineteenth century decadence, this appearance was misleading. A courageous boxer, he fought welterweight. Welterweight is heavier than lightweight but lighter than middleweight. Lacking an opponent of his own weight, he sometimes squared off against bigger men than himself and got punished. Nairac would have respected that. On 20 November 1969 he is described in a Press report as displaying "great gallantry" in an unequal match, which ended with his face "crimson with blood." He received his OUABC Panther Award for gallantry on this occasion. But did he ever, as Fallowell appears to suggest, engage in gallantry of a different kind with Nairac? Given that Nairac was now showing an interest in girls; at any rate in Irish girls, it seems rather unlikely. Unless new evidence comes to light, the Scottish verdict of "not proven" must be returned.

Having resigned himself to a fourth year at Oxford, Nairac pulled himself together. He would continue to box but would cease to be an office holder in the OUABC. He would endeavour to get as good a degree as was possible under the circumstances. A First was probably beyond his reach. Even a Second, after all that had happened, might prove very challenging, but at least the disgrace of a Pass degree could be avoided. He now finally looked at what he wanted to do after Oxford. He was already thinking seriously about the Army, for which he was well-suited. It would have to be a spectacularly distinguished Regiment, to compensate for his probable Third from Oxford. He aimed for, and achieved, a university cadetship with the Grenadier Guards.

The available evidence indicates that Nairac, most of whose friends had now departed from Oxford, settled down to work diligently for his Finals, while simultaneously starting to prepare for his future military career. He did not move back into College, with all its distractions, but shared lodgings with Shane Vane-Hervey, a younger Amplefordian and boxer, hawks and an owl. In the Hilary Term it was reported that:

"Mr Nairac has covered a good deal of ground this term and discussed a number of topics with enthusiasm. I hope that he may be able to repeat his work under exam conditions. But there is little doubt that his revision work has been serviceable."

In the Trinity term the verdict was:

"He has worked away well, and on some topics, mediaeval, his command of his material [is] admirable but his written work is often incoherent and I shall be surprised whether an appraisal [an assessment of course work, which can be used to upgrade the Honours Class awarded in Finals] will really bring him out of Third Class."

Nairac sat his Final Honours Schools in Army uniform, which the University Statutes permit to male undergraduates as an alternative to academic gown, white tie and subfusc. He received a Third Class Honours degree, which was not truly representative of his ability. It was less than Nairac had hoped for and it fell far short of his dead brother David's grades. (Nor did it compare well with T E Lawrence's results; he had scored a First, also in Modern History, in 1910. Lawrence subsequently won a postgraduate scholarship at Magdalen College and later became a Fellow of All Souls College). However Nairac's degree was still a respectable result, given the personal problems that he had faced. It was undeniably an Honours BA (Oxon), not a Pass degree. It was still worth having. It had also been attended by serious sporting and athletic achievement. That probably impressed the Army as much as, or more than, a brilliant First would have done.

Nairac left Oxford a few days after graduation. That was not the end of his association with Oxford, nor with the OUABC. Later he would lead Army boxing teams against Oxford. According to another soldier, who was with him, "he seemed rather chuffed that we were going to box the Oxford team". On the first occasion, in the course of the match he would experience a "clash of heads" and would require stitches. This was in the days before helmets. Nairac, with his usual guts and determination, wanted to continue the match, however bad the injury that he might have sustained. After the bouts, Oxford put on mouse racing. The mice ran through Perspex tubes. Wagers were taken. Injuries notwithstanding, everyone seems to have had a good time.

Fred Cook, then a Grenadier Guards Warrant Officer, recalls: "We were the boxing officers in Chelsea, when I had to throw the towel in the ring at Oxford Uni, after he had been head-butted and required a number of stitches over his left eye, if I remember rightly: a good officer. He also stayed with number three company when I was CSM for Christmas [1976], whilst we were in Middletown, Northern Ireland, shortly before he was murdered."

In 1975, seven years after his matriculation, Nairac was eligible to return to Oxford to collect the honorary MA which all Honours BA graduates can claim, provided that they formally apply for it and pay a fee. Most BAs do so. Once the formal MA degree conferment ceremony, in cap and gown, has concluded, this second graduation is an enjoyable and sometimes bibulous social occasion; above all, it is an opportunity to catch up with old friends. Nairac was on Regimental duties in London at the time and could easily have made the journey to Oxford for this purpose; it is only an hour away by fast train from Paddington Station. But he did not go. He remained a BA until his dying day, which by then lay only two years in the future.

One of Nairac's last public appearances in Oxford was when he attended the OUABC's 1976 retirement dinner for Alf Gallie, the club's coach, about a year before his own murder. Appropriately, given that Gallie was Welsh, the dinner took place in Jesus College. Gallie had been a Welsh Amateur Boxing Champion and the coach of the British Olympic boxing team at the 1952 Summer Olympics at Helsinki. He had devoted most of his life to the OUABC. Less than five years after Nairac's murder Gallie would receive the British Empire Medal (BEM) for his services to sport in the 1982 New Year Honours List. Interviewed at length by *The Oxford Times*, he spoke of his friendship with Nairac:

"He was a courageous sort of fellow. I never met a man like him. He seemed to be able to get the other men to do anything for him. He was one of the nicest men that I ever met."

Nairac would enjoy at least one further Oxonian moment before he was killed. On leave from his final duty tour in Northern Ireland, he attended the November 1976 Vincent's Club dinner in London. On this occasion some of Nairac's Oxford friends, including Julian Malins, saw him for the very last time: he disappeared six months later. Nairac seems to have paid a few fleeting visits to Oxford while on leave, even after this. He still had friends there, both Dons and undergraduates, one of whom he visited in 1977, shortly before his murder.

Robert Nairac's maternal uncle, Basil Dykes in a thoughtful mood soon after his escape from Dunkirk in 1940. Image kindly reproduced with permission. © Nicholas Dykes

Robert Nairac and fellow OUABC members with boxing trophies. Image kindly reproduced with permission. © *The Oxford Mail.*

Lincoln College, Oxford, where Nairac was an undergraduate from 1968 to 1972. Image reproduced with permission. © Photo by David Iliff. License: CC-BY-SA 3.0

Robert Nairac developed a keen interest in falconry. He is seen here with a peregrine falcon in Ireland. © The Honourable John Morris.

Above: Philip Glasier was Nairac's falconry instructor. He was to dedicate his work *Falconry and Hawking*, published in 1978, the year after Nairac's murder, to his memory. Image kindly reproduced with permission. © Jemima Parry-Jones MBE. *Right:* A contemporary photograph of Alderman Julian Malins Q.C., one of Robert Nairac's closest friends at Oxford. Image reproduced with permission. © Julian Malins Q.C.

Ampleforth College, North Yorkshire. Image reproduced with permission. © Ampleforth College.

The War Memorial Chapel at Ampleforth, where Robert Nairac is commemorated. Image used with kind permission. © North York Moors National Park Authority.

CHAPTER 8 | THE IRISH BACKGROUND

We are bound to lose Ireland in consequence of years of cruelty, stupidity and misgovernment and I would rather lose her as a friend than as a foe.
(W E Gladstone)

Whatever its exact political status, Northern Ireland has never really been treated by Whitehall as a constituent part of the United Kingdom, but as a post-colonial successor state. It has therefore been neither truly British nor truly Irish ... From 1921 to 1969 Britain washed its hands of Ulster. Since then, using the Army as a shield, it has been able to keep the worst of the problem at arm's length.
(Anthony Beevor, *Inside the British Army*)

Unlike most of the young British officers who were "blooded", and in some cases killed, in Northern Ireland between 1969 and 1998, Robert Nairac was well-informed about Irish history. It is an interesting but unhappy tale. It is also essential background. British people may have forgotten it, but the Irish have not. This history fascinated Robert Nairac – he became emotionally involved in the Irish tragedy: it drew him in and finally it destroyed him. Readers who are already well-informed may prefer to miss this chapter and proceed to the next one.

This book is not the place to rehearse the entire narrative of England's, and later Great Britain's, involvement in Ireland; a melancholy story that starts in at least Norman times, if not earlier. However some knowledge of the recent background, in the nineteenth and twentieth centuries, is necessary in order to understand how the late twentieth-century Troubles, which would claim many lives besides Robert Nairac's, came about in the late 1960s.

The presence in Northern Ireland, starting in 1609, of a large number of Protestants of English and (predominantly) Scots descent was the result of a policy decision by King James I of England and VI of Scotland. The native Ulster Irish, who spoke Gaelic, and their nearest Scottish neighbours, who also spoke Gaelic of a different but still inter-intelligible dialect, were far too friendly with each other and politically unreliable, in King James' eyes. Both sets of Celts tended to cling tenaciously to their ancient Catholic religion. They were always plotting rebellion or other mischief and were suspected of intriguing with foreign powers. They frequently intermarried. It seemed a good idea at the time to interpose a hostile buffer-state between them. This would best be achieved by dispossessing the native Irish from the six countries of what is now Northern Ireland – those nearest to Scotland – and "planting" them with politically reliable Protestant Lowland Scots and English settlers, who would also introduce the latest agricultural and industrial practices into that backward country. A further bonus could be achieved by clearing many of King James' most persistently rebellious Scots subjects, the Border Reivers, and transplanting them to Ulster where they could exercise their undoubted military skills on the King's enemies (the native Irish) instead of on their Scots and Northern English fellow-subjects: hence the presence in Northern Ireland today of many famous Scots Border and Galloway surnames like Armstrong, Elliot, McDowall, McClelland and Blair. These Scotch-Irish bequeathed their courage and warlike nature to their descendants. Unlike the more recent Highland Clearances, which are still the subject of bitter and maudlin ballads, the Border Clearances seem largely forgotten today; in Scotland, at any rate.

In the rest of Ireland there were relatively few areas where Protestants had settled in large numbers; mainly around Dublin, although there were other, usually urban, pockets of Protestant settlement, even in Nationalist strongholds like Cork. In Ulster, County Dublin and in these pockets there were Protestant middle and working classes, as well as gentry and nobility. George Bernard Shaw's family for example were from the Dublin Protestant lower-middle-class. Elsewhere, following a series of confiscations in the preceding centuries, particularly under King James I and VI, and Oliver Cromwell, a thin, sugary coating of Protestant Anglo-Irish gentry who imported their wives from the English shires, their guns and their claret from London and who mostly belonged to the Anglican Church of Ireland, dominated a countryside inhabited by a sullen Catholic peasant tenantry. Mrs Bernard Shaw, née Charlotte Townsend and herself the daughter of an Anglo-Irish squire, remarked in a letter to T E Lawrence that in much of Ireland before the twentieth century there had been only two classes: the gentry and the people. This was in contrast to England with its subtle gradations of social class. The gentry were mostly Anglican and the people were mostly Catholic (*Note 1*). Charlotte herself, the doctor's daughter, the Resident Magistrate, the Duke of Leinster and Provost Mahaffy of Trinity College were all equally gentry. Everyone else was of the people.

Queen Elizabeth I founded Trinity College, Dublin (TCD) to educate the sons of this Anglo-Irish Anglican élite, not all of whose fathers could afford to send them to Oxford or Cambridge. The Army and the British Empire, especially India, had provided them with careers. Nonconformist Protestants, like Catholics, were not initially eligible. For many years TCD was an exclusively Protestant university, more British than Irish. The ascendancy's lifestyle was amusingly described by Somerville and Ross in *Some Experiences of an Irish Resident Magistrate*. It was to this ascendancy that T E Lawrence's father, Sir Thomas Chapman, Baronet, belonged by birth. Mingled with the Anglo-Irish was a smaller number of native Irish noble families like the O'Conor Don (Ó Conchubhair Donn), Chief of the name of the Clan Ó Conchubhair, titular Prince of Connacht and senior descendent of the last High King of Ireland; the Barons Inchiquin who are the Chiefs of O'Brien; the McGillycuddy of the Reeks, directly descended from Mogh Nuaghad, King of Munster; the various branches of Fitzgerald, the

Guinnesses, the Considines and the McKinleys. These families had adjusted to changed times, become anglicised and had been permitted to keep some of their ancestral lands. However most of the old Celtic nobility had been dispossessed. They fled overseas and joined the armies of England's enemies; they became the original "wild geese". Their clansmen were reduced to being tenants of the new ruling class. Naturally, these native Irish people nursed a sense of grievance at this injustice.

In London a Secretary of State represented the Kingdom of Ireland at Cabinet level. In Ireland the Lord Lieutenant, sometimes referred to as the Viceroy, represented the British Crown. He was invariably English or Scots, not Irish. Over the centuries his role became increasingly formal and ornamental, as befitted the representative of a constitutional monarch. From the late eighteenth century the Chief Secretary for Ireland handled the day-to-day business of government (*Note 2*). He was "Prime Minister" to the Lord Lieutenant's "King". Latterly the Chief Secretary was also a British Cabinet Minister. There was a separate Irish Privy Council (which functioned until 1922), an Irish Peerage and an Irish College of Heralds, known as the Office of Arms, headed by Ulster King of Arms but located in Dublin Castle. There was an Irish Royal Household, whose members, hereditary or appointed, donned ornate Ruritanian uniforms and creaked into action on the rare occasion of a Royal Visit. Oscar Wilde's father, Sir William Wilde, was a member of this shadowy organisation. He was the Queen's Oculist in Ordinary in Ireland: like Robert Nairac's father, he was a distinguished ophthalmic surgeon. There was a special Irish Order of chivalry, the Order of St Patrick, whose motto was "Quis separabit?" or "Who shall divide us?" The Knights wore resplendent sky-blue mantles on ceremonial occasions. The Order is now extinct or dormant: the last Knight of St Patrick died in 1974.

Prior to 1801 Ireland had its own Parliament in Dublin, based on the Westminster model, with Houses of Lords and Commons, a Lord Chancellor, a Woolsack and a Speaker. The Anglican Church of Ireland Bishops sat in the Irish House of Lords, The standard of debate at Dublin was said to be noticeably higher than that at Westminster: the Anglo-Irish were more eloquent, witty and frequently better-educated than their English counterparts. For much of the eighteenth century the Irish Parliament sat in a purpose-built neoclassical palace designed by Edward Pearce and James Gandon, which was more beautiful and commodious than the former Palace of Westminster (an old mediaeval Royal palace adapted for Parliamentary use, which was burnt down in 1834 and replaced by the present neo-gothic Houses of Parliament). The foundation stone was laid in 1729. Edith Mary Johnston in her *Ireland in the Eighteenth Century* describes it as "incomparably the most splendid Parliament House in the Empire". Appearances, as is often the case in Ireland, were deceptive. For all its magnificent setting, the Irish Parliament had limited authority and was for most of its existence a subordinate legislature, whose most important work was to re-enact legislation already passed by Westminster, with adjustments to reflect local conditions. Still, it was better than no Parliament and, in the last years of its existence as "Grattan's Parliament", it achieved a good measure of autonomy or Home Rule.

Political activity was the preserve of the Anglican ascendancy. Catholics and Nonconformist Protestants could not participate directly in the political process, but latterly qualified Catholics and Nonconformists got the vote, although they could still only vote for members of the ascendancy. At the end of the eighteenth century the British Government decided to foreclose on the Irish Parliament, bringing Ireland under direct rule from London for various reasons, mainly the Great Irish Rebellion of 1798, which had been inspired by the American and French Revolutions and led by the Society of United Irishmen, whose leaders had included Protestants like Wolfe Tone and Lord Edward Fitzgerald, as well as Catholics. It had been aided and abetted by French revolutionary army officers. Ireland was now seen as England's Achilles heel.

The British Government achieved this outcome by the shameless bribery of Irish MPs and Peers, whom they induced to vote for union; even so, it took two attempts. In 1801 the Irish and British Parliaments merged; the Kingdom of Ireland ceased to exist; Ireland joined Great Britain to become the United Kingdom of Great Britain and Ireland, although some separate Irish institutions survived, including the offices of Lord Lieutenant, Chief Secretary for Ireland, the Office of Arms and the Irish Peerage. The office of Secretary of State for Ireland was abolished. The House of Commons in London expanded to admit approximately 100 Irish MPs, who became increasingly nationalist as the nineteenth century wore on and the franchise widened. On a basis of population, Ireland was over-represented at Westminster, but that had been part of the deal. A small number of Irish Representative Peers, elected for life, were admitted to the Lords. Those not seated in the Lords had the right to stand for election to the House of Commons. The Church of Ireland united with the Church of England. One Irish Archbishop and three Bishops, selected by rotation, would sit in the Lords until Disestablishment in 1871, when the Church of Ireland became separate once again.

Today Pearce and Gandon's architectural masterpiece houses the Bank of Ireland. It was extensively remodelled internally before being handed over to the Bank, so that it could never again serve as the seat of a legislature. Prior to 1801 the State Opening of Parliament by the Lord Lieutenant and the associated State balls, drawing rooms and receptions, had been the highlight of the Dublin social calendar. The Dublin State Opening was considered to be a more magnificent spectacle than its London equivalent. It attracted many of the nobility and gentry into the city, where they still maintained town houses, entertained in their turn and spent freely. Their seasonal presence in Dublin, along with large numbers of servants, provided a regular boost to the city's economy. Now that there was no Parliament and no State Opening any more, this no longer happened. Dublin became a ghost of its former self: a bourgeois provincial university city. It was still beautiful, still Georgian; still stuck firmly in the eighteenth century and haunted by the political and literary ghosts of its distinguished past but deserted by contemporary Irish politicians and by the nobility, who now spent most of their time in London. From time to time Vice-regal ceremonies at Dublin Castle: a ball, a State banquet, an investiture of the Order of St Patrick or a rare Royal Visit, would remind Dubliners that they still lived, at least in theory, in a European capital city.

There was one exception to this generalisation: the brilliant intellectual life that had characterised Dublin in the eighteenth century lived on. Dublin was a hotbed of genius. Despite the disappearance of its political focus, it continued to be a city of scholars, poets, writers, composers and artists who tended, as the nineteenth century wore on under the influence of the Romantic Movement, to become increasingly interested in Irish archaeology, folklore, culture and history, while remaining in touch with European thought. A prominent, but not untypical, Dublin citizen of this period was Sir William Rowan Hamilton. He was a mathematical prodigy; a Greek, Latin and Hebrew scholar; a poet and friend of Wordsworth; Professor of Astronomy at Trinity College at the age of twenty-two and later Astronomer Royal. This was the Dublin in which flourished Sheridan Lefanu, Bram Stoker, Sir William and Lady Wilde, Provost John Pentland Mahaffy of Trinity College, Lord Dunsany, Constance Markiewicz, W B Yeats, J M Synge, James Joyce, Lady Gregory and Robert Nairac's distant Protestant cousins. It saw the youth of George Moore, Oscar Wilde and Bernard Shaw before they migrated to England. Trinity College, later joined by University College, and learned societies like the Royal Dublin Society, the Royal Irish Academy and the Royal College of Physicians in Ireland, all throve. English visitors were impressed and speculated about where all this intellectual exuberance would lead. Would it eventually exhaust itself, fizzing away into the Empyrean and evaporating? Would the intellectuals follow the politicians and nobility to England? A certain number did. Or would they find a political cause? The answer was fairly clear: nationalism was the greatest, and potentially the most destructive, political force of nineteenth century Europe; and the apostles of nationalism – the Alfieris and Mazzinis – were the intelligentsia. As the nineteenth century wore on, many Irish intellectuals would become proponents of Home Rule or even of complete independence. That many of them were Protestants, and often monarchists as well, did not strike them as incongruous.

The Irish Potato Famine of 1845-52 horribly highlighted the lack of a separate Irish Parliament and Government. Sir Robert Peel's Conservative Government's response to it was characterised by a failure of comprehension. Ministers did not understand the full implications of what had happened until it was far too late. When they did finally comprehend, they had to get the necessary legislation through Parliament, which was to prove neither swift nor easy. At this period both the Conservative and Whig Parties adhered to market economics. The Whigs and their Liberal successors called this "laissez-faire" and it was a plank of their political platform. The Conservatives feared to disturb market equilibria. In this respect they were like modern neo-liberals. Neither Conservatives nor Whigs wished to upset the landed interest, which financed both Parties. There had been earlier failures of the Irish potato crop. They could have been almost equally disastrous, but they had occurred while Ireland still had its own Parliament and its own devolved Government, which, however unrepresentative of the majority it may have been, was still Irish; it understood the danger and knew what to do. This potato crop failure was much more serious, because it coincided with bad corn harvests everywhere, affecting the whole British Isles. Absentee Anglo-Irish landlords were exporting corn and livestock from Ireland to England to take advantage of the high prices paid there at the very time that they were most needed in Ireland. All over the United Kingdom consumers suffered. This led much of the British population to call for the repeal of the thirty-year-old Corn Laws, which prevented the import of cheap foreign grain. Unable to send sufficient food to Ireland to stem the famine, Prime Minister Peel decided that the Corn Laws must be repealed out of humanity. Most British people agreed with him. Most British people, however, did not have the vote. Landowners saw repeal as an attack on them, and fiercely protested in the House of Commons. Peel's Party would not support him and the debate lasted for five months. Eventually, in June 1846, the Corn Laws were repealed, at the cost of Peel's political career; he never held office again. His Whig successor, Lord John Russell, fared little better. He took much of the blame for the Government's failures in dealing with the Irish famine. Meanwhile one million Irish people had died of starvation and a further million had emigrated, mostly to the USA. The lesson that many of the surviving Irish drew from this nightmare was that despite its formal incorporation into the United Kingdom, Ireland was seen as a colony to be exploited. The next logical step was to demand independence or at least Home Rule. Peel and Russell, however unfairly, acquired a place in Irish demonology alongside Oliver Cromwell and King William III.

Another result of the famine was that Ireland acquired an international dimension. It could no longer be treated as a purely British internal matter. The children of the famine refugees flourished, grew rich and became a political force in the USA. There would soon be a bitterly anti-British Irish-American lobby at the heart of what was slowly evolving into the world's first super-power. Following the American Civil War of 1861 to 1865, in which many Irishmen served on both sides, the USA would become the main arsenal of Irish anti-British and anti-Canadian terrorism: the source of funds, guns, bombs, dynamite and battle-hardened Irish veteran soldiers. It still is.

Despite the loss of its Parliament, Ireland cannot truly claim to have been treated as a mere British colony in the nineteenth and early twentieth centuries, because Irish MPs sat in the British Parliament and often became very influential. No British colony or Dominion ever had that right. One prominent Irishman, Lord Palmerston, became Prime Minister on two occasions, dying in that office. He was in office in different Ministerial capacities almost continuously from 1807 until his death in 1865, initially as a Tory but latterly as a Liberal. Palmerston, as an Irish Peer with no British title, stood for election and sat as an MP in the Commons. The Irish Nationalist MPs formed a loose third Party – the Irish Parliamentary Party (IPP) – and tended to vote tactically in the Irish interest; as, for example, when in 1886 they held the balance of power in the Commons. By switching their support from the Conservatives to the Liberals they caused the fall of Lord Salisbury's government and the return to power of Mr Gladstone. On several occasions "the tail wagged the dog". The Irish and Scots MPs by their weight of numbers kept the Liberal Party in power when England had voted overwhelmingly Conservative. The IPP's main objective was the restoration of the Irish Parliament, with the important reform that Catholics should be allowed to stand for election, as well as to vote: Home Rule, in other words.

Liberal policy towards Ireland had evolved in the interval. Many members of the Liberal Party now concluded that Home Rule should be granted and was inevitable anyway; centuries of misgovernment by England had seen to that. In their eyes, it was simply a question of whether Ireland would achieve Home Rule under bitterly acrimonious or amicable circumstances. Prime Minister William Ewart Gladstone (a former Peelite Tory, later a Liberal) made it his life's work to deliver the latter. He did not succeed. Returned to office in early 1886, Gladstone brought in an Irish Home Rule Bill but this was defeated in the House of Commons in July. Gladstone resigned and the Conservatives returned to power. The resulting split in the Liberal Party, between advocates of Home Rule and Unionists, helped to keep them out of office, with one short break, for twenty years. In 1892 Gladstone formed his last government at the age of eighty-two. Again he introduced a Home Rule Bill. The Second Irish Home Rule Bill passed in the Commons but was defeated in the Lords. Gladstone resigned again in March 1894. He died three years later, his mission unfulfilled. The torpedoing of the Home Rule Bills was the work not merely of the Conservative and Irish Unionist MPs, but of their new allies, the breakaway Liberal Unionists led by Joseph Chamberlain, the father of Austen and Neville Chamberlain. Ironically, many of the Liberal Unionists were Radicals, on the left of the Party. They made strange bedfellows with the Conservatives. Both however considered that to grant Ireland autonomy would be the first step towards the break-up of the United Kingdom and of the British Empire. So, for them, Home Rule equated to Treason. Irish Home Rule proved to be one of the most emotive and divisive issues of the Victorian age. It is tempting to speculate that had Home Rule been granted then, Ireland could have remained British, although in charge of its own internal affairs.

That is not certain, however. There remained the "other" Irish Question: Ulster, which Mr Gladstone seemed to have overlooked. The focus now shifted from Dublin to Belfast. Belfast, while less visually attractive than Dublin, was distinguished by its modern Industrial Revolution dynamism, with coal mining, ship-building, linen mills and an international port. Belfast had its own university, founded as Queen's College in 1845. It became a university in its own right in 1908. Forward-looking and technologically-orientated from the beginning, Queen's was distinguished for scientific research. The next serious political challenge would come from Belfast. In the event that Home Rule was to be achieved, how would the progressive Protestants of Northern Ireland view the prospect of their inclusion in a devolved Ireland, ruled from Dublin, in which Protestants would no longer be in control? The answer, in many cases, was with horror. Their response, as it had been previously, was armed resistance. Many British people sympathised with them. In the words of Lord Randolph Churchill MP, the father of Sir Winston Churchill, "Ulster will fight and Ulster will be right". In the six Protestant counties a time bomb had now started to tick.

Meanwhile fate had granted the Unionists, and the Conservatives in mainland Great Britain, an unexpected twenty-year reprieve, which roughly coincided with the split in the Liberal Party. In 1890 Charles Stewart Parnell, the leader of the Irish Home Rule MPs, youthful, charismatic, a close associate of Gladstone and a brilliant Parliamentary orator, was caught up in, and discredited by, an adulterous sexual scandal culminating in a high-profile, high-society divorce. It damaged him irreparably at a time when Protestants and Catholics alike strongly disapproved of divorce and even more so of the remarriage of divorced persons. Parnell died young, four months after marrying his lover, Mrs Katharine "Kitty" O'Shea. Mrs O'Shea was the sister of Field Marshal Sir Evelyn Wood and a niece of Lord Hatherley, Gladstone's first Lord Chancellor. Parnell was buried in Glasnevin Cemetery in Dublin. He had split and seriously weakened the Irish Parliamentary Party, whose ageing, anglicised leaders bumbled on towards the next century. While they did so, younger and more intransigent Irish Nationalists began to look to men of action, often Irish-Americans, rather than Parliamentarians, for leadership and inspiration. Following the end of the American Civil War, in the last three decades of the nineteenth century the number of Irish terrorist incidents began to escalate.

The Conservatives and Liberal Unionists were neither happy with, nor complacent about, the status quo. They too wished to reach a solution to the Irish Home Rule Question. But unlike Mr Gladstone, who was an idealist, they subscribed to a pragmatic tradition. Their answer was not political but economic. They correctly perceived that the ownership of land was a major grievance. Over the centuries the native Irish had become tenants, often exploited ones, on the land of proprietors who were mainly of English and Scots descent. Some landlords were uncaring absentees, who used their Irish revenues to fund an agreeable life somewhere else: usually in England. If the Irish Land Question and its related grievances could be resolved, many of the grounds for Home Rule would fall away. The result was the Irish Land Acts, of which the most radical was Arthur Balfour's (Conservative Chief Secretary for Ireland 1887-91) Irish Land Act of 1887. It provided £33,000,000 Sterling for land purchase but contained so many complicated legal clauses that it was not put fully into effect until amended five years later. At that point only £13,500,000 had been used. It substituted smallholder proprietorship for tenancy as the principal form of land tenure. At the same time Balfour created the Congested Districts Board to deal with distress in the backward areas of the West of Ireland. The 1887 Act was amended by the 1896 Land Act, increasing the amount available for purchase and removing the clauses which had made the 1887 Act unattractive. The Land Courts were empowered to sell 1,500 bankrupt estates to tenants. In all, 47,000 holdings were bought out between 1891 and 1896. Purchase was mainly on the basis of willing seller, willing buyer. The Government bought large areas of land and sold them on easy terms to sitting tenants. In most areas landlordism, once the bane of Ireland, had ceased to be a problem well before Irish independence. This was not quite the end of the Anglo-Irish ascendancy, however. Many of them still retained a foothold in Ireland: a park, a shoot or a home farm, attached to the ancestral "big house". Some of them are still there, although now relegated to the margins of Irish life. Sporting estates, which did not usually have tenants, were not included in the land transfer scheme. A number of these still survive.

The attraction for landowners of selling out was, as a result of the repeal of the Corn Laws, by the late nineteenth century agricultural produce prices had been driven down by free trade and imperial competition: cheap food from the colonies and elsewhere. It followed that in Ireland and mainland Great Britain land was no longer seen as the supreme investment that it had formerly been, so it was a "win-win" situation, as A J Balfour astutely noted. It made sense for landowners to sell up and invest their money in other ways. Balfour also oversaw legislation for improved local government in Ireland. The other side of Balfour's legacy, during his time as Chief Secretary, was his ruthless enforcement of law and order, earning this elegant, highly-civilised philosopher, author and future Prime Minister the nickname in Ireland of "Bloody Balfour." Yet he came closer to resolving the Irish Question than anyone else. It may be coincidental, but during his time as Chief Secretary, Balfour's wavy brown hair turned grey. He had received a number of death-threats. Even for a calm and rational empirical philosopher who once said after careful reflection, that without having had any prior experience of it, he had no fear of death, it had been a stressful experience.

1910 proved to be Ireland's year of destiny. Two general elections that year had resulted in a hung Parliament in which the Liberal Party, now led by Herbert Asquith, won the largest number of seats. Asquith did not however command a majority in the House of Commons. A formal or informal coalition was now inevitable. Only with the support of John Redmond's 83 Irish Parliamentary Party MPs (the other 22 Irish MPs were Unionists) could Asquith hope to form a government. The price of Redmond's co-operation was Home Rule. Apart from Ulster, the prospect of imminent Home Rule caused great pleasure throughout Ireland and contributed to the success of King George V's Royal Visit to Dublin in 1911. The King himself expected that his next visit would be to attend the first State Opening of an Irish Parliament since 1800. Asquith presented the Third Irish Home Rule Bill to Parliament in April 1912. The Bill provided that purely Irish questions should be dealt with by a subordinate Irish Parliament in Dublin, but that the people of Ireland should still be represented by MPs at Westminster, who would play a full part in the formation of wider British and imperial policy. As the Conservatives were quick to note, Asquith proposed no reduction in the number of Irish Westminster MPs, because a majority of them usually supported the Liberals. To make it more palatable to the Conservatives, Irish Home Rule was represented as part of a sensible programme of reform conceding greater devolution to all parts of the United Kingdom that wanted it. A Scottish Home Rule Bill was passed at the same time. Like the Irish Home Rule Bill, it did not come into effect because of the intervention of the First World War. Some powers were also to be devolved to Wales. These included the controversial disestablishment of the Anglican Church in Wales, which was finally delivered in 1920.

The Conservatives and Liberal Unionists were not impressed. Apart from their furious opposition in Westminster, there was opposition to Home Rule within Ireland itself. This came mainly, but by no means exclusively, from the Protestants of Ulster, who considered that "Home Rule is Rome Rule" and was therefore unacceptable. Since the Ulstermen were prepared to defend their corner by force of arms if necessary, and had powerful backers in and outside Parliament, this could not be overlooked. Many Army officers had threatened to resign their commissions if Home Rule were to be forced upon the Ulster Protestants, using the Army to enforce it. Some of these officers were Irish and did not wish to be ordered out against the men of Ulster. The Commons nevertheless passed the Bill. John Redmond addressed the House with evident emotion: "If I may say so reverently, I personally thank God that I have lived to see this day." He spoke too soon. The views of the electors of the six Protestant counties of Ulster had not been properly taken into account. They believed that they had been sold out and were incandescent.

On 28 September the Ulster Covenant (to resist Home Rule) was signed by almost 250,000 men of Ulster. Eventually nearly half a million men would sign. 229,000 women signed a parallel declaration. Grimly, the Ulstermen started to prepare for armed resistance, as they had done in 1690 and 1798. Although the Bill passed the Commons in 1912, it was defeated in the Lords. However thanks to the passage of the Parliament Act of 1911, which had curtailed the veto powers of the House of Lords, the Lords were only able to delay implementation of the

Act for two years to 1914, so the Irish Home Bill secured the Royal Assent as the Government of Ireland Act 1914. The Act should have entered into force on 18 September 1914, but entry was postponed for the duration of the Great War, which the United Kingdom had entered on 4 August 1914. In 1912, however, the war was not foreseen. One advantage of the two-year delay imposed by the Bill's defeat in the Lords was that the Government now had some time in which belatedly to address the difficult question of allowing the six Protestant counties to opt out if they wished.

Through 1913 and 1914 Herbert Asquith's Ministers became more and more preoccupied with Ireland. It distracted their attention from sinister developments elsewhere in Europe. The memories of King James II's invasion in 1690, which had foundered at the Battle of the Boyne; of the bloody rebellion of 1798, when Protestants in Ulster and elsewhere in Ireland had been besieged and both sides had committed atrocities, leapt vividly back to life. The Irish past was making itself felt and visible through the increasingly blurred outlines of the present. It looked as though the Government of Ireland Act 1914, when it finally came into force, could prove unworkable and might well result in civil war. Whatever the Government did would be wrong. If it tried to temporise, for example by further delaying implementation of the Act, or by proposing special measures to safeguard Northern Irish interests, the Nationalists would regard it as reneging on a deal. Already some of the more extreme nationalists were calling for complete independence and a republic, into which Ulster should be forcibly incorporated. Until now the plan had always been for a united Ireland to achieve Home Rule within the British Empire. Now it was clear that most of the Protestants of Ulster would never under any circumstances accept to be ruled from Dublin; "No surrender!" as their charismatic leader, Sir Edward Carson QC MP, is widely believed to have said. The Ulster Unionists were furious at the absence of any definite provision in the Act protecting the position of the six Protestant counties. Asquith tried to defuse the Ulster Question with a vague promise of amending legislation, but the men of Ulster no longer trusted him. They knew that he could not deliver: Redmond and the Nationalists would never agree.

Almost overnight private armies came into being, like Cadmus' warriors springing fully-armed from his sowing of the dragon's teeth. Both sides, Nationalists and Loyalists, started to drill, train, arm themselves and prepare for battle. Meanwhile the March 1914 Curragh Incident had made it clear that the Government could not rely on the Army's loyalty in the event of the conflict escalating beyond the Royal Irish Constabulary's capacity to contain it.

In 1912 the embryonic Ulster Volunteer Force (UVF) had come into existence as a number of hastily-organised private militias. Their purpose was to block Home Rule or, if it went ahead, to ensure that the six Protestant counties should be excluded; if necessary by violent insurrection. In 1913 these militias were formally reorganised into a single body. By 1914 the UVF was at least 100,000 strong. On 25

April 1914 the UVF took over the town of Larne for a night, cutting communications and rendering the town authorities impotent as they unloaded 25,000 rifles and 3 million rounds of ammunition from a collier ship, the *Clydesdale*. She had also unloaded Loyalist guns at Bangor and other Ulster ports. The munitions, bought in Hamburg, had been loaded aboard the *Fanny*, and described as zinc plates, before being transferred to the *Clydesdale* at sea. The munitions unloaded at Larne were then driven away into the night in 700 cars and lorries for distribution. By the time the British Government found out, it was much too late.

The origins of the Irish Republican Army (IRA) (*Note 3*) also belong to this period. The IRA's historic ancestor are the Irish Volunteers, which Nationalists founded in 1913 to safeguard Home Rule and in reaction to the creation of the UVF. Some Irish Volunteers would stage the Dublin Easter Rising of 1916. The Irish Volunteers are also the ancestor of the modern Irish Army (*an t'Arm*), which has inherited none of the traditions of the old British Irish Regiments. As the IRA, the Republican minority wing of the Irish Volunteers would wage a guerrilla war against British rule during the Irish War of Independence, from 1919 to 1921. On the eve of the First World War the UVF and the Irish Volunteers were eyeing each other, ready to move the moment that the signal should be given. Ireland was moving ineluctably towards civil war and partition and no-one seemed able to prevent it.

The First World War was the catalyst that would lead to political polarisation and the partition of Ireland, although this was not immediately obvious. There now seemed to be other, more pressing, priorities than Home Rule. For the duration of the hostilities it seemed that the knotty Irish Question could be set aside, or so Herbert Asquith hoped.

One immediate benefit of the outbreak of war from Asquith's point of view was that the UVF, although it did not disband, almost vanished. Full of patriotic zeal, the men of Ulster, including most members of the UVF, hurried to volunteer for the Army; mainly for the 36th (Ulster) Division. Soon they would be on the Western Front, where they suffered appalling casualties but displayed the terrifying bravery for which they and their ancestors were famous, although their battle-cries would not have been reassuring to the Prime Minister, had he been aware of them:

Here are two pictures from my father's head –
I have kept them like secrets until now:
First, the Ulster Division at the Somme
Going over the top with 'Fuck the Pope!'
'No Surrender!' A boy about to die,
Screaming 'Give 'em one for the Shankill!'
'Wilder than Gurkhas' were my father's words
Of admiration and bewilderment.
(Michael Longley)

On that occasion, 1 July 1916, the first day of the Somme, the Royal Inniskilling Fusiliers sustained the highest number of casualties in a single day of any British line Regiment during the war. The First Battalion suffered 568 casualties while attempting to reach the German lines. But still the survivors fought on. Between 1914 and 1918, no less than seven Inniskillings would be awarded the Victoria Cross.

If Ulster's response to the 1914 call to arms was magnificent, so was that of the rest of Ireland. By 1915 about one-eighth of the total population of Ireland (half a million men) was serving in the Army. Political differences temporarily put aside, the Catholic Irish also flocked to join up. The Irish Volunteers were now split. A minority Republican group stayed in Ireland and would help to stage the 1916 Easter Rising. They would later form the nucleus of the IRA. The majority of National Volunteers supported the Allied war effort, joined up and fought in Irish Regiments on the Western Front and at Gallipoli. They hurried to volunteer for the Royal Irish Regiment; the Royal Dublin Fusiliers, the Connaught Rangers, the Royal Munster Fusiliers, the Prince of Wales's Leinster Regiment... These Regiments were all well-known for their dash and courage. They were all disbanded on 31 July 1922. Except for the South Irish Horse, whose ensigns are still in St Patrick's Cathedral in Dublin, their fading colours hang limply in Windsor Castle; unregarded now, except by the few who still remember their history and their bravery.

Prime Minister Herbert Asquith was not happy to enter the Great War. He was a man of peace; so were a majority of his cabinet. However he had little choice. The Liberal Party, fissiparous at the best of times, was about to experience another of its periodic splits: one that would ultimately prove so catastrophic as to keep the Party out of government forever afterwards, except as part of a coalition. Within the Party was a significant pro-war faction. This included Winston Churchill, the First Lord of the Admiralty, who was at that time a Liberal; his friend F E Smith, who would be appointed Solicitor-General and later Attorney-General in 1915; and David Lloyd George, the Chancellor of the Exchequer. Lloyd George's involvement in the "war party" was partly a matter of political opportunism and partly arose from a genuine sympathy for Belgium, which he saw as a small, defenceless country, rather like Wales, that was being bullied by a much bigger neighbour. Flamboyant men and brilliant Parliamentary orators, all three suffered from an excessive endowment of charisma: all were unreliable allies of Asquith. Churchill, Smith and their friends were also opposed to Home Rule, although despite this they had chosen to remain within the Liberal Party. If Asquith had declared neutrality, they would have acted; the Government would have fallen; the Conservatives would have returned to office. The UK would no doubt have been drawn into the war in any event. Asquith would suffer personally from the declaration of war. In 1916 he would lose his elder son, Raymond, a barrister; one of many brilliant young men lost on the Somme. Asquith never recovered from this blow. But, unlike most of his friends, Raymond had at least had time to procreate: in 1928 his twelve-year-old son would inherit from his grandfather the title of Earl of Oxford and Asquith.

Prime Ministers and other leaders who start wars tend not to finish them. Asquith, who had been a successful peacetime Prime Minister, an urbane and skilled negotiator, conciliator and fixer, was out of his depth as a war leader. He had no military experience. His wartime premiership of 1914-16 was characterised by muddle and delay, with Asquith himself becoming exhausted, depressed (especially after Raymond's death) and unable to cope. Conscription, introduced (to Great Britain only, not Ireland) in January 1916, bitterly divided the Liberal Party. It was becoming clear that Asquith would fall, although in the event he managed to hang on as Prime Minister until December 1916. In 1915 the "shell crisis" when the Artillery had seemed about to run out of ammunition – the high rate of fire lasting over a long period of time had not been anticipated and the stock of shells became depleted – and the failure of the Gallipoli expedition had forced him to invite the Conservatives to form a wartime coalition. They had accepted, but imposed conditions. These included the sacking of the renegade Tory Churchill, who as First Lord of the Admiralty was also the scapegoat for Gallipoli, and making concessions to the Ulster Unionists. Probably to Asquith's relief, Churchill departed for the Western Front, where he would serve as an Infantry officer for the next two years.

Now, however, Asquith had to accept the Ulster Unionists' leader, Sir Edward Carson KC, another dangerous and charismatic man, as his Attorney-General. Carson soon resigned on a point of principle and went into Opposition. In December 1916 Lloyd George, now Secretary of State for War, led a "palace coup" and, with the support of the Conservatives, ousted Asquith as Prime Minister. Asquith, who was still the Leader of the Liberal Party, went into Opposition and Sir Edward Carson returned to Government as First Lord of the Admiralty. The Liberal Party now split between the majority Opposition Asquithians and the coalition Lloyd George Liberals. The effect of the 1915 coalition, followed and accentuated by Asquith's fall, was that the opponents of Irish Home Rule now became the Government. It seemed increasingly likely that Irish Home Rule would be kicked into the long grass, to remain there indefinitely. (That is precisely what happened to the Scottish Home Rule Bill.) Irish Nationalists, inside and outside Parliament, viewed these developments with mounting concern.

It was against this evolving background that the 1916 Dublin Easter Rising took place. Seven members of the Military Council of the Irish Republican Brotherhood (IRB), a secret society, organised it. It began on Easter Monday, 24 April 1916. The rebels had received weaponry and other support from Germany, coordinated in the USA. Although it only lasted for six days, it was to be politically the most significant rebellion since 1798; at least in retrospect. Members of the minority Republican Irish Volunteers, led by Patrick Pearse, joined by the small Irish Citizen Army, led by James Connolly, and 200 members of the Cumann na mBan (a Republican women's paramilitary organisation), seized key locations in Dublin and declared an independent Irish Republic. There were a few minor sympathetic actions and demonstrations elsewhere in Ireland. The British Army quickly suppressed the Rising and Pearse surrendered unconditionally on 29 April. Most of the soldiers who did the suppressing were themselves Irish, including men of the Connaught Rangers. They showed little sympathy for the rebels.

The Rising had ended in fiasco. Other supporters, including Sir Roger Casement, had already been captured. Casement had been arrested days earlier on 21 April, hours after landing from a German submarine on the Kerry coast. Rather imprudently, he was wearing German Army uniform. The Royal Navy captured a shipment of German arms and ammunition that he had arranged to be landed on the same day. Due to navigational error it had failed to appear at its agreed rendezvous point. British intelligence had intercepted messages between the insurrectionists and the German Consulate-General in New York; the British authorities were expecting its arrival.

Contrary to Republican legend, initially there was little support for the rebels in Ireland. Patrick Pearse had made a serious error of judgement. There was no conscription in Ireland. The young Irishmen who had volunteered to fight in the Great War had done so willingly. Far from rising in support, Irish soldiers who were home on leave had reported to the nearest Regimental depot (in the case of Dublin, that of the Royal Dublin Fusiliers) to offer their services to help to suppress the Rising. They were not about to change sides. John Redmond and his moderate Home Rule movement still enjoyed far greater support than Pearse. Pearse, a fanatical promoter of the Irish language and Gaelic culture, was regarded in anglicised, Anglophone Dublin as wildly eccentric. The destruction of Dublin's main Post Office during the Rising was a major inconvenience and the destruction of other parts of the city was shocking to Dubliners. Many people in Dublin relied on the British Government and commercial firms for work. Many Dubliners had family members at the front and were outraged when they learned of the German support for the Rising. They turned out to insult and throw rubbish at the rebels as they were marched to prison.

At a time when moderation and leniency would have been prudent, Asquith reacted with something close to panic. His Government's extreme response to the Rising helped to turn Pearse, Connolly and their followers from oddball public nuisances into haloed martyrs. Pearse and the other leaders of the Rising were tried by court-martial, although they were technically civilians, holding no rank in any recognised army. Most of them were executed. This was a departure from previous British practice. Other rebels or potential rebels, e.g. the Maharajah Duleep Singh, King Kabarega of Bunyoro, King Prempeh of Ashanti or the Boer leaders of the Anglo-Boer War (1899-1902), had been deported for lengthy periods to cool their heels in places of exile like the Seychelles, Ceylon (Sri Lanka) or St Helena; or even in Great Britain itself. In the event Pearse, his brother William and fourteen others died by firing squad. General Sir John Maxwell, commanding the British forces in Ireland, sent a telegram to Asquith, advising him not to return the bodies of the Pearse brothers to their family, prophesying that "Irish sentimentality will turn these graves into martyrs' shrines to which annual processions will be made, which would cause constant irritation in this country". They became martyrs anyway. The fate of Pearse and his colleagues only became public knowledge after they had been executed and their bodies thrown into a pit in the prison yard without a coffin or a burial service. Many Irish Catholics found this extremely shocking. This was more or less what would happen to Robert Nairac's body sixty-one years later, and it provoked a similar reaction with many people. As with Nairac, it was in death that Patrick Pearse found real fame.

Sir Roger Casement received no mercy, either. He was tried for treason and executed in London the following year. Casement, as a former member of the Consular Service, had held the King's Commission. He had worked tirelessly to expose the human rights abuses of the rubber trade in the Belgian Congo and South America, which had won him a knighthood. He had also, however, defected to Germany in 1914; had tried unsuccessfully to recruit an insurgent force from among Irish prisoners of war in Germany and had reappeared on Irish soil in a German uniform. His body was thrown into a pit of quicklime in the prison yard after execution. He, too, became a martyr. Like the Pearse brothers, he now lies in Glasnevin Cemetery in Dublin.

Another leader of the Rising was not shot. This was Eamon de Valera. He was condemned to death by court martial, but saved by the fact that he was arguably a US citizen. The US Consulate in Dublin made representations before his trial, to the effect of: how would the United States react to the execution of one of its citizens? At that point Great Britain was trying to bring the USA into the war in Europe. When General Maxwell reviewed his case he said, "Who is he? I haven't heard of him before." On being told that de Valera was unimportant and had no known Fenian connection, he commuted the court-martial's death sentence to life imprisonment. De Valera, now the President of Sinn Fein, would soon escape from Lincoln Jail and would continue to cause trouble.

Thanks to the Easter Rising, the British Government had reluctantly to focus on Ireland again, and did so in July 1916. For discussion was a modified version of the Heads of Agreement of 1914 entitled "Headings of a Settlement as to the Government of Ireland." On 19 July 1916 the Ulster Unionists forced two amendments: the permanent exclusion of the six Protestant counties from Home Rule, and a reduction of Ireland's representation in the Commons. This represented a dilution of the Government of Ireland Act 1914. On 22 July 1916

Lloyd George informed Redmond, who was still Leader of the Irish Parliamentary Party. Redmond accused the Government of treachery. The Government bowed to the combined opposition of the Unionists and the Irish Parliamentary Party. On 27 July the Heads of Agreement scheme finally collapsed. This development helped to discredit Redmond and the moderates in the eyes of many Nationalists and left him personally demoralised. Asquith, by chopping, changing and vacillating, had cut the ground from beneath the moderate Home Rule men and infuriated the moderate Ulster Unionists.

Home Rule was debated at length in the Commons on 31 July. The Irish Nationalists and their supporters continued to demand that the Government of Ireland Act 1914 should be implemented in its entirety and called for senior officials in Dublin to be replaced by Home Rule supporters. Unionists countered that if the Act were to be implemented during the war, the six Ulster counties should be excluded and must not be forcibly incorporated in any devolved Irish settlement: Irish unity should only come about with their consent. Asquith wrote to Redmond on 28 July, "I think it is of great importance (if possible) to keep the *negotiating* spirit alive". But the breakdown of negotiations was now a distinct possibility, leaving the way open for the extremists to take the lead.

The apparently endless war in Europe; the heavy losses on the Somme of the two Irish Divisions; the threat of extending conscription to Ireland; and hardening attitudes in the British Government all combined to drive Irish people into the arms of Republican and Unionist extremists. On 18 October John Redmond introduced a motion in the Commons that 'the system of government at present maintained in Ireland is inconsistent with the principles for which the Allies are fighting in Europe, and has been mainly responsible for the recent unhappy events and the present state of feeling in the country'. It was defeated by 303 to 106 votes. Joseph Devlin, the moderate Ulster Unionist Leader, pleaded for Irishmen to "come together to seek agreement on resolving outstanding difficulties, which will receive the sanction of the Irish people." This plea for a conference was to lead to the later Irish Convention. It would be the moderates' last chance. After very lengthy consideration, Prime Minister Lloyd George agreed the following year. In May 1917 he wrote to Redmond that "Ireland should try her hand at hammering out an instrument of government for her own people."

The Irish Convention was announced in June 1917 and would be composed of representative Irishmen from different political parties and spheres of interest. It would sit in Regent House, part of Trinity College. It was a large and unwieldy assembly. Fifty-two delegates represented national interest-groups, including the churches. Thirty-two delegates were chairmen of county councils; eight were chairmen of urban district councils. The majority of the political delegates were connected either with the Irish Parliamentary Party or the Ulster Unionists. There were Southern Unionists and Ulster Unionists, who differed on some important issues. Sinn Fein, the main Republican Party, declined any involvement. It concentrated meanwhile on consolidating its hold on the Irish electorate, by various means. The All for Ireland Party, the Dublin Trades Council, The Cork Trade and Labour Council, the Gaelic and National League also refused to attend. The Convention sat in Dublin from July 1917 to March 1918 and addressed the challenges implicit in the imminent Entry into Force of the Government of Ireland Act of 1914. Its mandate was also to debate the wider future and to come to an understanding on recommendations as to the best way in which to implement the Act.

The Convention duly reported in March 1918. This report might have formed the basis of a future settlement but Lloyd George dealt it a fatal blow. Given the urgent need for men on the Western Front occasioned by Ludendorff's offensive, the British Government decided to introduce both Home Rule and conscription to Ireland simultaneously in the very near future, irrespective of the recommendations of the Convention. Again, this was an ill-considered panic decision, comparable to the decision to shoot the leaders of the Easter Rising. This "dual policy" was a mistake and was guaranteed to infuriate the spectrum of Irish opinion, from Republican to diehard Ulster Unionist. Until December 1917 Redmond had used his influence in support of a plan which had been put forward by the Southern Unionist leader, Lord Midleton. It proposed All-Ireland Home Rule with partial fiscal autonomy. All sides, including most Ulster delegates, seemed to be moving towards agreement. But Redmond was now a spent force. Already ill, he had been beaten up by a crowd of Sinn Féin supporters on his way to the Convention. On 15 January, when he intended to move a motion on his proposal to have the Midleton plan agreed, some Nationalist colleagues expressed doubts. Rather than split the Nationalist side he withdrew his motion. The opportunity had been lost. His last move was to support Bishop O'Brien's policy of accommodating Unionist opposition in the North and in the South.

On 6 March 1918 John Redmond died. He was interred, not in Glasnevin Cemetery, but in his family vault in the former Knights Templar churchyard in Wexford. With him died any realistic hope of a peaceful, negotiated settlement in Ireland. Ireland's future would not now be decided by reasoned debate and vote; certainly not on the floor of the House of Commons, but by emotion and firearms. Revolutions across Europe and the fall, or imminent fall, of great imperial and royal dynasties had emboldened the Irish revolutionaries.

The British Government, in particular Asquith and Lloyd George, had handled Ireland very badly. The combination of the knee-jerk shooting of the leaders of the 1916 Easter Rising and the 1918 Conscription Crisis would help to deliver the next election to the extreme Nationalists. Nor would the British cease from making further mistakes over the next three years. In December 1918 a long-delayed general election took place across the UK and Ireland. A Republican campaign of intimidation was already working. Republican Sinn Fein candidates won 73 out of 105 Irish seats on an independence platform. That looked like a strong mandate. Look again: in 25 of these seats the Sinn Fein candidate had been returned unopposed. Potential rival candidates had been scared off by threats and violence. Instead of taking their seats at Westminster, the new Sinn Fein MPs met in the Mansion House in Dublin on 21 January 1919; constituted themselves the Dail Eireann (*Note 4*), an Irish Parliament; and declared an independent "Irish Republic," with the Republican Irish Volunteers, soon to become the IRA, designated as its national army. It was an act of breathtaking audacity and without any legal foundation. A few streets away, the Lord Lieutenant, Lord Wimborne, still occupied his office in Dublin Castle. No State would accord diplomatic recognition to the "Republic," despite de Valera's energetic lobbying in Washington and the representations of influential Irish-Americans at the Paris Peace Conference in 1918-19. On the same day the Irish War of Independence began with the Soloheadbeg Ambush. Two Royal Irish Constabulary officers defending a cargo of gelignite were the first victims of the war. On 12 September the British Government would finally outlaw the Dail. On 19 September Michael Collins would found "The Squad", an IRA counter-intelligence and assassination unit. On 4 November the British Government proposed a new way forward, creating two Home Rule parliaments – one in Dublin and one in Belfast – with an umbrella organisation, the Council of Ireland, to provide a context for further reunification talks.

In mainland Great Britain the election had produced a different outcome. The Conservatives and Lloyd George Liberals had agreed to keep the wartime coalition in being and to retain Lloyd George as Leader. The Coalition won by a substantial majority. Asquith remained in opposition, leading the Asquithian Liberals – in other words, Britain still had a Unionist Government, which was willing to make some concessions to Home Rule but which had just had its mandate firmly renewed by the electorate, while in Ireland Sinn Fein was trying to assert independence unilaterally. On 31 January 1919 an editorial of *An t-Óglach*, a publication of the Irish Volunteers, stated that the formation of the Dáil Éireann "justifies Irish Volunteers in treating the armed forces of the enemy (i.e. Great Britain) – whether soldiers or policemen – exactly as a National Army would treat the members of an invading army." Fifty years later, in 1969, that would still be the IRA's position with regard to the British Army in Ulster, and the RUC.

The Irish War of Independence, also known as the Anglo-Irish War, lasted from 1919 to 1921. It broke out in January 1919, although seven months later a victory parade in Dublin on 19 July still attracted a lot of support. There were 20,000 in the parade, including 5,000 demobbed soldiers and sailors. Among those taking part were the Irish Guards Pipes and Drums; General Pagan, GOC, and Staff; a Detachment of the Royal Dublin Fusiliers; the Royal College of Surgeons in Ireland OTC and Trinity College OTC. While it would have been reasonable for the Irish of whatever persuasion to welcome their boys back from the trenches, the majority of servicemen taking part in the parade were in fact from English and Scottish Regiments, the Royal Navy, the Royal Marines and the newly-founded RAF. Nevertheless thousands of Irish men, women and children would flood the streets of the city in a show of support for the British Armed Forces, cheering and waving Union Flags. It was very much like all the other victory parades being held across the United Kingdom in 1918 and 1919. At times it was quite hard to work out what the Irish really wanted.

Detailed accounts of the Anglo-Irish War are available. The most important point is that both sides committed atrocities; the war left a residue of bitterness that even now can poison Anglo-Irish relations. The memories of 1919-21 are never far below the surface in Ireland. It was a guerrilla war that was also a civil war (since many Irish fought on the British Government side) and, like all civil wars, it was bound to be nasty. At the start of the war the IRA was concentrating its fire mainly on the Royal Irish Constabulary (RIC), whose members were all Irish. These men were now perceived as collaborators with the British. However the Army suffered too. In Michael Collins the IRA had a guerrilla leader approaching genius. His enormous personal charm was matched by his homicidal ruthlessness.

On 7 September 1919 an unofficial and unsanctioned reprisal took place in Fermoy, County Cork. Two hundred British soldiers looted and burned several commercial buildings in the town after 23 IRA Cork volunteers, under the leadership of Liam Lynch, had attacked members of the King's Own Shropshire Light Infantry on their way to a service at the Wesleyan Church. Four soldiers were wounded; one fatally. Fifteen rifles were captured. Lynch was also wounded and taken to a safe house.

1920 got off to a bad start. On 2 January IRA volunteers of the First Cork Brigade captured Carrigtwohill RIC barracks. On 17 January the IRA attacked Ardmore RIC barracks. On 20 January RIC Constable Luke Finnegan was shot dead in County Tipperary and RIC men attacked property belonging to Sinn Fein members. On 21 January RIC District Inspector Redmond of "G" Division DMP was killed by Michael Collins' The Squad. And so the gruesome litany of murder and reprisal continued. It was clear that the Royal Irish Constabulary would need reinforcement. Winston Churchill's answer was the Black and Tans. Churchill was back in Government as Secretary of State for War after an absence at the front as Lieutenant Colonel of a Scottish battalion. As such, he was a staunch interventionist.

The Black and Tans, officially the Royal Irish Constabulary Reserve Force, a paramilitary force, were mainly recruited in Great Britain, starting in late 1919. They started arriving in Ireland in March 1920. Most members were English or Scots, although there were Irish members. Many of them were war veterans. Their role was to help the RIC to maintain order and to fight the IRA. The nickname "Black and Tans" arose from the colour of the improvised uniforms they initially wore, combining Army khaki with black police caps and belts. Most

Black and Tans were former British Army "other ranks." They should not be confused, but frequently are, with the Auxiliary Division (the "Auxies"), which was a counter-insurgency unit of the RIC made up mainly of former officers. Temporary Constables were paid the relatively good wage of ten shillings a day, plus full board and lodging. With minimal police training, their main role was to defend RIC police posts, where they functioned as sentries, guards, escorts for government agents, reinforcement to the regular police, and crowd control officers and mounted a determined counter-insurgency campaign. They and the Auxies became known as "Tudor's Toughs" after the police commander, Major General Sir Henry Tudor. They were viewed by Republicans as an army of occupation because of these duties. They soon gained a reputation for brutality and, as the RIC campaign against IRA and Sinn Féin members was stepped up, police reprisals for IRA attacks were often condoned by the Government.

In January 1921 the British Labour Commission produced a report on the situation in Ireland which was highly critical of the Government's security policy. It said that the Government, in forming the Black and Tans, had "liberated forces which it is not at present able to dominate". Since 29 December 1920, the British Government had sanctioned "official reprisals" in Ireland. This usually meant burning down the property of IRA men and their suspected sympathisers. Together with an increased emphasis on discipline in the RIC, this helped to curb the random reprisals that the Black and Tans had been committing since March 1920 for the remainder of the war, if only because the reprisals were now directed from above, rather than being the result of a spontaneous desire for revenge. In reality many of the acts popularly attributed to the Black and Tans may have been committed by the Auxiliary Division; some were committed by Irish regular RIC men. Tomas Mac Curtain, the Mayor of Cork, was assassinated in March 1920 by local RIC men and – contrary to the legend – the shooting dead of 13 civilians at Croke Park, Dublin on the original Bloody Sunday of 21 November 1920 was also carried out by the regular RIC, although a small detachment of Auxiliaries was also present. But most Republicans did not make a distinction, and "Black and Tans" is still often used as a catch-all term for all Police and Army groups. The actions of the Black and Tans alienated public opinion in both Ireland and Great Britain. Their violent tactics encouraged the Irish public to increase their covert support of the IRA, while the British public pressed for a move towards a peaceful resolution. Edward Wood MP, later known as the Foreign Secretary Lord Halifax, rejected force and urged the British Government to make an offer to the Irish "conceived on the most generous lines."

Due to the ferocity of the Black and Tans' behaviour in Ireland, feelings continue to run high regarding their actions. "Black and Tan" or "Tan" remains a pejorative term for the British in Ireland. Their mention can still excite extreme reactions. The Irish War of Independence is sometimes referred to as the "Tan War" or "Black-and-Tan War." This term was preferred by those who fought on the anti-Treaty side in the Irish Civil War and is still used by Republicans today. The "Cogadh na Saoirse" medal, awarded since 1941 by the Irish Government to IRA veterans of the War of Independence, bears a ribbon with two vertical stripes in black and tan.

The Black and Tans were not the only out-of-control militia. So equally were the IRA. During the Anglo-Irish War and the Irish Civil War that followed in 1921-22, in many parts of Ireland it was open season on Protestants and other people, including Catholics, who were perceived as belonging to the ascendancy or connected, however vaguely or long ago, with the Government. Historic and beautiful houses – now belatedly recognised as part of Ireland's architectural heritage – were burned down. The IRA and their supporters attacked indiscriminately: they often attacked native Irish people and supporters of Home Rule. Both Lady Gregory and Mrs W B Yeats were threatened in their own houses. Yet Lady Gregory had been a leader of the Irish Renaissance of the late nineteenth and early twentieth centuries. She was an Irish literary heroine. Mrs Yeats, who was English by birth, was the wife of Ireland's foremost poet. Her husband, William Butler Yeats, would later become a Senator of the Irish Free State and win the Nobel Prize for Literature. George Moore, an influential Irish Catholic author, dramatist and critic, who had been arguing the case for Home Rule in London drawing-rooms for decades, was shocked and incredulous at the news that his family home, Moore Park in County Mayo, had been burned down. The Knight of Glin, one of Ireland's three hereditary Knights, was confronted by a mob of IRA supporters who demanded that he "get out back to England" while they burned down Glin Castle. He responded that, as a scion of the ancient Fitzgerald clan and a Gaelic speaker, he had no home but Ireland. The mob departed and Glin Castle is still standing but others were less fortunate. The McKinley family, likewise native Irish, but who had become gentrified, were notified that the IRA intended to burn down their home, the House of Cashel, in forty-eight hours' time – it was their decision whether they would be inside it. Prudently they packed what they could, fled to Dublin and then to England. The House of Cashel was duly burned down. IRA volunteers dragged Sir Arthur Vicars from his bed and shot him outside his house in front of his horrified wife, leaving a placard round his neck denouncing him as an "informer." They then burned down Vicars' home, Kilmorna House. Sir Arthur's real "crime" seems to have been that he had formerly served as Ulster King of Arms, the senior Irish Herald. Other IRA volunteers assassinated Field Marshal Sir Henry Wilson MP, a great Anglo-Irish soldier and former Chief of the Imperial General Staff, in London. At the time he had been acting as a security adviser to the Northern Ireland Government. There were numerous similar assassinations. A typical contemporary record for two days shows:

"An officer murdered leaving his hotel in Dublin, a bomb explosion in Amiens Street, a military lorry seized, a retired officer shot in County Cork, rioting in

Belfast, a Royal Irish Constabulary patrol ambushed and one man killed, an armoured car attacked, an attempt to derail a train, a raid by rebels on a farmer's house in Monaghan, a telephone office burnt and one man killed in Killiney."

And so it continued. The Anglo-Irish Treaty, agreed, signed and ratified in 1921 was likely to please no-one. For this reason Eamon de Valera, now the President of the Dail Eireann, future Prime Minister and President of Ireland, insisted that his chief rival, Michael Collins, who was then the head of the Irish Provisional Government, should head the Irish delegation to the Treaty negotiations in 1921. Collins would be the scapegoat if the die-hard Republicans did not like the outcome, which they did not. The Secretary of State for the Colonies, who was now, following a Cabinet reshuffle, Winston Churchill, also dealt with the Dominions: the Irish Free State was to become a Dominion, like Canada or Australia. In London to negotiate with Churchill and his Colonial Office team, Michael Collins found that one of his interlocutors was Lawrence of Arabia; another of Nairac's future military heroes. Lawrence was then a Colonial Office official, although hating the job and already contemplating re-enlistment. Collins and Lawrence evidently got on very well. In his biography of Collins, Tim Pat Coogan has suggested that Collins may have invited Lawrence to become head of military training for the new Irish Army. He also suggests that Churchill accelerated Lawrence's passage into the RAF in order to prevent any such appointment. This might be true. Lawrence was aware of, and proud of, his Irish heritage, although he never set foot in Ireland.

The outcome was that most of Ireland would become independent as a Dominion within the British Empire; the Irish Free State, retaining the monarchy, which would be represented by an Irish Governor-General. Northern Ireland would be separate, with its own subordinate legislature, and would be represented by MPs at Westminster. The Crown would be represented there by a Governor. The Governor of Northern Ireland and Governor-General of the Irish Free State would take the place of the Lord Lieutenant, whose functions would be terminated. The Prime Ministers of the two Governments would take over from the Chief Secretary, whose post would likewise be abolished. This was essentially the deal that the British Government had offered in 1919. It included the proposed umbrella organisation, the Council of Ireland, to which the Free State and Northern Ireland would both nominate MPs as members and which, it was hoped, would evolve into an all-Ireland Parliament, leading to reunification. The Council was duly established on the "Appointed Day", 3 May 1921, but it never met: it was dead in the water. The Free State increasingly claimed to legislate for the whole of Ireland. Northern Ireland did not trust the Free State. They could not work together. The final straw was the 1937 Constitution, of which Article 2 asserted that "the whole island of Ireland, its islands and the territorial seas" formed a single "national territory", while Article 3 asserted that the Oireachtas (the Irish Parliament) had a right "to exercise jurisdiction over the whole of that territory". These articles offended Unionists, who considered them an illegal extraterritorial claim to Northern Ireland. The trust between Belfast and London was also strained. From now on the Unionists' loyalty would always be conditional. The relationship might be easier when the Conservatives were in power, but they would never forget the occasions when British Liberals – of all varieties – had so nearly sold them down the river.

It is easy but unhistorical to demonise the Northern Irish Loyalists. Roman Catholic though he may have been, Robert Nairac never made that mistake, but the British Left habitually has, as Peter Hitchens puts it, "dismissed [our] Unionist cousins as concrete-headed fanatics who wore bowler hats and banged big drums". For the Left they have become totemic hate-objects, like General Pinochet, the white Rhodesians and the white South Africans. This was exemplified by the public displays of contempt and discourtesy with which Marjorie Mowlam (Labour Secretary of State for Northern Ireland 1997-99) would treat her Ulster Protestant staff, while clearly deriving a frisson from her cosy chats with IRA terrorists. Mowlam is now dead but this attitude still informs Labour thinking.

There is another factor, of which Robert Nairac was aware, but which tends to be forgotten by British and other people with only a superficial knowledge of Irish history. Before the First World War not all Protestant Ulstermen had been Unionists. There had been a vigorous, albeit definitely a minority, Ulster Protestant Irish Nationalist movement, which had supported Home Rule. Partition had left the Ulster Protestant Nationalists with nowhere to go. They soon came to dislike the Free State as much as the Unionists and for the same reasons as the disillusioned Dublin-based Irish Nationalists of the revolutionary generation like Hanna Sheehy Skeffington. The smug, stiflingly conformist, anti-intellectual, priest-ridden and very boring culture of the post-1922 Irish Free State was not the society for which they had struggled. The Ulster Home Rulers now merged with the Ulster Unionists and influenced their thinking. Their message was: "We must have Home Rule in Ulster; Westminster's role here must always be strictly limited; and in the last analysis we must decide our own future." British Governments disregard this other Nationalist tradition at their own risk. It is still very much alive.

There are no prizes in politics for being proved right if your predictions are unpopular, politically incorrect or inconvenient: Cassandra comes to mind. So do the Ulster Loyalists. Everything that Sir Edward Carson and his Unionist colleagues had feared and predicted now happened. While the Northern Irish Protestants looked on, the newly-emancipated citizens of the Irish Free State plunged excitedly into a civil war between the pragmatists who accepted Dominion status and Partition and the die-hard Republicans, led by Erskine Childers, who would agree to neither. Before the ink on the 1921 Anglo-Irish Treaty was dry they had flown at each other's throats. The IRA too was split, with the pro-Free State faction becoming the new Irish Army, while the opposition continued as the IRA, at war with both the Belfast and the Dublin Governments and recognising neither. The two Irish volunteer armies now fought each other. As T E Lawrence had predicted, and as Eamon de Valera probably hoped, Michael Collins was ambushed and murdered on 24 August 1922 for his part in negotiating the Treaty. By signing it, he had signed his own death-warrant – as he himself recognised, if Lawrence is to be believed. The circumstances of Collins' death have never been fully clarified. He was duly buried in Glasnevin Cemetery where, many years later, Eamon de Valera would join him.

In November 1922 the Free State authorities, having lost patience with him, arrested and tried Erskine Childers. A military court found him guilty of the charge of having a Spanish-made "Destroyer" .32 calibre semi-automatic pistol on his person in violation of the Emergency Powers Resolution. This pistol had been a gift from Michael Collins at a time when the two men had been friends, before Collins became head of the pro-Treaty Provisional Government. Very ironically, it now provided the pretext for Childers' execution. Childers was convicted and sentenced to death on 20 November. While his appeal against the sentence was still pending, he was executed on 24 November by firing squad at the Beggar's Bush Barracks in Dublin. Like King Charles I, Erskine Childers was a deeply flawed individual; in many people's view he was morally responsible for the Irish Civil War. But, like Charles I, he also knew how to die. Nothing in his life became Childers like the leaving of it. He left instructions to his son, Erskine Hamilton Childers, a future President of the Republic of Ireland, to seek out the men who had signed his death warrant and shake them by the hand, to make it clear that there were no hard feelings. On the morning of his execution, he displayed his usual courage and joked with the members of the firing squad. He was buried at the barracks, but in 1923 his remains were removed to Glasnevin Cemetery.

The Irish Civil War and attacks on high-profile members of the former ascendancy like Sir Arthur Vicars and Sir Henry Wilson naturally made British headlines. What did not, except in Ulster, was the systematic intimidation and violence against ordinary middle- and working-class Southern Irish Protestants. They were less newsworthy. After 1922 the Protestant population of the Free State shrank dramatically. Protestants remained numerous in and around Dublin, but elsewhere they dwindled rapidly and whole communities left. Most of them preferred to emigrate to Great Britain or elsewhere in the British Empire. Only about 2,000 of the total relocated to Northern Ireland, but that was enough. The tales that they brought with them, repeated in pubs and other social venues, lost nothing in the telling. One particularly gruesome account concerned the last Black and Tan wounded, who were awaiting evacuation in a Dublin hospital. A mob entered and hacked them to death with meat-cleavers and other makeshift weapons. The Dublin Veterans' Corps (DVC) was part of the Volunteer Training

Corps, the First World War equivalent of the Home Guard. It lost a number of men in the Easter Rising. Despite being unarmed, they were ambushed by the IRB on Mount Street Bridge. Their commander, Frank Browning, who had raised and organised the unit, and several of his men were murdered in the ambush. This murder would be mythologized as a blow for Irish freedom for generations to come.

The verdict in the six Protestant counties was "there but for the grace of God go we", and "that must never, ever happen here". As the Ulster Loyalists had predicted, Home Rule did indeed mean Rome Rule. The Roman Catholic Church was now in effect the established church in the Free State. Whole areas of the Law were turned over to the Church, including status and marriage. The Church now had vast powers to meddle in the lives of citizens and in public policy areas like education. Divorce was removed from the statute book. A form of censorship was introduced. The scintillating pre-war Dublin intellectual life was quickly suffocated. Because so many Protestants had departed, the population was soon more than 90 percent Roman Catholic. The gloating triumphalism of the Catholic clergy did not go unnoticed in Ulster.

The Unionists' disquiet was shared by the revolutionary pre-war Dublin Irish Nationalist generation, which had included many Protestants. They too were unhappy with the outcome. The Free State was not the kind of society that they had hoped for during the Irish renaissance of the late nineteenth and early twentieth centuries. Pre-war Ireland had been culturally diverse, bristling with exuberant personalities and intellectually rich. Not any more: after independence in 1922 one disillusioned former revolutionary, Hanna Sheehy Skeffington, wrote:

"Here we are rapidly becoming a Catholic statelet under Rome's grip – censorship and the like, with a very narrow provincial outlook, plus a self-satisfied smugness. Result of a failure of revolution, really."

Being Roman Catholic was not however a complete protection. Too close an association with the former Government could still lead to murder or ostracism. Irish soldiers returning from the Great War were often the victims of discrimination in jobs and housing. The IRA killed some of them. Soldiers whom the King had decorated for bravery were especially at risk. The same thing happened after World War II, in which once again many Irishmen from the Republic joined the British forces. The exception was the Connaught Rangers. In 1920 men from two Companies of the First Battalion, which was on garrison duty in India, had mutinied; probably as a result of Sinn Féin propaganda smuggled into their forts, although the unedited actions of the Black and Tans were provocative enough. They pulled down the Union Flag; hoisted a Republican Tricolour (presumably smuggled in with the propaganda); tried unsuccessfully to storm the armoury and refused to soldier any more until all British forces had been withdrawn from Ireland. A number of men were sentenced to death, but only one, Private James Daly, was actually executed. He is now the subject of a Republican ballad. Two more men had been killed by loyal troops while trying to storm the armoury. Others died later in prison during a typhoid epidemic. Many individuals in the two mutinous Companies, the entire Third Company of the 1st Battalion and the entire 2nd Battalion, had remained loyal to the Crown. However this detail is now forgotten. The Rangers all became Irish Nationalist heroes and the Free State Dail later voted special pensions for them. James Daly and his fellow-mutineers are now buried in that increasingly overcrowded Irish Valhalla, Glasnevin Cemetery.

From 1921 to 1969 Ireland existed in a kind of stalemate. The Governments of Northern Ireland and the Free State, later the Republic, did not talk to each other. The Abdication Crisis of 1936 gave Prime Minister de Valera the chance to "write the King out of the constitution" in 1937. The Free State became a republic in all but name. It changed its name to Eire. During the Second World War Eire stayed neutral, although many Irishmen from both Northern Ireland and the Republic again fought in the British forces. In the view of General Eisenhower, Ireland's neutrality was tainted by clear sympathy for the Axis powers. He seriously considered invading and occupying the Republic. He had his reasons. Prime Minister de Valera had paid a formal condolence visit to the German Embassy in Dublin after Hitler's death: he made no such gesture to the US Embassy when President Roosevelt died. In April 1949, less than a year after Robert Nairac's birth, Ireland left the Commonwealth and cut all remaining formal ties with the UK. It was now explicitly a republic. The rules of the Commonwealth had been altered so that republics could remain as Member States, but Ireland did not seek readmission. In 1948 Attlee's Government passed the Ireland Act, which entered into force simultaneously with Eire's Republic of Ireland Act in April 1949. It both recognised the Republic and confirmed Northern Ireland's separate status.

The IRA continued in existence, although its role tended to diminish after the end of the Irish Civil War. From time to time it would become active again. It hoped for support from Germany in World War II and seems to have received a little. In 1942 it attempted a bombing "blitz" of Belfast. However both in the Republic and in Northern Ireland the authorities acted firmly to suppress it. After 1948 the IRA began to rebuild itself and began a series of attacks on infrastructure and security installations in Northern Ireland. It also raided Cadet Force and Territorial Army bases in Northern Ireland and Great Britain to obtain rifles and ammunition. However, internment without trial, first introduced in Northern Ireland and then in the Republic, curtailed IRA operations and ultimately broke IRA morale. Eighteen people were killed during the campaign: of these, seven were members of the RUC and eight were IRA volunteers. The campaign was a failure. It flickered out in the late 1950s and ended formally in 1962. Thereafter the IRA seemed to become irrelevant until events in 1968 and 1969 started to favour it. These events took place in Northern Ireland, not the Republic. Meanwhile its leadership became ever more extreme, eccentric and overtly Marxist, which alienated many Catholic Irish Nationalists. From 1956 to

1969 the IRA killed no soldiers and only six RUC officers. Seven IRA men also lost their lives.

The Ulster Unionists were not complacent. They were well-aware that, because the partition of Ireland had been effected on a county basis, there were still significant Catholic and Nationalist communities, resentful of rule from Belfast, incorporated into Northern Ireland against their will. The best-known of these was in South Armagh, but there were also urban communities, like Ardoyne in Belfast and the Bogside in Londonderry. The Catholic population tended to grow over time, not simply because the Catholic birth-rate was higher than the Protestant, but because people came from other parts of Ireland seeking work in Northern Ireland's more dynamic economy. What the Unionists tended to overlook was that these people were by no means all Fenians. To this day the Unionist vote remains higher than the Protestant population would indicate. In the privacy of the balloting booth many Catholics continue to vote for Unionist candidates, although they wisely do not advertise their voting intentions. Never forgetting what had happened to the Protestant population of the Free State after 1921, many Unionists were determined to keep the Catholic and Nationalist population subjugated; if necessary by electoral gerrymandering, discrimination in jobs and housing and threats of violence. This would not be necessary so long as the economy remained buoyant and jobs were plentiful. But that ceased to be the case in the 1960s; unemployment then hit the Catholic population disproportionately. Starting in 1964, the Civil Rights movement, supported initially by some Unionists, was intended to address these grievances in a peaceful way. But once it had been infiltrated by the IRA, the protests became violent and law and order broke down. At that point the British Army became involved, starting in 1969. The first troops to arrive from mainland Great Britain, on 19 August, were from the Prince of Wales's Own Regiment. By 1972 some 20,000 British troops were deployed in Northern Ireland.

The Loyalists had not been idle. In March and April 1966 Republicans had held parades throughout Ireland to mark the fiftieth anniversary of the 1916 Easter Rising. The Loyalists saw this as a wake-up call. They revived the old Ulster Volunteer Force (UVF). On 8 March a group of IRA volunteers planted a bomb that destroyed Nelson's Pillar (*Note 5*), a well-known Dublin monument, which they saw as a relic of British rule. It was the Dublin equivalent of Nelson's Column in London. This was a provocative symbolic gesture, which annoyed many Dubliners, for whom it was a convenient and well-loved landmark. At the time the IRA was weak and not engaged in armed action, but some Loyalists warned that it was about to be revived and that it would soon launch another campaign against Northern Ireland. In this fear they proved to be correct. Loyalists led by the Reverend Ian Paisley founded the Ulster Constitution Defence Committee (UCDC). It set up a paramilitary wing called the Ulster Protestant Volunteers (UPV). Among its aims was to oppose the civil rights movement and to force the resignation of Terence O'Neill, the Northern Irish Prime Minister, whom they perceived as being too conciliatory to the civil rights movement and to the Republic of Ireland. There was considerable overlap in membership between the UCDC/UPV and the UVF. Once again the Irish past was coming back to life and would prove deadly.

Prime Minister O'Neill resigned following an inconclusive regional election in April 1969, having nearly lost his Parliamentary seat to the Reverend Ian Paisley. He left Northern Ireland, retired to the south of England and was later ennobled. James Chichester-Clarke succeeded him, both as Northern Ireland Prime Minister and as Leader of the Unionist Party. Later that year the NI Minister for Home Affairs, Robert Porter, would persuade the UK Home Secretary, James Callaghan, to send in the troops. He also personally authorised the first use of CS gas on rioters in the UK, after having tested it on himself. The stage was now set for confrontation.

The Army did not suddenly appear in Northern Ireland in 1969. There had historically always been a military presence there and it was not controversial; partly because the Army had not been directly involved in enforcing law and order since the early 1920s but also because there was a strong tradition of military service among Ulstermen. Irish Regiments of the British Army like the Inniskillings had their depots in Ulster. There were four Regular Army barracks in Belfast and other garrison towns. Palace Barracks, Belfast, was considered to be the best. Strange as it must now appear, in the 1950s and up to 1969, the Army looked on Northern Ireland as a desirable posting. There were abundant opportunities for sport, including angling, shooting, sailing, hill-walking and golf. The Border was just a line on the map. Trips to Dublin to watch international rugby matches were a normal part of Army off-duty weekends during the season. The natives, from aristocrats to ordinary citizens, seemed friendly and hospitable. Soldiers went out to drink in pubs; some adventurous ones even drank in Republican clubs. Local Northern Irish girls queued to be invited to NAAFI dances. Invitations for officers to private homes – including those with marriageable daughters – and to grand social events were plentiful. Nevertheless, under the smiling surface all was not well. The social round would continue right up to and even beyond 1969, but the days of peace were coming to an end. This period recalls RMS *Titanic*, steaming insouciantly towards disaster with its orchestras playing and the officers and passengers cheerfully dancing the night away. Only a few of them had the slightest idea of what was about to happen.

Northern Ireland was heading for civil conflict. From 1969 the Army's role was to back up the Royal Ulster Constabulary; to help to keep the two sides apart and to protect the Catholic population in urban areas. This was necessary because the Ulster Volunteer Force had been revived with the avowed aim of combating Irish Republicanism. From 1971 it would be eclipsed to some extent by the newly-formed hard-line Ulster Defence Association (UDA). The RUC, which was predominantly Protestant, did not act to protect the Catholic areas as it should have done, while its force of volunteer Special Constables ("the B Specials") was, not without reason, regarded by Catholics as just another Protestant militia. The B Specials were later disbanded and replaced by the mainly part-time Ulster Defence Regiment (UDR), which was subject to military discipline and which Catholics were actively encouraged to join. It was in its turn however penetrated by the UVF and the UDA. Latterly the Regular Army shared minimal information with it. This is one reason why Robert Nairac often used a false identity when liaising with the UDR.

Initially the Catholic community welcomed the arrival of the Army with relief and showed the British soldiers kindness and hospitality. With the exception of certain Scottish infantry Regiments, there is no reason to think that the Army particularly favoured the Protestant Loyalists at the start. As far as they were concerned, it was just another peacekeeping assignment. It should also be remembered that, while about 10% of the population of mainland Great Britain is Roman Catholic, 30% of the Army was at that time Catholic. Many Catholic soldiers, like Nairac, were horrified by the deep hatred that existed between the two communities in Ulster and felt sorry for the Ulster Catholics. The IRA was aghast at this development. This was not supposed to happen! It was not part of their plan that the Catholic population should look to the Army as their natural protectors. From 1970 they started to target the Army and to present themselves as the sole legitimate protectors of places like Ardoyne and the Bogside. The first British soldier to be killed was Gunner Robert Curtis, in 1971. Then three very young Scots soldiers of the Royal Highland Fusiliers, two of whom were brothers, were lured from a bar by girls and murdered by the PIRA while urinating at the roadside. *No*

> Now, with military honours of a kind,
> With his badges, his medals like rainbows,
> His spinning compass, I bury beside him
> Three teenage soldiers, bellies full of
> Bullets and Irish beer, their flies undone.
> (Michael Longley)

Republicans still frequently deface and dishonour the memorial at the site of their murder. The death toll of the Security Forces for 1971 reached 174. Relations steadily deteriorated until Bloody Sunday in 1972. If the Army appeared to swing round to favour the Loyalists, it was due to two factors; unlike the IRA, the UVF and the UDA relatively seldom targeted members of the Security Forces. They normally reserved their fire for Republicans. As mentioned already, in certain Scottish Regiments there was genuine sympathy for the Loyalists, whom they saw as fellow-Scots and fellow-Protestants. This feeling tended to grow, rather than diminish, with time. The Army's preparation for peacekeeping in Ulster was not ideal. Importantly, the Regiments' most recent experience of peacekeeping and low-intensity operations had been in colonial places like Aden, Borneo, Cyprus and Kenya. Northern Ireland was a new ball-game and they took time to adjust. This, from 1976, included the SAS, who were based in Hereford but had always hitherto been deployed outside the UK in places like Oman and Borneo.

The Troubles officially ended in 1998, more than 20 years after Robert Nairac's murder. By that time the total casualties had exceeded 50,000. This figure includes 705 Regular British soldiers killed; 7 Territorial Army soldiers killed; 301 Royal Ulster Constabulary officers killed; 1,936 civilians killed (including some ex-combatants); total dead 3,530; total injured at least 47,541. This butcher's bill puts Republican "grievances" in perspective. In the case of the 712 Regular and Territorial Army victims, only 93 of these killings resulted in a conviction for murder, with another 28 resulting in convictions on lesser offences. This means that for 87% of the killings of British soldiers, the killers have got off scot-free. What this also suggests is that, latterly at least, British politicians' priority was less to protect British soldiers, or to punish their killers, than to conciliate Irish Republicans and to reach a political agreement with them.

In the 38 years of Operation Banner (1969-2007) the British Army killed 301 people. They break down as Republican terrorists 121; Loyalist terrorists 10; Catholic civilians 138; Protestant civilians 20; other civilians 2; friendly fire 10. Republican terrorists killed 2,148 people – seven times as many as the British Army – of whom 162 were themselves Republican terrorists. So the British Army was responsible for only 40% of Republican terrorist deaths, other Republicans being largely responsible for the rest.

Two important factors in Anglo-Irish politics in the nineteenth and early twentieth centuries were the Monarchy and the Army. It took a long time for the Irish to become Republican. They are still immensely proud of their ancient native High Kings. However for much of Irish history the Lord or King of Ireland was the King of England. The affection in which many Irish held the Monarchy may be surprising, but there is plenty of evidence for it. King George IV's triumphal visit to Edinburgh in 1822, choreographed by Sir Walter Scott, is well-known. However George IV had made an equally successful, although less famous, Royal Visit to Dublin in 1821. Other successful and uneventful Royal Visits to Ireland took place in the first half of the nineteenth century. In 1861 Albert Edward, Prince of Wales, the future King Edward VII, was considered to be in so little danger that the Government allowed him to be stationed at the Curragh Army camp near Dublin with his Regiment (later also Nairac's Regiment), the Grenadier Guards. While there, he engaged in an enjoyable and indiscreet love-affair with a pretty Dublin actress, Nellie Clifden. She was his first lover. While it horrified the Queen and the Prince Consort when they found out, the affair seems to have made the Prince of Wales quite popular in Ireland; by favouring an Irish girl he had shown good taste. This lingering affection for the Monarchy was partly a matter of the (correct) Irish perception that the King or Queen was a constitutional monarch who had no direct say in Government policy, so that it was possible to be loyal to the monarch, while cordially detesting the British Government of the day, its Irish policy and the Anglo-Irish ascendancy. This was an important consideration for Irish soldiers serving in the British Army. Fierce loyalty to their Regiment was important to them for the same reason.

There was also a perception that members of the Royal Family were privately sympathetic to Irish grievances and would, had they been allowed to, have done something about them. This was indeed the case with certain members, including Prince Leopold, Alexandra Princess of Wales and her son Prince Albert Victor, the Duke of Clarence (J K Stephen's friend; George V's elder brother who died young and never reigned). So were Princess Louise and her Liberal politician husband the Marquis of Lorne. However Queen Victoria (*Note 6*) was not in this category. As her long reign wore on, her visits to Ireland became rarer. Between 1864 and 1900 she visited Ireland only four times. She preferred Scotland, speaking with pride about her distant Stuart ancestry and almost becoming a Jacobite; an odd position for a member of the House of Hanover. As a Dublin magazine put it in a satirical cartoon, "Her heart's in the Highlands, her heart is not here". Although they had made a number of private, military and official visits before becoming King, Victoria's successors, Edward VII and George V, only visited once each as King, in 1904 and 1911 respectively. Both visits were marked by displays of public enthusiasm, as well as some of dissent.

The reasons for Queen Victoria's preference are clear. She had not forgotten about the close links between the Irish Home Rulers and the English Chartists, whom she regarded as revolutionaries, early in her reign. She had come to believe that most Irish people were feral Fenians, whose supreme ambition was to assassinate her. A number of Irish terrorist incidents in the 1870s, 1880s and 1890s seemed to confirm this view. Yet, had Victoria overcome her misgivings and spent more time in Ireland or, better still, kept a residence there and visited annually, the emotional link with the monarchy might have survived. The private Victoria was quite loveable, her occasional tantrums and rudeness notwithstanding. Ordinary Scots who met her informally at Balmoral found her surprisingly down-to-earth. This favourable impression was shared by those of her Indian subjects who met her. They were impressed by her knowledge of their country, even though she had never visited it, and by her ability to speak (but not to read or write) Urdu, then the Indian *lingua franca*, which she had learned in order to communicate with them. The Irish might have warmed to her too, had they been given the chance. At the very end of her life she seemed to have relented, founding the Irish Guards in 1900 to honour the numerous Irishmen who had fought bravely for Britain in the Anglo-Boer War. Other Irishmen had fought, equally bravely, in the Boer army. She died in 1901.

Queen Victoria was neither stupid nor cowardly. However, unlike Hugh Dormer, she saw no special merit in martyrdom; especially not in a martyrdom whose consequence would be to place her scapegrace son, Albert Edward, Prince of Wales, on the throne one moment earlier than was absolutely necessary. In her own words, referring, as was her habit, to herself in the third person, in 1868:

"The Queen has now reigned nearly thirty years, is forty-eight years old, has lived in troubled times ... she has been shot at three times, once knocked on the head, threatening letters have been received over and over again, and yet we never changed our mode of living or going on..."

Also in 1868, a Fenian sympathiser had shot at and wounded Victoria's second son, Alfred Duke of Edinburgh, in New South Wales. This must have confirmed Victoria's worst suspicions.

On another occasion however she noted in her journal that "[the Queen] ... did not wish to have the kind of security that nervous monarchs throughout Europe insisted upon."

In all, seven physical attacks were made on Victoria. They all took place when she was out for a drive in her open carriage. Only two were by Irishmen, one of whom was judged to be insane and not responsible for his actions. On the last occasion, in 1882, the Queen wrote to her eldest daughter that "it is worth being shot at, just to see how much one is loved." Certainly, each narrow escape saw a temporary diminution in Republican sentiment.

The prolonged and painful divorce between Ireland and Great Britain was acutely felt in the Army. For centuries the British Army and the separate Indian Army had provided careers for Irishmen, both in the ranks and (especially in the case of the Anglo-Irish ascendancy (*Note 7*)) as officers. A third of Wellington's army was Irish. The Iron Duke himself had been born in Dublin and belonged to an Anglo-Irish ascendancy family. Much more recently, during the Second World War, a majority of the British Army's Field Marshals were still of Irish extraction. They included Alanbrooke (born in France, but the youngest child of Sir Victor Brooke, Baronet, of Colebrooke, Co. Fermanagh); Alexander (born in London, but a son of an Irish Peer, the Earl of Caledon, whose seat was in Co. Tyrone); Auchinleck (born in England, but his family were also from Co. Fermanagh); Dill (born in Lurgan, Co. Armagh); Gort (born in London, but a member of the Prendergast Vereker family, an old Anglo-Irish noble family); Templer (born in Ulster and first commissioned in the Royal Irish Fusiliers); and Montgomery (born in England but the family seat was at New Park, near Moville – Magh Bhile in Gaelic – in Co. Donegal).

Although the six Irish Regiments (*Note 8*) that had recruited mainly or exclusively in what was now the Free State were disbanded in 1922, Irishmen from the Free State and the Republic continued to serve in other Regiments like the Inniskilling Fusiliers, which recruited ostensibly only in Northern Ireland, but in fact drew their officers and men from all over Ireland. They are still serving today, in the Royal Irish Regiment and the Irish Guards, as well as in other Regiments and corps that are not explicitly Irish, and in the Royal Navy and the RAF. There are various reasons for this. The modern Irish Army is highly professional. It has high entry standards, but has always been small and has a small annual intake. It is much easier for a young Irishman from the Republic wishing for a military career to join the British Army. Given Ireland's stance of strict neutrality, its Army tends to be mobilised outside Ireland only in support of international peacekeeping and humanitarian relief operations. Aspirant soldiers from the Republic who want to do "proper soldiering", as opposed to being "social workers with guns", tend to opt for the British Army or the French Foreign Legion, where they are also quite numerous.

A further factor is family loyalty. Encountering the former Royal Irish Rangers in the UK in 1973, it was surprising to discover how many of them were from the Republic. The soldiers in question said simply that their fathers or grandfathers had been in the British Army. They would never have considered serving anywhere else. A century after the foundation of the UVF and the IRA, at a Buckingham Palace garden party in 2013, numerous soldiers of the Irish Guards and the Royal Irish Regiment were present, with family members, wearing newly-minted campaign medals from Afghanistan. Again, many of them turned out to be from the Republic. British Governments have not always recognised or requited the loyalty and contribution of their Irish soldiers. Brilliant soldiers though they may be, when cuts have had to be made the axe has fallen disproportionately heavily on the Irish Regiments.

Even after 1922 many of the men of the lost Irish Regiments would fight on. Their war was not yet over. At the moment of their disbandment the Free State was still gripped by civil war: a war in which former British Army soldiers would fight with the Irish National Army against the Anti-Treaty IRA. Following that, many would face rejection by a country that had changed significantly from the one that they had left in 1914. They were discriminated against in employment, housing and much else. Remembrance Day was not officially recognised and those marking it were subjected to abuse and attacks, often led by elected politicians.

Chapter 9 | In the Army Now

Many... have held and still hold the opinion that there is nothing which has less in common with another, and that is so dissimilar, as civilian life is from the military. Whence it is often observed, if anyone designs to avail himself of an enlistment in the army, that he soon changes; not only his clothes, but also his customs, his habits, his voice...
(Niccolo Machiavelli, *The Art of War*)

In the Brigade of Guards no moment is lost; everything is just right and in its place. The years I spent in the Guards taught me... how to manage one's day, how not to waste time, how to plan.
(Gavin Maxwell, author, cousin of David Stirling and former SOE officer)

In 1971 some of Nairac's friends and relations would be surprised when he announced that he had decided to make his career in the Army, especially given that he had shown little serious interest in doing so in the past.

If Nairac had set his sights on the Army from an early age, he would have organised his studies differently; incidentally saving his father a good deal of money. The normal course was to seek the sponsorship of a Regiment, sit the Regular Commissioning Board (RCB) and apply for a university cadetship before leaving school. Having secured a cadetship, a successful candidate would proceed to Mons Officer Cadet School at Aldershot for a two-week concentrated initial training course held in September, before starting at university in October. Alternatively he might negotiate a gap year for work experience, volunteering, travel or adventure and thereafter go to Mons and university. While he was an undergraduate the cadet would be commissioned as a Second Lieutenant. The Army would pay his matriculation and tutorial fees. During his time at university he would receive what in the late 1960s and 1970s was seen by fellow-undergraduates as a princely salary, although in reality it was less than the salary paid to a serving Second Lieutenant. He received a uniform allowance, but nothing else. In return, apart from passing his exams, he would be expected to involve himself actively in his university's Officers' Training Corps (OTC), to obtain the Certificate of Military Training (CMT, the former Cert B) and to pass much of his vacation time either training with his Regiment or doing other military activities. He would continue to be paid at the same rate, although he would receive any appropriate allowances, such as living overseas allowance (LOA) if undertaking an attachment with, for example, the British Army of the Rhine (BAOR). This relieved him of the need to seek vacation employment. After graduation he would undertake further training at Mons Officer Cadet School for six months or, starting in 1972, at the Royal Military Academy (RMA) Sandhurst for five months, join his corps or

Regiment and then serve in the Army for a minimum of three years. But that is not what happened in Nairac's case.

In 1966, when Nairac left Ampleforth, the Army was no longer fashionable as a career and he does not seem to have given it any serious consideration. An examination of his Leaving Report confirms this. Despite Ampleforth's military tradition, its CCF and Nairac's interest in military history, the Army was not one of the career options mentioned or discussed. Apart from the fact that Nairac was still undecided about what he wanted to do with his life, the reasons are not hard to guess. The Cavalry seems to have held no interest for him. The technical arms, like the Royal Electrical and Mechanical Engineers (REME), might still teach useful, marketable skills, but Nairac was not technologically-minded. As for the Infantry, following the loss of Empire and until August 1969, Army life for a young Infantry soldier, whether officer or other rank, consisted mostly of endless training exercises in armoured personnel carriers (APCs) in Germany and similar activities, mainly on foot, in the UK and, if he was a guardsman, ceremonial public duties in London and elsewhere. With the exception of emergencies like Aden, there was virtually nothing more challenging on the horizon, apart from duty tours in the few remaining dependent territories, including Hong Kong, Brunei and Belize, or in Cyprus with the UN or in one of the British bases; short adventurous training courses in places like Kenya or Canada, or secondments to Commonwealth forces, the Sultan of Oman's or the Abu Dhabi Defence Forces (spoken Arabic required). The most exciting postings were usually reserved for members of the Special Forces.

Probably not coincidentally, in the 1960s there was a sudden rise in the number of young British men without any criminal record and from respectable, even privileged, backgrounds, volunteering for the French Foreign Legion. It is not hard to see why: there was far more chance of action and excitement there. The Legion was more often than not engaged in conflict, usually in Africa. Simon Murray is a good example. In 1960, while Nairac was starting at Ampleforth, he joined the Legion and served for five years in the *deuxieme Regiment étranger de parachutistes* (2e REP), which still contains a good number of young British and Irish men. During his service Murray fought in the Second Algerian War. After rising to senior NCO rank he turned down an offer to undergo officer training and left the Legion in 1965. His military autobiography, *Legionnaire*, makes stimulating reading. Others would join the Rhodesian forces. A small number fought in the US Army in Vietnam. Yet others, having served for a short period in the British Army, would become mercenaries; especially in Africa and the Gulf, reviving an ancient and almost-extinct profession. Nairac however seems not to have considered any of these options.

Retention must have been a major headache for the Army in the 1960s, until in 1969 Northern Ireland changed everything. Suddenly almost everyone wanted to go there. In the early years, operations in Ulster might have been described as low-intensity compared with a "proper" combat environment, but at least it was "training with live ammunition." Northern Ireland, however, grew more challenging and dangerous by the year, as the Army quickly moved from being referee to "piggy-in-the-middle" to being one of the protagonists in a complex civil war, to becoming the main target for the terrorists. In 1970 a total of 15 RUC, civilians and terrorists were killed. There were 213 shooting incidents and 170 bomb incidents. 324 weapons and 0.4 tons of explosives were recovered. The 1971 figures show a sevenfold increase across the board and the totals would escalate in the coming years. Eventually some 700 soldiers would be killed. This was a positive incentive, if you welcomed the challenge and enjoyed living dangerously, as some people like Nairac clearly did. In addition, Nairac's almost obsessive interest in Ireland was never far below the surface. Added to this was the influence of his quietly heroic uncle, Basil Dykes, who had served in the Second World War both as a conventional soldier and undercover and had remained both an "old soldier" and an "old spook" thereafter. It follows that by 1971 the Army plus Northern Ireland would have presented an almost irresistible attraction to Nairac.

Another factor that would be highly influential in Nairac's choice of career was that he increasingly disliked the era in which he was growing to maturity. There were plenty of reasons for this. Consequently Nairac started to look around for a career that would as far as possible insulate him from it. Oxford and Vincent's Club could afford only a temporary refuge. Teaching in a good, traditional private sector boys' school might offer a solution, but for how long? From time to time the Labour Government would threaten on ideological grounds to abolish private education altogether and to impose the comprehensive school system across the UK. In the event this did not happen, although Labour did impose the comprehensive system on most of the grant-aided grammar schools, apart from those that opted out and went independent. An old private bank in the City, like Fleming's or Baring's, the Baltic Exchange or one of the learned professions might have provided a congenial, masculine and club-like environment, but they did not appeal to Nairac's adventurous spirit. Moreover, in most cases they would have required further years of study or vocational training after he had graduated from Oxford.

The Army, especially the older and more traditional Regiments like the Guards, seemed a much more attractive option, offering an atmosphere of security and permanence. The Army was also the most conservative (*Note 1*) of the three Armed Services. At Sandhurst and in the Officers' Mess the standards and etiquette of the Edwardian age still survived. The Infantry was the least technological of the "teeth arms" of the Army. The Guards Division was the most traditional and exclusive part of the Infantry; the Household Regiments were as delightfully out of harmony with the spirit of the age as Vincent's Club.

Why did Nairac choose the Grenadier Guards? Quite simply, for him it had to be either the Coldstream or the Grenadier Guards because they are perceived, at least in England, to be the premier Infantry Regiments in terms of antiquity. (In reality that honour belonged to the Royal Scots: see *Note 2*). These Regiments are normally based at Wellington Barracks in Birdcage Walk when they are stationed in London. They are in personal attendance on the Monarch and take part in State ceremonial. Men who attach high importance to symbols like uniforms, sporting teams, exclusive clubs or being at the right school or university tend to suffer from a slight status or identity anxiety. They need to belong, to be part of the establishment: the more prestigious the organisation, the better. Nairac seemed never to have felt that he had a proper home. He had spent most of his life in institutions: Gilling Castle and Ampleforth in Yorkshire, Lincoln College, Oxford, the RMA Sandhurst and various Army establishments. "For here we have no abiding city", as the author of the Epistle to the Hebrews reminds us. Where did he really belong: Gloucestershire, Northern England, London, Scotland, Ireland or Mauritius? Was he middle- or upper-class? The Army could settle that question decisively; a Regiment can be a good substitute for a home and family. The French Foreign Legion's motto "Legio Patria Nostra" or "The Legion is our Fatherland" applies to other Regiments, too. A good Regiment confers instant status. Being an officer in a Household Regiment like the Grenadier Guards conveys a message about who you are: one of the best, beyond a shadow of doubt.

In 1971 an introduction by someone who had a close personal or family connection with the Regiment was still helpful, even though by that time many illustrious Regiments were proactively seeking good officers, which they had not had to do in the past. It was Julian Malins' father who would in 1971 write on Nairac's behalf to the Grenadier Guards. The Reverend Peter Malins CF (Chaplain to the Forces) had the right connections. He had served in Palestine and Germany with the Grenadier and Coldstream Guards. He had been Chaplain to the Household Division at Wellington Barracks, where the Guards Chapel is situated, from 1951 to 1953. As he was promoted, he took on wider responsibilities. He would end his career as a full Colonel and Assistant Chaplain-General. He was therefore a senior, well-connected Army officer as well as a clergyman; an ideal person to make the introduction.

Because he did not feel able to ask him directly, Nairac asked his friend Julian to approach his father for a recommendation. Julian Malins was happy to oblige. He later said that, "I would not have done so if I had not thought that Robert was capable of it" (i.e. of making a success of the Army). He added that he believed that Nairac's man-management and leadership skills were of a high order and would serve him well up to about the rank of Lieutenant Colonel. He did not think that Nairac had what it took to progress far beyond that: in Malins' view Nairac lacked the breadth of vision, the political antennae and the ruthlessness needed for senior command. He was not devious or cynical enough. He was a good leader of men, which they appreciated. Malins may be right; he knew Nairac very well. Lieutenant Colonel is still a respectable terminal rank. However, some of Nairac's superiors in the Army differed and predicted a rapid rise to more senior rank. They included General Sir Jack Harman, who knew Nairac as a student at Sandhurst while he was serving as Commandant. These senior officers did not suggest that Nairac was a possible future Chief of the General Staff (CGS) or Chief of the Defence Staff (CDS), but they seem to have thought that he could nevertheless advance beyond Lieutenant Colonel. Who can now say whether they were wrong? Could he have eventually become Major General Sir Robert Nairac KCB, Commander of London District? One of his former Commanding Officers believes so, taking the view that he would have been a strong candidate because he was widely-liked and admired. We shall never know what might have happened if Nairac had returned safely from Ireland in 1977. But some well-qualified people evidently thought that he showed considerable promise and was likely to become prominent and well-known within the Army, if not in the wider world. And in Ireland, although not in the UK context, Nairac unquestionably did show political awareness.

A further attraction was that the Army offered, and still offers, the opportunity to engage in a wide spectrum of sport, including boxing and rugby. Serving soldiers who are star players are granted special leave to train for, and play in, important matches: their participation is seen as good publicity for the Army. There is usually at least one soldier in any given England or British and Irish Lions international rugby side; sometimes more than one, and quite frequently in the Scottish and Welsh national rugby teams, too. For some sports, like mountaineering and rock-climbing, which are seen as directly relevant to soldiering, the Army provides the facilities, the equipment and the professional instruction, for which a civilian enthusiast would have to pay large sums. Nairac would take to climbing in the Army. The Army continues to pay for the training and practice of chosen sports. None of this was to be sniffed at. The idea began to form in Nairac's mind that the Army might represent his best option.

In summary, the Army in 1971 offered Nairac almost everything that he could have asked for: the status, the outdoor life, the sport, the variety, the opportunity to teach, train and mentor. Added to that was the start of the Troubles in 1969 and his long-standing interest in, and understanding of, so many aspects of Ireland. What the Army could offer now must have seemed far more attractive than it had when he left Ampleforth in December 1966. By the spring of 1970 both Battalions of the Grenadier Guards had done duty tours in Northern Ireland. There would undoubtedly be further tours to Ulster soon.

On 1 September 1971 Nairac attended an interview with the Grenadiers. He made an excellent impression. Subject to medical and security clearance and his successfully passing the Regular Commissioning Board (RCB), he was offered a university cadetship for his last two terms (the Hilary and Trinity Terms of 1972) at Oxford. Despite his recent traumatic experiences, of which the Army seem to have been completely or largely unaware, he came across as "having strong ideals, confident and polite".

The next step was for Nairac to attend the RCB at Westbury in Wiltshire on 3 November. This was preceded by an intensive one-week military "cramming course" to give candidates the best possible chance of passing, and to ensure that those who had little or no military experience should not be seriously disadvantaged by comparison with those who had. There followed a series of tests, both written and practical, of candidates' leadership and problem-solving skills, and at least one tactical exercise with troops, using men of the long-suffering Training Battalion stationed at the School of Infantry. There was also a series of interviews, including one with the Course Commander, Major General David Lloyd Owen. Nairac passed with flying colours. This was the occasion on which Lloyd Owen wrote the very positive appreciation of Nairac previously quoted in Chapter 1.

Nairac was not quite home and dry. There followed a series of reference verifications and security checks. These probably caused him apprehension, given his LSD experiments at Oxford and other factors. However, nothing adverse came to light. On 23 December 1971 Nairac was taken on strength (TOS) as Second Lieutenant R L Nairac, 2nd Battalion Grenadier Guards. Later the same day he was also TOS by the Oxford University Officers' Training Corps (OTC), to which he would now be seconded until July 1972. He would start part-time military training with the OTC in January. That he joined the OTC is certain, but its records are incomplete; in 2014 they claimed to hold no material on Nairac – not even a photo – so we do not know whether Nairac took a very active role in it. This is strange, given that the OTC had supplied important evidence about Nairac's blood group for use in the trial of Kevin Crilly in 2011; not so very long ago. Evidently a file, presumably a slim one, on Nairac still existed in 2011, but it no longer does or it has gone missing like so much else.

After passing the RCB Nairac started to acquire his Grenadier Guards uniforms, although probably not all at once. For ceremonial Home Service Clothing with scarlet tunic, Nairac would have been fitted at Wellington Barracks and supplied according to whether or not there were second-hand uniforms available for alteration at the time. In the event no suitable second-hand tunic was available; Nairac's, which still exists, was cut for him by Meyer & Mortimer of Sackville Street, London. The Home Service Clothing uniform remained the Regiment's property. Nairac's other uniforms: No 1 (Blue Patrols), No 2 (Khaki Service Dress) and No 10 (Mess Dress) belonged to him. He might have had these uniforms made for him by one of a small number of Regimentally-approved London tailors, including Rogers, John Jones Ltd or Johns and Pegg of Savile Row, or he could have acquired them second-hand and had them altered. Nairac definitely possessed khaki Service Dress while still at Oxford and wore it when he sat Final Schools in the summer of 1972. Regiments tried to keep costs down by re-using second-hand uniforms wherever possible. When an officer left the Regiment he would normally hand in his uniforms for future re-use. (That eventually happened to Nairac's uniforms after his murder, apart from certain selected items, which are preserved as relics in the Guards Museum and at Ampleforth.) Nairac would also have owned suits of Disruptive Pattern (DP) Combat Dress, worn with the khaki Guards beret. Hats came from Lock or Herbert Johnson.

In September 1972 Nairac started the concentrated POSUC (Post-University Cadets Graduates Course) at the Royal Military Academy (RMA), Sandhurst. This course ran for five months to the end of January 1973. This was POSUC No 1; the very first course of its type to be held at Sandhurst. The reason for its introduction was the closure earlier that year of Mons Officer Cadet School and its amalgamation with the RMA. Mons had offered a much shorter course than Sandhurst: six months, as opposed to the two years of Sandhurst's Standard Military Course (SMC), which was intended for school-leavers; non-graduates who were seeking regular commissions. Prior to 1972 Mons had trained all Army graduate entrants and all Short Service Commission officers. It had also offered short courses for Territorial Army officers. Had Nairac graduated even one year earlier, he would have gone to Mons. Now it all happened at Sandhurst.

Nairac's five months at the RMA turned out to be happy ones. He was already familiar with Sandhurst, having boxed there on several occasions. He continued to box. He served in Salamanca Company, based in Victory College, and played in the Sandhurst First Rugby XV. He was awarded Full Colours for his rugby achievements; yet another sporting honour. Sandhurst rugby was then enjoying a renaissance in which Nairac played a part, albeit briefly. The main reason for this was Mons' amalgamation with Sandhurst: there was now a larger and more experienced pool of available players on which the RMA could draw. Graduate rugby players like Nairac, who had already represented their university or college, were now for the first time available and eligible to play in the Sandhurst First XV. According to an article in *The Wish Stream*, the RMA Journal for Spring 1973, their mature experience had "a very settling effect on the younger cadets", while Second Lieutenants Nairac, North and Whitley are described as a "veritable trio of demons" to any opposition, showing tremendous versatility on the pitch. A former brother officer commented that, even in "friendly" intra-Army matches, Nairac projected aggression and a fierce determination to win, which he expected his fellow team-members to share. On the sports field, as well as elsewhere, he often came across as a driven man, hungry for success.

Nairac did not pass out as Best Cadet of his intake, but he was not far behind. He received an above-average assessment from his tutors for academic and military studies and for his personal qualities, of which leadership was pre-eminent. Another young officer, who had been a fellow-student in Salamanca Company, speaking to the BBC's Roisin Macauley in 1978, recalled how Nairac, while at Sandhurst, had taken part in an infantry exercise in which he was given command of a platoon and the objective of taking a hill held by a detachment of Gurkhas. The Gurkhas, who had acted this role before, knew that an attack was most likely to come from a particular direction, which was good country for that purpose. Nairac, having thoroughly reconnoitred the ground, had worked this out for himself. He then chose an unorthodox route, which involved taking his men through very difficult, swampy country, to attack the hill from the direction that the Gurkhas least expected. Nairac and his platoon had to wade waist-deep through the mire. So did the umpires, who were assessing the students. Nairac achieved surprise and successfully took the hill. This independent thinking impressed the mud-covered umpires and reinforced their view that he was a winner.

Finally, it was time to join his Battalion, the 2nd Battalion Grenadier Guards, in early February 1973 (*Note 3*). The Battalion had recently returned from eighteen months' garrison duty in Belize. Nairac's military baptism would follow soon afterwards. The very next month he would be on the streets of Belfast for the first time, with his platoon.

Everyone who knew Nairac both before and after he joined the Army has remarked on how different he became following his five-month POSUC course at Sandhurst. The disorganised undergraduate had gone: in his place was a smart, efficient and motivated Army officer. They seemed like two different people and at twenty-four it appeared that he had finally grown up. One of Nairac's contemporaries has observed that at Oxford he had still been very young – less mature than his true age – and trying out different personalities to work out who he was. Almost everyone does this to a greater or lesser extent. A few very mature young men know exactly who they are early in life, but Nairac was not one of them; he was on a voyage to discover himself. Now, it seemed, he had arrived. Military life suited him; Nairac seemed very content.

Nairac was now in a world where, unlike Oxford, his day would be tightly structured and fully-occupied. His leadership and man-management skills would be used to the full. His physical strength and love of team games would be counted very much to his credit; he would be given every opportunity to practice them and other sports. He was in an all-male environment, which he preferred. He had got his confidence back. A contemporary remarked of Nairac a little later that, "He appeared no more mixed up than rest of us; but I *would* say that as another ex-Amplefordian who joined the Guards – one of many, of course!" In 2013, Malcolm Stewart, another former Guards officer and founder of Kensington Audio Visual (KAV), said: "The Army has given me lots of self-confidence and the discipline to go after what I wanted." Nairac, had he lived to hand his story down, would no doubt have said the same. But, having made it into the Grenadier Guards, after what, exactly, did he want to go next?

Nairac would take a little time to settle into the Grenadiers. Julian Malins has commented that Nairac was certainly not stupid, but that he was a physical person; more of a leader and man-of-action than an intellectual. At Oxford he had been perceived as a hearty. It was therefore slightly ironic that at the start of his military career certain of his brother officers, by no means all of whom would have been graduates, should have regarded Nairac as a closet intellectual and potentially unsound for that reason. Nairac's intelligence was never in question, although the uses to which he put it were sometimes suspect, and he might occasionally have displayed it with what was then perceived as an unbecoming lack of modesty.

Another factor may have been his age. When he joined the Battalion in 1973 he would be twenty-four. That was close to the then upper age limit for acceptance as an Infantry subaltern. His merits, including his high level of physical fitness, evidently outweighed this in the Army's eyes. But some of his fellow subalterns who were not graduates, but had followed the two-year Standard Military Course at Sandhurst after leaving school, were aged nineteen or twenty. They were of the age at which Nairac had gone up to Oxford in 1968, or younger. No doubt they seemed immature and "wet behind the ears" by comparison with Nairac, who was a well-travelled graduate who spoke at least one European language fluently and had a wide, varied and interesting circle of acquaintances. The other subalterns were only human: if you did not like and admire Nairac, you might easily end by envying and disliking him.

In the post-World War II British Army, being openly intellectual, as opposed to simply being astute, efficient or having useful, relevant experience and qualifications, was "not on": particularly not in smart Infantry or Cavalry Regiments. Intellect might be tolerated in the Chaplain; not in anyone else. If one were erudite, one would be wise not make a parade of it, as one would be more difficult to place (*Note 4*).

The perception of Nairac as intellectual seems to have arisen because Ireland was by then an unavoidable topic in military circles and Nairac turned out to know more about Ireland than almost anyone else. He soon acquired the reputation of being a "walking encyclopaedia" on that subject. He was happy to correct his colleagues' numerous misconceptions: for example, that Ulster comprised only the six counties of Northern Ireland. As Nairac was at pains to point out, the historic Kingdom of Ulster had consisted of nine counties. It also included Donegal, Cavan and Monaghan.

What the other officers could not have known was that there was a link between Nairac's fascination and affinity with Ireland, his nervous breakdown at Oxford in 1970-71 and his damaged self-confidence. Ireland was one of Nairac's "special subjects": one on which he was an acknowledged expert. The start of the Troubles in 1969 had rendered his in-depth knowledge of Ireland valuable and the Army valued him for it. Few officers, other than those who had been born and raised in Ireland, could match it. Nairac's fascination with Ireland began long before his 1970-71 nervous breakdown, and therefore well before he decided to join the

Army, but he had latterly developed his expertise on the subject; in part, at least, to restore and maintain his self-confidence. While most people seem to have found Nairac's conversation amusing and even fascinating, it is possible that some of his fellow-subalterns felt that he was talking down to them. In any case few of them would have shared his enthusiasm for the Irish and their culture, although they might have conceded that Ireland was, or had formerly been, a nice place in which to hunt, shoot, fish or go to the races.

In fairness to Nairac, Sir Michael Rose, writing in *The Tablet* in 1999, indicated that an important and practical way in which Nairac had hoped to make a difference in Northern Ireland was by helping to develop among his military colleagues a better awareness and understanding of the complicated origins of the British presence there. This was praiseworthy; such an understanding was often lacking, even among well-educated officers. Nairac was well-qualified, and lost no opportunity to do this. He was from time to time asked to lecture to his colleagues on Ireland, for example at the School of Infantry. Less formally, nothing pleased him more than to spend long hours discussing Irish history.

Nairac continued to read widely in the Army. A former brother officer in the 1st Battalion recalls that Nairac enjoyed Simon Raven's novels and had lent him Raven's first novel series, *Alms for Oblivion*, while they were serving in London in the 1970s. Raven, who died in 2001, was an erudite and stylistically excellent author who admired, and was influenced by, Evelyn Waugh and Anthony Trollope. Nairac's taste for his work is not surprising: Raven had been a regular Army officer before he turned to writing and journalism. Some of his novels (e.g. *Fielding Gray, Sound the Retreat, The Sabre Squadron, The Feathers of Death*) are set in a military context, which is accurately described. Nairac also knew the works of John Buchan. The same officer recalls Nairac and Adam Drummond (now Lord Strange, whose father was a famous falconer and author of books on falconry) having a running bet on which of them would first achieve a "McNab", which involves bagging a stag, a salmon and a grouse all on the same day. This refers to Buchan's light-hearted novel *John McNab*, in which the chief characters set out to accomplish this, while poaching on highland estates belonging to other people and getting away with it.

A less-predictable Nairac literary taste was for the works of Robert Smith Surtees (1805-1864). Although they are now attracting a wider readership, in Nairac's time they still tended be read mainly by equestrians. It is slightly surprising that Nairac should have taken to Surtees because, despite his enthusiasm for country sports, he seems never to have hunted – although some of his friends did – or even to have done much riding. However, the novels vividly recall a period, the early to mid nineteenth century, which Nairac preferred to the era in which he lived. Surtees' characters are memorable: Jorrocks, the sporting cockney grocer, with his unapologetic vulgarity and good-natured cunning, is impossible to dislike. He was a great success with the public, who loved him as much as they did Dickens' Mr Pickwick. Other likeable, scurrilous characters include "Soapey" Sponge and "Facey" Romford. Despite their excellence, Surtees' novels were not fashionable in the 1960s and 1970s; many of them were out of print. Nairac would have had to seek them from second-hand booksellers.

Surtees is addictive and can become a private cult for his readers, who like to banter Surtees in-jokes with each other. Snippets of Surtees ("multum in parvo" for example, which was one of Jorrocks' favourite expressions) peppered Nairac's conversation. David Sewell, a contemporary in the Grenadiers, was a fellow-devotee of Surtees: they would often bandy Surtees expressions and references. The young Siegfried Sassoon and his hunting friends had done exactly the same thing before 1914. So, somewhat earlier, did the young Rudyard Kipling and his schoolfriends. Surtees has a military relevance. Like war, riding to hounds is potentially dangerous. Hunting requires physical courage, which is impossible to fake. Like integrity, this is a supreme and uncommon virtue, which excuses a multitude of sins. As John Jorrocks memorably explained:

"'Unting is all that's worth living for. All time is lost wot is not spent in 'unting. It is like the hair we breathe; if we have it not we die. It's the sport of kings, the image of war without its guilt and only five and twenty per cent of its danger."

"The image of war" is a good description. Mr Jorrocks is talking about that adrenalin-fuelled state of heightened awareness that challenging, dangerous sports and war can deliver and which Nairac enjoyed above anything else.

An Army contemporary has observed that Nairac's devotion to most field sports was probably exceptional in the Guards at that time. A majority of Nairac's Regimental contemporaries, but by no means all, were game shooters to a greater or lesser degree. Even when serving in Northern Ireland they would sometimes manage to fit in a sortie with shotguns in counties Londonderry, Tyrone and Donegal. Nairac did so too. However only a minority of Guards officers were anglers; even fewer were keen on hunting or deerstalking. Very few indeed practiced falconry. Nairac seems to have done everything, apart from hunting.

In the Army Nairac would become a connoisseur of action films. As part of his lighter side, he was proud of his membership of the "Magnificent Seven Club", membership of which required an extremely detailed knowledge of that film.

Another aspect of Nairac that might not have gone down well with some Grenadier subalterns was his keenness and professionalism. At that period and still today, the Guards' public image was of effortless superiority: as Toby Harnden puts it in *Dead Men Risen*, "understated excellence." In the same book he quotes a Regimental Adjutant: "We don't shout about what we do, we just get on with it and people notice that". What the other subalterns might also have sensed instinctively was that Nairac was subtly subversive. Having satisfied one ambition by becoming a Guards officer, he would sooner or later revert and start doing un-officer-like things. These would include volunteering to coach boys in Ardoyne in boxing; general "hearts and minds" outreach work in Belfast, and later, his involvement in intelligence and undercover work that took him increasingly away from his Regiment. And, for all his humour, friendliness and charm, he was a hard man to know; a dark horse. What was he really like and where was he truly coming from? In Old French and Middle English, "charme" meant a magical spell or incantation. It can still have that sinister connotation in the British mind. Charm can be used as a disguise for something else; as a tool or the means to an end. Nairac knew that and understood how to use it, as do many Irishmen, Frenchmen and Italians. Most English and Scots people do not, and tend to be suspicious of it. Despite this, a large number of British people would prove to be susceptible to Nairac's personal brand of charm. What did it consist of? Vitality and enthusiasm are two qualities that his Army friends remember about Nairac. He was clever, funny and dashing. Most importantly, he had an intense love of life and an interest in human beings. Those two characteristics are probably the main ingredients of what Kipling called "it": charm, sex appeal or fascination. They no doubt explain why even casual acquaintances, who met him very briefly, still vividly recall Robert Nairac.

Nairac never took himself too seriously and loved playing practical jokes on those who did. Moreover he could be irreverent, including about things that most Regiments regard as sacred. For example, there was an unedifying incident at the Tower of London when Nairac turned a fire-hose on the unfortunate Commander of the Guard (another junior Grenadier officer), who was taking a leading part in the nightly Ceremony of the Keys. Nairac and some others were the Commander's guests for the ceremony and had got thoroughly drunk, so they remained in the Commander's flat in the White Tower, instead of joining the public downstairs and outside to watch the ceremony. The fire hose was mounted on the wall in the corridor outside the Commander's flat, which was at the back of the building, but the corridor ran from it to the kitchen and the guardsmen's accommodation; this looked out over the square where the Guard was drawn up for the Ceremony of the Keys. The fire hose caught Nairac's attention. It was apparently infinitely extendable and could easily be run along the corridor, through the kitchen or another room, and then directed out of one of the windows overlooking the square. It was then that Nairac had his brilliant idea... A jet of water directed from one of the windows drenched the Commander of the Guard. The outcome is long forgotten, but those present remember Nairac as being highly delighted with his misbehaviour and the resultant notoriety. "I fear that we all behaved appallingly in those days!" added his accomplice. What the members of the public who were watching the ceremony and the Yeomen Warders of Her Majesty's Royal Palace and Fortress the Tower of London (the Beefeaters) said is not recorded, possibly because it was unprintable; some of them must have got splashed. It was an episode worthy of a novel by Evelyn Waugh or Simon Raven. Under the circumstances, it is slightly ironic that Robert Nairac GC has himself posthumously become sacred: one of the tutelary heroes of Ampleforth and of his Regiment. An officer who had known Nairac at Warminster, where he undertook specialist training prior to one of his postings to Northern Ireland, commented that, "I do remember him as being great fun, attractive both intellectually and physically and very good company... He had a well-developed, but also cultivated, degree of unconventionality. It was I believe the cultivated bit that led to his ultimate downfall."

The foregoing, however, were minor teething troubles, or seemed so at the time. What is not in doubt is that Nairac was very good at his job: an excellent Regimental officer. In general he was admired and liked by other soldiers. He was very good at man-management and got on well with *almost* everybody. This is reflected in report after report on his Army file. There are numerous references to his "quick, analytical mind". "His staff work was quick and accurate", reads a 1976 report from the Staff College, Junior Division. The same report continues: "Tactically he was superb. He could always be relied upon for a really sound opinion and the others learned a great deal from him. In summary, an officer of considerable potential who will need careful guidance and encouragement... He was well above average overall".

Elsewhere he is described as: "An able and intelligent officer with a strong and attractive personality and an abundance of commonsense." A report from his time with 3 Brigade in Northern Ireland refers to him as "a determined, intelligent officer who has shown moral and physical courage in his tour with this unit. He has considerable leadership qualities, and his tact and patience in dealing with a wide variety of agencies and HQs has been most marked and has been the subject of favourable comment from both senior military and RUC officers... He writes well and his oral briefings are clear and concise". This represents a distinct improvement on his reports from Oxford, where his written work had often let him down. Obviously the Army's drafting courses, which had formed part of his training, had worked for him.

Amid this series of glowing appraisals, there are however a few criticisms or observations: small straws in the wind that could indicate trouble ahead. The Junior Staff College report mentioned above hints at this with "[Nairac] will need careful guidance and encouragement... he will require demanding appointments to tax his natural ability."

Lieutenant Colonel David Gordon Lennox reflected this in an annual confidential report written in 1976, noting that Nairac found it difficult to accept the routine of peacetime soldiering in England. Gordon Lennox's criticism refers to Nairac's professed distaste for administration, which, he said, had led him in 1975 to turn down the job of Adjutant of the 1st Battalion, for which he had been head-hunted, and to seek other more congenial work: initially training NCOs at Pirbright and then as Recce Platoon Commander for the 1st Battalion.

It is reasonable to infer that an officer who has "difficulty in accepting the more mundane life of soldiering" or "the routine of peacetime soldiering" will probably seek excitement and danger – "demanding appointments to tax his natural ability", in the words of his Staff College (Junior Division) report – in some theatre of unconventional warfare, whether serving on secondment with the aforementioned Sultan of Oman's Armed Forces (SAF), the Abu Dhabi Defence Force or other friendly forces, with the Special Forces or in the kind of undercover work towards which Nairac gravitated in Northern Ireland. Whether this would be a good career move was another matter. Moreover, by getting into special duties or unconventional work, Nairac would be depriving himself of the structure, support and discipline of Regimental life, which he had clearly found helpful and comforting, even though he might have found some of its obligations, for example administration, irksome.

Nairac's NCOs and guardsmen did not share the misgivings about him that a few of his brother officers evidently had. The survivors all speak very highly of him. They probably understood him no better than the officers, but they sensed that under the dashing and nonchalant exterior lay reserves of kindness and loyalty on which they could rely. He would lend a friendly shoulder to cry on if the occasion seemed to require it; they enjoyed his command of bad language; they liked his boxer's broken nose; they loved it when he scored tries at rugby. They admired his physical strength and prowess at sport: he was a proper man's man. One of Nairac's tricks at indoor Mess games was to cross the ante-room without touching the floor with any part of his anatomy. This was more difficult than mere handstands. The only aids permitted were a pair of champagne bottles, which were used like stilts. Nairac would "walk" across the floor bearing his whole weight on his arms and the champagne bottles. This feat requires great upper body strength and faultless balance in order not to come an undignified cropper and few people can accomplish it, even if they are very fit. When Nairac did it, he impressed the NCOs immensely. It may be significant that some of Nairac's best friends were officers who had been promoted from the ranks. In general he got on better with the WOs, NCOs and guardsmen than with commissioned officers; they appreciated his common touch. Very keen on being smartly turned out, they approved of Nairac's personal smartness, even when he was off duty in country clothes. There is a military perception that an officer who sets an example by applying "spit and polish" to himself, as well as demanding it from his men, is usually sound. Nairac not only was "the business"; he looked the business. The only cautious or dissenting note was struck by one or two of the older soldiers, who considered that he was a dangerous man. Why?

"If you're in his platoon, he'll get you killed. He has no fear of anything."

But they respected that, too. Nor was this favourable perception limited to the Grenadier Guards. Patrick Mercer, an officer in another Regiment, commented to the *Daily Mail* long after Nairac's death:

"I... had the chance to see him under fire. A patrol of mine to which he was attached was engaged by a gunman in Crossmaglen a couple of days before

Robert disappeared. Luckily, the rounds missed their mark, but it was as if a madly brave spirit had taken over Robert's body. One minute he was chatting away to one of the local farmers; the next, before the echoes of the shots had died away, he was issuing orders to the troops and charging straight for where he believed the enemy firing point to be, with his automatic shotgun ready to deal with anyone who got in his way. That in itself was remarkable, but even more fascinating was the way the men followed him. Such a powerful influence had he over the soldiers that they followed not just instantly but willingly – they would not have allowed him to go forward by himself. That is a tremendous tribute to any officer, particularly one from another Regiment." Nairac was leadership personified. Another friend, the retired SAS Major Brian Baty, describes him as "a brave man; even a dangerous man, in the right way".

Although he lacked a close connection with the Grenadiers, Nairac already had some friends among the officers and their number grew over time, in both Battalions, as they got more used to him. One close friend and fellow-subaltern was Lord Richard Cecil, a brother of Nairac's Oxford friend Viscount Cranborne. Both he and Nairac would serve as Commander of the Recce Platoon at different times. Cecil was a very similar character to Nairac. Born in the same year, 1948, he would be killed in 1978 in Rhodesia, where he was working as a war correspondent. Richard Cecil liked to accompany Rhodesian army units into action while wearing army uniform and carrying a rifle. His *Times* obituary of 22 April stated that he was "prepared to carry a rifle... and even to use it". He ignored warnings that this was inappropriate and dangerous behaviour for a journalist. Richard Cecil was a member of a twenty-strong group of correspondents known as the "Bang Gang". They were intimately associated with the Rhodesian cause and went about their journalistic work heavily armed. On 20 April Cecil and Nick Downie, a freelance film-maker and former officer in the SAF, landed by helicopter in North-East Rhodesia with an army Fireforce airborne unit. They were recording material for use in a TV documentary they were making about the Bush War. While moving through dense undergrowth Cecil encountered a ZANLA guerrilla fighter who fired at him at close range. He was hit by two bullets, first in the thigh and then in the chest, and died a few minutes later. It was pure Wilbur Smith. Cecil's body was repatriated to England. The Rhodesian Ministry of Defence reported him as having been "killed in action". P K van der Byl, the Rhodesian Foreign Minister, said, on being informed of his death:

"Lord Richard was the finest young man I ever knew and represented the best of everything that made the Englishman great, and built the British Empire."

But the Empire had gone. Richard Cecil and Robert Nairac were two of a kind; born too late into a world grown too old. Van der Byl's eulogy is very reminiscent of the kind of thing that was said and written about Nairac after his murder. Richard Cecil received a memorial service at the Guards Chapel on 9 May, less than a month after Nairac's; many of the same people attended both services. Like Nairac's death, Richard Cecil's had political repercussions. It caused many on the political Right in the UK, including Cecil's own family, to reconsider their support for the breakaway Rhodesian Government and to begin discreetly to urge Prime Minister Ian Smith to seek a negotiated settlement to the Bush War. Richard Cecil's death was a factor – albeit a minor one – in the end of a white-run Rhodesia.

Richard Cecil spent four years in the Grenadier Guards; he was in Northern Ireland, based in Creggan with his brother Valentine, in 1972-73 and with Nairac in Belfast on two duty tours in 1973. After leaving the Army to seek a political career, in July 1974 Cecil was adopted as the Conservative candidate for Barrow-in-Furness and contested the seat in the October 1974 general election. During the election campaign he complained about the restraints being placed on military action in Northern Ireland by politicians. He supported a proposal to make military incursions into the Republic of Ireland in order to track and kill IRA members sheltering there. Barrow is a very Labour area. Predictably, Albert Booth, the incumbent Labour MP, held the seat with a majority of 7,400 votes. However, Richard Cecil did not give up easily and continued to work in Barrow, nursing the Conservative vote. He managed to help reduce Albert Booth's majority to such an extent that the seat eventually went Conservative in 1983, five years after his death. It was a posthumous triumph for Cecil and a testimony to how hard he had worked between 1974 and 1978. Meanwhile he decided to become a freelance journalist while waiting to contest the seat again at the next election. But by the next election, which was held in 1979, following which the Conservatives returned to power led by Margaret Thatcher, he would be dead. It is possible to imagine that Nairac, had he survived Northern Ireland and become bored with garrison life, might have left the Army and progressed to fighting in some Rhodesian unit like the Selous Scouts or, like Cecil, worked as a war correspondent in dangerous hot-spots.

Lord Richard's younger brother, Lord Valentine Cecil, who had met Nairac through his brother, became a friend in his own right. He served with Nairac in Chelsea Barracks in 1975 and was also in South Armagh in 1977, just after he was killed. Valentine Cecil went over the ground where Nairac had been abducted and tried to reconstruct the events of 14-15 May, which led him to develop strong feelings about how Nairac had been managed – or rather had not been managed. Earlier, in 1976, he had begged Nairac not to return to Northern Ireland.

In early 1973 the 2nd Battalion was at Windsor and was preparing, among other public duties, to take part in the Sovereign's Birthday Parade in June. But before that they would briefly face the reality of Northern Ireland. There was to be a referendum there in March and the 2nd Battalion would be sent in for two weeks to help the troops already posted there and the civil authorities to keep the peace, while canvassing and voting took place. They would be based on a ship moored in Belfast Lough. The Northern Ireland Sovereignty Referendum of 1973 was held on 8 March, to decide whether Northern Ireland should remain part of the UK or join with the Republic of Ireland to form a united Ireland. Prominent Catholics and Republicans had indicated that they would boycott the poll and were encouraging others to do so.

The Referendum questions were simple:

"Do you want Northern Ireland to remain part of the United Kingdom?" and:

"Do you want Northern Ireland to be joined with the Republic of Ireland outside the United Kingdom?"

In the event, despite the call for a boycott, 58.66% of the Northern Irish electorate turned out and voted. This, by UK general election standards, was a high turnout: 44% or less being quite normal. A very small number spoiled their ballot papers. Of those who cast a vote, the overwhelming majority voted in favour of remaining in the UK. This also represented a majority of the total Northern Ireland electorate but, given the abstentions, a less dramatic majority than the arithmetical result of the poll might appear to indicate. We have however no way of knowing what proportion of the abstainers was actively boycotting the poll and what proportion, as usual, simply could not be bothered to vote. The British Government, considering that it now had a mandate, went ahead with the institution of a 78-seat Northern Ireland Assembly elected by proportional representation. This was thought to be more truly representative of Ulster public opinion than the Westminster "first past the post" election system in use elsewhere in the UK. The week of the Referendum was marked by two ominous incidents: the discovery of a boat carrying five tons of arms for the IRA from Libya, and an IRA bombing spree in London that killed one person and injured 250 others.

Following this brief early exposure to Northern Ireland, the 2nd Battalion returned, after a mere two weeks' training, to Belfast on 5 July for a regular four-month deployment to 31 October, taking over from the 3rd Battalion Parachute Regiment (3 Para): hard men, whose tough approach to Northern Ireland had not endeared them to the inhabitants. The Paras would be a diabolical act to follow, rather than simply a difficult one. There was an unhappy recent history behind this.

While Nairac had been preparing for his Final Schools at Oxford the situation in Northern Ireland had taken a turn for the worse. On 30 January 1972 the infamous Bloody Sunday confrontation had occurred in the Bogside, Londonderry, between demonstrating Republican civilians and soldiers. Thirteen men, seven of whom were teenagers, had died immediately or soon afterwards, while the death of another man four-and-a-half months later was attributed to the injuries he had received on that day. Two other protesters were injured when they were knocked down by Army vehicles. Five of those wounded had apparently been shot in the back. The incident occurred during a NICRA march;

the soldiers involved were members of the 1st Battalion Parachute Regiment (1 Para). According to the IRA the dead were all innocent, unarmed civilians whom the Paras had wilfully murdered after the march had degenerated into a riot. From this point the Parachute Regiment as a whole was demonised in the Republican mind. The media, including the BBC, tended to reflect the IRA line.

The Paras' perception was different. In their view it had been a mistake for the Northern Irish authorities to permit such a large-scale demonstration to take place at all: it was, or should have been, obvious that it would end in full-scale rioting – and it did. The Paras were ordered in to support the civil law enforcement authorities, who, totally foreseeably, had failed to cope with the disorder. Gunshots from among the crowd were heard. (Both sides agreed on this, although on little else.) At that point panic ensued. The Paras, believing themselves to be under attack, opened fire. Crucially, they had been given no contingency orders to follow in the event of a riot. When their Commander, Lieutenant Colonel Wilford, had asked during a briefing before the demonstration what he should order his men to do in that event, his superior officers gave him an unsatisfactory reply: "We'll face that when it happens". He later bitterly regretted not pursuing this and insisting on precise orders; not least because he had been made the chief scapegoat. The Para officers and men had been left with no option other than to use their own judgement and to open fire if they truly believed that they were in danger, which they did. It had arguably been a mistake to send in the Paras, of all Regiments, as back-up. The decision to use them was not military, but political, and made by the then Home Secretary, Reginald Maudling. His reasons for doing so are opaque. Apart from the SAS, the Paras are the hardest, most tightly-drilled Regiment in the Army. As Colonel Wilford later admitted, they would not simply stand there and be knocked down "like Aunt Sallies", as had happened to other units in Londonderry. They were not going to pause for a thoughtful or balanced reassessment, either. They had been trained to react quickly and instinctually to any perceived threat and they reacted: it was as simple as that.

A former SAS commander, Sir Peter de la Billiere, has written that: "It should be remembered at the time that civil society had almost broken down in much of the Province, which was close to anarchy or civil war. In the following May alone, 28 soldiers were killed and 110 wounded. Our soldiers feared for their lives while their officers feared a collapse of law and order. It is small wonder that events in Londonderry were chaotic that day."

As for the rioters, their innocence is questionable. Self-evidently most of them were voluntarily involved in a large scale riot and attacks on soldiers. At best, they were innocent only in the sense of not having thought through the probable consequences of their actions. If they were truly not aware of what they had let themselves in for, it follows that they were the dupes of the IRA leadership, some of whom were present; who had helped to provoke the riot and who would later exploit the event for propaganda purposes. The IRA at least would have known what the likely outcome would be. They regarded the civilian dead of that day as collateral damage; useful for creating a martyr legend and embarrassing the Army. The dead were the victims of hidden agendas.

Two investigations have since been held by the UK Government. The Widgery Tribunal, held immediately afterwards, largely cleared the soldiers and British authorities of blame. Widgery was inevitably the object of fierce criticism by the Left, Irish Republicans and the left-centre media. The Saville Inquiry was established under Labour in 1998 to reinvestigate the events. There followed an eye-wateringly costly twelve-year inquiry, which at times took the form of a political circus, with elderly Conservative former ministers, including the infirm former Prime Minister Sir Edward Heath, being publicly and disrespectfully interrogated like war criminals. The electorate was being given the impression that the Conservative Party as an institution was on trial and that was undoubtedly the intention. There was little justification for this, as the former ministers could add almost nothing to the Inquiry's information. Heath simply said that he had never sanctioned the use of unlawful lethal force in Northern Ireland, which came as no surprise to anyone. The one former Minister who might have made a serious contribution was not available. This was Reginald Maudling. He had been in office at the time of Bloody Sunday, had ordered the Paras to become involved and had defended their actions in the House of Commons. He had, however, inconsiderately died in 1979.

Saville's report was published on 15 June 2010. It contained findings of fault that could re-open the controversy, and potentially lead to the criminal investigation of former soldiers involved in the killings. The Saville Report found that that the Bloody Sunday killings were both "unjustified and unjustifiable". Many people in the Army thought and still think that Saville was politically inspired, to placate Sinn Fein. The exercise was expensive and its outcome inadequate. Emotions and grandstanding by the British Left and Irish Republicans have always prevented a calm, forensic examination of the event. By contrast with Saville's apparent willingness to facilitate the prosecution of former soldiers as part of a secret deal by Tony Blair's Labour administration with Sinn Fein, many PIRA terrorists who had been sought by the British authorities in connection with some 300 murders received comfort letters, mostly issued under Labour, formally exempting them from prosecution. It has been suggested in the Press that they may include two of Nairac's assassins. This special offer was limited to members of the IRA, who are the armed branch of Sinn Fein. Other terrorist suspects, Republican or Loyalist, could not expect the same treatment. Apparently without Ministers' knowledge, British officials issued further comfort letters even more recently, under the Conservative-Liberal Democrat Coalition Government. This secret deal led to the collapse of the prosecution related to the 1982 Hyde Park bomb atrocity, which killed four soldiers and a number of horses. The accused, John Downey, walked free from the court.

John Parker, in *The Paras*, published in 2000, puts it eloquently and succinctly: "...the new Bloody Sunday inquiry appeared to have been brokered in response to the IRA's agreement to point out the location of the bodies of Northern Ireland's 'disappeared' – those members of the community, mostly Catholic and dissident to the IRA cause (and including Special Forces liaison officer Captain Robert Nairac), who had been murdered in the intervening years. In the event, with the exception of perhaps three sets of remains recovered, the 'disappeared' are still exactly that, but the IRA had achieved its goal of a fresh inquiry into Bloody Sunday. The nature of the deals-on-the-side that Blair and his Ministers threw on the table in order to achieve the ceasefire and peace agreement soon became very obvious to all. The 'disappeared in exchange for Bloody Sunday inquiry' was one of the shoddier adjuncts to the peace agreement and Peter de la Billiere, among many, was forthright in his denunciation of it: 'As far as I can see, the reopening of this inquiry now is a political exercise, the effect of which is to appease the IRA and humiliate and embarrass the armed forces.'"

It is hard to disagree: the Saville Inquiry was not about establishing the facts. Whatever the rights and wrongs of Bloody Sunday, and it is now unlikely that we shall ever know the full truth, it represented a nadir in relations between the Army and the Republican and Catholic minorities. They were now convinced that the Army was there simply to shore up Unionist rule: the Army was no better than the Loyalist militias or the late, unregretted RUC "B Specials".

The IRA's immediate response to Bloody Sunday was to order all its combatants to kill every British soldier they could find. They had already killed 48 during 1971. They started by bombing the Paras' headquarters at Aldershot. Their victims also included nineteen-year-old Londonderry soldier, William "Geordie" Best, who had joined the Royal Irish Rangers. This, in the IRA's view, made him a traitor. Home on a visit to his parents, he was kidnapped ("arrested" in IRA-speak); "tried" by an IRA kangaroo court, and murdered ("executed"). By a strange coincidence Geordie Best had been the soldier-servant of a Royal Irish officer who would later become one of Nairac's closest friends. If there had still been any doubt, it was now clear that Britain was at war.

Bloody Sunday was an important background factor in Nairac's story, but since this book is about Robert Nairac and not about Bloody Sunday in which he played no part, since he was an undergraduate at the time, it is not necessary to consider it in any greater detail here.

In 1972, mainly as a result of Bloody Sunday, the British Government concluded that the devolved Unionist Northern Irish Government was incapable of maintaining law and order. It now proposed to take over responsibility for security within the Province. This was not acceptable to Stormont, so the Westminster Government rushed through the Northern Ireland (Temporary Provisions) Act 1972, imposing direct rule from London and closing down the Northern Irish Parliament. Northern Ireland continued to be represented by MPs at Westminster. The Act received the Royal Assent on 30 March. It was always intended to be a temporary measure, after which internal self-government would be restored on a more widely-acceptable basis. The necessary precondition for this was a measure of agreement between Unionists and Nationalists about the best way forward. This proved to be remarkably elusive through the 1970s, 1980s and early 1990s. Meanwhile the existence of barricaded Republican enclaves, the "no-go areas", was a challenge to the Government. On 31 July 1972 the Army demolished the barricades, in the teeth of spirited opposition, in Operation Motorman.

This was the situation that the 2nd Bn Grenadier Guards would inherit a year and a half after Bloody Sunday. They returned to Belfast to begin a tour of duty to run from 9 July to 31 October, preceded by a short handover from 5 to 9 July. Nairac was a member of the advance party, which arrived on 1 July. He showed himself to be able, enthusiastic and motivated during the handover arrangements with the outgoing 3 Para. Above all, he was tactful, diplomatic and politically-aware. It was on this occasion that he met Tony Clarke, who related their encounter in his book *Contact*:

"The Grenadier Guards advance party arrives and I have to show the platoon commander assigned to me the Shankill in all its glory. I'm still at the ops desk at ten in the morning, having had a brief respite for a wash and a shave followed by breakfast, when the OC comes in with the Grenadiers to introduce me.

"'Tony, this is Bob Nairac, who will be assigned to you for the handover period.' I shake hands with the stocky guy with curly black hair, far removed from the normal type of Guards officer you usually meet. I take in the broken nose and the cheerful grin and think 'Thank God I haven't got one of those guys with a mouthful of marbles.' The pleasantries over, he goes off and dumps his kit...

"Bob is the one with all the questions, insatiable for knowledge, expressing disappointment that his company is not in the Ardoyne, and is not convinced when I tell him that we, the Shankill Coy, have had far more finds and by far the biggest contact of the tour. He is no sooner in the place than he wants to go out on his first patrol. It just so happens that I'm due out with one of my sections in an hour's time so he goes away happy, to get his kit together. Clive and I look at each other in disbelief. There's no way we would be so keen to get out there and certainly not at this stage in the tour. In fact, the OC had to hound us to get us out onto the street. Well, each to his own... right now I want to stay safe.

"Out on the street, Bob is like a foxhound, digging into everything, questioning everything, wanting to cram five months' knowledge into one short, two hour patrol. The lads are working well, putting on their best performance to impress the 'crap-hats', and the two hours goes quickly past without incident."

The Catholics and Republicans had cordially detested 3 Para. This hatred was inherited by the Grenadiers, whose patrolling guardsmen would at the start of their tour of duty return from Ardoyne with their flak jackets slimy with saliva, having repeatedly been spat at. The 2nd Battalion was to change all that.

There was considerable physical danger. In many respects the IRA were better-equipped and better-informed than the Army. Over the years Ministers and civil servants in the Ministry of Defence and the Treasury have been morally responsible for the deaths and injuries of many soldiers through their parsimonious reluctance to fund the Army adequately, and to spend on the latest and best equipment that would have helped to keep them safe. This is far from being a modern complaint, although it has more recently come back into the headlines in the context of Helmand. It was particularly the case in Northern Ireland, for which the politicians continued to hope unrealistically that a political solution would be worked out sooner, rather than later. The corollary was that the Army's presence was hopefully temporary (although in the event Operation Banner was to last from 1969 to 2007) so that it was not worth investing in special kit for use in Ulster. In 1973 the Grenadiers were still wearing their khaki-coloured berets. Unbelievably, they did not receive helmets with visors until three years later. By that time a number of them had lost eyes or suffered head injuries from thrown bricks. They did receive flak jackets, but these only provided partial protection against low-velocity gunfire or shrapnel. Infantrymen on patrol carried 7.62 mm self-loading rifles (SLRs) – heavy weapons that weighed as much as the eighteenth-century Brown Bess musket – 9 mm Sterling sub-machine guns and in some cases Browning pistols. However the Army's confrontations with the local populace were not all fire-fights with the IRA. Good, old-fashioned riots and mob violence could also happen, so the soldiers also carried batons, weapons that fired rubber bullets and CS gas grenades for riot control. Soldiers moved around on foot or in Land Rovers, most of which were only lightly armoured. There were frequent casualties; the soldiers lived on adrenaline. Nairac seems to have been in his element.

Two separate Companies of the 2nd Battalion were deployed in the Protestant Shankill and the Catholic Ardoyne areas, so that most of the time they were dealing either with rebellious Catholics or with resentful Protestants, but not usually both. Nairac's Company was deployed in a backup role, so he served in both areas and with both communities. Nairac ended by befriending both: an almost impossible task, but he managed it. There is plenty of evidence for this. He was often to be seen in uniform, chatting to their leaders at street corners. He, amongst others, was good at defusing difficult situations before they got out of hand. He could not have done this if both sides had not trusted him and it may have been this experience that turned him towards intelligence work. He certainly started to turn in well-written intelligence papers, like the one on the Fianna, at this time. Four years later, in early 1977, the citizens of Ardoyne still had warm memories of Nairac and greeted him enthusiastically when he unexpectedly reappeared there with the Devon and Dorsets, two or three months before his death.

Nairac proved to be exceptionally good at chatting up both the Fianna (Catholic, Nationalist youth) and the Tartan (Protestant) Gangs. His personal "hearts and minds" initiative included boxing coaching for Catholic youths in Ardoyne in an existing sports centre. Nairac seems to have founded the boxing club, however. Although he greatly enjoyed doing this, it also allowed him to meet the boys' Republican parents, who were fellow-Catholics with whom he discussed Irish history and politics, about which he often proved to know more than they did, and sometimes sang Republican songs. He would warn them when their boys were being led astray. He was quick to realise that although most of the parents were Republicans, they were also in many cases respectable practising Roman Catholics, who were horrified at the prospect of their sons being recruited by the IRA. If Nairac could deflect their energies into other channels, like boxing, that was an outcome devoutly to be wished. This was helpful to him in gleaning information from them.

The Catholics of Ardoyne had numerous legitimate grievances. Belfast City Hall, which was very Orange, would not spend any money on the Catholic ghettos. Damaged street lighting was never repaired; crumbling roads were never resurfaced; drains were never cleaned out and an infestation of rats was not dealt with. Eventually the officers of the Battalion persuaded the City Hall to take the necessary action, starting with the elimination of the rats. After infesting Ardoyne for six years, the rats were gone in six weeks. Another grievance of the citizens of Ardoyne was the damage to property that the soldiers inflicted in the course of their raids. The Army was supposed either to repair the damage or to pay compensation. There was however a perception that 3 Para had not worried much about the damage that they had caused. One of Nairac's and other patrol leaders' roles was keeping in contact with families who had outstanding claims for damage caused by the previous Battalion, as well as for any inflicted by the 2nd Battalion Grenadiers, and ensuring that they received compensation. This scrupulous approach helped the Grenadiers to win approval in Ardoyne.

Despite his military profession, Nairac became personally popular in Ardoyne. Later, building on this, the Company Commander would call on leading Ardoyne Catholic laymen and exchange contact details, so that the Grenadiers could react fast if a community leader reported some problem or situation that he or she considered was threatening to get out of hand. Relations between Ardoyne and the Regiment improved beyond recognition. When the 2nd Battalion finally left Belfast, the senior Roman Catholic clergyman in the area thanked Lieutenant Colonel Richard Besly, stating, "The battalion has treated us in a courteous and gentlemanly fashion."

The 2nd Battalion's tour, which ended on 31 October 1973, was judged a success: 58 weapons, 9,000 rounds of ammunition and 693 lbs of explosive had been discovered and confiscated and 104 men jailed. The Battalion took no casualties and had no occasion to shoot anyone. When the Battalion moved back to England and then on to Hong Kong in late 1973, Nairac and four other Grenadiers volunteered to remain behind in Belfast to assist the incoming battalion, the 1st Battalion The Argyll and Sutherland Highlanders, as liaison officers. For this purpose they wore Argyll headgear; either glengarries or khaki tam o'shanters. Nairac would retain his for future use in other contexts. Soon after their arrival the Argylls suffered a baptism of fire, with Nairac and others narrowly avoiding violent death on their first patrol when a car bomb exploded on the Crumlin Road. Nairac seems to have remained on friendly terms with the Argylls thereafter and occasionally visited them in Scotland. Given that Nairac had a Scots maternal grandfather and loved to go hawking, fishing and shooting in Scotland, this connection would have appealed to him.

Nairac, while on friendly terms with the Loyalists for much of the time, did not achieve quite the same access with them. The Tartan Gangs were more stand-offish. A negative factor could have been his Catholicism, of which he then made no secret. Later, he would sometimes pose as a Scottish infantry officer, "Captain Charlie MacDonald of the Argyll and Sutherland Highlanders" and implicitly assumed a Protestant identity when talking to Loyalists. The Argylls' former recruiting area is a very Protestant and Presbyterian area of Scotland. With Loyalists he learned to play down his Catholicism; perhaps leading some people to think that he had lost his Catholic faith, but he was in reality just being tactful or prudent.

The custom of having a "handover party" from the previous Battalion to assist and familiarise the incoming Battalion was recent; 3 Para had initiated it. They had left behind a number of volunteers to operate as guardsmen with the incoming Grenadiers in Ardoyne and Shankill, in order to help the Grenadiers to identify any wanted men who had returned to the area when they assumed that it was safe to do so because the Paras had left. This innovation was judged so successful that the Grenadiers did the same for the Argylls when they left. It became standard practice.

Encouraged by his Battalion's success in Ardoyne in 1973, Nairac probably thought that a similar transformation in Army-local community relations might be possible in South Armagh in 1976-77. His warm reception, when he went back to Ardoyne in early 1977 with the Devon and Dorsets, is likely to have increased his confidence that he would be able to do it again. But he was wrong; South Armagh was a very different kind of place, like nowhere else in Northern Ireland.

Nairac seems to have visited South Armagh at this period; its rugged, merciless beauty – very reminiscent of his beloved Scottish Highlands and Islands – held a strong attraction for him. He was reportedly seen at Castle Dillon in 1973; possibly on a recce for his next Irish appointment. Nairac would be returning to Northern Ireland soon: he had volunteered for special duties in the Province.

Why did Nairac volunteer at that particular juncture? While there is no doubt that he intended to get back to Northern Ireland at some point, special duties in Ulster were not his first choice in early 1974. Nairac had intended to attempt SAS Selection that year. He said so to at least two brother officers and had made some preliminary inquiries. It was almost inevitable that with his drive to succeed and excel, he would wish to attempt Selection. Like climbing Everest, SAS Selection poses an irresistible challenge to a certain type of individual: it must be attempted it because it is there. Unlike Everest, only two attempts are permitted and most candidates are not successful. Exceptional physical and moral resilience, as well as intelligence and resourcefulness, are required; Nairac had already shown that he possessed most of the requisite qualities. In the final analysis, passing SAS Selection is about self-mastery. The hardest fight is against oneself; to transcend one's own physical and mental limitations. According to the SAS, "We do not fail you; you fail yourself".

Yet someone; apparently someone very senior and persuasive, induced Nairac to postpone his SAS ambitions and to volunteer instead for the Special Reconnaissance Unit (SRU), usually known as NITAT (NI): the Northern Ireland Training and Advisory Team (Northern Ireland), which was based at Castle Dillon. NITAT (NI) was a misleadingly-named undercover Army unit, which had been intelligence-gathering in Northern Ireland from 1973. It had taken the place of the former Military Reaction Force (MRF). It had a tough selection process, although it was physically less demanding than SAS Selection. NITAT (NI) was not part of the SAS, although some SAS personnel were serving in it on secondment. Nairac had evidently been informally "head-hunted" for his Irish expertise; we do not know on whose advice. Given his CV, from NITAT (NI)'s point of view the attraction of having him on the team was obvious. From Nairac's perspective, a posting to NITAT (NI) offered him the chance to return to Ireland much sooner than he had expected. Given his deep interest in Ireland, the offer must have looked irresistible.

Apart from the relatively small number of seconded specialists serving with NITAT (NI), the SAS did not at that time serve in Northern Ireland and would not do so until they were ordered in, against their better judgment, in 1976. Had Nairac, like a number of other Guards officers down the years, successfully attempted SAS selection in 1974, he would have been with the SAS for roughly three years, to 1977 or even 1978. He would probably have found himself in the later stages of the Oman counter-insurgency. The Dhofar rebellion was effectively defeated in 1976, although this was not immediately apparent; incidents continued to occur until 1979. It would follow from this that Nairac would not have been available for service as Liaison Officer/Military Intelligence Officer in South Armagh in 1976. Had he later been deployed to Northern Ireland, it would have been as a member of the SAS, under different circumstances, and he might still be alive today.

Nairac would not rejoin the Grenadier Guards until 1975, and then it would be the 1st Battalion, not the 2nd. He served, albeit briefly, in both Battalions. Although he spent so little time with the Grenadiers, many former officers and men from both Battalions recall him clearly, in most cases with great respect and affection. But Nairac's personal qualities and striking looks were not readily forgettable. This begs the question: was he the ideal person to engage in undercover work? Would not a more self-effacing character with unmemorable looks have enjoyed better cover? And did no-one think of this at the time? Apparently they did not.

The school of thought that maintains that Nairac was brawny, gung-ho and not very bright takes the view that when, in late 1973, Nairac volunteered for special duties in Northern Ireland, he had no idea of what was involved. This theory does not hold water. Not only had Nairac begun carving out an intelligence role for himself while serving in Belfast; he had also begun to make contacts within the RUC. If he was seen at Castle Dillon in 1973, that suggests that, even then, he was looking at the available options and briefing himself about the NITAT (NI) team's work there. It is an old military maxim that "time spent in reconnaissance is seldom wasted" and Nairac would have known that. In any case, his posting to NITAT (NI) would be preceded by several months of intensive training and briefing.

It has also been suggested that Nairac's Roman Catholic religion was a factor in his decision. This is possible, but hard to prove. At most one might suggest that he may have thought that, as an Army officer who was also a Roman Catholic and who knew Ireland well, he was especially well-placed to provide penetrating insights and to make a difference; he apparently spoke along these lines to one or two interlocutors. However Army contemporaries stress that Nairac's personal religion was "never an issue". He went to considerable trouble to be, or at any rate to appear to be, fair and even-handed between Catholic and Protestant. There is no reason to think that Nairac's revulsion at the hatred that divided the Northern Irish religious communities, and his wish to do something about that were anything other than genuine.

When they were first sent into Northern Ireland in 1969, the British Army had little recent and relevant experience of counter-insurgency, including urban warfare, in a developed country. Their most recent experience had been in distant former colonies like Malaya, Kenya, North Borneo, Cyprus and Aden. With the exception of Aden and particularly the Crater District, which was densely populated, none of these countries had been industrialised or heavily-populated. Some troops also had taken part in UN-led peace-keeping operations; again, usually in distant and exotic places. Although the situation in Northern Ireland bore little resemblance to insurgency in these countries and the "natives", however disaffected, were relatively sophisticated fellow-British people with MPs to speak up for them, initially the Army tended to follow the "colonial counter-insurgency" model, as set out in General Sir Frank Kitson's influential books, *Gangs and Counter-gangs* (1960) and *Low Intensity Operations: Subversion, Insurgency and Peacekeeping* (1971). Nairac was familiar with both books. They did this not out of an obstinate refusal to face the rather different facts of Northern Ireland, but because handling a colonial insurgency was the only relevant and applicable model that they knew.

Aden in particular was relevant to what happened in Northern Ireland. It was the most thoroughly urban counter-insurgency operation that the Army had faced prior to its involvement in Northern Ireland and it had ended less than two years earlier. The British Armed Forces had left Aden in November 1967; they were ordered into Northern Ireland in August 1969, while their memories of Aden were still fresh. 45 Commando of the Royal Marines, the Argyll and Sutherland Highlanders and different Battalions of the Parachute Regiment had all served in Aden, where they experienced close-hand urban fighting. Soon afterwards they found themselves in Ulster. In Aden the policy was very much "gloves off" and something of that attitude informed the Army's thinking in the early days in Northern Ireland. (Hence, perhaps, Bloody Sunday.)

Kitson himself, then a Brigadier, appeared in Northern Ireland at an early stage, in September 1970, as Commander of 39 Infantry Brigade, which covered Belfast and eastern Northern Ireland. He would exercise considerable influence over how the UK would handle the insurgency there in the early years. Kitson had served in several colonial campaigns, including in Kenya and Malaya. He now proposed to apply the lessons of these small wars to Ulster. A key phrase by Kitson is:

"Everything done by a Government and its agents in combating insurgency must be legal. But this does not mean that a government must work within the same set of laws during an insurgency that existed beforehand."

Put simply, this means that a government facing an insurgency may decide to introduce emergency measures like curfews, stop-and-search, tighter border controls and new legal procedures. It was, however, misinterpreted, probably quite honestly, by some officials, some parts of the Army, the RUC and the Security Service (MI5), as meaning that "government" in the broadest sense, including themselves, could make up and change the rules as it went along.

After the introduction of direct rule in 1972, Home Secretary Reginald Maudling became responsible for Northern Ireland. His policy was to distance himself as far as possible from Northern Irish issues and to let the Army get on with dealing with the insurgency. In other words he provided no leadership, or even a coherent policy-steer. He was, however, publicly supportive of the Army over Bloody Sunday. His comment after a rare visit to Northern Ireland was; "For God's sake bring me a large Scotch. What a bloody awful country!" Northern Ireland would soon cease to be Maudling's problem. On 18 July 1972 he was obliged to resign over his business links with John Poulson, a corrupt Danish architect.

Maudling's departure brought no improvement; surprisingly few decisive ministerial policy-steers would ever be given by his successor or by the subsequent Secretaries of State for Northern Ireland. It seemed to officials and the Army that they were expected to take policy decisions themselves, and effectively they did. Some of these decisions would provoke a highly-critical response from human rights organisations like Amnesty International. One example would be the use of "pseudo-gangs" and "counter-gangs," who appear to have enjoyed an unofficial licence to shoot to kill. This had worked in Kenya against the Mau Mau but was likely to prove problematic and controversial in Northern Ireland.

It is easy to be wise after the event. In the early 1970s the way forward was far from clear. It began to appear to the Army that they could do nothing right. Their relationship with human rights organisations became as bad as it already was with the Republicans. Whether they were British or non-British, these organisations tended to assume a moral equivalence between the Army and terrorist organisations like the IRA and the UDF. This was completely unacceptable and turned many soldiers against the "human rights industry". Typical are the remarks of another undercover soldier, Keith Johnson MM, the only British soldier to have survived (a very brief) IRA capture:

"It's a bit rich that they [the IRA] actually call themselves an army. They're Irish republican terrorists and that's about it."

Johnson despised the IRA for trying to bomb the Army's married quarters outside Londonderry. At the time most of the soldiers were out on duty and only wives and children remained in the quarters. Johnson himself was present and rescued a colleague's baby. The attempt was not successful; the families were evacuated before the bomb went off, but it blew the houses to pieces. Johnson commented further:

"They were going to kill wives and babies – and they call themselves soldiers."

An exceptional man, decorated for bravery, Johnson's view is shared by many soldiers and ex-soldiers. It is hard to argue with his conclusion.

What the Army lacked at this period (roughly 1969-74) was sophisticated intelligence. The RUC could have supplied this, but the Army and the RUC distrusted each other and did not share much information at that time. This lack of knowledge had led to simplistic judgements: for example, that all Catholics were allied to the IRA (they were not, or were not originally); that, when looking for weapons caches and bomb-factories, these were always to be found in Catholic areas; that it was therefore necessary to invade these areas from time to time, smash up houses, dig up gardens and intimidate the inhabitants (although compensation was paid and basic repairs would be carried out promptly by the Royal Engineers). This and other factors, like Bloody Sunday, had caused the Catholics' initial relief at the Army's arrival in 1969 to turn into visceral hatred.

The Army was equally slow to realise that the Loyalists' loyalty was strictly limited and conditional and that the Loyalist paramilitaries could be every bit as dangerous and extreme as the IRA. Horrific as many of the IRA's acts were, they were outclassed by those of the Loyalist Shankill Butchers, whose leader, Lenny Murphy, appears to have been a complete psychopath, enjoying the torture and murder of his enemies in well-equipped "romper rooms". When, to the Loyalists' anger, the UK placed Northern Ireland under direct rule in 1972, the Loyalist paramilitary organisations perceived this as the Government's first surrender to the IRA. They embarked on a spectacular killing spree that would cost hundreds of lives; mainly, but by no means all, Catholic – and many of them innocent. Their victims would include police and soldiers.

Chapter 10 | Ireland Again

Ireland, sir, for good or evil, is like no other place under heaven, and no man can touch its sod or breathe its air without becoming better or worse.
(George Bernard Shaw)

Robert Nairac's return to Northern Ireland in May 1974 followed a literally resounding event, with which his detractors have repeatedly sought to link him. On 17 May the Dublin and Monaghan bombings took place. These were a series of coordinated car bombings, which killed 33 civilians and injured almost 300. They constituted the single incident of the Troubles that produced the greatest number of fatalities. They were also the worst terrorist incident in the Republic of Ireland's history.

Nairac has often been accused of involvement in the bombings, but he arrived in Northern Ireland on 21 May; four days after they took place. Immediately prior to that date he had been on a training course in the UK with people who are still alive and confirm this. So there is no way in which he could have been involved in the two atrocities, even in the planning phase. In 1993 a Loyalist paramilitary organisation claimed responsibility for them. This was confirmed by the Irish Barron Inquiry, whose report stated that that the bombings had been the work of the Loyalist Glenanne Gang. This conclusion seems be based on good ballistic evidence. There continue however to be rumours of "collusion" or "collaboration" by the British Security Forces and inevitably Nairac's name is still mentioned in this context.

Should there be any remaining doubt as to the perpetrators' Loyalist identity, the bombings occurred during, and were linked to, the 1974 Ulster Workers' Council Strike, whose purpose was to wreck the 1973 Anglo-Irish Sunningdale Agreement. Loyalists believed that Sunningdale would give the Republic scope to influence Northern Irish affairs, leading eventually to reunification. It is clear that the British Government had nothing to gain from the bombings, had a great deal to lose, and had every interest in keeping Sunningdale alive. At the time that the bombings occurred, the Irish Government had been discussing new, tougher and extremely welcome measures against the IRA. Following the bombings their attitude changed: they became far less co-operative. The allegations of British Army collusion came not only from Republican sources but also from the mischievous Loyalists who were later proved to have committed the atrocities. Their aim was to sink Sunningdale beyond any hope of salvage and in this they were completely successful; the bombings delivered the *coup de grace* to the Agreement.

In 1974 no-one suggested that Nairac, a recently-arrived and obscure Lieutenant serving in an unknown unit, might have been involved. Those allegations arose only after his death in 1977, when he had become famous and had entered both legend and Republican demonology. Any unresolved crimes between 1973 and 1977 could be retrospectively attributed to him and often were; he was no longer alive to refute the rumours.

Apart from the bombings, Nairac had returned at a time of change. The "Kitson era" in Northern Ireland was coming to an end. Brigadier Kitson's approach had produced some results. However, a radical re-think was now required. The new policy would be marked by a move away from the "colonial" Kitson approach to something more sophisticated, based primarily on intelligence: the contacts, first-hand knowledge and experience of people like Nairac; still a relatively small number in the Army, who had made Northern Ireland, and Ireland in general, their special study. Nairac was in a position to make an important contribution. His third posting to Northern Ireland would last from May 1974 to April 1975. He would be based at Castle Dillon and would nominally be attached to 4 Field Survey Troop of the Royal Engineers (RE), which performed surveillance duties. A former RE Commander at Castle Dillon has explained their relationship, or lack of one:

"We had a number of 'spooks' as we called them, using Castle Dillon at the time. These folk wore plain clothes, never spoke about their work and we did not ask. They were not under my command."

In reality Nairac would be an intelligence-gatherer serving in one of three geographical sub-units of the Special Reconnaissance Unit (SRU) during its incarnation as NITAT (NI). The SRU would continue to exist for many years under different names, one of which was 14 Intelligence Company (14 Int) although the latter title was used at a period after Nairac's death. Nairac was also the Liaison Officer between the sub-unit, the local Army Brigade and the Royal Ulster Constabulary (RUC); especially their Special Branch.

The fact that Nairac has been confirmed as a former member of the SRU disposes of any suggestion that in 1974-75 or 1976-77 he was an innocent, an amateur, or dim. As already noted, the SRU had a very tough selection process, but Nairac had no difficulty in passing it and surviving members say that within the SRU he was highly regarded. The SRU's controllers and senior Liaison Officers were mostly SAS on secondment. Its approximately 50 members (perhaps as many as 130, if all the support staff were included) were highly-trained and very professional. They needed to be; their work was extremely dangerous. They all had an "official alias" by which they were known to their contacts and which they used at all times: if they were killed, that name would be announced on the radio or television and not their real one, so that their families should not learn of their death through the media before the Army or the police had time to break it to them. This policy had been adopted after Captain Anthony Pollen was shot dead in Londonderry in front of a crowd of more than 150 people, soon after his arrival in the Province, on 14 April 1974, while carrying out undercover surveillance of a Sinn Fein event. His parents first learned about it from a television news bulletin. Despite the ever-present danger, the SRU was a highly successful operation. More than once before 1998 it had brought the PIRA to the negotiating table, having penetrated and compromised it. Insofar as normal life has ever returned to Northern Ireland, the SRU deserves much of the credit.

The SRU did not become operative until 1973 and Nairac was one of its earliest recruits. Its role is now known to some extent from briefing documents released to the National Archives. Its primary task was to conduct covert surveillance of terrorists as a preliminary to an arrest carried out by Security Forces in uniform. The SRU was also used to contact and handle agents or informers and for the surveillance and protection of persons or property under terrorist threat. It relied to a great extent on RUC Special Branch (SB) information and the SB reportedly developed a high regard for the SRU. This was due to a great extent to Nairac's hard work and successful cultivation of key SB officers.

One important aspect of his job was to win the trust of, and to establish close co-operation on intelligence with, the SB. In this role Nairac was to be an unqualified success. His mixture of charm, brain-power and forcefulness would work in 1974-75 on the SB as effectively as it had in 1973 on the citizens of Ardoyne, despite the distrust that had existed since 1969 between the RUC and the Army. The evidence of this is the inscribed silver tankard that the SB presented to him in April 1975, shortly before he left the unlucky Province for the third time.

During the early stages of the Troubles, Brigadier Kitson had established his own highly secret intelligence group: this was the notorious Military Reaction Force or Military Reconnaissance Force (MRF). The SRU was its successor. Despite numerous allegations to that effect, Nairac was never a member of the MRF, although his future NITAT (NI) colleague and friend, Julian "Tony" Ball, was. It was small: numbering only about 40 men and women. It existed only for a few years: from roughly 1971-73. It operated without reference to the RUC and, for a surprisingly long time, remained unknown to it. It concentrated its investigations almost exclusively on the Catholic and Republican population, with a view to capturing or turning senior IRA figures of both wings. It also engaged in unconventional, clandestine forms of warfare. The MRF's personnel were volunteers from a spectrum of Army Regiments and corps and the Ulster Defence Regiment (UDR). Officers and NCOs of the Special Forces, including the SAS and the Special Boat Service (SBS), were involved in training the MRF. As noted earlier, the Special Forces have a training role towards the rest of the Armed Forces. A few of these specialist instructors volunteered to remain with the MRF as section commanders and in other capacities. That was the only SAS involvement at that early period.

The MRF could congratulate itself on a number of successes. These included the "Freds" (*Note 1*), who were former IRA volunteers now turned by, and recruited to, the British side in exchange for dropping charges against them, or some other bargain. This technique had worked well against the Mau Mau in Kenya. Their flagship projects had included the operation of a bogus laundry service, the Four-Square Laundry, and a massage parlour, the Gemini Health Studios, both in Belfast. The massage parlour was used to entrap Republicans and compromise them. For a while the laundry service was very successful: customers were apparently happy with its high standard of service. This allowed its male and female staff, who were in reality service personnel, to circulate freely around Belfast, including in staunchly Republican areas, collecting and delivering laundry and amassing information at the same time.

The MRF did not however confine itself to collecting information. The RUC were unaware of the MRF's existence until a drive-by shooting incident occurred on 22 June 1972, when some Catholics standing at a bus-stop in Glen Road were sprayed with machine gun bullets from a passing car. The police, who purely by chance were nearby, believed that they had witnessed a terrorist incident. They pursued and arrested the driver and his passenger, who turned out to be a British Army officer and an NCO, both from the MRF. The soldiers claimed that they had been returning fire. This two-man team later proved to have committed three or four similar drive-by shootings. They eventually stood trial but were acquitted for lack of evidence. We are unlikely ever to know the full facts, but it would seem to follow from this that the MRF did make some mistakes, or some elements of it were getting out of control.

The IRA, too, had begun to suspect the MRF's existence. Two of the "Freds", who had supposedly been turned, now turned back to their former comrades in the IRA and revealed the existence of the laundry and the massage parlour. On 2 October the IRA struck back and put both operations out of business for good. They also rounded up and murdered a number of other "Freds" who had been betrayed by their former colleagues. They became some of the Disappeared. Fortunately for him, Brigadier Kitson had left Northern Ireland several months earlier at the end of his tour. He was not murdered and his military career was not affected, although he incurred some criticism. In 1973 the MRF was wound up, although senior Army officers did not regard it as a failure. Despite criticism by human rights activists and politicians on both sides of the Irish Sea, lessons had been learned and they could be built on. There was, however, a further aspect of the MRF's activities; this was political. While they may have given a tactical advantage to the Security Forces, the MRF had not been helpful to the Conservative Government of the day, who were working secretly to promote a ceasefire in Northern Ireland. Drive-by shootings of Catholic civilians were not conducive to achieving this outcome. It was a case of the left hand not knowing what the right hand was doing: the MRF were completely ignorant of what the Government was doing, so secret were the ceasefire talks. There was a good reason for this secrecy: having said publicly that they would never talk to terrorists, the Government were now talking, through proxies, with the IRA.

In parallel with the Northern Ireland elections, discussions about new constitutional arrangements for Northern Ireland, the formation of a governing coalition and the bilateral discussions with the Republic about the proposed Council of Ireland, the British Government was following a secret agenda. The success of the new arrangements would depend heavily on a return to peace. Now the Government's first priority was to seek a ceasefire with the IRA, to permit a gradual return to normal political life in Northern Ireland. There seemed to be no alternative to talking directly with the terrorists, however distasteful this might be to ministers. To the Ulster Unionists, if they should find out, these talks would be completely unacceptable. But the Government believed that this was a risk worth taking.

There seemed to be a chance of success; British intelligence had penetrated the IRA; the Government had learned that the IRA was now under strong pressure from the Catholic community to work for a restoration of peace. Prime Minister Edward Heath authorised Northern Ireland Secretary William Whitelaw to open secret talks with the IRA leadership: both IRA wings responded favourably. Gerry Adams was released from Long Kesh prison camp to act as one of the leaders of the IRA delegation. A temporary IRA ceasefire was imposed, with immediate effect. The hope was that it would lead to a permanent, general ceasefire. On 20 June two of Whitelaw's senior officials met Gerry Adams and David O'Connell, a senior member of the PIRA, for secret talks in mainland Great Britain. So secret were the negotiations that the Army was not informed and nor were the RUC or Ulster officials.

Conspiracy theorists, including authors and journalists, have speculated that MI5, who reportedly resented MI6's growing involvement in "their" Province, had a strong motive for sabotaging any deal that the British Government might reach with Sinn Fein/the IRA. This is highly improbable, but if there could be shown to be any truth in these allegations, the almost certainly random drive-by shooting on 22 June 1972 in Glen Road might appear to be a deliberate, MI5-inspired attempt by the Security Forces to sabotage the talks. But even if that had really been the case, the attempt did not succeed; or not immediately. Too much was at stake for either side lightly to abandon the secret bilateral talks.

A former NCO who served in the MRF has proposed a far simpler and more plausible explanation: cock-up, rather than conspiracy. In his view the MRF had worked well and usually respected the law for as long as Brigadier Kitson was its Commander. His less-charismatic successors did not manage to keep as tight a control over its activities, so the MRF got out of hand. Given less-effective leadership, some MRF members had started to follow their own unofficial agenda; an important item of this was to discredit the Provisional IRA within the Roman Catholic and Republican community. The PIRA had successfully displaced the British Army as the Catholics' preferred protector and had killed a large number of soldiers. Their message to the Catholic and Nationalist areas was: "We are your natural and only legitimate protectors. Support us unconditionally and we will look after you. Everything will be fine. You will be safe." The unspoken subtext was: "And if you do not; if you inform on us to the SF, we will kill you, probably in a very unpleasant way." The message that the MRF wanted to deliver was: "The PIRA cannot deliver. Whatever they say, you will never be safe under their so-called protection." Drive-by shootings and other acts against Catholics were intended to convey and reinforce this message. All things being equal, these acts would automatically be attributed to Loyalist militias. It was the greatest bad luck that on 22 June 1972 the RUC should have caught one of the MRF hit teams.

The MRF had gathered much information which the SRU could and did use, so that by 1974 they flattered themselves that the IRA were now on the run, or soon would be. This was to prove wildly optimistic, but at the time there seemed to be grounds for hope. There had been many arrests and many key PIRA figures were now in internment. However the IRA were deepening their contacts with international terrorism and rogue States, including Libya, and becoming richer and much more dangerous as a result. Funding would shortly begin to pour into the IRA's coffers, now provided not only by naive Irish-Americans, but also by the sworn enemies of the West.

Despite the foregoing events, negotiations with the IRA continued. On 26 June Gerry Adams and Martin McGuinness met senior officials in London. The IRA's demands on this occasion were not acceptable. They included a commitment that British troops should be withdrawn by 1 January 1975. Although at the end of the talks there was no agreement, the two delegations expressed their intention not to give up, but to meet again soon. They clearly needed more time to achieve progress. Meanwhile they agreed that, above all else, the ceasefire should remain in force.

But time was running out. The next meeting did not take place because the situation in Northern Ireland suddenly deteriorated. Within days of the second meeting, violence had erupted as the UDA, still suspicious that a deal with the IRA was imminent and determined to sabotage it, embarked on a series of attacks on Catholic and Republican areas. By the end of June new barricades were going up. This effectively ended the Whitelaw peace initiative. 1973 would end amid a crescendo of violence. In the following year more than 3,000 acts of terrorism would be recorded in Northern Ireland and Nairac would return in 1974 to a Province that was in several respects less stable than the one that he had left several months earlier. Unionist political opposition, a Loyalist-inspired general strike and violence in Northern Ireland would cause the final collapse of the Sunningdale Agreement. The search for a political solution had failed; it was time to dust off the weapons. The scene was now set for further mayhem.

Mainland Great Britain was also looking politically unstable. In February 1974, following major disruption of the British economy by Trade Union industrial action, leading to power shortages and the imposition of a three-day week, Edward Heath called a snap election on the issue of "Who Governs Britain: the Elected Government or the Trade Unions?" He hoped for a strong mandate; however an increasingly nervous and demoralised British electorate hesitated to grant it. The Conservatives failed to secure a majority in the Commons, although they had won a majority of the votes cast (11.9 million, to Labour's 11.6 million). Labour returned to power, though without a Commons majority, in a hung Parliament. A further election in October 1974 would deliver a just-workable overall Labour majority of three seats. Ulster had played a major part in Edward Heath's debacle. The Ulster Unionists, who could normally be relied upon to support the Conservatives and who might have helped Heath to remain in office, withheld their support in February 1974 in protest at the Sunningdale Agreement.

Like the former MRF, NITAT (NI) has sometimes been described as an SAS unit. It was not – it was another name for the SRU – although SAS personnel had been seconded to it. One of them was Julian "Tony" Ball, Nairac's immediate superior, whose close friend he became. Tony Ball was to be a major influence on Nairac, interesting him in the kind of special operations soldiering which would lead indirectly to his early death in 1977. Ball himself was killed in 1981, so we do not have his impressions of Nairac. We do, however, have the impressions of Major, later Colonel, G of the SAS, given to John Parker:

"Meeting up with Robert, I certainly felt he was one of the most effective of our liaison officers. Not least because he had a lot of charm, but most particularly because he'd studied at the university in Dublin and had this very real love and understanding of the Irish people. That was abundantly clear, right from the beginning. He was very much a people person. He wasn't a bureaucrat and there was an evident rebel streak in his persona.

"He identified very strongly with the problems and the people whilst at the same time he was very much against the IRA and all the extreme elements. He probably had a better understanding than anyone I met of the IRA, their history and motivations and the Republican cause, along with the elements that supported it. He had studied it in great depth and by identifying with the south and the whole Irish situation, he had both the knowledge and, to some degree, empathy with the wider picture that confronted us.

"He also had that certain unique Guards smooth charm that works wonders in Army circles. He got along famously with the RUC, which was very, very important because the Army and the RUC were all too frequently at loggerheads. There were degrees of competition in all areas. Army units came and went. In the early years units were often trying to grab their own little share of glory to varying degrees, some more than others, and the RUC had been there forever and were constantly catching the flak of all concerned with security in the province. Robert did an extremely good job in the early days setting up the intelligence process down there."

That is a good summary, except for the mysterious assertion that Nairac had studied in Dublin, which was simply not true. However, Major G correctly identifies the key issues. One was the delicacy of the relationship between the Army and the RUC. It was very complex and contained elements of rivalry and competition for "assets". But what Nairac understood, and other Army officers often failed to grasp, was that in general the Regiments' interest, including their officers' interest, in the Province was limited and temporary; the RUC knew and resented this. They had also worked out that the soldiers usually grew to dislike the Northern Irish of both varieties. It was a case of "a plague on both your houses." If the soldiers hated the Republican Catholics more, it was because they were all supposed to be IRA supporters and the IRA had killed far more soldiers than the Loyalist militias. The Army, being non-political, tended to have a limited interest in the eventual outcome or in Northern Ireland's long-term future: they correctly saw that as being the job of the politicians. The most that the Army could do was to deliver a temporary peace, providing conditions in which a political solution might be worked out. In many cases, though not all, the Regiments' primary aims were to complete their tour of duty with no casualties, or as few as possible; to score a few successes involving the discovery of arms dumps; to arrest or kill some IRA; to win a few medals; not completely to alienate the civilian population in their area, leave behind a reasonably orderly situation for their successors and get the hell out again. During their duty tours they had the opportunity to take leave in the UK. Increasingly they preferred to leave their families there. As the war against the IRA prolonged itself, their allowance of short "breather visits" back to the UK would increase; often for as little as a weekend, but still helpful in de-stressing the soldiers.

None of this applied to the RUC. They could not be indifferent to, or neutral about, Northern Ireland's fate. Ulster was their home, to which they were fiercely attached. Whatever the eventual outcome of the Troubles should prove to be, it was certain that they, their spouses and children would be inescapably involved in it. While the Army could look forward to the end of their tour, the RUC could not. They could not take breather breaks – or not to anything like the same extent. They and their families would continue to be a target for the terrorists at all times. The stress that this placed on the RUC was enormous and not all soldiers appreciated this, although Nairac did.

Nor did the RUC initially trust the Army with their highly-sensitive intelligence. The distrust was mutual. On their side the Army were aware that the RUC and – still more – the Ulster Defence Regiment (UDR) had been penetrated by Loyalist militia. While they were keen for the RUC to share their intelligence with the Army, they were reluctant to reciprocate, for fear that it might end up in the wrong hands. So a situation of stalemate or "no deal" tended to develop. It would require all of Nairac's charm, his political skills, his deep knowledge of Ireland and his commitment to turn this around, but in due course he did; at least for a while.

The same considerations applied with even greater force to the Ulster Defence Regiment (UDR). The price paid by the UDR was high: 197 UDR soldiers were killed during the Troubles. UDR men and women were not safe anywhere, at any time: more of them were murdered while off duty, either at home or in the course of their civilian employment, than ever lost their lives in uniform. Even those who had left the Regiment did not always find safety; forty-seven former UDR soldiers were murdered after ceasing to be UDR personnel. Others, especially in the Fermanagh border area, were forced to move to safer areas and had to sell their homes and sometimes their land, as a result of terrorist threats.

Apart from that, there was a long and grim history about which most British people, including British soldiers, tended to be ignorant. Nairac however knew it well. Irish History was not widely taught in British universities at that time and Nairac's extensive knowledge was based almost entirely on his private study and first-hand experience of Ireland. In those British universities where it was taught, Irish History was treated as part of the British Empire History Course, which reinforced the perception of many British people that the conflict in Northern Ireland was essentially a late colonial one. That is how the Republicans liked to portray it; so did the British hard Left; and that is how the IRA's frighteningly ignorant but emotionally-involved and well-heeled Irish-American financial backers would perceive it. In Northern Ireland that history influenced contemporary attitudes. Older people still recalled the Easter Rising of 1916, in the middle of the First World War; the Anglo-Irish War of 1919-21; the Connaught Rangers' mutiny of 1920; the Irish Civil War of 1921-22; Partition; the flight of the Southern Irish Protestants and Eire's questionable neutrality during the Second World War.

Apart from his intelligence and diplomacy, one of Nairac's strengths was that he was an Oxford historian; the majority of his brother officers were not. The discipline of History teaches its students to analyse and understand the points of view of both or all sides in any given historical situation or conflict. He was able to bring this perspective to Northern Ireland. Nairac never seems to have favoured one side over the other, despite his Roman Catholic religion. While remaining deeply interested in Ireland as a whole, he took a balanced view. The fact that he knew the history, often better than the Northern Irish themselves, was a definite factor in his favour. It impressed them: so many British officers had only a superficial understanding. Nairac had done his homework and now it was paying off.

Major G also made the important point that, while Nairac might have empathised with the Republicans because he understood their history, he did not sympathise with them, their aims or their methods. If his occasional asides on the subject can be believed, Nairac hated all the paramilitaries and what they were doing, equally. It may be that he got too close to the issues and that at times he became emotionally involved, but Major G's comments, which are insightful, tend to dispose of any notion that Nairac was, or ever could have been, a double agent, or that he was anything other than impartial. If he spent less time tracking Protestant Loyalist paramilitaries and concentrated on the IRA and its splinter groups, that simply reflected the Army's thinking at that time; that the Loyalists seemed to pose less of a threat.

Whether or not Nairac really thought that he could personally infiltrate the IRA, as has been alleged, he achieved an unusual degree of trust and access with the local community, who probably perceived him as sympathetic but most of whom were nevertheless IRA sympathisers, or even IRA volunteers. At Castle Dillon he did not however enjoy the exceptional degree of trust and friendship that he had enjoyed in Ardoyne, partly because there were not the same opportunities. What he did achieve was some extremely good intelligence. This was like historical research; a matter of patience and sustained hard work, slowly assembling a jigsaw of very small pieces: gauging the mood of the locals; listening to pub gossip and picking up information about forthcoming IRA operations. Exercising his charisma, Nairac managed to get his interlocutors to relax and become indiscreet. His boisterous and humorous conversation, which they enjoyed, disguised the fact that they were being subtly interrogated. To do this, Nairac had to draw on his skills as an actor: to work out what his interlocutor wanted to see and then play this imaginary character back to them. As John Parker remarks in *Secret Hero*, Nairac must have been successful in this. If he had not been, he would have been killed in 1974.

Nairac's unusual ability as an actor is confirmed by an officer who knew him while he was in NITAT (NI). He seems to have had the ability ascribed to Sherlock Homes by his creator, to completely alter his appearance at will, with minimal effort. Another person who also had this gift was Sir Laurence Olivier. This was less a matter of changing his clothes than of altering his speech, manner, stance, or way of walking. The transformation could occur instantly, within seconds. Speaking to a senior Army officer Nairac would suddenly snap to attention and become very much the Guards Officer; even a senior Guards Officer, although he was in fact only an Acting Captain. Chatting with a local farmer, or drinking in a Fenian bar, he would seem a completely different person and would sound, look, act and walk differently.

Although Gerald Seymour's fictional Captain Harry Brown in his novel *Harry's Game*, published in 1975, was not based on Nairac, there is a strange, fortuitous, similarity between the ways in which the imaginary, but believable, Harry and the real Nairac operated. Few people in Northern Ireland knew about Harry Brown's existence or his activities, so secret was the mission that had been entrusted to him. As a result of this, he was inadvertently killed by his own side at the end of the novel. When Nairac was killed in 1977, inevitable comparisons would be drawn between them. From that it was a step to suspecting that Nairac had also been compromised or even killed by his own side, either accidentally or on purpose.

In the absence of official documentation, it has been necessary to fall back on the testimony of people who knew Nairac at this time. One who came to know him well was "Nicky Curtis", who was also engaged in intelligence work. Despite one or two incidents that were imaginary or much embellished in Curtis' Northern Irish memoir *Faith and Duty*, Curtis' former Platoon Commander, who appears under the name of "Chris Mather" in the book, has said that on the whole and with a few exceptions, those parts of *Faith and Duty* for which he can personally vouch are accurate. There is no reason to doubt that Curtis knew Nairac as well as anyone in the Army ever did, or that (with a few exceptions) his recorded personal impressions of Nairac are intended to be faithful, although they are suffused with an afterglow of hero-worship. He found Nairac brave, charismatic, intelligent but in the final analysis un-knowable and enigmatic. At one point he mistrusted him and feared that he might be a double-agent but later concluded that he could not have been. Nairac and Mather were almost the only two commissioned officers whom the NCO Curtis encountered in Northern Ireland, for whom he had any respect or about whom he had anything positive to say. He admired their leadership and physical courage, stating that they both had "balls of iron", forged in the same smithy.

One day Curtis was sitting in the outer office in Craigavon when someone entered the room. He had not heard him enter, but suddenly sensed his presence.

"He was a tall, dark-haired handsome bloke with an unusual air of confidence about him. He stuck in my mind because there was something about him that reminded me very much of my later impression of Chris Mather: the same natural officer-bred authority at odds with a squaddie's toughness in the eyes; the same kink in the nose that looked like a relic of boxing days and the same swagger of a soldier totally at ease with his own abilities. He strode past and disappeared into the [inner] office.

"I asked quietly of the officer beside me, 'Who is that?'

"'Oh that's Robert,' he said with a noticeable respect in his voice, as if the one name should be enough. 'He's part of the hush-hush operational guys that have been brought over' [*i.e. NITAT (NI)*]. This didn't really tell me a great deal more but added to the intrigue."

Lest any knowledgeable reader should be surprised at Nairac's being described as tall, encountered in the flesh he gave the impression of being taller than he really was. This was partly a matter of holding himself very straight and upright; partly the effect of his rather overwhelming personality. In fact, as his file confirms, Nairac was only five feet, ten inches tall. he had "presence"

Some weeks later Curtis, with others, was instructed to check a VIP though a military checkpoint situated near the border with the Republic. He was to pretend to search the man, so that no-one who might be watching should suspect anything, but to let him through without hassle. The man proved to be carrying false identity papers and a bogus driving licence that gave him an Irish name and address. Curtis and his colleagues searched the man, but not his car, as they had been warned that it would contain weapons. The man was Robert, the same handsome officer whom Curtis had seen earlier at Craigavon, now disguised by a beard. After the check, he drove away into the Republic and into the darkness.

A former member of NITAT (NI) has cast doubt on this account. In his view this is yet another imaginary episode that Curtis' ghost writer inserted in the narrative in order to "sex up" his narrative. He has stated that NITAT (NI) did not secretly cross the border. If they had to, there was some good official reason. At this distance in time, and without having Curtis' explanation, it is near-impossible to tell.

Later Curtis learned from a NITAT (NI) NCO that the mysterious officer was called Robert Nairac. He had already heard whispers about him. Nairac was highly rated by both NITAT (NI) and the RUC as an intelligence agent. His speciality was deep-cover infiltration and he reportedly had a great ability to mix with the locals, speaking with a credible Irish accent and passing himself off as Irish: not as an Armagh man, which would have been difficult or impossible, but as someone from another part of Ireland. His intimate knowledge of Belfast, Dublin and Galway allowed him to display credible familiarity with those areas. As Curtis remarks in his book:

"This was a very dangerous game to play. It was akin to tiptoeing through a minefield. One wrong step could blow your cover and the fallout from the blast would be your certain capture, torture and assassination."

The genuinely surprising part of this is not that Nairac was eventually abducted, tortured and murdered in 1977, but that this did not happen sooner. Yet he not only survived his 1974-75 special duties tour in Northern Ireland, but he almost survived his fourth and final tour. His murder would occur close to his end-of-tour date. This suggests that Nairac was in fact very good at his job and does not support the repeated claims by certain former SAS officers that Nairac was a liability; inexperienced, naive; "a lamb to the slaughter" in Clive Fairweather's words. On the contrary; in 1976-77 Nairac knew considerably more than most of the SAS. He had "been there, done that", long before them. Perhaps that had made him over-confident. But, this being so, why did Clive Fairweather and his friends continue to peddle this line of disinformation long after Nairac's disappearance; and especially given that it is so easy, with minimal research, to disprove?

Although the SAS were ordered into Ulster in 1976, there were, as Curtis remarks in his book, increasingly frequent rumours that the Regiment was already present in the Province well before that date. He adds that he was in no position to confirm or deny this. As Curtis knew, there were a number of SAS specialists training, assisting and advising first the MRF and later NITAT (NI). Rumours of their presence might have started to circulate and then been exaggerated; this possibility cannot be ruled out. Curtis, however, proposes an alternative explanation: that the rumours had been deliberately put about as part of a "black propaganda" exercise by MI5. Prior to 1980, the sinister legends surrounding the SAS, plus the perennial lack of hard information about their operations, were enough to trigger fear and paranoia in the ranks of the IRA. It hardly mattered that the SAS were not really present. Simply planting the belief that they were lurking somewhere in Northern Ireland would have the desired effect. The Unionist politicians, who in 1976 would press Prime Minister Harold Wilson to send the SAS into Northern Ireland, clearly did not think that the Regiment was already present. Had the SAS really been there, the Unionists might have asked that the SAS presence should be increased and strengthened, but they would hardly have made their request in the terms that they did; nor would Wilson have announced soon afterwards that the SAS were about to be sent in; nor would he have followed this with a number of unhelpful retrospective conditions. All of this suggests that Nicky Curtis' suspicion was correct.

Nairac was about to embark on another close and committed friendship that would have an important influence on his career and life. The new friend was an SAS officer, Acting Major Julian Antony Ball, usually known as Tony. Tony Ball was Nairac's immediate superior in NITAT (NI). He had risen from the ranks, which was probably a recommendation in Nairac's eyes. Ball was five years older than Nairac: he had been born in 1943 in Chelmsford, where he attended the King Edward VI School. He started to study at Welbeck, the Army's sixth-form college, in September 1959, but dropped out before the end of the two-year course. There is no record of his graduation or of any passes at A-level. He did not proceed from Welbeck to Sandhurst, which had presumably been his intention, but joined the Army as a Private. At different times Ball served in the Parachute Regiment and as a trooper in 22 SAS. Although he was not a Scot he was eventually commissioned, aged 27, into the King's Own Scottish Borderers in 1970, which was also Clive Fairweather's parent Regiment. He would be gazetted Major on 31 December 1976 and later returned to the SAS as an officer. While serving in Northern Ireland with the KOSB, Ball won the Military Cross (MC) for bravery.

There have been numerous allegations of Ball and Nairac's involvement in questionable activities, including murder, but no evidence that would satisfy a court has ever been produced. The most that can be verified is an entry in an Army Watch-Keeper log: a complaint by a member of the public in Turf Lodge, Belfast. The complainant refers to Tony Ball as "John Wayne" and his Sergeant as "Tonto". This suggests that they were perceived as cowboys and as having acted in an antisocial manner on that occasion. Turf Lodge is a housing estate that was built on the outskirts of Belfast following the Second World War and is a strongly Republican area.

According to another former officer:

"[Ball] strikes me as being extremely on edge – always 'operational'. During the 1972 KOSB tour of Northern Ireland he opened fire on a number of occasions, 'lifted' an extraordinary number of people (total for the Company was over 600; most of whom were subsequently released). Ball was in command of the 'squirrels'; a sub-unit of the Reconnaissance Platoon responsible for gathering intelligence and finding weapons/people. In some ways it is depicted as a forerunner of 14 Int – perhaps it was. He appears to have been, or at least was regarded as, very successful during this tour – even though he led a three man covert plain clothes patrol that shot two innocent men (the Conway brothers). He was definitely not psychopathic, but certainly aggressive and perhaps a little reckless though ultimately effective (I use this latter description not in a judgemental sense – effective, yes; but correct? – well that is another matter). Ball had been an SAS Trooper prior to his commissioning and the essence of the Watch-keeper log conveys a 'boys own' vision of a gung ho warrior who, because of his 'other rank' roots, was highly respected by his men. The number of entries attributed to 'Mr Ball' is quite extraordinary."

In addition to being his close friend, Nairac regarded Ball, a slightly older and more experienced soldier, as a mentor and an example: Ball influenced his thinking. But, for all his admirable characteristics, was the gung-ho ex-Para and SAS officer Ball the most helpful exemplar for someone like Robert Nairac to have followed? The previous quotation might suggest that possibly he was not. If Nairac was ever guilty of adopting a "Boys' Own" approach to soldiering, it is more likely to have been the result of Tony Ball's influence than that of Bulldog Drummond.

When considering allegations of murder, or even of "lifting" people, it is important to remember that Ball and Nairac's job in 1974-75 was not killing or kidnapping people, although they may occasionally have had to act in self-defence. It should not be supposed that they were involved in any dirty-tricks campaign. Their work, while definitely dangerous, was far less romantic than 007's: it was discreet and patient intelligence-gathering, research and analysis; putting together a complicated military intelligence jigsaw with many pieces. They were both very good at this. They made an excellent team and produced some impressive results.

Ball and Nairac would work together for almost nine months. They had much in common, both being original thinkers and very brave. Both were outstanding leaders and tacticians and had made themselves experts on Ireland, including Northern Ireland. They were also complementary; each had qualities that the other lacked. Ball was very organised, practical and exact. He could sometimes upset senior officers in the Army and the RUC by his directness. He could be abrasive, although he could also be great company. Nairac was by contrast tactful, suave and diplomatic. He could usually defuse any difficulty that Ball's manner had caused. Even so, despite his reputation for abrasiveness, numerous people including Nairac liked and respected Ball. They included many Northern Irish people. He has been described as "very tough and hard but a super chap to be with and completely admired by most of his contemporaries." According to his not-very-informative 1981 obituary in the SAS Regimental journal, *Mars and Minerva*:

"His loping figure will be missed in many areas of Belfast as well as in more familiar places... he made a considerable and long-lasting impact both on operations and training. Always restless, he elected to leave the Army and had just started to establish himself as a tough, uncompromising commanding officer of the Sultan of Oman's Special Forces when he was tragically killed in a road-traffic accident. He was only thirty-eight." In fact he was thirty-seven.

It is not strictly correct to state that Tony Ball resigned from the Army and the SAS because he was "always restless" and, by implication, had gone off to seek adventure in the Gulf. There was a simple, professional reason: Ball had not passed Staff College; furthermore, unlike Nairac, he had not passed, and had perhaps not even attended, any other British Army Staff course. This being so, he had correctly concluded that he would achieve no further promotion beyond Major. His last British appointment was as Commandant of PATA. This was the Pontrillas Army Training Area; formerly exclusively a SAS training area, later also used for the advanced training of SRU personnel who were preparing to go to Northern Ireland. In 1980 Ball chose to join the Sultan's Armed Forces.

Elsewhere Tony Ball's obituary states that:

"The personal contribution which he made to the fight against terrorism and his cool gallantry resulted in him being awarded a number of unique decorations for the campaign [*i.e. Operation Banner in Northern Ireland*]. He was also recommended for several others."

Those two sentences are intriguing. What were the proposed but undelivered decorations and why were the recommendations for these not acted upon? Did someone very senior veto the awards and if so, for what reason? It is not true that Ball had received "a number of unique decorations," although the medals that he did receive were enviable. They consisted of the Military Cross (MC); the MBE (Military), which is less often awarded than the civilian equivalent; the General Service Medal with clasps for Borneo, South Arabia (Aden) and Northern Ireland and an oak leaf, indicating that the recipient had been Mentioned in Despatches. There were also a UN decoration and the Oman Peace Medal, which was a Sultanate of Oman decoration. There was nothing unique about any of these medals, although some of them were awarded very sparingly. Tony Ball's family sold his medals after his death. Spinks Auctioneers offered them for sale, together with his cap and SAS beret, for sale as a single lot. The catalogue states:

"MAJOR BALL'S medals, [SAS] beret and, cap, expected to fetch up to £5,000, include the MBE, Military Cross, and Oman Peace Medal. He was commissioned as a subaltern into the [*King's Own Scottish*] Borderers in 1970, winning the MC with them after incidents with gunmen in Belfast. His work in the mid-70s as commander of a small undercover SAS team stationed in Northern Ireland is both controversial and mysterious. [*This is incorrect and refers to his work for NITAT (NI)*.] In 1980 he became commanding officer of the Sultan of Oman's Special Forces. He was killed soon afterwards when his Range Rover overturned."

In the event Major Ball's medals and memorabilia were to realise £12,000; more than twice Spinks' estimate.

A colleague described him simply as: "A good man to go to war with". "A great leader and a fine man, great sense of humour. Gone but not forgotten," said another. "I found him to be one of the most honest men I have ever served under", wrote a third. He evidently had a lot in common with Nairac.

Tony Ball, like Robert Nairac, remained to the end a man of mystery. Much of his Army career is known only in the barest outline. No-one knows exactly how he met his death in Oman in 1981, except that it appeared to have been a road traffic accident. There were no known witnesses and no survivors. Ball had been driving. His passenger, SAS Major Andrew Nightingale, another of Nairac's friends, died with him. No other vehicle was involved and there was no inquest. Although Ball had resigned from the British Army in order to work for the Sultan, the SAS claimed its dead. His body was repatriated to the UK in record time and he was buried in the SAS plot in St Martin's churchyard, Hereford, following a military funeral. Even Tony Ball's tombstone is intriguing and raises unanswered questions: it seems to be a standard Commonwealth War Graves Commission stone, bearing the badges of the KOSB and the SAS, although Ball did not die in either World War, nor was he even in the British Army at the time of his death.

Recent inquiries in Oman have revealed nothing. Apparently there was no record; no-one now recalled anything about Ball in his role as commander of the Sultan's Special Forces; or not officially, at any rate. Ball and Nightingale had known Nairac well in Northern Ireland. Had they survived, they might have provided important and informed insights into what he was doing in 1974-75.

Although almost all the legends that Nairac was at this period implicated in a series of illegal acts, including the Dublin and Monaghan bombings, have been disposed of because he was simply not there and not available to have taken part, nevertheless an exception is the murder in the Irish Republic of IRA Staff Captain John Francis "Benny" Green in January 1975. An undoubted terrorist, Green was also a personable and popular young man. He was a much-loved husband, father and a good friend to many Northern Irish Republicans. Nairac was in Northern Ireland at that time; he knew about Green's importance and that he had fled to the Republic.

However, at the time of Green's murder Nairac was engaged in a surveillance operation elsewhere. He was with (among others) his immediate superior, Tony Ball, who later confirmed this. An unreliable witness, Fred Holroyd, much later stated that during a meeting with Nairac in Portadown, Nairac claimed that he had killed Green. To support his claim, Nairac reportedly produced a colour Polaroid photograph of the dead IRA man, said to have been taken by him shortly after Green's murder. This photograph is the crucial piece of evidence on which Nairac's alleged guilt hangs. A reliable source, close both to Nairac and Tony Ball, has given assurances that the photo was authentic, but it had been taken by a member of the Garda, the Irish Republic Police; not by Nairac. The policeman who took it was one of those summoned to the scene of the crime. Nairac had legitimately requested a copy, or copies, through the RUC.

Also relevant is the comment in Martin Dillon's *The Dirty War* regarding the Polaroid photo. Dillon suggests that it was recovered from Holroyd's estranged wife by the RUC, rather than being handed over by him. Perhaps more significantly, he observes that forensic evidence suggests the photograph was taken some 18 hours after the victim's death. If this is true, it completely rules out Holroyd's suggestion that it was taken by Nairac or Ball at the time of Green's murder.

It has been argued that the Garda did not at that time possess Polaroid cameras. This was officially true. However the Gardai in question, based at Dundalk, possessed an unofficial Polaroid. It was an informal gift from the RUC: a camera that had been written-off as "lost" by the Newry RUC. More recently it has emerged that the real killer was a Loyalist, now dead, who believed that Green, or more probably his host, Gerry Carville, had been involved in his brother's murder. It is possible that Green was shot in mistake for Carville. Whatever Nairac might or might not have said to Holroyd, the truth is less exciting and scandalous than the legend.

According to Fred Holroyd, Nairac admitted his and Tony Ball's involvement in the murder and even parted with one of the Polaroid photos of the dead man lying in a pool of blood. This was a singularly incautious thing to have done if he had really been implicated in such an illegal act. The admission and provision of evidence would have amounted to an invitation to prosecute him. This photo is key to the thesis that Nairac must have been present; must have killed Green by himself or with Tony Ball; and must have taken the photo himself as a "trophy". But the argument collapses because Nairac was not there.

It has also been asserted that Nairac and Ball had personally kept the Carville farmhouse under surveillance for days before the shooting, noting the habits and movements of the inhabitants. The same source added that he would be "amazed if NITAT (NI) had ever conducted surveillance operations in the Republic".

Nevertheless an alternative Republican narrative is that, while Loyalists might have carried out the killing, Nairac, having carried out a detailed reconnaissance, "must" have revealed Green's whereabouts to them and the best time to get him alone. One way or another they seem determined to pin this crime on Nairac, in spite of there being no evidence.

It is impossible not to feel considerable sympathy for Fred Holroyd. He seems to have been unlucky in many ways. In the 1970s he suffered a succession of personal tragedies and career setbacks. These culminated in his return from Northern Ireland to the UK and his compulsory psychiatric referral by the Army. Given the strain and trauma that he had undergone, plus his growing addiction to alcohol, the referral seems to have been medically justified. However, he is not a totally reliable witness. He is a man with a grudge, who believes that the Army treated him badly and that his psychiatric referral, which occurred soon after Green's murder, was a politically motivated "dirty trick" to get him out of Northern Ireland and to discredit his testimony. Holroyd resigned from the Army in 1976. Nairac was taking over some of Holroyd's intelligence functions. That cannot have gone down well. However, the most serious flaw in the argument that Nairac "must" have been involved in the Green murder is that the allegations only surfaced long after Nairac's death. Tony Ball was also conveniently dead by then. Neither he nor Nairac was in any position to defend himself. Yet had Holroyd or others become aware of incontrovertible evidence that Ball and Nairac had been engaged in criminal activity in 1974-75, it was their duty to report it then. This suggests that firm evidence, as opposed to rumours, did not exist. It may be significant that Clive Fairweather, who also sought posthumously to damage Nairac's reputation, did not reiterate these particular allegations; probably because he knew them to be baseless and fairly easily disproved.

Another former officer who also served in Northern Ireland has made the following comment on the Green killing:

"It is on the one hand, in the sense that it would have been a covert penetration in a hostile area, the type of operation that Ball might have revelled in. But to commit a murder in such circumstances would go beyond reckless... If the John Francis Green incident was an out and out murder, then I would not have thought that Ball would have been involved. From what I now know of Nairac's background, I cannot imagine a conscientious individual like Robert Nairac participating in something so grotesque."

It is difficult to avoid the conclusion that, in an attempt to salvage his own reputation and credibility and perhaps to be reinstated or compensated by the Army, Fred Holroyd was prepared to cause extensive posthumous damage to Nairac's name and reputation.

Nairac's flair for self-dramatisation may have helped to muddy the waters; he might have taken mischievous delight in misleading and shocking Fred Holroyd.

This was not apparently particularly difficult to do: especially shocking him. It would have been in line with Nairac's known behaviour, while in "Mr Hyde" mode, of misleading other people. Nairac did discuss the Green murder with another person; one who remains attached to his memory. This was Nicky Curtis, who recorded that:

"I decided to test the waters with him about the killing of Benny Green. I didn't know if the whispers of his involvement were just of the Chinese variety, twisted in their travels beyond anything recognisably true. I said something like how it had been a good day's work by whoever had done the job and he just nodded and agreed. Then he looked at me with more than simple expectation of the next question, but with what looked like encouragement, too. It was the sign for me to jump in with both feet:

'I'd heard that you were involved in it, along with the SAS.'

He pressed his fingertips together in a cathedral arch, on which he rested his chin.

'I don't doubt, Nicky, that you've heard such a thing, but you and I have heard a lot of things in our time here. And no doubt we will hear a lot more.'

It was neither a denial nor an admission, but I realised that it was all I was going to get. He continued to look at me over his fingers but his eyes betrayed nothing either way. His face was as impenetrable as his answer."

If it has been correctly reported, this remark might be interpreted in more than one way. Most people would read it as: "If you believe that, you'll believe anything!" Curtis however was not sure:

"Was he cautiously admitting his involvement, but in such a way as not to compromise himself completely? Or was he just knowingly planting that thought in me as a way of further bolstering his own reputation – as an act of bravado? Maybe this was how the whispers had started in the first place, through Nairac's own carefully-worded hints. I didn't mention that I had been told outright of his liaising with the SAS... or that there was a widely held belief that he supplied information to the UVF and the UDA, enabling them to take out Provos. Perhaps this was the route that had led to the killing of Benny Green."

Two odd things, or simple errors, in this passage are that Nairac's role as a Liaison Officer was not secret. It was part of his official cover for his intelligence-gathering activities. Nairac was not at that time "liaising with the SAS", other than with a few SAS specialists, including Tony Ball, who were on secondment to NITAT (NI). His Liaison Officer's job was to improve co-operation and information-sharing between the Army (including NITAT (NI)) and the RUC's Special Branch. The SAS would not be ordered into Northern Ireland until 1976. Nairac could not have foreseen this in 1974-75. Curtis provides a further insight:

"It seemed to me that there was a side to him that secretly yearned for recognition of the undoubtedly brave and clever way in which he operated; wider recognition than that already given to him by the very select few who were privy to the whole truth of what he actually did here. During a previous briefing, when Nairac's name was mentioned, I'd already heard another officer say, 'He thinks he's Lawrence of bloody Arabia!' I now knew enough to know he would take that as a compliment."

Given Nairac's private cult of T E Lawrence, this was undoubtedly true. Curtis would encounter Nairac again and was clearly fascinated by him, although he continued to find him baffling. Here he is again:

"We talked about things, but he never really revealed to me exactly what he'd been doing or why. He still reminded me of Chris [*Curtis' former platoon commander*], though Nairac's confidence, unlike Chris', was tinged with arrogance. I didn't mind this, though; I'd found that arrogant, difficult men were usually the most interesting.

"It was odd; here I was trying to find out about him and all he was interested in was talking about me... It was a good way of him avoiding revealing too much about himself. But there was another reason behind his questions. I think when he knew I'd been through the mill, and seen some hard times and survived them, he knew he was safe with me. And that told me that he was a switched-on operator because I knew that just one of the many fears of undercover work was of someone else's incompetence blowing you out of the water. No king's reign would last long [*if he were*] surrounded by court jesters.

"I mentioned the time I'd passed him through the Aughnacloy checkpoint, but knew better than to press for details of the mission. He just nodded and then gave me a demonstration of his ability to adopt different Irish dialects: from the hard Belfast accent to the softer Derry brogue. This was a bloody difficult thing to do. The Irish could usually spot a stranger or a "faker" within seconds, particularly in the remoter provinces where unknown faces were treated with intense suspicion. I think his Irish background stood him in good stead on this score. His mother was a Protestant and his father was a Catholic. Like me, he had been raised as a devout Catholic and, again like me, he had gone through the same feelings on landing in Northern Ireland for the first time, his knowledge of the conflict's history giving him the belief that he might be able to do some good."

This is another interesting mix of fact and error: Nairac had no Irish blood, although he knew Ireland extremely well. If Curtis thought that Nairac was of Irish descent, it was because Nairac had told him so, or had implied this, or because he was so obviously knowledgeable about Ireland. Given Nairac's extensive travels in Ireland, it is also unlikely that his first experience of Northern Ireland was when the Army sent him there in early 1973.

Like Nairac, Curtis was raised as a Catholic. He was brought up in Yorkshire and served in a Yorkshire Regiment, the Green Howards, which historically had a good number of Catholic soldiers in its ranks. Unlike Nairac, Curtis, though born in England, genuinely has Irish ancestry. Yet, despite this, Nairac apparently

managed to fool Curtis, who seems to have found no fault with his assumed Irish identity and accent. Nairac's remarkable ability as a mimic is confirmed by another witness. Curtis and Nairac's wish, as Army Catholics, to make a positive difference in Northern Ireland by improving relations between the Army and the Catholic community, was genuine. In retrospect this now seems unrealistically optimistic, but on arrival they were both, in their quiet way, idealistic young men. One would become cynical, disillusioned and would lose his faith, but would survive. The other would not.

Curtis later commented: "I found that despite the obvious differences between us of class and rank, we had far more in common. He had that kind of savvy and natural, in-built bullshit-detector that was universal to all good soldiers. It was gratifying to meet someone who deserved the respect that they were given."

Coming from an NCO, there cannot be many higher badges of approval than the foregoing three sentences. The value of Curtis' account is less for the factual detail; he is sometimes inaccurate or just plain wrong. Rather it is for his snapshots, which bring Nairac vividly to life. Here, for example, is Nairac's comment following a dangerous brush with the IRA, in the course of which Curtis had to threaten someone with a revolver:

"On the way back Robert turned to me, smiling, and with reference to my treatment of Gurney said, 'So which charm school for advanced etiquette did you attend?'

As by now I was aware of his own reputation, I replied, 'Probably the same one as you.'

I eased back into the seat. I noticed Nairac's eyes in the rear-view mirror, narrowed slightly in a half-smile. I understood. You never planned near-misses or narrow escapes but when they did happen and you got away, you couldn't help but get off on the excitement."

Nairac all too clearly did get off on the excitement and could not get enough of it. The adrenaline was addictive.

"Despite my involvement with him, Nairac still remained something of an enigma to me. I had him down as one of those figures who revealed different sides of his character to different people, depending on who he was with at the time. This was part of the chameleon nature that made him so valuable as an undercover agent and so skilled at adopting various disguises. He was known to frequent rabidly Republican bars in the guise of a Belfast 'stickie'. It was even reported that he went so far as to jump on stage and join in drunken renderings of 'Danny Boy'. This kind of character submersion not only required balls of iron but a great self-confidence in your own abilities. I suspected that each person he worked with probably had his own personal and slightly differing view of Nairac."

Much less amusing, and illustrative of both the mischievous and mysterious sides of Nairac's character, was when he proposed to Curtis, following a

successful mission, that they should have a drink in a pub. This particular pub was a notorious Provo haunt in Coalisland. Curtis' reaction was incredulous:

"You're joking, aren't you? Have you gone totally fucking insane?"

Nairac was not joking, although Curtis' consternation obviously amused him. He replied that everything would be fine provided that Curtis stuck with him, did not speak and let him do all the talking and ordering of drinks. Anyway, if the worst came to the worst, both of them were armed with handguns in shoulder holsters. Curtis could think of no good reason why they should drink there rather than in a safe Protestant bar, except that perhaps Nairac wanted to show off his abilities as an undercover agent, but such was Curtis' faith in Nairac that he decided that this was inadequate: there had to be another reason. There was. While Curtis sipped his beer, Nairac had an absorbing conversation with the bar's owner, a notorious IRA sympathiser. In Curtis' book his name is given as McCrory, which is not his real name. Presently Nairac left the bar and did not reappear. McCrory too disappeared. Curtis became more and more agitated, fearing that Nairac might have been "jumped" by the PIRA in the men's lavatory and murdered. Finally he went in search of him.

Curtis eventually found Nairac and McCrory in another more private room, hunched over a table with drinks "like old pals". Curtis stood at the door and did not enter. They were deep in conversation and did not notice Curtis. It was clear that Nairac had established some kind of relationship with McCrory. Given the man's strong Republican credentials, it seemed unlikely that Nairac had recruited him as a source. If he had, it would have been an incredible coup. But whatever the truth may have been, they had evidently become close. So what were they up to? When pressed, Nairac said that he had "just been passing the time of day", which Curtis did not believe. "Whatever had passed between them, it was more than the time of day."

We shall never know what was said, but soon afterwards an RUC contact raised with Curtis the disquieting possibility that Nairac just might be a double agent. After all, he was a Catholic and his father was widely, although wrongly, believed to be Irish. The RUC contact had almost certainly picked up the rumour from the UDR or one of the Loyalist organisations. Curtis however concluded that Nairac was far too effective in his work against the IRA for it to be plausible. Had a double agent been at work, there would have been a number of significant security breaches on the British side; serious enough to have cancelled out any damage that the British had inflicted on the IRA and any advantage that they might have reaped from that. Nothing of the sort had happened. And in the final analysis Curtis trusted Nairac. All the available evidence suggests that he was right to have done so.

Some of these rumours evidently filtered back to the SAS in Hereford. Although they may present a united front to the outside world, in their private context soldiers talk shop, intrigue, gossip and whisper among themselves as much

as members of other professions. When Nairac returned to Ulster in 1976, he would find from Day 1 that certain SAS officers regarded him with suspicion as a potential double agent and general bad egg, and never really altered their view. Their unguarded recorded comments confirm this. In most if not all cases, they had come to that opinion without having met Nairac; when they met him they saw no reason to modify it. His charm offensive had no effect; it merely reinforced their prejudices. This *canard* of Nairac as possible double agent, and perhaps other bad things, was to have serious consequences. Not only does it seem to have been a factor in his murder in 1977; or rather in the inexplicably slow SAS/Army response to his abduction, but it has tarnished his memory. To his critics and enemies Nairac can still do no right. Either he was a scheming, thuggish SAS assassin of Irish Republicans; or he was a probable IRA sympathiser, a double agent and a traitor; or he was a naive, gung-ho would-be Bulldog Drummond, all brawn and no brain, whose antics and blunders put himself and others in danger: although logically he could not have been all of these things. In fact he was not any of them.

Other unverifiable exploits are attributed to Nairac at this time, including the recruitment and successful evacuation of an IRA informer, referred to as Jackie Lynch.

There is another dark element to this narrative. Although Nairac would leave Northern Ireland in April 1975 at the end of his tour with another very good confidential report under his belt and a silver tankard from the RUC in his baggage, and although he evidently enjoyed this kind of irregular soldiering, it was stressful. According even to well-disposed friends, Nairac, never exactly abstemious, drank quite heavily at this period; at least when he was on leave and off-duty. He nevertheless contrived somehow to remain physically very fit. He had become obsessive about information-gathering. He could not switch off. According to "Steve", a former Grenadier Guardsman, during 1974-75 Nairac, instead of spending his leave doing something therapeutic like angling, passed much of it in London, where he had numerous friends who were happy to put him up. They included Lord Salisbury's family, who had a house in Chelsea. Nairac's evenings and nights were spent in the Irish quarters of Kilburn and Cricklewood, sometimes with reluctant friends in tow; always looking out and listening for information. There, he would sometimes become violent, knocking people's lights out.

Afterwards he would often want to go into Chelsea Barracks, where the 1st Battalion Grenadiers were stationed, to use the Officers' Mess bar there. His brother officers of the 2nd Battalion were still in Hong Kong, so Nairac had relatively few close friends in the Mess at that time. There were incidents. Steve once witnessed Nairac knocking out a minicab driver outside the Barracks, following an altercation over the fare. Nairac stood looking thoughtfully at his fallen foe for a few moments. Then he carefully replaced the unconscious driver in the car. Usually Nairac would be scruffily dressed, which was advisable in Kilburn but not acceptable in Chelsea Barracks. Apart from the Picquet Officer, who wore uniform, the guidance for officers who were off-duty in the Mess in the evening was "dress as you would at home". In practice the young officers tended to err on the side of formality, wearing boating jackets (blazers) and flannels, with a tie. A few wore suits. At that period jeans and donkey-jackets would not have been seen as complying with the dress code.

Finally Lieutenant Colonel Bernard Gordon Lennox issued an order that Captain Nairac was not to be admitted to the Barracks if he turned up. Steve, who liked Nairac very much, hated having to carry out this order and queried it when it was first issued. More than once he had the embarrassing task of refusing Nairac entry when he was on Guard Duty. Nairac did not make a fuss: he just nodded and went away quietly, but he clearly minded this slight. It was very unusual for an officer to be treated in this way. It was also bad luck that the Army should meanwhile have decided that Nairac's next posting should be to the 1st Battalion, as Gordon Lennox's Adjutant. When, less than a year later, he was once more a dashing, dandiacal Guards officer, on Regimental duty with the 1st Battalion, the memory of this order created awkwardness; not merely between him and Gordon Lennox, but between him and one or two junior officers, who, Nairac discovered, had indicated publicly that they supported the ban on him. He found out who they were and let them know that he knew by treating them freezingly.

Bernard Gordon Lennox, however, probably had no choice. It is likely that a higher authority had instructed him to give this order. The Regimental grapevine correctly suggested that Nairac was spending too much time in Irish pubs in Kilburn and that he was still doing undercover work while on leave. It followed that he should not be having any contact with his Regiment. If in 1974 or 1975 he had been recognised going into Chelsea Barracks by an IRA sympathiser from Kilburn, his cover would have been blown and he could have been murdered. This was probably the real reason for his exclusion, but Nairac, after a few pints of Guinness, seemed to forget this; in the final analysis the ban was in his best interest. Whether he saw it in this light is another matter.

Steve left the Army in late 1976 and was working in Germany in 1977 when Nairac was murdered. He last saw him in South Armagh a few months earlier. While he was out on patrol, he suddenly felt a hand slap him hard on the back. Wheeling round, he saw grinning at him a scruffy, tough-looking fellow whom he recognised with difficulty as the once-dapper Captain Nairac. "Hello, Steve! Long time no see!" chuckled Nairac.

Steve has nothing but good feelings about Nairac. He attended his memorial service in 1978, keeps his portrait on the wall of his study and remembers him on Facebook on the anniversary of his death. This is fairly typical of the guardsmen who served under Nairac.

Let us conclude this chapter on a lighter note, with a typical Nairac exploit; one on which he used occasionally to dine out. The incident took place in 1974, soon after his arrival to start his third tour in the Province. In County Down there was a restaurant and bar that we shall call the Yew Tree. The family who owned it were staunch supporters of the Provisional IRA: their elder son was a local PIRA commander and the Army would shoot him dead later that year, in August 1974.

Prior to that distressing incident the restaurant had enjoyed a good reputation and attracted a large, loyal clientele. This is confirmed by a former regular visitor, a member of the old Anglo-Irish ascendancy. His family owned a property in the Republic of Ireland near Boyle, Co. Roscommon. Visiting Northern Ireland from the Republic, they often ate at the Yew Tree, whose cuisine they found excellent. They liked the owners, who they thought were a charming couple. Like most of the other diners, until the August 1974 shooting they had not the faintest idea that they had been lunching in a PIRA robbers' nest. Nevertheless, that was the case: the restaurant had an upper room in which the PIRA used to meet, which was accessed through the restaurant. This arrangement made it difficult for any Security Forces watching outside to tell which people entering the restaurant were customers, there for a legitimate gastronomic purpose, and which were going to attend an IRA meeting in the upper room. The Security Forces were naturally only interested in those who were going into the upper room.

Finally Robert Nairac volunteered to find out. When asked what his plan was, he said "I'll have lunch there!" So he did. It was not too difficult to work out on which days the PIRA were likely to be there. Nairac's backup team were concealed nearby. He arrived by car, parked outside, entered and secured a table with a good view of the doorway that led to the staircase to the upper room. He had a micro-camera concealed about his person. Whenever a visitor made for the door leading to the upper room, or emerged from it, pop! Nairac would take another photo.

That part went smoothly. Nairac was not suspected or detected. But the PIRA meeting went on for a long time. Nairac had to wait until the last PIRA members had come down from the upper room and had either departed or were having a post-meeting drink at the bar. Finally, after an extended lunch-break, Nairac headed for his car, which was parked outside, only to find that it would not start. This was not due to PIRA sabotage; the battery was flat. We do not know the reason, but Nairac, who was not technically-minded, was the kind of person absent-mindedly to leave the lights on when parking his car. He did not have the equipment or the expertise to re-charge the battery.

Nairac did not want to call the backup team to help him start the car, as this would have given his game away, and he was not a member of the Royal Irish Automobile Club. So, back in the restaurant, he called in his best Irish accent for volunteers to give him a push. There was no problem: many of those present were happy to assist. To the bemusement of his backup, who were watching concealed not far away, a group of known and suspected IRA operatives good-naturedly gave Nairac a push. The car started and off he drove, waving and thanking them profusely while carrying his concealed camera and its incriminating film. In spite of the problem with his car, Nairac's journey had not been wasted; it is fair to assume that it was no coincidence that the proprietor's elder son was shot dead the following August.

This story is confirmed by other people who were involved. Nairac would have recounted it with greater verve and humour than is possible in print: by all accounts he was a splendid raconteur and could imitate accents to enormous comic effect. But, with the wisdom of hindsight, it also seems to indicate potential trouble for the future: letting his car battery run down looks like dangerous carelessness. Forgetting to switch off his car lights, if that was what had caused the problem, suggests that he was so excited and eager to get *in situ* that normal caution was thrown to the winds – another bad sign. Nairac seems to have been lucky on that occasion; the escapade could easily have ended badly for him, in which case he would have needed his backup team. One can see how, having repeatedly got away with this kind of thing in the past, Nairac thought that it would be safe to go to the Three Steps in Drumintee on the night of 14 May 1977, on that occasion without backup.

This formal protrait of Robert Nairac shows him in December 1975, during his service with the 1st Battalion Grenadier Guards, less than eighteen months before his murder. The photograph forms part of the collection held by the National Portrait Gallery. © Copyright NPG 2015.

The 'Bloody Sunday' confrontation in the Bogside, Londonderry on 30 January 1972 between British paratroopers and Republican rioters marked a low point in relations between the Army and the Nationalist community. © Thopson/AFP/Getty Images

Lieutenant Colonel Derek Wilford, who commanded 1 Para on 'Bloody Sunday'. © Press Association.

Julian "Tony" Ball, an SAS officer, was Nairac's immediate superior and close friend in NITAT (NI) in 1974-75 Reproduced with kind permission. © www.specialforcesroh.com.

1st XV—AUTUMN 1972

Back Row (left to right): J.U.O. A. E. Whitley, O/Cdt. R. J. Knight, O/Cdt. J. S. Kerr, O/Cdt. L. P. M. Lyons, 2/Lt. I. A. Pender-Cudlip, R.A., O/Cdt. I. R. Savua, 2/Lt. B. C. Holt, I.G., 2/Lt. M. P. Gostick, R.E., W.O.II Hearne, W.G.
Centre Row (left to right): O/Cdt. R. K. G. Dutton, O/Cdt. P. H. Blundell, S.U.O. A. J. B. Edwards, Major D. E. King, R.A.P.C., S/Cdt. T. H. Eveleigh (Capt.), 2/Lt. R. L. Nairac, Gren. Gds., 2/Lt. R. North, R.E.
Front Row (left to right): O/Cdt. G. R. Wadsworth, O/Cdt. D. M. Santa-Ollala.

The Sandhurst Rugby 1st XV, with Robert Nairac seated centre row, second from the right. The photograph forms part of the Royal Military Academy (RMA) Sandhurst Collection, curated by Dr Anthony Morton. Reproduced with the kind permission of the Ministry of Defence/Crown Copyright, 2015.

SALAMANCA COMPANY, VICTORY COLLEGE, POST UNIVERSITY COURSE 1—SEPTEMBER 1972

Salamanca Company, based in Victory College. Robert Nairac is standing centre row, in the middle. The photograph forms part of the Royal Military Academy (RMA) Sandhurst Collection, curated by Dr Anthony Morton. Reproduced with the kind permission of the Ministry of Defence/ Crown Copyright, 2015.

Above: Robert Nairac during his time as a member of NITAT (NI), based at Castle Dillon in 1974-75. Naira appears to be dressed as a member of the IRA, with black beret, DP combat jacket, longish hair and a typica IRA firearm. Reproduced with the kind permission of a former brother officer and friend of Nairac's who wishe to remain anonymous. *Below:* Slieve Gullion, County Armagh. Used under free licence © Ring of Gullion.org

CHAPTER 11 | REGIMENTAL DAYS AND NIGHTS

Regimental soldiering... is a far higher and more arduous life than one of irresponsible adventure. (Hugh Dormer DSO)

I love any discourse of rivers, and fish and fishing. (Izaak Walton)

In the modern Army it is normal for officers to bid or volunteer well in advance for jobs that of interest to them, and which are likely to become vacant in the near to medium future. Competition for the more challenging ones and for those that are perceived to be a stepping stone to promotion is keen. In the 1970s, however, although some were proactive, most officers tended to wait for the Army to decide where to send them next. There was often no, or minimal, prior consultation with the officer concerned; especially if he was not married or a father. Officers were moved about like pawns in a chess-game.

The Household Division, however, did not operate in the same way as other Regiments. Normally a Guards officer would be told well in advance where he was being posted and when. If he did not like it for any reason (for example, a bad relationship), he could ask the Regimental Adjutant to send him somewhere else. If the Regimental Adjutant did not oblige, the officer could appeal further, to the Regimental Lieutenant Colonel (*Note 1*). So there was considerable flexibility, particularly at a time when three of the Regiments of Footguards still had two Battalions. This makes what happened to Nairac after he left Northern Ireland in early 1975 all the more mysterious, as it should have been avoidable.

The Army recalled Nairac from Northern Ireland in April 1975. This was not, say some authors, "a restful respite from Northern Ireland" conferred by a considerate Ministry of Defence. It was a normal posting back to the Grenadier Guards, from whom he had been absent for too long in career terms. It would be anything but restful; he had a lot of catching-up to do. It was not certain that he would be returning to Northern Ireland any time soon and, furthermore, there were strong career-related arguments that he should not do so; or not before his Battalion was sent there again, at which point they would all go together. At some stage before Nairac left the Province he learned that he had been selected to replace Captain Charles Fenwick as Adjutant of the First Battalion Grenadier Guards, which had recently returned from service in Germany. This was a position of considerable authority and responsibility; especially for an officer who had only graduated from Sandhurst two years earlier. During Nairac's absence in Northern Ireland the Army, as is normal with a prospective Adjutant, had conducted an in-depth security vetting of him. This had included a lengthy interview with Sir Walter Oakeshott, the now retired former Rector of Lincoln College. As had been the case in 1971, nothing adverse came to light; Nairac was selected.

For a few months Nairac would be understudying Charles Fenwick as one of two Assistant Adjutants, while he learned the ropes. Having done so, he would then take over as Adjutant. Fenwick is still remembered as an exceptionally good Adjutant; the ideal person to instruct Nairac, although he would also have been a hard act to follow. It appears that Nairac had accepted the nomination without knowing much about what an Adjutant did – he had done very little Regimental soldiering – and quickly changed his mind once he began to discover the reality. For, from an early stage in his London posting, Nairac was exercising considerable ingenuity to ensure that he should not in the event take over from Charles Fenwick.

On his return from Northern Ireland Nairac had taken a month's leave and reported for Regimental duties on Monday 19 May. He would not set foot in Ireland again for more than a year. For the next five months he would be based at Chelsea Barracks, carrying out duties in London, Windsor, and Pirbright in Surrey. At this period Nairac had a full diary, an active social life, a high public profile and was frequently seen in London and elsewhere on the British mainland by many people. This is important: the reason will shortly become clear.

Nairac had spent little time with his Regiment since the end of their second tour of duty in Northern Ireland on 31 October 1973. He had elected not to accompany the 2nd Battalion to Hong Kong, but to remain in Northern Ireland to assist the incoming Argyll and Sutherland Highlanders. Since then he had been almost continually either in training or on duty in Northern Ireland with NITAT (NI). Senior Grenadier officers had decided that Nairac, who was seen as a very bright officer and potentially destined for senior command, needed to return to mainland Great Britain to get some peacetime Regimental soldiering experience, including administration and public duties. He had been head-hunted for the post of Adjutant of the First Battalion Grenadier Guards because he had acquired a reputation for energy, enthusiasm, intelligence and problem-solving. His annual confidential reports confirm this. Being a successful Adjutant is still a recognised way of acquiring the administration "badge", which is one of the qualifications for higher command.

How could Nairac have wished to pass up such a sought-after appointment? The key lies in what Adjutants in the Infantry did in the 1970s. In the British Army an Adjutant is usually a Captain; very occasionally a Major. The word literally means "assistant" or "helper" and that is what he does; he assists the Commanding Officer. The Adjutant is therefore a man of influence and importance within his battalion. In the 1970s, as the Commanding Officer's personal staff officer, the Adjutant was in charge of all the organisation, administration and discipline of the Battalion. Today the bulk of the administrative work is carried out by the Regimental Administrative Officer (RAO), who is a professional; a seconded member of the Adjutant-General's Corps. Then, the Adjutant was also the Regimental Operations Officer, although this job, too, is now filled by a separate officer. Being Adjutant is still however an onerous and highly-responsible position. To reflect this, in the British Army Adjutants are given Field Rank; they outrank all other Captains.

The Adjutant's job is not a purely 'backroom' one. He accompanies his Commanding Officer at all times, including in combat. The Adjutant controls the battle while the Commanding Officer commands it. It follows that there has to be a close and trusting relationship between the Adjutant and his Commanding Officer. Because they spend so much time together, they have at least to be compatible; ideally, close friends. An example is Captain David Wood, the Adjutant of 2 Para, who was killed in action at Goose Green in the Falklands alongside, and a few moments before, his friend and Commanding Officer, H Jones, who had also been Nairac's close friend. Naturally they were together at the time; they died together and now they lie together in a small cemetery near the battlefield. It was part of being an Adjutant.

The vital phrase here is "a successful Adjutant". It seems clear from a conversation that Nairac had with a fellow gun during a shooting party at Eastnor Castle in the winter of 1976-77 a few months before his murder, that he thought that, had he accepted the job of Adjutant in 1975, success would have proved highly elusive. Whichever senior officer had identified Nairac as a potential Adjutant for the First Battalion Grenadier Guards must have been unaware that there was adverse history between Nairac and the then-Commanding Officer. The Commanding Officer of the First Battalion was still Lieutenant Colonel Bernard Gordon Lennox. As we have seen, Nairac had crossed swords with him and been banned by him from Chelsea Barracks during his 1974-75 posting with NITAT (NI). Neither of them would have forgotten this. It was not the most promising start to what would inevitably have to be a close collaboration. From the first day they seem to have eyed one another with suspicion and dislike; doubtless masked for most of the time by a facade of conventional good manners.

A former Grenadier officer has described Bernard Gordon Lennox as "a fanatic; I think it would be fair to say that some people didn't like him and made no bones about it, and it could be that's why he wasn't knighted (which he most certainly should have been, as he probably did more for the Household Division than any other person of his generation)." Even worse, he was reportedly allergic to Roman Catholics: "BGL absolutely could not stand Catholics and for that reason he might have had it in for Robert anyway, whatever he had or hadn't done." Nairac, as we have seen, was a devout Roman Catholic and would never have contemplated being anything else. Under these circumstances it seems unlikely that a close and efficient partnership could ever have evolved between Gordon

Lennox and Nairac, let alone a beautiful friendship. While Gordon Lennox is unlikely to have mentioned this prejudice directly to Nairac, he was probably already aware. It was inconvenient as well as regrettable; about thirty percent of the Army was Roman Catholic at that time. No-one seems to know the reason for Bernard Gordon Lennox's unfavourable view of Roman Catholics, but it may be relevant that some of his friends had been killed and injured while serving in Northern Ireland; not only by the IRA in firefights but also in the course of mob violence.

Knowledgeable military readers will point out that Charles Fenwick, the Adjutant whom Nairac was to have succeeded, is a Roman Catholic and an Amplefordian. He however seems to have been the exception that proved the rule. Exceptionally effective and dedicated, almost a workaholic, he was reportedly the ideal Adjutant, prepared to attend and support his Commanding Officer all day and then, after dinner, to work at his desk until 2.00 am if necessary to catch up on administration. Gordon Lennox admired his efficiency and drive and was evidently prepared to overlook his Catholicism. A parallel case is that of SAS Lt Col Robert Blair "Paddy" Mayne DSO, who has already been mentioned. Mayne, an Ulster Protestant, hated Roman Catholics, especially Irish ones. Nevertheless his best friend in the Army was an Irish Catholic. This friendship did nothing whatever to mellow his poor opinion of all other Catholics. The aforementioned eccentricity should not obscure the basic fact that Bernard Gordon Lennox was an able, distinguished soldier who, in the face of keen competition, achieved the rank of Major General. Whether they liked him or not, many who knew him greatly respected him.

For all the above reasons Nairac anticipated a personality clash with Gordon Lennox, whom he perceived as an irascible martinet and who was evidently a very demanding Commanding Officer. Other people's comments vary from "tough but fair" to "impossible". These factors, and the resulting, inevitable critical confidential reports, could have had an adverse impact on Nairac's Army career. It follows from this that not accepting that particular posting as Adjutant may have been a considered and tactical, rather than a capricious, decision. None of his former Army colleagues with whom I have spoken has any doubt that Nairac had the mental equipment to make a success of the Adjutant role under more favourable circumstances. Only one former colleague expressed a slight reservation. He commented that:

"He would have made a great Adjutant... although perhaps in a funny way [he was] a little too gentle and far too perceptive."

Inconveniently in an officer of the Household Division, and especially in a prospective Adjutant, Nairac also gave the impression that ceremonial public duties bored him. This is reinforced by the comment of one of Nairac's guardsmen; that he loved soldiering but hated public duties: a dapper officer, he liked wearing Home Service Clothing with scarlet tunic and Mess Dress and being photographed in them, but the business of Changing the Guard and Trooping the Colour just bored him. A former brother officer reportedly told General Sir John Wilsey:

"Robert was definitely not happy as a ceremonial soldier. He wanted something more and was considering taking SAS selection."

However, yet another former brother officer has said that, with his innate elegance and love of tradition, Nairac was a "natural for ceremonial." How to explain this contradiction?

There are two possible inferences to be drawn from this. One is that, while he might have enjoyed ceremonial at the start, for Nairac the novelty of public duties later wore off. Equally possibly, it could have been part of an act to help to ensure that he did not become the next Adjutant: Brigade of Guards Adjutants have to immerse themselves in ceremonial duties. The openly expressed view that public duties were a waste of time would have infuriated his Commanding Officer. In addition Nairac now adopted a cynical and flippant "Regency dandy" manner that was likely to irritate Lieutenant Colonel Gordon Lennox still more, and help to ensure that someone else got the job.

It was never in doubt, however, that "proper soldiering", including arduous training and demanding field survival exercises, had always appealed to Nairac far more than anything else. As one of his contemporaries, Tom Lort-Phillips, remarked in an interview with *Soldier* magazine in 1979:

"[Nairac] had a dislike of red tape and formality. He was a little unconventional, but he was very popular with the Guardsmen and an outstanding platoon commander... The closest image that I can think of is someone like [T E] Lawrence who is totally involved in the goings-on on the ground, but is not so concerned with spit-and-polish and that sort of thing."

Nairac might well have appreciated the comparison with T E Lawrence, but this tends to support the view that, had he reflected more carefully, Nairac might have concluded that he was more suited to the Royal Marines or the Parachute Regiment, who have a much smaller public duties commitment than the Brigade of Guards and whose work largely consists of proper soldiering. There was also the SAS: a very challenging option, to which Nairac evidently did give some thought.

Nairac won. He was not appointed Adjutant. Nor was this even counted to his discredit. The official reason given on his file is that since joining the Grenadier Guards in 1973, Nairac had spent too much time away from the Regiment, mainly in Northern Ireland, and not enough on Regimental soldiering. This was a fair comment: due to his absence on three duty tours in Northern Ireland, Nairac did not have much experience of peacetime Regimental soldiering in the UK; fairly essential background for any Adjutant. However, had Nairac been motivated to accept the job, he would have compensated for that; he was a fast learner.

The Army and the Grenadiers, who had no wish to lose Nairac, had reached a compromise with him. Nairac remained with the First Battalion. Initially he trained future NCOs at Pirbright. This was a success, despite his unorthodox training methods; for example he got to know his students by boxing with every man on the course. He and the aspirant corporals got along famously. Then the post of Recce (Reconnaissance) Platoon Commander fell vacant; Nairac got the job, for which he was ideally suited. When Battalions deployed to Northern Ireland their Recce Platoons were used for low-level covert surveillance; something on which Nairac was by now an expert. A Short Service Commission officer, Jonathan Forbes, who had been working alongside Nairac as an Assistant Adjutant, temporarily succeeded Charles Fenwick as Adjutant. John Rodwell, a regular officer, later replaced him.

Nairac was far from convinced that he would find Bernard Gordon Lennox congenial to work with, and admitted this to a few friends. He might or might not have been right; even if it was not apparent to him, and however annoying his Commanding Officer found some of Nairac's foibles, Gordon Lennox held a high opinion of him. But Nairac had to argue convincingly that being Adjutant was not right for him, or not at that time. He won that argument, but he was seen by not a few contemporaries and superiors as having turned down a brilliant opportunity on a whim. This, with his openly-expressed opinion, which may or may not have been sincere, that public duties were a waste of time, gave some of his superiors the impression that he was playing around: that he wanted to have adventurous Army fun and play a lot of sport; that he did not want to do "difficult" things like administration and was not serious about his career. That attitude might be admissible in a Short Service Commission officer, but not in the holder of a regular commission. This was evidently the view of Bernard Gordon Lennox's brother and successor, David Gordon Lennox, even though on a personal level he found Nairac, who was still the Commander of the Recce Platoon when he succeeded as Commanding Officer, charming and stimulating company. He also believed that Nairac had a very promising future in the Army, provided he could grit his teeth and overcome his aversion to the more mundane aspects of soldiering in the UK.

This episode shows, among other things, that Nairac had become good at office intrigue and getting his own way. To achieve this result, he must have got some senior officers on his side. It also highlights one of his more serious character flaws: impatience. An Adjutant is normally appointed for two to three years. A little research and discreet inquiry would have revealed that Nairac would be obliged to endure being Bernard Gordon Lennox's Adjutant for less than a year; part of which time he would anyway spend understudying Charles Fenwick. Bernard Gordon Lennox was due to leave the First Battalion on promotion during the Battalion's deployment to Kenya in early 1976. He and his wife had long-laid plans to take leave with friends in Kenya thereafter, immediately after handing over command to his brother. These leave arrangements would have had to be made well in advance, so it is likely that Colonel Bernard's transfer out of

Kenya was common knowledge, and that therefore Nairac should have known in advance that David Gordon Lennox would be taking over after ten months. Surely he could have kept the peace for that short time? Nairac evidently thought not. Bernard Gordon Lennox quickly moved on to higher things. His brother David would grow to like Nairac. It would have been in Nairac's best career interests to have put up with Bernard Gordon Lennox and get the "Adjutant badge" at that stage of his career, even at the risk of recording a temporary "blip" in his series of outstanding annual reports. There is another Nairac paradox here. There is evidence of his impatience in the military context; a visceral need to achieve results quickly, if necessary by cutting corners and ignoring procedures, which was probably a factor in his murder. Yet a dry-fly fisherman – any fisherman – must have limitless reserves of patience; which, in the angling context, Nairac displayed in legendary quantity.

In a generally favourable report on Nairac as Recce Platoon Commander, Colonel Greville Tufnell (the Grenadier Guards' Regimental Lieutenant Colonel) remarked that Nairac "undoubtedly finds difficulty in accepting the more mundane life of soldiering". Colonel Tufnell did not state precisely what he meant by this, but he seems to imply administration. He nevertheless continued that "He is an officer with considerable potential and he has a very promising future in the Army".

David Gordon Lennox, also reporting on Nairac as Recce Platoon Commander, noted that, "Although intelligent, he finds it difficult to accept the routine of peacetime soldiering in England. This he must learn to do, and allow himself to enjoy the other side of life when he has the chance; in particular as his distaste for inevitable routine duties is as transparent to the Guardsmen as is his enthusiasm for training".

David Gordon Lennox had a valid point: Nairac could not expect to enjoy challenging assignments all the time. He had to acquire administrative experience if he wished to achieve senior command. This comment was balanced by "He is now leaving the battalion again but I sincerely hope not for the last time, as he is not only a delightful and refreshing person but also one who loves soldiering and has a great deal to offer the Army". Those words were written in July 1976: Nairac had just returned to Northern Ireland for his fourth and final tour of duty. Less than a year later, he would be dead.

Meanwhile, on 31 July 1975, a notorious incident occurred in Northern Ireland. To this day many Irish Republicans and people on the British Left are convinced that Nairac planned and executed it; these allegations require examination. This was the Miami Showband Massacre. It claimed the lives of three members of one of Ireland's best and most popular boy-bands and of two Loyalist militiamen. Nairac has repeatedly been accused, not merely of having planned this atrocity, but of having been present when it happened. The known facts do not support this. As we have seen, the Army had recalled Nairac from Northern Ireland more than four months earlier. He had taken leave in April and started Regimental duties in May 1975. In June and July he was occupied as follows:

- 17 June - 11 July: Running an NCOs' course at Pirbright, of which there is photographic evidence. After this, Nairac took over as the First Battalion's Recce Platoon Commander.
- 13-26 July: Intensive field training and field firing on Salisbury Plain. The exercise was very important, as it was the Battalion's first major exercise since leaving Germany. Nairac was heavily involved. HRH the Duke of Edinburgh, the recently-appointed Colonel of the Regiment, visited on 22 and 23 July and met Nairac along with other officers.
- 29 July: Tactical debrief at Chelsea Barracks and a Conference on "Operation Trustee", a security exercise at Heathrow starting on 14 August.
- 30 July: Memoranda (Orders), probably the Commanding Officer's, at 2.30 pm.
- 31 July: From this day the Battalion was on block leave for two weeks. This was also the day of the Miami Showband Massacre. Northern Ireland was not, however, uppermost in Nairac's mind, but this was:

Now, with the challenging grouse and the sea-silver salmon,
August, of mountains and memories, comes into her own;
Would you gaze into the crystal and see the long valleys,
Braes of the north and the rivers that wander between?

These lines by Patrick Chalmers (1872-1942), Anglo-Irish poet, sportsman and author with whose works Nairac was familiar, are almost spot-on, except for the detail that Nairac would shortly be in pursuit of trout and not "the sea-silver salmon". On 31 July Nairac left London, not for Northern Ireland but for the Outer Hebrides of Scotland. He went there by road and MacBrayne's Ferry. His friend Captain David Sewell accompanied him. At that time he drove a red Alfa Romeo sports car. A few people still recall both this car and his using it for that journey. He spent his leave fly-fishing for sea trout and brown trout in South Uist with three friends; one brother officer and two civilians, two of whom are still alive and able to confirm this. The records of their expedition have survived, kept by the Lochboisdale estate office. From them we learn that Nairac favoured Black Zulu, Goat's Tail and Butcher flies. He and his friends experienced mixed weather; it was not possible to fish every single day. On bad days they would go hill-walking. The first day on which Nairac caught anything was 4 August. Thereafter they enjoyed good catches; as many as ten fish in one day. Rather oddly, Nairac signed himself in the fishing book "Captain" or "Capt." Nairac. This is not usual practice. His brother officer Sewell simply used his name. Nairac's observations include "Very large fish lost, probably over 5lbs – a Brownie?" and "Rainbows!!!" The second comment is unqualified and mysterious: it might refer to the weather, but would rainbows, however beautiful, merit mention in the log? It might equally refer to Nairac's or his companions' unexpected capture of some rainbow trout. That would have been surprising and arguably worthy of three exclamation marks, because at that time, apart from one small naturalised population in an isolated freshwater loch on Benbecula, the rainbow trout, an introduced American species, was not supposed to occur in the Outer Hebrides at all. The party's last angling day was 12 August: Operation Trustee would start on the fourteenth.

Nairac had a love affair with Scotland, or with certain parts of it, which was almost as strong as his romantic love for Ireland. He went there to shoot, to engage in falconry and to fish. Yet most of Nairac's biographers seem to ignore this, and his Scottish ancestry. When he returned to Scotland Nairac was reconnecting with his roots. His maternal grandfather, Dr David Dykes, had been a Scot and sometimes – in Northern Ireland – Nairac would pose as a Scots soldier. It is easy to see what drew him to that austere and unspoiled landscape. A later angling writer, Jon Berry, captures it perfectly in *Beneath the Black Water*:

"...we would at the very least be casting into relatively unfished waters on the periphery of British angling. The Highlands would be our big sky country, our wilderness... There we would find our last frontier, beneath our own big sky."

Sentiment apart, the other reason why Nairac and his friends chose South Uist in 1975 is that it offers some of the best sea-trout angling anywhere in the British Isles. In the two Uists the fish grow at a greater rate than almost anywhere else, and to a considerable size. In the Uists they will also take a fly, which many large sea-trout – in the Tweed, for example – refuse to do: they have to be caught with spinners or – even worse to a dry-fly purist like Nairac – with bait. When the weather is favourable, sea-trout angling in the Uists can be a deeply aesthetic experience. In the words of Viscount Grey of Fallodon (*Note 2*), it is the best sport of all, for that reason: there had been times "when I have stood still for the joy of it all on my way through the wild freedom of a Highland moor, and felt the wind and looked upon the mountains and water and light and sky till I felt conscious of a mighty current of life which swept away all consciousness of self and made me a part of all I beheld." No fish but the sea trout has ever enjoyed so lovely a tribute as this. This is Romantic writing at its best, reminiscent of Rousseau's meditation at Lake Bienne. Robert Nairac knew this passage and would have concurred heartily. It is good to know that Nairac spent what was destined to be his last long UK leave in that place and in that way.

Returning to the Miami Showband massacre, there is no window of time in 1975 in which Nairac could have gone back to Ireland and no reason why he should have done so. Given his busy schedule, it is impossible that he could have been privy either to the planning or the execution of this atrocity. If it had not been physically impossible and he really had been involved, it is difficult to believe that he would not have let fall something about going to Northern

Ireland to one or more of his brother officers, either at the time or over the weeks and months following that August leave. He did not. His friends do not recall Nairac as being remotely different in behaviour or personality after his leave, compared to prior to it. According to the friends who were with him in Scotland, Nairac was in great form. It was a happy time. Jonathan Forbes later remarked that "Robert came to Chelsea Barracks after leave (I was still around then as Adjutant) and normal day-to-day soldiering in London amongst a number of brother officers, and I have little doubt that some of us would have been aware sooner or later had he been involved in something unusual."

None of Nairac's accusers has ever deigned to explain what he, the Army or the British Government could have hoped to gain by wiping out the Miami Showband, a popular band whose music was enjoyed by Protestant and Catholic audiences alike and who supported the peace process. Unless, that is, they subscribe to the conspiracy theory of an "establishment plot", whose purpose was to escalate the situation in Northern Ireland into full-scale civil war, and that Nairac was one of its chosen instruments. There is no evidence to support this. Even more pertinently, it is difficult to believe that anyone in their right mind controlling Nairac would have put him in that situation; and why specifically Nairac for that "operation"? It makes no kind of military sense. The massacre was a Loyalist stunt that went wrong, carried out by Loyalist paramilitaries wearing UDR uniforms and perhaps prompted by ill-informed UDR gossip. Two Loyalists were accidentally killed, as well as members of the Band, when a time-bomb that they had been placing in the band's mini-bus went off prematurely. Surviving Loyalists then raked the surviving band members with bullets. Miraculously, not all of them were killed. It is difficult to imagine Nairac presiding over such a botched operation. The chief actor was John James Sommerville, who was arrested in September 1980 and jailed for 18 years for his part in the atrocity. He died in January 2015.

"An officer with a clipped English accent" was allegedly heard giving orders at the scene of the crime. Some writers have assumed that this must have been Nairac, and have said so. In reality, this person could not possibly have been Nairac, whoever else he might have been. Nairac was many miles away across the sea that night. According to one survivor's account, the "officer" had fair hair; Nairac's was very dark. The "officer" has been tentatively identified as a Loyalist paramilitary who had worked for a long time in England. He had acquired, or could put on, a convincing English upper-class accent. He is now dead, like many others in this event. Loyalist militia, all or most of whom were also part-time UDR soldiers, were manning the bogus checkpoint at which they stopped the band's mini-bus. All were wearing UDR-issued British Army combat kit with dark-blue berets. It was essential for the success of their plan that the driver and passengers should think that this was a genuine British Army checkpoint; that they were in no danger and that they should therefore co-operate peacefully when asked to get out and allow their vehicle to be inspected. An apparently

English officer giving orders in an Oxford accent would have been reassuring to them; someone shouting in an Ulster brogue might not have been.

One of the surviving band members, Stephen Travers, insists despite the strong evidence to the contrary that the "English officer" was Nairac. He has said so in media interviews and in his book, *The Miami Showband Massacre*. Consistently with this, he has called upon the British Government formally to apologise for what happened to his colleagues. However Travers had never met Nairac; he merely saw a photograph of him long after the event and after Nairac's death. Even later, he decided that this was the man whom he had seen on the fatal night. Travers still insists that Nairac was both the architect of the massacre and was present when it happened; He has described the "English officer" in this way:

"He had all the bearings (*sic*) of...someone used to being in command. He was dressed differently too. Unlike the soldiers in their UDR uniforms, he was in a pair of smart combat trousers with numerous pockets, and a combat smock. He was good looking and very cool. To me, he looked like 'action man'. I noticed that he was wearing a different coloured beret to the others. His was markedly lighter in colour, while the others were dark." [*This is presumably intended to imply that the "officer" was SAS, which Nairac is still widely believed to have been. The SAS's best-known uniform item is a pale fawn 'desert sand-coloured' beret.*] "However it was his English accent that really caught my attention. He spoke with an educated, curt military voice when he addressed the men standing around us. It was a commanding tone that demanded obedience."

This vivid description is deficient in detail. There is, for instance, no mention of the "officer's" nose having been broken. Yet his boxer's broken nose was one of Nairac's most noticeable features. The only points in common with Nairac are that the "officer" is described as being handsome and well-spoken, both of which Nairac was, but he was hardly unique in those respects. The evidence on the Miami Showband inquest file in the Public Record Office of Northern Ireland (PRONI) in Belfast does not support Mr Travers' construction. Apart from a single witness statement from one of the surviving band members that one of the soldiers "had an English accent", there is no evidence on the file that could link the crime to Nairac. The witness did not specify whether it was an Oxford accent: it might have been an English regional accent, which would tend to rule out Nairac. Numerous people with English accents live in Northern Ireland and many passed through the Province at that time.

There are details of the "officer's" appearance that, to anyone who had anything to do with the Army in the 1970s, do not seem right. These lead one to conclude that his smart combat kit had been purchased commercially. There are still stores where it is possible to buy uniform items over the counter or by mail order. The combat trousers with multiple pockets do not seem like any version of British Army combat kit worn in Europe at that time. Standard British Army DP combat trousers had only one trouser leg/map pocket, besides the standard trouser side pockets. The "officer" might have been wearing 1970s British DP tropical issue or American DP combat kit, both of which had more pockets than standard British combat trousers. The "smock" was presumably a Denison smock, originally designed to be worn by airborne troops in the Second World War. The Denison had been withdrawn from most of the Army in 1972 and by 1975 it was no longer on general issue. The SAS did not wear Denisons, preferring their own SAS Windproofs, which were shorter and lighter. By the time that the Falklands War broke out in 1982, the Denison had been consigned to military sartorial history. In 1975, however, Denisons could still be bought in many army surplus shops.

As far as that light-coloured beret is concerned, whatever may have been the case during World War II, the modern SAS normally only wear their sand-coloured SAS berets with No 1 or No 2 Dress, on formal or ceremonial occasions. One of these is Remembrance Day at Hereford. There have been a very few exceptions to this rule; one was in 1969 when they briefly appeared, ostensibly on a training exercise, in Ulster. On this occasion they wanted their presence to be known, so they wore their Regimental berets and drove "pink panther" Land Rovers. (The pink paint scheme was said to be highly effective desert camouflage, especially at dawn or dusk.) On a few occasions in Northern Ireland the SAS deliberately carried out vehicle and other checks while wearing their berets, which startled members of the public and was meant to. Operating in the field, however, the SAS normally wear neither the beret nor any other uniform items that could identify them as members of their Regiment. Whether the "officer" was a member of the UDR, or even a soldier at all, his uniform that evening seems to have been a disguise, and not even a flawless one. However the civilian Travers took it to be authentic, knowing no better.

Nicky Curtis has made the valid point that the Miami Showband members were Dublin-based and perceived as being Catholic, although at least one musician was in fact Protestant. As a result, they were taking a great risk by playing in Loyalist areas. Yes, they were popular; yes, they were well-meaning; yes, they were promoting tolerance, but in that war there was always "some blood-hungry bastard waiting to exploit someone else's good intentions". From Stephen Travers' book it is clear that, like Nairac, the band members chose to disregard the dangers; like Nairac they lived on adrenaline, and felt a compulsive need for "centre-stage visibility and approbation" and like Nairac, some of them paid for it with their lives. Apart from *requiescant in pace*, that is about all that there is to say about the Miami Showband Massacre.

Nevertheless, thanks to Travers, another Nairac myth has been born. The mention of Nairac was probably intended to help to sell his book, whose publication in 2007 coincided with the thirtieth anniversary of Nairac's disappearance and a resurgence of media and public interest in his fate.

Nairac's publisher friend, the late Martin Squires, has supplied some vignettes of Nairac at this period in his interviews with John Parker, quoted in full in

Death of a Hero. He was one of the quartet who went fishing in the Hebrides in August 1975 along with his friend John Hotchkiss. Nairac was accompanied by his brother officer David Sewell. A warm friendship grew up between the four of them. Squires provided some interesting insights:

"It was splendid – fishing by day or tramping over the wonderful countryside if the weather was too bad, then rollicking good evenings in the hotel."

Another member of the party confirms this. They had many fine evenings in South Uist, they drank too much and behaved badly. This is a recurrent theme with Nairac. The pledge of friendship and male-bonding was heavy drinking. Nevertheless, despite his consumption of alcohol and tobacco, Nairac was always far fitter than everyone else. He was never an addict of either drink or the weed. Oxford friends recall that he had the self-control to give up smoking and limit his alcohol consumption from October through to March so that he was fit for boxing and rugby. When training for, or carrying out, some tough military assignment, he applied the same discipline. Some Army friends have no recollection of Nairac's ever smoking; others have. The explanation is that he relaxed his non-smoking regime when on public duties in London or on leave. He would have done so on a fishing holiday. No Army "shop" was discussed during this vacation. Squires and Hotchkiss had only a vague idea of what Nairac's present or future military duties might involve.

"Fishing was banned on the Sunday between the two weeks. Not for Robert though – and this will perhaps give an insight into his character. 'We're bloody well going fishing and that's that!' So on the Sunday between the two weeks the four of us went to a secret loch he'd discovered six or seven miles from the hotel. He and Sewell were extremely fit, of course, and kept marching on at a pace that I and my chum had difficulty keeping up with. We were absolutely shattered after the first mile or so. I knew Robert was a falconer and so every time we needed a break I shouted 'Robert, over here! What's that bird of prey?' So he'd stop and look around. Couldn't find one of course, but it was the only way we could get him to slow down. And he absolutely had to have a look. He really was Mr Action Man."

On this occasion trout fishing held a greater attraction for Nairac than a vernacular Sunday Mass, which in South Uist in 1975 was celebrated in Scots Gaelic, which was unintelligible to him: according to the present parish priest, there was no service of Mass in English at that time. Fishing on Sundays was technically illegal in Scotland under the provisions of an old law that had never been repealed. The fine had never been increased either, and was by then negligible: two Pounds Scots, which would equate to about 20 pence or less in today's currency. However there were other sanctions: attitudes in the Highlands and Islands were still very sabbatarian, not only in Presbyterian islands but also in Catholic enclaves like South Uist. Nairac and his party could have incurred considerable disapproval if they had been spotted going fishing on a Sunday, so

Nairac led his friends to the loch across very rough moorland, avoiding roads. Unsurprisingly, Squires and Hotchkiss soon got exhausted. The loch in question was probably Loch an Dun. In Gaelic this means "Loch of the Fortress". There is a ruined broch nearby. Less than a year later Nairac would be based in another fort: Bessbrook Mill in County Armagh, where the last act of his tragedy would unfold.

Trout angling might shine some light on Nairac's mysterious personality. Trout anglers are notoriously inscrutable people; they have seemingly limitless patience; they display remarkable cunning; they strike without warning. They are very good at keeping secrets; especially the location of the best beats. As Jon Berry puts it: "I thought about... trout and the men who chased them, and how infuriatingly enigmatic both could be". It should follow from this that successful trout anglers ought to make good spies or intelligence officers and there is anecdotal evidence that this may be the case. One example is Colonel Peter Fleming, who was among other things a keen trout angler and game shot, a wartime Grenadier Guards officer and military spook *par excellence*. He was also Ian Fleming's elder brother and one of the originals of James Bond, who physically resembled him. Peter Fleming looked like a taller and even more handsome version of Sean Connery.

To many people the life of a Guards officer posted to London on public duties in the 1970s seemed enviable. It is true that there was a continual threat from the IRA, who had extended their campaign to mainland Great Britain and targeted the Army whenever they could. Public duties could prove tedious. However, unlike many garrison towns, London is seldom dull. It was an undeniable bonus to have the use of St James' Palace as a Regimental Mess if one was on public duties at the Royal palaces; there were limitless opportunities for sport; invitations were numerous, including invitations to shoot; there was racing at Ascot, Goodwood and other racecourses; and, for those who liked it, social life during the season was still glittering and attractive, notwithstanding the UK's economic difficulties. Even Nairac, who was a countryman at heart, would from time to time attend formal dinners and balls, at which he was expected to produce a personable lady. At this period of his life there seems to have been no shortage of female takers for Nairac's invitations, although none of these romantic occasions resulted in a romance. At the opposite end of the social spectrum there was slumming in the pubs of Kilburn, bare-knuckle fighting and other more basic pleasures.

In the words of Basil Dykes' former neighbour, W H Auden: "Sex was of course – it always is – /The most enticing of mysteries". For that reason a modern biographer is expected to do more than just touch upon his subject's sex life. This may be an important and absorbing study in the case of playboys like King Charles II, the Prince de Ligne or Metternich, for whom sex was so important that it influenced their political and military careers. It is more challenging if, as was the case with Nairac, the biographer's subject was not a playboy, sex was not the roof and crown of his existence and he probably preferred to go fishing or shooting. There is precious little surviving evidence of what Nairac's sexual preferences were, or with whom. In any case he had limited time for sexual adventures in the course of a short but very eventful life. A Victorian biographer's task was in some respects easier, because this consideration did not apply. He could, without incurring criticism, concentrate on his subject's literary, political or military legacy, while saying relatively little about his private life; often barely mentioning his parents, siblings, spouse and children unless they were independently famous in their own right, let alone any less formal connections.

We cannot be certain when Nairac started experimenting with sex, but the available evidence suggests that it was after he left Oxford and had joined the Army. While he was at university, and to the mystification of his friends, Nairac appeared to have no interest whatever in either sex or romance. Given the cauterising experience that he had endured at Ampleforth at the age of fourteen, this was understandable, always provided that you were aware of the background. Nairac did not however mention this to anyone. At Oxford in the late "swinging sixties" and early 1970s not a few of his contemporaries thought it odd that this strikingly handsome man, who was also famously charming and a sporting hero, never had a girlfriend while he was up at university. As Sir Mark Allen much later remarked: "Everyone else had a girl to bring to balls and dances, but not Robert. It's a bit of a mystery".

Although he evidently had sexual adventures, Nairac never had a regular girlfriend after Oxford, either. After his murder the tabloid Press hunted for one: find the lady and interview her! Surely the dashing Nairac – whom some journalists inevitably depicted as a James Bond figure – must have had a Bond girl or two hidden away somewhere? They came up with two: neither of whom was exactly what they had sought.

One, the aforementioned Mary Price, was a friend of Nairac's sister Rosemonde; not a sexy, uninhibited Bond girl but a respectable young upper-middle-class Catholic woman, whom Nairac had first met at Oxford, whose brother was a Guards officer and whom Nairac would invite by telephone, often at short notice, to Regimental balls and other social events. That however was the extent of the relationship: "He never even tried to kiss me!" said Mary later. Between balls, Mary never received so much as a postcard. She found Nairac attractive, but also a complete enigma; extraordinarily aloof, cold and ruthless. In her account he sounds like Mr Rochester. This is in total contrast to the memories of his male friends, who recall his attractive and lively personality, limitless enthusiasm, generosity and humour. After Nairac's death, Mary was surprised to learn that that he had sometimes produced a photo of her to Army friends, saying that she was the girl whom he intended to marry. This was the first that she had ever heard about it. Moreover, on the last occasion on which they were together, at a ball in 1976, relations between them had been strained because Mary had earlier told Nairac that she had finally met "Mr Right", the man whom she later married. As a result, she would no longer be available for "ball duty". Nairac received this news badly. He did not run Mary home after the ball; she had to find a taxi. Although she later tried to effect a reconciliation, he never saw her again. Mary was nevertheless greatly distressed by the news of Nairac's murder the following year.

The other candidate, Nel Lister, also known as Oonagh Flynn, has since been unmasked as a compulsive liar and fantasist. Even her close family take this view. She has more recently been in court and in the media in 2000 for attempting to blackmail Cherie Blair, and again in 2008 for making false allegations against Sir Cyril Taylor. Ms Lister claimed not only to have been Nairac's lover but also to have borne his child, who was her son Robert. In reality Nel Lister and Nairac never met. Her son, Robert Lister Jr, exasperated and embarrassed by his mother's claims, eventually underwent a DNA test which proved that he could not possibly have been Nairac's son but was – as he had always believed – the son of his mother's former partner, Robert Lister Sr. Although she is fluent and plausible, nothing that Ms Lister has said or written can be taken at face value. She provoked amusement in the Army with her claims. With the possible exception of Ken Livingstone, who appeared to attach some credence to her allegations in 1987, no-one now takes her seriously.

So there was never a serious girlfriend. This has led to speculation that Nairac was homosexual. There is, however, as little evidence of this as there is of heterosexual activity by him before he joined the Army. But in attempting to draw Nairac's portrait we cannot avoid all reference to the existence of these rumours, which are still circulating. This possibility only started to be aired publicly after Nairac's death. There was then no danger of a defamation suit arising, or of the authors of the allegations being put into Accident and Emergency by an incensed Nairac. They refer to two distinct periods of his life: his time as an undergraduate in 1968-72 and his time under cover in Northern Ireland in the mid- to late-1970s. These allegations that originally arose in the Oxford context seem to have been picked up by some people in the Army.

In the Oxford of Nairac's era, dominated as it still was by all-male colleges, it was possible for a man to ignore the existence of women for much of the time if he wanted to: it seems that is what Nairac wanted. But that might be all. If so, it would follow that Nairac was not active sexually at all, or hardly at all, while he was at Oxford. In support of this, Nairac's undergraduate friend, Julian Malins, says that he never got a homosexual vibration from Nairac; nor did any of his Oxford girlfriends, who inevitably met Nairac. Malins seems well-placed to comment: not only did he and Nairac see each other almost every day for three consecutive academic years, often boxing and playing rugby together, but for one of those years, living out of college, they shared a wing of a large country house on Boar's Hill with two other men.

Another friend, who knew Nairac well in the Army, has written that "I always assumed that Robert was 'red-blooded' and straight... My own view is that Robert was one of the world's great romantics and was passionate about many things; we were never short of finding things to do or talk about. I suspect that, like many of an earlier generation, he will have grown up with an extremely idealised view of women, and sadly never had the opportunity to learn differently in a real relationship." The same friend added that "I knew a fair number of gays (including a number in the Household Division) and suspect that Robert would have made a pass at me if he had been of that persuasion".

Nairac was carefully vetted at least twice by the Army: once in academic year 1971-72, after he had applied to join the Grenadier Guards and been provisionally accepted. He was vetted again in greater depth in 1975, when he was proposed for the job of Adjutant of the First Battalion. The Army vetting process was not completely infallible: some masculine homosexuals slipped through it undetected. Still, the fact remains that Nairac survived two in-depth Army positive vettings.

Another of Nairac's Army friends, who is also an Amplefordian, may have the correct answer:

"Although the 1970s had introduced many to the joys of sex, I suspect that many others, like Robert and me, will have been thoroughly naive and pretty innocent until we landed up in the Army. The big difference, and possible conundrum, being that I joined the Guards from School, while Robert went to Oxford, where he should have been romantically involved. My thought would be that he was either too busy or too noble [*i.e. too moral*] or just amazingly slow. However, if Robert's military adventures were anything like mine, he will have discovered rapidly that one's Guardsmen were splendidly uninhibited about sex – and they will have expected Robert to take part in their forays into every available red light district!"

Such evidence as we have suggests that this is correct: Nairac discovered the joys of sex in the Army and probably not before. He may well have been encouraged by the guardsmen in his platoon. There is evidence that as a soldier he had carnal knowledge of women through casual or commercial sex. This might not be the behaviour that one would expect of Chaucer's "verray, parfit, gentil knyght", which is how some people have viewed Nairac, but the Knight in *The Canterbury Tales* was a distinguished, middle-aged and married man. The Knight's son, the Squire, "A lovyere and a lusty bacheler", was another matter and possibly a more apt comparison. Boys will be boys and Nairac was a young officer on the loose in London. Given that his life was destined to be so short, and to end so brutally, no reasonable person would begrudge him whatever fun, of whichever variety, he managed to enjoy before the curtain fell.

So far as it has been possible to ascertain, Nairac avoided having a serious, committed or long-term relationship with any woman. That might have changed had he lived longer, but he was only twenty-eight when he was killed. This is confirmed by a friend who was formerly an officer in the Royal Marines:

"I seem to recall he brought a very pretty girl to the house one weekend, but on the whole he always seemed quite shy of such relationships. Robert's big love was his dog and the countryside. It was black and I think a St Bernard or similar." (The dog, "Bundle", was a Newfoundland. They look very like St Bernards but are even bigger.)

A former Grenadier brother officer added that: "[Nairac's] real interests were wildfowling and an outdoor life. His other passion in life was sporting weapons – he collected guns, particularly wildfowling guns".

A woman friend has made the interesting observation that: "I think this is the probable reason why men 'fell in love' with Robert: because he was a 'beautiful' man, as David Beckham is to so many people. Obviously good looks are part of it, but by no means all – much of it is to do with having a strong feminine side to their nature, and being in touch with their own femininity. Robert, for example, was clearly very protective of other people, both at school and in the Army – this may well be as a result of what he suffered at Ampleforth, but it also suggests a strong maternal streak; an understanding that a stiff upper lip isn't always the best way of helping people, and that things are not always cut and dried – as the Army would like them to be. This kind of man is often much more rounded as a human being because he can empathise with both sexes, and that is attractive. What I do think is that he was not a happy person and that he went to great lengths to hide from his insecurities."

The comparison with Beckham is a good one and puts the above remarks into perspective; many married, straight men cheerfully admit to having had a massive "man-crush" on Beckham in his soccer-star heyday. For an earlier generation it had been the former England rugby Captain, Will Carling. Like Beckham and Carling, Nairac was a sporting hero; that appeals to other men. One of Nairac's Oxford friends says that he had an "affective" nature. This means "concerned with or arousing the emotions or affection", which sounds accurate.

How to reconcile "not a happy person" with the high-spirited, funny friend whose perfectly-timed jokes detonated amid explosions of laughter? They were two sides of the same coin. John Keats, who was a medical man as well as a poet, often showed keen psychological insight:

> "Ay, in the very temple of Delight
> Veil'd Melancholy has her sov'ran shrine,
> Though seen of none save him whose strenuous tongue
> Can burst Joy's grape against his palate fine"

Nairac had often burst Joy's grape against his palate, but he definitely had a deeply melancholic side. The Black Dog was usually lurking somewhere nearby.

None of the foregoing amounts to irrefutable proof of Nairac's homosexuality, and does it matter anyway? Not now. Even if incontrovertible evidence of his homosexuality, bisexuality or something stranger were to emerge at some future date, it would signify very little. Nairac would be no less courageous; no less of a hero; no less deserving of our respect. But in the 1970s it mattered a great deal; that is the reason for mentioning it here. Any suspicion of unconventional sex would have set military alarm bells ringing. It was then seen as a security risk, rendering the soldier potentially open to blackmail by hostile intelligence agencies. Its detection could have resulted in Nairac's departure from the Army under a cloud: that at least was the theory. So indulging in it was risky and definitely not good for your career.

It is not in doubt that Nairac was capable of deep, committed friendships with other men. These friendships seem to have been indestructible and ended only with Nairac's death; if indeed they ever ended. In 2015 his male friends still miss him. "He is still sorely missed; a wonderful fly-fisherman and an amazing character. They don't make them like him anymore," says his angler friend John Hotchkiss.

It is important not to jump to sweeping conclusions based on Nairac's few known amorous adventures. That he evidently had some does not prove that he had lost his religious faith or abandoned all moral restraint. He just had slightly more to discuss in the Confessional. There is plenty of evidence that he retained both his ethical standards and his Catholic faith. He had simply learned to compartmentalise his life; as we all do as we grow up. Nairac, like Robert E Lee, in Stephen Vincent Benet's words, "Believed in God but did not preach too much". Equally, like Lee, he "Believed and followed duty first and last/ With marvellous consistency and force".

There is some evidence that Nairac went to church less often as an adult than he had while at Ampleforth, but this was unlikely to have been due to any loss of faith. There were other reasons. At Ampleforth Nairac had been obliged to attend church often: He would normally have been in the Abbey Church at 10 am every Sunday for High Mass. Once or twice a term there would additionally have been High Mass on a weekday which was a 'Holy Day of Obligation', which Roman Catholics treat as an extra Sunday. During the week Low Mass was served in all Houses on all or most weekdays, but the precise practice – at what hour; whether of the whole House or voluntary – would depend on the Housemaster. There were ten Houses and no uniformity of practice. Nairac is known to have been devout and regular, whether daily Low Mass was compulsory in St Edward's House or not. In addition to this, once a week each House had a day on which conscripts or volunteers went early, at 7.00 am, to serve individual priests' Masses in the Abbey crypt. This was before concelebration became the norm, which it did in 1965. People from that kind of very religious background, whether Protestant or Catholic, often allow themselves some leeway after leaving school. Having had a surfeit of church or chapel in early youth, they permit themselves to miss church from time to time, without abandoning their faith.

Another likely factor is that the sweeping reforms of Vatican II had begun to impact on the Roman Catholic Church in England. These included the widespread use of vernacular language instead of Latin in celebrating Mass; the revision of the Eucharistic prayers; the celebration of Mass with the priest facing the congregation instead of facing east toward the apse or wall behind the altar, and aesthetic changes affecting liturgical music and artwork, many of which remain divisive among Catholics to this day. Vatican II took effect after Nairac had left Ampleforth. Welcomed by many Catholics, for example in Africa, the modernised, vernacular and rather Protestant-sounding Mass deeply offended many English Catholics and especially those of the Recusant tradition, to which Nairac subscribed. They perceived the new liturgy almost as a betrayal. Apart from aesthetic considerations, there were historic reasons for this. During the years of the penal statutes, Recusant ancestors had taken risks, suffered and died to preserve and defend the Latin Mass and its holy mysteries in England. Now, apparently, it was being consigned to the rubbish-bin of history. Parish churches were often stripped of ornament at this time and redecorated in a more modern and "relevant" way. Evelyn Waugh's eldest son, Auberon, was vitriolic in his condemnation of the revisions in his autobiography, *Will this Do?*

"The new Mickey Mouse church of Cardinal Hume and Bishop Worlock is surely not a reduction of the old religion. It has nothing to do with it, being no more than idle diversion for the communally minded. Whatever central truth survives is outside it, buried in the historical awareness of individual members. Or so it seems to me. But whenever I have doubts, it is my father's fury rather than Divine retribution which I dread."

Robert Nairac's historical awareness was certainly well-developed. Luke Jennings thought much the same:

"A series of cringe-makingly inept translations as a thousand years of tradition bowed to the liberal orthodoxies of the Second Vatican Council."

And:

"Modern Catholic churches were uniformly hideous, essentially sports halls with altars, and the accompanying artworks, usually involving sheaves of wheat and staring, simplistic figures, depressing in the extreme."

We cannot know with certainty what Nairac thought about Vatican II. He did not confide his thoughts about it to anyone: not even to the monks of Ampleforth. His private views are likely to have been similar to those of his friend Jennings. Given his personal mysticism and his innate deep conservatism, it is impossible that Nairac could have viewed Vatican II with enthusiasm. He remained a committed Catholic, but he evidently allowed himself to skip church quite often as an adult, almost certainly as a result of what had happened following Vatican II.

In all this time Nairac never lost sight of his intention to get back to Ireland. In this respect he resembled Hugh Dormer, who had a similarly romantic view of France. This is what he wrote not long before his early death in battle in France during 1944:

"I realize that I could never sit back and rest till France is liberated, *so urgent are the ties that bind me there*" [author's italics].

Likewise, could Nairac ever have moved away from his emotional involvement – his fixation – with Ireland? This constituted a much greater potential danger to him than any amorous adventures that Nairac might have had in his spare time.

On 4 September 1975 Nairac sat and passed his Practical Promotion Exam in Edinburgh. Later that month he was confirmed Substantive Captain, with effect from 4 September, having been an Acting Captain for several months. On 19 September he travelled to Stanmore in Middlesex, to call on AG2, the manning branch of the Infantry. In those days the manning branches of all Regiments and corps were located at Stanmore, where officers could arrange to call and discuss their futures. Nairac wanted to find out what the future held for him if he pursued a certain line of work. What he discussed was a possible way of getting back to Northern Ireland. He had evidently learned that his paper recommending the appointment of a dedicated MIO in South Armagh had received favourable notice and that the SAS and RUC were apparently keen to have him back in the Province. This visit occurred some nine months before he joined 3 Brigade Headquarters as a Liaison Officer working with the various intelligence agencies (SAS, RUC-SB etc). There, he would be known as the SAS Liaison Officer (SASLO).

Here is Martin Squires again:

"Although he was in very good shape, he was I must say something of a conundrum as a person. I saw him up there in the wilds of the Outer Hebrides and he was wonderfully good fun, excellent company, full of charm and bonhomie, but there was below that something I could not quite identify. It was as if there were a darkness beyond the charming exterior that was quite impenetrable. I didn't give it a lot of thought at the time and anyway the holiday went marvellously."

People who disliked Nairac intensely and those who liked him very much both refer to this inner, unknowable darkness in his personality. What they may mean is that he was so complex and contradictory a character that you never really knew where you were with him; which is probably exactly what he wanted. He had several layers to his temperament and such people are hard to analyse. There must have been cunning in him – otherwise he could not possibly have done the type of work that he did, or survived as long as he did – and cunning people cause trepidation because we know that we might be being taken for a ride, but we are also under their irresistible spell. Cunning is not, however, a synonym for wisdom; nor is intelligence. Although his intelligence is not in doubt, the question is whether Nairac was a *wise* person. His Hebridean friendship with Martin Squires continued in London, where Nairac's wilder side began to show:

"We used to meet up several evenings a week if they weren't up to much. Then he began to go away again and our meetings were intermittent over the next year or so. There were a group of six of us in the end who were all rugby fanatics and we used to meet up at the Cross Keys in Chelsea, our main watering hole. Occasionally Robert would be in full mess kit and we'd have a formal dinner in St James' Palace. My actor friend and I would be in dinner jackets and all the others would be in full uniform. There were some dangerously wild evenings. One night at St James', Robert, after the fifth decanter of port, ran his dress sword through a Busby [*he meant a bearskin*] that was perched on a bust and a waiter who was coming out with the drinks got it in the ribs. It wasn't fatal, but I think that blood was drawn.

"That was Robert, so high-spirited; and, no doubt, that had something to do with his letting off steam after his experiences in Northern Ireland. Mad as a hatter."

Soon Nairac decided to involve Squires in his expeditions into Kilburn. "C'mon, put your old things on, we're going slumming," he would say. Adventure beckoned once more. Despite his considerable misgivings, and his clearly-expressed view that there were other safer, more convenient and congenial places in which to have evening drinks, Martin Squires seems never to have been able to resist these invitations. Other people have reported the same experience: Nairac was enchanting, disruptive and drew them into adventures in places where they would never have dreamed of going under normal circumstances or in their right mind. Over all of it he managed to spread such magical significance that the risk seemed well worth taking. Apart from that, just having his stimulating company outweighed the drawbacks and dangers. Like sea-trout angling in the Uists, Nairac's fellowship could be highly addictive: for many of his friends his loss was like an amputation.

"We would be standing at the bars, not saying a lot, just drinking. [*Squires could not put on an Irish accent, so Nairac had told him not to speak.*] We stuck to Guinness for the whole evening. When he spoke to order drinks or whatever, he did so loudly in an Irish accent.

"He had what I thought was a fantastic mimicry of the Irish accent and after several pints of Guinness he started singing these Republican songs. I felt quite uncomfortable. I mean, what was the man doing? Was he rehearsing for something or just trying to ingratiate himself? This was at a time when the IRA was bombing London again. I kept saying to him, 'This bloody place must be full of IRA'. I could not fathom it out, exactly. I was frightened out of my life a lot of the time I spent with him, you know, because the places we were visiting were pretty tough.

"He just carried on, encouraging others to join in his songs. It was quite an incredible scene. But, for all that, he'd be roaring with laughter on the way home and he was *such fun to be with*. You never knew what to expect and, meeting up with him, you'd think to yourself, 'What the bloody hell's going to happen tonight?'

"He could be pretty aggressive, especially with a few drinks inside him, and could knock anyone's lights out. It was another pretty worrying aspect of his make-up. You never quite knew if you were going to get into a fight. If you were, you'd want to be with him rather than against him. We made one or two hasty exists from the pubs in Kilburn, or at least I did, pulling at his arm to follow me out. Sometimes he stayed on for a bit of a knockabout while I was hiding round the corner... there was no denying that he had this thuggish side of him that I could not figure, very buoyant. Conversely there was nothing to compare with the elegance and charm of him in St James' Palace on a Regimental dinner. He was also a great sportsman, indoor and outdoor."

Back in Northern Ireland, a new wave of sectarian violence would engulf the Province over Christmas 1975 and into the New Year. On 5 January 1976 the Kingsmills massacre took place. On this occasion masked gunmen stopped eleven Protestant workmen travelling home on a minibus in South Armagh, lined them up beside it and shot them. A Catholic workman was unharmed. One of the shot men survived, despite having been shot eighteen times. A hitherto unknown terrorist group claimed responsibility and said the attack was in retaliation for the killing of six Catholics (the Reavey and O'Dowd killings) the night before. The Kingsmills massacre was the worst of a string of tit-for-tat killings in the area during the mid-1970s. The reality was that PIRA terrorists, posing as a separate organisation, the South Armagh Republican Action Force (SARAF), were responsible. What made this massacre particularly repulsive to many people was that most of the victims were not merely Protestants but Quakers; deeply religious pacifist Christians who would never have taken up arms, even to defend themselves. Nine of the men had lived in Bessbrook, a Quaker village which, because of the Troubles, hosted a major Army base. The SARAF orphaned fourteen children between them. The South Armagh PIRA has never admitted involvement and was supposed to be on ceasefire at the time, but there is no doubt that SARAF was simply the PIRA operating under another name. In 2011 the PSNI Historical Enquiries Team published a report that concluded that the PIRA were responsible for the atrocity and that the victims had been targeted because of their religion and for no other reason.

Once again, Nairac's name has repeatedly been linked to this atrocity. At the risk of repetition, it is worth reiterating that Nairac had left Northern Ireland in April 1975 and would not reappear there until June 1976. On 4-5 January he was at Pirbright, making last-minute preparations for the deployment of his Battalion to Kenya for arduous field-survival training while based at the military facility of Nanyuki. Numerous guardsmen saw him at Pirbright at that time. The Battalion moved to Kenya between 10 and 20 January 1976. They would remain there until mid/late March. As Commander of the Recce Platoon, Nairac had been heavily involved in planning and organising this training. He could not possibly have been present or involved in carrying out the Kingsmills massacre, or even in its planning.

Nairac enjoyed the field-survival training; Kenya was one of his favourite places. His later comments about it to family and friends were very upbeat. The training was tough. At times it involved living off the land, eating some unlikely animal prey species and plants. Although some writers such as Anthony Bradley have suggested that this was special training laid on for Nairac as part of his preparation to become an SAS assassin, it was in fact for the whole First Battalion Grenadier Guards; the SAS were not involved. Under a bilateral arrangement between the British and Kenyan Governments, a British Infantry battalion would come to Kenya every year during the UK winter to train for up to three months in varied terrain, from desert to savannah to mountain rain-forest to permanent snow on the upper slopes of Mount Kenya. This was normally followed by one or two weeks' rest and recuperation, usually at Malindi on Kenya's tropical coast. While some of the training might have been applicable in Northern Ireland, most of it was more relevant to out-of-area operations in non-European countries. It was during this deployment that Lieutenant Colonel Bernard Gordon Lennox left the Battalion and was replaced by his brother, David, who was to write about Nairac in Kenya:

"Captain Nairac made an admirable reconnaissance platoon commander in particular during a recent seven week period of training in Kenya. He organised thorough and imaginative training, showed a flair for this type of tactics and he is personally tough and fit. His enthusiasm for the rugged side of training is contagious and hence he is a real leader of men in this field."

It is hard to avoid concluding that this is the kind of work to which Nairac should have stuck.

While in Kenya, Nairac suffered a stroke of bad luck. He caught sleeping-sickness (African Tripanosomiasis): his life was in danger as a result. This disease is transmitted by the bite of the female tsetse fly. Being Nairac, he was reluctant to drop out of the exercise, even for a short time. One of his guardsmen recalls that:

"While we were on the training exercise we were split up into four camps at Nanyuki. Robert came to see us, driving his Recce Land Rover as he was in the Recce Platoon. He came out to us, as we could not get supplies from Base Camp because we had a rain storm and we were bogged in. I could see he didn't look good: when he stopped, he was just leaning on the steering wheel with his head in his arms and that's when I asked him if he was okay and he replied that he had sleeping sickness."

That was typical of Nairac: he would not let his men down under any circumstances, so he drove over with the supplies, even though he felt half-dead and risked having an accident. Without treatment Tripanosomiasis is invariably fatal, with progressive mental deterioration leading to coma, systemic organ failure and death. Nairac got treatment in time, in Nairobi. He recovered quickly and, being extremely fit, he bounced back and was able to continue with the training.

Nairac's next important career move was to attend the Junior Command and Staff Course at the Army Staff College (Junior Division) and graduate successfully. This was essential in order to progress from Captain to Major. In those days the Junior Division of the Staff College was situated at Warminster, Wiltshire. Most officers viewed it as an intensive and demanding course. Nairac, however, seems to have passed it without much difficulty, and even without much effort. He reportedly seemed remarkably relaxed and confident on this occasion.

The aim of the course was and is to "develop and assess the professional knowledge and understanding of junior officers in order to prepare them for appointments in command and on the staff, and for promotion to major". Regular Army officers are required to attend JCSC when they are about 28 years old. Subjects taught include:

- Military doctrine
- The organisation and Capability of the Arms and Services
- Operational and Non-Operational Staff Work
- Non-Operational Military Law
- Operations of War
- Operations Other Than War
- Operational Military Law

Many lectures are given by acknowledged experts in these fields, who may be senior military officers from the Ministry of Defence or civilian experts from universities and other teaching establishments. The method of instruction follows the traditional Staff College format of pre-reading, central presentation, syndicate discussion and confirmatory exercise. The course involves considerable homework. While there are some written exams, students are assessed on a continuous basis during the course. Although everyone who completes the course is deemed to have passed, the individual student report, written by the Directing Staff, is of great importance. It influences the JCSC student's immediate and near-future appointments within the Army. It is worth quoting the comments of Lieutenant Colonel Winder, GSO1, on Nairac in full:

"A powerful independent personality, who quickly established himself as one of the characters on this course. He is possessed of considerable natural gifts, so was able to coast through the course with some ease, relying on his good sense, experience, charm and ample cuff without ever really extending himself. He must realise, however, that there can be no substitute for thorough preparation and professional study; His approach to written work was too casual so his results were disappointing and did not reflect his true worth; it is a pity he did not make the best use of this opportunity to practise communicating succinctly on paper. By contrast he was particularly articulate orally, speaking quietly and persuasively and commanding the attention of his fellows. His nimble mind contributed handsomely to the success of the indoor exercises and his personal staff work was quick and accurate. Tactically he was superb. He could always be relied upon for a really sound opinion and the others learned a great deal from him. In summary, an officer of considerable potential, who will need careful guidance and encouragement and he will require demanding appointments to tax his natural ability. He was well above average overall."

A further comment by Colonel Andrew Myrtle, briefly quoted earlier in another context, reads in full:

"An able and intelligent officer with a strong and attractive personality and an abundance of commonsense. He is a natural leader who thrives on responsibility. He should now aim to match his ability to communicate orally with similar efficiency on paper. I have no hesitation in recommending him for a grade 3 staff appointment or as an Adjutant."

To return to matters in Northern Ireland, on 15 April 1976 the SAS shot a senior South Armagh PIRA Staff Officer, Peter Cleary, while he was trying to escape from SAS custody. He was the Regiment's first terrorist kill in the Province. Aged 26, he was among other things the PIRA South Armagh Brigade's treasurer. Once again, Nairac's name came to be attached to this killing. Although Cleary is celebrated in maudlin Republican ballads, one of which explicitly blames Nairac for his death, all the available evidence suggests that Cleary was a cold-blooded terrorist and probably a psychopath. The PSNI's Historical Enquiries Team (HET) believe him to have planned the massacre of the Quakers at Kingsmills. The journalist and author Joe Tiernan has stated that he was also implicated in the murder of Robert McConnell, a UDR Corporal and alleged UVF member, ten days before his own death. The SAS arrested Cleary at the home of his girlfriend near Forkhill and, according to the SAS, he was shot after trying to wrest the rifle from the single SAS officer who was guarding him while they waited for a helicopter to airlift him out. According to the IRA, Cleary was kidnapped from his mother's cottage in the Republic, brought back to Northern Ireland and shot there. Three of the SAS team attended the inquest, but a statement was read on behalf of the SAS officer, "Soldier A", who shot Cleary and who was allowed anonymity. The statement defended his actions, describing Cleary as "heavier and stronger" than him, as well as a "notorious killer", which was not in doubt. Soldier A continued:

"As he lurched at me my instincts as an SAS soldier took over. I released the safety catch on my weapon and started shooting. There was no chance to warn Cleary. I went on firing until the danger to me was over."

"My instincts as an SAS soldier" seems to rule Nairac out: he would not have described himself in those terms. The inquest returned an open verdict. Cleary's death is still an emotive subject in Ireland. Inevitably a legend has grown up there to the effect that Nairac was Soldier A. He was not. Support for the theory of Nairac's participation was, however, unexpectedly and strangely provided by Nicky Curtis, who says in *Faith and Duty* that Nairac was involved, although not directly.

A careful reading of Curtis' account shows that the evidence on which he relied was entirely hearsay; his conclusions were also wrong. The unidentified SAS soldier who shot Cleary, described by Curtis in error as a trooper rather than an officer, allegedly told Curtis that an RUC Special Branch (SB) officer with a strong Ulster accent had briefed his unit before the ambush. This SB officer told them unofficially that the RUC would be very happy if Cleary did not survive his abduction and arrest. It followed that they should ensure he did not. The SAS soldier therefore shot Cleary dead when he attempted to escape, using three bullets, instead of trying to restrain or merely wound him. From the soldier's description, Curtis decided that the RUC SB officer must have been Nairac in disguise. Except that he could not have been: Nairac was then in England attending the Junior Command and Staff Course. Once again, Nairac could not have been present or involved, even in the planning phase. Moreover, he was reportedly later critical of the SAS for killing Cleary. In his view, having secured such an important PIRA prisoner, their aim should have been at all costs to bring him in alive for interrogation. Instead, they had "slotted" him.

Why Curtis, who is supposed to have been Nairac's friend and admirer, should have written this about him is not clear. This might be one of several embellishments that his ghost writer added at his publisher's request to boost sales of the book, which was published in 1998, more than twenty years after Nairac's murder. It is however also possible that Curtis – who did not claim to have been present at the briefing – was genuinely mistaken in his identification of the RUC SB officer as Nairac; was not aware that at that time Nairac was no longer based in Ulster, and that he had failed, or been unable, to double-check his facts before meeting his publisher's deadline for going into print. Whatever the explanation, Curtis has done Nairac's memory a considerable disservice.

Apart from the fact that he was demonstrably elsewhere at the time, the various stories about Nairac's alleged involvement in crimes committed in Ireland in 1975-76 are not believable for another reason. It is hardly conceivable that an officer who was fully engaged in Regimental duties in the UK, Germany or Kenya, or attending important training, should be detached from time to time and sent to Ireland for a few days, for the sole purpose of killing suspected terrorists or committing other extra-legal acts. Even if the Army had been in that line of business, why import the hit-man? They had other good marksmen already present on the ground. Once more, it does not make sense.

However, Nairac would soon be back; he had been appointed as Liaison Officer between the RUC Special Branch, Brigade and the SAS in South Armagh. In reality he would be the first dedicated military intelligence officer (MIO) for South Armagh. The evidence on his Regimental file indicates that he went there in June 1976. He would have had very little time to prepare and brief himself between the end of the Junior Command and Staff Course and leaving for Northern Ireland. He may in any case not have considered that he needed much briefing for that particular job; he had written the MIO's job description himself. He was already acknowledged as one of the Army's Irish experts and he could not wait to return.

Nairac now had to let his family and friends know that he would be going back to Northern Ireland. He seems not to have told his parents that he was going to be on special duties and they therefore thought that it was another routine deployment. He was more truthful with his uncle, Basil Dykes. To Basil he entrusted a box a personal papers, to be kept in his law firm's offices until after Nairac should return safely in mid-1977. As noted earlier, it was still in existence in the law firm's archive 1992, but has since disappeared. Basil was also nominated as his next-of-kin. To his friend Martin Squires he said frankly:

"Martin, please do not attempt to contact me. I'm going back to Northern Ireland. I'm going back undercover."

It was impossible for Nairac to deceive his Army friends. They were dismayed for more than one reason. Lord Valentine Cecil feared the worst. He begged Nairac not to go back; he had become too emotionally involved and seemed no longer to see the dangers. Nairac strongly disagreed. He was determined to get back to the Province, apparently at any price. With his strength of character, he would have made sure that he got back, in one way or another. There are possible parallels between Nairac's experience as an officer who had seen active service in the uniquely dangerous environment of Northern Ireland, and those of officers who have been on active service more recently in Iraq and Afghanistan.

Such experiences affect different people in different ways, but a small number find themselves so absolutely in their element and so dedicated to the perceived justice of their mission that 'normal' life back in England – even normal Army life – can never again satisfy them; they can no longer conform to the accepted norms. This might explain why Nairac no longer appeared to be motivated by the prospect of a fast-track Army career, preferring to be on the front line and in the thick of the action.

Nevertheless, apart from personal safety considerations, there were good career-related reasons why Nairac should not have returned to Northern Ireland in 1976. One senior officer decided to act in Nairac's best interests and use his influence to stop the posting. This was Nairac's first Commanding Officer in the 2nd Battalion Grenadier Guards, Lieutenant Colonel Richard Besly, who believed that Nairac had the potential to achieve senior rank. He made it his business to encourage him and to look after his interests, which sometimes proved to be a frustrating experience; a brilliant mentor himself, Nairac did not always respond well to mentoring in his turn. Richard Besly was concerned about Nairac's obsession with Ireland, his wish to spend most of his time there, and in particular by the fact that Nairac had become too well-known in the Province and might therefore be in real danger. Nor did he fail to note Nairac's apparent disinclination to master the more mundane aspects of peacetime soldiering with the Regiment. In Colonel Besly's view, all this could have an adverse effect on his career; Nairac needed to spend more time on Regimental soldiering. Besly was therefore not happy when he learned in 1976 that Nairac had volunteered yet again for special duties in the Province, instead of staying with his Battalion. He had words with Nairac, who insisted that he had a personal mission to make a difference in Northern Ireland and was qualified to do so. He was going to do it and he would not be moved.

Colonel Besly then tried to intervene with the concerned Major General Commanding London District to get the posting rescinded. He was not successful, and ran into high-level opposition. Charles Guthrie, then the Brigade Major for the Household Division – later a notably political General, later still Field Marshal, Chief of the General Staff (CGS), Chief of the Defence Staff (CDS) and Baron Guthrie of Craigiebank – intercepted Colonel Besly and prevented him from seeing the Major General. It is not clear that the Major General was even made aware of the approach by Besly, who had to make his case to Guthrie instead. He said that the proposed Northern Irish posting was wrong for Nairac for two reasons: Nairac would be putting himself seriously at risk while, even if he survived, the posting would be taking Nairac in completely the wrong direction: it would be detrimental to his career.

Guthrie reportedly said that he had personally approved the posting. Apart from Nairac's own wishes, both the SAS and the RUC wanted Nairac back in Ulster; he had been swayed by the arguments that they had used. Besly and Guthrie had a long discussion about Nairac. According to Besly, Guthrie finally said, "Don't worry. He'll be looked after", without specifying what he implied by "looked after". He may have meant "I'll see to it that his career doesn't suffer", or "the SAS will ensure that he comes to no harm". If he meant the latter, Guthrie could not have been more wrong – certain members of the SAS would play a role in Nairac's death. However, Lord Guthrie could not have foreseen that; he would not have been aware of the rogue elements that were now operating in the SAS in Northern Ireland, whose actions would have horrified him and whom Nairac would soon encounter and clash with. Nor could he have foreseen the role that a former SAS officer, Major Clive Fairweather, would play in Nairac's last months. So when Guthrie told Besly that Nairac would be looked after, he genuinely thought that he would be.

In 2014 Lord Guthrie had no recollection of that conversation. He commented: "I am bound to say I am mystified. I do not think I have ever spoken to a Colonel Besly, although I do seem to recall there was a Colonel Besly who was a Grenadier. Robert Nairac's posting to Northern Ireland was nothing to do with me and I do not remember ever hearing about him until he was reported missing. I think he may have had some dealings with the SAS in which I served, but I had left them a long time before he would have become involved. One thing I am sure of is that I never said 'he will be looked after'. His length of tour and future were nothing to do with me. He was never under my command and the planning of his career would have been in the hands of The Grenadier Guards and the Military Secretary's Department. I was in South Armagh at the end of 1979 and Nairac's time there was discussed, but I do not remember anybody with me knowing any detail or expressing informed views as to what he had actually been doing or how long his posting should be. From the above you will understand I am not really in a position to comment, but I can understand Colonel Besly's views as expressed to you on Nairac's career, which you have outlined, and which sound sensible from the Grenadiers' point of view."

When I relayed this comment, Colonel Besly was surprised that Lord Guthrie's memory should be so selective. He added: "However, it confirms to me that Robert should not have been allowed to go back and I bitterly regret that I was not more forceful at the time. There is no doubt whatever in my mind that I went to see Guthrie and that he assured me that all would be well."

It must be assumed that the explanation of this seeming contradiction is the following: in the normal course of Army business, postings were definitely not a matter for the Brigade Major, but were the responsibility of the Regiment and the Personnel Branches. Lord Guthrie was correct to say this. At this distance in time, he might well not recall his meeting with Colonel Besly; especially if no note was taken. However, it is also undoubtedly true that, if Colonel Besly had succeeded in persuading either the Major General or the Brigade Major, they could easily have intervened to stop Nairac's posting to Northern Ireland. That Guthrie chose not to do so would indicate that he did not believe that there were strong enough grounds to do this when Nairac, and those in the Province who knew him, including the RUC and the SAS, wanted him to go back. It was only those close to Nairac, like Valentine Cecil, who had begged him not to go back to Ulster and who saw that he had become too close to the issues; who could see the looming danger. That danger would not have been apparent to the Brigade Major, who did not know Nairac, or at any rate did not know him well. To his enduring regret, Colonel Besly did not succeed in making his case.

Colonel Besly was not the only person who spotted the dangers. One of Nairac's Army friends commented: "I knew that he would not survive, I don't know why; I am not superstitious. I don't do feelings etc. I just knew that he wouldn't make it on the day that it was agreed that it should be him that went back... On a particular occasion when I was with Robert before he went back, I had a strong premonition that he would not survive. I... have only had that feeling that I can recall twice and sadly, on both occasions the premonition was to prove accurate. What had I sensed about Robert and his approach to life, I wonder? He was a romantic who wanted to make a difference."

So was Nairac the right man for the MIO South Armagh slot or not? Clearly he was, in the view of senior officers who were trying to utilise the resources at their disposal, including people, as best they could with considerable thought and care. He undoubtedly had ability and must have ticked a good number of boxes for the Army. Nairac himself wanted the job. The RUC and some of the SAS wanted him. Moreover, to the very last he was achieving exceptional annual confidential reports from his superiors in Northern Ireland; by 1977 his accelerated promotion to Major was assured, so he must have been doing something right. Many of Nairac's Army friends would have agreed: they expected him to have a distinguished career and achieve senior rank.

However Julian Malins, another person who is not superstitious, thought at the time and still thinks today that, despite his numerous qualities and accomplishments, Nairac was not the right choice and that the tragic outcome was foreseeable: he and one or two others, like Valentine Cecil, had foreseen it. Like Cassandra, they seemed unable to do anything to prevent it. While they were still at Oxford, as mentioned in Chapter 7, Malins had a premonitory fear of Nairac's early death: "I formed that impression from knowing Robert really well for our three years together at Oxford. This was before he joined the Army, let alone undertook dangerous undercover work." Malins and Nairac had never lost touch after Oxford. As noted previously, Nairac was an usher at Malins' wedding in July 1972. They managed to meet several times a year between 1973 and the end of 1976. In the few years that remained to them they attended a number of reunions with friends in common like John Leyden, and were both present at more than one Vincent's Club annual dinner.

In November 1976 Nairac attended the Vincent's Club Dinner, held at Lord's cricket ground. There for the last time he met his friends, Malins and Badenoch. To their surprise, he was wearing a Browning pistol in a shoulder holster under his dinner jacket. They were horrified when they learned that he was now working undercover and said so: he should return to Regimental duties as soon as possible. Nairac brushed aside their forebodings. He appeared cocky and confident; he was convinced that he was on the verge of an important intelligence breakthrough. In Malins' words:

"Robert was an Ampleforth and Oxford and Sandhurst educated Guardsman, romantic and with high ideals: it really does not take a super brain to work out that his chances of survival, working the pubs etc. in Northern Ireland to gather IRA intelligence, are just about close to zero. It was that obvious conclusion which so annoyed me with the Army; using him for those purposes. His senior officers (who were not themselves in harm's way) should NEVER for a moment have used Robert for plain clothes detective work in the bandit country of N.I It was... tantamount to murder because Robert was... obedient to orders and full of self-confidence! When I last saw him in the autumn of 1976 at Vincent's Dinner and he told me precisely what his work was... I instantly knew that I was looking at a dead man and really tried to get him, immediately, to stop... but no; he reported, he said, directly to the Secretary of State [Roy Mason] and lots of people "depended" on him etc. It was hopeless, so it was with real sadness that I said farewell. He was entirely unsuited to the particular work that he was being asked to perform."

While there is no consensus about this among Nairac's surviving friends, it is difficult to avoid the conclusion that whoever was really responsible for overruling Lieutenant Colonel Besly's and other people's well-founded objections to Nairac's fourth and final posting to Northern Ireland, they bear some moral responsibility for what happened to him in Ireland on 15 May 1977.

CHAPTER 12 | THE BIRD OF TIME

The Bird of Time has but a little way to flutter – and the Bird is on the Wing.
(Edward Fitzgerald, *The Rubaiyat of Omar Khayyám*)

The Special Air Service (22 SAS) is probably the most famous and, when given the option, the most secretive of all Special Forces. Although Robert Nairac was never a member of the SAS, he had a connection with it and that Regiment played an intimate part in his tragedy. Given that it is surrounded by as many legends as Nairac himself, it may be helpful to give a little of the historic background. The reality of the modern 22 SAS's work was largely unknown to the British public and the world until, three years after Nairac's murder, in 1980 – and under the eyes of the media – the SAS achieved the fast and successful rescue of Iranian diplomats who were being held hostage in their London embassy by terrorists claiming to represent "the Democratic Revolutionary Front for the Liberation of Arabistan". "Arabistan", an ethnically-Arab and oil-rich province of South-West Iran, is more usually known as Khuzistan. Its ownership had been a bone of contention between Iraq and Iran: Saddam Hussein had probably underwritten the hostages' seizure. In addition to the Iranians, the hostages included several British citizens: embassy employees, a Diplomatic Protection Squad police officer and some journalists who had been collecting visas from the Consular Section when the terrorists struck. When the SAS stormed the embassy they rescued all but one of the twenty hostages. The terrorists killed the sole hostage casualty. By contrast, only one terrorist survived. Prime Minister Margaret Thatcher personally congratulated the SAS team on this outcome.

This famous SAS operation was named Operation Nimrod. There followed intense public interest in the Regiment in the UK and around the world, which has never faded. The SAS, who had been accustomed to keeping a low profile wherever they operated, usually far from London, found themselves in a blaze of publicity. With the exception of Clive Fairweather, who welcomed the chance to work closely with the media, the Regiment saw this development as profoundly unhelpful. It had stimulated a flood of volunteers, some of them very good and others less so, from other Regiments. The public approval that they had gained might have been flattering to the SAS's collective ego, but their lives and work could never be the same again. Not only would the media continue to take a close interest in the Regiment; so would international terrorists and so would politicians. This political interest, whether in the UK or abroad, would sometimes be far from friendly. In future years former members of the Regiment would keep the interest alive with the publication of exciting – and profitable – war memoirs like Andy McNab's *Bravo Two-Zero* and an endless stream of realistic and revelatory SAS novels, which were often optioned for filming. Official attempts to gag the authors – even the threat of expulsion from the SAS Regimental Association

– would prove completely unsuccessful, probably because the potential profits were too great. But in 1976 this was still in the future. At that time what the SAS really did was not well-known. It was, however, sometimes the subject of ill-informed and occasionally wild speculation in the media, Parliament, and elsewhere on the infrequent occasions that the Regiment hit the headlines.

There is a perception that special operations and Special Forces date from the Second World War. In reality they have a long history and have been used whenever the resourceful commanders of small and irregular forces found themselves confronted by much larger conventional forces. They were usually raised to fight in unconventional campaigns and in response to a specific crisis, and then disbanded to save money as soon as it was over. What changed after World War II was that governments came reluctantly to realise that the need for Special Forces was now a fact of life; that many future wars would be low-intensity counter-insurgencies or guerrilla wars, which might go on for years, especially in colonial territories or post-colonial countries. As a result the Special Forces either remained in being or were disbanded soon after the war, only to be re-formed again a few years later. That is what happened to the SAS.

The original SAS Regiment was founded in 1941. It grew out of the Army Commandos and developed in response to the threat posed to Egypt, then part of the "informal British Empire", by the future Field Marshal Rommel in the Western Desert. The desert was its birthplace. Its wartime history is well-known, as several of the original officers, such as Major Roy Farran, later published readable accounts of the operations against the Germans and Italians in which they had taken part. Many of the early officers and recruits were Irish or of Irish descent; many of them were Catholic, like Farran. Scots and English Catholics were represented too: the Stirling brothers, David and William, who were two of the co-founders of the SAS, were Catholics and Amplefordians. As noted earlier, something in the English Catholic Recusant DNA seems to predispose the possessor towards unconventional warfare and covert operations. The non-Catholics included such men as the explorer and Arabist Wilfred Thesiger, Michael "Mad Mike" Calvert and Robert Blair "Paddy" Mayne. Mayne is regarded as the third co-founder of the SAS. The fourth, "Jock" Lewes, was an Oxford Rowing Blue with a keen analytical mind and great attention to detail. The modern 22 SAS looks back to "Stirling and Stirling" as its origin, but this earlier SAS Regiment, or "SAS Mark 1", was disbanded in 1945. Mike Calvert was its last Commanding Officer. Two Territorial Battalions would later be founded: 21 SAS (Artists' Rifles), recruiting in London, the South-East and Wales, was formed on 31 July 1947. 23 SAS, covering Scotland, Northern England and the West Midlands, was formed in February 1958. Both Battalions still exist. These volunteer reserve Battalions, in which former wartime SAS soldiers continued to serve, allowed the SAS ethos to continue in existence after the war. Good though they were, they were not a substitute for a regular battalion, as the Army eventually recognised.

The modern regular 22 SAS, or "SAS Mark 2", came into existence in 1950-52 under different circumstances from its predecessor. It was a development of the Army's response to the Malayan Emergency, the "jungle war" of 1948-60. There was an element of continuity between SAS Marks 1 and 2; for example, Mike Calvert played a role in re-founding the Regiment. In 1950 General Sir John Harding, Commander-in-Chief Far East, decided that he needed independent advice from an expert in jungle warfare. He called for Calvert, who had experience of jungle warfare in Burma, where he had commanded the 77th Indian Infantry Brigade. What Calvert advised was, in effect, the re-founding of the SAS (although the SAS name was not immediately revived) to confront the threat from the Chinese Communist insurgents. He was also the obvious person to command the new Regiment, which was initially christened the Malayan Scouts. In 1950 Calvert was formally appointed to command the Regiment and to engage in special operations against the insurgents. Despite their name, the Malayan Scouts were not recruited from the indigenous Malay population but from among the more adventurous British soldiers then serving in Malaya. Some of the specialists of SAS Mark 1 now returned to join them.

Two years later the Malayan Scouts would become the nucleus of the regular 22 SAS, which was officially founded on 16 July 1952. They never entirely lost a reputation for poor discipline and thuggish behaviour. This was said to be the result of highly informal selection procedures. If Calvert liked a candidate, he would be accepted. The SAS's critics have sometimes emphasised the Malayan Scouts' early bad reputation. It is nevertheless impossible for them to deny that the Chinese Communist insurgency in Malaya was defeated in 1960, in which the revived SAS played a key role. It was also in 1960 that the Regiment moved to what would become its permanent home: Bradbury Lines near Hereford.

The circumstances of the SAS's rebirth in 1952, when Robert Nairac was four years old, were to mark its character for the next quarter-century. Although based in the UK, the SAS were normally deployed overseas in distant locations, where they also undertook much of their training. In addition to Malaya and Borneo, the Regiment was deployed in the Arabian Peninsula. At this time they did not envisage or plan for being deployed in the United Kingdom, which was "not their patch". The SAS were involved covertly in the long North Yemen civil war; more openly in Aden and in the Oman counter-insurgency. In Oman the UK had also been involved in regime-change. The SAS provided training for friendly foreign forces and for other units of the British Army. Although the Regiment successfully kept a low profile through the fifties, sixties and into the seventies, a certain glamour clung to its name, inherited from SAS Mark 1 and its dashing raids in the Western Desert. Roy Farran's SAS memoir, *Winged Dagger,* had become a best-seller. Insofar as they were known, the SAS were still perceived as *hommes désertiques,* worthy successors of T E Lawrence. This was true up to a point; especially in the contexts of Oman and Yemen, although the jungles of Malaya and Borneo and the mountain rain-forests of Kenya, to give but three other examples, would not qualify as desert; nor did Germany.

The SAS is now generally recognised as an invaluable UK asset, but that has not always been the case: certainly not in the 1960s and 1970s, when its future once more became uncertain, and today the Regiment still has its detractors. These individuals are often motivated by political and ideological considerations rather than military arguments, although the SAS has its military critics too. However, if imitation be the subtlest form of flattery, the SAS's admirers must outnumber its critics. A number of other countries have modelled their Special Forces on the SAS, sometimes keeping the same name. The Australian SAS Regiment closely resembles its British equivalent, with which it maintains cordial relations. The New Zealand SAS, although smaller, is also formidable. The rebellious Rhodesian Republic had its own SAS Regiment and the US Navy SEALs were founded in conscious imitation of the SAS. They were placed under the Navy because their founder, John F Kennedy, was a former Navy officer. Nevertheless the SEALs are often found operating far from the sea, for example in Afghanistan.

For most of the period from 1964 to 1979 the Labour Party was in office and the SAS had always attracted criticism from the Left. Despite the Army's determinedly non-political stance, which dates from the eighteenth century, even today the SAS are sometimes depicted in the left-centre Press as right-wing thugs and assassins closely resembling Bulldog Drummond. Modern SAS soldiers do not really fit this profile. They tend to be enviably accomplished, especially in languages. The Territorial 21 and 23 SAS are equally distinguished and many of their members are high-achievers in civilian life; some belong to the learned professions. However – and very importantly – in the mid 1970s, before Sir Peter de la Billiere's reforms of 1979 had taken effect, the regular battalion's performance and its reputation suffered a sudden dip. A political decision had caused the Regiment to expand quickly, and temporarily to make its selection criteria less rigorous. As a result there were some rogue individuals present in 22 SAS in the mid-to-late 1970s. In 1976-77 Robert Nairac would find himself under attack from both the "respectable" SAS, who wished to do everything by their rule book and criticised him for not doing so, and the minority rogue element who had no intention of abiding by any rules and saw themselves as being in Northern Ireland to "mallet" or "slot" as many of the IRA and their sympathisers as possible. The Regiment was in a somewhat schizophrenic state in Ulster in 1976-78.

The SAS have played a political role in the past through their successful "hearts and minds" activities with local populations. These activities were a key element of the Army's success against insurgents in Malaya, Borneo and Arabia. The SAS proved themselves to be effective low-level and low-profile "ambassadors" for the UK and the British Army. They had even been involved in regime-change in a minor way. Although it now seems wildly unlikely, the suspicion arose back then among the Left: might the SAS start wanting to play a political role in the UK; including, perhaps, regime-change?

A more serious threat to the SAS was that by the 1960s it was becoming received wisdom in some parts of the Army that the Regiment was coming to the end of its useful life. Although it had always done other things, there was a perception that SAS Mark 2's main role was defeating insurgents in the colonies. But now the colonies had gone or were preparing for imminent independence. Admittedly the Regiment was still playing a helpful, low-profile role by supporting the UK's moderate Arab allies in Oman and the other Gulf States, but those countries would in due course develop their own Special Forces. (This duly happened and the SAS helped to set them up.) At that point the SAS's *raison d'être* must surely disappear? Would there then be any real justification for its continued existence? This view overlooked the SAS's potential role in defending the UK, as well as British interests overseas, and its value to NATO.

The Regiment's long-term future was once again in doubt. The Dhofar insurgency in Oman, which began in 1962 and lasted until 1979, probably saved it from a second disbandment. Nevertheless in 1964 the SAS was greatly reduced; pared down to an HQ and two Sabre Squadrons (Companies), plus the Territorial 21 and 23 SAS. No-one seems to have thought of this at the time, but in the event of any major emergency the Regiment would be severely stretched because SAS selection and training take time. Due to its highly-skilled and specialist function, the Regiment would not be able to expand quickly by training new SAS soldiers. If a very serious emergency – or an unforeseen change in Government policy – were to impose a sudden expansion of the Regiment, the SAS would have to lower their entry standards.

The SAS saw the warning signs and started to make adjustments. They set about transforming themselves into a modern, indispensible, flexible, multi-skilled unit, capable of being sent anywhere, to do anything, in any environment, at little or no notice. It was no longer acceptable to say "we don't go there" or "we don't do that". They would do everything that was asked of them, and more. Every member of the Regiment would now be a swimmer and a parachutist. They would all be trained in combat survival, escape and evasion, resistance to interrogation, battlecraft, close-quarter battle shooting, foreign weapons and jungle warfare. Every man should achieve either Basic, or preferably Advanced, Level in signals, medical skills and demolitions. Depending on their aptitude, they would acquire as many relevant languages as possible, including German, French, Swahili, Arabic, Malay and Thai. To these were added counter-terrorist training and, whenever possible, experience. This was to be achieved by rotating the Sabre Squadrons on "Pagoda duties" i.e. acting in turn as the SAS Special Projects Counter-Terrorism team. In 1976 Prime Minister Harold Wilson would compromise and dilute these praiseworthy plans by a policy change. The results would be serious, for Robert Nairac among others.

Meanwhile one factor was to remain unchanged. The SAS's normal areas of activity would still be outside the UK, although that would include the rest of Europe and anywhere else that NATO decided to operate. With the exception of certain remote and desolate training areas, the UK was still the nearest thing to a blank on the SAS's map of the world.

This started to change in the 1970s, when the PIRA decided to bring the war in Ulster to mainland Great Britain. At that point the SAS began to get involved domestically; initially by advising the civil authorities, who wished to make use of their counter-terrorism expertise. In the winter of 1975-76 a PIRA team attempted to assassinate former Prime Minister Edward Heath, but their bomb did not go off. This particular team was suspected of having committed a total of 40 bombings and 15 murders. A few days later the same team bombed Scott's restaurant in London, killing two people and injuring several others. Scott's very soon reopened, displaying a gritty "blitz spirit". Angered by this, the PIRA decided to hit the restaurant again. This time they raked it with fire from a 9-mm Sten gun, fired from a stolen car. That was a mistake, as the police now had Scott's under observation. They gave chase and the gang took refuge in a flat in Balcombe Street, St Marylebone, where they held the occupants, a married couple, to ransom. The Balcombe Street siege would last for six days, with considerable media coverage. Members of the SAS Special Projects Counter-Terrorism Team were called in. This information was leaked – possibly deliberately – and the terrorists heard on the radio that the SAS were now involved. They panicked and immediately surrendered. While the IRA might not know much about the SAS, they evidently regarded them as very dangerous indeed. In Northern Ireland the Loyalists noted this and nodded approvingly.

The Balcombe Street siege coincided with the start of a new wave of terror in Northern Ireland: a series of exceptionally vicious tit-for-tat killings. On 19 December 1975 Loyalists shot three Catholics in Silverbridge, County Armagh. Two weeks later the PIRA bombed a bar in Gifford, County Down, and killed three Protestants. At Whitecross, Loyalists killed five Catholics: the Reavey and O'Dowd killings of 4 January 1976.   GILFORD

The following day, 5 January, the Kingsmills massacre occurred. As noted in Chapters 1 and 11, numerous attempts have been made to link Robert Nairac's name to it. Recently, in June 2015, the Police Service of Northern Ireland (PSNI) Historical Enquiries Team (HET), which was set up in 2005 to investigate the unsolved crimes of the Troubles, announced that the leader of the eleven-man gang that carried out the murders was believed to have been Seamus Heuston, a senior South Armagh PIRA volunteer who had died in Dundalk in 1984, having fled to the Republic to avoid prosecution. The HET also believe that PIRA Staff Captain Peter Cleary planned the operation. As was the case with the Miami Showband massacre, there were reports that a mysterious man with an English accent seemed to be in charge of the terror operation. Alan Black, the sole survivor of the massacre, has recently reiterated that this was his firm impression. He has not been able to identify the man and has never suggested that he might have been Nairac, although others have suggested that. It should be borne in mind that the ambush parties in both atrocities were posing as regular Army checkpoints. In both cases the presence of an "officer" with an English accent would help to make the imposture more convincing. Apart from that, it is now independently clear that Nairac could not have been involved, since he was otherwise occupied in Pirbright.

The Northern Irish border area, especially South Armagh, was clearly out of control: the terrorist militias were acting with impunity. Unionist politicians demanded that Northern Ireland Secretary Merlyn Rees and Prime Minister Harold Wilson should do something urgently to curb the violence. Without consulting anybody, Wilson suddenly announced that the SAS were to be sent into South Armagh. Nearly 600 extra conventional "green army" troops were also committed to the Province at this time. Subsequent events showed that Wilson had not thought this decision through and that he had little idea of what the SAS really did, could deliver, or were doing at that moment.

The Prime Minister's announcement may have pleased and cheered the Loyalists, but it would cause Wilson political headaches, as he might have foreseen. The most likely explanation for his strange failure to consult is that the Unionists had pressed him urgently for this assistance and that Wilson, who hated confrontation, simply agreed, to get them off his back. Moreover, he had by this time decided to resign as Prime Minister and did so later in 1976: let his successor worry about the practical implications of Wilson's commitment. The second-in-command of 22 SAS, Major G, learned about it on 7 January 1976, when he heard Wilson's announcement reported on the television in his local pub, where he was enjoying a lunchtime pint. Apparently the SAS were to be deployed on "patrol and surveillance duties" in South Armagh. Major G was temporarily in command, as his Lieutenant Colonel was absent in Oman. The Director, SAS, Brigadier Johnny Watts, knew nothing about it either. (The SAS is technically a Corps, so it has a Director: at that time he was a Brigadier. Today the Director, Special Forces is a Major General.) The Chief of the General Staff, Sir Michael Carver, angrily accused Watts of intriguing with senior politicians to get the SAS into South Armagh without his knowledge. Watts denied this: he was as ignorant of the Prime Minister's thinking as every other soldier in the Army. Watts had been made to look either a fool, untruthful or uninformed in front of his superior. He would shortly be embarrassed again, for another reason.

In Northern Ireland the news caused surprise for completely different reasons. For months or even years rumour had been suggesting that the SAS were already present there. This might have been attributable to the presence of SAS specialists serving with NITAT (NI), news of whose involvement could have leaked. People who were aware of its existence sometimes wrongly suspected that NITAT (NI) was an SAS unit anyway, as there were close links between the two. Moreover, at the very start of the Troubles, when the Army's relations with both communities were still relatively good, L Detachment of D Squadron of 22 SAS had made a very public visit to Ulster. On Remembrance Day 1969 they had paraded in uniform through Newtownards to pay their respects to one of its most distinguished citizens and one of their original co-founders, the late Lieutenant Colonel Paddy Mayne, DSO and Three Bars, to fire a salute and lay a wreath on his grave. A few years later such a parade might have provoked a riot. The SAS's presence on that occasion had not been purely ceremonial, however; officially they were running a training exercise nearby. This was one of a very few occasions on which the SAS wore their sand-coloured berets in Northern Ireland. In reality they were there to intercept a rumoured shipment of weapons to Loyalist militia, but this turned out to be a false alarm and the SAS departed. They did not leave behind an undercover presence on that occasion, although some Northern Irish people who were aware of their visit tended to assume that they must have done so.

In *Faith and Duty*, Nicky Curtis proposes a possible explanation for the confusion over the date of the SAS's involvement in the Province. Although the SAS were only ordered into Ulster in 1976, well before that date there were frequent rumours that the SAS were there; he added that he was in no position to confirm or deny them. Curtis, however, credibly suggests that the rumours had been deliberately put about as part of a "black propaganda" exercise by MI5. The sinister legends surrounding the SAS and the perennial scarcity of hard information about them prior to 1980 were enough to trigger fear and paranoia in the ranks of the IRA. In that case, it hardly mattered that the SAS were not really present; simply planting the belief that they were somewhere about would still have had the desired effect. The Unionist politicians who in 1976 would press Harold Wilson to send the SAS into Northern Ireland clearly did not think that the Regiment was already present. Had the SAS really been there, the Unionists would have said something different. They might have asked that the SAS presence should be strengthened, but they would not have made their demand in the terms that they did; nor would Wilson have later announced that the SAS were about to be sent in. All of this suggests that Nicky Curtis' suspicion was correct.

Brigadier Watts was soon to be embarrassed again. It soon became clear that 22 SAS just did not have the men available to fulfil Harold Wilson's off-the-cuff pledge. The Regiment had grown again since the drastic cuts of the 1960s, but it was still small and it was fully-stretched. In 1976 22 SAS possessed four Sabre Squadrons and an HQ at Hereford. The HQ was deliberately kept small and lean. Of the Sabre Squadrons, one was currently deployed in Oman engaged in a counter-insurgency campaign; one was on an important NATO exercise in Europe; one was on "Pagoda duties," acting as the SAS Special Projects Counter-Terrorism Team, and the fourth, D Squadron, was dispersed on courses and secret small-group missions all over the world. Eleven men, mostly instructors and men on convalescent leave from Oman, were all that the SAS could produce at such short notice. They were designated as "an advance party" and packed off to Northern Ireland to save the Prime Minister's face. They went to South Armagh, where the resident Infantry battalion grudgingly made room for them in the already overcrowded Army base at Bessbrook Mill. When the media got wind of the deployment, it was written up as "hundreds" of SAS, but eleven was the true total. Nevertheless, there were now a few token SAS boots on the ground in South Armagh and, as far as Harold Wilson was concerned, he had now made his promised gesture to the Unionists. The advance party soon became self-contained: they set up their own exclusive SAS Mess and bar, into which few outsiders were ever invited. To the surprise of the resident battalion, there was no segregation of officers and other ranks.

From this it can be seen that the establishment of an SAS presence, as opposed to some experts on secondment, in Northern Ireland was not premeditated and that it predated Robert Nairac's arrival for his fourth and final tour of duty there in June 1976 by, at most, six months; much less in most cases. The difference between their respective levels of knowledge was vast. Apart from a small number of SAS who had previously served with the MRF, NITAT (NI), or in some other specialist capacity, the Regiment's knowledge of the Province was negligible. Nairac, by contrast, had done three duty tours already; he knew the whole of Ireland, especially the Republic, extremely well; he had been exploring it since his childhood; he had many Irish friends; he had studied Irish history and culture in depth; he had numerous potentially useful contacts, especially in the RUC, from his previous tours. It was not Nairac, but the vast majority of the SAS who would now be deployed to South Armagh who were absolute beginners and who would soon find themselves out of their depth.

Nairac was already an expert; the SAS had been lucky to secure his services. In 1976 they had much to learn from him and would have been wise to cultivate him; possibly even to recruit him. He was to be the SAS's, as well as Brigade's, Liaison Officer with the RUC Special Branch. Yet it appears that some, although not all, SAS officers and NCOs in South Armagh and elsewhere had a definite prejudice against him from the start; this prejudice persisted even after his abduction and murder and has been expressed since then in dismissive and defamatory interviews and articles.

Nairac was likeable; he was devoid of snobbery and so supposedly were the SAS. The SAS are a famously "democratic" Regiment in which officers and other ranks muck in together, which is what Nairac liked doing. Nairac was a notable boxer and rugby player and he radiated leadership. Even so, SAS Major G, who had personally requested Nairac as Liaison Officer, confirmed that there was feeling among some of the SAS against Nairac from the start. The following extracts are from John Parker's *Secret Hero*, where they are quoted in full:

"Robert... came for a briefing with us at Hereford. He was a bit resented by the boys: 'Who is this man?'... So Robert, appearing at Hereford, was treated initially with a touch of offhandedness."

Major G continued that Nairac "charmed his way into most hearts", but that he became "instantly suspect in the minds of some of the more cynical SAS hard-line soldiers."

Major G attributed this to Nairac's background as a Grenadier Guards officer; to inter-Regimental rivalry. However the SAS, the Brigade of Guards in general and the Grenadier Guards in particular, have had a history of successful co-operation and cross-fertilisation by exchanging personnel. At one time G Squadron of the SAS consisted entirely of seconded or former guardsmen.

There has to have been another reason – and there was. A former officer who served in Northern Ireland and knew Nairac reports that Harold Wilson's unreflecting commitment of the SAS to Ulster had placed the Regiment at a serious disadvantage. As we have seen, only eleven men had been immediately available for service there. Before the SAS could make an impact on the border security situation, their numbers would have to increase significantly. It would take months to build up the SAS detachment even to Squadron strength. The years of cheeseparing economy and run-down had had their effect: there were not enough trained SAS officers or men. More would start to become available later, as the counter-insurgency campaign in Oman began to move towards a successful conclusion. But meanwhile, to maintain Harold Wilson's credibility, SAS numbers in South Armagh had to be built up quickly: funding was made available and there was a rapid expansion. Men who had served in the SAS – or who had other relevant Special Forces experience – were brought back or brought in from elsewhere in the Armed Forces, from the Reserves and even from outside the Army. To make up the numbers there was a relaxation of standards. The new entrants or re-entrants included people who had left under a cloud; in some cases for good reasons. Rogue elements were being surreptitiously introduced by the back door and the results would soon start to be noticed. In particular there was the May 1976 border incident, in which eight SAS men were arrested in the Republic, apparently following a navigational error. As Michael Asher, who is himself ex-SAS, makes clear in his book, *The Regiment: The Real Story of the SAS*, the catalogue of errors that began with the border incident would continue with the shooting of innocent civilians who were in the wrong place at the wrong time; and of IRA volunteers who should have been arrested, interrogated and imprisoned but who instead were simply "malleted". Rogue members of the SAS seem to have applied their rules of engagement selectively, or not at all. It is difficult to imagine that Nairac could have felt remotely comfortable in the amoral psychological climate of 22 SAS as it was constituted at that time in South Armagh, or with its "canteen culture", which wrote off Northern Ireland as "a benighted Province of murderous shites", and which presumably influenced SAS troopers' conduct on operations. By contrast, they would not have appreciated Nairac's straight-arrow Catholic conscience and his empathy with the Irish. Responsibility for creating this situation lies firmly with Harold Wilson.

These errors were not typical of the SAS as a whole, but in 1976-78 there were disgruntled and rogue elements in the SAS stationed in South Armagh: Nairac as SASLO had to work with them. They would cause him serious headaches, for example because of their treatment of local civilians. The SAS's performance and reputation – in Northern Ireland but not necessarily anywhere else – continued to decline until in December 1978 Peter de la Billiere took over from Johnny Watts as Director. There followed a rigorous spring-cleaning, as a result of which the SAS today is a rather different organisation. They would redeem their reputation with the 1980 Iranian Embassy siege. But by that time it was a matter of indifference to Nairac; he was dead.

Major G further observed that "[Nairac] also faced some resentment from the more senior ranks of the SAS. He wasn't one of them, but he had a position of considerable power. People asked me whether he had ever done SAS selection. I had to explain that he wasn't with us for any SAS capability. He was not SAS. He was with us because he knew the score; he would make life easier for us; he would get us the vital intelligence we needed because no-one else was better equipped for that particular role than Robert Nairac. And he did just that."

This did not, however, satisfy some of the more disgruntled SAS, who would continue to snipe.

"He did on occasion wear a Regimental [SAS] beret, but he was given the choice to wear what beret seemed most appropriate to the task in hand, such as meeting Army personnel. Again, this also rankled with some of my people: 'Why is he wearing an SAS beret?' I had to explain that I trusted his judgement. He was not always going to be right but by and large it worked well and I still believe he did us very well."

This sensitivity about their beret on the SAS's part contains an element of blatant *chutzpah*: to confuse the opposition, they often wore the headgear of other Regiments (e.g. the RHF) when carrying out missions.

Although few or none of Nairac's former SAS colleagues and friends from NITAT (NI) were in Northern Ireland when he returned, they would reappear from time to time. One welcome visitor was Tony Ball. Major G records that Ball "came back to Northern Ireland for a tour, this time as SAS. Tony Ball took charge of our first detachment and again established an ideal working relationship with Nairac. They operated in South Armagh in a softly-softly capacity, and when we finally established the need to go looking for key IRA personnel in South Armagh, Robert and Tony Ball between them put together the early successes, which were absolutely critical to establishing more effective control and obtaining high-grade intelligence over that whole region".

Today Bessbrook Mill is silent, deserted and spooky, in the literal sense. In 2000 the British Government decided to close the base, following political pressure from the Republic of Ireland Government, Sinn Fein, the SDLP and former US President Bill Clinton, to which Tony Blair yielded. The base was finally closed down in 2007. Blair's security advisers warned him that the level of the terrorist threat there made any such move too great a gamble but, typically, he went ahead anyway. The advisers may yet be proved right; the story in South Armagh is not yet over. Bessbrook Mill is said to be haunted; whether by the ghosts of mill-workers or of twentieth century British soldiers, or both, is not clear. This was the base from which Robert Nairac would set out to a meet on the evening of 14 May 1977; the rendezvous from which he never returned.

In the mid-1970s Bessbrook Mill was by contrast a hive of military activity. The Army jokingly referred to it as the busiest heli-port in the UK. It had been a British Army base since early in the Troubles. Apart from the SAS, in 1976 it housed the 1st Battalion Royal Scots. The 1st Battalion Worcestershire and Sherwood Foresters would succeed them. The base was a large, fortified structure that had once been an important linen mill. The Army had acquired it and transformed it into a modern castle with its own helipad, watch-towers and anti-mortar screens; the twentieth century equivalent of the mediaeval curtain-wall. It glowered ogre-like over the immediate neighbourhood, the adjacent Protestant and Quaker enclave of Bessbrook village, which was well-disposed or neutral. The surrounding countryside was controlled by the PIRA; "bandit country" where almost everyone's hand was against the Army. So far, the South Armagh PIRA had killed 49 British soldiers without sustaining a single known casualty. The SAS aimed to change this; however their background and training were not ideal for Northern Ireland. Apart from the rogue element, some of them would come to Ulster directly from Dhofar, without any special training for Northern Ireland. In the deserts and mountains of Oman there had been few restrictions on the SAS's freedom of action. Now they were about to find themselves at the opposite extreme: on duty in the UK, hedged about by political and legalistic constraints. It was, in the slang of the day, "not their scene".

Ill-considered political gestures often have unintended consequences: the gesture often risks raising expectations that cannot be met. The people for whose benefit the gesture has been made – in Harold Wilson's case, the Ulster Unionists – expect to see results. If there are no early perceptible results, it will be seen as ineffective or fraudulent. Wilson's flippant decision to order the SAS into Northern Ireland created more problems, including political problems, than it solved.

To his chagrin, the immediate result of Wilson's announcement was to provoke a howl and gibber of dismay from his own side. The discretion and secrecy that the SAS regarded as essential to their work; the fact that they were rarely seen in the UK, apart from remote training areas like the Brecon Beacons or the Highlands of Scotland, because they operated mostly overseas; the fact that SAS soldiers never admitted to belonging to the Regiment and appeared in all official correspondence as though they were still with their original parent Regiments and that they did not always wear uniform, had allowed the media and the public to develop strange ideas about what they did. These ideas ranged from simply out-of-date notions, based on SAS Mark I's well-documented role in the Second World War, to sinister ones derived from thrillers, sensational action movies or an over-heated imagination. Insofar as the hard Left were aware of the SAS's functions, they treated it as a "given" that the Regiment was highly undesirable. They viewed it as an assassination squad, which had been brought in as a last resort to deal summarily with the IRA. This completely ignored the SAS's important "ambassadorial" work winning hearts and minds, which had greatly benefited the UK in the past, or its work for NATO. Civil rights groups, human rights organisations and journalists now prepared to subject the Regiment's work to close scrutiny.

Evelyn Waugh's naturalised Irish Marxist cousin, Claud Cockburn, wrote in *The Irish Times:* "Is South Armagh so short of terrorist gangs... that it needs a new one to be imported? Now the [British] Government is in the awkward position of... denying that it is waging war and yet defending the use of such forces as the SAS". Elsewhere in his article Cockburn prophesied that the SAS's actions would be "horrifying and illegitimate". Regrettably, the actions of a few members of the SAS over a very short period in 1976-78 would appear to give some substance to these alarmist predictions. The Government had never in fact denied that there was a kind of war in progress in Northern Ireland, although it tended to use euphemisms like "military action" or "peace-keeping".

Claud Cockburn, who died in 1981, was an erudite and eccentric journalist with a readable, elegant style. His articles appeared in a wide spectrum of newspapers and magazines, including *Private Eye*. He has been described as a colourful character; the colour being normally some shade of red. If he is remembered today, it is because his first wife, Jean Ross, was the original of the character Sally Bowles in Christopher Isherwood's novel, *Goodbye to Berlin* and the musical *Cabaret*.

In 1976 Cockburn was articulating the views of the British hard Left. At that period the hard Left showed strong support for the IRA, whom they perceived as native "freedom fighters" in a colonial territory, like Kenya or Rhodesia, which ought to be decolonised. They slid easily into their familiar "anti-colonial" rhetoric. In the case of Kenya the Left, for example Fenner Brockway MP, had openly supported the Mau Mau insurgents against the white Kenyans in the 1950s. After Kenya became independent in 1963, the white Rhodesians and South Africans became the Left's new totemic hate-objects. In 1969 the Ulster Loyalists joined them in this category.

Northern Ireland, however, was not like Kenya or Rhodesia; it was much more complicated. The white settlement of Rhodesia only dated from the nineteenth century and that of Kenya from the early twentieth. Relatively small numbers of colonists were involved. The plantation of Ulster was of far longer duration. The Protestant "white settlers" had lived there since the early seventeenth century. They predated many of the "native" Catholics, whose parents had arrived more recently from the South; in many cases seeking jobs after 1918. Protestants were still a majority of the population and were present at all levels of society from the nobility to the working-class. They regarded themselves as Irish, albeit of a special variety. Nevertheless the Left persisted in viewing the Ulster Protestants as an exploitative colonial élite who were not truly Irish; whose rights and views should be disregarded in favour of those of the Catholic and Republican "natives". It followed from this that the British Army must be an army of occupation propping up an indefensible colonial regime. This was a simplistic analysis of a complex historical and political situation.

British Army officers serving in Ulster learned to be circumspect when briefing visiting British parliamentary groups that included Labour MPs. There was an expectation that any information that they shared with the parliamentarians might later be shared with the IRA. The IRA and their supporters believed, or claimed to believe, everything that the British "loony Left" said or wrote about the SAS. Apart from that, they seem genuinely to have viewed the SAS's imminent arrival with consternation. Some Irish Roman Catholic clergy would routinely condemn terrorists in general in their public addresses – with varying degrees of sincerity – but would make a point of mentioning the SAS in the same breath as the terrorist organisations. The legends had begun to sprout vigorously, even before the SAS had arrived.

On the Loyalist side, too, there was an expectation that the SAS would adopt extreme methods with the IRA, although this was a cause for pleasure, rather than dismay. Loyalists saw them as a modern version of Wyatt Earp and his family posse (*Note 2*), who would now clean up the badlands of South Armagh. The Loyalists hoped that all the worst things that they had ever heard about the Regiment would turn out to be true and that these would now be visited upon the Catholic and Republican population. There was a perception that the SAS were not, or should not be, bound by any rules of engagement; were or should be immune from prosecution; and could enter the Republic in pursuit of their enemies. The expectations of both Republicans and Loyalists would on the whole be disappointed. Far from operating like terrorists, the SAS have their own operating rules and rules of engagement, which they normally observe strictly. The rules are different from those applicable to non-Special Forces, but they are "the Bible". One of certain SAS officers' numerous posthumous criticisms of Nairac was that he did not abide by these rules; although, given that he was not a member of the SAS, it was difficult to insist that he did so. The exception to this generalisation was the actions of rogue SAS members over a short period: 1976-78. Given the actions of this rogue element, the SAS were not well-placed to criticise Nairac, as he reportedly pointed out more than once.

Harold Wilson was embarrassed by the hornets' nest that he had unintentionally stirred up. Predictably, he made what almost amounted almost to a u-turn. He hurried to reassure Labour's supporters that their fears were misplaced. In a calming statement he specified that the SAS should patrol in uniform and should carry only the standard weapons used by the rest of the British Army. Since the SAS were already using other weapons of their own choice, this was a major inconvenience, to put it mildly. The SAS would have to abide by the same rules of engagement as everyone else.

This meant that the SAS could not use the aggressive tactics that had served them well in Arabia and Borneo. In Borneo they had never hesitated to attack and pursue deep into Indonesian territory. They now learned that they would not be allowed to enter the Republic of Ireland, which was the natural refuge of any terrorist fleeing from the Security Forces. They would only be permitted to open fire if they had reason to think that a suspect was about to endanger life and there was no other way of stopping him, or if he had just killed or injured someone and there was no other way of effecting an arrest. Even then, they had to issue a warning first. In other words, the SAS were expected to operate like any other Infantry unit, conforming to the same rules. They were expected to clean up South Armagh using the same methods as the conventional "green army"; methods that had already been shown to be ineffective.

Insofar as he had given it any thought, Wilson seemed to imagine that the mere name of the SAS would scare the terrorists into desisting from their activities, as had happened with the Balcombe Street siege. However, this was unlikely to happen with the South Armagh PIRA, who were a breed apart.

The SAS soon found that their presence was unwelcome. It was to be expected that Republicans should protest loudly against the arrival of this "killer élite" in the Province. Some Loyalists might have built up great, albeit unrealistic, expectations of the SAS, but the RUC, whose relations with the Army in general were often difficult, were both impressed by what they had heard about the SAS, and rather suspicious of them. They had not asked for the SAS to be sent in. Senior Army commanders in Northern Ireland had not requested the SAS's involvement either, and the "green army" of conventional soldiers resented their presence. Not being aware of the political background, the inference that the Army drew was that the Government saw them as having failed in their task and that the SAS experts were now being sent in to deal with the mess that they had not been able to clean up. They grudgingly made room for these intrusive cuckoos in the nest at Bessbrook Mill, and later elsewhere.

It did not take the SAS long to work out that they had been sent into the Province under false pretences and that their deployment had been a cynical political ploy. They soon discovered that apart from being hampered by the local rules of engagement, they would be denied some of their best tools; not just their preferred firearms. The most important of these was "hearts and minds." The SAS in diplomatic mode had enjoyed success in winning over such unlikely allies as the Saki in Malaya, Jebalis in Oman and Ibans in Borneo. For reasons already explained, they would have far more difficulty with the Catholic population of South Armagh, in whom was deeply ingrained strong resistance to any and all authority; above all to the British authorities and the British Army. Most of the SAS had joined the Regiment in the expectation of spending most of their time on challenging NATO and other overseas assignments; they were not pleased to find themselves in County Armagh. A rebellious and resentful mood developed. It might be summed up as: "What's the point of our being here? If we can't do it our way, we might as well go home".

As the months passed, the SAS began to suffer its own retention crisis. A growing number of SAS personnel in Northern Ireland started to consider taking early retirement. Used to an untrammelled existence in places like Oman, they decided that the very different conditions in which they now had to operate in Ulster were unacceptable: "If this is the future, we don't want it". They would find that their skills were better-appreciated elsewhere: some of the best SAS officers, including friends of Nairac, would soon return to their old stamping ground of the Gulf, but instead as contract soldiers working directly for Arab governments, which often proved to be very lucrative. After Nairac's death, his SAS friend Tony Ball would work for Sultan Qaboos of Oman and become Commander of the Omani Special Forces. Some became consultants; others started companies that would develop into fully-fledged private military companies (PMCs). Those who did not want to leave feared that if they did not score some major successes in Northern Ireland, the Regiment's future would soon be in doubt once more. Yet the Government seemed to be doing its best to stop them achieving anything of the kind. It was therefore with a disgruntled and slightly paranoid SAS, nursing a serious morale problem and a brood of uncooperative rogue members, that Nairac would be obliged to work with in 1976-77.

At first the small SAS advance party made the best of a bad job. They optimistically drew up a list of the eleven top PIRA leaders in South Armagh with a view to hunting them down and arresting them if possible or, if that were not possible, shooting them. Amazingly, given that they were initially so few, they eventually managed to score five out of their eleven targets. In some cases this would be thanks to intelligence supplied by Nairac after his arrival in June 1976. The troop patrolled the countryside of South Armagh, wearing camouflage combat kit and carrying Bergans. They set up hides in remote places where they could watch the movements of suspects for up to ten days; never cooking or smoking; always speaking in whispers. They left few traces behind them, bagging their excrement and bottling their urine. This cautious approach initially yielded few visible results, as the Unionist politicians began to notice.

At the start the SAS were hampered by small numbers, a lack of good intelligence and by the RUC's reluctance to share theirs with the conventional Army, let alone with the SAS. They could not easily assemble their own intelligence, given the unbroken hostility of South Armagh towards outsiders, especially those suspected of being connected with the Army. Any stranger seemed to stick out like a sore thumb. So the SAS could not simply go out, discreetly intelligence-gathering; or certainly not to begin with. Meanwhile they urgently needed someone who could – someone like Nairac. The essential conditions of SAS operations were and are "command at the highest level and intelligence at the highest level". These were not being given to them in South Armagh. There, they came under the authority of the Commanding Officer of the 1st Battalion Royal Scots, a very traditional Regiment dating from 1633. The available intelligence was provided by the Battalion's Intelligence Officer. This was not adequate for their purpose; Robert Nairac's contribution would now become not merely highly desirable but essential: he must be brought back soon to Northern Ireland to remedy this deficiency, and self-evidently the SAS must have their own chain of command in Northern Ireland. Meanwhile Harold Wilson's limiting strictures about the operating rules and rules of engagement should be discreetly jettisoned.

At this point the factors that were to lead to Robert Nairac's murder start to come together with the inevitability of a Greek tragedy. The elements are all there; now they start to move and advance towards what we in retrospect can see as a predictable, even inescapable, outcome, although not many people did so at the time. A very few, like Valentine Cecil, did and said so, but for excellent motives Nairac refused to listen and continued resolutely forward. His walk towards his rendezvous with death began not in South Armagh, but in London nearly two years before his murder, when he called on AG2 at Stanmore. In the best traditions of Sophoclean tragedy, the hero's character defects, and even his virtues, contributed to his downfall. Fate was not solely to blame, although Fate could be said to have played a part. There was already a "Nairac legend" growing around him although he was still in his twenties, and he had begun to be seen by some officers as having a personal touch that could resolve problems that had defeated others. He may even have started to believe this himself; he had achieved some remarkable results in Ardoyne in 1973 and at Castle Dillon in 1974-75. But in 1976 the exaggerated expectations placed on Nairac's shoulders, broad though they were, were not realistic.

The SAS's unforeseen 1976 deployment had made it even more likely that Nairac's services would be called for. During his service with NITAT (NI) in 1974-75 he had impressed seconded SAS officers, including Tony Ball, with his ability to charm local sources like the RUC into sharing intelligence; Nairac had also favourably impressed more senior SAS personnel, either by what they had read or heard about him, or in person. Nairac had attended courses held by 22 SAS at Hereford, although he had not so far attempted SAS selection. It was therefore extremely likely that, following their deployment to Ulster, Nairac would at the very least be mentioned as someone whose secondment should be sought to assist the SAS's work in County Armagh. Nairac had also made a favourable impression on the RUC's Special Branch. Given this circumstance, it was likely that the RUC too would request him as their preferred link-man with the Army. Both of these things happened, although the Grenadier Guards would not have been automatically obliged to release him. That would have required the intervention of senior officers. Again, that is what seems to have happened.

Although Nairac could not have predicted the SAS's sudden 1976 deployment to Ulster, he had in any case made a request for his own further posting there more likely to succeed by writing an Army paper in 1975, which is mentioned in the Prologue to this book. In this paper Nairac had advocated the appointment of a dedicated Military Intelligence Officer (MIO) to be based in South Armagh on a one-year posting. This officer would have to be "reasonably brave" and to possess imagination, determination and flexibility. Although he was only a recently-gazetted Captain, very senior officers had read the paper with respect and approval. Once the Army had taken up Nairac's recommendation, it became likely that he would be one of the first officers to be considered for the appointment; in describing his ideal candidate, Nairac had in effect described himself. The fact that his proposal was adopted and that he was appointed disposes of any notion that he was simply a Liaison Officer. Starting in June 1976, he was there in an intelligence role, whatever his official job-description may have been, and his appointment had been approved at the highest level. As noted earlier, in his paper Nairac had estimated this intelligence officer's chances of surviving his one-year tour of duty at less than fifty percent. Under those circumstances Nairac's determinedly bachelor status, with no dependents and no fiancée in sight, made him a particularly attractive candidate.

Major G, the aforementioned second-in-command of 22 SAS, who had met Nairac previously, confirmed in an interview with John Parker for *Death of a Hero* that he had personally requested Nairac. "We had to have someone out here with us who could establish access to the RUC and Special Branch and hopefully tap their intelligence... what we needed was an experienced, credible intelligence officer of our own who could liaise with them." The SAS could not provide such a person, so he called for Nairac. First of all, Major G had telephoned Nairac from Hereford. He reportedly "jumped at the chance" of an attachment with the SAS. Major G then made a formal request to the Household Division, who were "very helpful". Major G does not say with which helpful Household Division Officer he communicated, but we can work that out for ourselves. The RUC seconded the request. Unfortunately Major G would not be with Nairac in South Armagh for long. He was posted back to the UK later in 1976, although he would reappear in the Province from time to time.

Nairac was not the hapless victim of circumstances. He had been working towards this outcome. He had intrigued. He had discreetly sought the support of senior officers. His paper recommending the appointment of a MIO in South Armagh was part of this personal strategy. His interest in Ireland had latterly become an obsession and he was determined to get back there. He had convinced himself and others that he was unusually well-qualified to make a significant contribution towards defeating the IRA, restoring peace and normal political life to Northern Ireland, as well as supplying some of the deficiencies of the Army's intelligence operation. In the latter presumption, he was correct. The deficiencies, especially in South Armagh, were certainly numerous.

Nairac knew that it was now essential for him to score a significant success and he believed that a fourth tour in Northern Ireland, where he could use his Irish expertise to the full, besides being congenial, would provide that opportunity. He did everything that he could to achieve that result and he almost pulled it off. In Northern Ireland his confidential reports continued to be brilliant and, had he survived for a few more weeks, to the end of his tour in June 1977, early promotion and a medal were in the bag. He would have become a Company Commander, Acting Major Nairac MBE, before his twenty-ninth birthday.

In his biography of H Jones, Sir John Wilsey states that in 1974 Nairac had been keen to undergo SAS selection. In the event someone persuaded him to aim for NITAT (NI) instead. In NITAT (NI) he had met and befriended seconded SAS soldiers, including Tony Ball. He had been impressed with them, and they with him. Except for officers promoted from within the SAS's own ranks, at officer level the SAS does not offer a permanent career. An officer from another Regiment who passes SAS selection normally spends two to three years as a troop commander, which is what Nairac would have done, had he attempted and passed selection. In the next stage he returns to Regimental duties; most probably as a Battalion Operations Officer, a Company Commander, or possibly to do something at HQ DSF; on loan to some foreign army; working in the Special Forces Plans & Ops Cell, or in a formation HQ. There are a number of possibilities. Then, if he is lucky, he may return to the SAS as a Squadron Commander, OC Training Wing, or something similar. Then he returns to Regimental duties. If Nairac had attempted and passed selection in 1974 and then served as a Troop Commander with the SAS, he would still have been doing so in 1976. The chances are that he would have been in Oman or Germany and not immediately available for duties in Ulster. But if he had later gone to Northern Ireland with the SAS, he would have been bound by SAS operating rules. He could not have undertaken the duties that he did, and could not have operated in the way that he did, which was a factor in his murder.

Although it might appear that the SAS were homogeneous and unanimous: "the SAS wanted this" or "the SAS thought that", logically they could not have been so. They were a very varied bunch of men. So, although it might be true in a general sense to say that "the SAS wanted Nairac back in Northern Ireland", in reality not all of the SAS on the ground did want him. Equally, while most SAS men might be brave, brainy and team-spirited, there were those rogue individuals who pursued private agendas and had a toxic influence. Nairac had no doubt expected to enjoy as friendly a relationship with the SAS soldiers in 1976-77 as he had in 1974-75 when he was working in NITAT (NI). With some of them he seems to have done so, but by no means with all. A former NCO remarked that:

"Your comment about rivalry between Robert and some members of the SAS would be normal because no matter how good... others thought him; that would not count with members of the SAS for one simple reason: he had not been through the very tough selection process which is used to select personnel for training to join the SAS. This is very demanding and once you have passed this process you then have a gruelling training period in which individuals are assessed ... and can be rejected at any stage. This could be the reason why certain [SAS] personnel didn't like Robert."

A former officer has echoed this; adding that, however friendly you might become with individual SAS officers or soldiers, as Nairac obviously had become with Michael Rose and Tony Ball among others, this never translates into friendship with the SAS as a whole. You are either one of them, or you are not. Whether or not Nairac fully understood this, it would make the part of his job that consisted of acting as SAS Liaison Officer with the RUC difficult and challenging. He would have to walk a tight-rope: expected to act as though he were a member of the SAS for some purposes and at some times; expected also to abide by their operating rules, but at other times expected to keep his distance. He therefore was not, and could not be, one of them. Some SAS, however unreasonably, would come to resent his presence and the fact that they had to have a non-SAS man as their Liaison Officer. Because Nairac had been tipped for early promotion, interpreted the rules fairly elastically and tended not to hide the extent of his knowledge, it was easy for them to start disliking him.

In South Armagh Nairac unquestionably fulfilled his responsibilities; in one of the last Army reports ever written on him, it is recorded that:

"One of the major factors on which the success or failure of the Detachment stems, is the quality and quantity of exploitable source information provided by Special Branch. Before NAIRAC's arrival local Special Branch confidence was marginal and there was no intelligence available on the local PIRA Command structure. Over the year NAIRAC has steadily and systematically established an excellent working relationship with all the thirteen RUC Special Branch Officers in his area. As a result the Branch now have total confidence in the Detachment and any exploitable intelligence on the PIRA Command structure is immediately passed."

This was an impressive achievement, given the mutual suspicion and dislike that had existed between the Army, including the SAS, and the RUC before Nairac's arrival. In its way it is as impressive and unlikely as his achievement of befriending the Republican population of Ardoyne. The question remains: why were some SAS officers and NCOs unwilling to acknowledge this? Why were they so keen to believe the worst of him?

There is the question of Nairac's alleged "extra-curricular" activities. Speaking long after Nairac's death, Colonel Clive Fairweather referred to about 30 percent of Nairac's time that seemed to him to have been spent on unaccountable activities that were not easily explicable by his work for the SAS, the wider Army or with the RUC. Fairweather was not specific about what he meant by this. He speculated that Nairac was out of control and was "doing his own thing". Assuming that any reliance can be placed on anything that Fairweather said or wrote about Nairac, it is conceivable, although impossible to confirm, that he was unofficially assisting one of the Agencies; possibly the Secret Intelligence Service (SIS), also known as MI6. At this period the MI6 office in Northern Ireland was very small and probably needed all the help it could get, from whatever source. The MI6 representative at this time was a colourful and eccentric Scot called Craig Smellie, who often sported a Tam O'Shanter bonnet and no doubt appealed to Nairac for that reason. They were definitely acquainted. Among other eccentricities, it is reported that "Craig Smellie was a character. He would sit in the office, a satellite station in an elegant Georgian building, and shoot holes in the walls with his pistol" – much like Sherlock Holmes in moments of boredom in Baker Street.

There is not enough evidence on which to build a case: just curious scraps of information. Nairac was seen on one occasion speaking with, or perhaps briefing, an older man who has been tentatively identified as Sir Maurice Oldfield, who was then "C", the Director of MI6 from 1973 to 1978. In 1979, after Nairac's death, Sir Maurice would be appointed by Prime Minister Margaret Thatcher to overhaul and coordinate security and intelligence in Northern Ireland. As has been noted earlier, as an Army officer Nairac should not in theory have been doing any work for the Agencies but, as another former officer confirmed, at that time it was "all but officially encouraged". Quite a number of Army officers got involved – something that would not normally be permitted today. But then, the possibility of working with MI6 would have been irresistibly challenging to Nairac and it would not necessarily have done his career any harm. The attraction is obvious: Nairac's admired uncle Basil Dykes had worked as a "spook" during the Second World War. Nairac mentioned this to one or two Army friends with apparent pride, but without identifying Basil by name. Like his dead brother David, Basil Dykes was one of the significant others whom Nairac thought to emulate.

A possible alternative explanation is that Nairac was simply trying to do what Sir Maurice Oldfield would accomplish two years after his death: to get the various British intelligence agencies to talk to one another, to work together with himself acting as the intermediary. If so, it was a very ambitious project for a Captain, but it might explain the highly-classified and sensitive files from various sources that were found in his room at Bessbrook Mill after he disappeared.

The reason for Oldfield's 1979 appointment to Northern Ireland was that intelligence-gathering there had become chaotic, with Army Intelligence, the SAS, the RUC and the Agencies acting in an uncoordinated manner; even at times in apparent rivalry, competing for "assets." That was the situation while Nairac was in Ulster. It has been at least mooted (for example in John Parker's *Secret Hero*) that Nairac's death could have resulted from a deliberate betrayal by his own side: that he had become caught up in a bitter rivalry between MI6, for which he had been working, and MI5. There is no evidence for this, although the two Agencies' mutual ill-feeling at that period is not in doubt. MI5 resented MI6's intrusion into "their" territory, which had become justified by the IRA's increasingly complex links with international terrorist organisations and maverick States such as Libya. Whatever some members of MI5 might have thought, this international dimension was of legitimate interest to MI6 and its parent ministry, the Foreign Office, which at that date contained a large Republic of Ireland Department. (MI5, the Security Service, comes under the Home Office.) Despite this, it is unlikely that the Agencies' rivalry would have assumed a murderous form: we may leave speculation about that possibility to thriller-writers. In the final analysis the two Agencies still had to work together and would do so even more closely from 1979. Already in 1976-77 they were sharing office accommodation at Lisburn. A former senior MI6 officer agreed: "there was co-operation... we were all on the same side". The real problem was within the Army.

Whatever the reason, Nairac probably over-extended himself. More than one of his friends and family commented in retrospect on how tired and stressed he had seemed immediately before his murder; this could well have affected his judgement. However, it is now clear that his going to the Three Steps in Drumintee on the night of his abduction and murder was in connection with a legitimate SAS/Army intelligence matter, not MI6. It was on this basis that he had sought authorisation from Major H Jones. To his later regret, Jones granted the authorisation.

There is a link here with another of the Nairac legends, which is still believed by some people. As with the SAS, some members of the Labour Party, especially in Harold Wilson's time, entertained deep suspicions of the Agencies; especially of MI5, which they believed was working against them. The Left's narrative alleges that Nairac was really working for MI5, which had probably recruited him at Oxford. MI5's supposed aim was to sabotage the Anglo-Irish Sunningdale Agreement that Labour had inherited from the Conservatives; which, in the event, the Ulster Unionists derailed in May 1974 without any outside assistance, and then to sabotage the fragile agreements and cease-fires that Labour would from time to time negotiate with the IRA's representatives. To ensure that the carnage in Northern Ireland should continue and escalate towards civil war Nairac, on instructions from MI5, is supposed to have organised strikes and atrocities. The alleged purpose of all this was to embarrass the Labour Party so as to make it less likely to be re-elected, and to create a situation in which all-out war against the IRA, leading to its defeat by military means, could be countenanced.

There is no serious evidence for any of this, but there is ample evidence of Labour persecution mania. It has proved abundantly possible to show convincingly that Nairac could not have been involved in any of these incidents. If that were not enough, in order to have committed these acts, Nairac would have had to abandon all moral restraint; all his principles, including his deeply-held religious convictions, and his core integrity. As observed by American business leader and philanthropist Warren Buffett, "Look for three things in a person: intelligence, energy and integrity. If they don't have the last one, don't even bother."

From what we now know of Nairac, his integrity was not in doubt.

CHAPTER 13 | THE HUMAN FACTOR

He despises you yet he can't keep away from you. He's like a moth about a flame.
He despises you not because you snub him, but because he envies you.
(Gyles Brandreth, *Oscar Wilde and the Ring of Death*)

When Robert Nairac returned to Northern Ireland in mid 1976, changes were beginning to happen in the way in which Operation Banner was being implemented. These were developments which Nairac himself had foreseen and supported, although not everyone agreed. As new documentation has been released, there unfolds a picture of incompetence at the political level; of inadequate leadership and inappropriate tactical doctrine within the military; and a consequent sub-standard performance on the ground during the early years. The performance of the early covert units like the MRF and the turmoil between the rival or uncoordinated Intelligence functions (which Nairac had identified and was criticised for saying so) exposes some of this, but from about 1975-76 a more professional and coordinated approach began to be taken – an approach which, with a few significant caveats, was to lead to the eventual defeat of the IRA. Nairac played a role in developing this; his posthumous influence seems to have been quite profound, despite his junior Army rank.

After seven years of the Army's deployment in Northern Ireland, intelligence operations in the Province, especially in South Armagh, were still inadequate. This failing, including the lack of cross-border co-operation with the Garda and the Irish Army, brought about an urgent need to rectify the situation and created an opportunity for a person of Robert Nairac's unusual ability and character to take up this challenge. There can, in fact, have been few other suitable candidates. Nairac was capable of filling the new MIO South Armagh post, *if correctly supported in it*. This professional support must have been in place at the beginning, but from early 1977 it started to erode.

As time has passed, Nairac has proved to have been right about many things, although in the 1970s some of his views were controversial. Nevertheless some very senior officers did listen to him. The resistance that he encountered was lower down in the hierarchy. Nairac's views were important because he understood the vital causes, effects, failures and successes of the myriad processes that had fed into the Northern Ireland conflict in the early period. By background, and given his Irish experience, he was uniquely well-qualified to make this analysis: however he had not been there from the start.

The early years, roughly 1969-75, were the period that set the relationship between the Army and the Northern Irish communities, as Nairac clearly understood. Some SAS soldiers called him a potential double agent for his apparent empathy with the Republicans. But Nairac was right: taken together, the intelligence failures and the breakdown of relations between the Army and the Catholic community in 1969-75 would eventually result in more military casualties than the combined sum of the Falklands War, Iraq and Afghanistan. Anything that could be done to salvage the situation and reduce the butcher's bill, both to achieve better intelligence and to build better relations with the Catholic and Nationalist communities in particular, should be done. The fact that Nairac knew the history and understood the very complex bigger picture; that he could identify the failures, including political failures, their consequences and possible ways forward, at a time when few others did, seems to indicate that those senior Army officers who foresaw his rise to senior rank may have been correct in their view.

It is difficult to relate the last year of Nairac's life, because so much of it is still shrouded in secrecy. This is inevitable, given the type of sensitive undercover work that he was doing, but there is more to it than that. The official information issued at the time when Nairac disappeared was highly misleading. Just how misleading is only now beginning to become clear. Relevant Government files have meanwhile been shredded or are embargoed for many years into the future. Some MOD files containing information relevant to Nairac's disappearance, which had been released to the National Archives for researchers' use, have been withdrawn. Moreover, a good deal of disinformation has been spread about Nairac and his work at this period; not just by Republicans and the hard Left but also by former Army officers. In their case this was less for security reasons or to protect lives than to protect the reputation of individuals who had played a direct or indirect role at the time of Nairac's disappearance, and in the follow-up to it. Whether they deserved this protection is a moot point.

To make a biographer's task even more difficult in the absence of much official documentation, the verbatim accounts of Nairac's contemporaries often contradict one another. To give one example, there is even doubt as to what Nairac looked like at this period. Clive Fairweather describes Nairac in early January 1977, when Fairweather arrived in Northern Ireland, as looking more like a tramp or a hippie than a soldier: grubby, unshaven, scruffily dressed and with his curly hair hanging in ringlets to his collar. Fairweather later stated that he thought that Nairac "enjoyed being scruffy". However, shortly before this, a Grenadier brother officer met Nairac at his Portadown office. Nairac also attended the 3 Company of the 1st Battalion Grenadier Guards' 1976 Christmas celebration in Middletown, Co. Armagh, where he met one of his NCO former boxing partners. Both these men have emphasised that on these occasions Nairac was acceptably dressed and that his hair, while longer than a proper Regimental cut, was neat and clean. He had a motivated, confident air.

Patrick Mercer, who was one of the last people to see Nairac alive and liked him immensely, considers that he was latterly very scruffy. Mercer thinks, but is not 100 percent certain, that Nairac went on patrol with the Worcestershire and Sherwood Foresters in Crossmaglen on the morning of 14 May 1977, the last full day of his existence. If Mercer's recollection is correct, Nairac's fishing expedition into the Republic later that day must have been quite a short one. What Mercer does recall vividly is Nairac's appearance. Patrolling in Crossmaglen, Nairac had been conspicuous by being scruffy, carrying a non-standard weapon (a Wingmaster shotgun) and wearing a Foresters Private's beret with a large silver badge. The Army had long before stopped wearing metal beret badges, which were too good a target, in Northern Ireland. They wore dull black plastic badges or just collar-badges.

Civilian men's hairstyles in the 1970s were generally longer than what is now considered fashionable in 2015. Soldiers serving in Northern Ireland, whether undercover or in uniform, were permitted to keep their hair somewhat longer than the Army would normally allow elsewhere, so that they should not be too readily identifiable as soldiers when off duty. Many did this. They likewise tended when off duty to avoid wearing plain clothes that were too smart or that might give clues as to their military status. Nairac may simply have been following official advice. If so, he overdid it. Members of the SAS also tended to overdo it, with wild, long hair and beards. As a result, they were easily identifiable as SAS and were eventually told to smarten up. Even at his most casual, Nairac never looked that unkempt. For his undercover work Nairac often changed his appearance: sometimes disguising himself in working men's clothes. If he had to, he could also appear as a smart civilian in a dark suit. His hair length would vary. He would grow a beard or a moustache for a particular assignment and later shave it off.

The justification for the relaxation of Army haircut regulations had been tragically illustrated early in the Troubles when an IRA sniper shot dead a young Netherlands merchant seaman, who had gone ashore in Belfast to seek dental treatment. The Dutchman was smart, clean-shaven, walked with an upright carriage and had short hair. In the Netherlands, where long hair for men had never caught on to the same extent as in the UK, his neat appearance would not have been remarkable. In Belfast, he paid for it with his life. The IRA had mis-identified him as a British soldier.

In choosing to return to South Armagh in 1976, Robert Nairac knew that he was going back to the most dangerous theatre of operations anywhere for a British soldier. The danger was posed by the PIRA South Armagh Brigade, which was the most effective part of the PIRA. It was compounded by the Republic of Ireland Government's disinclination to do much about the IRA and by the fact that the Garda Siochana, even when well-disposed, was not then a credible anti-terrorist force. Relatively few IRA terrorists were ever convicted in the Republic. This was a reflection of a collective failure of political will on the part of successive Governments of the Republic to end the IRA campaign of the 1970s in the way in which previous Irish Governments had helped to terminate earlier IRA campaigns in the 1920s, 1940s and 1950s by cross-border co-operation with the British authorities. Although the public in the South would sometimes voice their fear that the Troubles might spread there, and although Irish politicians might publicly wring their hands or express indignation over the ongoing tragedy of the Troubles, it is impossible to exonerate the Republic from responsibility for their seemingly endless protraction after 1969; in reality until the present day. For Northern Ireland is not yet at peace: the volcano is only dormant, not extinct.

The most notable failure was in the Republic's policy towards South Armagh. The access routes from the Republic into what had become the most active terrorist zone in Europe should have been tightly controlled. However, security on the Republic's side was intermittent, sloppy and sometimes compromised by IRA sympathisers within the Dundalk Garda. The widely-publicised Breen and Buchanan murder in 1989 which hit the headlines was a particularly invidious example of this, but it was not unique. This failure to control the salient would cost hundreds of lives. The reasons were political; being hard on the IRA could cost a Minister, even a Prime Minister, his job. In 1979, two years after Nairac's death and following the Warrenpoint massacre of eighteen British soldiers by the PIRA, coinciding with Lord Mountbatten's murder in the Republic, Taoiseach Jack Lynch agreed a radical security review and greater cross-border co-operation with the new British Prime Minister, Margaret Thatcher. Elements of his Fianna Fail Party rebelled. Respected and popular statesman though he was, Lynch's position became untenable. He resigned as Leader of Fianna Fail on 5 December 1979 and was replaced as Leader and Taoiseach by Charles Haughey. The Republic's refusal to clamp down on the IRA prolonged the Northern Irish Troubles by decades and caused approximately a thousand people to die avoidably in the border areas: Robert Nairac was one of them. This factor should never be forgotten.

The last year of Nairac's existence was probably the most stressful of his life. That stress was not caused primarily by the PIRA or other terrorist groups – indeed at times he may have considered them the least of his problems. On a daily basis, he received more provocation from his own side: specifically from the SAS officers and NCOs whom he was trying to help, and in particular from Clive Fairweather. Despite this, throughout his last year, Nairac never showed less than 100 percent commitment and continued to deliver impressive results under far-from-ideal conditions. He overdid it, stretching himself to the limit.

In the words of SAS Major, later Colonel, G, who was well-disposed towards Nairac, quoted by John Parker:

"... new personnel [were] coming in who were not only totally inexperienced in the situation in Northern Ireland, but they themselves had just come though the rigours of many months of hard-fought guerrilla warfare in the mountains of Dhofar. That is not an excuse, it is just a fact. They came in, it must be said, with a hard-nosed attitude. Initially, with the speed of our commitment to Northern

Ireland by Harold Wilson (i.e. overnight!), they'd had only basic training for their new role on British soil. So our attitude, as much as anything, was seen as far too hard-line, compounded by media hysterics and the extraordinary speculation in newspapers in particular. [*Claud Cockburn's article in The Irish Times is an example of this.*] It wasn't so much what we did, as what we said; what we wanted to do; and how we saw the answer to the lawlessness in South Armagh. You must remember that at the time we were committed not to countering terrorism in the Province as a whole; just to restoring law and order in the no-go area, and particularly the border area of South Armagh.

"Looking back, the political aim was just to keep the hard-line Protestant element happy by giving them something they wanted. The Army was 'lumbered' with a military element [the SAS] that they did not want, found difficult to accept, with all the media interest and speculation – remember this was before the Iranian Embassy siege when the SAS became public property – and thought it best to keep us in a box with the lid nailed firmly down.

"Against this background there was Robert Nairac, who knew the area well and knew how far he could push something or, at least, he thought he did. He was the man in the middle who was doing his best to ensure that the SAS achieved its aim in a situation which he understood better than anyone amongst us. He was the meat in a strange political/military sandwich of contradictions. The fact is, he'd gone through a great deal in fulfilling this role. He didn't see it that way, I'm sure, but there had been enormous pressure on him in that last year or so, when he was working with successive SAS squadron commanders coming to a situation which they knew less about than Robert. There were officers who believed he was pushing it, particularly in the way he ignored some of the set SAS procedures, such as calling in at a set time or going out without back-up. The fact was, he wasn't a member of the club. He wasn't SAS and occasionally the veneer of the Grenadier and the Ampleforth lad would come through, and some of the hard-nosed Regiment people would say "We can do without this guy".

That view was not correct. The SAS could not do without Nairac. They could no more have dispensed with Nairac in South Armagh or Northern Ireland in general, than Dante could have dispensed with Virgil's services as a guide to the Inferno. Senior SAS officers, as well as the RUC, had requested him in the first place. The main reason was that the SAS deployed to South Armagh on short tours. Detachments, and later Squadrons, rotated frequently. This was important for morale: however bad their present situation might be, there was always a not-too-distant end-of-tour date in sight. However, it also meant that they had limited opportunity to build up local expertise and contacts. Nairac supplied the expert in-house knowledge and was "the corporate memory". If they had insisted on getting rid of Nairac, they would have had to operate in a different way, with longer duty tours, building up their knowledge and expertise, which would have been most unpopular.

One does not have to be a military genius to see that this situation was not satisfactory. Nairac had made himself indispensable but he had no dedicated support and no understudy. If he should be murdered or just invalided out without a proper, in-depth handover of at least two weeks to a fully-briefed successor, there would be a serious loss of information and contacts. Meanwhile, from his return from leave in September 1976 to the end of his tour, he was only able to take short "breather" leave breaks in the UK: he started to get tired and stressed. This would have happened anyway, even without the office intrigue and backbiting that he was experiencing. A few SAS officers noticed this and were concerned:

"Some officers who were coming back for second tours were critical that he had been allowed to remain for as long as we wanted him."

SAS Major G was so concerned that he recommended that Nairac should be withdrawn following one of his visits to Northern Ireland, roughly two months before Nairac was murdered. Speaking to John Parker, he said that he had approached his Commanding Officer on his return to Hereford:

"We've got to pull Robert out. He's a tired man. He's done the business, he's been effective. In my opinion he's going out on a limb these days and that's always a sign that you think you are untouchable."

In the event G was overruled. His Commanding Officer was adamant that Nairac was needed for one more SAS tour of duty. Major G did not, to his later considerable regret, insist on his recommendation.

Had Nairac survived to the end of his tour, he would have given his successor a full briefing about South Armagh before his departure. He would have left behind typed classified guidance notes. There would have been a handover, during which Nairac would have introduced the successor to his contacts. He would have done this with the usual Nairac efficiency and thoroughness. As it was, when he was murdered, his successor had been identified but they had not met. There would now be no opportunity for a handover, or for Nairac to write up handover notes. Nairac kept much of his knowledge in his head; that is what spooks, both military and civilian, do. As a result, an entire library of information on South Armagh, Ulster and Ireland in general was, metaphorically speaking, reduced to ashes when he died. Much of it was irreplaceable.

All 22 SAS officers serving in Northern Ireland held regular commissions, apart from some expert volunteers seconded from 21 and 23 SAS. The SAS in South Armagh had initially suffered from poor leadership. The first two Squadron Commanders appointed in 1976 were, by SAS standards, weak men and did not last long. Morale became steadily worse. At one point Brian Baty, the 22 SAS Adjutant, who was in Northern Ireland on pastoral Adjutant business, was ordered to put the current Commander on a plane to the UK and to prepare to take over the SAS detachment in South Armagh as Acting Commander for the next few months. He was still there in that acting capacity when Nairac arrived in

June 1976. His successor, Acting Major (Captain) John Sutherell, was only a year older than Nairac, with the same substantive rank and from the Royal Anglian Regiment. Two separate witnesses have said of Sutherell that he never got the measure of Nairac. As noted earlier, Nairac's closest friends and enemies alike were disconcerted by his unknowable "inner darkness". Like other colleagues, Sutherell was impressed by the fact that Nairac knew Ireland far better than anyone else. He also knew that Nairac had worked in NITAT (NI) in 1974-75. Sutherell quite reasonably assumed that Nairac knew what he was doing and decided that it was better to adopt a "hands-off" approach with him.

Perhaps importantly, according to a former colleague:

"Sutherell lacked confidence and needed always to be surrounded by stronger subordinates. None of this is critical – he's a good bloke." Another said: "He is a good bloke, decent and law abiding, wiry rather than strong; *not* your typical 22 SAS man: he is honourable, introverted, will always do his duty... He was confused about Robert: they were polar opposites, really."

Sutherell faced another difficulty: according to an officer who was serving in South Armagh at the time, Sutherell's Acting rank placed him at a disadvantage, with regard to both Nairac and Fairweather. The balance of power between Sutherell and Fairweather was very hard to gauge: the blurring of authority in which the SAS specialised made this and other things additionally difficult to assess. This officer commented further that: "My impression of the SAS Squadron was that it had got itself into a terrible bother over Nairac and didn't really know what to do. I suspect that exacerbated the already difficult command issues."

In wartime it is normally relatively easy to ensure that soldiers of all ranks pull together. Unlike in peacetime, camaraderie and devotion to the common cause tend to supersede careerism, which normally revives within weeks of peace being declared. Service in Northern Ireland however offered the worst of two worlds. Although it was in effect a war – one of the longest wars in which the British Army has ever been involved – it was dangerous and with frequent casualties; it was not "a proper war" against a clearly-defined enemy who fought under internationally-accepted rules of war. Many peacetime considerations still applied; especially political and career factors. It is probably correct to say that most regular officers saw service in the Province, far more than, for example, service in World War II, Korea, Malaya, Kenya or Borneo, as primarily a career opportunity: a chance to get ahead of professional rivals. The SAS were not immune from such thoughts; Clive Fairweather, a very ambitious man, certainly was not. Nairac was not immune to ambition, either. He was by nature competitive and impatient for success: if he did not get it, or if it did not come as quickly as he thought it should, he sometimes sulked and became depressed; as a result he would occasionally cut corners and take risks in order to achieve results. That he did usually achieve the desired result is not in question.

Nairac had returned to Northern Ireland at Major G's earnest request, explicitly, though not exclusively, to help the SAS. He had to rein them in on occasion and had been obliged to deliver some unpalatable lectures to them, but he was not responsible for the frustrating conditions under which the SAS had to operate in South Armagh; Harold Wilson was. It was a classic example of "shooting the messenger". Nairac was a man for whom loyalty and team-spirit were important and some of the SAS were not showing it.

There were disobliging comments that must have filtered back to him. Some of them were defamatory. These would include assertions that he seemed to empathise too closely with the Republicans; that he was too friendly with known IRA sympathisers. At that time the SAS regarded the IRA and Irish Nationalists in general simply as a despicable and savage enemy, to be defeated and preferably killed whenever the opportunity presented itself. Even Nairac's personal religion was seen as a "weakness". He was a Roman Catholic, so could he be trusted? Was he perhaps a double agent? Nairac's attempts to befriend the SAS were misinterpreted; perhaps wilfully. In the words of one of Nairac's most serious critics:

"Robert liked to cosy up to the SAS soldiers. He tended to be quite familiar with them, using their first names or their nicknames. He also liked swearing quite a lot. I got the feeling that when he was around the Special Forces soldiers they felt uneasy about him in the same way as I did... I got the impression that they didn't particularly respect him."

That critic was, of course, Clive Fairweather. These are strange remarks: not only was Nairac free from side or snobbery, but so supposedly were the SAS, with officers working and playing along with their men. Using first names and nicknames was normal for them, although it would not have been in the Grenadiers. As for swearing, admittedly Nairac used the f-word quite a lot, but which modern British soldier does not, and would any SAS soldier really have been offended by his using it? As for "feeling uneasy", that is presumably code for "they (or I or we) thought that he was homosexual". New rumours about Nairac's alleged homosexuality did in fact start to circulate within the Army in Northern Ireland at this time, although they only became more widely known later. They are reiterated for example in Anthony Bradley's *Requiem for a Spy*. These rumours are invariably attributed to a British military source, which is why they have been taken seriously. But should they be? They seem to have originated within the SAS or, more probably, with Clive Fairweather; they may also have been picked up and given legs by the UDR.

It has been proposed that Nairac's hypothetical "boyfriend" was his SAS friend Julian "Tony" Ball. Apart from the fact that Ball was apparently happily married and has at least one surviving child, it has been observed of Ball by another soldier who knew him well that: "Nothing about his behaviour suggests a gay *persona*. He was extremely active – perhaps herein lies the 'role model' that Nairac set out to model his own activity upon." In any case the gay rumours specified that Nairac's alleged affair was with another soldier who was still serving in Northern Ireland at that time; the affair was reportedly in full, passionate, committed and consummated swing at the time of his murder. It is a matter of record that Tony Ball was not serving in Northern Ireland when Nairac was murdered – he was back at Hereford. So the boyfriend, if indeed he ever existed, has to have been someone else; it has not, however, been possible to discover any trace of him. Had higher authority become aware of these rumours and taken them seriously, Nairac would have been investigated and, if the rumours had proved to be correct, he would have been removed immediately as a security risk. Because this did not happen, and because we now know that Nairac was due to leave Northern Ireland in June 1977 on promotion and with a medal, we must conclude that these stories had no factual basis. Whoever was the originator of the rumours, their purpose can only have been mischievous: to get Nairac replaced as MIO/SAS Liaison Officer in South Armagh. Only a very small number of people in the Army wanted this to happen: they were to be found among the SAS and at Lisburn.

Given that Nairac had been working hard to deliver successful duty tours for the SAS, he would have felt all of this keenly. In the past, the Army had provided him with moral and practical support. Now, in 1977, that support was conspicuously absent and he was being undermined, not even very subtly. He was not a quitter and would never have admitted this, even to himself; but his position as Liaison Officer was slowly becoming untenable as a result of the attitude of certain SAS officers and NCOs. Meanwhile their other sub-text: "and anyway we don't really want to be here; we hate it here", was being picked up by some of Nairac's RUC contacts; they were not impressed.

Even at an early stage in 1976, when Brian Baty, who was well-disposed towards him, was in command of the SAS detachment, there had been issues over booking in and out at Bessbrook Mill. Nairac was remiss about telling the SAS where he was going. He was not under Baty's operational control and he had his own agenda, which was acceptable, but the SAS Operations Officer needed to know his movements and where he would be. After Baty's departure Nairac gradually became isolated from the SAS. If the SAS distrusted him, he began to distrust them; not entirely without reason. He started to distance himself and kept his contact with them to a workable minimum. Although he still drank Guinness in the SAS bar at Bessbrook, his visits became rarer. Given that trust had broken down, he increasingly did not consult the SAS or keep them informed about what he was doing or proposing to do. If his "official" Liaison Officer role was proving disappointing and frustrating, he would concentrate on his "real" job as the first dedicated MIO for South Armagh. And he would do it with as little SAS involvement as humanly possible. They might benefit from the information that he was able to discover, but they should stay out of his way while he was gathering it. In the final analysis he did not need their backup; if necessary he would get it from other elements of the Security Forces, like the Worcestershire and Sherwood Foresters, now serving in South Armagh, or he could look after himself. Increasingly, that is what he preferred to do.

Predictably, the SAS did not like this, either. "He was out of touch and out of contact. We really had no idea what he was up to... only he knew. That was the nature of the man and we didn't like it... Quite frankly, we did not want him around us."

By early 1977 that feeling was mutual. The SAS had made it clear that Nairac was definitely "not one of us" and never could be, but they persisted in trying to impose SAS rules on him, which they lacked the formal authority to do: it was a grey area. The most important of these rules was "Never be out of contact". Given the state of relations between them, Nairac had an increasingly diminishing wish to be in contact with them. As a last resort there was a range of stiff fines for SAS officers and men who missed deadlines and otherwise broke operating rules. The heaviest fines – up to £1,000 – were imposed on people whose failure to communicate had caused helicopters or ground troops to be called out unnecessarily to search for them. Until the night that he disappeared, Nairac was never in this last category. However, if an officer was merely out of contact, missed a call-in or some other deadline, he had to give an explanation. If the SAS Squadron Sergeant Major did not think that the reason given was good enough, the officer would be fined, regardless of his rank or position. This did happen to Nairac. If officers repeatedly flouted this rule, they would be hauled before the Commanding Officer.

NCOs and Warrant Officers are the backbone of the Army: this is particularly the case with the SAS, because most of their commissioned officers are only there for about three years at a time. Unless they have been promoted from the SAS's own ranks, the officers return to their parent Regiments at the end of their tours, hoping to come back later in a more senior capacity after more Regimental soldiering and promotion, if they have really enjoyed their time with the SAS. The NCOs and Warrant Officers are there permanently. They are the SAS's corporate memory, so the SAS has a very "NCO" culture. Even their own officers, referred to as "Ruperts", are not treated with great respect or deference, at least initially: they have to prove themselves. The NCOs gave Nairac a hard time and he had frequent runs-in with them, running up quite a tab of fines. Usually he paid up – sometimes he did not – although, as a non-SAS officer, it is doubtful whether the fines could have been enforced. The important point to note here is that, contrary to popular impressions of how the SAS operate, they prefer to "go by the book". In a different way, their discipline is as strict as that of the Guards. That was the theory, but in 1976-77 some rogue members of the SAS definitely seem to have been trigger-happy; this was to cause Nairac concern and to lead to further disagreements.

Nairac hated the restrictions that the SAS tried to impose on him. And he had an SAS argument to use against them. Not only, as he was frequently reminded, was he not SAS anyway, but the SAS's own operating rules provided loopholes, which he was quick to identify. For undercover soldiers, a certain leeway is permitted. Depending on what they are doing at the time and where, checking in on time and respecting deadlines is not always physically possible. Adjustments have to be made to accommodate them. And Nairac was increasingly operating undercover.

At this distance in time it is easier to see the defects, dangers and challenges of Nairac's situation in South Armagh. In 1976, when the SAS and Nairac became engaged, or re-engaged, in the area, these would have been less obvious, especially on the ground. During their first six months in the Province, from January to June 1976, despite their lack of a dedicated Liaison Officer with the RUC Special Branch, the SAS had achieved some results. Before Nairac's arrival, on 12 March they had arrested Sean McKenna Junior, guilty of a string of terrorist offences and a future hunger striker. On 15 April, as we have seen, they managed to kill Peter Cleary, a serious terrorist and senior PIRA officer. It would, however, have been far preferable to have kept him alive and to have interrogated him, as Nairac pointed out when he returned. It is likely that certain members of the SAS had intended to "mallet" Cleary even before they caught him. As we have seen, the South Armagh PIRA would exact a dramatic revenge for Cleary's death: the murder on 21 July of the British Ambassador to the Republic of Ireland. Not long before, the Ambassador had made a familiarisation visit to South Armagh, which presumably brought him to the PIRA's attention; they may have considered his visit provocative. Even so, had Cleary remained alive, they would presumably not have murdered him.

South Armagh, while still a highly dangerous place, was quieter in 1976 than it had been in 1975. The main terrorist players had moved out; this contributed to the impression of quietness. This was due in part (but only in part) to the SAS presence; to that extent Harold Wilson had been right. Given their very small number at the start of their deployment, the SAS had probably achieved this result more thanks to the alarm and demoralisation that their appearance in an area could inspire among the terrorists and their supporters, than by their successes in the field. Now, however, they would soon be at Squadron strength and in a position to start going on the offensive. For this they were going to need Nairac. In particular they needed him to extract information from the RUC's Special Branch. This, Nairac was increasingly well-placed to deliver; several of his quite numerous RUC friends were moving up the command structure and into positions of authority and influence.

Nairac's position has been described by more than one former soldier as anomalous, and in some respects it was. He was the first independent MIO for South Armagh; he had drafted the job description; he was reporting to the GOC and other very senior officers and officials, although he also attended the regular Northern Ireland MIOs' meetings, at which he would, starting in January 1977, meet Clive Fairweather. Nairac's was a quasi-independent appointment – and that was how he liked it. Brian Baty has confirmed that Nairac was not under his operational control. His formal controller was based in Portadown and seems to have allowed him considerable leeway: put bluntly, Nairac was not being managed. Far from minding this, Nairac saw the opportunity of being on a less tight rein than he had been previously, and took it. There was no recent precedent, although similar quasi-independent MIO appointments could have been found in (and outside) British India during the period of the Anglo-Russian "Great Game", which had been played from 1813, with a break from 1907 to 1917, until Indian independence in 1947, as Nairac knew; he had read the relevant books. As he also knew, there were other intelligence officers in Northern Ireland who wanted to bring him under their control. He was potentially a very valuable asset. There was a lot of empire-building going on in Ulster at that time.

The more politically-aware SAS officers claimed to have been concerned about Nairac for another reason. They were aware of the media hype, positive and negative, that had resulted from their casual commitment to Northern Ireland by Harold Wilson. They were determined to play by the book – their book – and not to give their political enemies any pretext to start protesting. They expected Nairac to play by the book, too. Their aspiration was probably unrealistic, given that their book was different from that of the rest of the Army; that many of their critics objected to the SAS's presence in Northern Ireland in the first place and indeed to the Regiment's continued existence, so they could never be placated. The aforementioned political enemies numbered among their ranks IRA sympathisers, including the British hard Left in general; Irish-Americans, including the Kennedy clan; various journalists and a noisy international clique of human rights experts, lawyers and campaigners. They routinely described the SAS as terrorists, torturers and killers.

The SAS were not supposed to set foot in the Republic at all, although from time to time they did so; on one occasion with very unfortunate results. In May 1976 and not long before Nairac's arrival, Gardai, backed up by a platoon of Irish Army soldiers, had stopped and arrested two armed SAS men in a car inside the Republic. The Irish Army platoon, who out-gunned the SAS, forced them to hand over their weapons. The SAS men said that they had made a navigational error and were unaware that they had crossed the border. One of the former SAS soldiers involved has confirmed that they were telling the truth: they had made a genuine mistake, although very few people believed them, then or later. Although one does not expect the SAS, of all people, to make this kind of error, the mistake was easily made. The incident took place at night, but even by daylight in many places the border is poorly marked and hard to locate on the ground. It is an imaginary and usually invisible line that bisects woodland, roads, farms and villages. The Ordinance Survey maps of the area that were then available are now known to have contained confusing errors. Crucially, the maps appeared to show the road that the SAS were supposed to take as curving to the right; in reality the correct road went sharply to the left. Taking the wrong turning, the SAS ended up in the Republic. A second car-load of SAS men in a backup role followed the first – and took the same wrong turning. These men also got arrested after a further confrontation with the Irish Army troops and likewise had to hand over their weapons.

The SAS's true purpose was simple and unexciting, although they could not speak about it in an Irish court. Inside Northern Ireland, but still close to the border, two SAS men had been carrying out a surveillance mission for several days with a long-range camera, to obtain a photo of a particular person who operated out of a PIRA "safe house". They had been put into the area at night and were now due to be brought out again, also by night. As usual, the operation had been conducted with great secrecy, the two-man patrol taking care to make no noise and leave no trace of their presence. Their mission completed, an SAS car had gone to pick them up, followed by another SAS car with backup. Because they were using the same map, both drivers independently made the same error, missing the correct turning, continuing across the frontier and into the Republic. The driver of a third civilian car, which went to look for them and which contained the most senior SAS officer then serving in the Province, and a senior RUC Special Branch officer, made the same error too, but they escaped undetected; had they been caught, the political embarrassment would have been even greater. The arrested SAS men all appeared in court in Dublin the following day and were released on payment of £40,000 bail. Eventually they were fined £100 each.

At this point fact and legend collide. According to the legend, which is widely believed and set out as fact by authors such as Ken Connor, Brian Baty sent the eight arrested SAS men to Aldergrove to be interrogated by the Royal Military Police's (RMP) Special Investigation Branch (SIB), as though they had been guilty of disregarding or exceeding their orders. This allegedly provoked angry protests and a near-mutiny by the SAS in South Armagh. It required a flying visit by the SAS's Director, Johnny Watts, and 22 SAS's Commanding Officer to South Armagh to calm the volatile situation. Watts and the CO reportedly told the men that if their comrades were put on trial, they would both resign: this averted the mutiny.

The reality is that there was no question of a mutiny or even an argument. There had, however, undeniably been a serious international incident. Senior Army officers and Ministers urgently required accurate information and an explanation. The men involved immediately flew by helicopter to HQ at Lisburn to be debriefed by the RMP's SIB; a process that lasted for the rest of the night. This was a device to save time, because the GOC (Northern Ireland) and Cabinet

Ministers in London were not prepared to wait for an RUC Special Branch report. However, Brian Baty did recognise that the SAS did not want to be deployed in Northern Ireland and that there was a morale problem as a result. He gave them a brisk "pep-talk" to remind them that they were soldiers, albeit specialist ones, and that in the final analysis they had to go wherever they were ordered, however uncongenial that might prove to be. Visits by the Lieutenant Colonel from Hereford and the Director, SAS, did take place but later and separately. They had been scheduled long before and were not directly related to the border incident, although that was inevitably discussed during their visits.

The "navigational error" explanation was true and explicable, but because the full story could not be told at that time, in many people's eyes it made the SAS look incompetent. The Press thoroughly enjoyed the Regiment's discomfort. So did the SAS's fairly numerous Army critics, who included some members of the Parachute Regiment:

"If that's the élite, what the fuck must the rest of us be like?" wrote Tony Clarke of 3 Para. "I wouldn't give them the time of day... they are a joke."

There was a more serious aspect to this farce. This was not apparent to the public, but it was to well-informed members of the Army. Some of the names of the arrested SAS men seemed familiar. Tony Clarke noted that they included men who had previously either failed to get into the Parachute Regiment or had been dismissed from it. What, exactly, were they now doing in the SAS? "Cowboys the lot of them... how did they get in the SAS?"

Today we know the answer; they had been recently recruited or brought back to make up SAS numbers in South Armagh. The border incident was far from being the end of the story. The SAS's inadequate response to Nairac's disappearance also falls within their catalogue of failings at this period. The chief beneficiary on each occasion was the IRA, who made political capital out of it. When Peter de la Billiere took over from Johnny Watts as Director, SAS at the end of 1978, the Regiment's reputation was at an all-time low. The arrests following the border incident had necessitated a major damage limitation exercise, one of whose elements was the posting to Ulster of Clive Fairweather, who was ex-SAS and who had expertise in damage-limitation and media-management.

The SAS soon noticed that Nairac seemed to venture across the border whenever he felt like it. Following the May 1976 border incident, they considered that he should not be doing so; Nairac took no notice. The fact that he sometimes picked up interesting information in the South tended to be overlooked. So did the fact that, although he was armed, Nairac was never arrested or questioned. Some of Nairac's visits to the Republic were intelligence-related; to call on sources. The ease and frequency with which Nairac passed into and out of the Republic might suggest that the Garda and Irish border officials knew exactly who he was and had instructions not to interfere, although this is impossible to prove. Apart from information-gathering, what was Nairac really up to in the Republic? Sometimes he reportedly sang in pubs. Some of the time he was fishing. The trout-fishing was better in the Republic, so Nairac took his rods there. Apart from that there is frustratingly little evidence available, other than his own sparse recorded or remembered remarks, so we are free to speculate; and speculate is what Nairac's SAS enemies and critics increasingly did. Some of the SAS's speculations led them to alarming tentative conclusions: Was he conducting an illicit sexual liaison or acting as a double agent, or both? Nairac was known to have Irish civilian friends in the Republic from his school and university days. This, taken with his Catholicism and the incorrect rumours that he had studied at Trinity College, Dublin, was further evidence of his unsoundness in the eyes of some members of the SAS. (In reality Nairac had practically dropped his Southern Irish friends like the Morris brothers: for their protection, he hardly ever saw, telephoned or wrote to them after he joined the Army.)

From Nairac's point of view, a bonus of going to the Republic was that the SAS were highly unlikely to try to shadow him there, following the embarrassing border incident. The Republic must sometimes have appeared as a haven away from the backbiting and office intrigue that characterised Nairac's life at base. A number of factors now came together, the combined effect of which was to bring Nairac's murder closer. These were:

- The departure from Northern Ireland of Major G, who was Nairac's main point of contact within the SAS at the start of his posting in 1976. Nairac and G were already acquainted, liked and trusted one another, and had also shot wildfowl together. Nairac had been happy to accept a degree of management by Major G. Problems arose with his successor, as a result of which Nairac became determined to free himself from SAS tutelage. Given his relations with some members of the Regiment this may have been understandable, but it was still undesirable. He succeeded through intrigue, and from then onwards was hardly managed at all;

- A change in the SAS's terms of reference, which in January 1977 were expanded from South Armagh to cover the whole of the Province, stretching them and Nairac to the limit;

- The appointment of Major Clive Fairweather (KOSB and formerly SAS) as GSO2 Int/Liaison HQ NORIRELAND, based at Lisburn, from January 1977. Fairweather would conceive an emotionally-charged dislike of Nairac, which would become a factor in his tragedy;

- A decision, taken at very senior level, to withdraw Nairac from South Armagh in early 1977 and put him back on the streets of Belfast in uniform with the Devon and Dorsets as part of a secret military mission whose details are still not fully known. While Nairac was there, in late January – March, he was recognised and photographed in Ardoyne by the IRA;

- A further decision at senior level, whereby Nairac, now clean-shaven and short-haired, was then sent back to resume his undercover work in South

Armagh. Following his tour of duty in Belfast, he should not have gone back;

- The shooting of Seamus Harvey, a prominent PIRA volunteer, in a firefight with the SAS on 16 January 1977.

The killing of Seamus Harvey was the breaking point for Nairac's relationship with the SAS. The fault lay with the recently-recruited rogue element within the Regiment, who increasingly seemed to be – literally – calling the shots. This is the only high-profile PIRA killing with which Nairac is definitely associated, although it took place in disregard of his instructions. The SAS seemed to have wilfully misinterpreted them and Nairac was very angry. Relations with the local community, a subject on which Nairac had frequently lectured and admonished the SAS, to their annoyance, now suffered a major setback. Seamus Harvey soon became a canonised PIRA martyr and hero. The already obsessive fear and hatred of the SAS on the part of both the PIRA and its supportive local community in South Armagh intensified. Anyone whom they even suspected of being SAS could now expect to receive no mercy: Nairac's brutal murder would occur only four months later. The involvement of the SAS's rogue element was clear. Their decision to "mallet" Harvey in defiance of instructions tends to confirm this.

Nairac went "ballistic" and tore strips off the SAS, including their Commanding Officer, who was the same substantive rank as himself. He also invoked senior officers. The SAS were furious; they already resented Nairac's insistence on scrupulously observing the rules towards the civilian population. They complained about him to Clive Fairweather, the newly appointed GSO2 Int/Liaison HQ Northern Ireland. Nairac's relations with both became poisonous. That was still the situation in May 1977 when Nairac disappeared.

Soon after Seamus Harvey's death, Nairac was ordered to Belfast on temporary duty with the Devon and Dorsets. He would remain there until some point in March. His mission remains mysterious to this day. It is intimately linked to the "IRA photo" of Nairac that was released to the media by the PIRA and published after Nairac's murder. The photo is undoubtedly him; his broken nose is noticeable in profile. It shows him talking to young people in the Republican and Catholic Ardoyne district of Belfast. There is every reason to think that it was taken in early 1977, two or three months before Nairac's death. It had not previously been published in the UK or the Republic. In particular, it had not appeared in any Regimental magazine, which was where the IRA sometimes looked for photographs and information about officers' movements.

The two youths seen with Nairac who are face-on to the camera look shifty; they have been tasked to speak to Nairac and to detain him for a few minutes while he is out on patrol, so that an IRA cameraman can get a good shot of him. Nairac may have suspected this, as he is glancing cautiously round to his left, i.e. towards the camera. The youth to Nairac's right seems to be looking directly at the camera. This could this be a signal: "Now's your chance: you won't get a better shot than this", or "This is your man". If so, how did the two young men know who Nairac was? They almost certainly recognised him because they were among the boys whom he had taught to box three or four years earlier, or perhaps their younger brothers: the IRA photographer was presumably out of sight some distance away, and used a telephoto lens.

Nairac was an officer of the Grenadier Guards and served in no other Regiment. The Guards Regiments wear a khaki beret with DP combat kit. Nairac wore it in Belfast in 1973. According to Lieutenant Colonel Richard Besly, the Grenadier Guards only ever wore the khaki beret with the black grenade badge in Ulster. Although the photo is in black and white, Nairac is clearly not wearing a Guards beret. The commonest beret, worn by many corps and by some Infantry Regiments, is dark blue. That is what Nairac is wearing. It follows that this photo must have been taken by the IRA in 1977, as they stated, about two months before he was killed. This has been confirmed by other British Army sources.

Nairac had returned to Northern Ireland in June 1976, ostensibly as a Liaison Officer but also in a military intelligence role. For most of the time, he operated in civilian dress, sometimes further disguised by longish hair and facial hair. Nevertheless he was back in uniform in early 1977 in Belfast, disguised as a member of the Devon and Dorsets who were based there from January to May 1977. A former Devon and Dorsets officer has confirmed that Nairac wore their beret in early 1977 and that he went on patrol with the Regiment in Ardoyne. After four years, Nairac was back in Belfast, but to what purpose?

Nairac had not volunteered for this assignment; he had been summoned back to Belfast. He was there from mid-January 1977 until some point in March. This was a follow-up to "some previous problem, about which he had knowledge". This is believable; Nairac had made himself an expert on Catholic, Republican Belfast. The 1977 mission cannot have been a straightforward advisory role. If it had been, there would have been no need for Nairac to change his appearance or go out on patrol. However, for this assignment he had been specifically ordered to get back into uniform, shave off his facial hair and have a haircut. In the photo he looks smart; his hair is short and neat; he is clean-shaven and he is out on patrol. It is possible to draw another inference from this photo: that while he was of interest to the IRA, senior IRA commanders in Belfast, at any rate, were not interested in killing Nairac. If they had been, they could have done it on that day or any other day in Belfast. He would have seemed to be just another Army casualty, shot while patrolling. The IRA photographer could just as easily have been a sniper – and he probably was, at other times.

The initiative to bring Nairac back to Belfast came from the Devon and Dorsets' then Commanding Officer, the future Major General Colin Shortis CB CBE, a former Commander of NITAT (NI), who had read the 2nd Battalion Grenadier Guards' 1973 post-operation report, in which Nairac featured prominently. This persuaded him to request Nairac's temporary attachment to the Devon and Dorsets. This would have been a reasonable request, except for one extremely important consideration: Nairac was then working undercover in another part of Northern Ireland. If he had been based in the UK or Germany and not nearby in Ulster, there would have been no problem. But, under those circumstances, it was blatantly unwise and extremely risky. No-one, including Nairac himself, seems to have pointed this out.

Approval of the Devon and Dorsets' request would have been required at a more senior level. Whichever senior Army officer was responsible for approving the request to recall Nairac to Belfast in a uniformed role, he had put him and his intelligence work in South Armagh at risk. Nairac should have pointed this out, but he did not; that would have been out of character. The reason is that Northern Ireland is a small, gossipy place: only six counties and a total population of less than two million. Nairac should not have gone back to Armagh after that degree of exposure in Belfast. He had developed a high profile in Belfast in 1973, where he was still known under his real name by many people, especially in Ardoyne. Devon and Dorset soldiers who went on patrol with him in Ardoyne in early 1977 confirm this; the hostile stares would quickly morph into eager smiles when the locals recognised him:

"Hello Rabbert (Robert)! You're back! Where've you been?"

This was often followed by a pressing invitation to come in for a cup of tea. It was not the kind of reception to which the Devon and Dorsets were accustomed in Ardoyne – and it might seem incredible, but it is confirmed by other sources, including Nairac's Army obituary.

Did this seemingly foolish action by someone senior in recalling him to Belfast to serve in uniform early in 1977 and then sending him back to South Armagh cause Nairac's death two months later? It had made his identification easier, but was it the catalyst of his murder? This has been alleged, but to date there is no known reliable evidence that it was. Nevertheless it cannot be ruled out. SAS Major G certainly did not rule it out. In one of several conversations with John Parker he said:

"The mistake of leaving him there [in South Armagh] was only compounded by the fact that, as I understand it – and I could never fathom how this could have been allowed to happen – during his time with us and unbeknown to me, he had been asked to appear in uniform in the north by the Army for some previous problem about which he had knowledge. This opened up the possibility of recognition, regardless of whether he was miles from his normal patch. Those communities are very close knit. That was an extreme risk and one that, in my judgement, should not have been taken, because it was suggested that on the night [when he was abducted] suspicion had begun by someone saying that they had seen him in Army uniform. I don't know the detail and don't want to know now. It's too late..."

This is not confirmed by any other source, but Major G might have had access to now-suppressed classified information to that effect. Or it might just have been rumour.

There is a gap in March 1977 between Nairac's leaving Belfast and his starting again in South Armagh, during which he took leave to visit his parents in Gloucestershire for what was to be the last time. He returned to South Armagh in April and resumed his previous intelligence-gathering activities in civilian dress. He now had less than two months left to live. His local contacts would have noticed his absence from Armagh for several weeks. Some time would have elapsed before his hair grew even slightly long again and his facial hair (a moustache and sideburns, at this period) grew back. As he went about his business; talking to people, drinking and singing in pubs, his contacts would have noticed the changes in his appearance from scruffy to neat and short- haired, and then gradually back to scruffy again. That would have set them wondering. No doubt he had a plausible explanation for his transformation – a temporary job requiring him to smarten up, for instance, or an important job interview – but some doubts would have remained. Equally serious was Nairac's deteriorating relationship with some of the SAS and his determination to act independently whenever he judged it to be feasible.

Apart from the rogue element of the SAS, the most serious opposition that Nairac had to face was from Clive Fairweather. As the senior Army intelligence officer physically based in Northern Ireland, although technically a King's Own Scottish Borderer, Fairweather was closely involved with the SAS, in which he had served in the past and would serve again in future. The SAS in South Armagh were aware of his SAS past and treated him – unlike Nairac – as "one of us". They had a tendency to complain to him about Nairac, although he was not Nairac's immediate superior. Nairac was therefore caught between upper and lower SAS millstones. Indefensible as the SAS's actions towards Seamus Harvey might appear, in Clive Fairweather they had an able and influential defender: his expertise in news management and damage limitation is not in doubt. Fairweather was to play an important role in the last months of Nairac's existence, in his death and for years afterwards, when he did considerable damage to Nairac's posthumous reputation. For that reason, he occupies a prominent part in this narrative.

Quite apart from the SAS factor, Nairac and Fairweather had a personality clash: within five minutes of meeting they were enemies. This must have been largely Fairweather's doing, for it is clear that – with the exception of some SAS soldiers – Nairac usually got along well with most military men and indeed with most civilians, who found him charming and likeable. Some of the reasons for the clash lay in Fairweather's past.

When Fairweather died from a brain tumour in October 2012, he received laudatory obituary notices in the Press. There was much to commemorate: in the course of a thirty-four year Army career, Fairweather had risen from TA Private to full regular Colonel. He had served three duty tours with the SAS, and had been second-in-command of 22 SAS at the time that the SAS stormed the Iranian Embassy in 1980, although he had not been one of the soldiers who abseiled into the building. He had seen action in Borneo and had carried out operational tours in Sharjah, Northern Ireland, Oman, Iran, Dhofar and Jordan. After leaving the Army in 1994, he served for eight years as HM Chief Inspector of Prisons for Scotland; a role in which he made a number of influential friends, one of whom was the former Scottish First Minister, Alex Salmond. Latterly he was a fundraiser for, and Patron of, Combat Stress, a charitable foundation that supports war veterans with post-combat mental health problems. Fairweather used to joke that he, by some miracle, had never suffered from combat stress. This was not strictly truthful. He had suffered stress, quite possibly combat-related, and he had turned to alcohol as his therapy. In 2003 he had received the CBE (Commander of the Order of the British Empire) for his lifetime of public service.

Fairweather's memorial service, held in Edinburgh's historic Canongate Kirk the following month, was packed. This church has a strong military connection and is decorated with military heraldry; it is the "parish church" of Edinburgh Castle: the Governor of the Castle, who was at that time the GOC Scotland, has a decorative reserved pew, the Castle Pew. It is also the chapel of the Royal Regiment of Scotland and the current Minister is a former Army Chaplain. A formerly close female friend of Fairweather who attended the service reported: "The church was absolutely packed and, although the congregation seemed to consist of many, many Service chaps, of all ranks, I seem to remember that the tributes/eulogy dwelt more on his life after leaving the army (Combat Stress fund raising, Gardening Leave, his time as HM Inspector of Prisons in Scotland). Only about half a dozen women [were] in the congregation. (The atmosphere in the church before and after the service was that of an army (all ranks) reunion!) I did not go on to the wake, which was held at the Royal Scots Club."

Because this is a biography of Robert Nairac and not of Clive Fairweather, it is not proposed to comment extensively on Fairweather's career – except insofar as it impinged upon Nairac's career and his life – other than to acknowledge that by any standard Fairweather had an impressive CV. He appears as a figure traditionally admired in Scotland; the "lad of parts" who, by native intelligence and hard work, rose from obscurity to prominence; who became one of the Great and Good. Such people used to be held up to young Scots as exemplars. A famous example is Andrew Carnegie, the philanthropic working-class Scot who became a millionaire industrialist in the USA and whose generosity, long after his death, is still benefiting Scotland.

Clive Bruce Fairweather was the only child of an Edinburgh police constable. His parents sent him to George Heriot's School. Heriot, a rich Edinburgh goldsmith and proto-banker, had established the school as a charitable foundation in 1628 to provide an education for orphan boys and "fatherless bairns". By Fairweather's time it had become a grant-aided boys' school, equivalent to a grammar school in England. Having gone independent in order to avoid being forced into the comprehensive system, Heriot's is now an up-market co-educational fee-paying day school, although it still offers generous scholarships to pupils, whether orphaned, fatherless or otherwise disadvantaged, who need assistance with school fees. Throughout its evolution it has been noted for scholastic excellence, sending a respectable percentage of its pupils to university. It occupies an architecturally-distinguished building amid attractive grounds in central Edinburgh, near the university. However, little of its polish or its ethos can have rubbed off on the young Fairweather, as the Headmaster asked his parents to remove him; his disruptive behaviour had proved intolerable to both teachers and pupils. Lacking qualifications, it was unclear what he might do thereafter. He had some musical ability; he played the piano and had considered training to become a professional musician. However his parents' finances would not stretch to cover the tutorial fees.

Fortunately there was always the Army. Fairweather took a temporary job. He also joined the Territorial Army (TA) as a Private, training conscientiously on Wednesday evenings, at weekends and occasionally at other times, with the local TA Parachute Regiment battalion (15 Para). He successfully performed the requisite number of jumps and gained his Para Wings. The most professional parts of the TA (*Note 1*), which included the TA Paras, were a recognised "back door" into the Regular Army for those who, like Fairweather, lacked the requisite minimal educational qualifications, but clearly possessed leadership and organisational ability and were therefore seen as potential officers. In due course, following some favourable reports, Fairweather secured a place at RMA Sandhurst, where he studied as an Officer-Cadet from 1962 to 1964. At Sandhurst, as at Heriot's, there were reports of disruptive and bullying behaviour, one episode of which caused him to be excluded from the end-of-course Commissioning Ball as a punishment (or he attended it under escort; the accounts vary). He was nevertheless commissioned in the King's Own Scottish Borderers, an old and distinguished Scottish Infantry Regiment, originally raised in 1689. He was twenty years old when he left Sandhurst. Having secured a commission, Fairweather probably thought that he had confounded the critics of his early youth and was now officially an officer, a gentleman and an achiever. Life, however, is rarely that simple.

For all their antiquity and distinguished history, the KOSB were not fashionable or elitist in the same way as the Grenadier Guards. Unlike the Brigade of Guards or the Cavalry at that date, the Regiment did not expect that its officers should have a private income; with few exceptions, Scottish Infantry officers came from less opulent backgrounds than Guards or Cavalry officers and were expected to live within their Army pay. In the KOSB Fairweather would not be serving alongside the sons of dukes, millionaires or cabinet ministers. Nevertheless the old Scottish Regiments had their traditions, their ethos and their standards. At that period and for years to come, most Scottish Army officers, even clan chiefs of ancient Highland ancestry, spoke with cultured English accents or, at a pinch, with refined Edinburgh Scots accents. Privates and NCOs might speak with thick regional accents; officers did not. This applied across the Scottish élite.

This was the situation that Clive Fairweather encountered in 1964, when he joined his Regiment. A policeman's son, Fairweather had a strong Lowland Scots accent and probably spoke with a glottal stop. In other words, he sounded like an NCO. Prior to this, he had given no thought to his accent or his grammar. Now, however, he was gently mocked for it and for his general brashness and lack of *savoir-faire* by some of his brother officers. Sometimes the mockery was not so gentle. One day he was tasked to meet and look after a visiting English General. The General affected to be unable to understand a word that Fairweather addressed to him: "Bring me a proper officer!" he is alleged to have shouted. By implication a real officer in a good Infantry Regiment could not possibly have sounded like Fairweather, who never forgot this incident: in later life he sometimes dined out on it. The General is now unidentifiable and there is no independent corroboration of the story, but presumably some such incident occurred, possibly embroidered later by Fairweather as *raconteur*.

"Bring me a proper officer!" seems to have been Fairweather's defining moment. He developed a phobia about upper-class Englishmen; especially Englishmen who had attended Public Schools and élite universities like Oxford or Cambridge, or who served in aristocratic Regiments like the Grenadier Guards. Robert Nairac ticked all of these boxes. Fairweather was later to make exceptions to this blanket condemnation; usually for people with whom he had become friendly in the SAS. It has also been suggested that Fairweather, while not a noticeably religious person, probably shared a common, deep-rooted Scots Presbyterian dislike of Roman Catholics. This sentiment would have been reinforced in 1972 when an IRA booby trap blew up and injured him. Nairac, as we have seen, was an unapologetic Roman Catholic, who also loved Ireland. Finally, a retired senior officer who knew both Nairac and Fairweather relates that Fairweather had disliked Nairac's "flamboyance". Fairweather had told him so, without explaining how this so-called flamboyance had manifested itself. However, in Army-speak of that period "flamboyant" was often used as a well-understood code to describe someone who might be homosexual.

It follows that there were areas of potential disagreement between Nairac and Fairweather from the very start. Fairweather's dislike of people like Nairac was anything but straightforward or uncomplicated. Mixed with his dislike and disapproval were copious lashings of envy and admiration. The proof is that when he finally became comfortably-off, which he did as HM Chief Inspector of Prisons for Scotland, Colonel Fairweather reinvented himself quite convincingly as a "toff", with many of the same superficial characteristics as Nairac. This recalls Patricia Highsmith's novel, *The Talented Mr Ripley*, in which Ripley contrived to "become" his murdered, dashing preppy friend, Dickie Greenleaf, by stealing his identity. Fairweather did not go quite that far, but he would in due course acquire a country house near the picturesque county town of Haddington, East Lothian, where he could play the laird. Former visitors report that he displayed a connoisseur's appreciation of single-malt whiskies, which Nairac had also enjoyed. In television interviews recorded later in his life, usually on the subject of Nairac, Fairweather shows no trace of his earlier rough Scots accent. He is very much "the Colonel". His voice sounds English, educated and slightly plummy. A civil servant who met him on official business towards the end of his life was surprised when he later learned about Fairweather's modest origins. Their meeting had taken place in one of Edinburgh's best hotels. The impression that the civil servant received was that Fairweather must have come from an upper-middle-class military family, had attended a distinguished Public School and was probably a graduate. He had been well-dressed in tweeds like a country landowner. His conversation had been laced with casual references to deerstalking, shooting and fly-fishing; sports that Fairweather had latterly taken up and which Nairac had also enjoyed during his short life. It was a superb act, but it was still an act.

Aside from his complex feelings about people like Nairac in general, Fairweather developed an obsession about Nairac in particular. Again, the proof of the pudding is in the eating; although he had intensely disliked Nairac, to the end of his life he seemed unable either to forget him or to stop talking about him: Nairac haunted him. Given what was weighing on his conscience, this was not wholly surprising. More than two decades after Nairac's death, Fairweather was still obsessing about him, giving his opinion in interviews about Nairac's character and what might have happened to him. He seemed unable to leave the subject alone.

Fairweather was always willing to talk to researchers and journalists about Nairac. Apart from his irresistible compulsion to rattle on and to have the last word, he also had a practical interest in doing so: he had to ensure that his version of what had happened to Nairac on 14-15 May 1977 and of the events leading up to it should be widely disseminated and become accepted as the correct and accurate narrative. Eventually, following the publication in 1999 of John Parker's *Death of a Hero*, which contains lengthy transcripts of Fairweather's interviews with Parker, the Ministry of Defence ordered Fairweather to cease his public observations. By then a civilian, Fairweather took no notice. A review of *Death of a Hero* that appeared in the *Glasgow Herald* in 1999 under the byline of Ian

Bruce, the *Herald's* former Defence Correspondent, contains vitriolic and highly misleading remarks about Nairac and, for some reason, about his Newfoundland dog, "Bundle", which was described in the review as a savage, homicidal Pyrenean Mountain Dog. Although Ian Bruce has declined to confirm or deny this, the true author of these remarks was pretty clearly Fairweather, who continued to give media interviews, notably to the BBC in 2007, on the thirtieth anniversary of Nairac's murder. What appears to have been his last recorded media interview concerning Nairac was given in 2008; less than four years before his own death. Like his previous interviews it was factually misleading in a number of respects, as he must have known.

In January 1977 Clive Fairweather, then aged thirty-three, had reason to feel pleased with himself. Until recently he had been a Captain, the same rank as Nairac, but he was now a very recently gazetted Major. Better still, he had just graduated from the Army Staff College (Senior Division) at Camberley. This marked him as a potential future Lieutenant Colonel and meanwhile entitled him to put "psc" (Passed Staff College) after his name in official documents such as the Army List. His career was progressing well. This, however, did not make him any easier to work with. Fairweather at this period of his life has been described as "a balanced man, with chips on both shoulders". There seems to be some justification for this witty, unkind description; he managed to be both cocky and chippy at the same time. Although he was not the most tactful of men, it was relatively easy to offend him and he would take offence when none was intended. Thereafter he would bear a grudge.

This happened almost immediately with Nairac when he offered Fairweather a briefing about his work in South Armagh. No doubt this was intended to be a helpful introduction, but the prickly and sensitive Fairweather perceived it as an exercise in one-upmanship. "Robert very quickly tried to impress me... He was trying to make the point to me from very early on that he had a wealth of experience of working undercover in Northern Ireland... I think he thought that we [the SAS] were all a bit clodhopperish and he had a bit more experience because he had been there before, working with an intelligence organisation [i.e. NITAT (NI)] in civilian clothes on surveillance duties, and I think he felt that while on the one hand someone like me had quite a lot of SAS experience, he had done more on the ground in South Armagh and probably felt he knew the ground better."

Fairweather was inferring a great deal. How could he be so certain of what Nairac was thinking? He was also unintentionally telling the truth. Nairac did have a wealth of experience and knowledge to share. Although Fairweather had served in Northern Ireland previously, his service had not been in South Armagh and it had not been recent. The political and military situations had evolved since his time; his knowledge was not up to date. This was no doubt implicit in what Nairac told him but, given that this was correct, it would have been in

Fairweather's interest to cultivate Nairac and draw on his knowledge. Instead, he allowed his jealousy and resentment to get the better of him. This was to have fatal consequences.

CHAPTER 14 | THE AFTERMATH

He has the advantage of figuring in the memory of posterity as one eternally able and strong; for the image in which one leaves the world is that in which one moves among the shadows. (Goethe)

Nairac's actions on 14 May 1977 were typical of him: as we have seen, he much preferred operating on his own. Although on both 13 and 14 May he had in fact complied with Standard Operating Procedures (SOPs) regarding logging his intentions, whereabouts, timings and activities, he had not always consistently done so in the past and the SAS had criticised him for this. In his various statements Clive Fairweather gave the impression that Nairac had omitted to follow SOPs on 14 May, but this was not the case.

Despite Nairac's compliance with SOPs, the SAS and Fairweather showed surprising confusion and incompetence when he went missing: as indicated earlier, there was a definite possibility that he could have been rescued, using the Worcestershire and Sherwood Foresters COP platoon on Hill 799 or their COP backup, if the SAS had acted quickly. However, nothing was done within the window of time that presented itself. Many things that should have been done then were not done, or were done far too late.

All the evidence suggests that the SAS had no idea what to do. In particular, their Commanding Officer, Acting Major Sutherell, was evidently unsure. At no stage does he seem to have taken the lead. That task was initially ceded to Clive Fairweather; later "H" Jones, 3 Infantry Brigade's Brigade Major, would lead the search for Nairac, accompanied by his dog, Bundle. Presumably for this reason, Sutherell's name does not appear in any of the published accounts of Nairac's abduction and murder. There were standard procedures for when a soldier went missing, which the SAS should have activated by midnight at the latest, when Nairac missed the mandatory call-in, but they were unsure whether they ought to activate them in this case. Nairac was not one of them: he was an MIO/Liaison Officer on secondment. That evening they knew that he was at a sensitive, intelligence-related meet. They may have thought: "If we charge in, we might jeopardise some important project on which Nairac is working. Let's play it safe; let's ask Clive Fairweather first, before we do anything". Fairweather was, after all, the GSO2 Int/Liaison at HQ Northern Ireland and supposedly an expert. That, at any rate, is what they did.

It was a mistake: this was a time-critical emergency; decisions had to be taken and acted upon quickly. Fairweather was nowhere to be found and could not be reached immediately. When he was eventually located and contacted, his response was not helpful. He and the SAS managed to waste several hours; meanwhile the Foresters COP team on Hill 799 were never alerted. Nor were Brigade, the RUC or anyone else.

This begs the next unanswered question: rather than Clive Fairweather, why was Nairac's immediate superior not alerted at an early stage? It was true that in his Intelligence Officer capacity, Nairac often liaised directly with senior Army officers, police and civilian officials. In 2009 Brigadier Peter Morton, the former Commander of 3 Para in South Armagh – possibly trying to distance himself – told Liam Clarke of *The Belfast Telegraph* that "Robert was tasked directly from Headquarters Northern Ireland. So he wasn't really under my control", which was true as far as his intelligence-gathering was concerned. However, on day-to-day matters Nairac would not have reported directly to HQNI, although he might have given the impression that he did; less for self-aggrandisement than to confuse his superiors.

Nevertheless, there was an officer at Brigade, based in Portadown, who had formal responsibility for Nairac in his capacity as Liaison Officer and who wrote his confidential report. This was the Brigade Major, H Jones. It was Jones who had authorised Nairac to go to the Three Steps on 14 May. As Jones is dead, we cannot now discover from him whether Nairac told him that he would not be taking backup. Jones probably assumed that he would, as he had done so the previous evening. This, and the inexplicable delay in sounding the alarm, explains why Jones was so horrified when he was finally informed that Nairac had gone to a meet without backup and was now missing. According to Sir John Wilsey, the effect on Jones of Nairac's disappearance "was significant. H was highly charged at the best of times; on this occasion he was 'chewing the carpet' with anxiety." He felt personally responsible and never forgave himself. Jones had trusted Nairac's judgement – believing that he knew the land better than anyone else and knew best. Latterly he had allowed him considerable liberty, which in retrospect he now bitterly regretted. Apart from that, Jones and Nairac had become close friends. Jones' brother, Tim Jones, a retired Royal Navy officer, confirms that "H had a lot of time for him". In fairness to him, Jones had not been alerted until much too late: 5.43 am. By that time Nairac had been dead for over three hours. But Jones was a dynamic man; had he been notified when he should have been, at 11.45 or midnight, he might have been able to do something practical to rescue Nairac. This preyed on his mind; it must have been a relief for him to leave the Province four months later.

We come to other questions: firstly, what happened to Nairac's body? His remains have never been found, despite intensive searches and numerous appeals for information. A lot of ink has been expended in discussing the possibilities, without any result. Clive Fairweather, who in later life constituted himself an instant Nairac expert – good for a quote or a media interview whenever the fate of Captain Nairac GC returned to the headlines – muddied the water on this issue too. Until recently Fairweather was taken seriously as an authoritative source. It has latterly become clear that, although in reality he knew little more than anyone else, he was happy to speculate, pontificate, recycle rumour and gossip to interviewers about what might have happened. In the process he rendered later researchers' work more difficult. For example, in interviews he mentioned (unconfirmed) reports that Nairac's body had been dumped "in water", which might have referred to the discredited "flooded quarry" story; or in a peat bog in central Ireland, which certainly happened to the remains of some other Disappeared PIRA victims; or had been brought back to the North and buried somewhere near Belfast. None of these scenarios is what happened; nor were they even very likely, given the circumstances.

Normally, when the IRA murder (or, as they would say, "execute") someone, with the intention that he should disappear without trace, preparations for the disposal of the body are made while the victim is still alive. The grave will be dug in a remote place that is accessible by vehicle. Ideally, the land will belong to an IRA sympathiser, which, in South Armagh and adjacent areas of the Republic, means almost everybody. The access route should be by an unclassified road, farm or forestry track; the grave is dug near the track and the turf carefully saved. Usually the grave is about four feet deep, sometimes less. Much depends on the local geology, the soil type and the time available. A six-foot-deep grave is the exception. The victim is brought close to the burial site by car, usually by night, blindfolded and with his hands tied. He is made to walk the short distance to the graveside and forced to kneel at the foot of the grave. He will then be shot in the back of the head, using two bullets. He falls into the grave and is buried immediately, with his hands still tied and usually dressed in some or all of the clothes that he was wearing when he was kidnapped. This is how some of the Disappeared, whose burial sites have been found, have been identified. Friends or family have recognised a familiar belt buckle, a bunch of keys or a pair of shoes. The grave is quickly filled in and the surface disguised as well as possible. The grass grows quickly in Ireland's mild, rainy climate. In a few weeks there will be nothing on the surface to indicate a corpse underneath.

However, the PIRA had not authorised or planned Nairac's abduction and murder. No grave had been prepared. Nairac's killers ran away, leaving his body in the field where he had been murdered. The PIRA were faced with a *fait accompli*. Without their authorisation, a man suspected of being an SAS soldier or a Loyalist militiaman had been abducted and murdered by a group of their South Armagh supporters, only two of whom (Fearon and O'Rourke) were authentic, signed-up PIRA volunteers; very junior recent recruits. The other genuine PIRA volunteer who was involved, Liam Townson, was also very junior. A low-grade hit-man, he had been drinking like the others: unlike them, he had been doing so all day. When summoned to the scene, he had compounded the mess by shooting the abducted man dead. At no stage in his clumsy and brutal "interrogation" by McCormick and Townson had Nairac revealed anything even vaguely useful or interesting to the PIRA. It was still not clear who or what he had really been; that would emerge later, from media reporting. The driving licence and other papers on his body indicated that he was Danny McErlean and gave a Belfast address. In support of this, Martin Dillon states in *The Dirty War* that Fearon met O'Rourke, Crilly and McCormick in the Border Inn the following day to discuss the killing. They agreed that their victim must have been either "an Army man" or a member of the Ulster Volunteer Force. However they were by now reportedly "nearly 100 percent sure that he was a soldier". Their uncertainty disposes of any suggestion that Nairac was the victim of a premeditated trap. At Crilly's trial in 2011 the lawyers argued at length about how much he had actually known and understood at the time. In the event the judge dismissed the Prosecution's case and Crilly walked free from the court. Dillon's account, if it is correct, would however suggest that Crilly was implicated in the abduction and murder from start to finish.

Meanwhile the PIRA were being asked to clear up the mess of a crime that they had not authorised and to dispose of the body. It was inconvenient and embarrassing, but it would have to be done. The day would break early; the weather was fine. 15 May was a little over a month away from Tuesday 21 June, the longest day and shortest night of the year. Time was short: if the murdered man had genuinely been a soldier, the chances were that the alarm would already have been raised. It should have been – but it had not, thanks to the SAS and Clive Fairweather, although the PIRA could not have known that. Even so, the search operation would begin soon enough. Once that happened, the Garda would become involved too. The PIRA had to act immediately. Senior PIRA officers, far from wishing to pat McCormick, Maguire and the others on the back, were furious; they had been put in a difficult position. They would grow still more furious when details of the abduction and killing and the true identity of the murdered man started to become known over the next 48 hours.

Later Gerard Fearon would tell the police that he had no idea what had happened to Nairac's body. He and his friends had definitely not conveyed it back across the border into the North for fear of running into Garda, RUC or Army patrols. Once more Maguire and McCormick had taken the lead and contacted the PIRA for assistance. A few days after the murder, Fearon had encountered either Maguire or McCormick in Jonesborough (he could not recall which), and had been told that the body "had been taken care of". When pressed, he said that he did not know what had been meant by that – he had not asked. He speculated that it might have been moved back to the North, but none of Nairac's abductors knew what had been done with their victim's body and they had not inquired; it was preferable not to know.

Fearon's guess that the body had been brought back to the North after the murder in the South was wrong, although the IRA are said to have done this in a few other cases to render the police investigation, which then had to be conducted on both sides of the border, more difficult. There seem however to be no recent known examples of this. (In the unlikely event that it had been moved back to Ulster, the burial would have been somewhere just north of the border, not near Belfast, but why take the risk?) By the time that the PIRA had located and collected the body, the search for Nairac was under way in Northern Ireland and was about to start up in the Republic. There was now no question of moving the body any great distance, and certainly not in a vehicle. The risk of encountering a Garda or RUC patrol or checkpoint was now too great. Indeed, the use of any public road was too risky. Likewise, taking it to the meat-processing factory – if that had ever been seriously considered – was not a practical proposition: in the event, the factory was one of the first places that the Garda would search.

Equally, the corpse could not be left where it was. As Eamon Collins later wrote, the PIRA did not want the public to know about the appalling injuries that Nairac had sustained, and with good reason. For centuries the exposure of a mutilated murdered body, a realistic effigy, a gruesomely accurate painting or latterly a photograph accompanied by a vivid Press report, has been a well-known and effective way of stirring up public indignation against the murderers. It followed that Nairac would have to be secretly buried. The body must be spirited away discreetly and immediately; moved and buried by hand. Muscle is significantly heavier than fat, and Nairac was a very hard, muscular man. He would have been heavy, so his body could not have been moved far by this method. Even moving it a short distance by hand was risky, given that the burying-party might be spotted by a police ground search-party or from a helicopter. A hastily-organised party of PIRA volunteers, none of whom had participated in the murder, moved Nairac's body across the fields onto land belonging to a farmer who was a known IRA supporter. Either because time was short, or because he could not easily be contacted – farmers are out and about early and there were no mobile phones at that time – the farmer was not consulted. His consent was taken for granted – wrongly, as it later turned out. A shallow grave, about two feet deep, was hastily excavated and the body was interred in it. But, according to a reliable former PIRA source, it was not destined to rest there for very long. Meanwhile the search for Robert Nairac, dead or alive, continued and intensified on both sides of the border.

A few days later, while the search for him was still in progress, animals dug up the fresh grave and partly exposed Nairac's body. The farmer found it and guessed whose it was. He was not happy but, since he was indeed a PIRA supporter and did not wish to assist the searchers for Nairac, he notified the PIRA, not the Garda, and asked them to move the body off his property. He was not willing for it to be reinterred elsewhere on his land: another location would have to be found. If they did not act promptly, he would inform the Garda. This time the PIRA entrusted the task to a different party of more carefully selected volunteers, led by a local smallholder called Liam Fagan, who died in 1989. It is not likely that the body was reburied on Fagan's own land – he was a potential suspect – but it was reportedly reinterred not far from the murder site, either on farmland or inside Ravensdale Forest. For all these reasons it was still neither safe nor practical to attempt to move it far, or in a vehicle. Once more Nairac's body, which was now starting to decompose and to smell badly, was moved by hand across the fields and interred in a more secluded location close to or inside Ravensdale Forest. This information comes from Terry McCormick, who is not, however, sure of the exact location. This time Nairac's body was buried more deeply, about four feet below the surface, and there it remains. The precise location was known to a very few people. Although Fagan is now dead, he was assisted by fellow PIRA volunteers. Some of them are still alive and they have reportedly shared their secret with a few others, including members of their families. Fagan was also Liam Townson's host. Townson was on the run, living in Fagan's house because he was wanted in Northern Ireland. It was on Fagan's farm that Gardai arrested Townson in late May 1977. It is difficult to believe, since he had been Fagan's lodger both before and after the murder, that Townson has no idea at all where the body is buried, although that is what he maintains.

The next question is: why has there been no response to the various appeals for information about the whereabouts of Nairac's body? In May-June 1977 Robert Nairac's family made no direct public appeal for information through the media. Maurice Nairac had discussed the possibility by letter with Brigadier David Woodford, who advised against this action in his letter dated 9 June, because a suspect (Townson) had just been arrested and there was the prospect of further arrests. Others, including Cardinal Basil Hume, the then Archbishop of Westminster and former Abbot of Ampleforth, appealed on their behalf to the PIRA to return Nairac to his family or, if he were dead, to allow his remains to receive Christian burial. More recently, on 27 April 1999, the Independent Commission for the Location of Victims' Remains (ICLVR) was established by treaty between the Governments of the United Kingdom and the Republic of Ireland. It, too, has repeatedly appealed for information; in vain, as far as the PIRA are concerned. Twenty years after Nairac's disappearance and following a BBC *Spotlight* programme about him, on 20 June 2007 Martin McGuinness, now the Deputy First Minister of Northern Ireland, made an appeal for information. Once more the PIRA took no notice.

The explanation lies in the nature of the beast: of the South Armagh PIRA, to be precise. Even within the IRA, the South Armagh PIRA Brigade is regarded as "a republic within a republic", a dissident group that makes its own rules, takes its own decisions and is not in effect answerable to anybody else; even the IRA's high command. It is the only PIRA Brigade that still retains the Brigade structure. The other Brigades were split into self-contained cells after being penetrated by British Intelligence. The South Armagh Brigade do not seem to regard themselves as being bound by the 1998 Good Friday Agreement. They have never co-operated with the ICLVR. For that matter, they have never admitted to having "disappeared" anyone, although they have undoubtedly frequently done so. By contrast the Belfast IRA, for example, have made admissions and co-operated with the authorities to locate the remains of some of their Disappeared victims. When the IRA agreed in 1999 to reveal the whereabouts of some of their victims, those of South Armagh were left off the list. They included Robert Nairac, Charlie Armstrong and Gerry Evans. An IRA statement indicated that no information about these bodies would ever be given. The IRA killed more than 700 British soldiers during its failed 1970-97 campaign to force Northern Ireland out of the United Kingdom. The remains of all the others were recovered.

In the event, the IRA statement proved to be wrong in two instances. These were the aforementioned Gerry Evans, disappeared and murdered in 1979, and Charlie Armstrong, disappeared and murdered in 1981. Both were Catholics from Crossmaglen. In 2011 a coroner's court finally recorded verdicts of death by unlawful killing in both cases, after the two families had run an intensive campaign to shame the PIRA into revealing where they were buried. This was reasonably successful; the South Armagh PIRA Brigade were eventually shamed into co-operating, but only up to a point. They indicated by indirect means roughly where they "thought the bodies might be found". The remains of Armstrong and Evans were duly found in that area. The PIRA did not, however, admit to having put them there, nor did they express contrition or sympathy for the families. Although the Evans and Armstrong families were now able to give their dead relations Christian burial, no-one would ever be charged in connection with the murders. Nor does anyone know to this day why the two men were abducted and murdered. Neither was politically active. It has been suggested that one of them, at least, was simply in the wrong place at the wrong time and witnessed an incident that he was not supposed to see, so he was silenced. A third probable South Armagh PIRA victim was found by accident in 1986 inside a car in Dundalk harbour, which was being dredged. This was Sean Murphy, the son of John Murphy, whose band had been playing at the Three Steps on the night of Nairac's abduction. No information about his murder has ever been forthcoming. The other Disappeared attributable to the South Armagh Brigade remain disappeared. No-one even knows how many they were: "What happens in South Armagh stays in South Armagh".

By contrast with the Armstrongs and Evanses, Robert Nairac's family maintained a dignified silence, never making any direct public appeal or statement. Apart from giving a moving, strictly factual, televised interview to the BBC's Roisin McAuley in 1978, Nairac's parents broke their silence only twice more: in 1984, when a Channel 4 television programme allowed Fred Holroyd publicly to air his claims that Nairac had murdered John Francis Green in the Irish Republic, and again in 1987, when Ken Livingstone MP articulated the same theories and attacked Nairac's record, character and memory in the House of Commons. (He also attacked the reputation of another victim of terrorism, Airey Neave.) Others had appealed on the Nairac family's behalf, but had met with no response. It is not hard to guess why: there was far less sympathy in South Armagh for Nairac's family than for the Armstrong and Evans families. Nairac was English, not Irish; he is still widely and erroneously believed to have been SAS and therefore a dangerous enemy undeserving of any sympathy. The fact that he was a committed Catholic, to whom the last rites, a proper burial and a requiem would have been important, seems not to matter. In South Armagh, Nairac is still seen as a traitorous Catholic who helped Protestant Loyalists to kill other Catholics, although an Irish judicial inquiry, the Barron Inquiry, found no evidence to support such allegations. The late Paddy Short (*Note 1*), whose Republican bar in Crossmaglen Nairac had sometimes frequented – where he was apparently well-liked and where he quite often sang and had acquired the nickname "Danny Boy" – said afterwards that there were "no regrets" locally about what had been done to Nairac. The deep, corrosive subterranean hatred is still active.

South Armagh is not Ireland, however. Elsewhere in Ireland, as the sickening details of Nairac's last hours, and the courage that he had shown when faced with his own death, began to become common knowledge; once information about Nairac's personal character and his work in Ardoyne had become public property; after it had been made clear that he had been a devout Catholic who was committed to the peace process, the IRA suffered a reputational setback. Ordinary Irish Catholics, including the better sort of priest, in whose name the murder had supposedly been committed, were alienated: not only by the murder, but even more by the fact that Nairac's body had been treated with so little respect; had reportedly been destroyed in the meat-processing plant and had definitely been denied Christian burial. Even Eamon Collins, another Catholic, who was at that time a PIRA volunteer and not one of Nairac's admirers, found this shocking and "unbelievable". Many Catholics were also shocked by the later revelation that McCormick had posed as a priest to try to extract information from the doomed man under pretence of taking his Confession, and that the last rites had been denied to him.

Some of the Republic of Ireland media condemned the murder. On 17 May RTE Radio broadcast a long interview with Seamus Mallon (SDLP), in which he condemned the Provisionals as cold-blooded and cowardly killers. *The Irish Independent* newspaper bore the banner headline "Murder Again". The *Independent's* reporting assumed (correctly) that Nairac was already dead and bitterly attacked the PIRA. The murder had been carried out by "thugs whose barbarity knows no bounds and who have no right to claim any affinity with Republicans or Nationalists". Nairac was described as "the unfortunate soldier who was so bravely ready in risking his own life in taking part in an action which is common to both sides of the border – trying to stamp out the Provisionals". The *Independent* argued that, by making the majority in the North clamour for greater security, the Provisionals' action in murdering Nairac could benefit only one person: the Reverend Ian Paisley, the Leader of the Democratic Unionist Party, and would make the lives of the SDLP far more difficult. Even the photo that the IRA had released to the media, showing Nairac talking to young people in Ardoyne, was an "own goal", because it showed him in a sympathetic light. Had he been depicted looking mean, arrogant, or charging civilians in a riot, it would have better supported the PIRA's narrative.

The UK media in general condemned the murder, although there was also criticism of the Army for permitting Nairac to be alone in the Three Steps. Because of their geographical proximity, the historical ties between Scotland and Northern Ireland and the fact that the Scottish Infantry were increasingly being deployed – and suffering casualties – the Scottish Press in Ulster took an especially close interest. *The Scotsman's* editorial on 17 May 1977 is fairly typical:

"Though they are a murderous gang, the Provisional IRA claim to be soldiers and award themselves high military rank. But in their kind of warfare there is no Geneva Convention about the treatment of prisoners. Their statement that the kidnapped British officer, Captain Robert Nairac, has been executed is typical of their cold-blooded ruthlessness. During the [recent] Loyalist strike the IRA kept quiet, but with its failure they have lost no time in resuming their assassinations and bombings, as if to remind the world that the Loyalist paramilitaries have no monopoly of murder and intimidation".

These were valid points, albeit the Editor of *The Scotsman* could not have known that senior PIRA commanders had not authorised the murder, although they now had to pretend that they did.

The PIRA began to lose sympathy and support. Their response was to launch a disinformation campaign to blacken Nairac's memory: given that it was a work of fiction, it was to be surprisingly successful. The PIRA now insisted that Nairac had deserved to be "executed" because he had been in effect a British Government-sponsored assassin: he had planned and participated in high-profile killings, including the 1974 bombings in Dublin and County Monaghan, in which civilians had died; the 1975 murder of IRA Staff Captain John Francis Green in the Republic; the 1975 Miami Showband Massacre and the 1976 killing of IRA Staff Captain Peter Cleary while he was in SAS custody; that Nairac was both a cold-blooded professional murderer and a member of the SAS, which amounted to much the same thing; and that he had colluded with Loyalist paramilitaries in their campaign against the Catholic population. Nevertheless, as Toby Harnden observes in his *Dictionary of National Biography* entry for Nairac, despite the widespread repetition of these allegations against him, particularly by Irish Republicans, no convincing evidence of Nairac's involvement in any of these events has ever emerged (*Note 2*).

There is evidence, not least from official inquiries, of British collusion with Loyalist violence, ranging from active participation by the RUC and UDR, through to turning a blind eye to and tolerance of Loyalist violence by the military, intelligence and other arms of Government. In these circumstances it might seem reasonable to assume that Nairac "must have been" implicated. However this assumption leaves out of the equation Nairac's "straight-arrow" Catholic conscience and his very clear ideas about how life should be lived. Much as he loved the Army, had he been ordered to do anything that he considered seriously unethical, Nairac would have refused. Faced with extreme pressure to do so, he would probably have resigned his commission – this is the view of his surviving Army friends.

The fact that these allegations will not stand close scrutiny does not carry any weight. For the reasons cited above, many people in Ireland and elsewhere still firmly believe them. Every successful Loyalist strike against IRA or Catholic targets – and a few IRA strikes against Protestant or Loyalist targets – in the 1970s, up to May 1977, is apt to be attributed to Nairac, even if he was not physically present in Ireland at the time. Any potentially discreditable scrap of evidence, however trivial, is eagerly seized upon. For example, much has been made of a souvenir handkerchief decorated with Loyalist emblems, which was found among Nairac's effects after his death and later displayed in the Guards Museum. This handkerchief is regarded by some Republicans as conclusive proof of Nairac's collusion with Loyalist paramilitaries. The reality is that paramilitary prisoners of both persuasions in HM Prison Maze made such handkerchiefs and sold them to raise cash. Some soldiers who served in Northern Ireland made collections of them. Soldiers have always collected souvenirs of their campaigns and travels: as a result their Regimental museums tend to become cluttered with the most unlikely objects. Nairac's handkerchief was a souvenir of this kind; he had probably bought it from a Loyalist detainee whom he had questioned.

Even before joining the Army, Nairac seems to have been a magpie, accumulating items and not passing them on or throwing them away, including books and sporting equipment. When, a year after his death, his parents permitted the BBC's Roisin McAuley to visit the family home in Gloucestershire to interview them for a *Spotlight* documentary on Nairac, his rooms were still preserved as they had been during his lifetime. He had never thrown anything out: alongside a small forest of silver trophies – mostly sporting ones, but including the silver presentation tankard from the RUC's Special Branch – were boys' adventure novels by authors such as G A Henty; even childhood toys, including a rocking-horse and model soldiers. They were all still there, waiting for someone who would never come back.

The PIRA were able successfully to market their narrative of "Nairac the psychopathic killer" in Ireland and also in the USA, among Irish-Americans, who still funded the IRA's terrorist activities through the purportedly "humanitarian" Noraid and other nominally charitable front organisations. For many of these expatriate Irish, Nairac became and remains a demonic, Moriarty-like homicidal figure, who might even still be alive, although this conflicts with the other narrative which makes him out to be brawny, dim and stupidly brave, almost inviting his own death by his antics. He cannot have been both of these things and in fact he was neither.

The British public had for many years been aware of, and bitterly resented, the uncritical and generous Irish-American support for the IRA. When, on 11 September 2001 (9/11), Al-Qaeda terrorists struck at the heart of Washington and New York, there was a strong feeling in the UK of "serves them right" and "now they know how it feels", at least until the substantial British death-toll from the destruction of the Twin Towers had been announced. There was a knock-on effect: 9/11 forced the IRA, who had agreed a cease-fire in 1996, had negotiated the Good Friday Agreement in 1997 and agreed in principle to decommission their weapons, to start decommissioning earlier than they would otherwise have done. The flow of funds has, however, continued; if anything it has increased, but now to Sinn Fein, rather than directly to the IRA.

For complicated political reasons, the PIRA's anti-Nairac narrative began to find takers in England too, on the political Left. This was despite the fact that in mainland Great Britain, Nairac's murder had initially provoked something akin to the popular revulsion and indignation evoked by the more recent murder of Drummer Lee Rigby by Islamists in 2013. One of these takers would be "Red" Ken Livingstone, the future Labour MP for Brent East from 1987 to 2001; a man on the hard Left of his Party. Livingstone would use his maiden speech in the Commons to attack Nairac and others for alleged criminal acts against Irish civilians. He did so secure in the knowledge that Nairac had been dead for ten years; in any case, speaking in the Commons, he was protected by Parliamentary privilege. Livingstone's sincere sympathy for the IRA and advocacy of a united Ireland at any cost are well-known. The sincerity of Maurice Nairac's reaction, when he expressed to the media his disgust at Livingstone's attack on his much-loved son, was equally clear. For other reasons the rumours and controversy that came to surround Nairac's name, starting in 1984, suited Nairac's former enemies and rivals within the Army, including those who had played a role in the events leading up to and surrounding his murder and who had incurred criticism, or risked doing so, as a result. One of these enemies, Fred Holroyd, was also Livingstone's constituent.

As more information about Nairac's abduction and murder appeared in the media, ironically both the British Army and the Provisional IRA became frantically engaged in parallel exercises in damage limitation and reputation management. It is hard now to judge which of the two was more firmly on the back foot. As Eamon Collins wrote, Nairac's abduction had certainly not been sanctioned by the PIRA: all but two of the men who had snatched him were simply IRA sympathisers who had happened to be drinking in the pub that evening. None of them were people of any account within the IRA. If they were thinking clearly at all, they no doubt hoped to win the IRA's approval and to acquire local notoriety by beating up, or killing, an enemy of the people: "an SAS man", "a spy" or possibly "a Loyalist paramilitary"; they were not sure which.

A valid comparison might be drawn with Gavrilo Princip (*Note 3*), the teenage ethnic Serb terrorist who assassinated the Archduke Franz Ferdinand and his consort in Sarajevo on 28 June 1914 and precipitated the First World War. As Ben Macintyre (the historian and *Times* columnist) has pointed out, Princip is the prototypical twentieth-century terrorist assassin: not because he was some powerful mastermind who knew exactly what he was doing, but because he manifestly was not. Princip was callow, manipulated and amateurish. He was motivated as much by personal disgruntlement as by politics. Most of the prominent political, and even non-political, assassins of the past hundred years, from Princip to Lee Harvey Oswald to Mark David Chapman (who killed John Lennon in 1980) to the Islamist killers of 9/11, were of a similar bent: small, angry people who believed that a single act of violence would make them big. They are human failures; nobodies who long for one spectacular, elevating success. This applies equally to Nairac's murderers, and with particular force to the 24-year-old PIRA hit man, Liam Townson.

What they all failed to understand until it was too late was, far from becoming folk heroes like Redmond O'Hanlon, they had severely embarrassed the PIRA and would now be punished. Their insignificance made them expendable. McCormick, Maguire, Townson and the rest had disobeyed a cardinal PIRA operating rule. Having captured a potentially interesting suspect, they should have reported the fact to senior PIRA officers, sat back and waited for instructions. They should not have tried to interrogate their captive – still less, murdered him. As Eamon Collins wrote in *Killing Rage*, the PIRA would have wished to interrogate someone like Nairac for weeks; furthermore, they might well have used their prize as a valuable bargaining-chip. Instead, by the time that the PIRA at a senior level came to hear about Nairac's capture, neither option was open to them; the unfortunate officer was just a bloody mess lying in a field.

There was damage to the IRA's credibility with its overseas supporters and suppliers. Apart from the Irish-Americans, anti-Western Governments and organisations had begun to assist the IRA with funding, arms and military *matériel*. This was the reason for MI6's growing involvement in the Province and its "turf war" with MI5, the Security Service responsible for homeland security in the UK and therefore Northern Ireland. MI6, the Secret Intelligence Service, operates in foreign countries. It covers the Republic of Ireland. Normally they do not overlap. Now they would do so increasingly often.

The PIRA's senior commanders had every reason to be angry. They never managed to capture a genuine British undercover operative other than Nairac (and Keith Johnson MM, who was only briefly in their hands before being rescued). Nairac's captors had not only murdered a potentially extremely valuable prisoner; they had learned nothing from him and they had become the catalyst of the largest-ever joint search operation in recent Irish history. The PIRA could not move a muscle for as long for as it lasted. Their strategy to get it wound down was threefold; firstly they would convince both the Republic of Ireland and British authorities that Nairac's body had been destroyed, so there was nothing left to search for. Secondly, the IRA would pretend to have authorised Nairac's abduction and murder; they would imply that they had learned valuable information from him under interrogation and would make use of this lie in their psychological game with the Security Forces. Thirdly, they would deliver up every one of their own murderous, bungling supporters to the aforesaid authorities in record time, through tip-offs to the RUC and the Garda. That would help to hasten the end of the search for Captain Nairac and, as a bonus, would result in exemplary punishment being meted out by the authorities to Townson, McCormick and the rest. The lesson would not be lost on any other over-enthusiastic amateur terrorists who might in future be tempted to step out of line and "freelance". In the event, after being interviewed by the police, three of the men fled to the United States. Two of them are still there. The British Government has never tried to extradite them and *The Daily Mail* has recently suggested that they may have received letters of comfort guaranteeing immunity from arrest or legal action, issued under Tony Blair's premiership as part of a deal with Sinn Fein.

The speed with which most of Nairac's abductors and assassins were identified and pursued, both in the Republic and in Northern Ireland, leaves no doubt as to the IRA's involvement. The first to be picked up was Liam Townson, the IRA hit man (*Note 4*). Townson was a 24-year-old unemployed joiner and known junior PIRA volunteer from the village of Meigh outside Newry. He was arrested in the Republic, on Liam Fagan's farm near Dundalk, on 28 May and charged with Nairac's murder by Gardai, who had acted on a tip-off. Townson appeared before a special criminal court in Dublin in June and was remanded in custody. On 8 November three judges at Dublin's Special Criminal Court convicted Townson of the murder of Captain Nairac on or about 15 May and of the separate charge of possession of a .32 revolver and ammunition with intent to endanger life, on the same date, both offences being committed in County Louth. Much of the information used in this book came out in the course of this trial, which some British officers attended, including Clive Fairweather, who said that he spoke briefly with the prisoner Townson afterwards.

Fairweather had muddied the water on Townson, too. In one of his interviews he described Townson as being "from Yorkshire" and in another, with John Parker, as "an Englishman who had gone to Ireland" and as a local IRA Commander, none of which he was. "Like all Englishmen he had to show how much more Irish he was". (Fairweather, a Scot, had his prejudices about both English and Irish people.) The reality was this: Townson's father had been an Englishman.

Many years before these events, during the Second World War, the Army had posted him to Northern Ireland: he had fallen in love with and married a local Northern Irish girl in Meigh and had returned there later, becoming a Northern Ireland civil servant, serving as a sanitary inspector with the Department of Health. He had retired and in due course died in Meigh. A not-very-religious Protestant, Townson Senior appears to have settled down contentedly in his wife's home area of South Armagh, despite its being a hotbed of Republicanism. As was usual with mixed marriages in those days, including that of Nairac's parents, the children were brought up as Catholics. His son Liam, having been brought up in South Armagh as a Catholic Irishman and one-hundred percent Irish in his loyalties, perceived himself as being at a disadvantage as "the son of the Englishman". He compensated for this by becoming an outspoken Republican and an IRA volunteer; in the process denying everything British in his heritage. This included his father's nationality and wartime service in the British Army. He probably saw the brutal torture and murder of Robert Nairac, a suspected British soldier, as expiating the fact of his paternity and constituting his own apotheosis as an Irish Nationalist hero. Like Princip – a small, angry person who believed that a single act of violence would make him big.

Townson's behaviour when he was arrested was anything but heroic. He made a total of seven statements to the Irish detectives; later retracted all of them, claiming that they had been made under duress or subject to other procedural irregularities; but two were in the event ruled admissible as evidence in court and were used against him. On the second occasion he got out of control, became distressed and hysterical. He screamed:

"I'll swing for nobody! They'll never put a rope around my neck. They can shoot me if they like. I will kill myself tonight. I will tear my heart out. Nobody's going to hang me for a British soldier!"

A policeman firmly told Townson to cease these histrionics, pull himself together and have a strong cup of tea. This was in contrast to Nairac's demeanour when faced with death at Townson's shaky hand. Townson's behaviour contrasted equally unfavourably with that of the Irish nationalist heroes who were presumably his inspirational role models. In fairness, his fear of execution was not completely groundless. Capital punishment for murder was still theoretically possible in the Republic of Ireland in 1977 and would not be formally abolished until 1990. However, nobody had been executed since 1954. From then until 1990, for as long as capital punishment remained on the statute book, the practice arose whereby every death sentence was commuted by the President, using his prerogative of mercy.

His dual heritage is the key to Townson's otherwise not very interesting character. Some of the most ardent Irish Nationalists have been the offspring of mixed marriages: typically, of a British father and an Irish mother. Psychologists can happily spend years discussing the possible oedipal significance of this, but there is definitely a pattern. Patrick (or Padraig) Pearse who, with his brother Willie, died by firing-squad after the 1916 Easter Rising, is one example. Another, whose father was of Manx, rather than English, extraction, although he had been brought up in England, was Sir Roger Casement (*Note 5*). Like T E Lawrence, Robert Nairac appears to have been an admirer of Casement, who had many admirable qualities, as well as a number of serious weaknesses. One was his promiscuous homosexuality: this should not be criticised *per se*, as it was hardly his fault, but the flamboyant, high-adrenaline risks that Casement ran to satisfy his needs were potentially very dangerous. Evidently taking the risk was part of the fun from his point of view; but had Casement been compromised, this could have left him vulnerable to blackmail and the discrediting of his important humanitarian work in the Congo and Brazil. He was hanged for treason in 1916. Robert Erskine Childers (*Note 6*), the author of the spy thriller *The Riddle of the Sands,* was ironically executed by the authorities of the nascent Irish Free State in 1922, during the Irish Civil War. Like Pearse and Casement, he showed great courage at the end. Childers had been born in London and educated at Haileybury and Cambridge. His father was English; his mother (née Barton) was from the Anglo-Irish Protestant ascendancy. His fierce, sentimental love of Ireland had been kindled on boyhood holidays passed on the Barton family estate at Glendalough in County Wicklow. In that respect Childers had something in common with Robert Nairac, whose love of Ireland was likewise awoken during holidays spent in Dublin and in another Irish country house: Lord Killanin's house at Spiddal in Galway. Childers had won a major British military decoration, the Distinguished Service Cross (DSC), while serving with the Royal Navy at Gallipoli.

We do not know exactly when Townson became an IRA volunteer. A further possible factor in his adherence to the PIRA might have been that he had been arrested and interrogated by the RUC some months before the murder. According to an officer who was involved, these interrogations of suspects, which were bitterly resented, were often the best recruiting officer for the IRA. It was following this interrogation that Townson fled to the Republic and became Liam Fagan's lodger. Townson was the only one of Nairac's assassins to be arrested and tried in the Republic. He was found guilty and sentenced to life imprisonment with hard labour (penal servitude). But in the Republic of Ireland "life" rarely means life, and he was released after thirteen years. He moved back to Meigh and has resumed his position in society. He has never consented to speak about Robert Nairac's murder to any journalist.

Five more men were awaiting trial in Northern Ireland. Their trials were delayed until November 1978 – because important evidence might emerge in the course of Townson's trial in the Republic – and ran until 15 December. They were Gerard Patrick Fearon, the young recent recruit to the IRA, who received life for murder and 22 years for grievous bodily harm; Thomas Patrick Morgan, who was detained at her Majesty's pleasure and awarded 22 years for possession of a firearm and kidnap; and Daniel Joseph O'Rourke, the other IRA member, who received 10 years for manslaughter and membership of the IRA. Michael Joseph McCoy received 5 years for kidnap. Owen Francis Rocks received two 3-year sentences, to run concurrently, for withholding information. The trial made legal history, as it was the first occasion on which defendants had ever faced trial in a UK court for a crime committed (mainly) in the Republic of Ireland. As mentioned earlier, McCormick, Maguire and Crilly had fled to the United States. None of the prisoners served more than the minimum term of their sentences. All of Nairac's killers are now at liberty, except for McCormick and Maguire, who are still on the run, and Thomas Morgan, the teenager who had kicked the wounded Nairac in the genitals. After the murder, Morgan had twice attended Mass on 15 May, which was a Sunday. He killed himself a year after his release from prison by crashing his car into a cement mixer. It appears to have been a drunk-driving incident. The car was a write-off, as was its driver.✓

Following the trial and sentencing of Townson, the Dundalk Coroner, Thomas Scully, held an inquest on Nairac, despite the fact that still no corpse was available for examination. It is unusual in any jurisdiction for a death certificate to be issued under these circumstances, but it happened in this case. The inquest took place in early October 1978. Scully had to rely heavily on court records and witness statements. The Irish Death Certificate, issued on the basis of information supplied by Scully to Sean McCormack, the Registrar of Births and Deaths for the District of Ravensdale, states that Nairac's death occurred on 18 May 1977: three days after Townson shot him. Was this simply a clerical error? Likewise, the date on which the death was registered is given as 16 October 1978, although the inquest had been adjourned on 5 October. But there is a strange alteration in the Registrar's handwriting: "October Twelfth" has been firmly crossed out and replaced by "October Sixteenth". Like the alteration of the date, the delay in registration might be significant. It probably is not, but it is still very questionable. Under "Certified Cause of Death and Duration of Illness," the certificate simply states: "Unknown – body not available for post-mortem examination". That part at least was true.

Meanwhile a memorial service, entitled "A Service of Thanksgiving for the Life of Robert Laurence Nairac" had taken place in the Guards Chapel (*Note 7*) on 18 April 1978. The standard of church music at the Chapel is high, so it draws good congregations on Sundays, often including numbers of tourists. The choir is surpliced, worship is traditional Anglican and an Army Chaplain preaches the sermon. A small Guards or other Army Band chamber orchestra supplements the organ music. Guardsmen and Guards NCOs hand out the Order of Service to worshippers, take the collection, walk in procession as crucifers and serve at the altar. They wear Home Service Clothing with scarlet tunics. The Picquet Officer reads the lesson.

The Grenadiers organised a grand and dignified ceremony for Nairac. The Regimental Band provided much of the music. The service was military and therefore basically Anglican, although Father Edward Corbould, Nairac's former Housemaster at Ampleforth, officiated with Army clergy. This was not inappropriate: Nairac, although a practicing Catholic, had not been bigoted: he was the offspring of a happy, loving Catholic-Anglican union. As Picquet Officer at Chelsea Barracks, he had attended divine service in the Guards Chapel and read the lesson in his turn; it was his chapel. Representatives of HRH the Duke of Edinburgh, the Colonel of the Regiment, and of the Secretary of State for Northern Ireland attended, with other notables. Nairac's parents were present: for them the service, held less than a year after his murder, must have been an ordeal. Many of Nairac's numerous friends, from all the different phases of his life, were also there; they included Amplefordians and former Oxonian boxers and rugby players. Vincent's Club was well-represented; Julian Malins was there. Luke Jennings sat near the newly-installed Robert Nairac memorial window. Some combat-hardened soldiers admit to having lost control and having shed tears at certain moments, one of which was at the Bidding:

"We have come here today to remember Robert and to thank God for his friendship. We remember with affection his sense of fun, his love and enthusiasm for life, and his joy in all things living; we give thanks to God for his outstanding courage and devotion to duty, and we commend his soul to the everlasting care of God the Father of All."

At this point the extent of their loss finally sank in. Even if they had never truly understood him or got the measure of the man, Nairac had been a fantastic friend to those lucky enough to win his regard. As one of his friends, another Guards officer, said later: "He was fun, charismatic and different, and a loyal (if unreliable) friend." There had been nobody like Robert and now he had been taken away forever, with brutal suddenness. Another such moment was provided by an anthem, when the choir sang to the *Londonderry Air* (*Danny Boy* was one of Nairac's favourite songs) these words by Howard A Walter (1883 – 1918) (*Note 8*):

I would be true, for there are those who trust me;
I would be pure, for there are those who care;
I would be strong, for there is much to suffer;
I would be brave, for there is much to dare;
I would be friend of all—the foe, the friendless;
I would be giving, and forget the gift;
I would be humble, for I know my weakness;
I would look up, and laugh, and love and live.

The incidental music and the closing voluntaries, performed after the *Nunc Dimittis*, were suitably bracing and martial: they included part of Sibelius'

Finlandia, *The Grenadiers March*, the March from Handel's *Scipio* and Schubert's *Marche Miltaire*.

It was now time to consider which posthumous award to confer on Nairac. Although MPs of all parties had signed a petition in November 1977 strongly recommending that Nairac should receive the George Cross, his parents received it from the Queen in February 1979, nearly two years after his death. The reason for the delay has been explained in the Prologue.

If the posthumous GC, like the memorial service and other events that had been held in Nairac's honour, had been intended symbolically to lay Nairac's ghost and to draw a line under the messy tragedy, it did not succeed. Too many questions remained unanswered. As any classical scholar could confirm, a memorial service is not the same as a proper funeral. No-one, especially not a hero, can be at rest until the prescribed funeral rites have been performed: in classical antiquity it was the funeral rites – in Nairac's case, a Requiem Mass – that were important. These alone allowed the deceased to pass into the Underworld. Wherever he had really been buried, Nairac's ghost did not long remain dormant. He would continue to trouble the British and Irish political scene, reappearing in the headlines like Pepper's Ghost. He still does. He remains a controversial and divisive figure to this day.

In the Northern Irish context, the pious hope expressed in his official Army obituary, which was drafted by his first Commanding Officer, Lieutenant Colonel Richard Besly was admirable but unrealistic:

"Perhaps his tragic loss at such an early age will not have been in vain if it helps to create a better understanding between the two communities in Northern Ireland. Robert would have wanted this more than anything."

Nairac's death was to have no such effect. As we have seen, soon after his death he was being demonised both by Republicans and by some Loyalists. The carnival of murder, mayhem, rioting and revenge that was the Troubles would continue for more than two decades after that date, and is even now not completely at an end. Again, classical antiquity comes to mind: as Elpenor says to Odysseus from the Underworld: "Do not go home, leaving me unwept and unburied, in case I bring down the Gods' curse on you". The Army has gone home – for the moment – leaving Nairac's remains behind, without a requiem, somewhere in Ireland. And although that would not have been Nairac's wish, the Gods' curse could be said to have been well and truly visited upon Northern Ireland since his murder. Even now sporadic terror continues and political normality is absent. The wounds are slow to heal. Over 3,500 people were killed during the Troubles, including over 700 members of the Armed Forces and over 300 police. Like the Nairacs, the grieving families and friends of those who lost their lives, were maimed or crippled, or who have completely vanished, still await justice – or simply official recognition of their loss and grief. However, there is no equivalence of treatment between those who served the State and those who fought it. The official inquiries into Bloody Sunday, Finucane, Rosemary Nelson and others probe the actions of the Security Forces, but never those of the terrorists. ✓

Later, Lieutenant Colonel Besly tried to promote a project to create a Robert Nairac Memorial Outward Bound Centre on a site near Lough Neagh. It would be a place at which Catholic and Protestant boys could be based, to hike, climb, kayak and engage in other sports together; hopefully leading to better community relations. Initially there was interest in Northern Ireland and funding from various sources seemed likely to become available. A helpful Northern Ireland civil servant identified a suitable property. It was the kind of project that Nairac would have enjoyed. Then Richard Besly consulted the RUC. Their response was unequivocal:

"Forget it. The IRA would blow it up or burn it down." Too right.

Then there was the British Army: however accurately they may have reflected the feelings of his parent Regiment, in both of whose Battalions Nairac had served, the loving and elevated sentiments expressed at his memorial service were not shared equally across the Army. Nairac's critics had already begun to surface. Unsurprisingly, most of them were to be found in the SAS. In many cases their criticism took a distinctly defensive line, spiced with definite, albeit publicly unacknowledged, guilt.

The dismay and damage to morale that Nairac's disappearance had caused among the Army in Northern Ireland and indeed elsewhere was only partly inspired by the sorrow and anger felt by the many soldiers who had known and liked him. There was a minority, including some SAS soldiers, who had not liked him at all and were prepared to believe the worst of him. Such was the uncertainty about his death that some SAS personnel openly expressed their suspicion that his kidnapping could have been staged and that Nairac might have defected to the IRA. In their view he had always shown far too great an empathy with the Republicans and he was a Roman Catholic to boot. Ridiculous as this must seem in retrospect, it was a view that was also shared by some Loyalists and by at least one RUC officer. There was speculation that Nairac might sooner or later show up at an IRA Press conference in the Republic.

When considering this kind of reaction, it should be borne in mind that the Special Forces have a different mindset from the rest of us. This was put forcefully by a former friend of Nairac: "The idea that Robert was a double/triple agent working for the IRA is ludicrous. Frankly there was/is more chance of Elvis Presley turning up in London than of Robert turning up at an IRA press conference! The spy/SAS world is full of complete cranks and idiots... (The work they do requires that kind of person)".

Allowing for military humorous exaggeration, there may be something in what he writes but, in fairness to the SAS, they had little reliable information on which to base their speculations. Some of them must have looked at "worst case scenarios", of which Nairac as a defecting double-agent would have been one. Even so, it is extraordinary that these suspicions should have been aired so openly outside the Army context, unless this was part of a deliberate attempt to discredit Nairac posthumously.

Nicky Curtis, a Green Howard who had liked and respected Nairac when working undercover with him, had also worried that he seemed to be on very good terms with known IRA supporters and likewise wondered whether he might turn out to be a double agent. Curtis eventually concluded that he could not be, because the damage that the Army and RUC had managed to inflict on the IRA as a result of Nairac's intelligence-gathering had not been counterbalanced by any obvious improvement in the IRA's own capability. Whether his disappearance had been voluntary or not, there was also a widespread and reasonable concern that he might have compromised Army security and placed lives in jeopardy. We now know that this was not the case, but they could not have been certain of this at that time.

Nevertheless there is something unnerving about the speed with which some soldiers and officials now hurried to distance themselves from Nairac. The relationship between the RUC and the Army was strained at the best of times: Nairac's disappearance added to the stress. This animosity would come to a head two years later. Meanwhile one senior RUC officer, who was presumably not aware of Nairac's real intelligence function, tartly remarked:

"He was a liaison officer and certainly he had not been tasked by the RUC Special Branch as all those operations were supposed to be. He was a bit of a cowboy!"

An SAS officer expressed similar views: "Robert Nairac was either incredibly brave or bloody stupid. Quite frankly I choose the second option. He did a lot of silly things... Half the time the Ops Officer didn't know where the fuck he was!" (This was certainly not true of the night when he disappeared, however.)

Another former SAS soldier told Ken Wharton in an off-the-record conversation: "When I met [Nairac], I could see that he was arrogant and reckless; he was a disaster waiting to happen."

Another officer said: "It's simple: Nairac didn't just stick his head into the lion's mouth – that wouldn't have been enough for him. Instead, he had to go and stick it right up the lion's arse."

Yet another officer described him as having "another element which made me think that I couldn't quite trust the guy or begin to work him out". (This could be code for "I feared that he might be a double agent", or "I suspected that he might be gay".)

However a fellow MIO, quoted in *Soldier* magazine in 1979, did not agree:

"He was a fairly strong-willed fellow with a confident knowledge of the area – a guy with a lot of common sense and well aware of what the risk was. By and large he was a very careful man."

Clive Fairweather, who was not a fool, would temper his remarks about Nairac over the years. As time went by and Nairac's posthumous reputation endured and grew, rather than fading, he became warmer and more generous in his comments; never denying Nairac's courage, dash and charm; describing him as a "brave maverick", while continuing to sow subtle doubts about his sexuality, sanity and common sense. Even his last media interview, given in 2008 to *The Scotsman*, was factually misleading. He also claimed on one occasion to have written Nairac's GC citation, which was in fact a "committee job". Fairweather, as G2 (Int) at the time, undoubtedly saw it in draft and contributed language to it. It has since emerged that he did so against his better judgement and only because his superiors had instructed him to do so. At the time his reaction was along these lines, as reported by John Parker:

"...we had made a fool of ourselves in front of the RUC. Back in Hereford the SAS feeling was 'Christ, we really have blown it here and someone who is not part of the Regiment has let the side down...' It was a mixture. There was puzzlement and there was horror among people like myself that it had happened, and if we could have seen the overall picture we could probably have stopped Robert from doing this sort of thing, but we hadn't seen the complete picture until too late. I think that in the end he was out of control. He had bitten off more than he could chew".

"Steve", a retired Grenadier guardsman who knew Nairac well, does not concur:

"The SAS knew damned well what he was doing; that he was going out alone; frequenting pubs, just as he had in London, and they could have stopped him if they had wanted to."

The hostile attitude of some SAS officers was at least partly related to professional jealousy. They were always a "club" and he was an outsider. They were irritated by Nairac's apparently casual attitude to his role and probably to his own safety. More than anything else, his romantic love of the Irish and their culture grated with their view of them as a savage and despicable enemy.

On a practical level Nairac's disappearance and death would cause many of his former colleagues, including the SAS, considerable extra work over many months. Some of them, especially those who had not personally known and liked Nairac, were infuriated by this. Their lives would have been vastly easier if he had just taken a few more precautions, stayed alive, completed his tour of duty in June 1977 and returned to Regimental duties in the UK. Some of the most unpleasant comments about him seem to have originated around this time.

Guilt there certainly was: the Army had not properly managed Nairac in 1976-77; it had not responded as it should have done when he went missing and this had made his death certain. The majority of military cock-ups and tragedies happen because of problems at some level in the chain of command. This is brought out clearly in Major General Christopher Elliott's book, *High*

Command, which concentrates on the failings of the British higher command in Iraq and Afghanistan, but the lessons have a broader application. If the chain of command at the level that was responsible for Nairac had been clearer about who was in control and who had formal responsibility for him, Nairac would not have been alone in the Three Steps that night, without backup. Somewhere, at Major or Lieutenant Colonel level, there was a lack of clarity, partly for the reasons already given and partly because the relevant people at Bessbrook Mill were new and inexperienced. Initially there were bound to be mistakes, while the RUC, SAS and Brigade worked out the liaison, command and control issues of who reported to whom, and who was primarily responsible for whom; a most important detail, when Nairac's personality is taken into account.

Although Clive Fairweather was an accomplished man who rose from humble origins to eminent positions, both military and civil, his selective loyalty, office intriguing and persistent disinformation do not make edifying reading. Nor were they good for the Army. For integrity, a quality that Nairac possessed in abundance, is not just admirable but vital in an army or any other large organisation, including commercial organisations and government departments. Integrity leads to trust and trust leads to greater effectiveness. Put simply, in organisations where people trust their leaders and colleagues trust one another there are better business outcomes and there is more innovation. That plainly was not the case in the military environment in which Nairac was working at the end of his life. Mistrust and office politics are at the very least time-consuming, dispiriting and costly. In an army, they can be lethal. When a company has a reputation for fair dealing, its costs drop: trust cuts the time spent second-guessing, worrying, and (in extreme cases) litigating. Trust strengthens every part of any deal: its durability, its potential profitability and its flexibility. Like most other organisations, an army works better when the energy expended on doubt, fear and suspicion is minimised. It was written of the explorer Sir Ernest Shackleton that:

"Many people think that loyalty is something that the members of an organisation owe to the leadership... but loyalty always starts at the top and is reflected [we would now say 'cascaded'] down to the bottom. It seems to me that Shackleton understood this".

Nairac understood this, too, but not everyone else then serving in the Army in Northern Ireland did. The explicit dislike and distrust of many Warrant Officers and NCOs towards their commissioned officers at that time was a symptom of this. But the real deficiency was at the top: a failure of political leadership by successive British Governments of both the major Parties.

It is hard not to sympathise with the NCO who was shocked at the relentless emphasis on damage limitation and reputation management after Nairac's disappearance. Officers like Fairweather seemed far more concerned about that "than they were about Bob never being seen again".

Possibly the common soldiers should be allowed to have the last word:

- "I once met Bob Nairac in Belfast. We gave him the pre ops 'Grand Tour.' The GDG were taking over from 2 Para, and he was in the advance party. Never saw a Rupert with so much get up and go. Sadly missed. RIP."
- "Unfortunately it was that 'get-up-and-go' that got him killed."
- "I knew him personally as I was in the Int Sect at Portadown at the time. Always affable and charming with a determination to make a difference over there."
- "Yes, I served under Robert Nairac (Lieutenant at that time), during our tour in the Ardoyne. I can't give enough praise for the man, an approachable, down to earth officer (not the stereotypical Guards officer), who unselfishly put others before himself. He did so much for Catholic credence [credibility], unlike those who would murder and maim in the name of their religious beliefs. It's a small world, but there would be easily enough room for men like Robert Nairac."
- "Bob was my platoon commander in Recce Platoon in the UK and Kenya. He told us he was leaving us, but never said why or where. The next time I seen him was in Keady [Co. Armagh]. He was a lovely man who loved to sing rebel songs. Sadly missed by all that knew him. A true brave man. RIP BOSS."
- "Even the people who took his life had enormous respect for him. Nuff said. I would have loved to have had 40% of his guts. He loved the Irish in his own way. Very sad, but never, ever forgotten by people from all sides of the conflict."
- "I knew Bob as a close friend. He cared passionately about Ireland; North and South. He worked tirelessly to help bring peace to a country he loved. In my opinion it was his love of this country which caused him to visit the [Three Steps] Bar and led to his death."

It would be possible to cover many pages with this kind of testimony.

"SAS Captain D" speaking at length to John Parker, revealed that he had searched Nairac's room at Bessbrook Mill for clues soon after his disappearance, although Nairac's destination and the purpose of his meet were known in advance, because he had informed SAS Captain Collett, the SAS Operations Officer. Not only did the room contain a number of highly-classified files that arguably should not have been there, but it was in chaos: "a tip, very untidy, a real mess". Captain D presumed that this mess reflected the fact that Nairac had been under considerable stress latterly and that "the immaculate procedures of Guards discipline had waned considerably". Others commented that the disarrangement of the room was explained by "Nairac was a slovenly, untidy bugger who didn't mind living in a tip", although this view has been contested by people who knew him. However, the state of the room could equally well have reflected the fact that it had been very recently ransacked: it sounds like the scene of a burglary. Conspicuous by its absence was Nairac's Filofax.

As already mentioned, Clive Fairweather's misleading claim that Nairac had left his Service handgun in his car when he entered the Three Steps Inn, and had later tried desperately and unsuccessfully to retrieve it when he was attacked by the mob, did Nairac's reputation great damage. Fairweather's words on this subject were:

"It would appear that when he got there, having locked his car in the car park, he didn't walk in wearing his pistol. It would appear that he left his pistol either in the glove box or under the car seat. You would normally wear it in your waistband, but he deliberately left it behind because I think he knew he was going to be up on the stage singing. He had it in his mind that if he was going to stand up on the stage and sing and put his arms out, then a waistband holster or a shoulder holster was going to show."

"It would appear" nothing of the sort. Nairac had his gun on him in a shoulder holster all the time. That is why he kept his jacket on. Fairweather's account is not supported by the testimony of Nairac's assassins, nor by the police evidence, nor by the findings of serious investigative journalists like Roisin McAuley and Darragh McIntyre.

The second Fairweather fiction: that Nairac had taken a Filofax containing highly-sensitive information to a potentially hazardous meet and had lost it, did further damage to Nairac's credibility and reinforced the perception that he was a rogue agent: irresponsible, reckless, out of control and a danger to his own side. It successfully deflected the military authorities from consideration of what had gone wrong with the Army's response when it became clear that Nairac was missing, and why nearly six hours had been allowed to elapse before the SAS alerted Brigade and the RUC. It is a mystery why this narrative has remained unchallenged for so long, because it is so implausible. Even stranger was the SAS's apparently laid-back attitude over the disappearance of the Filofax. They had delayed reporting its alleged loss, just as they had delayed reporting Nairac's disappearance for several hours after they should have done so. A possible inference is that they knew that it was not with the IRA, but that it was convenient for them that others should think so, should panic and be diverted from consideration of other matters as a result.

A murder inquiry was now under way, but Nairac's room, which should have been left untouched, had already been searched and disarranged by SAS Captain D and probably by at least one other person before him, before the Royal Military Police's SIB or the RUC ever had a chance to look at it. According to Captain Collett, the room was soon declared to be out-of-bounds and no-one was allowed to enter without prior authorisation, but by that time the damage seems to have been done.

It was not until 19 May that Captain Collett showed the room to RUC Detective Sergeant Swanston. DS Swanston searched it and removed evidential items, which included a hairbrush that Collett confirmed had belonged to Nairac. Some of Nairac's dark hair was adhering to the bristles. It seemed to match hair found at the sites associated with Nairac's murder and on a pullover belonging to Liam Townson. DS Swanston also took hair samples from Nairac's black dog. It is unclear whether this was the black Newfoundland, "Bundle", or his black Labrador.

Soon afterwards, with almost indecent haste, the room was cleared. Space was always at a premium in overcrowded Bessbrook Mill and the room was needed for someone else. Nairac's uniform items and some personal effects were packed up and eventually returned to his family. A lot of "rubbish", which might have had evidential value, was thrown out. In summary, at least three pieces of vital evidence had apparently been suppressed, while other evidence was probably lost and destroyed. Whether this was deliberate or not, it was very unhelpful.

According to Toby Harnden, yet another SAS officer, Major C, cleared Nairac's room. His explicitly hostile comment was:

"He [Nairac] was a Catholic. He almost believed in the [IRA] cause. His room was an absolute shit tip and amongst all the rubbish was a collection of Gaelic language tapes."

SAS officers would later cite the Gaelic language tapes as final conclusive evidence of Nairac's general eccentricity and lunacy. This was Clive Fairweather's openly-held view. He had earlier rejected Nairac's request for Army funding to buy the tapes, claiming that this was yet another manifestation of Nairac's foolish and foredoomed attempt to be taken for an Irishman, which the Army had no interest in assisting. Fairweather's comment was either wide of the mark or, like other comments by him, was disingenuous.

There was a simple reason for Nairac's request: he wanted to be able to understand what the locals were saying in Gaelic. Despite the 1609 plantation of Ulster and despite some premature announcements of its death, in the 1970s the Irish Gaelic tongue was still alive, although not flourishing, in a few rural areas of Northern Ireland, one of which was South Armagh. Moreover Gaelic was taught in all schools in the Republic: its study was compulsory to O-Level. It followed that many Irish people who had been educated in the Republic, even if they did not come from the *Gaeltacht*, had a basic acquaintance with the language and were able to speak it to some extent. The inhabitants of South Armagh used Gaelic when they did not wish to be understood by the Security Forces, just as contemporary Gaelic-speaking Scots and Welsh-speakers will switch from English to their Celtic languages when they wish to be rude about Lowland Scots or English tourists in their hearing. This is confirmed both by Lieutenant Colonel Richard Besly and by Lord Valentine Cecil, who remarked that, "It would have been very useful to Robert... and I did hear it [used] in the circumstances that Richard Besly has described." He added that the use of Gaelic was promoted by the Republicans because it was a fairly secure means of communication. Gaelic is a medium-hard language with a complicated grammar, although not insuperable to someone like Nairac, who was a good linguist. A few Scots Gaelic speakers in Highland Regiments might have been able to grasp the gist when they heard it spoken, but no-one else.

Among the mess in Nairac's room were also found highly-classified official files, not all of them Army ones, which should have been kept in secure conditions, even if he had legitimate access to them. It was reasonable that these should be removed as soon as possible and returned to their filing cabinets. However, no-one, including SAS Major C, seems to have made a note of the files' titles and contents. They could have given some indication of what Nairac was up to. This might have been important evidence, but it was in effect suppressed or disregarded.

It is still unclear what Nairac had been doing with the files. If he had indeed been working unofficially for one of the Agencies, this might explain their presence in his room. There could have been a simpler and less exciting explanation. Nairac was abducted and murdered in mid-May 1977. He was due to leave Northern Ireland at the end of his tour in June. In May he should have been starting preparations for briefing his successor, who had been named. As far as is known, Nairac had not yet met him. Some of the briefing would have been oral and delivered after the successor's arrival, but Nairac could reasonably have borrowed the files to refresh his memory before starting work on the handover notes.

There was an additional problem with the RMP SIB. A former RMP Regimental Sergeant-Major (RSM) believes that the RMP SIB of the early-to-mid 1970s in Northern Ireland had been discreetly infiltrated and augmented by members of the Security Service (MI5), who were acting as investigators on especially controversial cases. Nairac's disappearance would have fallen into this category. The RSM cited two instances where members of his RMP SIB unit, of whose background he knew little, had been involved in events of which he had no prior knowledge – people who subsequently disappeared from the nominal role or, on one occasion, were killed in circumstances about which he was ignorant. Yet he, as the RSM, would normally have expected to be high on the 'need to know' list. In effect the RSM was saying that controversial cases were not being properly investigated, either in terms of process or of personnel. This seems to have happened in Nairac's case and, conveniently, it would appear that there was no 'suitable or acceptable' investigating team available at short notice.

An SAS officer, probably Major C, told a BBC Northern Ireland journalist that "something very significant" had been found in Nairac's room at Bessbrook after he disappeared. The officer refused to say what this was and remained silent. He could have been referring to the highly-classified files, or possibly to Nairac's private handgun. But it was probably something completely different.

Knowledgeable people have made intelligent and informed guesses as to what the "something very significant" might have been. One is that it was an extensive list of informers or "touts" as the IRA called them, in South Armagh, giving their real names and code names. That is possible, given that Nairac was on his way, as he thought, to meet a potentially important new tout at the Three Steps Bar. Any such list would have been suppressed, for obvious reasons. The second suggestion is that it was a Polaroid photo of the dead John Francis "Benny" Green lying in a pool of his own blood on the floor of the Carville farmhouse. This is also plausible. As we have seen, Green had been murdered in the Republic in January 1975 by Loyalists, but his murder is still frequently attributed to Nairac and Tony Ball. In 1977 Fred Holroyd's "revelations" to the media and his MP were still well in the future. The discovery of this Polaroid would have been startling to an SAS officer who had probably heard the rumours – traceable to Fred Holroyd – about Nairac's involvement in the killing. Two factors make this story possible: Nairac would hardly have given away his only copy of the Polaroid to Holroyd. He would have possessed other examples (which he had obtained quite legally from the Garda through the RUC). Secondly, as recorded previously, the SAS officer who cleared Nairac's room had found a collection of photos of dead terrorists and other individuals, which he thought morbid and unhealthy. A Polaroid of Green's corpse would have been worthy of a place in that collection. Whatever the case, this mysterious piece of evidence seems to have disappeared, along with so much else.

Was the tragedy avoidable? Even if he had been disinclined to accept the MIO/SASLO post in South Armagh, Nairac would have come under strong pressure to accept. Prior to his arrival, Military Intelligence in South Armagh was adrift: the PIRA were able to operate freely, had inflicted numerous deaths on the Army, but had suffered very few of their own. The previous twelve months had been desperate for the military authorities, with 3 Para and 40 Commando of the Royal Marines taking serious casualties, while the Royal Highland Fusiliers had been shocked by the death of the popular Lance Corporal David Hind at the hands of a PIRA sniper in Crossmaglen. The 1976 Border Incident and similar errors had caused 22 SAS to become regarded in Northern Ireland, however unfairly, as "a busted flush", in the words of one of their most mordant Army critics of that period. Robert Nairac was seen as the answer to the South Armagh PIRA. Despite the fact that he was only a Captain, his reputation was enormous and "higher formation" seemed to be in awe of him. If Nairac could not meet the South Armagh intelligence challenge, it was not clear who could. Nairac was not exaggerating when in November 1976 he had told Julian Malins and David Badenoch that many people depended on him. It might have been even more accurate to say that several more senior officers had bet their shirts on his success. Nairac was spared much of the stultifying burden of military risk-aversion; he lived in a twilight zone between the Army and the RUC and he sometimes played the two sides off against each other. He enjoyed this situation, but it made him enemies, especially among the SAS. Very few people in the Army understood just how dangerous Nairac's type of work was. They knew about being shot up in uniform in Crossmaglen, but Nairac had moved around for months with impunity; why restrict a man who was getting results? Moreover no-one else had ever been abducted until then. In summary, Nairac was given unprecedented freedom of action, which in the end proved fatal.

CHAPTER 15 | UNFINISHED BUSINESS

It was a death that caused many ripples and left many feeling uncomfortable.
Like everybody else, [we] felt badly about Robert's death. (One of Nairac's former
colleagues in NITAT (NI))

Ach cá bhfuil uaigh Robert Nairac?!
(But where is the grave of Robert Nairac? David Wheatley)

The fragile 1998 Good Friday Peace Agreement has not been totally successful.
Sporadic violence has continued and a number of civilians have been murdered
in the succeeding years. Operation Banner finally ended in 2007, 38 years after
the first "temporary" deployment of British troops to Northern Ireland and 30
years after Nairac's murder. Only 5,000 troops are now stationed in Ulster, but
they are no longer deployed in support of the police to enforce law and order.
Nevertheless, on 7 March 2009 a Republican paramilitary group, the Real IRA,
shot dead two off-duty Royal Engineers outside Massereene Barracks in Antrim
Town. They wounded two other soldiers and two civilians. These were the first
British military fatalities in Northern Ireland since 1997. Two days later another
group, the Continuity IRA, shot dead a Police Service of Northern Ireland (PSNI)
officer. The PSNI, which is the RUC's successor, has to date lost 24 officers. There
have been no recent IRA terrorist incidents on the British mainland, which was
the main concern of British politicians in 1998. The British public has lost interest
in Northern Ireland but the story there is not yet over; the Troubles could start
up again at any time and, as Lord Randolph Churchill famously warned, "The
Irish Question will never be solved."

Meanwhile in 2015 Robert Nairac's body remains undiscovered and there
are many other unanswered questions. Their resolution has been made more
difficult by the determined secrecy of the South Armagh PIRA and by the Army's
obfuscatory damage limitation exercise in 1977, which resulted in the suppression
of evidence and an incomplete, misleading picture of what had happened, or
might have happened, being presented to Ministers, Parliament and the public.

Sean O'Callaghan, a former volunteer in the PIRA Tyrone Brigade who is now
an active supporter of the Peace Process, adds an interesting perspective to this
story. The Tyrone PIRA is the closest to the South Armagh PIRA – insofar as
anyone is close to them. He has commented that Thomas "Slab" Murphy, a farmer
who was widely believed to be the former PIRA Chief of Staff in South Armagh,
would have been livid when he learned the full facts of Nairac's abduction and
murder. The PIRA had been made to look both barbaric and stupid: "It was a
monumental cock-up". So the word went out: "We won't ever speak about it;
it's too embarrassing". Even within the PIRA, if O'Callaghan ever asked about
Nairac, a curtain of silence would descend. The subject is never mentioned or

discussed, even internally. This is a contributory reason why Nairac's body has never been found.

There are certain other difficult subjects, which the PIRA has banned from even internal discussion or reference. Again, the curtain of silence descends. One is the theft of a top-secret British Army document on the PIRA, in which General Sir James Glover gave a forthright and realistic view of its capabilities. He prepared it soon after taking over command in Northern Ireland in 1979. Nairac had anticipated many of Glover's conclusions in his own writings. Although it was a highly-classified and sensitive document, a copy somehow found its way into the PIRA's hands, embarrassing the British Government which tried to play down its pessimistic and disturbing conclusions when the PIRA published them. Glover reported that in ten years the PIRA had progressed from being an amateur organisation to a well-equipped, financially strong body of some 500 activists who were talented, dedicated and "possessed the sinews to wage war for the foreseeable future". To this day the PIRA does not permit discussion of, or comment on, the theft of General Glover's report. The reason for this is not known.

Another sensitive subject with the PIRA is the bungled kidnapping and subsequent slaughter by PIRA supporters of the valuable former racehorse and stud stallion, Shergar, in 1983. Their intention had been to hold the horse to ransom to raise funds for arms purchases. O'Callaghan said that the PIRA had demanded a £5 million ransom from the Aga Khan, whom they believed to be Shergar's owner, which was never paid. Unknown to the PIRA, he really belonged to a consortium. One of the gang later indicated that Shergar had been killed within hours of his theft. The thieves, who had no prior experience of highly-strung thoroughbred stallions, were unable to control him; he became hysterical in the horsebox and injured his leg, so they panicked and killed him. According to one of the thieves, "Shergar was machine-gunned. There was blood everywhere and the horse even slipped on his own blood. There was lots of cussin' and swearin' because the horse wouldn't die. It was a very bloody death." His remains were secretly buried and have never been found. It was a sickening and pointless death, rather reminiscent of Nairac's.

There are further mysteries which at present remain unexplained. One concerns Nairac's blood group (*Note 1*). Although his body was never found, teeth, hair and copious dried blood were discovered at the three places where he had fought for his life. At that time no DNA testing was available, but blood groups could be identified. Both the RUC and the Garda asked the Army for information about Nairac's blood group to assist their investigations. However, the Army stated firmly that it did not hold any record of it. This was literally unbelievable; it is mandatory to record all soldiers' blood groups in case an emergency transfusion should ever be necessary. Admittedly Nairac was detached from his Regiment, but his basic medical information would have been transferred to the HQ of wherever he was posted. Moreover, Nairac's Army identity card (No 493007), which for obvious reasons he did not carry with him on undercover operations, has survived. It had been in his room when he disappeared; it, too, disappeared, but it re-surfaced long after the murder, far too late to be used in evidence. It still exists, somewhat damaged; apparently chewed by his dog. It records Nairac's blood group (O, Rhesus Positive) and this information also turns out to have been stored elsewhere. (*Note 2*) So who was responsible for this failure of co-operation – which infuriated both the RUC and the Garda in 1977 – and why? As a result of it, the blood found at the Three Steps car park, at Flurry Bridge and at the murder site was never positively identified as Nairac's, although undoubtedly much of it was his. Likewise, the tufts of hair were never certainly identified as his, although there is little doubt that they were.

Apart from Nairac's ID card, his three metal ID discs, which are issued on commissioning or joining, would have been in his room. The soldier's name, initials and religion are stamped on the front of each one and his blood group on the back. Nairac did not wear them to the Three Steps. They, too, seem to have disappeared. His undercover work, however, would have made it more, not less, essential that HQ NI, or whoever administered Nairac in Ulster, should have all his medical details to hand. The 1st Battalion Grenadier Guards, as his parent Regiment, had them on file. So, it later transpired, did the 2nd Battalion and the Oxford University OTC. Even if they did not have the information ready to hand, it should not have taken long for someone in Army HQ in Northern Ireland to contact Nairac's parent unit, or units, for the information. It appears unnecessarily obstructive simply to "deny".

This perplexing withholding of information has lent colour to persistent claims by Liam Townson's Defending Counsel, Patrick McEntee, that his client's conviction had been secured on the basis of insufficient and flawed evidence. This begs the question: was someone in the Army keen to sabotage the whole criminal justice process in order to cause the collapse of the Prosecution's case and avoid Townson and his fellow participants being convicted? Were they afraid of what might come out either in Court or at the Coroner's inquest? What other possible explanation could there be?

What happened to Nairac's Filofax? This was a preoccupation of nightmare proportions for the Army and the RUC in the days following his disappearance. In addition to his engagement diary, which could have been revelatory or even compromising, it contained, among other things, numerous notes and the private contact details of RUC and Army officers – including some who lived off-base, like Clive Fairweather – as well as those of many other useful local contacts and sources. These people's lives would now be in danger if the Filofax had fallen into the PIRA's hands. Given that they knew about the Filofax's existence, the SAS's lack of urgency in seeking it when Nairac disappeared is, on the face of it, very odd. When they later let it be known that the Filofax was missing, there was panic; the RUC waited anxiously for the inevitable massacre of agents and others whose contact details were recorded in it. This did not happen; we now know that the IRA never had it: its fate remains unknown. We can, however, draw some legitimate inferences. According to people who served with Nairac, he was very firm about the need to protect contacts, sources and their identities. He was no more likely to have taken his Filofax (which was probably Army issue) to a rendezvous than he was to have carried his Army ID card, worn his Army ID discs under his shirt or carried a bleeper. Any of these would have been an obvious giveaway. Apart from the danger of its theft, putting the lives of his contacts at risk, the Filofax would have identified him as a member of the Armed Forces. At most, he might have taken a few notes with him, or a few relevant loose-leaf pages from the Filofax, in his wallet. It could have been one of these that he disposed of down the lavatory in the Three Steps on the night of his murder, but we shall never know.

No trace of the Filofax has ever been found; not even its durable leather cover. Security considerations aside, it could have been an important piece of evidence, possibly providing clues as to whom Nairac had planned to meet on the evening of 14 May. It is now clear that the Filofax never left Bessbrook Mill; it was in Nairac's room along with his other personal effects. Several people had legitimate access to the keys in Nairac's absence; it therefore follows that someone stationed at Bessbrook must have recovered the Filofax and the ID items soon after it had become clear that Nairac was missing, and suppressed any record of their removal. All of these items should have been kept as evidence for use in the investigation and in the trials of Nairac's assassins, and there is no telling what else might have been removed or destroyed when the room was ransacked and subsequently cleared.

In case of a suspected mistake, the Filofax in question is likely to have been an Army green ring-binder. These were issued in more than one size; some were standard Filofax-sized but had a different arrangement of rings. There was also a Northern Ireland Special Operations version, which had an eyelet so that it could be attached to the owner's person by an "idiot cord". This is probably the version that Nairac used. It is also possible that he used a genuine Filofax, bought commercially. A few categories of extremely busy and highly organised people, including Army officers and parish clergy, had adopted the Filofax long before anyone else did. Indeed, at that period Filofaxes were an Army affectation: an almost universal, albeit unofficial, officer's badge. This was so much the case that some officers had slightly enlarged pockets in their barrack dress trousers to fit them. Whatever its provenance, Nairac was highly unlikely to have taken his Filofax to any clandestine meeting.

A further question: why did Nairac, an experienced soldier and skilled user of firearms, drop his gun in the Three Steps car park? Nairac's handgun was an Army Browning 9mm pistol. To cock this type of pistol, the breech cover is moved to the rear. It ejects any unused round that may be present and pushes a fresh round from the magazine, which is inserted in the pistol grip, into the breech. This action briefly requires the use of the other free hand. Most people are right-handed, so the left hand would normally move the breech cover. The safety-catch is positioned on the left-hand side of the pistol grip and the right-hand thumb can move the catch to on/off. If unimpeded, an expert like Nairac can perform this operation very quickly. Nairac was carrying his pistol in a concealed shoulder-holster. While the magazine would have been in the weapon, it would not normally have been cocked, so the aforementioned procedure would have been necessary in order to do this.

If one of Nairac's hands or arms was being restrained, cocking would be very difficult. Even if the pistol had been pre-cocked, but was being held in the 'wrong', i.e. the left, hand, it would be more difficult to move the safety-catch. We can speculate that perhaps Nairac had no choice but to draw the handgun with his left hand as the right hand was incapacitated in some way: held by an assailant; trying to simultaneously open the car door, or perhaps injured. Having drawn the 9mm, especially if it were un-cocked, it would be awkward to use: hence, perhaps, Nairac's fumbling and dropping the weapon. He might also have been overwhelmed by numbers.

However, that might not be the correct scenario: Nairac's Q car had been fitted with a panic button. Possibly his first reaction was to get to it. He would presumably have tried to use his car keys to open the door, which would have been difficult, given the predicament in which he found himself. When that failed, as a last resort he might have drawn the Browning 9mm. (The keys were never found; probably they were buried with him, along with anything else that he was carrying.)

An alternative scenario is that the Browning 9mm had jammed. If this had occurred, either in the Three Steps car park or at Flurry Bridge, the next action would have been to re-cock it, which would eject the unfired round. However, no contemporary report mentions any unfired 9mm rounds (possibly part-struck by the firing pin) having been found at any of his last locations.

Nairac or one of his assailants would have cocked the pistol in the Three Steps car park. Apart from the one round that Nairac is reported to have fired when he briefly regained possession of the weapon, all shots would have been fired by his assailants. The pistol would continue to fire each time that the trigger was pulled, until the magazine was empty. Nairac managed only the one shot, presumably because of his physical state or the action of an assailant. Both Nicky Curtis and Lord Ashcroft (writing in *Special Forces Heroes* and *George Cross Heroes*) believe that Nairac's own gun was used to kill him. Empty Browning shells were reportedly found near the murder site. Yet the evidence given in court indicates that Liam Townson used his own revolver to murder Nairac. The IRA apparently have a custom or superstition: unless there is absolutely no alternative, a victim's own firearm should never be used to murder him.

It is conceivable that two guns were used in Nairac's murder: that his Browning 9mm was in good working order and that it was used either to incapacitate him prior to the use of Liam Townson's .32 to kill him, or to deliver the *coup de grace* afterwards. This theory reads strangely and it is pure guesswork. It could explain some of the evidence found at and near the murder site. It does not, however, accord with Nairac's assassins' testimony, given when all but three of them – who had fled to the USA – were charged later in 1977 in the Republic and in Northern Ireland, with offences ranging from withholding information from the police, to murder.

That Nairac's Browning jammed – which is what appears to have happened – is one of the most perplexing parts of this mysterious story. Nairac was experienced in the use of both military and sporting firearms. He was a very good shot and did his own cleaning, oiling and minor repairs. It has been suggested that Nairac might latterly have become careless with his weapons and had not been maintaining and checking them as he should have done. From everything that we know about him, this would have been out of character. Brought up with guns from an early age, he would not have made that error; even with a sporting gun which, if not properly maintained, can be a danger to its user and to others. Luke Jennings maintains that Nairac "was highly conscientious in the cleaning and maintenance of his sporting guns". He would have been no less so with his Army weapons. Julian Malins supports this view. He has commented that:

"It is impossible to imagine Nairac not having his weapon with him and not keeping it in good order. This is because there is time available to attend to the weapon at the end of an assignment, but, faced with sudden calls out at any time, there might not be any opportunity to clean and oil the weapon [before] rushing out [on the next occasion]. He would therefore have oiled and cleaned his handgun at the end of his last outing with it and simply collected it for the next assignment on the assumption that it was as he had left it."

This seems reasonable and logical. It is one thing to take daring but calculated risks such as visiting Republican bars and singing in them; quite another to neglect a weapon upon which, in extreme circumstances, one's life and the lives of others may depend. By analogy Malins adds: "He was, like me, a fisherman and we never put our tackle away after an outing, however late or tired we were, without putting it into good order ready for the next trip." In other words, the conscientious care of his equipment was part of an ingrained behaviour pattern. We can dismiss the suggestion that Nairac had been careless with his weaponry. He would have assumed on the evening of 14 May that, when he picked it up, the Browning was in perfect condition.

Both guns are now held by the PSNI, along with the rest of the evidential material received from both the former RUC and the Garda. They are not available for inspection, so we have little hard evidence on which to base any theory. What are the other possible explanations?

One potential explanation, which deserves consideration, is sabotage. Nairac had made some enemies, notably among the rogue element of the SAS detachment based in Bessbrook Mill. This was confirmed by their openly disparaging comments about him after he disappeared. Later Clive Fairweather would repeatedly say, to John Parker among others, that some of the SAS had regarded Nairac as a liability, did not like him and did not trust him. An SAS officer was to claim that Nairac had been a security risk and had put his men's lives in danger, although without stating how. Given the presence of the rogue SAS men, and knowing their mindset, the sabotage of Nairac's Browning pistol is theoretically possible. It is just conceivable that, as a result of the Seamus Harvey incident in January 1977 and Nairac's reaction to it, certain SAS personnel might have determined to put an end to Nairac. So, could some of them have been mad enough to sabotage his handgun? In practice it was extremely improbable. Moreover, and despite Fairweather's assertions, a majority of the SAS soldiers evidently did like Nairac: they had after all allowed him, and very few others, the privilege of access to their private SAS bar at Bessbrook Mill.

What were the other possibilities? During the Vietnam War "fragging" (derived from "fragmentation grenade") entered the American-English military lexicon. It refers to the act of murdering a fellow soldier in battle. The term now covers any method of deliberately causing the death of fellow military personnel, including sabotage. In addition, it can be applied to manipulating the chain of command in order to have an individual killed by deliberately placing him in harm's way or to betrayal by his own side. The last possibility has certainly been mooted in Nairac's case by other biographers. So might he have been "fragged" by some other means and if so were certain SAS soldiers the fraggers? Again, in the final analysis this looks highly unlikely.

The most compelling argument against fragging is that Nairac was shortly to leave Northern Ireland, so – for anyone at all who had a problem with him – the "Nairac problem" was about to resolve itself. It was now mid-May; Nairac's tour of duty was due to end in June; there was no possibility of extending his posting, because a successor had been identified. It follows from this that there would have been no point in anybody fragging Nairac at this stage, because he was about to rejoin the Grenadiers and become a Company Commander: good riddance, in the eyes of his SAS critics. These considerations would apply equally to any other Nairac critics, including Clive Fairweather.

Much of the uncertainty about what actually happened, and when, was caused by disinformation: by Fairweather's successful attempts to cover his own back and avoid the blame that should rightfully have been his. He lied repeatedly about Nairac, but that was to save his career, not to cover up a fragging murder. His actions may be understandable, but why did other people in the Army, who were in a position to know, go along with this?

The SAS probably felt some loyalty to Fairweather, who was "one of them". They, too, risked incurring criticism for their late, dithering and inadequate response to Nairac's disappearance. Senior Army officers could have incurred criticism over the fact that Nairac had been sent back to Ulster in 1976 at all; over the way in which he had not been managed in South Armagh; because he had been allowed too much freedom of action; over his mysterious and potentially fatally compromising mission in Belfast in early 1977 and because he should have been relieved much earlier. Nairac had remained in Northern Ireland for too long because he had been allowed to become indispensable. He was an exhausted man in the last weeks of his life but he would never have asked to be relieved; someone more senior should have made the case. SAS Major G had tried to do so, but he was overruled by his superior.

Most importantly, it was definitely not in Fairweather's or the SAS's interest that the PIRA should capture and interrogate Nairac. Early on 15 May, once it had become clear that Nairac really was missing, everyone at Bessbrook Mill and later at Lisburn, Hereford and elsewhere, was panic-stricken at the thought that he was probably being tortured and interrogated somewhere in the Republic. As noted earlier, Nairac had unrivalled knowledge of everything that the Security Forces, including the SAS and the RUC, were doing in South Armagh. He was also well-informed about what was happening elsewhere in the Province. Once the PIRA had broken him, it would all come out. At that early stage in the drama, Nairac's former colleagues could not have known that he had been abducted by thuggish amateurs; that they would shortly murder him and that he would die without revealing anything.

There is a further argument against the fragging theory. The PIRA would certainly have known, or would soon have worked it out, if Nairac had been deliberately betrayed by someone on his own side. They would have had no hesitation in going public with this information, presented in the most dramatic and damaging way possible. Individuals would have been embarrassed but so, too, would the institution of the Army as a whole. This would have been irresistible to the PIRA, but it did not happen.

Finally, fragging is relatively alien to British military tradition. Whatever may be the case in other armies, officers and soldiers of the Regular Army are intensely loyal, even to people whom they do not like, who may be professional rivals, but who are nevertheless "part of the family". Fragging has certainly happened in the British Army, but comparatively rarely and usually in wartime. The people involved were often conscripts or wartime volunteers, not regular soldiers.

It is, however, possible to argue that Fairweather was guilty of negligence, or at the very least of poor judgement. His lack of action and complete disregard for Nairac's safety on the night of the murder was tantamount to fragging by accident or negligence. He realised this when he began groggily to focus on what had probably happened in the early hours of 15 May. The cold facts were that although he was the GSO2 Int/Liaison HQ NORIRELAND, the previous evening he had gone out without his bleeper, without giving anyone an indication of where he was going and without leaving telephone numbers on which he could be contacted. No-one had been asked to cover for him in his absence. This was further complicated by the fact that he lived off-base. Ringing his house was of no use because no-one was there; he was not married and he lived alone. Had he been living in a Mess, he might have been more readily traceable. Consequently he was not contacted until after midnight, by which time Nairac was being beaten up, bundled into a car and driven away. To judge from his history and his own testimony, it is a racing certainty that Fairweather was not completely sober. His reaction, when he finally answered the telephone, was dismissive and along the following lines:

"That bastard Nairac's always missing call-ins and deadlines. Never fear: the bad penny will turn up sooner or later. I'm definitely not going to haul senior officers out of their beds or alert Brigade and the RUC for what will certainly turn out to be a false alarm. Do nothing. I'm going to bed now. We'll speak about this in the morning."

So nothing was done: the Worcestershire and Sherwood Foresters COP team on Hill 799 were not alerted, nor were their COP backup team. The SAS were not willing to involve them without Fairweather's authorisation and this had evidently not been forthcoming. Fairweather might well have added: "Let's keep this within the SAS".

Although he had a distinguished Army career, followed by a second career as a reforming Chief Inspector of Prisons for Scotland, Clive Fairweather does not appear in a sympathetic light in this narrative. One of the reasons is his alcoholism, to which he admitted in later life after he had left the Army. This was bound to affect his personality, and it did. A now-retired senior Scottish civil servant met Fairweather after he had become HM Inspector of Prisons for Scotland. On this occasion Fairweather had candidly – even courageously – admitted that he had had a drink problem: he still had one, but he claimed that he now had it under control, although not completely beaten. He said that it had started while he was in the Army. It had become worse in Northern Ireland – a stressful posting – and it had eventually cost him his marriage. (Fairweather would marry in 1980, three years after Nairac's murder. The union produced three children, but did not last.) On the evening of Nairac's disappearance it is reasonable to assume that he had consumed some alcohol, if not a lot. If, as seems highly likely, Fairweather was still under the influence of alcohol when he assumed the lead of the search operation, that might explain a good deal; including some of the decisions that he took. Whatever the explanation, they probably cost Nairac his life.

While it is unlikely that Fairweather wanted Nairac dead, his decision not to inform the Foresters COP team, Brigade or the RUC, and to keep the knowledge of his disappearance within the SAS for several crucial hours, taken with some of his later remarks, suggests that he hoped that Nairac had got himself into a scrape; specifically, into a sexual one. We know that Fairweather thought that Nairac was an unpredictable and out-of-control maverick who, as he said to more than one interlocutor, had probably been "screwing some lady". He did not add, but almost certainly thought, "Better still, if it turns out that he has been screwing a soldier!" Give Nairac enough rope and, with any luck, he would hang himself. Nairac had been in scrapes with authority before but he usually got out of them by charm and cleverness. Fairweather, who did his homework, knew about them. But this time Nairac seemed to have become seriously unstuck. This latest scrape should give Fairweather the chance to severely reprimand Nairac and to demand that the GOC should subject him to tighter supervision; ideally to Fairweather's supervision. If he succeeded in this, he could make Nairac's life very difficult and disagreeable for the remainder of his Northern Irish posting. Depending upon what Nairac had been doing and with whom, Fairweather might get him sent back early to his Regiment or even dismissed from the Army. He had probably been working towards this outcome for months.

But towards 1.00 am Nairac had still not reappeared. The SAS Operations Officer reported that he had not returned to Bessbrook Mill, nor had there been any radio contact; not even at midnight, when a radio check was mandatory. Maybe something bad *had* happened after all? It did not look good: Fairweather, who had started to sober up, began to get worried but still, he did not want to involve the Foresters COP team. He sent up an SAS helicopter team at about 1.00 am, who reported that Nairac's red Triumph Toledo Q Car was standing alone and damaged in the Three Steps car park. Now at last it began to dawn on both Fairweather at Lisburn and the SAS detachment at Bessbrook Mill that the worst had happened: Nairac was not out having fun; he had been captured and taken south of the border. He was presumably now in the PIRA's hands. They would soon begin interrogating him, if they had not already started.

Now thoroughly alarmed, Fairweather went into damage limitation mode. Although Nairac was still alive at this point, rescuing him was not a high priority: Fairweather had his career to salvage. He next sent in an SAS ground team, still without telling the Worcestershire and Sherwood Foresters COP team and risking a friendly-fire incident as a result. They confirmed Fairweather's worst fears. He now held a frantic telephone conversation with the SAS at Hereford. By bad luck Tony Ball, Nairac's trusted friend, took the call. He was very worried and wanted to come immediately to help to find Nairac. That was the least of Fairweather's concerns: Ball was told to stay out of it. Fairweather continued the telephone consultation with someone else. This conversation was mainly concerned with face-saving and damage limitation. Fairweather no doubt put it to the SAS that they could be damaged, as well as him. Following the embarrassing 1976 border incident only a year earlier, they could not afford more bad publicity; there could be more political fallout. Either Fairweather or the SAS belatedly informed Brigade, who informed the RUC. Then the RUC informed the Garda, who later still contacted the Irish Army.

To Army colleagues and later to journalists, Fairweather began systematically to demolish Nairac's reputation. Among other things he accused Nairac of:

- Doing his own thing, without reference to anyone else, including engaging in unauthorised intelligence missions;
- Exceeding his humble terms of reference, which were those of a simple, and very junior, Liaison Officer;
- "Putting our men's lives in danger";
- Unforgivably leaving his Service handgun in his car when he went into the Three Steps and then being unable to retrieve it when set upon by the mob;
- Taking his Army Filofax, containing a wealth of sensitive information, to a hazardous and unauthorised meet at the Three Steps. The Filofax was now feared to be in the PIRA's hands;
- Trying to pass for an Irishman and requesting official funds to buy Gaelic language tapes. This showed that he was completely barmy and living in a parallel universe.
- Being generally naive, ignorant, rash and unreliable; a loose cannon, brawny but not very bright: in Fairweather's view, "a typical Public School boy" reared on Biggles and Bulldog Drummond.

Fairweather's thesis, that Nairac was a foolhardy, dim man; brave no doubt, but the main author of his own death, has found wide acceptance: it is reiterated, for example in Adrian Weale's *Secret Warfare* (1997), including the "gun in the glove compartment" canard. It deflected attention from what really happened, from what had gone wrong with the Army's response, and especially with Fairweather's, when it became clear that Nairac really was missing. The availability of backup from the Worcestershire and Sherwood Foresters COP team on the spot has never been publicly mentioned, except *en passant* by Ken Livingstone in 1987.

Over the years Fairweather would nuance his comments on Nairac. In 2007 he even added his voice to those urging the PIRA to reveal where Nairac had been buried. *The Belfast Telegraph* reported that Fairweather, incorrectly described as "Nairac's former SAS superior", believed that it was time that the PIRA gave up its grisly secret. (Nairac had never reported to Fairweather and neither of them was at that time a member of the SAS.)

"Times in Ireland have changed very much for the better. With all the dramatic political developments and power-sharing, surely someone can now give some indication of how his body was disposed of. They owe it to many other families whose relatives' bodies have never been recovered after abduction by the IRA," said Colonel Fairweather. There was no response.

Fairweather's lack of urgency when Nairac first went missing had left him open to criticism, much of which he successfully deflected at the time by denigrating Nairac; however the past might still catch up with him at a later date. More than twenty years after Nairac's murder, Fairweather, who by this time had left the Army, was reprimanded by the Ministry of Defence for his lengthy, unauthorised and indiscreet interviews with John Parker, who was researching for his book *Death of a Hero*, published in 1999. These interviews are reproduced verbatim in Parker's book. Fairweather is also said to have been threatened with expulsion from the SAS Regimental Association, presumably for the same reason. Neither warning seems to have had much effect.

The two circumstances are connected. Given his acts and omissions, it was vital for Fairweather to get his version of what had happened (for example, the "gun in the glove compartment" story) included in John Parker's narrative and laid before the public. Parker is a respected author and journalist who specialises in Defence subjects; his books sell well. There was therefore a good chance that *Death of a Hero* would come to be seen as the definitive account of Nairac's fate. This was an opportunity not to be missed and Fairweather took it. It proved, from his point of view, to be the right course of action. Despite Sir Michael Rose's scathing 1999 review of it in *The Tablet*, *Death of a Hero/Secret Hero* is now widely regarded as the best available account of Nairac, although – due in part to restrictions imposed on him by Nairac's family – it is not Parker's most accomplished book. Apart from that, Fairweather appears to have had a compulsive need to give his view on everything and above all to have the last word, whether or not he was well-qualified to opine. As a result, he seems to have been an interviewer's delight.

In 2008 Fairweather gave the last of his media interviews about Robert Nairac to *The Scotsman* newspaper, which had taken a close interest in Nairac's disappearance from Day One. This was couched – by his standards – in warm language and seemed to imply that he and Nairac had been quite friendly. But later in the same year, Fairweather had an unusually frank conversation with a member of an international organisation. Speaking in private with this senior official, it was another story. The subject of Nairac came up and Fairweather's mask came off: his enduring hatred of Nairac became obvious. According to him, Nairac was a fool, "a loose cannon" and wasted space. He said that when he was informed that Nairac was missing, he had assumed that he was "with a woman", and he "was not going to haul senior officers out of their beds over that". He seemed to imply that this had happened before. It had not, and it conflicts strangely with his other hints about Nairac's alleged homosexuality. He also claimed falsely that "we had absolutely no clue where Nairac was that evening". As we have seen, Nairac had formally sought authorisation from H Jones, the Brigade Major, and had notified the SAS Operations Officer, Captain Collett. Everyone who needed to know did know exactly where and when his meet would be taking place.

Finally, Fairweather made it clear that he did not think that Nairac had deserved the George Cross. He had indeed contributed language to the draft citation, but that had been on his superior officer's orders, not of his own volition. He had not been in favour of any award to Nairac. He had been "utterly astonished and disgusted" when he learned that Nairac was to receive this posthumous recognition: "He was not worth the GC". Earlier, in conversation with a former brother officer, Fairweather had dismissed Nairac as "a cowboy".

One of Fairweather's former brother officers and friends, who had also been close to Nairac, has said that in his view Fairweather had been "worried about the command and control of [Nairac] and where responsibility for him lay" while Nairac was alive, and that "I know he felt badly about [Nairac's fate]" after his murder. This might simply have reflected Fairweather's awareness that his interlocutor had been deeply attached to Nairac; he had therefore been making tactful but insincere remarks about him. Or it may have been an oblique way of saying that Fairweather had a lot on his conscience.

Fairweather's role has never, to anyone's knowledge, been closely scrutinised, still less criticised, presumably because he was such a distinguished man. Yet we cannot ignore the fact that Fairweather clearly disliked Nairac and had clashed with him on more than one occasion. Nairac might not have been deliberately fragged, but if the SAS had promptly activated the nearby Foresters COP team or their COP backup team at 11.45 pm or midnight, as Orders said that they should have, he could have been saved. They did not, because they were uncertain what to do and because Fairweather, when they finally reached him, gave orders to do nothing. By the time action was taken at 4.30 or 5.43 am, depending upon which narrative one accepts, Nairac was dead.

As noted earlier, the SAS Operations Officer broke the rules; his CO was careless and Fairweather's response, probably clouded by alcohol, was negligent. By telling the SAS to do nothing and contact nobody, he effectively sealed Nairac's fate. Later, panicking and concerned about his own career, Fairweather undertook some investigations and a damage limitation exercise, which did nothing to help Nairac, who was murdered at some point after 2.00 am. To suggest that Fairweather would have been completely sober is to do him no favours. If it should ever emerge that Fairweather was *not* affected by alcohol when he returned from his convivial evening in Saintfield, that would imply that he took the flawed decisions that led to Nairac's murder while thinking clearly and deliberately. On balance, Fairweather's apologists would be well-advised to choose the alcohol option.

One person who understood Nairac well was General Sir Jack Harman, who had been the Commandant of RMA Sandhurst when Nairac had been a student there in 1972-73, and later NATO's Deputy Supreme Allied Commander, Europe (DSACEUR). In 1979, shortly after the announcement of Nairac's posthumous George Cross award, he was quoted in *Soldier*, the Army's in-house magazine:

"Of course I knew that Robert Nairac would do great things. It was therefore utterly tragic that his life was cut short so soon. Obviously supremely courageous – I do not say without fear for it is only the truly brave who act courageously but who also know fear. Service before self was Robert's lodestar and his death is an eloquent mockery of happenings in the UK today. There are certainly few like him. It is only when one meets a Robert Nairac that life suddenly seems so very much worthwhile."

That could almost have been a Victorian writer describing General Gordon. At that moment the UK presented an unedifying spectacle. On 16 March 1976 Harold Wilson had suddenly announced his resignation as Prime Minister with effect from 5 April. The media speculated excitedly about Wilson's real reasons, but it was clear to anyone working in Whitehall at the time why he resigned at that moment. Like a car in a Hammer House of Horror movie, possessed of an evil spirit and careering out of control, the British economy was about to crash. An application for an IMF loan was now inevitable. The IMF's conditions would be very unpalatable; especially to the Trade Unions and many other Labour voters, who continued to live in a parallel universe. They were bitterly, even fanatically, opposed to any austerity measures: disbelieving in the parlous state of the economy, they were convinced that there was really plenty of money out there. It was just a matter of "squeezing the rich" – and commercial companies – to balance the books and achieve a more equitable redistribution – in their own favour. That was wishful thinking.

Harold Wilson did not live in a parallel universe: he saw what was going to happen and did not want to be in charge when it did. He refused the earldom that is customarily offered to Prime Ministers who retire while in office, but accepted the Order of the Garter; the most ancient and prestigious order of chivalry in the UK. For his first Garter ceremony at Windsor, Wilson would don recycled robes formerly worn by Field Marshal Viscount Montgomery, who had recently died. A few years earlier, in an interview with *Life* magazine, W H Auden had acidly observed that "Harold Wilson radiates conceit". Certainly he did so on that occasion. Sir Harold Wilson KG now prepared to assume the mantles of elder statesman and (he hoped) special adviser to The Queen, although this latter role did not materialise. Nevertheless in due course Wilson would become, among other honours, an Elder Brother of Trinity House, Privy Councillor, Fellow of the Royal Society and Baron Wilson of Rievaulx. In the nick of time Wilson had taken retirement amid fanfares and tributes, which in retrospect seem extremely ironic.

The "happenings in the UK today" to which Jack Harman was alluding in 1979 were the endless strikes being orchestrated by the Trade Unions for increased wages. Predictably, the Unions were reacting badly to the austerity programme that the IMF's economic rescue plan had imposed. "Service before self" was not being conspicuously practiced. While the Unions were clamouring for cash and threatening yet more mayhem if they did not get it, Army pay had lagged behind. People like Nairac were meanwhile giving their all in the Army. Not only that, but they would often be fiercely criticised for doing so. Given his selfless service ethic, Nairac did indeed belong to another, very different, era.

Robert Nairac was not the only brave and committed young man whose life was sacrificed to military incompetence and political expediency during Operation Banner; he was simply the best-known. The people who controlled him were drawing on a special reserve of human quality and courage, which Britain had once possessed in abundance, but which had been squandered in two World Wars. It was this kind of commitment and bravery that had won the Empire, but now the Empire had vanished and the lives of its grandsons were being wasted. That process would continue in Iraq and Afghanistan.

This book refers to Nairac as "a late Edwardian", given his tastes, interests and his views on a range of subjects. One might however argue that with his flamboyant bravery, his falcons, his military vocation, his code of honour and his love of adventure and espionage, Nairac could also be seen in some respects as a Renaissance man born out of time. Taking the comparison further, there are strange parallels between the lives of Robert Nairac and the Elizabethan poet, dramatist, dandy and under-cover secret agent, Christopher Marlowe. Marlowe, a Cambridge graduate, had been engaged in undercover work for Mr Secretary Walsingham and had likewise died at the height of his powers, violently and mysteriously – allegedly in a tavern brawl – at almost exactly the same age, nearly 400 years earlier:

"There is something in the meteor-like suddenness of his appearance..., and in the swift flaming of his genius through its course, that seems to make inevitable his violent end. He sums up for us the Renaissance passion for life, sleepless in its search and daring in its grasp after the infinite in power, in knowledge, and in pleasure."

This quotation from *A History of English Literature*, Seventh Edition, by Moody, Lovett and Millett, refers to Marlowe, but it could equally well describe Nairac. Like Marlowe, Robert Nairac has passed into legend and, although he was murdered well within living memory, many questions remain unanswered.

It is equally correct to call Nairac a Romantic, provided that we are clear about what that means. It is often incorrectly used to designate someone who is impractical, other-worldly or unrealistic. However Romanticism is really a life philosophy that rejects pure rationalism in favour of intuition, imagination, and emotion: the embrace of nonconformity and sincerity; a tendency towards nostalgia and the celebration of curiosity, spontaneity, and wonder. These qualities Nairac possessed in abundance. Romantic artists sought to create original works that sprang from their lively imagination. Nairac never did much painting, but he had the soul of an artist or a poet. He refused to see the world as dull and constrained, but rather viewed it as a magnificent landscape of possibilities, where the forces of good and the forces of evil did battle. Any man who possessed the necessary courage and will could join the fight and become a hero. In the words of the American author Thoreau, "Whoso would be a man must be a nonconformist." Not conforming did not exclude a love of history and tradition. That was indulged to the full, for example at Oxford, at Regimental dinners or formal balls in Mess Dress, and in church. Such rituals were essential for a rich, meaningful life. However, like Winston Churchill, Nairac "venerated tradition, but ridiculed convention". If he thought there was a better way of doing things, he followed that inspiration, and to hell with the approved procedures. He has been criticised, as well as praised, for this.

But in the end, he wins the argument. In Luke Jennings' words,

"I understand now why Robert was absolutist in his method, and why he spoke of honour and the dry fly in the same sentence. Because the rules we impose on ourselves are everything... It's not a question of wilfully making things harder, but of a purity of approach without which success has no meaning. And this, ultimately, was his lesson: that the fiercest joy is to be a spectator of your own conduct and to find no cause for complaint."

Not many of us can truthfully claim this. To achieve that, it is necessary to have great, diamond-hard integrity, like Nairac.

Nairac was one of the most interesting and complex soldiers whom the British Army had the good luck to attract in the twentieth century. Had he been born earlier and had the chance to serve in the Second World War, he would have surely found a place in the SAS as it was then constituted, the Army Commandos or the Chindits, and would probably have ended the war as a still-youthful Colonel or Brigadier. The Special Operations Executive (SOE), which conducted sabotage, espionage and reconnaissance in occupied Europe and aided local resistance movements, would have suited Nairac very well. Leaving speculation aside, the SOE had made successful use of the Amplefordian Hugh Dormer's talents; he and Nairac were very similar men, even to their common love of Kenya and falconry. Born earlier still, Nairac could have had a satisfying career in the Indian Army or the Indian Political Service. As it was, born in 1948 at the end of the Empire, he got caught up in the nastiest of the UK's savage little wars of peace, in Northern Ireland. In some respects he was very like his boyhood hero, Lawrence of Arabia. Had he lived longer, he might have become as celebrated an unconventional soldier as Lawrence, David Stirling, Billy McLean, Orde Wingate or "Mad Mike" Calvert. We may never know Nairac's full story: he took many secrets with him to his grave, wherever exactly that is. The best that we may be able to achieve is something akin to an almost complete jigsaw puzzle, of which Nairac himself will always hold the important final pieces.

Real heroes, unlike legendary ones, are fallible and have feet of clay; Nairac was no exception. Nevertheless, despite all his scrapes, follies and foibles, after all the legends have been exploded; when all his enemies have finished throwing their brickbats at him; when the smoke and dust have finally cleared, somehow Nairac is still standing. His integrity, intelligence, humour and courage trump everything and can never be taken away. Perhaps that is the greatest tribute we can pay him.

THE EPITAPH

On 14 May 2002 42 Commando of the Royal Marines held a short memorial service for Robert Nairac at Bessbrook Mill on the twenty-fifth anniversary of his murder. The reading was from the Book of Wisdom. This was a worthy epitaph for Nairac:

"The souls of the righteous are in the hand of God, and no torment will ever touch them. In the eyes of the foolish they seemed to have died, and their departure was thought to be a disaster, and their going from us to be their destruction; but they are at peace. For though in the sight of others they were punished, their hope is full of immortality. Having been disciplined a little, they will receive great good, because God tested them and found them worthy of himself; like gold in the furnace he tried them, and like a sacrificial burnt-offering he accepted them. In the time of their visitation they will shine forth, and will run like sparks through the stubble. They will govern nations and rule over peoples, and the Lord will reign over them forever. Those who trust in him will understand truth, and the faithful will abide with him in love, because grace and mercy are upon his holy ones, and he watches over his elect."

And even now the earth stands sentinel,
reaching back into itself for reminders of what happened
like a wound working a foreign body to the surface of the skin.

– extract taken from 'Mametz Wood' by Owen Sheers
from *Skirrid Hill* (Seren, 2005).

APPENDIX 1 | NAIRAC TIMELINE

1945-47: Prelude

1945: The end of World War II. British General Election: Labour majority 146 seats; "the Labour landslide". Clement Attlee Prime Minister.

1946: Robert Nairac's parents and three elder children move to Maurice Nairac's native Mauritius.

15 August 1947: The end of the British Indian Empire: India and Pakistan become independent within the Commonwealth.

20 November 1947: Wedding of HRH Princess Elizabeth and Lieutenant Philip Mountbatten RN in Westminster Abbey. Household Division Regiments revert to Home Service Clothing for this event.

22 June 1948: HM King George VI ceases to be Emperor of India.

1948-59: Early Youth

1948-60: The Malayan Emergency.

31 August 1948: Robert Laurence Nairac is born in Mauritius.

21 December 1948: Eire passes the Republic of Ireland Act.

18 April 1949: Eire becomes the Republic of Ireland, leaves the Commonwealth and cuts all remaining formal ties with the UK. The British Ireland Act of 1949 also enters into force.

July 1949: The Nairacs move back to the UK, settling in Sunderland. Maurice Nairac begins practice as an ophthalmic eye-surgeon at Sunderland Infirmary.

1950: British General Election: Labour majority 5; Clement Attlee remains Prime Minister.

1950-53: The Korean War.

1951: British General Election: Conservative majority 17: Sir Winston Churchill Prime Minister.

6 February 1952: Death of King George VI. HM Queen Elizabeth II returns to the UK from Kenya.

1952-1960: The Mau Mau insurgency in Kenya.

2 June 1953: Coronation of HM Queen Elizabeth II. Most non-Household

Division regiments restore Full Dress uniform for this event; in some cases only for the Regimental Band and a Colour Party.

September 1953: Robert Nairac starts primary day school in Sunderland.

5 April 1955: Sir Winston Churchill resigns as Prime Minister and is succeeded by Sir Anthony Eden.

26 May 1955: British General Election: Conservative majority 60.

1956-60: The Cyprus Emergency.

26 July 1956: Nasser nationalises the Suez Canal: start of the Suez Crisis.

September 1956: Robert Nairac starts boarding school at Gilling Castle, a feeder school for Ampleforth College.

5 November 1956: British and French troops land at Port Said: intervention aborted two days later under US pressure. This marks the end of the Suez Crisis: the UK's role as a great international player is now also at an end.

9 January 1957: Sir Anthony Eden resigns as Prime Minister, citing a health problem and is succeeded by Harold Macmillan.

8 October 1959: British General Election, Conservative majority 100.

1960-68: Ampleforth and Adolescence

September 1960: Robert Nairac enters College, the junior school of Ampleforth College.

31 December 1960: Call-ups for National Service formally end. Conscription continues for those whose call-up has been deferred for any reason.

1962-67: The Aden insurgency.

1962: Dr David Laurence Nairac, Robert Nairac's elder brother, dies suddenly at the age of 24. Nairac enters St Edward's House, Ampleforth College.

1963: Last full year of Conservative government. Kenya becomes independent within the Commonwealth.

1963-66: The Borneo Counter-Insurgency.

May 1963: Last National Servicemen leave the British Armed Forces, ending 24 years of conscription.

5 June 1963: Secretary of State for War John Profumo resigns, having knowingly misled Parliament over his relationship with Christine Keeler.

26 September 1963: *The Denning Report* on the Profumo Scandal is published.

It concludes that there has been no security breach.

18 October 1963: Harold MacMillan resigns as Prime Minister and Leader of the Conservative Party, citing a health problem, and is succeeded by Sir Alec Douglas-Home.

1964: Maurice Nairac becomes a Consultant at the Royal Gloucestershire Hospital. About this time the Nairacs move from Sunderland to Master's Keep in Standish, Gloucestershire.

1 April 1964: Unified Ministry of Defence created: abolition of the historic Cabinet Ministerial posts of First Lord of the Admiralty, Secretary of State for War and Secretary of State for Air. Peter Thorneycroft becomes the first Secretary of State for Defence. The Chief of the Imperial General Staff (CIGS) changes his title to Chief of the General Staff (CGS).

15 October 1964: British General Election: Labour majority of 4. Thirteen years of Conservative rule end. Harold Wilson becomes the first Labour Prime Minister since 1951.

January 1965: Sir Winston Churchill dies and receives a State funeral.

1965-66: Nairac is Head of St Edward's House, Ampleforth College. He sits his A Level exams. He is now a Cadet Under-Officer in the CCF, Captain of Boxing and a member of the First XV rugby team. He applies to several universities.

March 1966: The prelude to the Troubles: Irish Republicans celebrate the fiftieth anniversary of the Dublin Easter Rising with marches and ceremonies. They blow up Nelson's Pillar in Dublin.

September 1966: Nairac returns to Ampleforth for an extra term to prepare for the Oxford entry exam and interviews.

December 1966: Nairac attends entry exam and interviews at Oxford.

1967: The Falconry Centre opens at Newent, Gloucestershire.

January 1967 – July 1968: Nairac works as an uncertified Assistant Master at Avisford School, teaching History, French and Games. He applies again to Oxford, giving Lincoln College as his first choice.

November 1967: The UK abandons Aden, which plunges into civil war.

December 1967: Nairac again attempts the Oxford entry exam and interviews. Lincoln College accepts him.

1968: The only year since 1945 in which no British soldiers were killed in battle.

24 March 1968: Nairac's native Mauritius becomes independent within the Commonwealth.

May-June 1968: "Les événéments de mai", a volatile period of civil unrest in France marked by demonstrations, large-scale strikes and the occupation of colleges and factories throughout France. There are copy-cat events in other countries, including Northern Ireland, where civil unrest escalates.

1968-71: Oxford Undergraduate

Early October 1968: Nairac goes up to Lincoln College, Oxford, to study Modern History. He becomes Captain of the Oxford University Amateur Boxing Club (OUABC) and plays for the Greyhounds (Second XV) rugby team. He becomes a Boxing Blue.

1969: The Army is ordered into Northern Ireland. The Troubles begin in earnest.

1969-70 (academic year): Nairac lives out of college on Boar's Hill with Julian Malins and two other undergraduates.

18 June 1970: British General Election. The Conservatives, led by Edward Heath, return to office.

1970-71 (academic year): Nairac moves back into college.

6 February 1971: An IRA gunman shoots Gunner Robert Curtis in Belfast. He is the first soldier to be killed in the Troubles.

Late 1971: Nairac applies for, and is accepted by, the Grenadier Guards. He passes his Regular Commissioning Board (RCB). He is awarded a university cadetship for his last two terms at Oxford.

23 December 1971: Nairac is taken on strength (TOS) by the Grenadier Guards. He is now 2/Lt R L Nairac. He is also TOS by Oxford University OTC.

30 January 1972: The Bloody Sunday incident in Londonderry.

June 1972: Nairac graduates from Oxford with a Third-Class Honours BA degree in History. This is balanced by numerous sporting and athletic distinctions.

31 July 1972: Operation Motorman: the Army demolishes barriers round Republican enclaves in Londonderry and Belfast.

1972-74: Sandhurst and Soldiering in Belfast with the Second Battalion Grenadier Guards

September 1972 – January 1973. Nairac attends the POSUC No 1 Course at the Royal Military Academy (RMA), Sandhurst. He continues to box and plays in the Sandhurst First XV rugby team. He is awarded Full Colours for rugby. He passes out with a "well above average" marking.

February 1973: Nairac joins the Second Battalion Grenadier Guards as a Lieutenant.

February – June 1973: Nairac on Public Duties in London.

March 1973: Nairac's first Northern Ireland (NI) tour of duty. Nairac and his Battalion are on duty in Belfast for two weeks, immediately prior to and during the Northern Ireland Constitutional Referendum.

June 1973: Nairac takes part in Trooping the Colour (The Queen's Birthday Parade).

1 July: Nairac's second NI tour. Nairac arrives in Belfast with the Second Battalion Grenadier Guards Advance Party.

9 July – 31 October 1973: Nairac on duty in Belfast with the Second Battalion Grenadier Guards.

1-14 November 1973: Following the departure of the Battalion to Hong Kong, Nairac remains *in situ* to assist the First Battalion The Argyll and Sutherland Highlanders.

1974-75: Service with NITAT (NI) at Castle Dillon

Early 1974: Nairac trains for a new role with NITAT (NI), based at Castle Dillon.

28 February 1974: British General Election. Hung Parliament: Labour minority Government (-33), led by Harold Wilson.

17 May 1974: the Dublin and Monaghan car-bombings take place.

21 May 1974: Nairac returns to Northern Ireland, having completed his training. His third NI tour of duty begins. He joins NITAT (NI)'s Castle Dillon "spook" detachment.

10 October 1974: British General Election: Labour majority of 3. Harold Wilson remains Prime Minister.

10 January 1975: Murder of John Francis Green (IRA) in the Republic.

11 February 1975: Margaret Thatcher replaces Edward Heath as Leader of the Conservative Party and Leader of the Opposition.

1975-76: Regimental Duties with the First Battalion Grenadier Guards

Mid-April 1975: Nairac returns to the UK and takes a month's leave.

19 May 1975: Nairac reports for duty with the First Battalion Grenadier Guards, based mainly at Chelsea Barracks in London. He is initially Joint Assistant Adjutant of the First Battalion.

17 June – 11 July 1975: Nairac runs a training course for NCOs at Pirbright.

12 July 1975: Nairac is appointed Commander of the First Battalion Grenadier Guards Recce Platoon. He is now Acting Captain.

13-26 July 1975: Nairac and his Battalion train on Salisbury Plain. He meets HRH the Duke of Edinburgh, the new Colonel of the Regiment, during a visit.

29-30 July 1975: Nairac attends various conferences and meetings in London.

31 July 1975: The First Battalion is now on block leave for two weeks. Nairac departs for a fishing holiday in South Uist.

31 July 1975 (late evening): The Miami Showband Massacre in Northern Ireland.

13 August 1975: Nairac returns to London.

14 August 1975: Operation Trustee begins at Heathrow in which Nairac is involved.

4 September 1975: Nairac passes his Practical Promotion Exam in Edinburgh. He is confirmed as Substantive Captain w.e.f. this date. About this time Nairac belatedly receives the General Service Medal (GSM) with clasp for Northern Ireland.

19 September 1975: Nairac visits AG2 at Stanmore, to discuss his future.

12 December 1975: Nairac is photographed in Full Dress uniform with his GSM by Bassano, a London Court photographer.

December 1975 - January 1976: Nairac is heavily involved at Pirbright in final preparations for deployment of his battalion to Kenya for field survival training.

5 January 1976: The Kingsmills Massacre in Northern Ireland.

10-20 January 1976: Nairac's Battalion moves to Kenya for training.

2 March 1976: Sterling falls below $2 US.

16 March 1976: Harold Wilson announces his imminent resignation as Prime Minister.

March – May 1976: Nairac on Junior Command and Staff Course at Warminster. He is assessed "well above average", with a recommendation for early promotion. He receives briefing and relevant SAS training at Hereford.

5 April 1976: James Callaghan is elected as Labour Leader and becomes Prime Minister.

15 April 1976: SAS kill Peter Cleary (IRA) in Northern Ireland, apparently while he is attempting to escape from their custody.

5-6 May 1976: The "SAS Border Incident", in which eight SAS men are arrested in the Republic.

May 1976: Nairac attends retirement dinner for Alf Gallie (OUABC boxing coach) in Oxford.

1975-76: Final Tour of Duty in South Armagh

June 1976: Nairac's fourth NI tour. He returns to South Armagh, this time based mainly at Bessbrook Mill, officially as SAS Liaison Officer (SASLO) but really in an intelligence role.

November 1976: Nairac attends the annual Vincent's Club Dinner in London. He meets Julian Malins and other Oxford friends for the last time.

December 1976: Nairac attends the 3 Company, First Battalion Grenadier Guards Christmas celebration in Middletown, Co. Armagh.

December 1976/January 1977: Nairac is a shooting guest at Eastnor Castle.

January 1977: Clive Fairweather arrives in NI as GSO2 Int/Liaison in Northern Ireland. The Devon and Dorsets start a tour of duty in Belfast (Jan – May). H Jones becomes Brigade Major of 3 Infantry Brigade, based in Portadown.

16 January 1977: SAS ambush and kill Seamus Harvey (IRA) near the border with the Republic.

Late January – early March 1977: Nairac is in Belfast attached to the Devon and Dorsets. While he is patrolling in Ardoyne, an IRA photographer identifies and photographs him.

March 1977: Nairac takes a short leave break in the UK, when he visits his parents in Gloucestershire for the last time.

Late March/early April 1977: Nairac returns to South Armagh.

April-May 1977: Nairac makes tentative contact with a possible informer, though an intermediary. He visits the Three Steps Bar in Drumintee more than once.

Friday 13 May 1977: Nairac meets a representative of the potential informer near Newry courthouse. He waits for the informer in the Three Steps Inn, Drumintee.

Saturday 14 May 1977: Nairac goes trout fishing in the Republic and returns about 4 pm. He takes a telephone call and again agrees to meet in the Three Steps.

9.25 pm Saturday 14 May 1977: Nairac travels by car from Bessbrook Mill to the Three Steps, making radio contact three times during the journey.

9.59 pm: Nairac makes his fourth and final radio contact from the Three Steps.

00.00 Midnight 14-15 May 1977: Nairac misses a mandatory radio check.

00.15-00.30 am Sunday 15 May 1977 (approx): Nairac is abducted by IRA supporters and taken to a location in the Republic near Ravensdale Forest.

01.00 am – 02.30 am Sunday 15 May 1977 (approx): Nairac is interrogated, tortured and murdered.

05.43 am Sunday 15 May 1977: The alarm is raised. Brigade, the RUC and the Garda are notified. The search for Captain Nairac begins. Nairac's parents are informed that he is missing.

Monday 16 May 1977: The IRA announce that they have interrogated and "executed" Captain Nairac.

18 May 1977: Anglers lead Irish police to two sites near Ravensdale Forest where evidence of Nairac's torture and murder is found.

21 May 1977: An article appears in the PIRA newspaper and others, with the photograph of Nairac taken in Ardoyne in early 1977. His assassins, apart from three who flee to the USA, are arrested.

1978 – 2015: The Aftermath

1978: The first edition of Philip Glasier's authoritative book *Falconry and Hawking* is published, dedicated to Captain Robert Nairac.

18 April 1978: Nairac's memorial service is held in the Guards' Chapel.

16 October 1978: Nairac's death certificate is issued in the Republic.

15 December 1978: The first BBC NI *Spotlight* programme on *The Search for Captain Nairac*, by Roisin McAuley, is broadcast.

13 February 1979: Nairac's parents receive his posthumous George Cross from HM the Queen.

1981: Michael Cunningham privately publishes *The Nairac Affair*.

4 May 1984: The *New Statesman* publishes an article, "Dirty War: An ex-Northern Ireland Army Officer Tells All".

1987: Ken Livingstone MP makes his maiden speech in the Commons.

1989: Fred Holroyd publishes *War Without Honour*.

15 June 1991: At The Queen's Birthday Parade the massed bands perform a new slow march *Nairac GC*, composed by Colonel Stuart Watts.

1992: Basil Dykes, Nairac's uncle, dies. Anthony Bradley's *Requiem for a Spy: The Killing of Robert Nairac* is published in Ireland.

1993: Nairac's father dies.

Early 1999: John Parker's biography of Nairac, *Death of a Hero*, is published.

17 April 1999: Sir Michael Rose's review of *Death of a Hero* is published in *The Tablet*.

27 April 1999: The Independent Commission for the Location of Victims' Remains (ICLVR) is established by an intergovernmental agreement between the Irish and British Governments.

24 November 1999: Nairac's mother dies.

6 May 2000: On behalf of The Royal Society of St George, the Rt. Rev. Michael Mann KCVO, Dean of Windsor, dedicates a stained-glass window in memory of Nairac in St Mary de Lode Church, Gloucester.

14 May 2002: The 25th anniversary of Nairac's murder. The resident Royal Marines garrison hold a service for Nairac in Bessbrook Mill.

2004: John Parker's Nairac biography *Death of a Hero* republished with new material as Secret Hero. Toby Harnden's short biography of Nairac published in *The Dictionary of National Biography*. Eoin McNamee's "faction" novel about Nairac, *The Ultras*, is also published.

19 June 2007: A BBC NI *Spotlight* programme on *The Search for Captain Nairac* by Darragh McIntyre is broadcast.

7 March 2009: A Republican paramilitary group, the Real IRA, shoots dead two off-duty Royal Engineers outside Massereene Barracks in Antrim Town. They are the first British military fatalities in Northern Ireland since 1997.

9 March 2009: The Continuity IRA shoots dead a Police Service of Northern Ireland (PSNI) officer; the first Northern Irish police officer to be killed by paramilitaries since 1998.

2010: Luke Jennings' angling memoir, *Blood Knots*, is published.

2011: Kevin Crilly is tried for complicity in Nairac's murder, but is acquitted.

13 October 2012: Colonel Clive Fairweather dies.

November 2012: Memorial Service for Fairweather in the Canongate Church, Edinburgh, followed by a Reception.

2015: Robert Nairac's remains have still not been discovered.

APPENDIX 2 | LAST PORTRAITS

*All photographs are memento mori. To take a photograph is to participate
in another person's (or thing's) mortality, vulnerability, mutability.
Precisely by slicing out this moment and freezing it, all photographs
testify to time's relentless melt.* (Susan Sontag)

The last photographs known, or alleged, to have been taken of Robert Nairac
before his abduction and murder in May 1977 may offer clues as to what he was
doing and how he came to meet his death. These are:

"The IRA Photo" of Nairac and Young People in Ardoyne

Reproduced with kind permission. ©PA Photos.

A fuller account is given in *Chapter 13: The Human Factor*. This is the well-
known image of Nairac talking to young people in the Republican and Catholic
Ardoyne district of Belfast, which appeared in the PIRA newspaper *Republican
News* and in the Irish and foreign Press shortly after his murder. It was supplied
by the IRA, who stated that they had taken the photo. This may be the last photo
ever taken of Robert Nairac. It is certainly one of the last, taken in early 1977,
probably February or March: two to three months before Nairac's death. Several
of Nairac's former friends and colleagues have attested that it definitely depicts
him; his broken nose is noticeable in profile.

On this occasion Nairac was disguised as a member of another regiment, which
was serving in Belfast at that time – he was going on patrol with them and he

wanted to blend in. The regiment was the Devonshire and Dorsetshire Regiment (The Devon and Dorsets); Major H Jones's regiment, which was based in Belfast from January to May 1977. It looks as though Nairac is wearing a Devon and Dorsets beret. A former Devon and Dorsets officer has confirmed that Nairac did indeed wear their beret in early 1977 and that he went on patrol with them in Ardoyne. This is fairly conclusive proof that the photo was taken in early 1977, as the IRA maintain.

It has been suggested that the initiative to bring Nairac back to Belfast early in 1977 might have come from the future Lieutenant General Sir Cedric Delves KBE DSO, then a high-achieving young Devon and Dorsets Captain, already marked for fast track promotion like Nairac himself. This is certainly plausible. Delves had successfully persuaded senior officers to adopt a scheme to bring knowledgeable officers back to areas where they had formerly served and where they knew from experience whom and what to look for, to assist and advise the regiment currently stationed there.

"The SAS Party Photo", said to be Nairac in scruffy civilian clothes

Reproduced with under licence. ©Press Eye, Belfast.

This photo has frequently been reproduced – in *Soldier* magazine in March 1979, among other places – and has long been accepted as the last photograph of Robert Nairac. The photograph is stated to depict a very scruffy undercover Nairac drinking at a party in the private SAS bar at Bessbrook Mill shortly before his disappearance. It appears to show him with his hair worn long and a full moustache. A copy of it, with a slightly inaccurate short biography, now hangs in the Special Forces Club in London. However, its authenticity is now disputed. It is definitely not Nairac's last photo and might not be of him at all. For example, the man's nose does not appear to be broken, whereas Nairac's unquestionably was. But it has been suggested that this is an old, grainy photo and it could be a trick of the light that the nose appears unbroken.

Nairac was allowed to drink in the SAS bar; he was one of the few non-SAS people to whom the SAS extended this privilege. However, the SAS do not usually permit photographs to be taken in any SAS bar or other establishment. Moreover the photo might have been taken in an Operations Room, not a bar: the 1:25,000 Ordinance Survey Map of Northern Ireland is visible pinned on the wall behind the man.

An alternative explanation has been proposed by a former brother Grenadier Guards officer: he thinks that it might be Nairac. He commented that if it is, he looks younger than he did in 1977. So it might have been taken during his 1974-75 tour of duty, when he was slimmer and much less stocky and muscular than he later became. A drawback to this theory is that undisputed photos of Nairac taken in 1974-75 exist and they do not resemble this photo. Almost all of them show him with prominent sideburns and a shock of curly hair which is still too long by Army standards but shorter than, and unlike, the hair of the man in the "SAS Party" photo. An examples of this is reproduced here. They resemble the picture on his Army ID card, also taken in 1974.

Reproduced with kind permission of a brother officer and friend of Nairac's who wishes to remain anonymous.

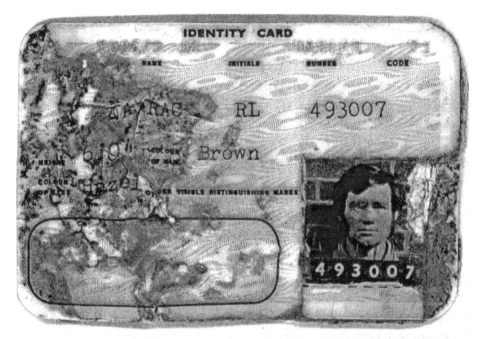

Julian Malins is characteristically forthright: "I do not think it is Nairac. The eyes are wrong. If it is him, then he is wearing a wig, has had a false nose fitted and is maybe under the influence of drink and/or drugs which could just about explain the eyes. But as I say, I do not believe it is Nairac."

If the photo is not of Nairac, who could it be? The mysterious photo's copyright belongs today to a small Belfast Press agency, Press Eye. They were unable to give much information about its provenance, whose copyright they had acquired in good faith, on the understanding that it did depict Captain Nairac. If it genuinely dates from the 1970s, as it appears to, it predates the birth of the present owner of the company. The copyright has changed hands more than once. It would now be difficult, if not impossible, to locate the original photographer even if he were still alive.

The Formal Photographs

This formal portrait of Robert Nairac shows him in 1975. The photograph, by Bassano of London, forms part of the collection held by the National Portrait Gallery. © Copyright NPG 2015.

Formal photographs exist of Nairac, taken during his last UK posting in 1975-76. Some are regimental group photos, including those taken while he was running the Grenadier Guards Corporals' Cadre in 1975. The best ones are a series of formal portraits, taken in December 1975 by Bassano, a fashionable London Court photographer. None of the photographs described above is very revealing, nor are the regimental groups. However Bassano's portrait photographs of Nairac in his Grenadier Guards Home Service Clothing are good character studies. They could have been taken to celebrate Nairac's substantive Captaincy, which was confirmed in September 1975, or his General Service Medal with Northern Ireland clasp, which he received in late 1975, or both. These give a better idea of the formidably tough, intelligent, humorous man whose friends still miss him today. They were used as the basis of the posthumous oil paintings of Nairac that hang today in Wellington Barracks, the Guards Museum and Sandhurst. In the Sandhurst and Guards Museum oil portraits a smile has been painted onto his rather stern features. When Bassano's business was wound up, the National Portrait Gallery in London acquired those photos and negatives that were considered to be of historic interest; Nairac's portraits were among them.

Jonathan Forbes commented on these portraits, "This is basically how I remember Nairac, (at) that brief meeting in Portadown in (?) late Oct: or early Nov: 1976, when some of us from 1GG went up one morning to meet relevant RUC/SB individuals for our N Armagh tour. I recall talking briefly (I think in the passage outside his office) with Robert and that, if correct, his office door had 'SASLO' on it. I don't think he had lunch with us that day and I did not attend the Grenadier Guards 1976 Christmas lunch in Northern Ireland that someone said he attended. My recollection [on that occasion] was that he was casually dressed, and although his hair was longer than a 'regimental' cut, it was nothing like the SAS party... photograph shown here. To me, he was his usual self, with the confident air that you tell me his friends had noted at the 1976 Vincent's Club dinner."

Conclusions

What can we learn from these photos? If there were still any doubt, the "IRA Photo" indicates that Nairac had come to the notice of the IRA's senior commanders in Belfast. He admitted as much to friends in unguarded conversations in London, which caused them great concern. However it is not clear that he was ever the object of a kidnap or murder plot by the IRA. A former IRA volunteer has implied that he was not yet trusted, but was seen as being of potential interest and possibly sympathetic to their cause. They were using people to talk to him and draw him out. For the IRA his appearance in Belfast in uniform must have been very helpful, laying to rest any lingering doubts that they may have had that he was indeed an undercover soldier and an important operative; in other words, someone worth talking to. They managed to get a good photo of him while he was there.

Nairac's undercover work was stressful. This is confirmed by the available evidence: the increasingly serious and preoccupied demeanour of a normally exuberant and humorous man during the last two months of his life; the sporadic contact with his family. Friends in Gloucestershire recall that during the last home leaves he spent there, from mid-1976 to March 1977, he would often drive for long distances; not using the most direct route, between his home and the houses of friends, to shake off anyone who might be following him, and avoid endangering the friends on whom he was calling.

This was not paranoia. At that time Gloucestershire had quite a large expatriate Irish population, some of whom had Republican sympathies. There are still enough of them to support a St Patrick's Gaelic Athletic Club in Gloucester itself. Nairac would have known this. He had boxed and taught boxing at a club in Gloucester during the academic vacations: no doubt he met young Irishmen there. It is just possible that his match against Martin Meehan, if it ever happened, happened in Gloucester at the boxing club. Nairac's last home leave with his family was in March 1977. When he drove him to the airport, his father asked him to be especially careful. Nairac promised that he would be, and added that his chief concern was that his father should approve of what he was doing. Maurice Nairac replied, "If you are doing what you see as your duty... then I approve."

APPENDIX 3 | SEX AND THE SINGLE SPOOK

Ever since his life was taken suddenly and brutally in the County Louth countryside nearly four decades ago, rumours about Robert Nairac's sexuality have been part of the story, along with the who, where and why of his terrible death. Rather like Lawrence of Arabia, a figure in English history with similarities to Nairac – and some important differences – the question of his sexuality appears to have become inseparable from his extraordinary career in the service of Queen and country; even though it played no evident part in the violent interaction with those who took his life in the early hours of 15 May 1977. In the somewhat irrelevant and unseemly debate that has ensued about whether Robert Nairac preferred his own or the female sex, one thing is beyond dispute: the opportunity for sexual dalliance of any sort for a single and unattached military officer engaged in the delicate and dangerous intelligence war in Northern Ireland was almost non-existent, except when he was on leave in the UK or somewhere else outside Northern Ireland.

Whatever Nairac might have done in Northern Ireland, one of his former "spook" colleagues there offered this crucial testimony:

"I have no evidence of Robert's sexuality in either direction. But having said that I should perhaps write a line or two on the subject of 'Sex and the Single Spook'!

"For someone in Robert's position (or indeed mine), access to girls was not easy. The army had very few females in NI and none at all in field intelligence work since the Four Square Laundry incident. Workwise, this was a lack we felt very strongly indeed. A man and a woman can go places and do things that would make a lone man or worse two men very conspicuous. I was only ever able to "borrow" a woman once for a very low risk job. This was a RN Sub-Lt attached to 45 Commando RM and I think she got a mega bollocking as a result.

"Socially, how was one to meet a civilian girl? There was the house of beauties who worked for the civilian spooks, but they were increasingly in purdah. You could hardly go to a pub and pick someone up – look what happened to the three Scots kids. If you had good local contacts outside work you might meet some singles there. My cousin worked quite hard to set me up. The COs of the SMIU sometimes had parties in their quarters in Lisburn and would invite single female soldiers – but girls on short tours could no more go out of an evening than males on OP Banner tours. There were of course female RUC officers, but not many. Female UDR soldiers? Well yes, but there were serious security issues there too. There were some long tour women with the RMP [Royal Military Police] but dating a WRMP was fraught with career danger, especially if there was a rank difference.

"And if you did meet someone would they be happy going out with a chap who always carried at least a pistol, spent quite a lot of time on anti-surveillance drills and wouldn't sit with his back to a door? I met someone who would, but she had six brothers in the RUC and thought looking under a car before you got in and sleeping with a pistol under the pillow was something everybody did. I met her at an officers' mess party.

"During my first tour of two years I had one brief fling with a local girl I met at my cousin's house. She was a civil servant, but in the end the guns and uncertainty were too much for her.

"In the same tour I 'picked up' one girl only and she was an object lesson in danger. She was a very nice kid and very pretty – but she lived in the Falls Road and it transpired she knew all the players (and hated them). I bailed out very rapidly.

"On hows and wheres, I think it would be virtually impossible to carry on a sexual relationship in a NI barracks. In Bessbrook it would be impossible. All the officers' rooms were soft board cubicles, some of which didn't reach the roof. Soldiers were in huge dorms. So where else? How would they get away to be alone together off duty? And again where?

"Again as an example, my nephew, a major in the RA, was courting a fellow officer (female) who was in the HQ in which he worked. They believed they were so careful that nobody had any idea. When the Brigade deployed to Afghanistan they were living in adjacent cabins made from steel shipping containers. A week or two into the tour they went off duty to discover on their return that the soldiers had cut a "secret" door between their two containers. *The Boys always know*!!!"

Three authors in particular have chosen to make an issue out of Nairac's sex life, or rather of his alleged sexual interests. One is Anthony Bradley (born 1932); a former freelance journalist who is apparently still alive and living in Belfast. He wrote a bitterly unjust and inaccurate book about Nairac entitled *Requiem for a Spy: the Killing of Robert Nairac*, published by Mercier Press (Cork) in 1993. In it he writes: "Running alongside that are persistent rumours from various quarters that the ultra-masculine Nairac was a man who battled against homosexual leanings. At times their pull was too strong for him and his resistance crumbled, so they say. In at least one case, according to one man who was close to both parties, that resulted in a passionately committed gay affair which was still going on at the time of Nairac's death."

The truthful part of this assertion is the reference to the "persistent rumours". The rumours do indeed persist to the present day. So do a lot of other rumours, despite that fact they do not usually stand up to scrutiny. Elsewhere, Bradley states that Nairac's keenness on boxing and other macho sports was explicable by his alleged orientation:

"There are those who claim that the magnet here was the need to demonstrate his own ambiguous manhood and, if that be so, then it is something that he shared with the homosexual warrior Alexander the Great and the Second World War SAS hero, Colonel Blair Mayne, the Belfast lawyer who was also an Irish [and British Lions] rugby international. He [Mayne] was a man whose heroism rested on a degenerate framework of homosexual sadism."

Bradley does not say who his sources in "various quarters" were. Nor is it clear whether he actually spoke to the man who was "close to both parties", or whether he is, as seems often to be the case, merely repeating double-hearsay. I suspect that Bradley eagerly seized upon any rumour, however insubstantial, that was potentially damaging to Nairac. I tried to contact him through his publishers, but Bradley never responded. Given that Bradley is passionately anti-British and anti-Nairac, and that his book is inaccurate about many things; even getting basic CV details like Nairac's age at the time of his death (28, not 29) and place of birth (Mauritius, not Sunderland) wrong, he cannot be relied on. He seems to assume that there is an ineluctable read-across from Blair Mayne to Nairac. There is not: there might just possibly have been, if they had known each other or had been genetically related, like T E Lawrence and Orde Wingate, but that was not the case.

John Cassidy, another freelance writer who also lives in Northern Ireland, repeats a similar story in his article "Nel of a Liar" in *The Sunday Mirror* in 2001. This concerns Nel Lister/Oonagh Flynn, a compulsive liar and fantasist, who has since been discredited, who claimed among other things to have been Nairac's lover and to have borne his child. In it Cassidy states that former soldiers laughed at the suggestion:

"But those who knew Nairac from his days working in South Armagh said the Grenadier Guards Captain was known to be gay. 'We all knew Nairac was a homosexual. He was having a relationship with a member of the Armed Forces in one of the camps,' said a former soldier last week."

I have spoken with Mr Cassidy, who, frustratingly, cannot now recall his "former soldier" source. He promised to look through his 2001 notes for me, but came up with nothing. He put me in touch with a former UDR soldier, who he thought might have been the source of the story, but the man denied it, although he had known Nairac (under the *nom-de-guerre* of "Captain Charles Johnston") and had liked and respected him. He had not been aware of the rumours.

In addition, the late Colonel Clive Fairweather (GSO2 Int/Liaison at HQ Northern Ireland), who disliked Nairac intensely, dropped tantalising hints of homosexuality in his numerous interviews about him with the media and researchers; for example with John Parker, the author of *Death of a Hero*. I suspect that at least some of the defamatory stories about Nairac can be traced to Fairweather, who died in 2012.

In *The Irish Times* and the now defunct *Hibernia* magazine, there appeared in 1977 a curious story that a soldier who was apparently very close to Nairac had killed himself soon after he disappeared. This, we were implicitly invited to understand, was the alleged "Army boyfriend". The author was a respected Dublin journalist, Niall Kiely. I have not been able to discover a death among the numerous deaths in Northern Ireland about that time that are not attributable to terrorist action, which would exactly fit the description. However further inquiry indicated that the young man was probably killed in a drunk-driving accident. This might or might not have been suicide and might or might not have been connected with Nairac. Mr Kiely does not now recall his source, or even having written the story, but he commented that:

"I've a vivid enough memory of hitting the Three Steps Inn in Dromintee the morning after [Nairac's] abduction; and my local contacts in the area at that time were pretty good. I'd come across his spoor earlier, and almost couldn't believe what I was told he'd been up to; it turned out he had been (up to it). I suspect there were *more than a few suicides or self-harming cries for help from the poor divils climbing the walls in various barracks/compounds in the 1970s* [author's italics], but Irish reporters tended to hear only scuttlebutt, and the B-Army fed us flannel and fluff; we understood why."

Virtually all of the assertions about Nairac's private life made thus far appear to fall into the category of double-hearsay. Unless a credible witness comes out of the shadows, perhaps in response to having read this book, and says: "You are quite wrong: I was Robert Nairac's lover between (dates)," we shall never know the answer to this riddle.

In conclusion, although one can never be dogmatic about someone else's private life, it seems that Robert Nairac's chances of having an amorous affair of any kind in Northern Ireland, and of keeping it secret, were slim. There is no reliable evidence to suggest that he did, or that he even had the time or inclination for such activities.

APPENDIX 4 | *THE NAIRAC AFFAIR* BY MICHAEL CUNNINGHAM

I have made a few references in the text to *The Nairac Affair,* which Michael Cunningham self-published in 1981. This author also wrote as Micheal O'Cuinneagain. His book, which is long out of print and hard to obtain, is of historic interest, if only because it was the first book, as opposed to article, ever written about Robert Nairac, only four years after his murder. For that reason some other authors (e.g. Anthony Bradley in *Requiem for a Spy*) have used it and referred to it.

They would, however, have been unwise to have relied on it as a source. *The Nairac Affair* bristles with inaccuracies, a few of which are unintentionally quite funny. For example, Cunningham quoted "a Sub-Rector in Lincoln" as having said something kind about Nairac after his murder. He seemed to infer that a Sub-Rector was some kind of Anglican clergyman, like a Curate or Minor Canon. In reality Nairac had no connection with Lincoln or Lincolnshire. The author of the quotation was the Sub-Rector of Lincoln *College,* Oxford, which was Nairac's old college. The Head of Lincoln College is known as the Rector and his deputy is the Sub-Rector. Heads of other Oxford colleges are called the Warden, the President, the Master, the Principal, the Provost or the Dean (of Christ Church only): there is no uniform usage.

The Nairac Affair is a bitterly anti-British and anti-Nairac Republican rant, starting with the Foreword, which sets the tone. The book is stated to be:

"... a brief examination of some of the events in South Armagh and North Louth in the period 1976-1977 involving Captain Nairac of the 22nd Special Air Service (SAS) Regiment. This Regiment caused untold suffering on both sides of the Irish Border. The unjust conviction of two young Catholic men, for murder, bears testimony to the evil influence of Captain Nairac and his fellow SAS men. This evil appears to have permeated every sector of the legal process, North and South."

The "two young Catholic men" who were allegedly unjustly convicted were John Anthony McCooey, who was convicted of the five 1975 Tullyvallen Orange Hall murders and Nairac's murderer, Liam Townson. Cunningham tried to link the Nairac murder with Tullyvallen Orange Hall. There was no connection. He saw it as his mission *inter alia* to clear the name of Liam Townson. This was a hopeless task, in which he did not succeed.

Cunningham also suggested – in 1981 – that Nairac might still be alive somewhere; that the man killed at Ravensdale was not Nairac and that the Army's strange refusal to release any information about his blood group proved this (they denied holding any relevant data, which was not true); that Nairac was not really the son of his parents, Maurice and Barbara Nairac; that Nairac (or whoever he really was) was SAS, which he was not. The author further insisted that Nairac was involved in the killing of Peter Cleary in April 1976, although he could not have been: Nairac did not set foot in Ireland between mid-April 1975 and some point in June 1976, when he started his fourth and final tour of duty in the Province.

However *The Nairac Affair* contains a few tantalising statements of potential interest, which might bear further investigation if they could ever be corroborated: Cunningham claimed to have interviewed some or most of Nairac's kidnappers and assassins; he mentioned them all in his narrative, but under false names. They are however easily identifiable;

- He believed that Nairac's apparently rash act of singing with the band on 14 May could have been a recognition signal to identify himself, and to let his contact know that he was present. Also:

- That Nairac was almost certainly under the impression that Terry McCormick (still on the run in the USA) was the potential informer whom he had to meet that evening, or his representative;

- That Nairac's potential informer was "a prominent member of the Provisionals", which McCormick was not. He was merely a PIRA sympathiser. This leaves open the question as to which prominent Provo was his contact. One name has been suggested to me more than once, but that person is still alive and does not give interviews;

- That there was some kind of discussion or argument with McCormick in the car park before the fight began;

- That Nairac had gone into the Republic and to Forkhill before he went to Drumintee. This could have been partly true: Nairac had been in the Republic on a fishing trip earlier in the day and could have returned via Forkhill. He returned to Bessbrook Mill at about 4.00 pm;

- That Nairac had told the SAS that he was going to Forkhill and not to Drumintee when he set out on the evening of 14 May. This would explain the SAS's uncertainty about where to look when it became clear that Nairac was missing and the resultant delays in taking action. Nairac on past performance probably used a circuitous route – perhaps passing through Forkhill on his way to Drumintee. Apart from that, this anecdote is completely wrong, although it bears some resemblance to the SAS/Fairweather false narrative of Nairac's last hours given to Ministers in May 1977, which would have been public knowledge by 1981;

- Cunningham gave circumstantial detail about the fight in the car park, which, if it could be shown to be true, might explain why Nairac, an experienced soldier, dropped his handgun. Cunningham alleged that someone who remains unidentified, drove up a metallic silver Ford Escort and turned on the main beam. By doing so he blocked any attempt by Nairac to escape in his own car; this action also distracted and dazzled him at a critical moment, which allowed McCormick (whose back was to the light) to knock the gun from Nairac's hand. It was found under his car behind one of the wheels. No other account mentions the silver car and McCormick has not confirmed this narrative;

- That the late Desmond McCreesh, the bar owner, might have been lying when he claimed to have gone indoors before the fighting started. His story, as he recounted it later, contains inconsistencies. He could easily have witnessed much of the drama and might have informed Eamon Collins about it. He was inaccurate about timings and detail in his statement to the police;

- That Cunningham had apparently picked up the rumours, probably traceable to the SAS or Clive Fairweather, of Nairac's alleged homosexuality. He describes him as "a queer sort of man".

- That Nairac had used the alias "Buckley" while working in Belfast. He might have done. He undoubtedly did use aliases, including Danny McErlean, Captain Charlie Macdonald and Captain Charles Johnston, but no-one now recalls Buckley. However, Father Sigebert Buckley was the name of the last Benedictine monk of Westminster Abbey who, by professing some English monks in France, ensured the survival of the ancient English Benedictine congregation and became the spiritual ancestor of the monks of Dieulouard and Ampleforth. Nairac would have known that and might have chosen Buckley as one of his aliases. It would have appealed to his sense of history.

APPENDIX 5 | NAIRAC AND THE SAS

Given Nairac's difficult relationship with the SAS, it is ironic that many Irish Republicans still firmly believe that he was an SAS officer. Initially Nairac did not know much about how they operated, but he had admired the Regiment and in 1974 had shown serious interest in attempting SAS selection; it was the kind of challenge that he relished. He was, however, deflected towards NITAT (NI) instead. His encounters in 1976-77 with the rogue SAS intake must have tempered his enthusiasm and, despite his friendships with several individual SAS officers, by the time of his murder his relationship with the SAS in South Armagh had become bad; almost unworkable. Nairac's evident relief at the prospect of returning to the Grenadier Guards in June 1977, leaving the SAS behind, was unfeigned.

It had become clear that any tentative plans that he might have had for attempting SAS Selection in the near future were pointless; he would almost certainly be blackballed. After his death SAS personnel were to voice some of the harshest criticisms of Nairac, including some outright defamatory statements.

One of the rocks on which Nairac's relationship with the SAS foundered was their attitude towards the local community in South Armagh. Had they read Nairac's paper, *Talking to People in South Armagh*, the SAS would have understood why. Nairac, who often had to read them the Riot Act over their behaviour towards local people, had emphasised the importance of studying and understanding the historical and religious background and of behaving scrupulously towards local people at all times, as he had done in Ardoyne in 1973.

As far as the SAS rogue element were concerned, he was wasting his breath. As we have seen, they saw their aim in Northern Ireland as being to "mallet" or "slot" as many of the IRA and its supporters as possible. They had no interest in the history or culture. Nairac was aware of the SAS's unauthorised crossing of the border in 1976, which had caused a diplomatic incident and made co-operation with the Republic's authorities much more difficult. He had been critical of the SAS's shooting of Peter Cleary before they or anyone else had extracted any information from him.

The killing of Seamus Harvey on 16 January 1977 was the last straw for Nairac. As usual, the fault lay with the recently-recruited or re-engaged rogue element within the Regiment, who increasingly seemed to be – literally – calling the shots. This is the only high-profile PIRA killing with which Nairac is definitely associated, although it took place in blatant disregard of his instructions. It also illustrates the difficulty, especially at this distance in time, of cutting through rumour and falsehood to discover what really occurred. There are at least two versions of what happened:

The PIRA Version: The SAS murdered Harvey. He was lured to a lonely spot near the border with the Republic following reports of a car mysteriously abandoned in suspicious circumstances. He went there with a small PIRA detachment. The car was a decoy: soldiers concealed nearby opened fire without any warning or challenge while Harvey was cautiously investigating the car. At the time they were thought to be Royal Highland Fusiliers (RHF), because they were wearing RHF bonnets, but it later emerged that they were really SAS. They shot Harvey several times, fatally. After a fierce firefight the other PIRA men beat a retreat, leaving their leader's body behind.

The SAS version: Harvey was killed in a firefight, probably by friendly-fire. The SAS had received intelligence that a consignment of arms for the PIRA would be left in an apparently abandoned car at a lonely spot near the border with the Republic. Their orders were to intercept the shipment, ensure that the arms should not fall into the PIRA's hands and arrest or otherwise neutralise those who came to collect them. The SAS found the car and staked it out. They saw the PIRA detachment arrive. It was led by a man wearing a black beret, a combat jacket and a cartridge belt, his face and masked by a black balaclava. He was clearly up to no good and later proved to be armed. The man began to open the boot of the car, obviously with a view to taking out the guns. When the SAS – who were wearing RHF headgear and accompanied by some genuine RHF soldiers – challenged him, he pulled out a sawn-off shotgun, so they shot him, but not fatally. Then an unseen, presumably PIRA, gunman opened fire on the SAS patrol: a short, fierce firefight began. According to former SAS soldiers who were there, Harvey was wounded, but still alive when the firefight started. He was caught in the crossfire and was finished off by a burst of PIRA friendly-fire. 3-4 PIRA bullets landed in his body. He died within minutes, but the other PIRA men escaped, leaving their leader's body behind.

It is impossible to say which of the two foregoing accounts is closer to the truth but, significantly, Harvey's family reportedly did not regard him as having been murdered; to them he fell in battle.

What probably really happened: The SAS's intelligence, supplied by Robert Nairac, was correct. There was a consignment of arms. What neither of the above accounts mentions is that the car in question was a Volkswagen Type 1 ("VW Beetle"). In this model the boot was at the front and the engine was at the rear. Harvey was indeed wearing a black balaclava, but pushed down scarf-like round his neck, so his face was not covered. He should have been recognisable through binoculars. He was, for reasons known to himself, investigating the VW's engine; possibly because he feared that the car might have been booby-trapped. The SAS, who had apparently forgotten about the VW Beetle's eccentric construction, although it was then a common model in the UK, thought erroneously that he was opening the boot to get at the guns and ammunition. The SAS challenged and then deliberately shot him; 2-3 SAS bullets hit him. He fell wounded to the ground and was soon caught in the crossfire. Although this is impossible to establish beyond doubt, he was probably finished off by a burst of PIRA friendly-fire. After a brisk firefight the other PIRA men escaped, leaving their leader's body behind. No-one else was killed. The SAS strapped his body underneath a Scout helicopter and flew it back to base.

What should have happened: Limited intelligence can be obtained from a corpse. Nairac was less interested in the consignment of arms than in Seamus Harvey, whom he wanted arrested and brought in alive and undamaged for interrogation. The SAS seemed to have wilfully misinterpreted these instructions: Nairac was very angry; relations with the local community now suffered a setback.

Despite his family's wishes, Seamus Harvey soon became a PIRA martyr and hero. His family gave him a simple religious burial at which the local Gaelic Athletic Club football team, the Rangers, provided the guard of honour. Harvey had formerly played for them. He was buried in a 'civilian' grave at Crossmaglen, but he has more recently been ceremoniously reinterred in the official Republican plot; the local equivalent of that Irish Republican Valhalla, Glasnevin Cemetery in Dublin.

If the SAS had intended to give two fingers to the IRA by shooting Harvey instead of arresting him, they had also given two fingers to Nairac; this, too, may have been intentional. The involvement of the SAS's rogue element was indicated by their apparent ignorance that the engine of a VW Beetle was at the back. In Nairac's eyes this was of a piece with the "border incident": their incursion into the Republic the previous year and, more importantly, their getting caught. Their seeming determination to "mallet" Harvey in defiance of orders tends to confirm this. There were foreseeable consequences: the already obsessive fear and hatred of the SAS on the part of both the PIRA and the supportive local community in South Armagh intensified. Anyone whom they suspected of being SAS could expect to receive no mercy. Nairac's abduction and brutal murder by PIRA supporters, some of whom suspected that he was SAS, would occur four months later.

Meanwhile Nairac went "ballistic" and tore strips off the SAS, including their local Commander. He invoked senior officers. The SAS were furious; they resented Nairac's insistence on scrupulously observing the rules towards the civilian population; they hated his empathy with the Irish; they were very suspicious of his Catholicism; they suspected – or hinted that they suspected – that he was a double agent. They complained about him to Major Clive Fairweather, the newly appointed GSO2 Int/Liaison HQ Northern Ireland, who was based at Lisburn. Nairac's relations with both became poisonous and this was still the situation in May 1977 when Nairac disappeared.

The SAS had reason to be wary of Nairac, because he knew about the not infrequent occasions when they had bent their own rules and broken Army ones. One example was the use of Territorial and Army Volunteer Reserve (TA) SAS soldiers in Northern Ireland. Volunteer Reservists are only mobilised when absolutely necessary. Their legal status differs from that of regular troops, except when they are called up in wartime. Because Operation Banner was never officially to be declared a war, Volunteer Reservists were not called up or deployed, apart from the Ulster Defence Regiment, which was a special case. Only regular troops were supposed to be deployed to Northern Ireland.

The SAS, however, did not scrupulously observe this rule. In the 1970s specialists from the TA 21 and 23 SAS were from time to time discreetly brought into Ulster to carry out specific tasks if no suitably qualified regulars were readily available. That might seem reasonable, if of questionable legality, but SAS non-specialist Reservists went there too.

One day, a dapper Infantry officer in a distinguished English country Regiment stationed in South Armagh was unexpectedly confronted by a troop of extremely scruffy soldiers, some with long hair and facial hair, and clad in a motley collection of uniforms which included numerous non-regulation items. He correctly assumed that they were SAS. They asked to be permitted go out on patrol in Crossmaglen and the officer arranged for this to happen on two occasions. The SAS were escorted by men of his Regiment and the patrols passed off without major incident. It only later emerged that all of the visiting SAS troop were Territorials. They had come over to do some field training in order to qualify for their annual bounty. Others came simply to join in the fun and if possible to pot a few of the IRA. All of this was unauthorised and illegal. Had any of them been killed or been shown to have killed anyone else, questions would have been asked in Parliament.

The "Green Army" did not welcome the SAS's involvement; especially not that of the TA SAS. According to the aforementioned former Infantry officer:

"The 'troop', or whatever it was called, in XMG were so self-consciously 'tuff' that it was painful. My platoon was deeply amused by their amateurishness..."

This puts into perspective the dismissive comments by some SAS officers and Clive Fairweather about Nairac's amateurism and raffishness. The Infantry officer added that the SAS should never have been sent to Northern Ireland. They were out of their depth, bored, under-employed and being asked to do duties for which they were not suited; a view with which many of the SAS themselves would have concurred. The blame lay with Harold Wilson.

ACKNOWLEDGEMENTS

Whatever I have managed to achieve would not have been possible without the help and encouragement of many other people, which I gratefully acknowledge here. It should not however be assumed that they endorse everything that I have written. They supplied factual information; I drew conclusions from it. The conclusions are my own, as are all errors.

I am especially grateful to:

Sir Mark Allen KCMG; Lieutenant Colonel Richard Besly, Nairac's first Commanding Officer; Colonel John Blashford-Snell OBE DSc DEng (hc) FRSGS, RE (Retd); Captain Cliff Burrage, aka "Chris Mather", formerly Green Howards; Colonel Andrew Campbell, formerly Argyll and Sutherland Highlanders; John Cassidy, journalist; Count Alexandre de Castellane; Lord Valentine Cecil, formerly Grenadier Guards and a brother officer of Nairac; Fred Cook, a former Grenadier Guards WO; Father Edward Corbould OSB, Nairac's former Housemaster at Ampleforth; Father Anselm Cramer OSB, Archivist of Ampleforth College; Ralph Dempsey of the British Association for Shooting and Conservation (BASC, formerly WAGBI); Dr Ruth Dudley Edwards, historian; Nigel Fish of the Worcestershire and Sherwood Foresters Regimental Association; the Hon. Jonathan Forbes, formerly Grenadier Guards and a brother officer of Nairac; Trevor Galtress, formerly of the RAOC; John Gooding, historian and my former Director of Studies; Daphne Guinness, journalist (whose idea it was); The Rt. Hon. Dominic Grieve QC, MP; Stan Halford, a former Grenadier Guardsman; Toby Harnden, *The Sunday Times* Washington Bureau Chief; Terry Hissey, a fellow author on George Cross recipients; John Hotchkiss, an angling friend of Nairac; Luke Jennings, dance critic of *The Observer*, author and youthful friend of Nairac; Martin Jones, falconer and friend of Nairac; Dr Peter Jones MBE, academic and classicist; Lieutenant Colonel Gerald Lesinski, Master of Lord Leycester's Hospital, formerly Grenadier Guards and a brother officer of Nairac; Nic Ling of the Gloucestershire Wildfowlers' Association; Roisin McAuley, journalist and author; Dr Alexander McCall Smith CBE, author and (many years ago) fellow Officer-Cadet, who encouraged me; Alderman Julian Malins QC, Nairac's close friend at Oxford; Colonel Patrick Mercer OBE, formerly Worcestershire and Sherwood Foresters; Stephen Marriott, a former Grenadier Guardsman; the Hon. John Morris, falconer and a former friend of Nairac; Dr Anthony Morton, Royal Military Academy, Sandhurst; Andrew Mussell, Archivist of Lincoln College, Oxford and the Rector and Fellows of Lincoln College; Charles Nairac, Robert Nairac's cousin; Sean O'Callaghan, former IRA Volunteer; Robin Oliver, television critic of *The Sydney Morning Herald*; Mrs Jemima Parry-Jones MBE, falconer; Major Pat Ralph, formerly Green Howards; the Most Hon. The Marquess of Salisbury; Lieutenant Colonel Conway Seymour, the former Grenadier Guards Archivist; Dr Andrew Sanders of University College, Dublin; Peregrine Solly, formerly Irish Guards, who knew Nairac at Ampleforth and in the Army; Captain Jeremy Tozer, formerly Duke of Edinburgh's Royal Regiment (Berkshire and Wiltshire); General Sir John Wilsey; Ian Wood, historian; Major Robert Woodfield, formerly Grenadier Guards and a brother officer of Nairac.

I am also extremely grateful to Andrew Young and Ken Sewell of Cambridge Media Group, my publishers, who took a gamble on my book, despite my lack of a track-record as a writer or of a literary agent. Their encouragement and support helped enormously.

Finally, I should thank my copy-editor, Virginia Besly, for her tireless help with spelling, grammar and punctuation, as well as weeding out deviation, repetition and potentially libellous remarks.

If I have inadvertently omitted anyone, I apologise unreservedly. Likewise, if I have unintentionally missed out anyone's Doctorate, Order of Chivalry or other distinction.

Others prefer not to be named, because they are still considered to be at risk due to the work that they did in the 1970s, or because they live in Ireland, or for other reasons. They know who they are. I am extremely grateful to them, too.

NOTES BY CHAPTER

Prologue | The Citation

<u>Note1: Available Military Decorations</u>. *In 1979 very few decorations could be awarded posthumously. They were: The Victoria Cross (awarded for wartime service only); the George Cross; the Queen's Commendation for Brave Conduct; and Mentioned in Despatches (MID). The rules have since been changed. The George Cross (GC) is the equal highest award for gallantry in the UK honours system, being second in the order of wear, but of equal precedence, to the Victoria Cross (VC). The GC is the highest gallantry award for civilians, as well as for members of the Armed Forces in actions for which purely military honours would not normally be granted. Nairac's was the third GC to be awarded to Armed Service personnel in Northern Ireland. The previous awards were to Sergeant Michael Willetts, the Parachute Regiment (posthumous), and Major George Styles RAOC, a bomb disposal expert.*

<u>Note 2: HM The Queen</u> *was to suffer personal loss in Ireland later in 1979. On 27 August the PIRA would murder Lord Mountbatten, the Duke of Edinburgh's uncle and a relation of the Queen, while he was on holiday in the Irish Republic. Others, including one of his grandsons, died with him. On the same day the PIRA detonated two explosions at Warrenpoint in Northern Ireland, in which 18 British soldiers died. The dead at Warrenpoint included the most senior Army officer to be killed in Northern Ireland: the Commanding Officer of the Queen's Own Highlanders, Lieutenant Colonel David Blair.*

<u>Note 3: The RUC Special Branch Tankard</u>. *This silver trophy is almost the only remaining tangible evidence that, having arrived in Northern Ireland as a soldier, Robert Nairac had latterly been working closely with Special Branch.*

<u>Note 4: The Legends</u>. *SAS Major C, who arrived at Bessbrook Mill a few weeks before Nairac's disappearance, later stated that "there was already a Nairac myth growing up after his time in the Det and with G Squadron before us." Since then Nairac has achieved another kind of legendary immortality: he appears as a character in a Triple Nade video war game: "Captain Robert Nairac (MOD, UK)," doing appropriately dashing and dangerous things. The war game bears no relationship to anything in Nairac's real career.*

<u>Note 5: Jim Thompson</u>. *This distinguished American went out alone for a walk while on holiday with friends in the Cameron Highlands, Malaysia, in 1967 and was never seen again. He had been a member of the CIA's predecessor organisation, the OSS, and may later have also been in the CIA. Scraps of evidence suggest that*

his disappearance was planned; he could have been spirited away, presumably by his CIA controllers. There were sporadic reports of sightings, especially in Cambodia, in the succeeding years. In the late 1980s Thompson's elderly houseboy, Yee, was still alive and was firmly convinced that his near-nonagenarian master was also alive, somewhere. Thompson's house, now a museum, was then being kept exactly as he had left it, in the hope that he would one day return.

Chapter 1 | The Myths

Note 1: Anthony Bradley *was a journalist in Belfast for many years. His book, "Requiem for a Spy: the Killing of Robert Nairac" (1993, Mercier Press), is an anti-British and anti-Nairac tract. While it contains some interesting insights, it also bristles with inaccuracies. Bradley has a parallel career as a landlord with rental property in Belfast (Antrim Road), Dundalk and elsewhere.*

Note 2: Fred Holroyd and Colin Wallace. *Both of these former officers accused Nairac, after his death, of complicity in crimes. Fred Holroyd, the author of "War Without Honour" was the MIO of J Division. He struck colleagues at the time as unstable and his treatment by the RUC Special Branch led to a nervous breakdown. His files make distinctly odd reading; there were many contributory factors to his breakdown. While we may sympathise, this hardly makes him a reliable witness. Colin Wallace was only ever an officer in the UDR; not in the British Regular Army. He was a locally-employed Public Relations Officer at HQ Northern Ireland without any access to intelligence material. He was not, as described in Wikipedia, "a former British soldier and psychological warfare specialist who was one of the members of the [probably imaginary] Intelligence-led 'Clockwork Orange' project, which is alleged to have been an attempt to smear various individuals, including a number of British politicians, in the early 1970s".*

Note 3: The Little Owl. *According to the eminent classicist, Dr Peter Jones MBE, the Little Owl was definitely associated with Pallas Athene. Its scientific name is Athene noctua. However the superstition – that if an owl hooted from the roof of a building it signified a death – is thought to have been Roman, rather than Greek.*

Note 4: Loyalist Crimes. *A former soldier has observed that, "as Nairac was a colourful, idiosyncratic individual, a bit of a character and possibly SAS, it seems irresistible to some that they must associate him personally with any and all of the atrocities associated with Loyalists before 1977. Did he kill the Reavey brothers? Perhaps he even was a double agent at Kingsmills? I'm just awaiting his being blamed for something that happened after May 1977 – but then again, some may attribute that to his survival even unto the present day..."*

Note 5: The Film "Kes." *Ken Loach, the Director, wrote in 2014: "I can categorically confirm that Robert Nairac had absolutely nothing to do with the kestrels in 'Kes'. The birds were found and trained by the writer Barry Hines and his brother, assisted by David Bradley, who played Billy Casper. There were three young kestrels, which we called Freeman, Hardy and Willis. Two were good, though which I can't recall. I never met Robert Nairac. He had nothing to do with the film in any shape or form".*

Note 6: Head Boy at Ampleforth. *I have been informed that this was apparently offered to Nairac in 1966, but that he turned it down because he did not want to remain at Ampleforth beyond Christmas 1966.*

Note 7: Newfoundland Dogs. *Byron's Newfoundland was called Bo'sun; Nairac's was known as Bundle. "Newfies" are known for their gigantic size, intelligence, tremendous strength, calm dispositions, and loyalty. They make great life-savers thanks to their muscular build, thick double coat, webbed toes, and swimming abilities. They also make good retrieving dogs for wildfowl, which was Nairac's reason for acquiring Bundle. He was one of the great loves of Nairac's short life; they adored one another. (Nairac possessed at least one other dog, a Labrador retriever).*

Note 8: The Edwardian Age. *I have used "Edwardian" loosely, as a synonym for "la belle époque". King Edward VII died in 1910. However his son, George V, who was Britain's first true constitutional monarch, made little impact on the age in which he lived; he was not a style-setter. The Edwardian age, lasting to August 1914, was followed by the Great War. After Edward VII, no British monarch's name would be attached to an era, although there were attempts to do so, as in "Georgian Poetry", published in 1911 and 1912, and a "Second Elizabethan Age", proclaimed and quickly forgotten when Elizabeth II was crowned.*

Note 9: Edwardian Notions of Masculinity. *Dr Callum McKenzie of the University of Strathclyde has explored this theme in an article in The Sports Historian (No 20.1, of May 2000 pp 70-96): "The British Big-Game Hunting Tradition, Masculinity and Fraternalism with Particular Reference to the Shikar Club". I have drawn on this article for background.*

Chapter 2 | The Murder Part 1

Note 1: Adjutant of the 1st Battalion Grenadier Guards. *It has been suggested that Nairac's main motive for serving a fourth tour in Northern Ireland was simple ambition: he wanted promotion and a medal, both of which he would have received had he lived. But while he was certainly competitive and career-minded, it would have been preferable for his career (and his life) to have spent less time in Ireland and more on conventional Regimental soldiering.*

Note 2: Nairac's Four Tours of Duty in Northern Ireland. *Nairac served briefly in Northern Ireland in March 1973, when the 2nd Battalion Grenadier Guards reinforced the Security Forces at the time of the Constitutional Referendum of 8 March. He returned for a normal duty tour in July-October 1973. He and four others from 2nd Bn Grenadier Guards remained after his Battalion had left, to assist the incoming Battalion. In May 1974, following training in the UK, Nairac was attached to 4 Field Survey Troop, Royal Engineers, in one of the three sub-units of a Special Duties unit known as NITAT (NI). This was an intelligence-gathering unit. In April 1975 he was posted back to the UK on Regimental duties in London. He returned to Northern Ireland in June 1976 and remained there, apart from short "breather" leaves in the UK, until his death in May 1977. He passed most of his military service in Northern Ireland, detached from his Regiment for the last two tours. This amounted to a total of four NI duty tours.*

Note 3: Nairac's Last Tour in Northern Ireland. *Nairac's final duty tour, lasting one year during which he served as SASLO, was due to end soon after the date of his murder. His Army records indicate that he was posted back to Northern Ireland in June 1976. Letters from Nairac to his Regiment towards the end of his life confirm that his return to the UK and to Regimental soldering was imminent.*

Note 4: Nairac's Triumph Toledo Q Car. *The messy state of the car's interior was fairly typical of Nairac. A woman friend whom Nairac drove to a dance in the Officers' Mess at Victoria Barracks in Windsor recalls his picking her up in his MG sports car. She vividly remembers that the foot-well on the passenger's side was carpeted with a lush crop of bright green grass.*

Note 5: The Filofax. *According to one former officer, "Very many officers had one and Filofax actually printed military pages, but they were not an issue item." However the Filofax in question could have been an Army green ring binder, some of which were Filofax size but had a different arrangement of rings.*

Chapter 3 | The Murder, Part 2

Note 1: Captain David Collett. *Captain Collett has been variously described as Worcestershire and Sherwood Foresters, SAS and Parachute Regiment. From Army records it appears that he served with The Parachute Regiment, having been commissioned in 1966, when he was 20. He became a Captain in 1972 and Acting Major January to March 1977. By May 1977, when Nairac disappeared, he was definitely in the SAS, as a Captain. In 1982 he is recorded as having served in the Parachute Regiment in the Falklands but was later 2IC of 22 SAS. As is standard procedure, Collett did not identify as SAS when giving evidence in Dublin at Liam Townson's trial. In court, normal SAS practice is always to state the original*

Regiment, and not the SAS, as the parent unit. However the Paras were nearly as unpopular as the SAS in Ireland, so Collett gave the Worcestershire and Sherwood Foresters as his Regiment.

Note 2: Acting Major John Sutherell. *John Sutherell held Acting rank from December 1975 to December 1979. He would be gazetted Substantive Major on 31 December 1979. Later he became Major General John Sutherell CB CBE DL. A year older than Nairac, he had been commissioned in the Royal Anglian Regiment, which he would later command. He went on to become, among other appointments, Commander of the 8th Infantry Brigade in Northern Ireland, Deputy Military Secretary and Director, Special Forces. He retired in 2002.*

Note 3: Kevin Crilly. *Kevin Crilly, wanted by the RUC, fled to the USA like McCormick and Maguire. He lived there for nearly 30 years. Unlike them, he returned clandestinely to Northern Ireland and resumed his life in Jonesborough under an assumed name. He was recognised, arrested and tried in 2011 for his part in Robert Nairac's murder. A judge at Belfast Crown Court acquitted Crilly of involvement in the murder. As well as the murder charge, Crilly was cleared of four other charges, including kidnapping and false imprisonment. Mr Justice Richard McLaughlin said that in his view, while it was clear that Crilly had been present on the night; had driven Nairac in his car to the murder location; and had picked up the man who murdered Nairac – Liam Townson – it had not been proved that he knew what was going to happen. The judge also said that forensic evidence did not establish Crilly's guilt beyond doubt. "The prosecution has not proved beyond reasonable doubt the state of knowledge or intention necessary to transform the transporting of (Liam) Townson (who was convicted of the murder) by Crilly to an unspecified place at an unspecified time into a knowing participation in a potential murder. For these reasons I find the accused not guilty," the judge said. Mr Justice McLaughlin added: "The admissions by Crilly to the journalists from the [BBC Northern Ireland] Spotlight programme prove he was involved to some degree in the events surrounding the death of Captain Nairac. He was present at the Three Steps Inn where what he described as a 'battle' took place. This can only mean that what he witnessed was the abduction of Captain Nairac, but it does not prove his active participation in it," said the learned judge.*

Note 4: Julian "Tony" Ball. *The incident in 1981 in which Tony Ball and Andrew Nightingale were killed seems to have been a road traffic accident. There were no survivors and no witnesses. Apparently no other vehicle was involved.*

Note 5: Basil Dykes, *Nairac's maternal uncle, was a solicitor. He became a part-time soldier, commissioned into the 7th (Territorial) Battalion, the Worcestershire*

Regiment in 1936, as a Second Lieutenant. In May 1940 he took part in the advance into Belgium and the subsequent withdrawal of the British Expeditionary Force (BEF) to Dunkirk.

Note 6: PIRA Statements. *There were at least two announcements. At 11.45 am the RUC received an anonymous telephone call to the effect that a body could be found near Newtownhamilton. This was assumed to be Nairac's, but no corpse was ever recovered, there or anywhere else. At 12.30 pm Downtown Radio Belfast received a message purporting to come from the 1st Armagh Battalion PIRA to the effect that they had arrested, interrogated and executed Captain Nairac and that he had admitted to being a member of the SAS. The PIRA also briefed selected media in the Republic.*

Note 7: Eamon Collins "Killing Rage". *An example of Collins' unreliability, when uncritically repeating hearsay, is that he also related that he had spoken with a man who claimed that he had been sitting in his car in the car park of the Three Steps Inn on the night of 14-15 May 1977. This man claimed that he had witnessed the assault on Nairac. In his opinion, Nairac could not possibly have survived the ferocious beating that he received in the car park. Later he saw Nairac's limp form being loaded into a car. This is at variance with all other accounts of the abduction. Nairac did survive the initial attack; was abducted to the Republic while still alive; and fought hard for his life until almost the last moment. This leaves the question: how many men were sitting in their parked cars that night? Who was this mysterious man? Could this have been McCreesh, telling a different story from that which he had related to the police? I suspect that this story is imaginary. By extension it calls into question the meat-processing plant story, which is also hearsay and was also uncritically repeated by Collins. Desmond McCreesh is now dead. I have reservations about the value of his testimony. On 14 May 1977 he was on the lookout for anything odd, as he feared a Loyalist car bomb or other attack. He reportedly had no suspicions of Nairac. Yet he later stated to police that he had noted the fact that the number plates on Nairac's car were partly obscured by "mud." He even guessed that it was really cement. Did this set no alarm bells ringing and did he not mention it to anyone else? If he did, could it be this that sparked McCormick's initial hostile interest in Nairac? And could McCreesh be the mysterious man who gave a strange account of Nairac's abduction to Eamon Collins? We shall never know.*

Note 8: Nicky Curtis. *Nicky Curtis is the pseudonym of a former NCO in the Green Howards, a winner of the Military Medal (MM) and one of the most highly-decorated non-commissioned soldiers to have served in Northern Ireland. "Curtis" is the author of a book about his military service in Northern Ireland during the Troubles: "Faith and Duty." The book, which is well-written, falls neatly into two halves: firstly the "Corporals' War" on the streets of Belfast, and secondly Curtis' time undercover, including in South Armagh. He seems to have known Nairac well; to have liked and been fascinated by him. Occasionally he worried that he might be a double agent. I have tried in vain to contact Curtis, who lives a very reclusive existence, with a view to clarifying some of his statements.*

Note 9: Which gun was used to murder Nairac? *We cannot be absolutely sure unless and until Robert Nairac's remains are recovered. If they are, the bullet injuries to the skull might yield conclusive evidence. It is quite clear that Nairac had his Browning on him in its shoulder-holster when he was attacked in the car park at Drumintee.*

Note 10: Company Commander. *I have been told by several former senior Grenadier officers that Nairac would definitely have become a Company Commander, Acting Major on his return to Regimental duty after June 1977: Company Commanders were not chosen by seniority, but by suitability and Nairac was an ideal choice. However, although he had been designated Fit for Immediate Promotion (FIP), and although Companies are normally commanded by Majors, this does not mean that Nairac would have received his substantive promotion immediately. This was because of the system then in operation in the Army. Substantiation in the rank of Major was decided on an Army-wide basis: as a result, this would often come too early/too late to meet the Regiment's requirement for Company Commanders. So it was not unheard of for a battalion to have only the Senior Major actually substantive, while the Company Commanders were all Substantive Captains, Acting Majors.*

Note 11: *In manus tuas, Domine. Lord, into your hands I commend my spirit. Based on the last words of Christ on the cross, it forms part of a Latin prayer.*
In manus tuas, Domine, commendo spiritum meum.
Redemisti me Domine, Deus veritatis.
Sancta Maria, Mater Dei, ora pro nobis.

Chapter 4 | New to Earth and Sky

Note 1: The Sartorial Influence of the Brigade of Guards. *It was not only middle-class men who took their lead from Guards officers in plain clothes. Teddy boys, who were part of a 1950s working-class subculture closely associated with Rock'n' Roll and with attacks on ethnic minorities, also wore clothes that were distantly inspired by the styles worn by Edwardian dandies and more immediately by off-duty Guards officers, including velvet-collared overcoats. Even their Brylcreem hair oil may have been distantly copied from Guards officers, who would have used the equivalent from George F. Trumper.*

Note 2: Presentation at Court. *The ceremony of presentation of débutantes, and of recently-married young women, to the Monarch was discontinued in 1958. Debutante balls, however, persist to the present day.*

Note 3: The New Statesman. *Founded in 1913, this left-leaning magazine is affectionately known as "The Staggers" because of its numerous crises of funding, ownership and circulation. Kingsley Martin edited it from 1931-1960. He and Richard Crossman (1970-1972) are the only former editors who are household names. It still (2015) staggers on. Sometimes a colourful public figure is invited to be guest editor. On 4 May 1984, The New Statesman was to publish an article, "Dirty War: An ex-Northern Ireland Army Officer Tells All", in which Nairac featured in a most unpleasant light, as the probable murderer of IRA Staff Captain John Francis Green. The article was based on the allegations of Fred Holroyd. By this time Nairac had been dead for seven years and could not reach for his lawyer.*

Note 4: Kipling's *Kim. Peter Hopkirk's book, "Quest for Kim", gives the historic background to Kipling's novel. Some of it was straight reportage. Kim is believable because he was based on a real person.*

Note 5: Bulldog Drummond and the SAS. *Persons on the Left of the political spectrum tend to attribute Bulldog Drummond-like political attitudes to members of the SAS – and by extension to Robert Nairac. In reality Nairac showed little interest in British, as opposed to Irish, politics.*

Note 6: Nairac's IQ. *Army reports refer to his quick, analytical intelligence. There is no doubt that Robert Nairac was an intelligent man; although he had difficulty in applying himself to subjects that did not interest him. Army gossip suggests that for a bet Nairac once successfully sat the Mensa exam, which would imply that he had an IQ of 148 or over: within the top 2% of the population. Mensa were unable to confirm this to me, but pointed out that many people, having taken the tests successfully, do not bother to join Mensa, which involves payment of an annual subscription, and therefore Mensa retains no record of them. Nairac could have been in this category.*

Note 7: Philip Glasier (1915 – 2000). *There is another Proustian coincidence here. During World War II Glasier was an instructor at RMA Sandhurst, where he set up a falconry mews. He became acquainted with Hugh Dormer, who was a Sandhurst cadet before joining the Irish Guards, and taught him falconry. Glasier therefore knew both Dormer and Nairac.*

Note 8: The Patience of Job. *Training a hawk is never easy. Much, however, depends on which species you choose. Kestrels are recommended for beginners. North*

American Harris Hawks are now popular. In the wild these sociable birds hunt cooperatively in small groups of 2-6. They readily adapt to hunting co-operatively with humans, and dogs too. Other raptors, like gyrfalcons, peregrines, goshawks and eagles, are more challenging. Brimstone, the Hawk Eagle, made headlines in The Daily Mail in the 1980s when she recovered from bad frostbite, having lost two toes and all her talons:"Pet bird of Murdered Army Hero is nursed Back to Health".

Note 9: No Sentimental Narrative. Luke Jennings correctly observes that, "nature, for all its outward poetry, is a slaughterhouse." It may be possible to ignore this unpalatable fact in the UK, which now has few large predators, and especially if one is completely ignorant of natural history, as the opponents of field sports tend to be. However, when living in Africa, for example, where gruesome kills are easy to spot – just follow the vultures – this horrid truth is glaringly, bloodily, obvious.

Chapter 5 | Ampleforth, Setbacks and Achievement

Note 1: The Cardinal of York. Henry Benedict Stuart (1725 – 1807), titular Duke of York, was the younger brother of Prince Charles Edward Stuart and the last of the Royal Stuart dynasty. In theory he became de jure King Henry I of Scotland and IX of England following his brother's death in 1788. He was also Dean of the Sacred College, Bishop of Frascati, later of Ostia, Archbishop of Corinth in Partibus Infidelium and Abbot of numerous wealthy monasteries, most of which were in France. After the death of Pope Pius VI in French Revolutionary captivity, he organised the election of Pius VII in the teeth of strong French opposition. The French Revolution had ruined him, so George III granted him a Civil List pension. The Cardinal bequeathed some historic Stuart jewels to George III.

Note 2: Catholic Recusancy. A Recusant is one of the English Roman Catholics who, between the sixteenth and late eighteenth centuries, incurred legal and social penalties for clinging to the old religion and refusing to attend services of the Church of England. The word can be translated as "obstinate in refusal." Once a pejorative expression, it is now a source of pride to old English Catholic families, who use the term unselfconsciously. Members of old Recusant families have in the past tended to set the tone for other English Catholics. The fictional Crouchback family in Evelyn Waugh's war trilogy, "The Sword of Honour", were Recusants. So in real life were William Shakespeare's parents. In 1559 the fine for Recusants who failed to attend Anglican Church services was 12 pence. In 1581 this was raised to a ruinous £20. 1587 saw the introduction of cumulative fines and the forfeiture of two-thirds of a defaulting Recusant's estate.

Note 3: Ampleforth and the Armed Forces. This theme is developed more eloquently in Madeleine Bunting's book, "The Plot", in which she explains, inter *alia, how Ampleforth's War Memorial Chapel came to be built. I have drawn freely on her informed insights.*

Note 4: English Catholics in the Service of Foreign Catholic Sovereigns. *A good example is Sir John Acton, 6th Baronet, of Aldenham Hall, Shropshire ((1736 – 1811). Acton served under his uncle in the navy of Tuscany. In 1779 Queen Maria Carolina of Naples persuaded her brother, the Grand Duke Leopold of Tuscany, to release Acton to undertake the reorganisation of the Neapolitan navy. He rapidly became Commander-in-Chief of both the army and the navy of the Kingdom of Naples, Minister of Finance and finally Prime Minister. Acton remained a patriotic Englishman: he worked closely with the British Minister, Sir William Hamilton, and with Admiral Nelson to frustrate Napoleon's ambitions in the Mediterranean. His Catholic religion alone had prevented Acton from performing similar services for Great Britain. Acton's grandson became the first Lord Acton, the Victorian historian.*

Note 5: Sir David Stirling and the SAS. *In view of their originally strong Irish connection, it is ironic that the SAS were latterly regarded with an almost superstitious hatred and dread by Republicans in Northern Ireland. The wartime SAS had contained a high proportion of Catholics, many of whom were Irish, or of Irish origin. One was Major Roy Farran DSO, a devout Catholic whose book, "Winged Dagger", is a readable account of the early SAS. Protestant Irishmen, like Blair "Paddy" Mayne, also served. Mayne's personality has been judged borderline psychopathic, but totally stable and sensible people do not volunteer for the kind of war service with the SAS that Mayne performed so efficiently. The same might possibly be said of Robert Nairac's undercover work.*

Note 6: Lawrence of Arabia. *An extreme example of self-dramatising half-truth in T E Lawrence's case is the story, related in The Seven Pillars of Wisdom, of Lawrence's torture and sexual violation by Turkish soldiers at Deraa in Syria. It is now known that this episode did take place, but in what is now Saudi Arabia, and the participants were Arabs, not Turks. The instigator was not a sadistic Turkish Pasha but an ally and friend, the handsome Sharif Ali, who was a cousin of Lawrence's friend Prince Faisal. And Lawrence enjoyed it. Thereafter he would employ fit young men, including soldiers and airmen, to flog him and in that and other ways help him recall that shocking but liberating experience.*

Chapter 6 | Getting to Oxford

Note 1: Michaelmas Term. *The Oxford Terms are:*
- *Michaelmas term – (autumn-winter) 13 Sundays before to 5 Sundays before the feast day of St Hilary*

- *Hilary term – (winter-spring) 1 Sunday to 9 Sundays after the feast day of St Hilary*
- *Trinity term – (Spring-summer) 15 Sundays to 21 Sundays after the feast day of St Hilary.*

The terms originated in the legal system. At the University of Oxford, Hilary Term begins on and includes 7th January and ends on and includes 25th March or the Saturday before Palm Sunday, whichever is the earlier. In Hilary Term, as in Michaelmas Term and in Trinity Term, there is a period of eight weeks known as Full Term, beginning on a Sunday, within which lectures and other instruction prescribed by statute or regulation are given. Oxford has shorter terms than most other universities.

Note 2: The Profumo Scandal. *John Profumo resigned on 5 June 1963. It was never shown that his relationship with Miss Keeler had led to any breach of national security. A rich man of independent means, he spent the rest of his life working in the voluntary sector in the East End of London, for which he received the CBE. There had been earlier scandals, none closely linked to the Conservative Party, but which nevertheless caused the Government and the public concern at the time, such as the defection to Russia in 1951 of the diplomats Guy Burgess and Donald Maclean and the John Vassall affair in 1962. In 1952 William Marshall, an employee of the Diplomatic Wireless Service, was convicted of offences under the Official Secrets Act: he had been spying for Russia. These unconnected spy scandals allowed Labour to seethe with synthetic indignation, and the media cynically to whip up mass hysteria about moral turpitude in "the Establishment" and scare-mongering "concern" about national security. Although there was no link between these scandals, or between them and John Profumo, false connections were made. The Profumo scandal was the last straw for many credulous voters. I refer interested readers to Richard Davenport-Hines' intriguing book, "An English Affair: Sex, Class and Power in the Age of Profumo".*

Note 3: Harold Wilson. *Although Wilson was an undistinguished Prime Minister, presiding over a period of muddle and decline, he was not as bad as he was depicted by his numerous right-wing critics. He was not corrupt: he left office a comparatively poor man. He was not in the pay of the Soviet Government or of anyone else. His Socialism owed much to John Wesley; little to Karl Marx. He resisted American pressure to commit British forces to the Vietnam War, which the British Generals had told him (correctly) was unwinnable. Wilson was a poor judge of character. His appointment of the tactless Marcia Williams (later Baroness Falkender) to his private office and some of his ministerial appointments (Arthur Bottomley, George Brown), showed this. But the application of reason was not one of Wilson's strong points. Underneath his pipe-smoking "common man" image, Wilson was an eccentric oddball: some of his notions now seem very strange.*

Note 4: Harold Wilson's Associates. *Although Wilson may have been clean, some of his associates were not. Wilson rapidly established a "kitchen cabinet"; a coterie of cronies with whom he conferred privately and frequently. East Germany was then a pariah state, yet two of Wilson's intimates visited regularly, ostensibly for trade talks, and were treated with fawning sycophancy. Another of the kitchen cabinet, and among those lurking around the East German politburo, was Austrian-born, bilingual Sir Rudy Sternberg, later Lord Plurenden.*

Note 5: The Commonwealth. *The Heads of Government Meeting (CHOGM) of July 1964 is a good example. CHOGM was split over the ending of white rule in the self-governing British colony of Southern Rhodesia. Seven African Heads of Government, including Hastings Banda (Malawi), Kwame Nkrumah (Ghana) and Jomo Kenyatta (Kenya) – all of whom presided over undemocratic one-party States characterised by endemic corruption, varying from moderate to phosphorescent – clashed vociferously with Duncan Sandys, the Commonwealth and Colonial Secretary and Sir Robert Menzies of Australia, who supported the UK, for not imposing a timetable for independence leading to majority rule in Rhodesia. The Press reported excitedly that the Commonwealth was now "dangerously split". In reality the Commonwealth, and therefore the split, had by this time ceased to be of any importance.Since those days the Commonwealth has reinvented itself and has admitted countries that were never part of the British Empire. It now counts for more than it did in the 1960s.*

Note 6: McAlpine Building Sites. *An Irish friend writes: "I spent the summer of 1974 working on London building sites as an undergraduate student... and we ventured up Kilburn Road a few times. You are correct in your observation that few students had the fitness/strength requirement for the job; my initiation on the concrete gang almost prepared me! A friend and I moved up into an apartment in Cricklewood for the final month. It was there I wrote my first piece of paid journalism – a new feature on the demise of the "Lump" system that had operated on building sites. I worked the lump that summer, an under the counter system whereby I was paid cash in hand each Friday [and so presumably was Nairac], most often in the pub frequented by the gang. We went a few times to pubs such as the 'Crown' in Kilburn, celebrated in the song 'McAlpine's Fusiliers'. It was dreadful! I don't recall any fights, however. I suspect that fights may have occurred with frequency at the Irish dance halls. So it is quite possible that I might have had a drink with Nairac on one of my occasional forays up Kilburn Road".*

Note 7: The IRA and Kilburn. *Kilburn and Cricklewood were IRA strongholds in London. In "Secret Hero", John Parker refers to an account that he had received from "a former IRA member who maintained that he had been briefed on Nairac". This man claimed that Nairac had first made contact with the Republicans in North*

London. "Nairac had been mixing with Republicans for some time. He had contact with Republicans but he had not yet come close to the actual active service unit. He did know the workings of the unit and would have known some of the actions that individual volunteers had carried out. He was beginning to be trusted but he was not yet trusted as much as he needed to be." John Parker's tone in reporting this is sceptical: this is one of many Nairac stories that circulated after his death. Read in one way, it might almost seem to confirm rumours that Nairac had been a double agent. If it contains any element of truth, it tends to confirm that senior IRA commanders had no reason to want Nairac dead and had every interest in keeping him alive. However, given the enduring ban by the IRA on discussion of Nairac, even within the organisation, this account, while plausible, also seems rather unlikely. There are former British soldiers who like to dine out on their slight or non-existent acquaintance with Nairac; these Army raconteurs probably have their IRA equivalent.

Note 8: "The Men Behind the Wire." *This pro-IRA song by Paddy McGuigan refers to those held at Long Kesh prison camp and elsewhere. McGuigan himself was detained in a later round of internment, which some saw as the British State's revenge for writing the song.*

Chapter 7 | This Side of Paradise

Note 1: OU Amateur Boxing Club. *The first Varsity match with Cambridge was not held until 1897 and was a joint affair with the fencing team. Victories in the four boxing bouts were split evenly between the two teams, but overall victory was awarded to Oxford on the fencing score. The Annual Varsity Boxing Match has long been separated from the fencing event and has expanded over time to include nine bouts in total, with a full gamut of weight categories ranging from featherweight (57kg) to heavyweight (91kg). Boxing became a full blue sport in 1937 (and remains one of the fourteen 'full blues' today) but the OUABC disbanded in 1968 due to a lack of interest and financial problems. The club was only saved from folding and the match took place because Robert Nairac and Julian Malins knocked on doors around the university during the week before the start of the 1968 Michaelmas term, to find enough willing brawlers to make up the numbers at short notice. Oxford lost that match, but by a surprisingly narrow margin.*

Note 2: Boxing and the Army. *Although boxing and the Army may go together like bacon and eggs, not all Commanding Officers favour it, being aware of the physical and mental damage that it can inflict, especially on inexperienced soldiers who get coerced into joining the boxing team to make up numbers and then get injured. For this reason Nairac's first Commanding Officer, Lieutenant Colonel Richard Besly, was against boxing and would not allow the Second Battalion Grenadier Guards to have a boxing team. Nairac managed to continue boxing in other contexts.*

Note 3: A W Lawrence *was one of five brothers, the illegitimate sons of Sir Thomas Robert Tighe Chapman, Baronet (aka Thomas Lawrence) and his mistress, Sarah Junner (aka Mrs Lawrence). The brothers were, in order of seniority: Robert (Bob), who became a medical missionary in China; Thomas Edward (Ned), who was Lawrence of Arabia; Will and Frank, who were killed in the First World War, and Arnold, who became Professor A W Lawrence and later acted as his elder brother's literary executor. Arnold Lawrence, like several other people in this story, worked in secret intelligence; in his case for MI5 during World War II.*

Chapter 8 | The Irish Background

Note 1: The Gentry. *Although the majority of the Irish gentry were Protestant and Anglican, there were Catholic and Presbyterian gentry too. In general the Catholic gentry identified more closely with the Anglican ascendancy than with the Catholic peasantry. They were sometimes derided as "Castle Catholics," from their habit of accepting invitations from the Lord Lieutenant to functions at Dublin Castle. Even worse, they sent their sons to Trinity College, Dublin, which was then seen as an evil Protestant stronghold where they might pick up unsuitable ideas. Catholics were supposed to request a Dispensation from their Church in order to study there. John Redmond MP was a TCD graduate.*

Note 2: Chief Secretary for Ireland. *This was a key British Government political appointment during the years of direct rule (1801-1921). The last holder of the office, which was abolished in 1922, was Sir Hamar Greenwood, Baronet.*

Note 3: The Irish Republican Army (IRA). *The IRA was originally a non-sectarian Irish revolutionary organisation. It is the successor of the Irish Volunteers, established in 1913, some of whom staged the 1916 Easter Rising. In 1919 an Irish Republic which had been proclaimed during the Easter Rising was proclaimed again and the Irish Volunteers were recognised by the "Irish Parliament" (Dáil Éireann) as its legitimate army. Thereafter, the IRA waged a guerrilla war against British rule in Ireland in the 1919–21 Irish War of Independence. Following the signing of the Anglo-Irish Treaty in 1921 which ended the war, permitted the six counties of Northern Ireland to remain part of the United Kingdom, and established the Irish Free State as a self-governing Dominion (monarchy) within the British Commonwealth, a split occurred within the IRA. Members who supported the Treaty formed the nucleus of the new Irish National Army founded by Michael Collins. However, much of the IRA was opposed to the Treaty. The result was the Irish Civil War of 1922-23. Having lost the war, the IRA remained in existence with the aims of establishing a fully-independent all-Ireland Republic and of overthrowing both the Irish Free State and the Government of Northern Ireland. In August 1969, following an Apprentice Boys of Derry march, a confrontation between mainly Catholic residents of the*

Bogside and police in Londonderry (Derry) led to a large riot sometimes referred to as the Battle of the Bogside: three days of fighting between rioters throwing stones and petrol bombs at the police. The Provisional IRA emerged from yet another split in the IRA in 1969, partly as a result of the Marxist Official IRA's (OIRA or "Stickies") perceived failure to defend Catholic neighbourhoods from attack. The Provisionals ("Provos") gained credibility from their efforts to physically defend such areas in 1970 and 1971. They are explicitly nationalist and overwhelmingly Catholic. From 1971–72, the IRA took to the offensive and conducted a relatively high-intensity campaign against the British and Northern Ireland Security Forces and the infrastructure of the state. The British Army characterised this period as the 'insurgency phase' of the IRA's campaign. The IRA should not be confused with the Irish Republican Brotherhood (IRB, 1858-1924), which was an oath-bound secret society dedicated to the creation of a republic in Ireland. (Many individuals belonged to both.) It had a counterpart in the USA called the Fenian Brotherhood. Both branches tended to be referred to as Fenians. This term was and still is also used to designate Irish nationalists in general; especially in Ulster. Patrick Pearse was a member of the IRB.

Note 4: The Dail Eireann of December 1918. One of the MPs elected in 1918 was the Irish Nationalist, Constance, Countess Markiewicz. She thus became the UK's first woman MP, but she never took her seat at Westminster, sitting instead in the illegal Dail in Dublin. As a result Lady Astor, who was elected in 1919, is erroneously believed to have been the first woman MP.

Note 5: Nelson's Pillar. When the IRA blew up this Dublin landmark, they caused annoyance to Dubliners and damage to surrounding buildings. Even more damage would result when Irish Army engineers later blew up the truncated stump and seriously overdid the explosive. The pillar had been a useful reference point – everyone knew it and at one time it had marked a tram terminus. The City Fathers discussed what to do. Nelson's broken statue could not be replaced on the column; the IRA would destroy it again. Alternatives discussed included a statue of the Virgin Mary which was vetoed because many Dubliners are Protestant and would have objected. St Patrick was another possibility but it was pointed out that he had been British. Today the site is marked by an apolitical monument, the Spire of Dublin, alternatively titled the Monument of Light. It is a large, stainless steel, pin-like object, 398 feet high.

Note 6: Queen Victoria. Fenian terrorist incidents that alarmed the Queen and everyone else include the following:
1865: IRB coup attempt in Dublin backed by Irish-American Civil War veterans.
1866: American Fenians try to invade Canada.
1867: A Fenian rising in Ireland is easily crushed.

1870: A second American Fenian invasion of Canada is defeated in a day.
1882: The Phoenix Park Murders. On 6 May 1882 in Dublin's Phoenix Park, Lord Henry Cavendish, Chief Secretary for Ireland, and Thomas Henry Burke, his Permanent Under-Secretary, are stabbed to death by members of the "Irish National Invincibles", a splinter group of the IRB.
1883: Irish bombers are arrested in Cork, Liverpool, Birmingham and London.
1884: Irish bombs left at four London railway stations. Only one explodes. Other bombs explode around Whitehall, including one at Scotland Yard.
1885: Irish bomb attacks on the Tower of London and the House of Commons (which was empty, as it was not a sitting day).
1887: Fears of a Fenian bomb attack during the celebrations of Queen Victoria's Golden Jubilee. The Jubilee passes off without incident but evidence is found of an abortive bomb plot. The bombs were supposed to be placed in the crypt of Westminster Abbey and detonated during the Service of Thanksgiving.

Note 7: The Anglo-Irish Ascendancy. *Despite the assassinations and castle-burnings of 1918-22, a number of them are still in Ireland. They keep a low profile but can be spotted at events like the Punchestown and Leopardstown Races. Occasionally they return to the headlines: as for example on the occasion when in 1974 Lord and Lady Donoughmore were kidnapped from Knocklofty House, Clonmel by the IRA and held as political hostages for a week.*

Note 8: The Irish Regiments. *These are the lost Regiments that formerly recruited in what is now the Republic, and which in 1914 were inundated with recruits:*
The Royal Irish Regiment
The Royal Dublin Fusiliers
The Royal Munster Fusiliers
The Connaught Rangers (aka "The Devil's Own")
The Prince of Wales' Leinster Regiment
The South Irish Horse

They were all disbanded in 1922. The British Government of the day was happy to do this, as it was under pressure to make cuts to the Armed Forces for economic reasons. Had the Irish line Regiments not been axed, the Irish and Welsh Guards were under threat and might have been disbanded.

The Northern Irish Regiments:
The Royal Inniskilling Fusiliers
The 8th Kings Royal Irish Hussars
The 4th Royal Irish Dragoon Guards,
The 5th Royal Irish Lancers
The Royal Irish Fusiliers

The Royal Ulster Rifles
The 6th Inniskilling Dragoons

These have vanished more recently, the victims of swingeing cuts and mergers, as has the Ulster Defence Regiment (UDR), which was raised specifically in response to the Troubles. The only Irish line Regiment that is left is the Royal Irish Regiment (Mark II), which still draws many recruits from the Republic. The Irish Guards still exist, although they are part of the Household Division, and so do one or two ghostly Territorial units, like the Liverpool Irish, now reduced to "A" (Liverpool Irish) Troop, within 208 Battery, 103 Regiment, the Royal Artillery, and the London Irish Rifles, which survive at Company strength.

Chapter 9 | In the Army Now

Note 1: The Most Conservative of the Three Armed Forces. *The Royal Navy is the Senior Service. However, as the authoritative "Official Sloane Ranger Handbook" by Ann Barr and Peter York, originally published in the 1980s, makes clear, the Army is the true Sloane Service, and Nairac aspired to Sloane Ranger status.*

Note 2: The Premier Infantry Regiments. *The Coldstream Guards predate the Grenadier Guards, but had been part of Cromwell's New Model Army and therefore take second place to the Grenadier Guards, founded by Charles II.*

Note 3: Nairac's Commission. *Intriguingly, Nairac's entry in the Army List for 1977, the year of his murder, reads as follows: "NAIRAC, Robert Laurence, B.A. Born 31/8/48. (Univ. Cadetship). Gren Guards. 2-Lt 1/8/69 (14/8/72). (A/Capt 29/6/74 to 3/9/75). Capt. 4/9/75. (P/493007)." Readers may suspect an error, because in 1969 Nairac had not been thinking about joining the Army, let alone been commissioned. A helpful military friend has given the following explanation: "I believe it is common practice to alter commissioning dates for the purpose of establishing seniority. In RLN's (i.e. Nairac's) case you are probably correct in that the eventual date (1969) would refer to his University period. There is also an issue of moving between categories – for example, at one point, while still at University, RLN is listed in the 'Special Regular Commission' category which, in his case, referred to his University status (see Army List 1972 where is 2/Lt date is different again). I believe that these dates or seniority ultimately depended also on achievement. In all probability the different dates will refer to the category in which the officer is listed at the time, but may change when he has completed the formalities that allow for a permanent seniority date for the specific rank. You will see from the Army List 1973, that RLN's seniority in this version is given as 1/8/71 – I think this reinforces that the 1/8/69 date is correct as it provides for the two year period from 2/Lt to Lt to be fulfilled. The dates given in any version of the Army List refer not to the original commissioning, but to the substantive rank held at the time the version was published. It can all be a bit confusing, but I think your assumptions are correct." It is logical when fully explained: Although the Army could not retrospectively fund Nairac's university studies when they awarded him a university cadetship, they could at least give him the three years' seniority that a full-time university cadetship would have conferred. Because he had repeated a year, they could only backdate it to 1969; not to 1968, when Nairac first went up to Oxford.*

Note 4: the Army and Intellectuals. *This passage describes attitudes in certain prominent Regiments in the 1970s. Patrick Hennessey's books on Afghanistan, "The Junior Officers' Reading Club" and "Kandak", suggest that intellect and serious literary interests are a fact of life among today's junior Army officers and no longer something to conceal or apologise for. Elsewhere in the Services intellect has always been prized: for example in the Royal Navy and the Royal Marines. The latter were feared by the IRA because they were seen as "too clever by half." The Royal Military Academy, Sandhurst, has a respectable intellectual tradition, with distinguished academics instructing in subjects like History,alongside military specialists.*

Chapter 10 | Ireland Again

Note 1: "Freds". *"Research" was one of the euphemistic labels used to describe the British Army's activities around the recruitment and handling of HUMINT (human intelligence) sources: Freds - or Touts, as the IRA would say - in Northern Ireland in the 1970s and early 1980s.*

Note 2: NITAT (NI). *There were three NITATs, whose full name was Northern Ireland Training and Advisory Team. NITAT (UK) genuinely was a training and advisory centre for soldiers about to be posted to Northern Ireland. It was located in southern England. The training included training in urban warfare. There was an equivalent, located in Germany, known as NITAT (BAOR). NITAT (NI), located in Northern Ireland, was deliberately misleadingly named. It was unconnected with NITAT (UK), and was an intelligence-gathering agency. It continued in existence over many years, changing its name from time to time. Circa 1980 it was known as 14 Int. NITAT (NI) was issued with a number of non-standard military weapons. They included Ingram M10 9 mm sub-machine guns and Remington Bushmaster 12G shotguns with an extended magazine and a folding stock.*

Chapter 11 | Regimental Days and Nights

Note 1: Regimental Lieutenant Colonel and Adjutant, Household Regiments. *The terms "Regimental Lieutenant Colonel" and "Regimental Adjutant" may require explanation. Unlike other Regiments, Regiments of the Household Division have been permitted to retain separate Regimental Headquarters (RHQs) located at Wellington Barracks, which comprise a combination of ceremonial and real Commanders. The Sovereign continues as Colonel-in-Chief. The Grenadiers generally have a member of the Royal Family as the Colonel of the Regiment – which is primarily a ceremonial role: the current holder is HRH The Duke of Edinburgh. The Regimental Lieutenant Colonel (any senior rank) is the senior officer who actually commands the Regiment; he is assisted by the Regimental Adjutant, another senior officer, who acts as his chief executive. Below them, each Battalion is commanded by a Commanding Officer (a Lieutenant Colonel), who has his own Battalion Adjutant, who is usually a Captain. (The Grenadier Guards now have only one Battalion.)*

Note 2: Viscount Grey of Fallodon (1862-1933). *Viscount Grey of Fallodon, better known as Sir Edward Grey, was a kindred spirit to Nairac: a serious dry-fly fisherman and ornithologist who wrote lyrical, readable books about both subjects. It is likely that, through the medium of his books, it was he who interested Nairac in angling in the Outer Hebrides. Two of his books in particular, "Fly Fishing" and "The Charm of Birds", became best-sellers. "Fly Fishing" was in the school library at Ampleforth, while "The Charm of Birds" was a book that Fr Edward Corbould would recommend to pupils. Nairac read both at Ampleforth and acquired his own copies then or later. Although Grey, who died in 1933, was never a soldier, his life has some parallels with Nairac's. They fished in some of the same places. Both were very friendly with the Cecil family. They both experienced more than their share of misfortune. Grey was a Liberal politician and a pessimistic, civilised man. Asquith's Foreign Secretary from 1905 to 1916, he is now best remembered for his remark at the outbreak of the Great War, which he had tried hard and vainly to prevent: "The lamps are going out all over Europe. We shall not see them lit again in our lifetime".*

Chapter 12 | The Bird of Time

Note 1: Wyatt Earp. *The truth about Wyatt Earp is less romantic than the Hollywood legend. In addition to being a lawman in the Wild West, Wyatt Earp was also (among other things) a buffalo hunter, night-club bouncer, saloon-keeper, gambler, brothel-owner and pimp. The true hero of the OK Corral gunfight was his brother Virgil, who was the Tombstone City Marshal and regional Deputy U.S. Marshal at that time. He seems to have been a much more respectable citizen than Wyatt. Virgil Earp also had more experience as a soldier in battle and also as a Constable, Sheriff and Marshal.*

Chapter 13 | The Human Factor

Note 1: The Most Professional Parts of the TA (now The Army Reserve). *Regular troops are battle-ready and have a short deployment time. By contrast, different*

Reserve units are trained to different levels of battle-readiness. The best and most professional Reserve units, which include the Paras, 21 and 23 SAS, can be battle-ready and deployed in 48 hours. Other units however require more time; up to 30 days' extra training to reach battle-readiness.

Chapter 15 | The Story Continues

Note 1: Paddy Short. *Apart from other claims to notoriety, the late Paddy Short was the uncle of Clare Short MP; briefly one of Tony Blair's Cabinet Ministers.*

Note 2: The Dictionary of National Biography (DNB). *Everything that I have discovered supports what Toby Harnden has written in the DNB, apart from the meat-processing factory story, to which he refers. This DNB entry is the best available short account of Nairac.*

Note 3: Gavrilo Princip. *The First World War would have happened even without Princip's involvement, or even if he had been caught and disarmed before he could shoot the Archduke Franz Ferdinand. Sooner or later there would have been another incident producing the same result. As Ben Macintyre correctly points out, Princip triggered history, but he did not control or mould it. He pulled the trigger to make a point, set off a chain of events he could never have predicted, and then disappeared for ever. Even in former Yugoslavia, he seems totally forgotten. Today Princip's tomb in Sarajevo is neglected and ruined.*

Note 4: Liam Townson. *Townson's story parallels that of Seán Mac Stíofáin (born John Edward Drayton Stephenson, 1928 – 2001), who was an Irish Republican paramilitary activist born in London. He became associated with the Republican movement in Ireland after serving in the RAF. He was the first chief-of-staff of the Provisional IRA, a position he held between 1969 and 1972. His much-disliked father was British; his mother was of Protestant Irish origin, from East Belfast.*

Note 5: Sir Roger Casement. *T E Lawrence shared Nairac's interest in Casement and had planned to write a biography of him. This project never materialised due to Lawrence's death in 1935, but he had apparently begun his research. There is still controversy over the authenticity of the "Black Diaries," copies of which were circulated selectively by the British authorities following Casement's conviction and which, if accepted as genuine, portrayed Casement as a promiscuous homosexual with a fondness for fit, muscular young men. Given prevailing views on homosexuality at the time (Oscar Wilde had been dead for less than 20 years), circulation of the diaries to influential people helped to undermine any support for clemency. Some Irish Nationalists assert that the diaries are a forgery. However even Mr and Mrs Bernard Shaw, who were sympathetic to Casement, believed them to be genuine and said so to Lawrence. All the available evidence suggests that they are genuine.*

Note 6: Erskine Childers. *Winston Churchill, who knew him, wrote a damning epitaph of Childers: "No man has done more harm, or shown more genuine malice, or endeavoured to bring a greater curse upon the common people of Ireland, than this strange being, activated by a deadly and malignant hatred for the land of his birth".*

Note 7: The Guards Chapel. *Strictly speaking, the Royal Military Chapel. The Chapel is the spiritual home of the Household Division. In recent years the Chapel has held numerous funerals and memorial services for soldiers who have made the ultimate sacrifice in Iraq, Afghanistan and around the world. An engraved window commemorates Robert Nairac. It is decorated with a representation of a falcon on a gloved fist.*

Note 8: Howard A Walter, *"I Would Be True." This hymn was written in 1906, when Walter, an American, was living in Japan. He only wrote the first two verses. Later his friend S Ralph Harlow added other verses. The hymn was also sung at Princess Diana's funeral.*

Note 9: Nairac's Blood Group (1). *At Kevin Crilly's trial in 2011 it was revealed that Nairac's blood group was recorded as O Rhesus Positive. This was based on a sample taken on 4 February 1973, about the time that Nairac left Sandhurst and joined his Battalion. A list of ten officer cadets included "2 LT NAIRAC," whose blood grouping was marked as "O Rhesus Pos". This was confirmed by Thomas Worthington, a clerical officer attached to the Officers' Training Corps (OTC) at Oxford University, who had examined their records from 1972, which also showed the same information. The reason why these records were not produced in 1977 is still unknown. Nairac's OTC file disappeared at some point after 2011.*

Note 10: Nairac's Blood Group (2). *Questions were asked about this in the Press after Nairac's disappearance. Writing on 16 December 1978, after the trial of some of his assassins, Colin Brady curiously referred to "bloodstains and hair on grass and stones that indicated that they belonged to Capt. Nairac, whose blood group was similar to only one in 500 people in Northern Ireland." This is not correct. Nairac's blood group was O Rhesus Positive which is a fairly common group, especially in Ireland: about 47% of the Irish population have it. However another group, O Rhesus Negative, is very rare and only belongs to about 8% of the Irish population. But the "O Rhesus" is common to both. It would appear that someone had obtained information about Nairac's blood group, mistakenly understanding that he was O Rhesus Negative. The source of the misinformation remains a mystery.*

Appendix 1 | Four Last Portraits

Note 1: Major H Jones' Regiment. *People who served in Northern Ireland in the 1970s may think that there is a mistake here, because they will recall H Jones wearing a maroon Para beret, rather than Devon and Dorsets headgear. There is a reason for this. Officially, H remained badged as a Devon and Dorset until he took command of 2 Para in 1981. However it was known well in advance that he would be getting a Para Battalion to command, so the pressure was on to identify publicly with the Paras and to demonstrate his new allegiance. In H's case it was slightly easier, as he had retained his maroon beret from his time with 3 Para. The difficulty was: what would the Devon and Dorsets think about his premature change of allegiance? H Jones had to clear his lines with the Colonel of the Regiment, General Archer, who had anyway offered H up for command elsewhere. H was therefore wearing the Para badge before he took command. He was very conscious that the whole question of his allegiance dogged his transfer and thought that the Paras would be irritated that a 'crap-hat blow-in' should command them rather than one of their own. He was right: this is why, even in death, H has been criticized for his final action, which his detractors believed would not have been taken by a proper Para officer. It is however fairly clear that by his almost suicidal bravery, H had helped to turn the tide of the Falklands War in favour of the British forces; moreover he undeniably achieved a posthumous Victoria Cross. In the process of losing his own life, H had probably saved a great many other people's lives. I am indebted to Sir John Wilsey for this explanation.*

Note 2: Ampleforth, Oxford, Sandhurst and the Guards. *Julian Malins reportedly thought that no disguise could conceal what Nairac really was. He may or may not be right: although Malins is from an Army family, he is a Silk (QC) and not a soldier. His view is echoed by one of Nairac's Royal Marine friends: "Guards officers stand out at the best of times!!! RMs are a little more subtle on the whole!" However other people cited in this book thought that Nairac's disguises were effective.*

SELECT BIBLIOGRAPHY

Books about Nairac, including Biographies

As far as I know these are the only biographies of Nairac currently available.

Bradley, Anthony: *Requiem for a Spy: the Killing of Robert Nairac*, published 1993 by Mercier Press (Cork). This book gets many basic facts, e.g. Nairac's place of birth and other details of his CV, wrong.

Cunningham, Michael: *The Nairac Affair*, privately published in 1981 and long out of print, although second-hand copies may be sourced online. A pro-IRA polemic, but not without interest to researchers.

Harnden, Toby: *The Oxford Dictionary of National Biography*: Nairac, Robert Laurence (1948–1977), army officer. First published 2004; online edition, May 2010, 903 words, with portrait illustration. The best short biography of Nairac.

Jennings, Luke: *Blood Knots: Of Fathers, Friendship and Fishing*, published 2010 by Atlantic Books. This is a highly readable angling memoir in which the young pre-military Nairac occupies a prominent place.

Parker, John: *Secret Hero: The Life and Mysterious Death of Captain Robert Nairac*, published in 2004 Metro Publishing Ltd (originally published as *Death of a Hero* in 1999). This is mainly concerned with Nairac's military career, 1973-77.

Books about the Troubles that mention Nairac
There are many books about the Troubles, most of which mention Nairac; sometimes quite briefly. Here is a selection, which I have used for reference.

Bowlin, Mark: *British Intelligence and the IRA: The Secret War in Northern Ireland 1969-1988*, published September 1998. Postgraduate Thesis, US Naval Academy, Monterrey.

Cadwallader, Anne: *Lethal Allies: British Collusion in Ireland*, published 2013 by Mercier Press (Cork)

Collins, Eamon (with Mick McGovern): *Killing Rage* published by Granta 1997 (an account of the Troubles from an IRA perspective)

Clarke, Tony (A F N) *Contact: The Brutal Chronicle of a Para's War on the Battlefield of Ulster*, published by Secker & Warburg 1983

Curtis, Nicky: *Faith and Duty: The True Story of a Soldier's War in Northern Ireland*, published 1998 by Andre Deutsch

Dillon, Martin: *The Dirty War,* published 1990 by Random House

Hamill, Desmond: *Pig in the Middle: The Army in Northern Ireland 1969-84,* published 1985 by Methuen

Harnden, Toby: *Bandit Country: The IRA and South Armagh,* published 2000 by Hodder & Stoughton

Sander, Andrew (with Ian S Wood) *Times of Troubles: Britain's War in Northern Ireland,* published 2012 by Edinburgh University Press

Thornton, Chris (with Kelters, Brian Feeney and David McKittrick): *Lost Lives: The Stories of the Men, Women and Children Who Died as a Result of the Northern Ireland Troubles,* published 1999 by Mainstream

Urban, Mark: *Big Boys' Rules: the SAS and the Secret Struggle against the IRA,* published 1992 by Faber & Faber

Wharton, Ken: *Wasted Years, Wasted Lives, Vol 1: The British Army in Northern Ireland 1975-77,* published 2013 by Helion & Company Ltd

Wilsey, John: *The Ulster Tales: A Tribute to Those who Served 1969-2000,* published 2011 by Pen & Sword Military

Other Books that mention Nairac

Ashcroft, Michael: *George Cross Heroes* published 2010 by MAA Publishing Ltd. (Short biographies of winners of the George Cross. It includes chapters on Nairac and other GC winners who served in Northern Ireland.)

Bunting, Madeleine: *The Plot: A Biography of my Father's English Acre,* published 2009 by Granta

Green, the Rev. Dr Vivian HH: *The Unpublished Memoirs of Dr Vivian H H Green,* Fellow, History Tutor and Chaplain of Lincoln College, later Sub-Rector and Rector

Harnden, Toby: *Dead Men Risen: The Welsh Guards and the defining story of Britain's War in Afghanistan,* published 2011 by Quercus

Weale, Adrian: *Secret Warfare: Special Operations Forces from the Great Game to the SAS,* published 1997 by Hodder & Stoughton. This contains a short but not wholly accurate account of Nairac, reflecting Clive Fairweather's narrative.

Wilsey, John (with John Keegan): *H Jones VC, The Life and Death of an Unusual Hero,* published 2002 by Hutchinson

Other relevant books

Anglim, Simon: *Orde Wingate: Unconventional Warrior,* published 2014 by Pen and Sword Military

Asher, John: *The Regiment: the Real Story of the SAS*, published 2007 by Viking Press

Dillon, Martin (with Roy Bradford): *Rogue Warrior of the SAS: the Blair Mayne Legend*, published 1987 by John Murray

Dykes, Basil David Woosnam: *Dunkirk: A Memoir*, privately published. The author was Robert Nairac's uncle.

Glasier, Philip: *Falconry and Hawking*, first published 1978 by Batsford. Dedicated to Nairac.

Macdonald, Helen: *H is for Hawk*, published 2014 by Jonathan Cape. This book contains valuable background on falconry.

Novels in which Nairac appears
Nairac is often mentioned en passant in tough action thrillers, whose heroes are frequently ex-Army; most recently in :

Kerr, Philip: *Research*, published 2014 by Quercus.

He also features prominently in:

McNamee, Patrick: *The Ultras*, published 2004 by Faber & Faber (readable but factually inaccurate)

Voss, Wilfried: *The Bleeding Hills*, published 2009 by Copperhill Media Corporation (The author is sympathetic to the IRA. Nairac appears briefly in a walk-on, walk-off role).

Press Articles about Nairac
There are literally hundreds of Press articles about Nairac, and there will no doubt be more in future. Of interest are :

Cassidy, John: *Nel of a Liar* in *The Sunday Mirror* 2001

Fairweather, Clive: *Brave Maverick who paid ultimate price for one risk too many in a personal spy game* in *The Scotsman* 2008

Holroyd, Fred: *Victims of the Dirty War*, based on an interview with Fred Holroyd, *The New Statesman* of 4 May 1984

O'Neill, Eamonn: *Shadow Man: An Investigation into Robert Nairac* in *Esquire* Magazine 2010

Rennell, Tony: *Heroic Undercover Soldier Robert Nairac was savagely executed by the IRA* in *The Daily Mail* 2008.

INDEX

(Note: Robert Laurence Nairac is referred to here as RLN; Northern Ireland as NI; Grenadier Guards as GG; British Army as BA; All army ranks have been abbreviated; Commanding Officer as CO. Illustrations are indicated by the use of italic page numbers. References to notes are indicated by the use of 'n' after the page number.)

Map used in accordance with free licence. © Atlas and Cyclopedia of Ireland, p.36

COUNTY OF
ARMAGH

English Miles

Sta. ____ Roads ———— Canals ————

...ies thus , UPPER ORIOR
...d by P.W. Joyce, LL.D, M.R.I.A.